LAT

T0283548

PAUL BRUMMELL

www.bradtguides.com

Bradt Guides Ltd, UK
The Globe Pequot Press Inc, USA

Bradt GUIDES

TRAVEL TAKEN SERIOUSLY

Admire elegant Art Nouveau architecture in Rīga, Latvia's attractive historic capital
page 63

Enjoy a traditional Latvian sauna at the Ziedlejas wellness resort
page 152

N

Bradt

| 0 | 75km |
| 0 | 50 miles |

Nynäshamn, Sweden

Slītere National Park

Ventspils

Talsi

Kandava

Kuldīga   Sabile

Pāvilosta

Tukums

Kurzeme

Aizpute

Kemeri National Park

Saldus

Dobele

Liepāja

Travemünde, Germany

Baltic Sea

Gulf of Riga

Ainaži
Salacgrīva

Saulkrasti

Rīga
Jūrmala
RĪGA

Salaspils

Jelgava

Sēlija

Bauska

LITHUANIA

The compelling port town of Liepāja is preparing to be European Capital of Culture in 2027
page 269

Stroll through Kuldīga's delightful UNESCO-listed Old Town
page 259

Don't miss Jūrmala – Latvia's best-known beach resort – with its fine white sand and elegant wooden architecture
page 122

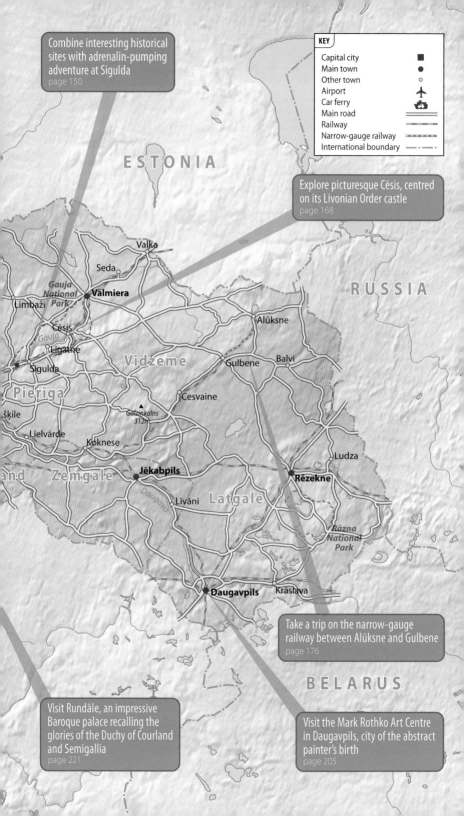

Combine interesting historical sites with adrenalin-pumping adventure at Sigulda
page 150

Explore picturesque Cēsis, centred on its Livonian Order castle
page 168

ESTONIA

RUSSIA

Valka

Seda

Gauja National Park

Valmiera

Limbaži

Cēsis

Gauja

Līgatne

Alūksne

Sigulda

Vidzeme

Gulbene

Balvi

Pieriga

Cesvaine

škile

Gaiziņkalns 312m

Lielvārde

Koknese

Ludza

and

Zemgale

Jēkabpils

Rēzekne

Daugava

Līvāni

Latgale

Rāzna National Park

Daugavpils

Kraslava

Take a trip on the narrow-gauge railway between Alūksne and Gulbene
page 176

BELARUS

Visit Rundāle, an impressive Baroque palace recalling the glories of the Duchy of Courland and Semigallia
page 221

Visit the Mark Rothko Art Centre in Daugavpils, city of the abstract painter's birth
page 205

LATVIA
DON'T MISS...

ART NOUVEAU
Rīga boasts one of the finest collections of Art Nouveau buildings in Europe PAGE 106
(LB/S)

FORESTS
The Gauja National Park provides superb opportunities for hiking, kayaking and simply enjoying Latvia's forests PAGE 6
(JK/S)

CASTLES
Turaida Castle dates from the 13th century: one of many reminders of the German crusaders PAGE 156
(EF/S)

SONG AND DANCE
The Song and Dance Festival, held every five years, is Latvia's greatest cultural event, but there are opportunities to see massed choirs and folk dancing at summer festivals around the country PAGE 54
(S/S)

LEGACIES OF SOVIET OCCUPATION
A huge head of Lenin stands at the abandoned nuclear missile base at Zeltiņi PAGE 184
(EB/S)

LATVIA
IN COLOUR

above
(PP/S)

One in three of Latvia's inhabitants live in Rīga, the country's vibrant capital
PAGE 63

below
(PZ/S)

The House of the Blackheads is arguably the showiest building in the capital
PAGE 93

The Swedish Gate is the only surviving gate of Rīga's old city wall PAGE 91

above
(S25/S)

One of the most striking remnants of Rīga's medieval defences, the Powder Tower today houses the Latvian War Museum PAGE 91

above right
(AKa/S)

The Freedom Monument – a symbol of both independence won and independence regained PAGE 101

right
(RVB)

A welcoming pocket of greenery, Bastejkalns Park centres on the City Canal PAGE 100

below
(T/S)

AUTHOR

Paul Brummell is currently British Ambassador to Latvia. A career diplomat, who joined the then Foreign and Commonwealth Office in 1987, he has served in Islamabad and Rome, and as British Ambassador to Turkmenistan (2002–05) and Kazakhstan (2005–09), and concurrently non-resident Ambassador to Kyrgyzstan. He then served as British High Commissioner to the eastern Caribbean (2009–13), British Ambassador to Romania (2014–18), and head  of soft power at the Foreign, Commonwealth and Development Office (2018–21). He took up his present post in Latvia in 2021. He has written Bradt Guides to Turkmenistan, Kazakhstan and (with Lucy Mallows) Transylvania, and is the author of *Diplomatic Gifts: A History in Fifty Presents* (Hurst, 2022).

AUTHOR'S STORY

At the start of 2021, I was in London preparing for my new diplomatic posting to Latvia. Those pre-posting weeks are always exciting, a period of intensive learning about the history, politics, language and culture of my future home, as well as about the role, and the diplomatic relationship to be nurtured. In 2021, as the world started to emerge cautiously from Covid-induced lockdowns through which none of us had travelled at all, the prospect of moving to another country felt all the more thrilling. My wife, Adriana, and I looked eagerly online for books to help us explore the attractions of Latvia we were so itching to discover. Yet it seemed that the country had disappeared, covered only as a chapter of guides to the wider Baltic region, or restricted to its capital, Rīga, with nothing on the lands beyond. The best guide available was an earlier Bradt Guide to Latvia, a lovingly prepared work by Stephen Baister and Chris Patrick, but this had last been updated in 2007, and Latvia had moved on. The idea of a new guide to Latvia was born.

Researching the guide took Adriana, our son George and I to every corner of the country, meeting Latvians who may be natural introverts but who are above all intensely proud of their country, and of the way it has maintained a strong identity through centuries of occupation and war. We met a student from the Latvia University of Life Science and Technologies gamely sporting the costume of a European spruce bark beetle in an effort to draw attention to its dangers for Latvia's spruce forests. We met the organisers of private museums showcasing their passions, from antlers to bicycles. We were invited to sing folk songs by the fireside on Midsummer's Eve and to go mushrooming in the forest – even if our hosts on the latter expedition kept their best spots secret, in true Latvian tradition. We failed in our quest to find the fabled blue cows of Latvia, a rare breed with a blueish tint to their hides. We did, though, meet some cattle bred to resemble the extinct auroch, slept in a camel park, and fed carrots to a village of rabbits at the Rīga Christmas market. We ate a great deal of cottage cheese and of foods doused with dill. I hope you enjoy the fruits of this research.

Sixth edition published June 2024
First published 1995
Bradt Travel Guides Ltd
31a High Street, Chesham, Buckinghamshire, HP5 1BW, England
www.bradtguides.com
Print edition published in the USA by The Globe Pequot Press Inc,
PO Box 480, Guilford, Connecticut 06437-0480

Text copyright © Bradt Travel Guides Ltd, 2024
Maps copyright © Bradt Travel Guides Ltd, 2024; includes map data © EuroGeographics 2022
and © OpenStreetMap contributors
Photographs copyright © Individual photographers, 2024 (see below)
Project Manager: Susannah Lord
Copy editor: Gina Rathbone
Cover research: Pepi Bluck, Perfect Picture

ISBN: 9781804690406

British Library Cataloguing in Publication Data
A catalogue record for this book is available from the British Library

Photographs Adriana Ivama Brummell (AIB); Alamy Stock Photo: sanga park (SP/A); Jānis
Bautra (JB); Latvia Travel (LT); Olga Kuzmina (OK); Reinis Vilnis Baltiņš (RVB); Shutterstock.
com: ako photography (AP/S), AlenKadr (AKa/S), Alvydas Kucas (AKu/S), anmiiv (A/S),
Bargais (B/S), Diana Sklarova (DS/S), Diego Grandi (DG/S), Edgars Butans (EB/S), EvijaF
(EF/S), Igor Shoshin (IS/S), Ingus Kruklitis (IK/S), Julija_Kumpinovica (JK/S), Konstantin
Tronin (KT/S), Kristine_K (KK/S), Lana B (LB/S), Lorens-Lorens (LL/S), Pandora Pictures
(PP/S), Papik (P/S), Peter Zachar (PZ/S), Sergei25 (S25/S), shulers (S/S), StockPhotosLV
(SPLV/S), Studio MDF (SM/S), trabantos (T/S), Viesturs Jugs (VJ/S), yegorovnick (Y/S);
SuperStock (SS); Valmiera Tourist Information Centre (Valmieras Tūrisma informācijas centrs)
(VTIC); Vita Balckare (VB)

Front cover Kemeri National Park bog trail (SP/A)
Back cover, clockwise from top left Gauja National Park (JK/S); Art Nouveau architectural detail,
Rīga (VB); Traditional Latvian woven fabric (KK/S)
Title page, clockwise from left Cesvaine Palace (AP/S); Sunset over the White Dune at Saulkrasti
(DS/S); National Song and Dance Festival, Rīga (SPLV/S)

Maps David McCutcheon FBCart.S. FRGS

Typeset by Ian Spick, Bradt Travel Guides Ltd
Production managed by Page Bros; printed in the UK
Digital conversion by www.dataworks.co.in

Acknowledgements

First of all, thanks to everyone in Latvia who has shared with me something of the history, traditions, culture and surprises of the country. And thanks to great colleagues at the British Embassy in Rīga for their insights, in particular Aldis Celms, Aleksejs Mihejevs, Dace Černišova, Ieva Indriksone, Oskars Urtans and Paulis Grinhofs. I am grateful to Jānis Rozitīs and Ints Mednis of Pasaules Dabas Fonds for their introduction to the Lake Pape rewilding project and to Intra Liepiņa for her invaluable help, both on the Latvian language section of the guide and on the attractions of the Dobele region. Neil Taylor, author of Bradt's *Estonia* guide, encouraged me to write a guide to its southern neighbour. Linda Ziedina-Ergle, Andra Brice and colleagues at the Investment and Development Agency of Latvia have been helpful and supportive. My gratitude to the authors of earlier editions of Bradt's *Latvia*: Ināra Punga, William Hough, Kārlis Cerbulis, Stephen Baister and Chris Patrick. While this edition is an entirely new guide, their work in highlighting the rich attractions of a country then emerging from the shadows of Soviet occupation played an important role in helping to support Latvia's developing tourism offer.

I also wish to thank the wonderful team at Bradt, in particular Claire Strange, Susannah Lord and Anna Moores. Above all, my thanks go to my wife, Adriana, for being such a wonderful travelling companion, for her insights and advice, and for her great work on the Latvian language section. And to our son, George, for road-testing the more child-friendly attractions, and for being reasonably patient over the amount of time his Dad spent in museums.

The comments presented herein do not necessarily reflect the views of the Foreign, Commonwealth and Development Office.

FEEDBACK REQUEST

At Bradt Guides we're aware that guidebooks start to go out of date on the day they're published – and that you, our readers, are out there in the field doing research of your own. You'll find out before us when a fine new family-run hotel opens or a favourite restaurant changes hands and goes downhill. So why not tell us about your experiences? Contact us on ☏ 01753 893444 or e info@bradtguides.com. We will forward emails to the author who may post updates on the Bradt website at w bradtguides.com/updates. Alternatively, you can add a review of the book to Amazon, or share your adventures with us on social:

f BradtGuides
𝕏 BradtGuides & @PaulBrummell
◎ BradtGuides & pbrummell

Contents

Introduction

While all countries are a product of their history, Latvia's experience over many centuries of occupation and war is at the heart of its identity and its understanding of its place in the world. A fair share of Latvia's sights and tourist infrastructure speak to the exercise of control by occupying powers. The castles of the Livonian Order at the centre of many Latvian towns were built by German crusaders to subjugate and convert the native Baltic tribes, used and remodelled by later occupying forces – Polish, Swedish and Russian – before abandonment and conversion to the romantic ruins of today. The manor houses, today revitalised into charming rural hotels, with storks' nests on their roofs and spa treatments in remodelled outbuildings, were once home to a German Baltic nobility controlling the lives of their ethnic Latvian peasantry. Sights today that echo with the ghosts of the Soviet Union, like the secret bunker complex under a sanatorium in Līgatne or the large radio telescopes near the Baltic coast at Irbene, are part of the detritus of a period of occupation that for Latvians meant deportations and depredations.

To couch Latvian history through the actions of a series of occupying powers ignores the Latvian agency in preserving their heritage and forging their destiny. The Latvian Song and Dance Festival, held every five years, is a vibrant symbol of a collective national resilience and determination to preserve and celebrate Latvia's language and culture. This is at the heart of so much else in Latvia: the story told so movingly in the Museum of the Occupation of Latvia; the impressive modern building of the National Library of Latvia, a temple to the country's literary heritage; the candles placed on the external walls of Rīga Castle on 11 November each year in commemoration of those who gave their lives to secure Latvian independence; and the Freedom Monument in Rīga, which has come to celebrate both the securing and restoration of Latvian independence.

Latvia's capital is one of the great European cities, combining a medieval core with elegant Art Nouveau apartment blocks, a vibrant nightlife, packed cultural programme and enticing restaurant scene. Latvia is though far more than Rīga. With more than half its territory covered by forest, supplemented by the added natural attractions of lakes, raised peat bogs and near-deserted sandy beaches, this is a country in which nature exerts a strong call. From the passage of migratory birds around Cape Kolka to the wild horses introduced as part of imaginative rewilding projects, Latvia's wildlife will enchant. Latvians themselves love to be immersed in the energising power of the natural environment, whether in foraging for mushrooms or berries or in hiking, running, kayaking or skiing through wild terrains. The historic towns and cities across Latvia's regions contain much to detain the visitor.

Latvia's tourist infrastructure has developed rapidly in quality, and the offer continues to grow in sophistication. In 2023, the Max Cekot restaurant in Rīga earned Latvia's first ever Michelin star. Museums are jettisoning tired, text-heavy displays for the latest in interactive technologies. Spas are reinventing the traditional Latvian sauna for a more discerning clientèle. Chefs are creating an identifiable new Latvian cuisine, with attention to locally sourced, seasonal products. Latvians may be slow to display emotion, but they love their country, and they love it when visitors appreciate what they have to offer. There has not been a better time to come to Latvia and experience that offer at first hand.

HOW TO USE THIS GUIDE

PRICE CODES Throughout this guide we have used price codes to indicate the cost of those places to stay and eat listed in the guide.

Accommodation price codes Average price of a double room in high season.

€€€€€	Over €200
€€€€	€120–200
€€€	€80–120
€€	€40–80
€	Less than €40

Restaurant price codes Average price of a main dish, including sides.

€€€€€	Over €25
€€€€	€15–25
€€€	€10–15
€€	€6–10
€	Less than €6

MAPS
Keys and symbols Maps include alphabetical keys covering the locations of those places to stay, eat or drink that are featured in the book. Note that regional maps may not show all hotels and restaurants in the area: other establishments may be located in towns shown on the map.

Grids and grid references Some maps use gridlines to allow easy location of sites. Map grid references are listed in square brackets after the name of the place or site of interest in the text, with page number followed by grid number, eg: [77 C3].

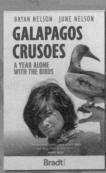
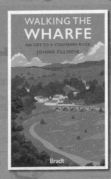

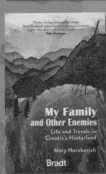

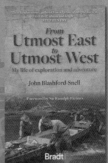

Part One

GENERAL INFORMATION

LATVIA AT A GLANCE

Location The eastern shore of the Baltic Sea

Neighbouring countries Estonia, Russia, Belarus, Lithuania

Area 64,559km²

Climate Temperate, with snowy and dark winters and mild summers with light evenings

Status Parliamentary republic

Population 1.83 million (2023)

Life expectancy 75.7 years (2023)

Capital Rīga (population 615,000)

Other main towns Daugavpils (population 79,000), Liepāja (67,000), Jelgava (55,000), Jūrmala (51,000), Ventspils (33,000), Rēzekne (27,000)

GDP Around $40bn (nominal), $70bn (PPP) (2022 estimates). GDP/capita around $25,000 (nominal), $37,000 (PPP).

Official language Latvian

Religion The three major Christian denominations are Lutheran, Roman Catholic and Latvian Orthodox

Currency Euro

Exchange rate £1 = €0.85, US$1 = €1.07 (May 2024)

National airline Air Baltic

International telephone code +371

Time Eastern European Time (EET): UTC +2. Daylight saving time (1hr ahead to UTC +3) is observed from final Sunday in March to final Sunday in October.

Electricity 230V, 50Hz

Flag Three horizontal stripes: the upper and lower stripes are carmine red (a deep red), each twice the depth of the central white stripe

National anthem 'Dievs, svētī Latviju!' ('God Bless Latvia!')

National flower Ox-eye daisy (*Leucanthemum vulgare*)

National bird White wagtail (*Motacilla alba*)

National sports Ice hockey and basketball are the most popular sports

Public holidays 1 January (New Year's Day), Good Friday, Easter Monday, 1 May (Labour Day), 4 May (Restoration of Independence Day), 23 June (Midsummer's Eve – Līgo), 24 June (Midsummer's Day – Jāņi), 18 November (Independence Day), 24–26 December (Christmas), 31 December (New Year's Eve)

1

Background Information

GEOGRAPHY

On the eastern shore of the Baltic Sea Latvia, like the other Baltic States, has a predominantly flattish terrain, its highest point just 312m above sea level. While most of the land comprises undulating plains, there are also several upland areas of low hills. This topography was fashioned in the last Ice Age, shaping the pattern of uplands in the west and east where glaciers pushed up morainic debris and a central lowland area. Its total area, 64,559km², is slightly smaller than Ireland.

The major river is the Daugava. It rises in the Valdai Hills in Russia, where the river is known as the Zapadnaya Dvina. It heads southwestwards into Belarus before curving northwestwards and flowing through Latvia to the Gulf of Rīga. Other important rivers include the Gauja, measuring 460km, the longest river flowing entirely in Latvia, which makes a picturesque course through the Gauja National Park. The Venta runs northwards for 346km from Lithuania, discharging into the Baltic at Ventspils. The Aiviekste in central Latvia, 114km long, is the largest tributary of the Daugava within Latvia. And the Lielupe is formed at Bauska from the confluence of the Mēmele and Mūsa rivers, heading northwards through Jelgava and finally sandwiching the town of Jūrmala between its left bank and the sea before discharging into the Gulf of Rīga. Latvia also has a large number of lakes – more than 1,200 in the Latgale Region alone.

Latvia comprises several historical regions, taking the names of tribes inhabiting the area before the arrival of the German Crusaders. They are Kurzeme (or Courland) in the west, Zemgale (or Semigallia) and Sēlija (or Selonia) beyond the left bank of the Daugava, Vidzeme beyond its right bank, and Latgale (or Latgalia) in the east. While these regions have no formal role in Latvian local government, which is based around the smaller district, or *novad*, regional identity is nonetheless important, not least because regional boundaries in several cases marked the boundaries between different countries for protracted periods, for example, that between Latgale and Vidzeme.

CLIMATE

Latvia has a temperate climate with four distinct seasons. In winter, days are short and cold, with a daily mean temperature of –2°C in Rīga, and several weeks of snow cover. Extreme winter temperatures, dropping to –30°C, are possible. The first snows may arrive in November, and flurries of snow may be recorded in April. Summer days are long and light, with a daily mean temperature in Rīga of 19°C in July, though temperatures above 30°C may be recorded. Summer runs from June to August. Spring and autumn are generally fairly mild, though changeable. Proximity to the coast brings regional variation, with a more maritime climate in

3

the west, especially along the Kurzeme coast, characterised by cooler summers but milder winters, while the climate further inland is more continental in character, with warmer summers and cooler winters. The differences are a matter of just a few degrees.

NATURAL HISTORY AND CONSERVATION

A little more than half of the total land area is covered by **forest**, and forests have a huge cultural significance for Latvians. Access is encouraged, with everyone having the right to move freely through both state and private forests, unless there are specific signs announcing 'no entry', or if the forest lies in a specifically protected nature reserve. Foraging in forests is a national pastime, and entirely legal in the state-managed forests. Mushroom picking (see opposite) is taken particularly seriously, but foraging for berries is also highly popular, and in spring, birch trees are tapped for their juice.

Forest cover in Latvia has more than doubled over the past century: in 1923, just 23% of the land area was forested. A growth in forested areas accompanied abandonment of fields during the Soviet occupation, resulting from both the reduced focus on agriculture and the negative impact of collectivisation. Following the restoration of independence, both abandonment of former agricultural areas and planned afforestation continued. With the collapse of the collective farming system and the restoration of land property rights, many new landowners chose not to continue with agricultural production. With support from European Union funding, afforestation proved a financially attractive option, with a particular focus on the planting of silver birch and Norway spruce.

Latvia sits in the mixing zone between belts of deciduous and boreal coniferous forests, giving Latvian forests charm and variety. Scots pine (*Pinus sylvestris*) is the most common species, accounting for around 34% of cover, followed by birch (*Betula*) at around 31%, Norway spruce (*Picea abies*) at 18% and grey alder (*Alnus incana*) at 7%.

Between 5% and 10% of Latvian territory is covered by **bogs**, depending on how these are defined. The most iconic of Latvia's wetlands are raised peat bogs. These typically originated from shallow glacial lakes. Reeds grew along the edge of the lakes, nurtured by nutrient-rich groundwater. When they died, the wet environment where lack of oxygen hindered breakdown of the plant material slowed decomposition. Their remains gradually built up as a layer of peat on the lake bed. Over time, as the peat thickened, it became increasingly difficult for plant roots to access the calcium-rich groundwater below the peat. The only source of minerals for plants on top of the thick peat was nutrient-poor rainwater. In these poorer, acidic conditions, few plants could survive, and Sphagnum mosses became dominant. A raised bog had formed, its flattened dome slightly higher than the surrounding ground. Raised bogs are also associated with plants such as cloudberries and cranberries, as well as on drier patches dwarf pine trees, often taking on twisted forms.

The Latvian **coast** stretches for 500km, some 300km around the Gulf of Rīga and almost 200km abutting the Baltic Sea. Nearly half is characterised by white, sandy beaches, one of the jewels of the country. There are also stretches of pebble and boulder beach. Behind the sandy beaches typically lie lines of dunes, those closest to the beach characterised by shifting sands and scattered vegetation. Dunes further back are more stable and more heavily covered by plants, typically with an intermediate band of so-called grey dunes, colonised by plants tolerant of dry conditions, and then black dunes, covered by pine forest.

MUSHROOM PICKING

One of the defining sights of a Latvian autumn is that of locals heading into the forest, a wicker basket over their arm and a knife close at hand. By some estimates up to four Latvians in five go mushroom picking at least once a year. There can be a furtiveness involved, and it is said that the last thing a Latvian will reveal to others is their favoured mushroom spot.

Top of the wanted list is the **porcini** (*Boletus edulis*), also known as the penny bun. They are characterised by a brown cap, and in common with other boletus mushrooms have a spongy surface with tubes rather than gills on the underside. The stipe, or stem, is notably thick in relation to the size of the cap. They have a strong, nutty flavour, and may be eaten sautéed with butter. Another prized variety is the **chanterelle**, which with its yellow or orange colour, funnel shape and stipe tapering from the cap, is among the best known. A common mushroom in Latvian forests, the **brittlegill** (*Russula*) tends to have bright coloured caps and, as the name suggests, brittle gills. Not all make for good eating, and Latvians will often nibble at a brittlegill before putting it into their basket to check against a bitter taste.

While many Latvians confine themselves to collecting a few varieties of whose edibility they are confident, more experienced mushroom pickers will add all manner of intriguing fungi to their baskets. Like the **amethyst deceiver** (*Laccaria amethystine*), whose deep lilac colour is common to cap, gills and stipe, though fades with age, making the mushroom more difficult to identify – hence 'deceiver'. It retains its colour when cooked, so can add a distinctive purple tone to your omelette. And what are often referred to as **butter mushrooms** (*Suillus*), like the slippery jack (*Suillus luteus*), whose brown cap is typically slimy in wet weather, which while edible is disdained by some pickers, as the requirement carefully to remove the slimy coating before eating is a pain.

Not all Latvia's mushrooms are edible, however, and there are poisonings every year from the **death cap** (*Amanita phalloides*), greenish in colour with a white stipe and gills. Its toxins target the liver, and death may follow. The **spring destroying angel** (*Amanita verna*), white in colour throughout and unusually found in spring rather than autumn, has similarly serious effects. The **fly agaric** (*Amanita muscaria*), everyone's image of a poisonous toadstool, with its red cap covered in white spots and white gills and stipe, is indeed poisonous, though less deadly than the death cap.

Given the challenges of discerning edible from poisonous varieties, particularly if not accompanied by an expert local collector, you may decide to forego mushroom collecting in favour of mushroom spotting, the simple enjoyment of the amazing range of mushrooms in Latvia's forests. You may spot a **cauliflower mushroom** (*Sparassis*), a creamy-white mass of folds resembling a cauliflower, or perhaps a brain. Or a **milk-cap** (*Lactarius*), which exudes a milky fluid if damaged.

Those large expanses of forest house a diverse range of **mammals,** including elk, wild boar, lynx, European badger, racoon dogs, European pine marten, beech marten and polecat. There are also a few brown bears, mainly in the north and east. The casual hiker is unlikely to encounter any of these. Mammals you are more likely to see, in forests or more usually on adjacent meadows and farmland, include red and roe deer, European hare and red fox. The Eurasian beaver can even be spotted in the City Canal in Rīga, particularly in the early morning or at the last of the evening light.

The expansion of forests over the past century has also favoured **bird** populations, with the country providing nesting grounds for many migratory species. White storks are emblematic of summer. Households consider a storks' nest a sign of good fortune, and may attempt to entice storks by erecting a pole with a ring on top as the foundation for a nice nest. Electricity providers are less impressed, as the storks' tendency to build nests on utility poles is dangerous for the birds and disruptive for the power supply. The old story about storks bringing babies receives additional relevance in Latvia where their arrival at the end of March comes nine months after the uninhibited festivities of Midsummer. Another migratory bird arriving for the summer is the corncrake, which turns up from its African wintering grounds in early May. Favouring the long grass of floodplain meadows, the species is easier to hear than to see. More straightforward to spot is the common crane, a resident of Latvia from March until October, often found in bogs. The red-backed shrike, which favours nesting in thorny bushes, is another summer resident.

Cape Kolka and Lake Pape in the west are good sites from which to observe the passage of migratory birds in spring and autumn, when thousands of birds nesting further north cross Latvia along the Baltic Sea Bird Migration Route, joining those nesting locally.

LATVIA'S NATIONAL PARKS

GAUJA NATIONAL PARK Covering 917km², the Gauja National Park is the oldest of Latvia's national parks. It is centred on a stretch of the Gauja River as it cuts through sandstone rocks in a hilly and forested area of Vidzeme. Encompassing the hinterlands of Sigulda and Cēsis, as well as Līgatne, it is perhaps Latvia's greatest tourist draw outside Rīga. Designated a national park in 1973, the promotion of sustainable tourism and recreation has always been part of its ethos, in an area which drew hikers from Tsarist times.

ĶEMERI NATIONAL PARK West of Jūrmala, covering 361km², it was established in 1997. Its origins lie in the sanitary protection zones set up around the spa resort of Ķemeri in Tsarist times to protect the sulphurous waters critical to the resort's operation. In 1989, ornithologist Māris Strazds set up a project to research black storks here, his work underpinning efforts to establish a national park. The park is particularly known for its raised bogs, black alder swamps and fens.

SLĪTERE NATIONAL PARK Located on the northern Kurzeme peninsula, this was established as a national park in 2000, though based on a protected area created in 1923, which in turn evolved into the Slītere State Reserve in 1977. The smallest of Latvia's national parks, at 265km², it is focused on a ridge, known as the Blue Hills, the ancient shoreline of the Baltic ice lake. Seaward of this is a terrain of alternating forested dune bands and marshy depressions.

RĀZNA NATIONAL PARK The youngest of Latvia's national parks, Rāzna covers 532km² in the eastern Latgale region. It was established in 2007, based around an existing nature park, to protect a lakeland environment including Lake Rāzna, the second largest lake in Latvia.

Latvian forests are home to nine species of woodpeckers, of which the most frequently seen is the great spotted woodpecker. There is a similar number of owl species.

With its extensive forests and a tradition of **nature conservation** dating to the early 20th century, Latvia has many strengths as regards protection of the natural environment. There are challenges too. Eutrophication is a problem in the Baltic Sea, resulting from pollution from agricultural run-off. Grassland pastures and meadows are among the most biodiverse landscapes in Latvia, but are threatened both by encroachment of forests in lands abandoned by grazing and by more intensive agricultural land use elsewhere. There are challenges around management of both forestry and peatlands, where habitat deterioration has all too often been the outcome of poor decisions. Among invasive species, the most notorious is the Sosnowsky's hogweed, known in Latvian as latvānis. Introduced in the early Soviet period from the Caucasus region as cattle fodder, this distinctive plant, with umbrella-shaped clusters of white flowers, can grow more than 2m high and has spread across the country. It is a phototoxic plant, whose sap can cause severe burns. Latvia has a complex network of protected areas, together comprising 18% of the surface area, including four national parks (see opposite), nature parks, nature reserves, marine protected areas and the North Vidzeme Biosphere Reserve. Following Latvian accession to the EU in 2004, its approach to nature conservation has largely been guided by the EU, and around 12% of the country is included in the Natura 2000 network.

HISTORY

History matters to Latvians. The country has been independent for just two short periods, between 1918 and 1940 and again since 1991. It also looks back to a time before the 13th century when the place was inhabited by Baltic tribes who were the ancestors of Latvians today. The rest of its history has been a matter of preservation of Latvian language and culture in the face of successive occupations: German, Polish, Swedish and Russian. A basic understanding of its often challenging, sometimes tragic, history will help you better appreciate Latvia as it is now.

EARLY TIMES As the ice covering present-day Latvia receded around 12,000 years ago, the land was gradually occupied by hunter-gatherers during the Palaeolithic and Mesolithic Ages. In the Neolithic, the Narva Culture developed among a people who were the forefathers of the Livonians, a Finnic people, whose pottery displayed a distinctive comb-ware style. This group was followed in the late Neolithic by Indo-European migrants, the ornamentation of whose pottery has given them the name of the Corded-Ware Culture, who possessed the domesticated horse and wheeled vehicles and were seemingly altogether more warlike in nature. These were the forefathers of the Latvians.

In ancient times, the Baltic region was the only known source of amber, the fossilised tree resin highly prized for its warm colour and natural beauty. Trading routes brought amber to the Mediterranean, and it is as the source lands of this valuable product that Greek and Roman historians knew the Baltic.

Baltic tribes gradually emerged across present-day Latvia. In the west, the Curonians, or Kurs, lived on the shores of the Baltic Sea. They were renowned sailors and pirates. The Latgalians expanded across present-day Vidzeme, displacing the Finnic Liv tribe to the eastern side of the Gulf of Rīga. The Semigallians and Selonians lived south of the Daugava River.

These tribes faced Slavic expansion in the east and Viking incursions in the west. The Baltic relationship with the Vikings was, though, not all about raids and fighting. In more peaceful periods the Vikings would negotiate safe passage to use the Daugava as part of trading networks that ran as far as the Black Sea.

THE CRUSADERS While there had been some inroads from the east by Orthodox Christianity into pagan Latvia, the region would be changed immeasurably by a Christian invasion from the west: that of the Catholic Church. A German Augustinian priest named Meinhard arrived in the late 12th century, with a mission to convert pagan Baltic tribes to Christianity. He built a church at Ikšķile on the Daugava, southeast of Rīga, where he was named bishop. Meinhard initially sought to secure conversions by peaceful means, but made little progress. The church quickly turned to force.

Meinhard died in 1196, and his replacement, Bishop Berthold of Hanover, was killed almost immediately in battle. Pope Innocent III, best known for the instigation of the Fourth Crusade in the Holy Land, declared a crusade in the Baltic too. Albert von Buxhoeveden, a canon in Bremen, was given the title of Bishop of Livonia, a name used by the Germans for the region, deriving from the Finnic Livs, the people they had encountered where the Daugava entered the Gulf of Rīga. Von Buxhoeveden established Rīga as his capital. The military order established during the Livonian Crusade was known as the Livonian Brothers of the Sword, their members hailing mostly from northern Germany. While the objectives of the crusade were posited around conversion, the goals also included conquest and economic control. By his death in 1229, Albert had subjugated not only the Livs but also the Latgalian principalities of Koknese, Jersika and Tālava.

The conquest of lands south of the Daugava was to prove a more difficult proposition. In 1236, at the Battle of Saule, a combined force of Semigallians and Samogitians, whose lands lay in present-day Lithuania, soundly defeated the Livonian Brothers of the Sword. This hastened the assimilation the following year of the Livonian Brothers of the Sword into the Teutonic Order, the broader crusading military order, becoming an autonomous branch of the latter known as the Livonian Order.

The Semigallians continued to resist the order through much of the 13th century. Their leader Namejs even launched an attack on Rīga in 1280. The order responded with a major campaign against the Semigallians, burning their fields to induce famine, and the conquest of the area by the Livonian Order was completed by 1290. Many Semigallians departed to Lithuania, where they continued to oppose the German crusaders.

Alongside the Germanic military conquest of the region came the German-led confederation of merchant guilds and market towns across northern Europe known as the Hanseatic League. Rīga joined in 1282, and other Latvian towns becoming part of the network included Kuldīga, Limbaži, Cēsis, Ventspils and Valmiera. The relationship between burghers of Rīga and knights of the Livonian Order was always rocky and sometimes descended into violence, as at the end of the 13th century, when a civil war broke out. More friction surrounded the relationship between the Livonian Order and the Archbishopric of Rīga. The order formally owed the archbishop obedience but, holding both the bulk of military power and land, saw itself as the dominant partner. The archbishop frequently found himself in alliance with the city of Rīga against the order.

The establishment of the Livonian Confederation in the early 15th century was an attempt to end the feuding. It brought together the Livonian Order, Baltic bishoprics and the Hanseatic cities, including Rīga. But mutual distrust undermined it. By the early 16th century, both the Livonian Order and the Hanseatic League were weakening. The Protestant Reformation was taking hold. Muscovy was eyeing the Baltic. The order's decline was delayed by the selection of the capable Wolter von Plettenberg as its master in 1494, but his successors were unable to maintain the order's fortunes.

POLAND In 1558, Ivan the Terrible launched an invasion from the east, initiating the Livonian War, which would last until 1583. With the Livonian Order in no condition to hold its territory, the local nobility sought protection from Poland–Lithuania, precipitating the order's demise. Its last master, the shrewd Gotthard Kettler, was in 1561 created the Duke of Courland and Semigallia, establishing a new political unit, albeit formally subordinated to Poland. Transylvanian Prince Stephen Báthory became Polish ruler in 1576, proving an able leader, freeing Livonia from Russian forces in alliance with Sweden. Ivan the Terrible ceded defeat. Much of present-day Latvia was left in Polish hands. Báthory persuaded Rīga, which had remained a free city, to join Poland–Lithuania in 1581, on the proviso that its existing rights were maintained.

SWEDEN Swedish ambition for territory and power brought that country into conflict with Poland–Lithuania, and a series of Polish–Swedish wars were waged between 1600 and 1629. The outcome was Swedish control over much of present-day Latvia save for Latgale, which remained under Polish rule, and the Duchy of Courland and Semigallia. Following years of war, compounded by disease, many Latvian towns suffered drastic declines in their populations. Swedish rule did, however, usher in a relatively enlightened period. The courts were reformed, the rights of landlords to judge their peasants were abolished, there was investment in education, and strong support was provided to the Lutheran church.

Swedish rule was brought to an end by the Great Northern War of 1700–21, when the victorious Peter the Great secured Livonia, ushering in a period of Russian rule that would last two centuries.

THE DUCHY OF COURLAND AND SEMIGALLIA The observant reader will recall that back in 1561 we left Gotthard Kettler ruling over the new Duchy of Courland and Semigallia, loosely subordinated to Poland. On his death in 1587, the duchy was split between his two sons – Wilhelm became Duke of Courland and Friedrich Duke of Semigallia. Wilhelm became embroiled in a power struggle with his nobles, who forced him out, Friedrich then becoming duke of a reunited Courland and Semigallia. He defended the interests of the duchy, protecting its Lutheranism against Polish Catholicism, and proved more adept than his brother at placating the nobility. But he had no heir. There was a risk that the duchy would revert to the Polish monarchy. Friedrich proposed that Wilhelm's son Jacob be recognised as his heir, and Jacob duly became duke upon his death in 1642.

Jacob would preside over the duchy's golden age. He developed local industries, built up Courland and Semigallia as a maritime force through an ambitious shipbuilding programme, and even dabbled at colonialism. He at one point held the Caribbean island of Tobago – it still possesses a 'Little Courland Bay'. And he built Fort Jacob on an island at the mouth of the Gambia River. He was, however, taken prisoner by the Swedes in 1658 during the Second Northern War and deported with his family to Rīga and later Ivangorod. He remained in captivity until 1560, when he was released back into a restored duchy, the Swedes contenting themselves with the island of Ruhna in the Gulf of Rīga and territories close to the Daugava strategically important for the defence of Rīga.

Jacob died in 1682. The wisest move of his son, Friedrich Casimir Kettler, was to accord a warm welcome to visiting Tsar Peter I in 1697. Friedrich Casimir died in 1698 and was succeeded by his young son Friedrich Wilhelm. In 1701, Swedish forces occupied the duchy, and Friedrich Wilhelm fled to Prussia, where he remained until 1709, when the Russians ousted the Swedes. It was at that point that the hospitality his father had offered Peter the Great paid dividends. Peter not only restored Friedrich Wilhelm to the dukedom, but also arranged a marriage between Friedrich and his niece, Anna. Everything was going well for Friedrich Wilhelm. Except one thing. He died on his way back to Mitau after his sumptuous wedding in St Petersburg. Ferdinand, brother of Friedrich Casimir, was heir, but reluctant to return to Courland, where the duchy was ruled as regent by Anna until her elevation to be ruler of Russia in 1730. On the childless Ferdinand's death in 1737, the Kettler dynasty was over.

As a widow in Mitau, Anna had been charmed by a local man, Ernst Johann Biron, who, under her patronage, rose to become her most trusted advisor. Anna determined to offer Ernst Johann the dukedom on Ferdinand's death, and the Polish king, anxious to maintain Russia's goodwill, agreed that notwithstanding the end of the Kettler dynasty, the Diet of Courland could elect a new duke. Ernst Johann was duly chosen. Under Anna's patronage, he continued to wield considerable influence in Russia itself. Anna's death in 1740 ended all that. Ernst Johann lost his dukedom and was deported to Siberia. Biron's fluctuating fortunes dramatically reversed again in 1762 when Empress Elizabeth of Russia was replaced by Peter III, who promptly restored him to the duchy. He abdicated in 1769 in favour of his son Peter.

The weakening position of Poland through the late 18th century was, though, to mark the end of the line for the Duchy of Courland and Semigallia. As part of the Third Partition of Poland in 1795, Russia annexed the duchy. Duke Peter retired to exile in Prussia. Russia had secured Latgale under the First Partition of Poland in 1772, which meant that by 1795 the whole of modern-day Latvia fell under Russian rule.

RUSSIA AND THE LATVIAN NATIONAL AWAKENING The German-Baltic nobility retained their position under Russian rule. Many Swedish reforms were halted or reversed, and life in Latvia reverted to a more reactionary feudal system. Successive Russian emperors alternated between repressive and mildly reformist rule.

In the second half of the 19th century, something was stirring in Latvia. What has been termed the Latvian National Awakening was underway, led by young intellectuals keen to embrace their Latvian heritage, suppressed by centuries of foreign occupation. Key figures included Krišjānis Barons, a collector of *dainas*, the rich Latvian cultural repository of four-line poems; Krišjānis Valdemārs, who encouraged Latvians to discover a maritime vocation, founding schools of seamanship; and linguist Atis Kronvalds, who set out the aspirations of the Latvian people in his 1872 manifesto *Nationale Bestrebungen*. The phrase 'Latvian National Awakening' is sometimes used in relation to three different revival movements: that of the late 19th century, also sometimes termed the First Awakening; that leading up to the proclamation of independence in 1918, sometimes described as the Second Awakening; and that ahead of the restoration of independence in 1991, also known as the Third Awakening. In this guide, I use the term National Awakening to refer to the first of these movements, and National Reawakening to refer to the third.

Tsar Alexander III launched a programme of Russification in the mid-1880s, its targets including both nascent Latvian national consciousness and German-Baltic nobility. The Russian economy was sluggish, its administration cumbersome and its international standing tarnished by defeat in the 1905 war with Japan. A spirit of discontent was ignited in 1905 when troops in St Petersburg opened fire on demonstrators, and the 1905 Revolution burned brightly in Latvia, where protests were targeted at both Imperial Russia and the local German-Baltic overlords. Manor houses were set ablaze. Russian troops, supported by the local nobles, put down the revolution. Many Latvian intellectuals fled to the west.

WORLD WAR I AND THE LATVIAN WAR OF INDEPENDENCE Latvia fought against Germany in World War I as part of the Russian Empire. But in an important development for the mobilisation of Latvian national consciousness, the Tsar authorised the establishment of units of Latvian Riflemen within his army, fighting under Latvian insignia. Germany occupied Kurzeme in 1915, but the front line stabilised across Latvia roughly along the Daugava. Following the February Revolution in Russia in 1917 and the end of Tsarist rule, the tide of war turned in Germany's favour, and by September, Rīga had fallen. Amid the turmoil, some Latvians sensed an opportunity to realise independence. In Valka on the border with Estonia, a town still unoccupied by the advancing Germans, the newly formed Latvian Provisional National Council proclaimed the unity of a Latvia comprised of Vidzeme, Kurzeme and Latgale. Under the Treaty of Brest-Litovsk in March 1918, Soviet Russia gave up its territorial claims to the Baltic, save only Latgale. The German-Baltic nobility envisaged the creation of a United Baltic Duchy, a new monarchy that would be a client of the German Empire.

On 18 November 1918, at the building in Rīga now housing the Latvian National Theatre, independence was declared by the People's Council of Latvia, a body formed out of the Latvian Provisional National Council. The declaration of independence was one matter, but securing it was another, given the number of powers with designs on Latvian territory. The Allies, concerned about Russian ambitions, had provided that German troops remain in place until local forces could be built up. Indeed, in December 1918 Soviet forces invaded Latvia, capturing Rīga at the beginning of January. A Latvian Soviet Socialist Republic was proclaimed, headed by Pēteris Stučka.

German and Latvian forces launched a counter-attack against the Soviets, but the picture was further complicated in April 1919 when, at the instigation of members of the German-Baltic nobility, a German coup established a puppet government under Andrievs Niedra, forcing the Latvian Provisional Government under Kārlis Ulmanis to seek refuge off Liepāja on the steamship *Saratov* under British protection. The tide of war started, however, to turn in favour of the Provisional Government, thanks to a combined force of the Estonian Army and Latvian units loyal to Ulmanis, who notched up victories against Soviet forces in Vidzeme and then, at the Battle of Cēsis in June, against the Germans. The Ulmanis government was restored to Rīga and German forces were ordered to leave Latvia. Instead, many German troops were simply turned over to the West Russian Volunteer Army, headed by Cossack general Pavel Bermondt-Avalov. This army, supported by Germany, had been established to fight the Bolsheviks, initially mainly comprising former Russian prisoners of war released from German camps. The injection of German troops allowed Germany to pursue its interests in the Baltics without suffering the wrath of the allies. Bermondt's forces captured Zemgale, much of Kurzeme, parts of Lithuania and sought to enter Rīga, but were defeated by a combination of Latvian,

Lithuanian and Estonian forces, with the support of British naval artillery during fighting in Rīga. Bermondt's troops withdrew to Germany by December 1919.

Latvian troops ousted the remaining Russian forces from its territory, and an armistice was signed between Latvia and Soviet Russia at the start of February 1920. Under the Latvian–Soviet Peace Treaty of 11 August, Russia recognised Latvian independence.

THE FIRST PERIOD OF LATVIAN INDEPENDENCE Latvia had secured its independence, but was shattered by war. The new government acted against the landed German-Baltic nobility, long viewed by Latvians as oppressors. Under

KĀRLIS ULMANIS

Ulmanis was the best-known political figure of Latvia's first independence period from 1918 to 1940, but the assessment of his political legacy continues to divide opinion today.

Kārlis was the youngest son of a well-off agricultural family, owners of the Pikšas farm in the Courland Governorate of the Russian Empire. He had no prospect of inheriting the farm, which would go to the eldest son, so his parents focused on his education. Kārlis studied agriculture in Zürich and Leipzig and later, during a political exile engendered by his support for the 1905 Revolution, in Lincoln, Nebraska. He returned to Latvia in 1913, founding the Latvian Farmers' Union in 1917, a conservative political force agitating for Latvian independence, and was one of the leading lights of the People's Council that on 18 November 1918 declared Latvia an independent country, with Ulmanis prime minister of its Provisional Government. Following the April coup in 1919 when German troops installed the government of Andrievs Niedra in Rīga, Ulmanis and his Provisional Government were forced to take refuge on the steamer *Saratov* off Liepāja. Returning to Rīga later that year, the Provisional Government consolidated their power as the tide of the independence war turned in their favour. The achievements of the Provisional Government were considerable, in simultaneously waging war, securing public support and initiating reform.

Ulmanis played an important role in the Latvian parliamentary democracy, commencing with the election of the Constituent Assembly in 1920 in which his Latvian Farmers' Union emerged as the second largest party. He served as prime minister for brief stints in 1925–26 and 1931. He was elected again prime minister in March 1934, but just two months later led a coup d'état, declaring a state of war, abolishing parliament and all political parties (including his own Latvian Farmers' Union), arresting political opponents and restricting press freedom. While constitutional reform and return to democracy were promised, no activity was taken in that direction, and Ulmanis acted only to strengthen his own power, adding the role of president in 1936 on the expiry of the term of office of Alberts Kviesis, who had meekly accepted Ulmanis's seizure of control.

Ulmanis argued his coup was necessary because of the hopelessly fragmented parliament; because the economic crisis needed to be addressed in a way that a government beholden to parliament was unable to manage; because far-right and far-left radicals were plotting to secure power; to weaken the influence of Germans, Jews and other foreigners over the country; and to strengthen the place of farming in Latvia. But the coup seems to have been more a response to Ulmanis's own travails. His position had weakened from his heyday as Prime the Latvian Land Reform Act, the lands of the large manors were expropriated, leaving landowners with 50ha each. The land was distributed among landless peasants, transforming the country into a nation of small farmers. Many German-Baltic nobles packed up and left for Germany. The government embarked on the challenging process of economic reconstruction and a national currency, the Lat, was introduced.

In February 1922 the Latvian Constitution was passed, providing for a unicameral parliament, the *Saeima*, a government headed by a prime minister, and the election of a president by the *Saeima*. It was a political system grounded in liberal democracy, but generated numerous political parties which grouped together in shifting

Minister of the Provisional Government. His Latvian Farmers' Union was gradually losing support. The Latvian Farmers' Bank, with which he was closely associated, was in debt. The coup was a means of averting what otherwise looked set to be a gradual political decline.

Ulmanis's authoritarian regime was a paternalistic dictatorship, in which he claimed to be acting in the interests of the Latvian people. It shared some features of the corporate state model of Mussolini's Italy, based around Chambers of Professions. It was strongly nationalistic, identifying the state of Latvia with the Latvian people, and moving against businesses with German or Jewish ownership. The number of state monopolies increased. Advertising campaigns promoted the consumption of state monopoly products like sugar. Smaller private companies were amalgamated into state enterprises. This was the era of the development of the Minox miniature camera, radios and even aeroplanes by the State Electrotechnical Factory VEF. Large-scale state construction projects included the Ķegums hydroelectric power station on the Daugava. There was a focus on agricultural output, with stronger state support for farmers. Education was emphasised, but focused on the Latvian language, and used as a device for the assimilation of minorities.

Following Latvia's occupation by the Soviet Union on 17 June 1940, Ulmanis, realising that war with the new occupying power was unwinnable, asked Latvians not to resist. Little over a month later, Ulmanis was arrested, and sent to Stavropol in Russia. In 1942 he was sent further to a prison in present-day Turkmenistan, contracting fatal dysentery on the way. His final resting place is unknown.

In Latvia, differing assessments of Ulmanis's rule are represented by two very different statues. A monument erected in central Rīga in 2003, funded by private donations, embodies the views of those who see him as an architect of independent Latvia, viewing even his dictatorship nostalgically when set against the traumas of war and occupation to follow. They argue that, as dictatorships go, his was a benevolent sort, in which political opponents were arrested but not killed, which kept extremism at bay, which oversaw economic growth, and which had the interests of Latvian people at heart, set against centuries of occupying governments which did not. Supporters of Ulmanis fumed at an exhibition by students of the Latvian Art Academy, in which they had fashioned a monument to the dictator out of margarine, offered for making sandwiches during the opening ceremony. This edible monument, *Food for the People*, embodied the views of those who argue that the undoubted horrors of what was to follow cannot excuse the totalitarian wrongs of Ulmanis's rule.

coalition parties. The fragmented parliament and global economic downturn of the early 1930s provided the backdrop to the coup of 1934 and the authoritarian rule of Kārlis Ulmanis (page 12). The independence period did, though, emerge as a golden time for Latvian culture.

WORLD WAR II A secret protocol to the Molotov–Ribbentrop Pact of 23 August 1939 assigned Latvia to the Soviet 'sphere of influence'. On 5 October, Latvia signed under duress the Soviet–Latvian Mutual Assistance Treaty, providing for the establishment of Soviet military bases in Latvia. Ethnic Germans were repatriated to Germany, largely ending the presence in Latvia of a group that had been a significant force for close to 700 years.

In June 1940 the Soviet Union occupied Latvia, and a puppet government was set up to formally request that Latvia be admitted to the Soviet Union. Overseas, the Latvian diplomatic service in exile refused to recognise Soviet occupation and would continue to lobby against it until 1991. Key foreign powers like the USA and UK never recognised *de jure* the Soviet takeover. On the night of 13–14 June 1941 came the mass deportation to Siberia of 15,000 Latvians, with a focus on former government officials, army officers, professionals and the minority intelligentsia.

Further deportations were cut short by the Nazi invasion of the Soviet Union a week later. Rīga was occupied by German troops on 1 July. While some Latvians welcomed the arrival of German troops as liberators from Soviet occupation, it soon became clear that this was swapping one form of occupation for another. The extermination of the Jewish population commenced almost immediately (page 118). From early 1943, Latvians were forced to enlist in the German armed forces, as part of a 'volunteer' Latvian Legion.

Following Germany's defeat at Stalingrad, the fortunes of war changed. By August 1944, Latvia had become the theatre of battle, with fighting between the Russian army and Latvian Legion, in some cases pitting Latvian brother against brother. The Red Army took Rīga on 13 October 1944, though German forces in the 'Courland Pocket' held out until May 1945. Ahead of the advancing Russians, many Latvians headed west, as refugees. Latvian exiles in western Europe, North America and Australia would play an important role during the subsequent Soviet occupation in sustaining Latvian cultural traditions and lobbying host governments against recognition of the occupation. Within Latvia, partisans known as 'Forest Brothers' waged a guerrilla war against the Soviets for several years.

THE SOVIET OCCUPATION As Soviet occupation returned to Latvia, the country was devastated by war, having lost a fifth of its population, including much of the professional elite. The country's economy was restructured to meet Soviet goals of industrialisation. Latvia was chosen for advanced manufacturing facilities, all at the expense of agriculture and small-scale manufacturing. Because the population was not sufficient for the labour requirements of the new factories, a process of Russianisation commenced as new workers were brought in, also serving the regime's goal to dilute the Latvianness of the republic. While ethnic Latvians had comprised 77% of the pre-war population, by 1989 that was down to just 52%. Collectivisation of agriculture was accompanied by further deportations in March 1949, involving 43,000 people, and focused on farmers resisting the process. Collectivisation was marked by a sharp decline in agricultural production.

Latvia and the other Baltic States had some of the highest living standards in the USSR, although well below those enjoyed in the west. Jūrmala became a favoured holiday resort for the Soviet Union. The country was more urban in feel, with the majority of the population living in cities and towns for the first time. Latvians developed a duality of character, with outward compliance to the regime while also trying to preserve Latvian language and culture.

The liberalising policies of *glasnost* and *perestroika* launched by Gorbachev in the mid-1980s accelerated the development in Latvia of a nationalist critique of Soviet ideology. Protests against the construction of a further hydroelectric power station on the Daugava led to the project's cancellation in 1987. Moscow appeared to be on the back foot. On 14 June 1987, the anniversary of the deportations of 1941, a demonstration was held at the Freedom Monument in Rīga. On 23 August 1989, the 50th anniversary of the Molotov–Ribbentrop Pact, the Baltic Chain was formed, with 2 million people joining hands to link Tallinn, Rīga and Vilnius.

On 4 May 1990, the Supreme Soviet of the Latvian Soviet Socialist Republic, its members elected in March that year in the first elections in Soviet Latvia in which multiple political parties had been permitted, adopted a declaration on the restoration of independence of the Republic of Latvia. But with Gorbachev dismissing the declaration, there were constant fears of a Soviet backlash, which came at the start of 1991. The move of Soviet forces to secure key sites around Rīga was seen off by the peaceful defiance of ordinary Latvians in protecting them by the erection and staffing of barricades (page 94). Through 1991, contacts between Rīga and Moscow took place against the gradual disintegration of the Soviet Union itself. A renewed flare-up of tension in August, during the coup d'état against Gorbachev, came to an end on the failure of that reactionary move. In the aftermath of the failed coup attempt, Latvia claimed de facto independence, recognised by the Soviet Union on 6 September.

THE RESTORATION OF LATVIAN INDEPENDENCE Latvian independence had been restored, but disentangling itself from decades of life in the Soviet command economy was hugely complex. The new government looked for its authority to interwar Latvian independence, which meant a return to the 1922 Constitution. Issues around citizenship were difficult, given the legacy of decades of in-migration from across the Soviet Union. Under new citizenship rules, criteria around Latvian language competence were applied for residents not born in Latvia, resulting in the creation of a category of non-citizens, who were, however, granted permanent residential status. Russian troops remained in Latvia until 1994, with a Russian presence at the radar station at Skrunda until the end of the 1990s.

Latvia set its sights westwards, building a free market economy, and aspiring to membership of the EU and NATO. The country elected as president in 1999 Vaira Vīķe-Freiberga, a former professor of psychology at the University of Montreal, who embodied and encouraged this western orientation. During her tenure, Latvia and the other Baltic States secured membership of NATO in March 2004 and the EU on 1 May. On 1 January 2014, Latvia joined the Euro.

GOVERNMENT AND POLITICS

Following the restoration of independence in 1991, Latvia in large measure re-implemented its 1922 Constitution. This provides for elections to its 100-member parliament, the Saeima, every four years. A proportional representation system requires parties to pass a 5% threshold to enter parliament. The latter provision has encouraged parties to form mini-coalitions to contest elections, but in no election has any one party or group come close to securing a majority of seats, and coalition governments have been the norm. There have been numerous changes

1

in the political party landscape since 1991: many parties have been essentially political projects linked with individuals, to be discarded or merged into new formations. The ethnic split between the majority of native Latvian speakers and a sizeable minority of speakers of Russian as a first language has been an important conditioning factor to the party landscape, as few parties have transcended these constituencies, most seeking to appeal to either Latvian or Russian speakers.

In parliamentary elections held in October 2022, the New Unity (Jaunā vienotība) party of incumbent prime minister Krišjānis Kariņš was the most successful, securing 26 of the 100 seats available. A broadly centre-right liberal conservative party, it entered into a coalition with the National Alliance (Nacionālā apvienība), a right-wing nationalistic party, and the United List (Apvienotais saraksts), a political alliance of largely centre-right regional and green conservative parties. Maintaining a pattern of recent Latvian elections, the governing coalition consisted of parties appealing to ethnic Latvian voters. In the wake of the Russian invasion of Ukraine, the voting pattern of native Russian speakers was fragmented, with many opting for populist groupings. The more moderate party traditionally supporting ethnic Russians, Harmony (Saskaņa), failed to reach the 5% threshold.

However, during 2023, Prime Minister Kariņš became frustrated with his coalition partners, whose more socially conservative standpoints blocked reforms the prime minister was keen to put forward, including a more progressive approach to civil partnerships. Throughout summer 2023 Kariņš led negotiations to attempt to broaden his coalition, but when these failed amid objections from his current partners that they would prefer things as they were, Kariņš resigned. This paved the way for a new government, again headed by New Unity, whose prime minister, Evika Siliņa, brought together two new coalition partners, the centre-left Progressives (Progresīvie) and rural conservative Union of Greens and Farmers (Zaļo un Zemnieku savienība). The incorporation of the latter engendered some controversy given that party's links with oligarch Aivars Lembergs, former mayor of Ventspils, convicted of corruption-related charges in 2021.

Latvia's head of state is the president, elected for a four-year term by the Saeima. While the post often seems ceremonial, it is not entirely so. The president has some important functions, such as chair of the National Security Council, and the role can become particularly important at times of political perturbations. The president can also carry considerable moral authority. Currently in the role is Edgars Rinkēvičs, previously a longstanding foreign minister. On taking office in July 2023, he became the first openly gay head of state in an EU country.

ECONOMY

On the restoration of independence in 1991, Latvia embarked on the challenging tasks of transition from centrally planned to market economy, and reorientation of its economic space from former Soviet Union to western Europe. The transition involved much pain, as former state industries collapsed and unemployment rocketed. Privatisation of state-owned enterprises was often opaque. There was a substantial economic contraction in the early 1990s, though by 1994 the economy had stabilised.

The structure of the economy changed, with the collapse of heavy industries at the heart of the Latvian economy in Soviet times, and a decline, too, in agriculture, while there was a growth in light industry and financial services. Inadequate financial service regulation, however, dogged Latvia in the post-independence years.

Through a combination of economic reform and a still relatively low-cost but skilled workforce, and fuelled by the prospects and then reality of EU membership,

Latvia and the other Baltic States grew rapidly in the first few years of the new millennium, attracting foreign investment and earning themselves the label 'Baltic Tigers'. Problems were, however, brewing. Latvia was hit hard by the global financial crisis of 2008. The credit boom had been particularly pronounced, with a real estate bubble fuelled by exuberant financing. Its downturn was among the sharpest in the world, and by December 2009 unemployment stood at over 22%. The economy, though, bounced back relatively quickly. By 2012 Latvia registered the highest growth rate in the EU. In 2014, the country joined the Euro area.

The Russian invasion of Ukraine in 2022 intensified efforts to remove Latvia's remaining dependencies on Russia, including an end to the importation of Russian natural gas. This westward shift in Latvia's economic orientation has confounded those who envisaged the country as a bridge between east and west. It has also underlined the challenges faced by a country with a small domestic market at the periphery of the European Union, experiencing depopulation through a combination of low birth rates and the exodus of young people in search of better wages elsewhere in the EU.

The Latvian government is looking to develop higher value-added industries in the tech and digital fields to confront these challenges, in the manner adopted by neighbouring Estonia. There have been success stories, like print on-demand companies Printful and Printify, and networking software company MikroTik. Traditional sectors like forestry remain, though, important Latvian exports. Wood and other timber products are Latvia's principal export products to the United Kingdom. The same would have been true in Hanseatic times.

PEOPLE

The Latvian people, descendants of the Baltic tribes populating the country before the arrival of the German crusaders, and speaking Latvian as their native tongue, form a little over 62% of the population, though that proportion has been growing since the restoration of independence in 1991. Many Latvians are reserved by nature, and this tendency towards introversion was at the heart of a self-deprecating campaign devised by the Latvian Literature organisation for the London Book Fair in 2018. The #iamintrovert campaign included a comic series in which writer Anete Konste identified the perfect weather for an introverted Latvian writer as involving temperatures below zero – meaning reduced risks of a random encounter. Rīga even has a suburb called Solitude (Zolitūde).

The origins of Latvian introversion may lie in the traditional rural settlement, with households dispersed in isolated wooden homesteads. Farmhouses were surrounded by barns and other outbuildings providing rural self-sufficiency separated from their neighbours. Living in isolated farmsteads is today, of course, the exception rather than the norm. The Soviet occupation, with its emphasis on industrialisation and collectivisation, put paid to it, and most Latvians live in apartments. But personal space is still cherished, and you should not expect to be greeted in the street with cheery acknowledgements from strangers.

There are, though, some regional differences at play. The different history of the eastern region of Latgale, long under the rule of Catholic Poland rather than Lutheran Sweden and with a historical greater preponderance of poorer and smaller farms, has been accompanied by marked differences in language, with Latgalian predominating, and outlook, with a reputation as the most welcoming part of the country. But the reserved Latvian character does not mean they are uncaring towards visitors. Latvians are proud of their country, and keen to ensure that all

1

who come have a rewarding time. When in a small town in Vidzeme, struggling to find an open café, we asked a passer-by for advice; she walked 20 minutes out of her way to ensure we arrived safely at the one place open. It is just that she accompanied us silently.

Most of the remainder of the population are native Russian speakers. Ethnic Russians form around 23% of the population, down from 34% at the restoration of independence. Ethnic Russians formed only 10% of the Latvian population during the interwar period. Their numbers rose sharply during the Soviet occupation, brought in to work in military service and in the new large industrial enterprises. There was a political motive here too: an attempt to dilute the ethnic composition of Latvia to bind it more firmly within the USSR. The native Russian-speaking minority also includes non-ethnic Russian groups such as Belarusians and Ukrainians, many of whom also arrived during the Soviet period.

The division between native Latvian speakers and native Russian speakers is a challenge to social cohesion. The question of citizenship was a highly charged one on the restoration of Latvia's independence. Citizenship was automatically granted to those who held it before the Soviet occupation of 1940 and their descendants. But citizenship was not automatic for those, mostly Russian speakers, who settled in Latvia during the Soviet period. Citizenship could be obtained through naturalisation, but this required passing an exam in the Latvian language. Many Russian speakers in Latvia opted to settle instead for non-citizen status. Ethnic Latvians have sometimes questioned the loyalty of this group, whose status facilitated travel and work in Russia.

Deteriorating relations with Russia following its invasion of Ukraine in 2022 prompted Latvia's government and parliament to accelerate moves away from reminders of past ties. The use of Russian language in schools is being phased out, and the government announced in 2023 that the 25,000 residents of Latvia holding Russian citizenship would henceforth need to pass a Latvian language proficiency exam to secure a continued residence permit. Monuments linked to the Soviet occupation were another target, with a 2022 law providing for the removal of monuments perceived as glorifying the Soviet regime. The tall obelisk in Rīga dedicated to the liberation of Soviet Latvia from the Germans was the highest profile casualty. Such actions have fuelled disaffection among native Russian speakers, some of whom feel marginalised in their country of residence and often birth.

One historically important minority, ethnic Germans, dominated the ruling nobility for some 800 years, from the Crusades until the creation of an independent Latvian state. In 1897, Germans comprised more than 6% of the population, and they were still more than 3% in 1935. But following the Molotov–Ribbentrop Pact in 1939, the German Balts were resettled into Germany or Poland ahead of the Soviet occupation, and this group is now essentially absent from Latvian society. The Jewish minority, which represented 7% of the population at the 1897 census, already subjected to persecution and emigratory pressures in the early 20th century, was largely wiped out during the Holocaust, and now numbers just a few thousand people.

LANGUAGE

Latvian is a member of the Baltic group of Indo-European languages. The other principal surviving member of this group is Lithuanian. The group also includes Latgalian but not Estonian, which is part of the Finno-Ugric language group. Many former members of the Baltic language family died out during long centuries of foreign occupation, among them Selonian, Semigallian and Old Prussian. Latvians regard their language as sitting at the heart of their identity, and have drawn the lesson from their experience of centuries of resisting pressures of Germanisation or Russification that their language must, at all costs, be protected and nurtured.

While German was long the language of nobility and power in Latvia, German pastors helped propagate written Latvian in their efforts to provide religious materials in the language, better to engage with their flocks. Lutheran pastor Johann Ernst Glück provided the first translation of the Bible into Latvian at the end of the 17th century. This activity extended to secular texts. Another Lutheran pastor, Gotthard Friedrich Stender, wrote the first German-Latvian and Latvian-German dictionaries in the late 18th century, as well as the first illustrated alphabet book. The first Latvian-language recipe book dates from 1795, the work of Lutheran priest Christoph Harder.

The Latvian language was at the core of the mid-19th-century National Awakening, its use popularised by the intellectuals who led the movement. They not only promoted the language, but also developed it. Juris Alunāns, for example, created around 500 words, many still in use. The modern Latvian alphabet was crystallised by Kārlis Mīlenbahs and Jānis Endzelīns in 1908. These two linguists were also responsible for the magisterial *Dictionary of the Latvian Language*, a Latvian-German dictionary commenced by Mīlenbahs in the 1890s while a schoolteacher in Talsi.

During the Soviet occupation, Latvia was subjected to an official focus on the Russian language. In the dying years of the USSR, amid the National Reawakening, Latvian was declared the state language of the Latvian Soviet Socialist Republic, and following the restoration of independence, it has been enshrined as the official language, its role fiercely defended. New parliamentarians must, for example, promise to strengthen Latvian as the only official language.

A 2012 referendum, initiated by political groups within the Russian-speaking minority, which sought to add Russian as second official language, was roundly defeated, a mark of Latvian desire to distance their country from the Soviet and Russian occupation. This does, however, mean that Russian speakers in Latvia are among the largest linguistic minorities in the European Union whose language lacks any official status. In Latvia today, you will hear a great deal of spoken Russian, especially in Rīga, Liepāja, Jūrmala and much of Latgale. But you will see little written Russian. From street signs to museum displays, Latvian prevails.

Latgalian is spoken daily by around 9% of the population, concentrated mainly in Latgale. There is much debate on whether Latgalian should be considered a dialect of Latvian or a separate language. Under the Latvian Language Law it is regarded as a 'historical variant of the Latvian language', which gives a degree of official protection, and you will encounter in Latgale road signs in both Latvian and Latgalian. The Livonian language has an entirely different root, one that is within the Finno-Ugric language family, which also includes Estonian. Historically centred on the northern coast of Kurzeme, this language almost died out, with just six native speakers identified in 2007. It is, however, being promoted enthusiastically by the Livonian Institute at the University of Latvia and the Livonian Cultural Centre. Some road signs in northern Kurzeme have both Latvian and Livonian text.

Many young Latvians speak English, and you will rarely find problems of communication in Rīga or other large towns. Restaurants often have English-language menus. Some knowledge of Latvian is, however, an appreciated courtesy, and may be of practical importance in rural areas where knowledge of English is more patchy. Basic words and phrases are listed on page 283.

RELIGION

PAGANISM Prior to the arrival of the German Crusaders, Latvia was a land of pagan Baltic tribes. Their paganism was polytheistic, based on nurturing female deities like Saule, the sun, Māra, goddess of living creatures, and Laima, goddess of fate. They ruled in counterposition with masculine deities like Dievs, the sky god, who following the arrival of the Crusaders would take on attributes of the Christian God, Mēness, the moon god, and Pērkons, god of thunder. From the evidence provided in the *dainas*, folk songs transmitted orally through the generations, as well as that from ancient burial sites and other archaeological traces, it is clear that harmony with the natural environment was at the centre of the faith, with emphasis, too, on changes wrought by the seasons and the human lifecycle.

Growing interest in the *dainas* and other folk traditions provided the backdrop to the creation of the **Dievturība** movement during the first period of Latvian independence in the 1920s, an attempt to recreate the pagan religion of old. Under its

LATVIAN ETHNOGRAPHIC SIGNS

Geometric symbols representing pagan Latvian deities are in vogue. You may see them decorating Latvian-made clothing, in the branding of shops and restaurants, fashioned into jewellery or chosen as tattoos. Some are considered to have protective qualities, others promote prosperity or fertility, or act as sources of positive energy. You may hear Latvians interpreting specific signs in very different ways, and many signs possess a range of meanings according to context, but the following is a brief account of a few of the best known and their main associations.

LAIMA The goddess of fate, whose cult gradually merged with that of Mary under the influence of the Catholic religion, has a symbol of a sequence of chevrons, pointing in the same direction. The pattern is considered to mimic the needles of a pine tree, an evergreen, as Laima is always with us. There is no specific limit to the number of chevrons in the pattern: the length varies according to the length of life lived. The Laima sign has long been used in decorating ceramics, clothing and jewellery.

A related sign is **Laima's broom** (Laimas slotiņa), typically consisting of two horizontal lines of chevrons converging on three central vertical lines, or sometimes on a central diamond shape. The broom sweeps out all that is undesired. When adorning clothing, it will protect the wearer.

AUSEKLIS The morning star, a male god, has the sign of an eight-pointed star, said to have protective powers in symbolising victory of light over darkness, and hence a popular feature of Latvian clothing. Three such signs, one representing each of the three principal Latvian regions, were woven into the jumper knitted by Anastasia Runkowski presented in 1988 to Dainis Īvāns, first chair of the Latvian Popular Front, and both jumper and Auseklis sign became symbols of the Latvian National Reawakening and the restoration of independence.

JUMIS The bearer of fertility, the Jumis sign, which looks like a pair of inverted and crossed 'L' shapes, represents crossed ears

20

founder, Ernests Brastiņš, it bore some similarities with Christian practices, including its focus on a trilogy of deities – Dievs, Māra and Laima – and forms of services that would not have been unfamiliar in a Christian context. Dievturība was suppressed during the Soviet occupation, though revived in the National Reawakening of the late 1980s. Few Latvians attend Dievturība ceremonies, but beliefs and practices derived from paganism remain widespread. Midsummer celebrations, with their traditions of weaving floral crowns and jumping over fires, are one example. So, too, are the popularity of talismanic ethnographic Latvian signs, the frequency of references to ancient deities appearing in Latvian song lyrics, and the widespread belief in energy-enhancing properties of certain natural features.

CHRISTIANITY The three major religious groups in Latvia by number of adherents are all Christian denominations: the Evangelical Lutheran, Roman Catholic and Latvian Orthodox faiths. According to the overall membership reported by the Latvian Ministry of Justice, the Evangelical Lutheran church is the largest, though

of wheat. Latvian barns often feature the Jumis sign as crossed beams of wood on their top, ensuring the abundance of the crop stored below. The Jumis sign is the symbol of the Riija store in Rīga, purveyor of ethnography-inspired handicrafts.

ZALKTIS The grass snake, whose sign is like a stylised, inverted letter 'S', was considered a symbol of wisdom. The sign is also associated with Māra, the highest ranking of the Latvian goddesses, as the snake was among her incarnations, and is particularly associated with women's clothing. The sign is also regarded as a bestower of prosperity.

ŪSIŅŠ The god of spring, a symbol of flowering and light, and guardian of horses, the Ūsiņš sign looks like two capital letter 'E's, placed back to back. The sign is frequently seen as an adornment on gloves, considered to bestow good fortune on the wearer during journeys.

PĒRKONKRUSTS The 'thunder cross', one of a family of signs collectively known as a fire-cross, or Ugunskrusts, is an ancient sign, associated with the thunder god Pērkons. It is today the most controversial of Latvian signs because the symbol is a swastika. The hooks at the end of the cross are said to symbolise the motion of the sun. While traditionally the sign would be carved above the front door as protection against lightning and is still to be seen from time to time, there is a degree of self-censorship around the sign today. Dressmakers tend either not to favour it, or to adopt more complex depictions of the Pērkonkrusts that look less swastika-like. Uses of the sign continue to fuel controversies, as around an album cover by Latvian folk-tinged heavy metal band Skyforger, depicting the god Pērkons wearing a belt buckle with a swastika. Many Latvians argue that the correspondence between the Pērkonkrusts and the Nazi swastika is simply an unfortunate coincidence, which has led unfairly to the vilification of the sign. This argument is, however, muddied by the fact that Pērkonkrusts was the name of a nationalistic and anti-Semitic political party founded in Latvia in 1933.

opinion polls generally place the three main churches rather more equal in size, with the Evangelical Lutheran church slightly the smaller of the three.

Evangelical Lutheranism The Evangelical Lutheran Church is heir to the powerful impact of the Reformation in 16th-century Latvia. That movement was initially focused on the German-speaking Latvian elite. The church began to gain ground among Latvian speakers through the Moravian Brethren in the 18th century, though was still dominated by German speakers in the following century. An Evangelical Lutheran Church of Latvia focused on Latvian-speaking congregations was a creature of the first period of Latvian independence, but the church was heavily persecuted during the Soviet occupation. In the late 1980s, the Evangelical Lutheran Church sought to identify itself as providing a spiritual context to the Latvian National Reawakening, and the church has grown since the restoration of independence. Its leader, the Archbishop of Rīga, has since 1993 been Jānis Vanags, who has adopted a theologically conservative approach, refusing to ordain women and taking a critical approach towards LGBTQIA+ relationships.

Roman Catholicism The Catholic Church, the religion of the German Crusaders, is today strongest in Latgale. From 1621, with much of the rest of Latvia under the control of Lutheran Sweden, Latgale remained part of the Inflanty Voivodeship, within the Catholic Polish–Lithuanian Commonwealth. The life of Bishop Boļeslavs Sloskāns, arrested by Soviet secret police while serving in Minsk in 1927 and then incarcerated for several years in a Soviet prison camp, is an example of the bravery of which the church was capable in standing up to the Soviet system. Overall, though, the Catholic Church fared relatively better than the Evangelical Lutherans during the Soviet occupation, in part because of external support from the Vatican. The current head of the Catholic Church in Latvia is Zbigņevs Stankevičs, metropolitan Archbishop of Rīga, born into a Latvian family of Polish descent.

Latvian Orthodox The Latvian Orthodox Church is linked with the Russian-speaking minority. Its primate, the Metropolitan of Rīga and All Latvia, has since 1990 been Aleksandrs Kudrjašovs. The Orthodox presence developed following the incorporation of the country into the Russian Empire in the 18th century. The vicariate of Rīga was established in 1836, part of the Russian Orthodox Church, upgraded in 1850 to the diocese of Rīga, as conversions of Latvians had increased the size of the Orthodox community. In 1921, following the establishment of Latvian independence, the Latvian Orthodox Church was created, recognised by the Russian Orthodox Church as autonomous, but still subordinate to the Moscow Patriarchate. Its Archbishop, Jānis Pommers, was assassinated by Soviet agents in 1934, at which point the Latvian Orthodox Church requested to join the family of the Ecumenical Patriarchate of Constantinople. In 1941, following the Soviet invasion, its autonomy was essentially abolished by the Russian Orthodox Church. In 1992, the Latvian church was again granted autonomy from the Russian Orthodox Church, though remained under the Moscow Patriarchy. Following the Russian invasion of Ukraine in 2022, the Latvian parliament adopted amendments to the law governing the Latvian Orthodox Church to provide for its full independence from Moscow, and indeed from any church authority outside Latvia, defining the Latvian church as autocephalous.

Old Believers Another Orthodox group, though much less numerous, has played a significant role in Latvia's history. Old Believers are Eastern Orthodox Christians who refused to accept the liturgical reforms of Patriarch Nikon of Moscow in the 17th century, who had sought more closely to realign the Russian Orthodox Church with the Greek one. Among Nikon's reforms was to alter the way that the sign of the cross was formed, proposing the use of three fingers rather than two. Following the public denunciation of these reforms by the Old Believers, a period of persecution began. Old Believer families fled Russia, many arriving in Latgale, then part of the Polish–Lithuanian Commonwealth.

Comprising 1.7% of Latvia's population, Old Believers are the fourth strongest religion in the country, but well behind the first three in numbers. They are still concentrated in Latgale, but are found across the country, and the Grebenščikov House of Prayer in Rīga claims to be the largest Old Believer church in the world. They are mostly native Russian speakers. Because the Orthodox Church hierarchy was associated with Nikon's reforms, Old Believer communities are priestless, relying on an elected lay spiritual leader they call *nastavnik*. Old Believers have preserved a singing tradition known as the Znamenny chant, associated with a form of notation using special marks. Old Believer houses of prayer are typically decorated with lines of icons standing on shelves. Other artefacts of the faith include the eight-pointed cross (with three bars, rather than the single bar of the Latin cross), the 'step'-like leather prayer rope known as *lestovka*, and the *podruchnik*, a small cushion used during the prostrations that accompany Old Believer services. Old Believer families tend to be conservative, with men sporting long beards and women avoiding make-up, though younger generations are less likely to observe such rules.

JUDAISM The Jewish community today is small, standing at little more than 8,000. But Jews have played an important role in the development of Latvia. It was only following the collapse of the Livonian Confederation in the late 16th century that Jews were allowed to settle here. In the Duchy of Courland, educated Jews from Germany were encouraged in by the dukes, seeking capable managers of the financial affairs of the duchy. A community of poorer Yiddish-speaking Jews, mainly occupied in farming and small-scale trade, arrived in Latgale in the mid 17th century, many fleeing the persecutions of Bohdan Khmelnytsky in Ukraine. As the territory of Latvia came under Russian control, the establishment of the Pale of Settlement under Catherine the Great in 1791 played an important role in the geography of the Jewish people. The Pale defined those territories in which the permanent residency of Jews was allowed. Latgale was included within the Pale, while Vidzeme was not. Even within the Pale, Jewish rights were circumscribed by many laws and regulations.

By 1914, there were 190,000 Jews in Latvia, comprising more than 7% of the population. But the following year many Jews were deported, especially from Courland, into interior parts of the Russian Empire around fears that their loyalties might lie with Germany. By 1920, the Jewish population of Latvia was down to 80,000, though this figure increased over the next few years as more Latvians returned from Russia. Jews made an important contribution to the economic, political and cultural life of the interwar independent Latvian Republic, although the authoritarian regime of Kārlis Ulmanis was accompanied by growing restrictions on Jewish activity in economic life, as well as a more restrictive attitude towards minority education.

Following the Soviet occupation in June 1940, Jews were included in the targets of the new regime. Thousands of Jews were among those deported to Siberia on 13 and 14 June 1941. Many died in their first harsh winter in Siberia. It is an appalling testimony of the savagery of the Holocaust in Latvia (page 118) that the fate of those who remained would be even worse, its legacy a community that is today just a few thousand strong.

EDUCATION

Pre-school education is available from 18 months, but mandatory only for a two-year pre-primary education programme for five- and six-year-olds. There then follows a compulsory nine-year basic education programme, corresponding to primary and lower secondary years, for children from the age of seven to 16. A complex structure of schools provides all or part of the basic education programme. Thus, a *pamatskola* provides the full programme, while a *sākumskola*, or primary school, tends to cover only the first six years. A *vidusskola*, or secondary school, also covers the full basic programme. A certificate of basic education is secured through exams at the end of the process.

The basic education programme is then followed by three years of secondary education. This takes one of two forms. The academic programme is for students looking to enter university. There is the option of a general education programme, or one oriented towards either humanities and the social sciences or mathematics and science. There is also a tailored programme for students focused on the arts, music or sports. The programme is provided either through the *vidusskola*, or a *ģimnāzija* (gymnasium), a school which offers the secondary education programmes only, or in some cases also covers the last few years of the basic education programme. Entry to the highest-rated gymnasia is fiercely competitive.

The other form of secondary education is vocational, geared towards students looking to enter the labour market after school. Programmes tend to be delivered through vocational secondary schools named *arodskolas* or *tehnikums*.

Entry into higher education institutions is based on the results of secondary education exam results. Higher education is provided through a *koledža* (college), *augstskola* (literally 'high school', but actually a higher education establishment) or university. Programmes are defined as academic or professional. The former usually lead to a bachelor's degree. The latter are more vocational.

The genesis of Latvia's modern university system lies in the establishment of the Rīga Polytechnical Institute in 1862, the first such institute in the Russian Empire, offering technical degrees as well as courses in agriculture and commerce. In 1919, following Latvian independence, the University of Latvia was formed from the Polytechnical Institute, and still occupies the grand former main building of the Polytechnic on Raiņa bulvāris.

First in the 1930s and then during the Soviet period, several specialist universities were developed from faculties separating out from the University of Latvia. Three of these now rank among the top Latvian universities. The Latvia University of Life Sciences and Technologies emerged out of the agriculture faculty when, as the Academy of Agriculture, it was moved into the grand Jelgava Palace. It acquired its current name in 2018 to reflect its broader focus, covering food technology, forestry, IT and environmental engineering, as well as agriculture. The Rīga Technical University was established in 1958 as the Rīga Polytechnic Institute out of the engineering department of the Latvian State University, its name and focus aping the original Polytechnical Institute of 1862. It focuses today on engineering, materials science and IT. Rīga Stradiņš University was formed in 1950 as the Rīga Medical Institute from the Latvian State University medical faculty, with a continued focus today on medicine, dentistry and pharmacy, though also faculties of law and social sciences. These four universities represented Latvia in the Times

Higher Education World University Rankings 2024 list, though none quite made it into the top 1,000.

Current challenges facing education in Latvia include the management of a phased transition towards teaching in schools solely in Latvian rather than also Russian, and pressures to amalgamate rural schools as pupil numbers decline through depopulation.

CULTURE

PAINTING The most famous Latvia-born artist, **Mark Rothko**, left the country as a child, but artists based in Latvia have created a significant body of work. Until the mid 19th century, painting in Latvia was dominated by foreign artists, fulfilling commissions for the local German-Baltic aristocracy. But local Latvian painters gradually emerged. Towards the end of the 19th century, young Latvian artists studying in St Petersburg, influenced by the Latvian National Awakening, founded the student group Rūķis (Gnome) in a conscious effort to establish a national school of painting. They would develop their careers in Latvia. Among their number were three notable artists. **Janis Rozentāls** was one of the first artists to capture Latvian peasant life. **Vilhelms Purvītis** became known for landscape paintings, capturing the changes of seasons. Latvians today are prone to describe a scene of snow melting in the spring sun as a 'Purvītis landscape'. **Johann Walter**, influenced by Impressionism, also produced landscapes, as well as paintings highlighting reflections on water, as seen in his most famous canvas, *Peldētāji zēni* (*Bathing Boys*). Following the traumatic years of war, a group of young Latvian artists formed in 1920 the Rīga Group of Artists, embracing new movements such as Cubism. The first chair of the group was **Jēkabs Kazaks**, a modernist whose choice of themes included refugees. He died of tuberculosis in 1920 at the age of just 25. His near contemporary, **Jāzeps Grosvalds**, fell victim in Paris to the Spanish flu in the same year. Grosvalds is known for canvases depicting the lives and battles of the Latvian Riflemen. Another noted member of the Rīga Group of Artists was **Aleksandra Beļcova**, who focused on portraits and still lives with a style moving from Cubism to realism.

Also in the interwar period, Latvian Constructivist artist **Gustavs Klucis** worked in Moscow, combining expressive photographs with slogans, increasingly in the service of the Stalinist regime. Not that this protected him from Stalinist terror: he was executed in 1938 as part of an operation against Latvians in the USSR. His contemporary, painter **Aleksandrs Drēviņš**, was another victim.

During the Soviet occupation, there was pressure on Latvian artists to conform to the dictates of Socialist Realism, though some worked imaginatively and often bravely at the edges of the permissible. The husband and wife team of **Miervaldis Polis and Līga Purmale** broke with Socialist Realism in the 1970s, adopting instead the style of Photorealism from western currents in art. Polis later turned to performance art, dressing in 1987 as a Bronze Man in reference to the Soviet statues that dotted Rīga. Following the restoration of independence, Polis was chosen to paint the official portraits of presidents of Latvia. In the last years of the Soviet Union, artists helped promote the Latvian National Reawakening. **Džemma Skulme**, born into a family of artists, was chairman of the Union of Artists in the late Soviet period and became one of the founders of the Latvian People's Front in 1988.

Latvia today has a thriving contemporary art scene, well presented in festivals such as the Rīga International Biennial of Contemporary Art (RIBOCA) and the annual Survival Kit festival in Rīga. The offering might range from Ritums Ivanovs' large canvases of cultural icons, through Frančeska Kirke's parodies of Old Masters to Kaspars Podnieks' photographs of villagers apparently levitating against the background.

APPLIED ART The development of distinctively Latvian decorative applied arts owed much to a group of Latvians studying at the end of the 19th century at the Stieglitz Central School for Technical Drawing in St Petersburg, who formed part of the Rūķis group. There were disagreements from the outset around the balance to be struck between replication of the traditions of Latvian folk art and the use of these simply as inspirations to be adapted to the major artistic currents of the time. Thus **Rihards Zariņš**, a graphic artist who became director of the government printing house following Latvian independence, argued that applied art should follow folk traditions, utilising ethnographic patterns extensively. In contrast, **Jūlijs Madernieks**, designer of furniture and textiles, opposed the simple repetition of ethnographic patterns.

In 1924, a group of young artists established the **Baltars** ceramics painting workshop in Rīga, its name a play on the Latin *ars Baltica* – Baltic art. The three leading lights were Romans Suta, his wife Aleksandra Beļcova and graphic artist Sigismunds Vidbergs. The workshop sought to combine Latvian ethnic traditions with the modernist styles in vogue, including Art Deco, cubism and constructivism. Before it folded in 1930, the workshop's output included ceramic plates painted with designs ranging from Latvian weddings to foreign travels.

Following the establishment of the Ulmanis dictatorship, the use of a distinctively Latvian style in all forms of art was encouraged as part of the government's focus on nationalism and patriotism. The furniture designed by **Ansis Cīrulis** in 1937 for the Latvian Chamber of Agriculture, following its move to Jelgava Palace, was an example, inspired by Art Deco, but with distinctively local touches, such as inlaid motifs of wheat sheaves reflecting the regime's obsession with agriculture.

Under the Soviet occupation, applied artists were confronted with different ideological priorities. For example, in the 1960s **Marta Staņa** and **Erna Rubene** designed modern furniture sets in a light and cheap style, appropriate for the new high-rise apartment blocks going up all over Latvia. A chair made of wickerwork, looking rather like a deckchair, is typical.

The applied arts are vibrant today in Latvia and continue to express debates about the right balance between the reflection of Latvian traditional motifs and the embracing of modern styles that have been continuing for more than a century. Note, for example, the traditional folk costumes made by **Anna Aizsilniece** using recycled textiles.

LITERATURE The story of Latvian literature is entwined with that of Latvia's National Awakening. The German-Baltic aristocracy long regarded Latvian as the language of the peasantry, unsuited to great literary works. **Juris Alunāns**, a member of the Young Latvian movement, sought to prove them wrong, publishing a collection of poems in 1856 to demonstrate the beauty of the Latvian language. In 1888, **Andrejs Pumpurs**, who combined a career as a Russian army officer with a vocation as a promoter of Latvian culture, wrote the epic *Lāčplēsis* (*The Bear Slayer*) based on local legends. In its climatic battle between our hero Lāčplēsis and the sinister Dark Knight, the story emphasises Latvia's struggle to free itself from foreign occupiers, in this case the German Crusaders.

A husband-and-wife couple known by their pen names **Rainis and Aspazija** are among the writers best known to Latvians. Rainis' birthday, 11 September, is the focus of the annual poetry days commemoration in Latvia, with readings at the foot of his statue in Rīga. Both Rainis and Aspazija were born in 1865. Aspazija, born Elza Rozenberga, was the first to achieve fame. Her play *Vaidelote*, staged in 1894, launched a new age of Latvian romantic drama. She met Jānis Pliekšāns, editor of the *Dienas Lapa* newspaper and a leader of the leftist New Current (Jaunā strāva) movement, who wrote under the name Rainis. His political activities led to his arrest in 1897, and the couple married that year so Aspazija could accompany Rainis into his forced exile. Returning to Latvia ahead of the 1905 Revolution, in which he would be closely involved, Rainis wrote the play *Uguns un nakts* (*Fire and Night*), which takes Pumpurs' epic *Lāčplēsis* as its starting point, but draws clearer parallels with Latvia's contemporary situation.

With the failure of the 1905 Revolution, Rainis and Aspazija were forced to flee Latvia, emigrating to Switzerland, where they settled in Castagnola just outside Lugano. Both continued to write. Rainis' dramatic ballad *Daugava*, written in 1916, was among the first literary works specifically to call for a Latvian state. Rainis and Aspazija returned to a newly independent Latvia in 1920, getting a heroes' welcome for the literary support they had provided for the Latvian cause. Rainis immersed himself in political and cultural life, becoming both director of the Latvian National Theatre and Minister of Education. But both his political and literary dreams were unfulfilled – he never secured either the presidency of Latvia or the Nobel Prize for Literature. He died in 1929 at the age of 64. Aspazija outlived him by 14 years.

Rūdolfs Blaumanis was a novelist and playwright, regarded as a master of realism. Among his best-known works is a 22-page 1899 novella *Nāves ēnā* (*In the Shadow of Death*), which was made into a critically acclaimed film in 1971. It tells the story of a group of fishermen who become stranded on a floating iceberg. Some do not survive, but with their hope fading, a small boat arrives. This is not, however, the end of the drama, as the boat lacks the space to take them all. Ailing with tuberculosis, Blaumanis shared a flat in Rīga with his friend, painter Janis Rozentāls, in the last years of his life. He died in 1908 at the age of 45.

During the first period of Latvian independence there was a flourishing of Latvian literature. Among the best-known writers from this period was **Aleksandrs Čaks**, one of the first major Latvian literary figures to embrace an urban, and specifically Rīga, setting, rather than the then typical accounts of village life. During the Soviet period, Čaks's health suffered under the strain of accusations of political incorrectness in his works, and he died in 1950, aged 48.

During the Soviet occupation, writers navigated the pressures exerted by the Soviet authorities in varying ways. Some largely thrived. The poet, novelist and literary critic **Andrejs Upīts** received the USSR State Prize in 1946 for his novel *Zaļā zeme* (*Verdant Land*) and became president of the Latvian Writers' Union. Poet **Ojārs Vācietis** was more questioning, and he was unable to publish for an extended period in the 1960s, though the attitude of the authorities towards his work later changed, and he received many awards towards the end of his career. **Vizma Belševica** attracted the opprobrium of the Soviet authorities for her 1969 poetry collection, *Gadu gredzeni* (*Annual Rings*), interpreted as critical of the Soviet occupation although ostensibly about the fate of those subjugated by the German crusaders. As a result, Belševica was banned from publishing from 1971 to 1974.

Another poet, **Imants Ziedonis**, similarly navigated the difficult path between dissidence and being able to work. His 1971 work *Epifānijas* (*Epiphanies*) is based around short prose poems, often allegorical, which illuminate the challenges of everyday life. While he never broke with the regime, he was increasingly active in environmental movements, notably the 'Great Tree Liberation Group', formed in

1976 to protect the great trees that have a particular significance to Latvian identity. Elected to the Latvian Supreme Soviet, Ziedonis was among the parliamentarians voting to restore Latvian independence on 4 May 1990.

Today, the Latvian Literature platform seeks to promote international recognition of Latvian literature. Among recent works available in English translation, two very different novels worth searching out are, first, *Mātes piens* (*Soviet Milk*) by **Nora Ikstena**, which tells the story of the Soviet occupation through three generations of Latvian women, involving aversion to both breast milk and the Soviet school milk. And second, *Maskačkas stāsti* (*Dog Town*) by **Luiže Pastore**, a delightful children's book involving a lonely small boy, the talking dogs of the Maskačka district of Rīga and a legend that says the city will flood if anyone should dare to say that its construction is complete.

CINEMA The oldest surviving film made in Rīga dates from 1910 and portrays the visit of Tsar Nicholas II. Since then, film studios in Latvia have produced some interesting work, ensuring that Latvia means more to cinema than as the birthplace of celebrated Soviet director Sergei Eisenstein.

The first major attempt to produce a full-length feature in independent Latvia was the silent film *Lāčplēsis* (*Bearslayer*), directed in 1930 by Aleksandrs Rusteiķis, based on Andrejs Pumpurs' epic poem.

In the Soviet period, the Rīga Film Studio was founded, and its output would grow to ten or more films per year by the 1970s. While many of its products were standard Soviet fare, some Latvian directors pushed at the boundaries of the censors' acceptance. One notable example was the 1967 film *Četri Balti krekli* (*Four White Shirts*), the work of director Rolands Kalniņš, centred on telephone repairman Cēzars Kalniņš, the singer in a rock-and-roll band by night. The band is reported to the authorities over their 'indecent' lyrics, and a conflict ensues between band members willing to accommodate the demands of the authorities and the idealistic Cēzars. The plot of the film mirrored its experience in real life. The authorities didn't like the title, which mocked the tendency in Soviet life to change opinions as frequently as shirts in response to the views of different bosses, and forced a change to *Elpojiet dziļi* (*Breathe Deeply*). They introduced so many other restrictions around the film that it was essentially suppressed for two decades, until *glasnost* in the 1980s allowed it to be screened as intended. With music by noted Latvian composer Imants Kalniņš (yes, there were a lot of people called Kalniņš associated with the film) and a style reminiscent of the French New Wave, it was an immediate hit, albeit 20 years late.

A 1981 film, *Limuzīns Jāņu nakts krāsā* (*A Limousine the Colour of Midsummer's Eve*), holds a position in Latvia not dissimilar to that of *It's a Wonderful Life* in the USA, except that instead of being broadcast every Christmas it is shown each year at Midsummer. Directed by Jānis Streičs, it tells the story of an old lady living in the countryside who wins a car in the lottery, providing the occasion for relatives she has not seen for years to turn up and try to win her favour. A number of lines from the film reverberate culturally, for example, the pleas of a spoiled young woman to the object of her affections to take her to Munamägi, the highest point in Estonia, a phrase used by Latvians to refer to naïve youthful dreams of escapism.

Documentary film making is an important component of the cinematic history of Latvia. The Rīga School of Poetic Documentary would prove influential, through such output as *Vecāks par desmit minūtēm* (*Ten Minutes Older*), a film just 10 minutes long, directed in 1978 by Herz Frank, which portrays a group of children watching an (unseen) puppet show. The viewer watches their emotions as they grow, quite literally, 10 minutes older. A 2002 project dedicated to Frank and to his cameraman Juris Podnieks, entitled *Ten Minutes Older: The Trumpet* and *The Cello* involved fifteen filmmakers from Jean-Luc Godard to Spike Lee, exploring their own versions of the passage of time through 10 minutes of film.

During Latvia's National Reawakening, the documentary films of Frank's cameraman Juris Podnieks played an influential role in both reporting on and promoting social change. His 1986 film ***Vai viegli būt jaunam?*** (*Is It Easy to Be Young?*) interviews young Latvians, capturing their alienation from Soviet expectations. The film includes footage of a concert of Latvian rock group Pērkons, as well as the aftermath of the concert in which youths were sentenced for their involvement in the vandalism of the compartment of a train taking them back to Rīga. Two members of Podnieks' film crew, including cameraman Andris Slapiņš, were killed in January 1991 during the assault by OMON forces on the Ministry of the Interior building in Rīga. Podnieks himself died in 1992 while scuba-diving at a lake in Kurzeme.

Another influential documentary of this period was the 1988 film *Šķērsiela*, directed by Ivars Seleckis. This takes as its theme the inhabitants of a street named Šķērsiela on the outskirts of Rīga, a superficially picturesque place of dilapidated wooden houses between districts of high-rise tower blocks. The inhabitants are muddling through a period of rapid social, political and economic change. Seleckis returned to the street a decade later to film *Jaunie laiki Šķērsielā* (*New Times on Šķērsiela*) and again in 2013 for *Kapitālisms Šķērsielā* (*Capitalism on Šķērsiela*).

Following the restoration of Latvian independence, film output in Latvia declined, as the Soviet film infrastructure was broken up, and the country faced straitened economic times. It has gradually increased, with the National Film Centre of Latvia set up in 1991 to provide public support to Latvian films. The 2019 historical drama ***Dvēseļu putenis*** (*Blizzard of Souls*), directed by Dzintars Dreibergs, became the most watched Latvian film since the restoration of independence. Marketed in the UK as *The Rifleman*, it tells the story of young Artūrs, who joins the Latvian Riflemen within the Russian army, later joins the Bolsheviks, but disillusioned with that cause ends up fighting for Latvia in the War of Independence.

MUSIC Traditional Latvian folk songs based on short, usually four-line poems called *dainas* are central to Latvia's national identity. Their themes are often centred on the trials and tribulations of rural life, or the stages of the human life cycle. Many also refer to pre-Christian deities and the worship of natural phenomena. The exhaustive work of Krišjānis Barons in compiling Latvian *dainas* was important in the development of Latvian consciousness.

Among the traditional musical instruments of Latvia, the most important is the *kokle*. This plucked stringed instrument is part of a family known as Baltic psalteries, found across the Baltic States, Finland and northwest Russia, and including the Finnish *kantele*. They are usually played in a horizontal position, either on the lap or laid on a table, but are occasionally seen played vertically, for example, in the statue of a *kokle* player in the town of Talsi. Strings are strummed by the index finger of the right hand and muted by the left. *Kokles* dating to the 13th century have been found in archaeological excavations. The instrument became popularised in modern times with the Latvian folklore revival in the later Soviet period, part of the National Reawakening, and is now widely performed. The traditional *kokle* has 11 strings, but performances often use a 32-string concert *kokle*, which stands on legs, the player seated behind it.

The most distinctive Baltic musical form is the massed choir, whose performances reach their exuberant peak in the five-yearly Song and Dance festivals (page 54).

The Latvian Song and Dance Festival has been performed on a roughly five-yearly basis since 1873, initially as the All-Latvian Song Festival, and has long been a major event in the development and celebration of Latvian national identity (page 54). Performed by massed choirs of several thousand singers, the songs, speaking to Latvia's struggles and achievements, are spine-tinglingly evocative, their lyrics familiar to all Latvians. These are six of the most important. Performances of all are readily available on YouTube.

PŪT, VĒJIŅI! (BLOW, WINDS!) A traditional Livonian wedding song, which eventually also acquired Latvian lyrics and was first published in 1872, this tells of a young man urging the winds to blow harder so his boat will return to Courland and he will marry his love. Without, however, her parents' knowledge, as her mother believes him to be a drunkard and reckless horseman. The song was associated with the Latvian Singing Revolution and the re-establishment of independence. Rainis wrote a whole play based on it, which was made into a Soviet feature film in 1973. The score of that film, by Imants Kalniņš, is itself enduringly popular in Latvia, and in the final concert of the 2023 Song and Dance Festival *Pūt, vējiņi!* had the distinction of being performed twice, in both an instrumental version from the film score by massed brass bands, and as the original folk song by the choir.

DIEVS, SVĒTĪ LATVIJU! (GOD BLESS LATVIA!) A song written by Kārlis Baumanis, specifically for the first Latvian Song Festival in 1873, though Tsarist censorship meant that it was not sung by the full choir. It earned that accolade only in 1895, when to smooth the path past the censors some references to 'Latvia' were replaced by the more generic 'Baltics'. In 1920, with all references to 'Latvia' restored, the song was selected as the national anthem of the newly independent Republic of Latvia, and it is in that capacity that it continues to be sung at festivals today.

GAISMAS PILS (CASTLE OF LIGHT) The work of Jāzeps Vītols, the first rector of the Latvian Conservatory and a father figure of Latvian choral music, *Gaismas pils* was written in 1899 and first performed at a Song Festival in 1910. Based on a poem by Latvian writer Auseklis, it tells of a great castle where the gods of the

Derived from a choral tradition brought to the region by German Balts, but mutated into a symbol of burgeoning Latvian national consciousness during the National Awakening of the 19th century, many of the most popular compositions of the festival draw from *dainas* and other traditional folk songs.

Among the most important figures in the development of Latvian classical music stands **Jāzeps Vītols**, who remained as a teacher at the St Petersburg Conservatory following the completion of his studies, counting among his pupils Sergei Prokofiev. Vītols returned from Russia following the establishment of Latvian independence, and set up in Rīga the first Latvian Conservatory of Music, which today bears the name Jāzeps Vītols Latvian Academy of Music. Vītols adopted a national romantic style, drawing inspiration from Latvian folk tunes, and was closely associated with Latvian choral music and with the Song and Dance Festival. **Emīls Dārziņš** also composed choral works that have become mainstays of the Song and Dance Festival, as well as a beautiful orchestral piece, *Melanholiskais valsis* (*Melancholic Waltz*). Dārziņš' life was tragic.

nation's fathers lie. In the wake of war and the loss of its heroes the castle has disappeared, but will rise up again. The song speaks to Latvia's troubled history of occupation and is closely associated with the story of the festival. Its performance in 1985, despite having been removed from the festival programme by the Soviet authorities, was among the acts of defiance marking the Latvian National Reawakening that presaged the re-establishment of independence in 1991.

JĀŅUVAKARS (MIDSUMMER EVENING) Composed in 1926 by Emilis Melngailis, and first performed in the 1931 festival, this is part of a particular genre of Latvian choral song: the Midsummer song. They characteristically feature the refrain 'līgo', in reference to Midsummer, and carry associations with fertility and good fortune. Melngailis was one of the composers and folksong collectors most closely associated with the genre of Midsummer songs, and *Jāņuvakars* is the second most frequently performed song at the festivals after *Gaismas pils*.

SAULE, PĒRKONS, DAUGAVA (SUN, THUNDER, DAUGAVA) Composed by Mārtiņš Brauns, with lyrics based on the 1916 poem *Daugava* by Rainis, this song was first performed at the 1990 Song and Dance Festival. In a 2018 radio poll, it was voted by listeners as the most popular Latvian song of all time. Its lyrics are nationalistic, identifying the sun as the mother of the Latvian nation, thunder as the father, and the Daugava as the nurse of Latvia's pain. Sung by a massed Latvian choir, it is mesmerising. With Catalan lyrics, Brauns' composition was adopted in 2014 as the anthem of the Catalan independence movement.

LĒC, SAULĪTE (RISE, DEAR SUN) Composed by Raimonds Tiguls, with lyrics by Rasa Bugavičute-Pēce, this was first performed at events linked with Rīga's European Capital of Culture celebrations in 2014, and has been a standout success at the Song and Dance Festivals in 2018 and 2023. It is another of the nationalistic songs that draws from Latvia's pre-Christian faith, with references to sun and thunder, as well as to Laima, goddess of fate. Long pauses before the rendition of the last two lines of the song, which call on the sun to rise and tear down the darkness to unite the Latvian nation, have added to its impact at the festivals.

He battled poverty and alcoholism, as well as a hostile attitude from other Latvian composers, including accusations of plagiarism that led him to destroy all his orchestral works. *Melancholic Waltz* was restored only after his death in 1910 when he fell under a train, though whether this was by accident or suicide has never been determined. The prolific **Jānis Ivanovs** composed 21 symphonies, drawing inspiration from the musical traditions of his home region of Latgale, his career stretching from the first period of Latvian independence into the Soviet period, when he became a People's Artist of the USSR.

The best-known living Latvian composer is **Raimonds Pauls**, almost invariably addressed as 'Maestro Raimonds Pauls'. A pianist from a working-class Rīga family, he is the composer of a huge number of popular songs of the Soviet and post-restoration of independence periods, combining Latvian folk influences with the worlds of rock 'n' roll and easy listening. His *Manai Dzimtenei* (*My Homeland*) is an enduring favourite of the Latvian Song and Dance Festival and a popular Latvian anthem. He served as Latvia's Minister of Culture from 1988 to 1993. Many of his songs were recorded in Russian, and he collaborated with popular Russian singers such as Alla Pugachova, giving him a recognition across the former Soviet Union.

Songwriter **Imants Kalniņš** played a significant role in the lives of many young Latvians growing up in the Soviet period. His song *Viņi dejoja vienu vasaru* (*They Danced One Summer Long*), with lyrics from poet Māris Čaklais, from the 1967 film *Four White Shirts*, is a much-loved evocation of summer romance. His *Fourth Symphony* from 1973 incorporated rock elements as well as lines from American poet Kelly Cherry, with whom Kalniņš had an affair, though the latter were deleted in the version passed by Soviet censors. From 1976, his name day was marked by a concert, performed by his band Menuets and subject to harassment from the Soviet authorities. The tradition has been reintroduced, and the Imantdienas festival still takes place in Cēsis at the start of July.

Imants Kalniņš was also one of the composers of the rock music that accompanied Latvia's National Reawakening in the 1980s and emerging discontent with Soviet rule. Another key figure was Zigmārs Liepiņš who, with writer Māra Zālīte, composed the rock opera *Lāčplēsis*, performed in 1988, based on the Latvian national epic. Among the most influential rock bands of the time were **Līvi**, founded in Liepāja in 1976, who have undergone many changes of style and line-up during their career, with an output including patriotic ballads such as *Dzimtā valoda*, about the importance of the Latvian language. **Pērkons**, a hard rock band whose name means 'Thunder', faced frequent run-ins with the Soviet authorities. Vocalist Nauris Puntulis served as Latvia's Culture Minister from 2019 to 2023. **Dzeltenie Pastnieki**, 'the Yellow Postmen', are a new-wave band whose early albums during the Soviet period were home-recorded on tape recorders and distributed in bootleg fashion to avoid the censors.

Bands to emerge following the restoration of Latvian independence include **Prāta Vētra**, also known as Brainstorm, formed in Jelgava in 1989, whose song *My Star* secured third place in the 2000 Eurovision Song Contest, Latvia's first outing in the competition. Latvian singer **Marie N**, the stage name of Marija Naumova, won the contest in 2002, with the song *I Wanna*, a song that thereafter achieved the unfortunate and unusual feat for a Eurovision winner of being a commercial failure. In an entirely different vein, **Olive Mess** is a progressive rock band that performs mostly in English. Their name, incidentally, plays homage to French composer Olivier Messiaen.

SPORT

The sport most strongly associated with Latvia is **ice hockey**. It gradually supplanted the sport of bandy in the 1930s, another game involving ice-skating teams wielding sticks, but with a ball and a much larger playing surface. The Latvian experience of ice hockey was helpful to Soviet sporting authorities following World War II when they decided to focus on ice hockey rather than bandy, as it was an Olympic sport. The most important club during the Soviet period was Dinamo Rīga, known as Daugava Rīga during the 1950s, which participated in the elite Soviet Championship League. Goaltender Artūrs Irbe became a popular figure in Latvia's reassertion of independence for his refusal to play for the Soviet Union and his participation in the Barricades of 1991. He then moved to North America, to play with the San Jose Sharks. His departure paralleled that of many top Latvian players during the economic challenges following the restoration of Latvian independence. Dinamo Rīga was refounded in 2008, to take part in the Kontinental Hockey League, based around Russian clubs and playing its games at the 10,000 capacity Arēna Rīga. The club, however, withdrew from that league in February 2022 following the Russian invasion of Ukraine. The other major Latvian teams compete together with Estonian and Lithuanian counterparts in the Latvian Hockey League, though using smaller capacity venues. The strong performance of the men's national team in securing a third-place finish in the 2023 IIHF World Championship, whose early rounds were held in Latvia, was a cause of national celebration, and marked by the impromptu declaration of a national public holiday.

Basketball is also highly popular, helped by the tall stature of many Latvians. The most glorious moment for the men's national team came early, in 1935, when Latvia were the winners of the first ever European basketball championship, defeating Spain in the finals. In the Soviet period, the Rīgas ASK basketball club was a major force in the USSR Premier League. The exploits in the late 1950s of their 220cm centre, Jānis Krūmiņš, helped lead ASK to the top of that league, as well as bringing him membership of the Soviet national team. The TTT Rīga basketball club, founded in 1958, established Rīga as a dominant place for women's basketball in the Soviet period, as ASK had done for the men's game. Their iconic figure was another giant, Uljana Semjonova. Some 213cm tall, she was regarded as the best women's basketball player in the world in much of the 1970s and 1980s, securing Olympic gold medals as part of the Soviet team in 1976 and 1980. Latvia's performance in the 2023 FIBA Basketball World Cup provided a more recent moment of celebration – a highly creditable fifth place.

Sporting pursuits that allow Latvians to enjoy their forests and fens are popular, from orienteering in summer to cross-country skiing in winter. The construction in 1986 of the Sigulda bobsleigh, luge and skeleton track to provide for the needs of the Soviet teams has facilitated ongoing Latvian strength in those winter sports. Given the bracing climate, one perhaps more unexpected arena of Latvian sporting strength is beach volleyball, the men's pair of Jānis Šmēdiņš and Mārtiņš Pļaviņš securing bronze at the London Olympics in 2012.

In some bars and other venues in Latvia you may see a wooden table with pockets in each corner, marked with lines. This is the board for **novuss**, a game that, like billiards, involves a cue stick. Here it is used to propel a puck at small discs, which you are trying to get into the pockets. Novuss is associated with Latvia and Estonia, developing here in the 1920s from a pastime of British sailors – a good shipboard game as the flat discs were less prone than billiard balls to move across the table in rough seas. The game in Britain had, in turn, been adapted from an Indian game known as carrom.

2

Practical Information

WHEN TO VISIT

The summer months between late May and early September are peak tourist season in Latvia. Days are long, with delightful light evenings, temperatures are warm but rarely oppressive, and this is also the time of year when Latvia's festivals tend to cluster. Latvian school summer holidays are long, typically covering the three months of June, July and August, and many Latvians choose summer holidays domestically, to take advantage of the climate, reserving foreign getaways for the cold winter months. The Midsummer celebrations in late June are a particular domestic tourism peak. While accommodation prices are higher and availability tighter than at other times of the year, you should have no difficulty finding somewhere to fit your pocket if you book in advance.

Autumn, from late September until mid-November, offers lower prices, colourful displays of autumn leaves (the Gauja National Park has a well-deserved reputation for a vibrant display), and traditional pastimes such as mushroom picking. Latvia's weather is, though, at its most unpredictable, and you should be prepared for some cold and rainy days.

Winter offers days ranging from fairytale panoramas of sunny skies and freshly dusted snow to gloomy, dark and cold. Nights draw in early, and ensuring that you bring suitably warm and water-resistant clothing becomes an essential part of your enjoyment of the experience. While winter is the low season for tourism in Latvia, there are some draws. These include a welcoming Christmas market in Rīga, a city billing itself as the birthplace of the decorated Christmas tree, and opportunities to enjoy winter pursuits from husky dog sledding to descending the Sigulda bobsleigh track in a soft bob.

In spring, from late March to early May, Latvia emerges with relief from the long, cold months, people shedding drab winter colours in favour of a polychrome wardrobe. Celebrations of Easter, and of flowering blossoms, such as the lilac festival in Dobele, mark the optimism of the season, though the weather can be unpredictable, with late snows still possible. Both spring and autumn are good seasons for birdwatching in Latvia, as this is the time of the bird migrations.

HIGHLIGHTS

For many visitors to Latvia, Rīga is the only place they see. Latvia's capital does indeed make a delightful destination, with the combination of its Old Town and the Art Nouveau buildings across the city centre the main draw. But there is a great deal more to Latvia. Easy day trips from Rīga include the beach resort of Jūrmala, with its finely carved wooden villas, and the Baroque palace of Rundāle. Further afield, the Gauja National Park in Vidzeme offers a winning combination of natural beauty, as the Gauja River cuts through Devonian sandstone amid undulating forests, and the historic towns of Cēsis and Sigulda. Top destinations in Kurzeme in the west include the charismatic port city and forthcoming European Culture Capital of Liepāja, and the laid-back UNESCO World Heritage-listed town of Kuldīga. To get well away from the usual tourist routes you could head to the eastern region of Latgale, home to the largely Russian-speaking city of Daugavpils, birthplace of abstract painter Mark Rothko, whose work can be admired in an innovative gallery within the city's Tsarist fortress. Latvia is a fine destination for those looking for history and culture, for those wanting to immerse themselves in the great outdoors of forests, peat bogs and long expanses of often deserted sandy beaches, and for those looking to do a bit of both.

SUGGESTED ITINERARIES

A WEEKEND Rīga is a great option for a weekend break from Europe, with good flight connections to many European capitals. Spend the first day wandering the Old Town, combined with a visit to the salutary Museum of the Occupation of Latvia, and take in the city centre on the second, including the Art Nouveau showcase of Alberta iela and the National Museum of Art. A performance at the Latvian National Opera and Ballet or dinner at one of the restaurants helping to develop a distinctive Latvian cuisine provides a fine end to the day. Make it a long weekend and add in a trip to the beach at Jūrmala or a visit to the Baroque palace of Rundāle.

ONE WEEK You could base yourself for the first half of the week in Rīga, with a day trip to Jūrmala and another combining Rundāle Palace and Bauska Castle. For the second half of the week, one good option would be the Gauja National Park. You could plump for a mix of nature and history, with a day in Sigulda, taking the bus to Turaida Castle and walking back into town via Gutman's Cave, another in the picture-postcard town of Cēsis, and a third exploring the diverse attractions in and around scenic Līgatne. Or you could head west to Kurzeme, visiting the port towns of Liepāja and Ventspils, both boasting attractive beaches and plenty of historical interest, as well as the UNESCO-listed town of Kuldīga, where in spring you may enjoy the spectacle of fish leaping up Europe's widest waterfall.

TWO WEEKS A couple of weeks gives you time to do all the above, and additionally take in one of the less known regions of Latvia. You might opt for eastern Vidzeme, combining the attractive town of Alūksne with a trip on the narrow-gauge railway to the neighbouring district capital of Gulbene. Or you could explore the eastern region of Latgale, including Latvia's second city, Daugavpils, and the Catholic Basilica in the village of Aglona.

THREE WEEKS Three weeks gives you time for an in-depth visit covering all regions of the country.

TOUR OPERATORS

AUSTRALIA
Utracks w utracks.com. Walking & cycling specialists, offering guided & self-guided regional cycling packages.

LATVIA
Baltic Country Holidays w celotajs.lv. Will help put together tailored programmes with rural accommodation across the country, including

If your interests lie in an energetic holiday in the midst of nature, one option would be to walk one or more sections of one of the two long-distance footpaths, the Baltic Trails, which traverse Latvia as part of long European routes. The **Forest Trail** (Mežtaka) is part of the E11 hiking route. It enters Latvia north of the Lithuanian town of Skuodas, running through Kurzeme to Kuldīga, and thence eastwards along the Abava Valley to Rīga, the Gauja National Park and Valmiera, running eastwards just south of the Estonian border, before finally crossing into Estonia. The total trail length within Latvia is 674km, which amounts to a trip of between 31 and 38 days if you opt for the whole trail, using the recommended sections which divide the route into chunks of approximately 20km a day, and which aim to generate overnight stops close to accommodation options. The **Baltic Coastal Hiking Route** (Jūrtaka) is part of the E9 long-distance path running, as the name suggests, the full length of the Latvian coast as part of the 10,000km European Coastal Path, the longest coastal trail in the world. It stretches for 581km within Latvia, a walk of 30 days if you take the recommended section a day. An excellent website (w baltictrails. eu) provides detailed information on both trails, with section-by-section coverage including accommodation and catering options, as well as details of public transport to allow you to get there and away if your ambitions run to just one section.

The route is marked by signs painted on trees along the forest trail of three horizontal bands, respectively white, orange and white, or orange trail stickers in urban areas. For the coastal trail, the corresponding signs have white, blue and white bands, or blue stickers. A 'hiker-friendly' (Gājējam draudzīgs) sign provides an indication that the establishment may offer the kind of services hikers need, like drinking water, the opportunity to charge electronic devices or to wash clothing.

Another long-distance trail is the **Camino Latvia** (w caminolatvia.com), running from Valka on the Estonian border, through Valmiera and Sigulda to Rīga, and thence south to Lithuania in one of two routes – a western option through Dobele or an eastern one via Ķegums and Skaistkalne. This is the Latvian stretch of the Camino de Santiago, the great pilgrimage route terminating in Santiago de Compostela in northwestern Spain. This trail has also been divided up into sections of approximately 20km, with accommodation suggestions listed on the website, though at the time of writing some stretches were not yet fully signposted on the ground. On those that are, the yellow seashell symbol of St James on a blue background guides your path. That and GPS.

options for birdwatching, hiking & visiting local artisans.

Baltic Travel Group w baltic.travel. Can set up tailored programmes in Latvia for groups & individuals.

RigaTours.lv w rigatours.lv. Provides tailored itineraries, as well as small group scheduled tours (May–Oct).

UK

Baltic Holidays w balticholidays.com. Specialists in tailored itineraries in the Baltic States. Also offer small group tours to the Baltic capitals.

Exodus w exodus.co.uk. Offers a 12-day guided group tour of the Baltic States & an 11-day cycling itinerary.

Explore w explore.co.uk. Offers 1-week & 2-week Baltic highlights tours, as well as walking & cycling programmes.

Kirker Holidays w kirkerholidays.com. Offers high-end short breaks in Rīga & a tailor-made programme to the 3 Baltic capitals.

Martin Randall Travel w martinrandall.com. Cultural travel specialists, offering a 2-week group tour of the history, art & architecture of the Baltics.

Naturetrek w naturetrek.co.uk. Offers birdwatching tours to Latvia, to capture the spring migration at Cape Kolka.

Regent Holidays w regent-holidays.co.uk. Highly regarded UK operator offering private &

group tours & itineraries to Latvia and the other Baltic states.

TravelLocal w travellocal.com. A UK-based website where you can book direct with selected local travel companies, allowing you to communicate with a ground operator without having to go through a 3rd-party travel operator or agent. Your booking with the local company has full financial protection, but note that travel to the destination is not included. Member of ABTA, ASTA.

USA
Vytis Tours w vytistours.com. Offers small group tours of the Baltic States.

RED TAPE

Latvia is both a member of the European Union and one of the countries of the Schengen area. If you are a national of a fellow Schengen country, which includes most EU member states plus Iceland, Liechtenstein, Norway and Switzerland, there is little red tape involved in a visit beyond the strong recommendation to have your passport or identity document with you as proof of identity. This will be needed, for example, when registering at a hotel. Note that a driving licence is not considered an acceptable personal identity document in this context. If you are crossing into Latvia from another Schengen country there are no border checks, except in the unlikely event of a temporary reintroduction of border controls around a serious threat to security. Driving into Latvia from Estonia or Lithuania you will barely notice the border crossing at all.

EU citizens wishing to stay longer than 90 days in Latvia are able to do so, but must register with the Latvian authorities.

Nationals of countries outside the Schengen area wishing to travel to Latvia need a passport, which must be valid for at least three months after the date you will be leaving the Schengen area. Note also that the passport must have been issued within the last ten years. This catches some travellers out: even if the expiry date quoted in the passport has not been reached, if the issue date is more than ten years ago it will not be accepted.

VISAS In addition to the above, a visa may be required. Countries whose citizens may enter Latvia as tourists without a visa include the United Kingdom, United States, Canada, Australia and New Zealand. The full list of countries is on the Latvian Ministry of Foreign Affairs website (w mfa.gov.lv). You are only able to stay in the territory of Latvia (and the Schengen area) for up to 90 days in any 180-day period. Your passport will be stamped when you enter and leave the Schengen area. It is important to ensure your passport is stamped to avoid any risk that you may be considered to have overstayed your 90-day limit. When entering Latvia, the border authorities may ask you to demonstrate proof of your accommodation, a return or onward ticket, travel insurance and proof that you have sufficient funds for your stay, though you are unlikely to get this level of questioning. From mid-2025 it is anticipated that travellers in the visa-exempt category will require an ETIAS travel authorisation in advance, obtained via the ETIAS website (w travel-europe.europa.eu).

If you need a visa because you are a national of a country not on the exempt list, but intend to stay in Latvia or the wider Schengen area for less than 90 days in a 180-day period, you can apply for a Schengen visa. You can fill out the Schengen visa application online. Further details are available on the Schengen visa website (w schengenvisainfo.com). You must, though, submit the printed application form together with supporting documents at the Latvian diplomatic mission in your country. If there isn't one, in some countries the embassy of another Schengen member state has agreed to represent Latvia for Schengen visa purposes. Otherwise, you will need to apply to the Latvian diplomatic mission covering your country remotely. If you want to stay in Latvia for more than 90 days, you will need a Latvian national visa rather than a Schengen visa. This is a requirement also for nationals of countries exempt from the requirement for a Schengen visa, including the United Kingdom. Full details of all the arrangements are given on the Ministry of Foreign Affairs website. Information about how to apply for a visa, including required documents, is also set out on the website of the Office of Citizenship and Migration Affairs (w pmlp.gov.lv). That organisation is also the place you will need to apply to if you want to extend your visa.

EMBASSIES The website of the Latvian Ministry of Foreign affairs (w mfa.gov.lv) offers a list of Latvia's diplomatic missions overseas with their contact details, as well as a list of both resident and non-resident foreign diplomatic missions in Latvia.

GETTING THERE AND AWAY

BY AIR Rīga International Airport (w riga-airport.com) is the largest international airport in the Baltic States and the major gateway to Latvia. Following the demise of a scheduled domestic service between Rīga and Liepāja it became the only airport in Latvia offering scheduled services. At the time of writing, the main scheduled services on offer were as follows.

Aegean Airlines w aegeanair.com. Operates a twice-weekly service to Athens.

airBaltic w airbaltic.com. The Latvian flag carrier, with a majority ownership from the Latvian government, airBaltic uses Rīga as its main hub, with additional bases in Tallinn, Vilnius & Tampere. It operates a fleet of Airbus A220 aircraft, with a lime-green-&-white livery (other than 3 planes painted each in the flag colours of Latvia, Lithuania & Estonia). It operates direct flights to many major European capitals, with a growing network of routes including a particularly strong range of destinations in Scandinavia and Germany, as well as 1 or 2 flights daily to London Gatwick. Aberdeen is also served as a seasonal destination.

British Airways w britishairways.com. Flies 3 times a week to London Heathrow.

Finnair w finnair.com. Operates 4 direct flights a day to Helsinki.

LOT Polish Airlines w lot.com. Operates between 1 & 3 flights daily to Warsaw.

Lufthansa w lufthansa.com. Operates 1 or 2 flights daily to Frankfurt.

Norwegian w norwegian.com. Operates scheduled services to Copenhagen & Oslo, as well as seasonally to Stockholm & Trondheim.

Ryanair w ryanair.com. After airBaltic, offers the most comprehensive range of destinations from Rīga. In the UK & Ireland there are scheduled services to London Stansted, Bristol, Dublin, East Midlands, Edinburgh, Leeds/Bradford & Manchester. Other destinations include Barcelona, Berlin, Prague, Rome, Stockholm, Vienna & Warsaw.

Transavia w transavia.com. Flies twice a week to Amsterdam.

Turkish Airlines w turkishairlines.com. Operates between 1 & 3 flights daily to Istanbul.

Uzbekistan Airways w uzairways.com. Flies 3 times a week to Tashkent.

BY TRAIN AND BUS If your desire is to arrive in Latvia by **international rail**, you are currently destined for disappointment, though change is in the air. The **Rail Baltica** project (w railbaltica.org) aims to provide a high-speed rail service running through the Baltic States from Tallinn to Warsaw, connecting the region with the wider European railway infrastructure. Crucially, the trains will run on the 1,435mm European standard gauge found in most of the rest of the EU, rather than the 1,520mm Russian gauge characteristic of the existing rail networks in the Baltic States, which date from the Tsarist Empire. There will be stations at both Rīga and Rīga Airport, as well as destinations in Estonia and Lithuania, including Tallinn and Vilnius. Construction is underway, with a target completion date of 2030.

Until the Rail Baltica project is complete, options for international rail travel to and from Latvia are modest. There are no longer passenger rail connections from Latvia to Russia or Belarus. The one train operating from Rīga to Estonia at the time of writing was the service from Rīga to Valga, the station for the town of Valka/Valga, which actually sits just across the Estonian border. From Valga, there are onward connections on Estonian Railways (Eesti Raudtee; w evr.ee). There were, though, discussions underway on a possible additional service from Rīga to the Estonian university city of Tartu. One daily train between Vilnius and Rīga via Jelgava, operated by Lithuanian Railways (w ltglink.lt), commenced operations in December 2023. By contrast, **international bus** services are well developed, and there are several options.

Ecolines w ecolines.net. Offer services from Rīga to European destinations including Amsterdam (3 a week; 33hrs 20mins), Berlin (3 a day; 20hrs 30mins), Prague; (daily 23 hrs 30mins), Tallinn (4 a day; 4hrs 30mins) & Vilnius (7 a day; 4hrs). At the time of writing, they were also offering services to Moscow & St Petersburg despite the difficult bilateral relationship with Russia. Buses are equipped with onboard toilets & Wi-Fi, & journeys longer than 350km have an onboard steward.

FlixBus w global.flixbus.com. Options include Kraków (14hrs 45mins), Tallinn (4hrs 30mins), Vienna (22hrs), Vilnius (4hrs), & Warsaw West (10hrs), with many onward connections from the latter. With its lime-green coaches, this is a low-cost (particularly if you book early), low-frills option.

Lux Express w luxexpress.eu. Offers frequent services between Rīga & both Vilnius & Tallinn (via Pärnu), as well as from Rīga Airport to Tartu via Rīga Bus Station & Valga. Buses have onboard toilets & Wi-Fi. They provide good value & a comfortable option for travel between the Baltic capitals. Rīga to Tallinn is around 4hrs 30mins, Rīga to Vilnius from 4hrs.

BY CAR If **driving** to Latvia, you will need a valid full driving licence, motor insurance and the car registration document. You must also be over 18. Drivers from some countries additionally require an international driving permit, but this does not include the UK, unless you still have a paper driving licence. The car must display the national identifier (eg: 'UK' for vehicles registered in the UK). If this is not included within your number plate you will need to affix a separate sticker. If your car is registered in the UK, note that if your number plate incorporates the old 'GB' identifier or the Euro symbol you will need to display a separate 'UK' sticker. If bringing your car from the UK, you will need headlamp converters for driving on the right. A warning triangle is also compulsory, and a fire extinguisher, first-aid kit and reflective jacket are recommended, as are spare bulbs for all external lights. When crossing by road from fellow Schengen area members Lithuania and Estonia you will often barely be aware of the border at all. Crossing into Russia and Belarus is a different story, and at the time of writing the UK Foreign, Commonwealth and Development Office advised against all travel to Russia and Belarus.

BY SEA There are currently no scheduled ferries serving the Latvian capital. However, **Stena Line** (w stenaline.com) operates ferries to the two main ports in Kurzeme. There are one or two sailings daily between Ventspils and Nynäshamn in Sweden (around 10hrs), and a daily service between Liepāja and Travemünde (around 22hrs) on Germany's Baltic coast.

Rīga is, however, visited by **cruise ships**. The Baltic Sea is an important cruise ship destination, ringed by historic port cities a short sailing distance apart. In the wake of the Russian invasion of Ukraine many operators have removed St Petersburg from their Baltic itineraries. Rīga has in some cases been added, as operators sought out alternative destinations to compensate for the loss of St Petersburg. The following companies are among those cruise operators offering packages including Rīga.

Azamara Cruises w azamara.com. Offers tours of Baltic capitals commencing in Copenhagen & finishing in either Stockholm or Southampton.
Crystal w crystalcruises.com. Rīga is one of the stops on a 10-night Stockholm to Copenhagen cruise.
MSC Cruises w msccruises.com. A Baltic cities & Copenhagen cruise, starting from the Danish capital, including Rīga.

Norwegian Cruise Line w ncl.com. Cruises incorporating Rīga including Baltic cities itineraries starting in both Oslo & Stockholm.
Oceania Cruises w oceaniacruises.com. Rīga is covered in Stockholm-to-Copenhagen & Southampton-to-Stockholm cruises.
Princess Cruises w princess.com. If the open waters are really your thing, you can take in Rīga as part of a mammoth 110-night world cruise starting & finishing in Sydney.

HEALTH   *with Dr Daniel Campion*

The standard of public health in Latvia overall is generally good and tap water is safe to drink.

PREPARATIONS There are no legally required **vaccinations** to enter Latvia. You should, however, ensure that you are up to date with routine vaccinations recommended in your home country, including influenza and Covid-19. As everywhere, it is sensible to ensure that you are protected against tetanus. In the UK, this is provided in a single vaccine that also covers diphtheria and polio. Other vaccinations that may be recommended depending on your length of stay, lifestyle and planned activities when in Latvia include hepatitis A, hepatitis B, rabies and tick-borne encephalitis. If you are a national of an EU member state or Iceland, Liechtenstein, Norway or Switzerland, you should obtain the (free) **European Health Insurance Card** (EHIC). This allows you to receive medical treatment on the same basis as locals if this becomes necessary during your visit. UK residents can apply for the UK Global Health Insurance Card (UK GHIC), which is also free. Note, though, that these cards are not an alternative to travel insurance and do not cover such health-related costs as medical repatriation or any private treatment, so it is still important to take out travel insurance appropriate to your needs.

Travel clinics and health information A full list of current travel clinic websites worldwide is available on w istm.org. For other journey preparation information, consult w travelhealthpro.org.uk (UK) or w wwwnc.cdc.gov/travel (USA). All advice found online should be used in conjunction with expert advice received prior to or during travel.

MEDICAL PROBLEMS

Insect- and tick-borne diseases While mosquitoes can be an annoyance in summer, those in Latvia are carriers of neither malaria nor dengue fever, and the creature you should be more worried about is the **tick**. Usually found in forests and long grass they are, less frequently, even found in city parks, and can be encountered from April to October, although as the climate changes, the tick season has tended to lengthen. Ticks in Latvia can carry a range of diseases, and some local estimates suggest that at least 5% of tick bites may result in a disease.

Tick-borne encephalitis is a disease of the central nervous system: if you are planning to spend a lot of time in forests and rural areas while in Latvia you may well wish to consider the vaccine against it. In the UK, this is a three-dose vaccine given over 6–12 months. If time is short, two doses 14 days apart can give good short-term protection.

There is, however, currently no vaccine available for other tick-borne diseases such as Lyme disease, which is why it is important to do all you can to avoid tick bites. When walking in the forest or areas of long grass, wear long-sleeved shirts, long trousers, boots and socks, and a hat, and use insect repellent which should contain either DEET or picaridin. Inspect yourself and your clothing after your walk for any ticks. A hot shower and use of a washcloth may help remove any unattached ticks.

If a tick has embedded itself in your skin, it is important to remove it as quickly as possible in the correct way (see below). The risk of infection increases the longer the tick is in place. Devices specifically designed to assist in the removal of ticks – such as metal tweezers and a notched plastic card about the size of a credit card – are available in Latvian pharmacies.

Rabies Rabies virus is not found in domestic pets in Latvia and was last detected in wildlife in 2012. However, bats can still carry rabies-like viruses and other mammals could reintroduce rabies from neighbouring countries: foxes in Latvia are considered high risk by the UK Health Security Agency.

Rabies is spread through the saliva of an infected animal and is usually transmitted through a bite or a scratch. If this unlikely event should occur, wash the wound with soap and water for at least 10 minutes and then immediately seek medical advice.

TICK REMOVAL

Ticks should ideally be removed complete, and as soon as possible, to reduce the chance of infection. You can use special tick tweezers, which can be bought in good travel shops; or failing this, with your fingernails, grasp the tick as close to your body as possible, and pull it away steadily and firmly at right angles to your skin without jerking or twisting. Applying irritants (eg: Olbas oil) or lit cigarettes is to be discouraged as a means of removal since they can cause the ticks to regurgitate and therefore increase the risk of disease. Once the tick is removed, if possible douse the wound with alcohol (any spirit will do), soap and water, or iodine. If you are travelling with small children, remember to check their heads and particularly behind the ears for ticks. Spreading redness around the bite and/or fever and/or aching joints after a tick bite imply that you have an infection that requires antibiotic treatment. In this case seek medical advice.

MEDICAL TREATMENT Rīga is home to several private clinics, offering English-speaking doctors, as well as diagnostic services and vaccinations. These include the **ARS medical centre** (Skolas iela 5; w arsmed.lv), **Capital Clinic Rīga** (Duntes iela 15A; w capitalclinicriga.lv) and **Veselības Centrs 4** (Krišjāņa Barona iela 117; w vc4. lv). The best-known hospital is the **Pauls Stradiņš Clinical University Hospital** (w stradini.lv) in Rīga. There are many pharmacies in Rīga and other main towns: Mēness and Benu are among the best-known chains.

The number to call in the event of a medical emergency is ☏113.

SAFETY

Latvia is on the whole a safe country for visitors, with levels of street crime lower than in many European countries. You should, though, take the same safety precautions you would employ elsewhere. Be alive to the risks of pickpocketing, including on public transport, and the snatching of bags from bars and restaurants. To avoid the risk of drink spiking, do not accept drinks from strangers, and make sure not to leave your own drink unattended in bars and nightclubs. Use a guarded car park when parking, especially overnight, and avoid leaving bags and other belongings in visible locations in your car. Also avoid unlit areas at night, both for the risks associated with crime and those linked to uneven surfaces.

It is sensible practice to leave your passport in a trusted hotel safe where you can, but to carry a photocopy around with you.

Winter poses physical hazards. Icy roads and pavements represent significant risks. If you are driving in Latvia in winter, make sure your car is fitted with appropriate winter tyres. If on foot, ice grips worn over your regular footwear are helpful in providing a sureness of step. Icicles falling from rooftops present another winter risk, particularly during times of thaw. Be alert to the roofscape above you, and avoid walking too close to the side of buildings. In the warmer months, e-scooters and bicycles can constitute an additional danger on Rīga's pavements.

Latvia is a relatively safe destination for solo **female travellers**. Street harassment is uncommon. You should, though, adopt the same precautions you would take in any major European city.

TRAVELLING WITH A DISABILITY

The cobbled streets of Rīga Old Town and paucity of wheelchair-accessible lifts in many historic buildings present challenges to travellers with mobility problems. Outside the Old Town, most pavements are wide and smooth, with lowered kerbsides at crossings. Many city buses and trolleybuses in Rīga are wheelchair accessible, via an electronic ramp at the centre door, deployed by the driver when you press the button displaying a wheelchair icon on the side of the bus. Older-style trams in Rīga are, however, not wheelchair accessible. Public transportation in Rīga is free for people with a disability. The picture in other Latvian cities is variable. Most railway stations are not wheelchair accessible, and for those that are, you need to book assistance in advance. Finding a wheelchair-accessible toilet is a challenge everywhere in Latvia.

There is a useful guide titled 'Disability and Travel Abroad' prepared by the UK government and available on its website (w gov.uk/guidance/foreign-travel-for-disabled-people), offering much practical information. The website Wheelmap (w wheelmap.org) has an interactive global map showing accessible and partially accessible properties, including museums, hotels and restaurants. The Society for Accessible Travel and Hospitality (**w** sath.org) is another good source of general information.

LGBTQIA+ TRAVELLERS

Both male and female same-sex relationships are legal in Latvia, and the age of consent was equalised at 16 in 1999, regardless of sexual orientation. The appointment in July 2023 of Edgars Rinkēvičs as president meant that Latvia became the first EU country with an openly gay head of state. Nonetheless, LGBTQIA+ people in Latvia still face challenges. Same-sex marriage is not recognised, and indeed Latvia amended its Constitution in 2006 to specify that marriage represented 'a union between a man and a woman'. A 2020 ruling of the Constitutional Court in favour of parental leave rights for same-sex couples paved the way for legislation in November 2023 to legalise civil partnerships. The legislation covers social security, medical benefits and pensions, but does not tackle adoption or inheritance rules, so the LGBTQIA+ community in Latvia regards it as the beginning rather than the end of the story. Tolerance for the LGBTQIA+ community remains patchy, given social conservatism in Latvian society, criticism from some church groups, and the influence in the Russian-speaking community of homophobic content in Russian-language social media.

The **LGBT House Rīga** (Stabu iela 19-2; **w** lgbthouse.lv) is a centre for the LGBTQIA+ community, housing the non-governmental organisation Mozaīka and other support groups, as well as free HIV testing. They organise the **Rīga Pride** (**w** rigapride.lv) event every June. Every third year this is subsumed into the larger Baltic Pride, which rotates between the three Baltic capitals. There are few specifically gay venues in Latvia, and most of those are to be found in Rīga, but providing discretion is exercised outside these, LGBTQIA+ tourists are unlikely to face significant problems.

TRAVELLING WITH KIDS

Latvia is a good destination for travellers with children. Almost every town seems to boast a smart new playground, and there are plenty of more adventurous attractions for older children, like ziplines and rope walks. Many museums have child-friendly interactive exhibits. If driving, note that children under the age of 12 (or under 150cm in height or 36kg in weight) require child seats appropriate to their age and weight.

WHAT TO TAKE

Enjoyment of a winter holiday in Latvia requires ensuring that you have adequately **warm clothing**, including gloves, hat and boots. There are plenty of clothing stores in the country with the right gear, but a good outdoor adventure store in your home country will have what you need to ensure you are properly insulated from the outset. Boots with built-in reversible spikes, or ice traction devices you fit over your ordinary shoes or boots, such as Yaktrax (**w** yaktrax.com), can help tackle icy roads and pavements in winter. In summer, **insect repellent** is an important addition to your baggage, particularly if you are planning to spend time out of town. Make sure you come with adequate stocks of **prescription medicine**.

Latvian electrical sockets are the two round pin variety, common in much of northern and central Europe. They fit both the type C and 'Schuko', or type F plugs.

If your appliances are based on a different system, such as that in the UK, remember to take **plug adaptors**. The standard voltage is 230V.

MONEY AND BUDGETING

MONEY The Latvian currency has been the **euro** since 2014, replacing the Latvian lats. The latter is still viewed nostalgically, as a symbol of Latvia's hard-won independence. The designs of the first lats coins and notes, introduced in 1922, owed much to Rihards Zariņš, head of the national printing press. The five lats coin, portraying a rural maid, known as Milda, was particularly loved. In the 1980s, surviving 'Milda' coins, often preserved as pendants or brooches, became a symbol of the Latvian National Reawakening.

The use of **debit or credit cards** has increasingly become the default means of making payments in Latvia, and both Visa and MasterCard are widely accepted. Nonetheless, you will still need some euros in **cash** for the increasingly small but still relevant number of outlets that do not take cards, including on some types of public transport when buying tickets from the driver and because of a quirk of the tipping system in Latvia. Restaurants are generally unable to accept tips added to the bill on a card. Instead, you should leave a tip in cash. **Tipping** is not necessary if a service charge is included, and should in any case not be lavish, perhaps up to around 10% of the bill.

ATMs are reasonably plentiful, especially in main towns, and accept both Visa and MasterCard credit and debit cards. Banks and exchange offices can also be used to exchange money, though check the rate on offer. Note that outside the main towns, many banks have restricted opening hours. The website w xe.com is a good place to find the latest exchange rate.

BUDGETING While holidays in Latvia are cheaper than many European locations, the country is increasingly Nordic in aspirations and expectations, and it is no longer accurate to view Latvia as a low-cost destination overall.

If you are travelling on a shoestring, you might budget €30 a day on a mix of hostel dormitory beds, cheap hotels and guest houses and camping, €25 for food and drink, and €15 to cover public transport, museum charges and the like, to a total of €70 a day. A mid-range budget might average €70 on hotels, €55 on food and drink, and €25 on other costs, to a total of €150 a day. A higher-end budget might average €100 on hotels, €70 on food and drink, and €50 on other costs, to include a concert or other evening entertainment, to a total of €220 a day. As ever, these are just vague guidelines, as the amount you spend will depend on the number and type of activities you plump for, whether you are travelling alone or

AVERAGE PRICES	
Litre of bottled water	€0.60 (including €0.10 deposit, redeemable by feeding the empty bottle into collection machines in large supermarkets)
50cl beer	€2.20 (including €0.10 deposit)
Loaf of bread	€1.50
Pastry	€1.50
T-shirt	€16.00
Litre of petrol	€1.75

accompanied, and how much time you are planning to spend in Rīga. Costs of both accommodation and food tend to be higher in the capital than elsewhere. There is also a seasonal price differential, with accommodation rates typically lower outside the summer peak.

GETTING AROUND

Latvia's generally flat terrain, good network of footpaths and picturesque, gently flowing rivers all favour more active travel options. Tourist information offices offer up-to-date advice on local **bicycle hire** and other adventurous travel possibilities, and some of the tour operators listed on page 35 offer walking and cycling packages.

BY TRAIN The railway network in Latvia is managed by the state-owned Latvijas dzelzceļš. The network is based on the 1,520mm Soviet gauge, reflecting its origins in the Tsarist Russian Empire, save for a stretch of narrow-gauge track connecting the towns of Gulbene and Alūksne and the forthcoming Rail Baltica high-speed link, which aims to connect the three Baltic States. Passenger services are operated by Pasažieru vilciens (w pv.lv), a separate but also state-owned company.

Rīga is the hub of passenger train routes in Latvia, which offers a widely differing frequency of service. Among the most useful is the electric line from Rīga to Tukums, stopping at various stations through the long resort of Jūrmala, with departures every 30 minutes at peak times. The northern coastal route from Rīga to Saulkrasti, with some trains going further to Skulte, is another helpful service, with at least one departure hourly through the day. Jelgava is also well served from Rīga. The route southeastwards from Rīga along the Daugava maintains a frequent service as far as Aizkraukle, to which point electric trains operate, but the service to stations further east is patchier. Routes to Daugavpils and Kraslava, Rēzekne and Zilupe and Madona and Gulbene, are covered by infrequent services requiring careful planning. The frequency on the onward route through Kurzeme from Jelgava to Liepāja is particularly poor. The route from Rīga to Valga, just across the Estonian border, helpfully takes in key towns around the Gauja National Park, including Sigulda, Cēsis and Valmiera.

You can purchase tickets at ticket offices in railway stations, online through the Pasažieru vilciens website or Mobilly (w mobilly.lv) and Bezrindas (w bezrindas. lv) apps, and also on the train. If you buy onboard, however, note that you pay a small additional fee if the ticket office was open at the station at which you boarded. If travelling with a bicycle, or particularly large items of baggage, you need to purchase a baggage ticket. Wheelchairs, prams, skis and fishing rods are exempt. Coaches fitted with bike holders have a label on the door. Some long-distance trains, particularly those serving Rēzekne, Daugavpils and Krāslava, have a 'comfort class' option, with assigned seating, a table to work at and an electricity socket. While not a huge step up in terms of comfort, the additional fee is modest (€1.40 at the time of writing). Ticket prices are low by European standards. At the time of writing, a single ticket from Rīga to Sigulda was €1.89, to Valmiera €3.96 and to Daugavpils €6.53. Journeys are stately rather than speedy, and generally don't offer a significant time saving over bus travel.

BY BUS Latvia has an extensive bus network, reaching out into small villages around the country. The frequency of service to smaller places is, however, understandably limited, so you need to pay particular attention to timetables to avoid getting stranded at that scenic spot. Tickets can be purchased at ticket offices at bus stations, from the driver if there are still seats available, and online through the Mobilly and Bezrindas apps. Ticket prices are typically higher than the equivalent journey by train. Thus at the time of writing, a single ticket from Rīga to Sigulda was €3.00, to Valmiera €5.48 and to Daugavpils €10.21. One advantage of travelling by bus, though, is that railway stations are often peripherally located, while bus stations tend to be more central. The 1188 (w 1188.lv) website has timetable information.

BY CAR Bringing your own car, or renting one, gives you the freedom to explore the country as a whole. Many country manors and other rural destinations simply do not lend themselves to public transport. Roads are generally good quality, though forest roads are usually unmetalled and can become muddy after rain. Driving in Latvia is on the right-hand side of the road. You are required to drive with your lights on at all times. There are no road tolls in Latvia, other than the fee to enter the resort town of Jūrmala during the summer. Speed limits are typically 50km/h in urban areas (and just 20km/h in designated residential areas), 90km/h in the open countryside and 100km/h on certain dual carriageways. Driving in winter requires winter tyres and special care.

Car rental At Rīga airport, there is a cluster of **car rental** offices waiting for you in the arrival hall for flights from within the Schengen area. If you are arriving from the UK or another destination outside Schengen, you need to go to arrival gate E to find car rental. At the time of writing, Avis (w avis.lv), Budget (w budget. lv), EasyCars (w easycars.lv), Enterprise (w enterprise.lv), Europcar (w europcar. lv), Greenmotion (w greenmotion.com), Hertz (w hertz.com), Sixt (w sixt.lv) and TopRent (w toprent.lv) all had a presence at the airport.

Several of these also offer other collection and delivery points in Latvia, including Rīga bus and train stations. To rent a car, you need a full, valid driver's licence and another form of ID, like your passport. You generally need to be at least 21 years of age, though rules vary by provider, and many companies apply a young driver surcharge to drivers under 25. Some companies additionally insist that you have held your licence for a minimum period, usually one year. Travellers from some countries need an international driving permit, but many do not, including other EU countries and also the USA and UK (unless you only have the old-style paper licence). Note that seatbelts are compulsory for all passengers. Car rental companies will provide child seats or boosters if needed (page 43) for an additional fee.

ACCOMMODATION

Rīga offers a good range of **hotels**, from well-known international chains to stylish Old Town boutique offerings, and there is a strong selection in Jūrmala and Liepāja too. In all three places, the selection is richer at the top than the budget range. Outside these major destinations, the hotel offer is thinner. Most towns of any size boast a centrally located concrete block, dating from the Soviet era but having undergone various degrees of modernisation, and which provides a functional if unexciting place to stay.

One more-interesting accommodation option found across rural Latvia is the restored **manor houses** (muižas), once the country homes of the German-Baltic aristocracy. The best combine good accommodation in rooms redecorated to recreate their 19th-century heyday with fine restaurants and spas. The Covid-19 pandemic was tough on these places, and some had closed their doors at the time

ACCOMMODATION PRICE CODES

Average price of a double room in high season.

€€€€€	Over €200
€€€€	€120–200
€€€	€80–120
€€	€40–80
€	Less than €40

of writing, among them the manors at Dikļi and Mežotne. But others have emerged on the scene. Note that these buildings typically had a hard time during the Soviet occupation, when many were put to work as schools, sanatoria or even warehouses. In most cases, all original interior furnishings have been lost. Restoration work is a gradual business, and some are far less grand as accommodation options than their aristocratic exteriors might suggest. Of the smarter options, some are geared to weddings, so you might find you are sharing your idyllic rural retreat with a noisy party. Almost all are poorly served by public transport.

Given the relative paucity of hotel accommodation in many places, **house and apartment rentals** are another option, with a range of possibilities normally available through the main websites, particularly Booking.com (**w** booking.com) and Airbnb (**w** airbnb.com). Rooms in private **guesthouses** can provide a more homely option than the standard central hotel and are generally advertised on the Booking.com site. Guesthouse accommodation in Latvia covers a range of establishments, from what are essentially small hotels to homestays, where you find yourself in the spare room of the owner's house. Bathrooms and toilets may be shared. Some places offer a home-cooked breakfast for a usually modest extra charge. For stays at the more rustic end of the range, **Baltic Country Holidays** (**w** celotajs.lv) is focused on farmhouses and other rural retreats.

The death of nine people in a fire in 2021 at the Japanese Style Centrum hostel in Rīga highlighted failings at the bottom end of the **hostels** sector. There are, however, some welcoming and friendly hostel options, particularly in the capital, although the country is not part of the Hostelling International network. **Campsites** are often in fine locations along the coast or in a lakeside setting, and, in addition to places to pitch your tent or hook up your trailer, often offer self-standing accommodation options such as little wooden cottages. These range from places that appear to have been unrenovated since their Soviet-era heyday to sophisticated 'glamping' offers.

Latvia also offers good opportunities for **wild camping**, though there are some restrictions to bear in mind. It is permitted to pitch a tent or hang up a hammock in one of the public forests managed by the Latvia's State Forests (Latvijas valsts meži) organisation, accounting for around half of all forests in Latvia, other than those under special protection (identified by a green sign bearing an oak leaf). Yellow signs with the Latvian State Forests logo and a painted yellow band around trees indicate that you are on their land. You need of course to obey the rules of the forest, such as to avoid littering, and must apply in writing for permission if you plan to camp in one spot for more than a week or are coming in a group larger than 50. Camping in privately managed forests requires the permission of the owner. The rules around pitching tents on the coast are determined by the local municipality concerned and are generally less liberal.

Hammock camping offers an unrivalled opportunity to experience life in a Latvian forest, though the attentions of mosquitoes can be a significant nuisance. Attaching a mosquito net to a line strung above the hammock is recommended, as well as using plenty of repellent. Make sure, too, that you are not hanging your hammock beneath any potentially unsafe branches.

Hotel prices are highest in summer and in Rīga, where a high-end hotel room in high season will cost upwards of €150. In low season, expect to pay €100 upwards. Smarter coastal hotels in places like Jūrmala, Liepāja and Pāvilosta charge summer prices similar to Rīga. The renovated but functional main hotel of a district capital off the main tourist beat might set you back €80 in the summer, €60 in low season. At the other end of the scale, a dorm bed in Rīga in high season is around €20 and €12–14 in low season.

EATING AND DRINKING

FOOD Latvian cuisine draws from two main sources: the dishes of the Latvian peasantry, and the influence of occupying powers. It is focused on the crops and livestock that thrive in these temperate northern climes. The long winters encourage a diet high in butter and fat. They also stimulated the Latvian practice of conserving vegetables, with gherkins, tomatoes and mushrooms pickled in the autumn glut, to last through the tough winter months.

TEN CLASSIC LATVIAN DISHES

BLOOD SAUSAGE (ASINSDESA) This rich sausage, typically served with lingonberry jam and sour cream, often crops up on the menus of Medieval-themed restaurants. The sausage is usually made from pork blood and fried in a pan. A similar dish is the groat sausage (putraimu desa), where the blood-soaked sausage filling is made of barley groats.

BUKSTIŅBIEZPUTRA A warming dish typically served in the winter, this is made from barley groats, potatoes, onion and milk or cream, mixed into a porridge. It is served with bacon and onion, and dill sprinkled over the top.

COLD BORSCHT (AUKSTĀ ZUPA) This distinctive pink-coloured cold soup heralds the arrival of summer. Ingredients include kefir or soured milk, beetroot, radishes, cucumbers, boiled eggs and loads of dill. Meat is sometimes also added.

GREY PEAS WITH BACON (PELĒKIE ZIRŅI AR SPEĶI) This hearty dish is centred on Latvia's big grey peas, a much-loved local product, holding EU Protected Designation of Origin status. They are cooked with bacon and onion, making a heavy winter meal, particularly associated with Christmas. Eat every one of those peas to safeguard your good luck in the New Year. It is typically served with kefir or sour milk to leaven the greasiness.

HERRING IN A FUR COAT (SIĻĶE KAŽOKĀ) A salad involving diced pickled herring smothered with layers of potatoes, beetroots, eggs and carrots, plus onions and mayonnaise. A top layer of grated beetroot and mayonnaise is typically used to give the salad a pleasing purple colour. It is a dish found across the former Soviet Union.

Bread has a vital place in the Latvian diet. Dark **rye bread** (rudzu maize) holds centre stage, made with rye flour, malt and caraway seeds. Another popular bread is **saldskābmaize**, literally 'sweet and sour bread', made from finely ground rye flour, with caraway seeds. Bread made from wheat was traditionally regarded as a delicacy. There are numerous variations, and Latvians love to experiment with their bread by adding fruit, nuts and seeds. Bread was so important in the traditional Latvian diet that there are various superstitions associated with it. Thus if you accidentally drop a piece of bread on the floor, pick it up and kiss it so as not to offend God. Fried rye bread with garlic (ķiploku graudziņi) served with mayonnaise is a common pub snack. Little savoury pies known as **pīrāgi** or **pīrādziņi** are widely available in Latvian bakeries. The classic form is a crescent-shaped pie filled with cubes of bacon and onion, sometimes referred to as speķrausi, but there are many other fillings, including sauerkraut and cottage cheese.

In 2021, the Latvian Investment and Development Agency produced a promotional video devoted to the importance of the **potato** in Latvian culture, featuring two young men enjoying potato-related meals around the country. Potatoes served with herring and cottage cheese, garnished with dill, makes for a simple but classic Latvian dish. Beets and other root vegetables are also popular, as is cabbage. Plants foraged from forests, including berries and especially mushrooms, are ingredients of many classic Latvian dishes. **Soups** are popular, including mushroom soup (sēņu zupa) and the greenish sorrel soup (skābeņu zupa), the latter

LAYERED RYE BREAD (RUPJMAIZES KĀRTOJUMS) This dessert involves layers of toasted rye breadcrumbs, flavoured with cinnamon and sugar, interspersed with jam and whipped cream. The dessert is then topped with sprinkled rye breadcrumbs or sometimes fresh berries. The overall effect is something like a trifle, but distinctively Latvian.

POTATOES WITH CHANTERELLE SAUCE (KARTUPEĻI AR GAILEŅU MĒRCI) A simple but tasty dish of boiled potatoes covered with a sauce of mushrooms foraged from the forest, and typically dressed with a sprinkling of dill.

POTATO PANCAKES (KARTUPEĻU PANKŪKAS) A ubiquitous dish, made with grated potatoes, flour and eggs, which are then fried. They may be served elaborately, for example, with smoked salmon and sour cream or duck and lingonberry jam, or as a simple savoury or sweet dish.

RASOLS A variant of a dish found across the former Soviet Union, this is a rich salad of potatoes, eggs and pickled vegetables, immersed in sour cream and mayonnaise. Every family has their own recipe, and many add cooked ham or sausage. There are regional variations such as the Valmiera Salad, which features cheese and tomato sauce, the latter giving the dish a pink hue. Just don't describe rasols as 'Russian salad'.

RYE BREAD SOUP (RUPJMAIZES ZUPA) Despite what the name might suggest, this is a dessert, not a savoury dish. Soggy rye bread is put through a sieve. Spices, sugar and dried fruit are added, and the dessert is served cold, topped with whipped cream.

sometimes described as 'green borscht', involving beef broth, pork, barley, onion, potato and sorrel, typically served with a halved boiled egg floating on the top. Among **meat** products, pork takes an important place, with the breaded and pan-fried **karbonāde** a central feature of more modest Latvian restaurants. Other meat dishes include **galerts**: a pork aspic, incorporating vegetables like carrot and celery. It is typically served with vinegar and horseradish.

Dairy products play a significant role in the Latvian diet, including the ubiquitous cottage cheese (biezpiens). Sour cream and soured milk appear in many recipes. Smoked cheese (kūpināts siers) makes a good snack with beer. Among **fish** dishes, seek out the smoked fish (kūpināta zivs) sold at small huts along the Baltic coast. Canned sprats in oil (šprotes eļļā) have been a noted Latvian export since the 19th century.

Latvian cuisine makes little use of spices, other than caraway and black pepper. Among herbs, **dill** takes centre stage. It is used to flavour almost everything, from fish to meat to salads.

Latvia offers many sweet pastries. Pride of place goes to the **kliņģeris**, shaped like a large pretzel and made with raisins, cardamom and saffron. It is typically served at festive occasions. Some bakeries also make savoury versions, flavoured with bacon and onions. **Alexandertorte** (Aleksandra kūka) involves two strips of pastry with raspberry jam in the middle, often topped with pink icing. It was created to commemorate Tsar Alexander III's visit to Rīga. **Gingerbread** (piparkūkas) is a staple of Christmas markets.

Many dishes on Latvian menus reflect the period of Soviet occupation, and Latvia's place in the Tsarist Empire before that. **Shashlik** (šašliks) is a dish originally from the South Caucasus, found across the former Soviet Union, involving cubes of meat, marinated in vinegar, skewered and grilled over a barbecue. Soups such as **borscht**, originating in Ukraine, and **solyanka**, a sour soup involving pickled cucumbers, meat, tomatoes, onions and dill, are popular. The **curd snack** (biezpiena sieriņš), a dessert known in Russian as a *tvorozhniy syrok*, is a bar of curd cheese mixed with sugar, and coated in chocolate or another sweet glaze. They were mass-produced in the Soviet Union from the 1950s. The best-known Latvian variety is *Kārums*. They are available in a huge range of flavours, though the chocolate-covered vanilla variety is the classic version.

DRINK The most popular alcoholic drink in Latvia is **beer**. Breweries typically offer a lager (gaišais) and dark beer (tumšais). The best-known varieties include Aldaris, Cesu and Lacplešis, but Latvia also has many smaller breweries with dedicated local followings and a more interesting range of products. Among those to look out for are Valmiermuižas from Valmiera, Užavas, made at a brewery south of Ventspils, and Tērvetes, from the village of that name in Zemgale. **Cider** production started to develop following the restoration of independence, and there are several good craft producers, among them Abavas, Abuls, Mr Plūme and Tālavas. The Abava valley claims to possess the world's northernmost vineyard, and Abavas, which uses the dragonfly as its symbol, is perhaps the best-known Latvian **wine** producer. Their output is by no means all derived from grapes: among their most interesting products is a semi-sweet rhubarb wine.

A liqueur that is something of a calling card for Latvia, although an acquired taste, is **Rīga Black Balsam**. This bitter herbal drink was created in Rīga in 1752 by apothecary Abraham Kunze and initially viewed as medicine rather than alcohol. Legend has it that black balsam administered to Catherine the Great, who had fallen sick while visiting Rīga, proved most efficacious, bolstering its popularity as a curative. A merchant named Semyon Leluchin refocused the drink for general

RESTAURANT PRICE CODES

Average price of a main dish, including sides.

€€€€€	Over €25
€€€€	€15–25
€€€	€10–15
€€	€6–10
€	Less than €6

alcoholic consumption at the end of the century, and the popularity of black balsam continued to grow. Disaster nearly struck during the exodus of ethnic Germans ahead of the first Soviet occupation in 1940, when the secret recipe was apparently lost. Fortunately for balsam lovers, it was carefully recreated in the Soviet period. The drink is said to contain 24 ingredients, including various roots and herbs. It is now available in additional flavours designed to appeal to a wider range of palates, including blackcurrant, cherry and even a chocolate and mint flavour. Sold in a distinctive ceramic bottle, it is one of the best-known Latvian souvenir gifts, though one destined all too often to languish at the back of the recipient's drinks cabinet.

Other drinks worth looking out for include **kvass**, traditionally made from fermented rye bread, typically having an alcohol content of no more than 1%. In spring, you will find plastic bottles of **birch sap** (bērzu sula) for sale in markets, its taste rather like a slightly sweet water when consumed fresh.

EATING OUT A **restorāns** is, logically enough, a restaurant, though this category of eatery is by no means the only place to get a meal, particularly if you are looking for a cheaper bite. The **kafejnīca** is the most confusing category of places to eat, covering simple cafés serving only hot drinks and pastries, through places that additionally serve simple lunches of sandwiches, soups and salads, to those that are essentially restaurants, with full menus. The latter tend towards simpler and heartier dishes than those found in a restorāns, but there are no hard rules. A **konditoreja** will certainly stick to cakes and pastries.

If you are on a tight budget, one type of place to look out for is the **ēdnīca**. This is a canteen, where you take your tray and choose from the ready-cooked options behind the counter. Typically, a server will ladle out your chosen stew and potatoes, or hand you a karbonāde, while you simply take a small ready-prepared bowl of mayonnaise-heavy salad or dessert such as rupjmaizes kārtojums. They can be fairly soulless places but are cheap, and are often good spots to find traditional Latvian dishes that rarely grace the menus of fancier joints. A **pusdienotava**, or lunchery, is typically a smarter ēdnīca. The Lido chain in and around Rīga deserves a special mention: essentially upmarket ēdnīcas. A **krogs** is a pub. Again, this category covers both places offering no food other than bar snacks, and establishments offering a full menu, with restaurants putting the accent on beer rather than wine.

MEALS **Breakfast** (brokastis) is not a big deal in Latvia. Your hotel will typically serve a standard international affair of bread, sliced cold meats and cheese, smoked salmon and perhaps pickled herring, cereal, fruit and a couple of dishes in warming pans. Eating out, the challenge can be to find somewhere serving breakfast, but those kafejnīcas that do often feature omelettes, pancakes, toasted sandwiches and porridge. At **lunch** (pusdienas), particularly during the working week, look out

Practical Information   EATING AND DRINKING

2

for restaurants and cafés serving set lunches. Designed to attract a local working clientele, the price of these is usually substantially lower than the standard menu. Menus otherwise rarely differ as between lunch and **dinner** (vakariņas).

There is a wide choice of eating options in Rīga, offering Latvian and numerous international cuisines. Jūrmala, Liepāja and Cēsis all have a strong range of good places to eat, and in other major tourist centres like Ventspils, Kuldīga and Sigulda, you will have no difficulty finding a pleasant place to dine. Outside the main centres, the range of options reduces markedly. If you spend much time in less touristy small towns, you will find yourself eating an awful lot of karbonāde. Be aware that in smaller centres, eating options tend to close early in the evening.

PUBLIC HOLIDAYS AND FESTIVALS

The calendar of public holidays draws on three main influences: religious and other internationally observed festivities, events linked to the changing seasons, and commemorations of significant events in the securing and restoration of Latvian independence. Outside of the key events on the annual calendar, listed below, the most important and impressive Latvian celebration is the Song and Dance Festival, held every five years (page 54). Almost every town commemorates its City Day with concerts, parades and other homespun fun. These tend to cluster in the warmer summer months, which is the peak period for festivals of all kinds, from political discussion fora like the LAMPA conversation festival in Cēsis, to music festivals like Positivus in Rīga and Summer Sound in Liepāja.

NEW YEAR'S DAY (Jaunais Gads; 1 Jan; public holiday) As elsewhere, New Year's Day in Latvia mainly involves sleeping off the night before.

REMEMBRANCE DAY OF THE LATVIAN LEGIONNAIRES (Leģionāru diena; 16 Mar) One of the most controversial commemorations in Latvia, and not a public holiday. It remembers those who fought in the Latvian SS Volunteer Legion, established on Hitler's orders early in 1943. The choice of 16 March marks the date in 1944 when both divisions of the legion fought alongside each other in defending a hill on the bank of the Velikaya River in Russia against the advancing Red Army. Critics of the commemorations argue that they glorify the SS and Nazism, and point to the presence in the Latvian Legion of individuals earlier involved in the atrocities of the Holocaust in Latvia, including members of the auxiliary police unit the Arajs Kommando. Supporters contend that the 'Volunteer Legion' contained few volunteers: most were conscripted in defiance of international law. While nominally part of the SS, the two Latvian divisions were in practice subordinated to the high command of the Wehrmacht. They argue that the Latvian soldiers conscripted into the Legion were in their hearts not fighting for Nazi Germany but against the Soviet Union, whose occupation of Latvia in 1940–41 had been marked by deportations and terror. Commemorations on 16 March centre on the laying of flowers at the Freedom Monument in Rīga and the Brothers' Cemetery in Lestene.

EASTER (Lieldienas; Good Friday & Easter Monday are public holidays) This is celebrated enthusiastically in Latvia, as the country shakes off the last days of winter cold. Sprigs of pussy willow appear in the markets ahead of Palm Sunday, and also making an appearance at celebratory events are decorated wooden swings. A good swing at Easter will ward off the mosquitoes all through the summer, they say. Which has to be worth a try. Egg-related activities are popular, particularly the colouring of eggs using natural dyes such as onion peel, and then egg 'battles' – the egg that cracks is the loser.

LABOUR DAY (Darba svētki; 1 May; public holiday) A holiday that evokes mixed emotions in Latvia. The enthusiasm with which 'International Workers' Day' was celebrated across the Soviet Union is off-putting to Latvians anxious to put that chapter of occupation behind them. On the other hand, 1 May has coincidentally local political significance as marking the day in 1920 when the first parliament of independent Latvia met to start drafting a national constitution. The Latvian parliament has mulled the removal of 1 May from the list of public holidays in favour of Lāčplēsis Day, but Labour Day is so far still on the list, perhaps because May is more convivial a time for a holiday than November.

DAY OF THE RESTORATION OF LATVIAN INDEPENDENCE (Latvijas Republikas Neatkarības atjaunošanas diena; 4 May; public holiday) This marks the anniversary of the vote by the Supreme Soviet of the Latvian Soviet Socialist Republic on 4 May 1990 to restore independence on the basis of the 1922 Constitution on the grounds that the Molotov–Ribbentrop Pact and Soviet occupation of Latvia were illegal. The day is marked by a military parade, which by tradition is held in one of the Latvian district capitals outside Rīga.

MIDSUMMER EVE AND ST JOHN'S DAY (Līgo & Jāņi; 23 & 24 Jun; both public holidays) The Midsummer holidays are the most distinctive events on the Latvian calendar. They are celebrated with gusto and show normally introverted Latvians at their most uninhibited. Public institutions and the majority of shops are shut. Latvians head out of town on Līgo day for family celebrations in the countryside. In Rīga, a Līgo Fair on Dome Square offers everything required for the event, including yellow Jāņi cheese, flavoured with caraway seeds, usually consumed with beer. Another essential component of the event is a floral crown. Ladies wear elegant wreaths of many varieties of wildflowers, while men sport sturdy crowns of oak leaves, giving the wearer the appearance of a creature of the woods. While the crowns should by tradition be fashioned by the wearer, using plants gathered from a walk in the fields, many Latvians buy them expertly made by sellers in the Līgo Fair or from vendors stationed on roadsides.

The festival centres on the night between 23 and 24 June. Having found their spot in the countryside or on the beach, a fire will be built. One common sight is a container in which a fire is lit, on the top of a long pole fixed into the sand. This is called a *pūdele*. You may see boys chucking sticks, trying to land them into the container to keep the fire going. As the eating and drinking commence, folk songs will be sung, invariably with a midsummer theme, usually featuring the repeated singing of the word 'Līgo'. Which makes them easier to remember after all that beer. Jumping over the bonfire is said to release the participant of their burdens, though this is best done when the fire has burnt down. Celebrations continue through the night, with couples heading away from the fire to search for the mythical fern flower (*papardes zieds*), which is said to bloom only on the night of 23 June, bringing fortune to the finder. 'Going to look for the fern flower' is a euphemism, and for that reason, Papardes Zieds is the name of a Latvian non-governmental organisation promoting sex education.

MIĶEĻI Also known as Miķeļdiena, this is Latvia's harvest festival, celebrated at the autumn equinox. The name derives from archangel Michael, and it is related to the festival of Michaelmas observed in other Christian countries, though the roots of the Latvian festival are pagan. It is commemorated in Rīga through a fair in Dome Square, with stalls selling honey, bread, sausages, hemp butter, gingerbread cookies decorated in the image of Homer Simpson, jars of pickles and ethnographic jewellery. There is a stage. Expect folk dancing.

LĀČPLĒSIS DAY (Lāčplēša diena; 11 Nov) is a memorial day for soldiers killed while fighting for Latvian independence. The choice of 11 November has nothing to do with the Remembrance Day observed in many countries to mark the end of hostilities in World War I. In Latvia, hostilities were far from over. Rather, it recalls the battles in autumn 1919 when the Latvian Army was defending Rīga against the West Russian Volunteer Army under Pavel Bermondt-Avalov. The decisive engagement, in which Bermondt's forces were driven away from the capital, took

LATVIAN SONG AND DANCE FESTIVAL

The Latvian Song and Dance Festival is a major event not just of Latvian culture but as an expression of Latvian identity. Together with similar song festivals in the neighbouring Baltic States of Estonia and Lithuania, it is inscribed as a UNESCO Masterpiece of the Oral and Intangible Heritage of Humanity. The festival in Latvia is currently held every five years. Its focus is around a massed choir, involving several thousand singers dressed in traditional costumes. The singers have been practising the repertoire for months within their local choirs across Latvia and among Latvian Diaspora groups worldwide. These choirs come together for the week of the festival, for combined rehearsals under the direction of professional conductors, culminating in a grand concert on the final evening of the festival that will form an event to be talked about for years thereafter.

Spurred by the growing popularity of choral singing, the song festival tradition emerged in Switzerland and Germany in the mid 19th century and was brought to the Baltic States by German Balts. Latvia provided fertile ground for the propagating of song festivals, as the Moravian-Brethren movement and the later establishment of seminaries to prepare future teachers and choir leaders had already encouraged the growth of a choral singing tradition. This German import fused with the emerging Latvian National Awakening and the work of figures such as Krišjānis Barons, collector and compiler of Latvian folk songs. The first song festival held in Latvia was a local affair in Dikļi in Vidzeme where in 1864 pastor Juris Neikens gathered together 200 singers from local congregations.

The first All-Latvian Song Festival was held in 1873 in Rīga's Kaisergarten (now Viesturdārzs) and brought together 1,003 singers. Composer Kārlis Baumanis sent in his compositions from St Petersburg. One of those, 'Dievs, svētī Latviju', performed at this first festival, was chosen in 1920 as the Latvian national anthem. By the third edition of the festival, held in 1888, with attempts to Russify the Baltic provinces of the Tsarist Empire underway, the Latvian Song Festival had already taken on an important role in strengthening Latvian national identity. Performers sported Latvian folk costumes, and young composers like Jāzeps Vītols celebrated their Latvian roots.

Following the establishment of Latvian independence, the scale of the festival grew, with more than 10,000 singers at its seventh edition in 1931. The ninth festival in 1938 was closely controlled by the paternalistic dictatorship of Kārlis Ulmanis, with a patriotic repertoire. Authoritarianism of a different kind was on show at place on 11 November. Latvian writer Kārlis Skalbe compared the efforts of the Latvian forces to the deeds of epic Latvian hero Lāčplēsis. The day is marked by a commemoration in the Rīga Brethren Cemetery, and by the tradition of the placing of a candle outside the walls of Rīga Castle. This has taken on to such a degree that the municipal authorities fix metal grilles with little shelves along the castle wall facing the Daugava, to accommodate better the thousands of red and white candles placed here during the evening. A torchlight procession is also organised between the cemetery and castle.

PROCLAMATION DAY OF THE REPUBLIC OF LATVIA (Latvijas neatkarības pasludināšanas atzīmēšanas diena; 18 Nov; public holiday) Latvia's Independence Day, marking the anniversary of the declaration of independence in 1918 by the People's Council of Latvia. There is a flower-laying at the Freedom Monument in

the next edition, in 1948, following the interruption of World War II, when the programme featured the necessary praise of Stalin's regime. Dance performances were included for the first time, and have thereafter grown in importance. The festival had hitherto been held in different locations in Rīga (and once, in 1895, in Jelgava), but since the 1955 festival it has been held at a purpose-built outdoor amphitheatre in Rīga's Mežaparks.

Through the 1960s and 70s, the Soviet authorities continued to seek to control the content, removing nationalistic pieces such as 'Gaismas pils' from the repertoire. The festival of 1970 was dedicated to the centenary of Lenin's birth and the 30th anniversary of Soviet Latvia. In 1980, 'Gaismas pils' returned to the festival, the audience demanding that the song be repeated three times in an early mark of the National Reawakening. At the next one in 1985, 'Gaismas pils' was removed from the repertoire just ahead of the festival, but in an act of defiance following the final performance, choir and audience stayed on to perform it anyway. The 20th edition in 1990, bringing together more than 20,000 singers and 10,000 dancers, incorporated exiled Latvian choirs and dance groups in a foreshadowing of the restoration of independence. The national anthem, 'Dievs, svētī Latviju', was performed again. The festival of 2003 was the first in which more dancers than singers participated, dance events taking an increasingly important role in the festival programme. A brass band element was also introduced for the first time. The 2018 festival involved some 43,000 participants.

Getting to see the most important concerts within the festival as a tourist is not, however, straightforward. The choral concert on the final night of the festival in Mežaparks is a central event in the Latvian cultural calendar. Choir and audience typically continue to sing together informally for hours until daybreak, long after the concert programme has wrapped up. Tickets sell out as soon as they are released. The main dance concerts, held in Rīga's Daugava Stadium, also book out within hours of going on sale. But tickets can be obtained more easily for some events during the week-long festival, including rehearsals of the main choral programme on the nights preceding the finale. The opening parade through the streets of Rīga is a major spectacle in itself, and all week the city is buzzing with choirs, dressed in traditional costumes. The Latvian Song and Dance Festival is the very reverse of those international festivals that embrace diversity: it is about Latvian identity, a celebration of national resilience.

Rīga in the morning, then in the afternoon a military parade along 11 novembra krastmala, with torchlight processions later in the evening.

CHRISTMAS (Ziemassvētki; typically 24–26 Dec are public holidays) Christmas celebrations are an eagerly awaited leavening of the long Latvian winter, and indeed Rīga lays claim to being the birthplace of the decorated Christmas tree, a claim contested by northern neighbour Tallinn. Latvian families are allowed to fell one Christmas tree free of charge from state forests. Latvian Christmas decorations encompass more than decorated trees, including intricate hanging mobiles made of straw, known as *puzurs*, to dispel negative energy from the room. The Rīga Christmas market in Dome Square offers a compelling mix of gingerbread, mulled wine and Christmas gifts as well as Santa. At the winter solstice, log dragging events are held across Latvia, involving the hauling around town and eventually burning of a large log, which represents the misfortunes of the year past. In Rīga, the event takes place in the Old Town, with the log burned in Town Hall Square.

The evening of Christmas Eve is traditionally the most important time of the Latvian Christmas celebrations. A large meal should include nine dishes. Grey peas with bacon usually numbers among the nine. Christmas presents are given at this time, with children required to sing a song or recite a poem to receive them.

NEW YEAR'S EVE (Vecgada vakars; 31 Dec; public holiday) As in many countries, New Year's Eve in Latvia involves friends, drink and merrymaking, though large public firework displays are less of a feature than in some places. There are plenty of traditions to mark the passing of the year. For example, you should eat sauerkraut on New Year's Eve, to consume away the sourness of the year past. But on no account eat sauerkraut on New Year's Day, or you will generate sourness for the year to come.

SHOPPING

The iconic souvenir from Latvia is **amber**, just as it was in ancient times. The fossilised tree resin, washed up on the beaches of Kurzeme, is fashioned into jewellery, from necklaces of partially worked stones to finely polished pendants. It is found in many colours, from the warm orange tones usually associated with the word 'amber' to darker browns and pale yellows. While you will see amber on display at every souvenir store in Old Rīga, you need to be mindful of fakes. The craft houses (Amatu mājas) supported by local authorities across the country, particularly those in Ventspils and Liepāja, are a good place to look for authentic local amber jewellery, and indeed for locally made handicraft items more widely.

Silver jewellery, with designs based around Latvian ethnographic signs (page 20), makes another worthwhile souvenir. The Namejs rings, named after a Semigallian chieftain and incorporating three entwined strands representing the three main Latvian regions, are a distinctive item, worn by many Latvian men. While traditional folk costumes are expensive, a major outlay for Latvian families who purchase them to perform in song and dance festivals and as a symbol of their national and local identities, smaller items of clothing can make great souvenirs. Knitted **woollen mittens**, many incorporating traditional ethnographic signs, are a staple of Christmas markets. Intricately woven belts, though pricey, are eye-catching. Linen tablecloths decorated with Latvian symbols, woven blankets, wooden toys, colourful scarves and imaginative ceramics are among the **handicraft**

items making excellent souvenirs. The Saturday market at Kalnciems Quarter in Rīga attracts high-quality providers, as do markets in Vērmane Garden or Dome Square in Rīga marking Midsummer and other festivities. Good-quality handicraft stores such as RIIJA in Rīga or KUULD in Kuldīga (what is it with handicraft places and capital letters?) showcase local artists.

A bottle of **Rīga Black Balsam** makes a distinctive souvenir, but as the drink is an acquired taste, it is not a gift that will be fully appreciated by everyone. You are on safer ground with **chocolates**: Laima is the best-known Latvian brand and even has a chain of its own stores across Rīga, but there are also some newer names on the block, such as the Kurzeme-based Pure Chocolate, which specialises in round truffles. A celebrated Latvian sweet treat is a soft **fudge** known as *gotiņa*. The best-known brand is produced by the Skrīveru Saldumi factory. Sold in colourful bags, this can make a fine gift for children. Other edible giftable products include Latvian honey or even a loaf of rye bread.

For **general shopping**, many Latvians head to malls. The major supermarkets are Rimi, a Rīga-based but Swedish-owned chain, and the Lithuanian-owned Maxima. Both have large out-of-town superstores and in-town convenience stores. The size of a Maxima store is revealed by the number of 'X's on the storefront: a Maxima XXX is particularly grand, while a Maxima X is a local grocery. The latter used to be called, rather wondrously, Minima. Smaller Rimi stores are named either Rimi Mini or Rimi Express. Other retailers, which fill the gap outside the main centres, include Mego, LaTS, CITRO and Top! The German discount retail chain Lidl is also growing its presence in Latvia.

ARTS AND ENTERTAINMENT

Song and dance are central to Latvian national identity: every town has a cultural centre at which local choirs and dance groups practise, both in readiness for the Song and Dance Festival and at humbler local performances. Rīga offers the widest range of entertainment options, from first-rate performances at the Opera and Ballet Theatre at a fraction of the price you would pay in some European cities to visiting international acts at the Arena. There has been considerable investment in recent years in concert halls in Latvia's regions, too, and venues like the Great Amber Concert Hall in Liepāja and GORS in Rēzekne are among the finest in the country.

The most prestigious performances sell out quickly, and it is a good idea to purchase tickets in advance through the venue websites to be sure of getting a seat. Theatre productions tend to be in Latvian, but surtitles are being used at a few venues, including the Dailes Theatre in Rīga and the New Rīga Theatre. The websites of the theatres concerned make clear where surtitling is available. Rīga also has a lively contemporary art scene, with venues like Kim? and Zuzeum offering high-quality exhibitions. The Survival Kit festival organised by the Latvian Centre for Contemporary Art is worth checking out if you are in Rīga in the early autumn.

OPENING TIMES

Office hours in Latvia are typically 09.00–17.00 Monday to Friday. **Banks** are typically open on this timetable, but there is much variation around this, and in smaller towns, bank branches may not be open every day during the week. Conversely, some branches, particularly in shopping centres in larger cities, remain open until 18.00 or 19.00, and some banks also open on Saturdays. **Shops** tend to open from 09.00 or 10.00 until 18.00 or 19.00, Monday to Friday, and to 16.00 or 17.00 on Saturday. Supermarkets and convenience stores generally adopt longer hours, from 08.00 or 09.00 until 20.00, 21.00 or 22.00 daily, including Sundays, with some hypermarkets open from 07.00 to midnight. A few stores are open 24 hours.

The most likely **museum** closure day is Monday, and some museums close on Tuesdays as well, but there is no standard pattern. Museums and other attractions often operate reduced opening hours outside the summer season, and some attractions (especially those involving an outdoor component) are closed altogether in winter. **Restaurants** in Rīga and other major centres typically open from noon to 23.00 or even midnight. Canteen-type ēdnīcas usually close earlier, at 20.00 or 21.00 in Rīga. Generally, the smaller and less touristy the town, the earlier eateries tend to close, and in some places getting a meal at eight o'clock in the evening can be a challenge. In many places there is a limited choice of venues outside hotels open for breakfast: kafejnīcas and bakeries are often your best bet. **Bars** in Rīga may stay open into the small hours, particularly on Friday nights and at the weekend. Again, closing times tend to be earlier in small towns.

MEDIA AND COMMUNICATIONS

PRINTED MEDIA Latvia's **newspapers** have been suffering from declining circulations. The main Latvian-language dailies include *Latvijas Avīze* and *Diena*. *Segodnya* is a Russian-language daily. The *Baltic Times* (w baltictimes.com) is an English-language monthly. A good source of English-language news about Latvia is provided by the English version of the official news portal of Latvian Radio and Television, *ENG.LSM.lv* (w eng.lsm.lv).

TELEVISION AND RADIO The State-owned public-service **television** broadcaster Latvijas Televīzija (LTV) operates two channels, LTV1 and, curiously, LTV7. They broadcast almost entirely in Latvian, save for a small amount of Russian content on LTV7. Also in the Latvian language are commercial channels owned by the TV3 group, which has its headquarters in Lithuania. They run the TV3 and TV6 channels, alongside the children's TV3 Mini, TV3 Plus for Russian-speaking audiences and film and sports channels. Most hotel TV packages include a few international news and entertainment channels in English. Russian-language channels transmitting Russian state propaganda previously popular among the Russian-speaking minority were banned following the Russian invasion of Ukraine in 2022.

The public-service **radio** broadcaster Latvijas Radio offers six channels. LR1 is news and current affairs. LR2 is focused on pop music and easy listening in the Latvian language. LR3 is classical music. LR4 broadcasts in Russian and, to a lesser extent, other minority languages. LR5 plays youth-oriented music, and LR6, also known as Radio NABA, started out as a student station of the University of Latvia. There are also many commercial radio stations, of which the pop-oriented Radio Skonto is currently most popular.

INTERNET Access to high-speed internet in Latvia is among the best in the EU. Almost all hotels and many bars and restaurants offer free Wi-Fi access.

TELEPHONE Latvia's country code is +371. Phone numbers have eight digits, other than numbers for emergencies and certain special services. Landlines generally start with a 6, with the next two digits identifying the geographic location (630 is Jelgava, for example). Payphone numbers start with a 7, and mobile telephones with a 2.

If you have an EU/EEA SIM card on your mobile phone, you will not be liable for international roaming charges in Latvia. If you do not, to avoid these charges, you may wish to purchase a local SIM card. There are three main options, each linked to a different network: LMT, Zelta Zivtiņa (on the Tele2 network) and Bite. All offer pretty good coverage. Cards are available in the stores of the companies concerned, as well as convenience stores such as Narvesen, petrol stations and supermarkets. You do not need to show your passport or register the SIM to purchase a card. Note, however, that to be able to use a Latvian SIM card, you must have an unlocked (SIM-lock free) mobile phone. If your mobile phone is locked, you are unfortunately consigned to international roaming (or buying another phone).

POST The main postal-service provider is the state-owned Latvijas Pasts, its symbol a yellow envelope. There are post offices in most towns, and the service is pretty efficient, although you may have to queue behind locals paying their utility bills.

CULTURAL ETIQUETTE

The characteristic Latvian introversion translates into a reserved approach when interacting with those outside family and immediate friends. Don't expect cheery 'good mornings' when passing strangers in the street. Latvians are by inclination private people and tend to keep business and personal lives separate. Punctuality is highly valued. Latvians arrive on time for meetings and expect you to do the same. They tend to keep business meetings business-like. Small talk is kept brief, and personal questions should be avoided. Formality in business meetings is expected, and the honorifics 'kungs' after the surname when addressing a man, and 'kundze' for a woman, are useful to know.

Invitations from Latvians are more often to a restaurant than to their home. At such occasions, and when attending cultural events, Latvians make the effort to dress smartly, and you should do the same, as a mark of respect for your host. If invited to a Latvian's home, you should bring a gift. Pre-eminent here are flowers: florists are everywhere, reflecting the national obsession with flower-giving. The key rule is to give an odd number, as even numbers are associated with death. Your flowers can be supplemented with a box of chocolates or that bottle of duty-free you bought on the plane over. Be prepared to take off your shoes when entering the house, though your host will usually make clear whether this is necessary. For invitations in the depth of winter, it is a good idea to bring indoor shoes with you if you will be arriving in snow-covered boots.

TRAVELLING POSITIVELY

With so many visitors confining themselves to Rīga, the individuals and organisations across the rest of the country working to develop restored manor houses, restaurants using local ingredients, and innovative attractions need every appreciative guest they can muster. Taking the time to see the country in depth, getting beyond international chain hotels, and bringing to your travels an interest in understanding how modern-day Latvia has been forged from its often-tragic history, is a great way to travel positively in Latvia.

There are many non-governmental organisations doing fine work that welcome support, and would be delighted to brief interested visitors on their activities. They include:

Allaži Crisis Centre Stārķu iela 4, Allaži, Siguldas nov.; w allazukrizescentrs.lv. A centre providing support for children who have suffered from violence.

Centrs Marta Matīsa iela 49A-11, Rīga; w marta.lv. Dedicated organisation supporting victims of domestic violence & helping to change the approach of the police and judicial agencies towards these crimes. They also have offices in Liepāja & Rēzekne.

Pasaules Dabas Fonds Elizabetes iela 8-4, Rīga; w lv-pdf.panda.org. The Latvian arm of the WWF. For more on their innovative rewilding project at Lake Pape, see page 278.

Zvannieki Home 'Vecrogas', Vaives pag., Cesu nov.; w zvannieki.lv. A privately funded alternative family home providing care for children who have been abused.

Part Two

THE GUIDE

3

Rīga

With a population of around 615,000, Rīga is more than seven times the size of the next largest city in Latvia. Some one in three residents of Latvia live here. It is the country's transport hub, the centre of government, home to most of the country's top universities and many of its most vibrant entertainment venues. A visit to Rīga should be part of any Latvian itinerary, and many visitors to the country go nowhere else. Its historic centre received UNESCO World Heritage status in 1997, for a combination of its historic Old Town, once a major trading city of the Hanseatic League, and its more recent rich architectural heritage of Art Nouveau buildings, constructed during a period of urban expansion at the start of the 20th century. These two themes help shape touristic explorations of the city.

Within the Old Town, its squares, cathedrals and churches are all major draws, but there are compelling museums too, such as the Museum of the Occupation of Latvia, which tells the often-harrowing story of war, occupation and Latvia's struggle to restore its independence. The modern city centre around the Old Town offers charming parks; Art Nouveau showcases, such as the flamboyant Alberta iela; the Freedom Monument, a symbol of Latvian independence; and a selection of contrasting museums. Sights further out include the extensive Latvian Ethnographic Open-Air Museum, the glitzy Rīga Motor Museum and the natural attractions of Rīga's forested lung, Mežaparks. Rīga's markets, particularly the large Central Market and more upmarket Āgenskalns, are not to be missed, and the city has by far the fullest programme of concerts and other events, widest range of restaurants and liveliest nightlife in the country.

HISTORY

Reindeer hunters arrived on the territory of modern-day Rīga in the 9th millennium BCE as the waters of the Baltic Ice Lake receded. The area has been inhabited since then, with the Livs arriving in the lower Daugava in the 10th century. Rīga's year of birth is, however, traditionally considered to be 1201, when Bishop Albert von Buxhoeveden, leading the crusade in Livonia, determined that the existing seat of the diocese at Ikšķile was in a militarily unpropitious location, and decided to move the centre of the bishopric to a sheltered natural harbour in the lower reaches of the Rīga River, now long silted up, as it emptied into the Daugava. Construction of its fortifications commenced in 1207.

The rapid development of Rīga owed much to its emergence as a major trading centre of the Baltic, a hub for trade between Russia and western Europe. Wax, fur, flax and hemp were brought from the east, while from the west came salt, herring, wine, silver and other luxury goods. Rīga became a member of the Hanseatic League, that medieval confederation of north European market towns and merchant guilds, in 1282. Much of the early history of the city involved a three-cornered power struggle between the townspeople and two competing overlords: the Bishop (later Archbishop) of Rīga and the Livonian Order. Rīga's merchants had acquired in 1221 the right to self-administer Rīga. A Town Council would become the administrative authority, with the right to collect taxes and command the city's military forces. Disputes between the Town Council and the powerful Livonian Order, however, developed into a full conflict ending with the defeat of the citizens of Rīga in 1330. Further friction between the city and the order in the late 15th century included the destruction by the Rīgans of the Livonian Order Castle in 1484, a somewhat fruitless activity as the city was forced to rebuild it under the terms of the peace treaty between the groups.

The Reformation during the 16th century played a major role in Rīga. Opposition to the Catholic Church was bound up with opposition to the overlords of the city, the Livonian Order and the Archbishop, and this mobilised the townsfolk, chafing for greater autonomy, to the Reformation cause. The Town Council grew in power as a result. With the Livonian War, and the collapse of the Livonian Order, Rīga became essentially independent for two decades from 1561, before, in 1581, being forced to submit to the control of the Polish–Lithuanian Commonwealth. Polish rule over the city lasted until 1621. The Poles allowed the city to retain many of its former privileges, though imposed a tax on Rīga's trade. In 1621, Rīga was taken by Swedish king Gustavus Adolphus. The Swedes retained the city during the Russo-Swedish War of 1656–58, despite a determined Russian attack, and the trading importance of Rīga provided an essential source of revenue for the Swedish coffers. During this period, as the city developed economically, and under the influence of humanist ideas from western Europe, the social and cultural life of the city took on an increasingly secular tone. Schools were opened. The first newspapers and printing presses were founded.

If the Russians had failed in their bid to secure Rīga in the 1650s, their time would come half a century later, under Peter the Great. Rīga fell to the Russians in 1710, replacing control from the west by that from the east. Russian control of Rīga and Vidzeme was formalised through the Treaty of Nystad in 1721. After St Petersburg, the city became the second port of the empire, focused on the export of agricultural products and industrial raw materials. The monopoly of trade rights by the merchants of the Big Guild was increasingly an obstacle to the development of trade, and from the second half of the 18th century the Tsarist authorities chipped away at the guild's privileges, until they were removed altogether by the mid 19th century.

From the latter part of the 18th century, factories started to develop in the suburbs, focused on industries falling outside the monopolies of the guilds, such as wood processing, paper, textiles, bricks and ceramics. In 1769, an esplanade free of development was created around the ramparts of the city. Beyond this, the suburban area outside the city walls rapidly expanded, although its buildings were all of wood. Suburbs were deliberately set on fire during the war of 1812, when Napoleon's troops appeared to be menacing Rīga. In the late 18th century, almost half of the population of the city was ethnic German. Latvians comprised around 30% of the townsfolk, engaged in craftwork, fishing, auxiliary work in trade and domestic service. There were also Russians, Poles and merchant communities of Englishmen, Dutchmen, Swedes and others. Rīga was becoming a vibrant cultural centre, fuelled by the ideas of the Enlightenment.

A key moment in the city's development came in 1856, when with the fortifications around the historic centre no longer serving a clear military use, the tsar agreed to their demolition. This had two important consequences. First, until that point, only timber buildings had been permitted outside of the fortified centre, a stipulation with its root in Russian defence planning. It was now possible to build in brick across this wider area. Second, the chief architect of Rīga, Johann Felsko, set to work on the development of a new city layout, with an elegant arc of parks and boulevards surrounding the medieval core. Beyond these, apartment buildings several storeys in height were erected and, with economic boom years around the turn of the century accompanied by marked rural to urban migration and the rapid growth of the city's population, an acceleration of this process coincided with the peak in fashion of the Art Nouveau style.

In the late 19th century, a new form of city administration was established in Rīga, with the creation of an elected City Council. The first mayor of Rīga, Ludvigs Kerkoviuss, was elected in 1890. The most celebrated mayor, however, was George Armitstead, a member of a British merchant family of the city, in office from 1901 to 1912. He oversaw the rapid transformation of Rīga as an increasingly important port and industrial centre. With a large in-migration of ethnic Latvians from rural areas, the German-Baltic community occupied a smaller share of the urban population, but continued to dominate the city's social and economic life. Rīga played a central role in the Latvian National Awakening of the late 19th century. The Rīga Latvian Society, founded in 1868, gave voice to Latvian aspirations, organising the Latvian Song Festivals that played such an important role in building Latvian feelings of unity. In 1901, the city celebrated its 700th anniversary with an Industrial and Handicrafts Exhibition on the Esplanade, with more than 40 pavilions showcasing its achievements and positioning Rīga as the centre of the Baltic region. Just four years later, Rīga was a major centre of the 1905 Revolution.

In 1917, Rīga fell to the advancing Germans. While the Baltic countries had been allocated to Germany under the Treaty of Brest-Litovsk of March 1918 with Soviet Russia, the armistice of 11 November 1918 superseded that treaty, allowing Latvia to declare its independence on 18 November 1918. This newly proclaimed republic was, however, promptly invaded by Soviet Russia, with Rīga falling to the Red Army in January 1919. In May, the city was retaken by pro-German forces, but the German defeat at Cēsis in June 1919 at the hands of Estonian and Latvian troops turned the tide of the war, paving the way for the restoration of the Latvian government under Kārlis Ulmanis, which returned to Rīga on 8 July 1919. This was not, however, the end of the Latvian War of Independence, or of the dangers facing Rīga: the pro-German West Russian Volunteer Army under Pavel Bermondt-Avalov attacked the city during the autumn, until their defeat by the Latvian army, with Estonian, British and French support, on 11 November, a day still celebrated as Lāčplēsis Day.

During the first period of Latvian independence, Rīga's status as Latvia's capital was underlined by new public buildings such as the iconic Freedom Monument. World War II was marked by successive Soviet, German, and again Soviet occupations, all traumatic for the city, with the deportations of the Soviet occupations and the Holocaust of the Nazi one. During the latter, the Jewish community was first crammed in the Rīga ghetto and then mostly executed in the massacre at Rumbula just outside the city. The Red Army captured Rīga from the Germans on 13 October 1944. The Soviet occupation was marked by immigration into the city from other parts of the USSR to support the Soviet programme of military and industrial development of Latvia. New suburban micro-districts of identikit housing blocks accommodated the new arrivals. This had a dramatic effect on the ethnic composition of the city, and by 1989, only 36% of the population of Rīga was ethnic Latvian.

Since the restoration of independence in 1991, the population of Rīga has fallen, through emigration westwards to better-paid employment and low birth rates. From a population of 900,000 in 1991, it has now dropped to a little over 600,000, eclipsed by Vilnius as the largest city in the Baltic States. Ethnic Latvians make up around 48% of the urban population, with ethnic Russians comprising 35%. The city remains the pulsating heart of the country, generating more than half the country's GDP. There have been challenging times for the city since the restoration of independence, none more so than on 21 November 2013 when a supermarket roof collapsed in the suburb of Zolitūde, killing 54 people. But when Rīga celebrated its stint as European Capital of Culture in 2014, it did so as a proud and confident city.

GETTING THERE AND AWAY

BY AIR **Rīga International Airport** (Starptautiskā lidosta Rīga; w riga-airport. com) is around 10km west of the city centre. Arrivals from the Schengen area bring you out at arrival gate E; those from outside it, including the UK, at arrival gate C. To get to the centre by **bus**, follow the signs 300m to the number 22 bus stop. You can purchase your ticket at the ticket machine at the bus stop, through the Mobilly or Rīgas satiksme apps, or at the Narvesen store adjacent to the exit from arrival gate E, all at the standard charge of €1.50 for a 90-minute ticket. The number 22 bus only also allows you to buy your ticket direct from the driver, but drivers do not accept cash and a ticket purchased this way will cost you €2. The 22 bus runs at time of writing from 05.25 until 00.40, at a frequency between half-hourly and every 10 minutes. The journey time is around 35 minutes.

There are also **taxis** outside the arrivals gates. Ensure you take one of the licensed taxis here rather than accepting any 'taxi driver' who seeks to approach you: these are unofficial taxis and you risk being scammed. The cost will be around €25, and the journey time about 20 minutes, more at peak hours on weekdays. You can also book a ride through the **Bolt** app, though since Bolt drivers are not allowed in the arrivals parking, you will have to go to the departures area above to meet your car. The **car rental** offices are in the E arrival hall, where you will also find a **visitor centre** and **baggage storage** (€5/24hrs).

BY TRAIN The **railway station** [77 C8] (Rīgas Pasažieru stacija; Stacijas laukums 2; \6723 2122) is at the southern end of Merķeļa iela, wrapped up in the complex that houses the Origo shopping mall. It is the hub of the Latvian railway network: save for the Gulbene to Alūksne narrow-gauge railway, all domestic rail routes depart from here. There are strong services to stations in the Jūrmala resort, with some trains going on to Tukums, as well as good services to Saulkrasti, Jelgava, and along the Daugava to Aizkraukle. Other useful services include the line to Valga just across the Estonian border, passing through Sigulda and Cēsis. There are less frequent services to Daugavpils, Krāslava, Rēzekne, Ludza, Gulbene, Dobele and Liepāja. At the time of writing, the only international connections from Rīga were a daily service to Vilnius in Lithuania and the hop into Valga, but this picture should change with the high-speed Rail Baltica line under construction, involving a new Rīga station building.

BY BUS The **bus station** [87 G8] (Rīgas Starptautiskā autoosta; Prāgas iela 1; w infobus.eu/en/bus/station/info-757) sits southwest of the railway station, across the railway tracks. It is separated from Rīga Central Market by the City Canal.

Both international and inter-city domestic bus services depart from here, and international operators Ecolines and Lux Express have offices in the station.

GETTING AROUND

Walking is the best option around Vecrīga and the city centre, where sights are close together.

BY PUBLIC TRANSPORT For further-flung destinations, Rīga's **public transport network** (Rīgas satiksme; w rigassatiksme.lv), which contains a mix of buses, trams and trolleybuses (the latter looking like buses but running on overhead wires) is efficient, comprehensive and good value. Tickets give you a specified amount of time on the network and allow changes between all three forms of transport. At time of writing, a 90-minute ticket cost €1.50, €5 for 24 hours, €8 for 3 days, €10 for 5 days and €30 for a month. You must register the ticket every time you enter a bus, tram or trolleybus. If you have a 90-minute ticket, provided you register the ticket before the 90th minute on your final bus or tram, it remains valid until your destination. You can buy tickets at stores such as those of the Narvesen, Rimi and Maxima chains, as well as the automatic machines found at some stops. You can also pay using the Rīgas satiksme or Mobilly phone apps. Note one quirk of the Rīga public transport system is that route numbers for each of the bus, tram and trolleybus networks are unique to that form of transport. Thus, the route of the number 2 tram is not the same as the route of the number 2 bus.

Some routes have entered the Latvian national consciousness. **Trolleybus 15**, which runs from the central University of Latvia, eastwards through the Maskavas forštate to the Ķengarags suburb with its Soviet-era housing, has developed an exaggerated reputation for drunkenness, petty crime and eccentric conversations. This is fuelled by its clientele, a mix of students and the mostly Russian-speaking residents of some of the city's poorer neighbourhoods. There was even a Twitter account devoted to the route at one point. **Tram 11**, which runs from the city centre to Mežaparks, is known during the five-yearly Latvian Song and Dance Festival as the 'singing tram' from the habit of choir members and spectators, returning from performances in Mežaparks, to keep the singing going on their journey back into town.

BY TAXI Licensed **taxis** have yellow number plates. Reputable companies include **Baltic Taxi** (w baltictaxi.com), whose taxis are lime green, and **Red Cab** (w redcab. lv), which operates a fleet of red-and-white taxis. As ever, ensure that the meter is switched on before you start your journey.

The popular **Bolt** (w bolt.eu) works in essentially the same way as Uber in other cities – you need to download their app, and then you can order cabs and track their progress. The cost usually works out cheaper than taxis. Bolt also offers a pay-as-you-ride **electric scooter** service, through the same app. At time of writing rides cost an initial €1, then 10 cents for each additional minute.

BY BIKE Places to rent **bicycles** in Rīga include **Rīga Bicycle Rental** [87 D5] (Rātslaukums 7; w rigabicycle.com), based at the House of the Blackheads. They also offer bike tours around Rīga and to Jūrmala. The sports equipment store **Gandrs** [69 D7] (Kalnciema iela 28/Kapseļu 7B; w gandrs.eu), in Pārdaugava not far from the Kalnciems market, offers rental of bikes, as well as winter sports gear. **Nextbike** (w nextbike.lv) is a bicycle sharing service. Having registered, you collect

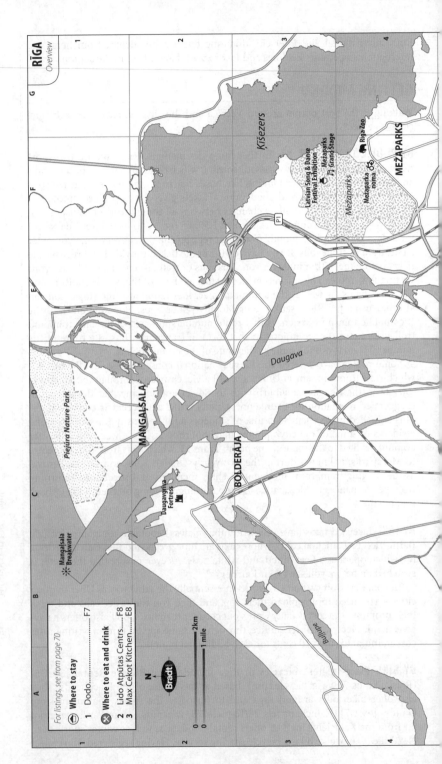

G 1
F 2
3
4

For listings, see from page 70

Where to stay
1 Dodo.................F7

Where to eat and drink
2 Lido Atpūtas Centrs....F8
3 Max Cekot Kitchen.......E8

Piejūra Nature Park

Mangaļsala
Breakwater

MANGAĻSALA

Daugavgrīva
Fortress

BOLDERĀJA

Daugava

Buļļupe

Ķīšezers

Latvian Song & Dance
Festival Exhibition

Mežaparks
Grand Stage

Mežaparks

Mežaparka
noma

Rīga Zoo

MEŽAPARKS

P1

N

Bradt

0   2km
0   1 mile

1
2
3
4

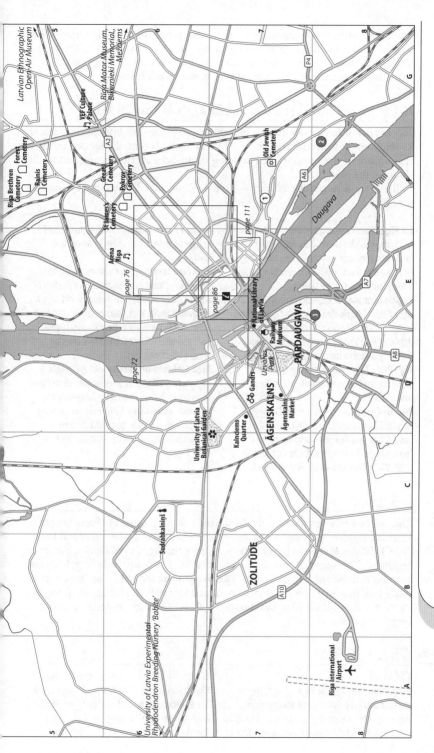

Latvian Ethnographic
Open-Air Museum

Rīga Motor Museum,
Biķernieki Memorial,
Mežciems

VEF Culture
Palace

A2

Rīga Brethren
Cemetery   Forest
             Cemetery

Rainis
Cemetery

Great
Cemetery

Pokrov
Cemetery

St James's
Cemetery

Old Jewish
Cemetery

Arena
Rīga

A6

Daugava

page 111

page 76

page 86

page 72

National Library
of Latvia

Railway
Museum

PĀRDAUGAVA

Uzvāras
Park

A7

A8

Gandrs

ĀGENSKALNS

Kalnciems
Quarter

Āgenskalns
Market

University of Latvia
Botanical Garden

Sudrabkalniņš

ZOLITŪDE

A10

University of Latvia Experimental
Rhododendron Breeding Nursery 'Babīte'

Rīga International
Airport

P4

your bike from base stations across town, and pay for each 30-minute period. There is an additional €1 charge for returning the bike outside a base station. The service is supported by Lidl stores, and base stations tend to be outside their branches.

Use bicycle lanes where these are available, and wear a helmet.

TOURIST INFORMATION AND LOCAL TOUR OPERATORS

The **tourist information centre** [87 D5] (Rīgas Tūrisma informācijas centrs; Rātslaukums 6; w liveriga.com; ⏱ 10.00–18.00 daily) is centrally located in Town Hall Square in the reconstructed building of the Schwab House, adjacent to the House of the Blackheads.

There are a range of city tour options by foot, bicycle, bus, canal boat and river boat.

Eat Rīga Tours w eatriga.lv. The name stands for Experience Alternative Tours, & they offer small-group tours of roughly 2hrs duration. They also offer bike tours, a Rīga craft beer tour & a food tasting tour at the Central Market.

Kuģītis Jūrmala w kugitisjurmala.lv. From a pier on the 11 Novembra krastmala the river boat *Jūrmala* offers a 1hr Rīga Panorama trip (adult/child €15/5), a 2½hr cruise to the Gulf of Rīga & (Sat–Sun only) a river passage to Mežaparks.

Rīga River Tour (w rigarivertours.lv) offers rather similar fare: neither operates in the winter months.

Rīga by Canal w rigabycanal.lv; ⏱ Apr–Oct. Circular 50min tours from Bastejkalns of the City Canal & Daugava River on one of 4 canal boats. The veteran of their fleet is the *Darling*, built in 1907. **River Cruises Latvia** (w rivercruises.

lv) has a similar offer from Bastejkalns, as well as river boat departures from 11 Novembra krastmala.

Rīga Free Tours w rigafreetours.com. Offers free walking tours (though donation expected) of around 2hrs, covering such themes as Old Rīga, Art Nouveau & Soviet Rīga. Tours generally start from St Peter's Church or the Latvian National Opera. They also offer (charged) bike tours, covering around 10km over 3hrs.

Rīga Sightseeing Service w riga-tour.lv. A hop-on hop-off tour on a red double-decker bus, covering both city centre & Pārdaugava, with an audio commentary. A more expensive 2-day ticket is also available. Buses circulate every 30mins in high season (Jun–Aug); every hour outside of this.

FESTIVALS

Rīga offers a busy events calendar, with frequent fairs, often in Dome Square or Vērmane Garden, marking out major celebrations such as Midsummer and Easter. The **Christmas Market** in Dome Square, running through December, is a particular highlight. The summer months are packed with activity, including Rīga city birthday activities in August, and the **Positivus music festival** (w positivusfestival. com), held over two days in July, which attracts international names. In spring and autumn, watch out for **Rīga Restaurant Week**, when many top restaurants offer a bargain set menu.

 ## WHERE TO STAY

VECRĪGA

Grand Hotel Kempinski Rīga [86 G4] (141 rooms) Aspazijas bulvāris 22; w kempinski.com. This venerable hotel started out life in the late 19th century as the Hotel Rome, was damaged in World War II & rebuilt in the Soviet period as the Hotel Rīga. It is now part of the Kempinski chain, offering a spa, restaurants on both rooftop & ground floor, & for those truly demanding personal space, a Presidential Suite covering 278m². **€€€€€**

Dome Hotel [86 C3] (15 rooms) Miesnieku iela 4; w domehotel.lv. Housed in a smartly restored 17th-century building in the Old Town, this is a good upper-end option with nicely furnished rooms, a spa & a great restaurant (€€€€€), with a rooftop option in summer. €€€€

Grand Palace Hotel [86 B3] (56 rooms) Pils iela 12; w grandpalaceriga.com. The only Latvian hotel affiliated to the Leading Hotels of the World group, this place close to Rīga Castle boasts a '5-star superior' rating & smart rooms & facilities to match. €€€€

Hotel Neiburgs [86 D4] (55 rooms) Jauniela 25/27; w neiburgs.com. This Art Nouveau building, its entrance watched over by a stern female head, was the property of entrepreneur Ludvigs Neiburgs. Restored to his heirs following the restoration of Latvian independence, it has been converted into a tastefully decorated 'mindful hotel'. Rooms have a kitchenette & there is a good restaurant (€€€€). €€€€

Hotel Gutenbergs [86 B4] (38 rooms) Doma laukums 1; w hotelgutenbergs.lv. This place takes its name from Johannes Gutenberg, German inventor of the printing press, who has no connection with Rīga. One of the 2 adjacent buildings did, though, once accommodate a printing house, & there is a bust of Gutenberg atop the arched gateway on the façade. The hotel is laid out in Olde Worlde style, though the cheaper rooms can be cramped. The restaurant (€€€€€) is pricey: its best feature is its roof terrace aspect. €€€–€€€€

Hotel Justus [86 C4] (45 rooms) Jauniela 24; w hoteljustus.lv. Nicely located on picturesque Jauniela, the Justus is housed in a smartly restored building with lots of exposed brickwork & comfortable rooms. €€€

Konventa Sēta Hotel [86 F4] (161 rooms) Kalēju iela 9/11; w keystonecollection.com. This hotel occupies several buildings in the 'Convent Courtyard', site of the first castle of the Livonian Brothers of the Sword, later acquired by the Convent of the Holy Spirit, hence the name. Commercial uses took over from religious ones, and the buildings served as warehouses, gradually falling into disrepair until their modern-day restoration. Rooms have parquet floors & are smartly renovated, even if the style is blander than the historic location might warrant. Their restaurant, **Two More Beers** (w twomorebeers.lv; €€€€) is as much pub as

dining option, with a menu heavy on burgers, though also offering local dishes. €€€

Naughty Squirrel Hostel [87 G6] (15 rooms) Kalēju iela 50; w naughtysquirrelbackpackers. com. Centrally located Australian- & British-owned backpacker hostel, offering both private rooms & shared dorms of 4–8 beds, a kitchen & common rooms. They organise social activities, including both Latvian beer tasting & rifle shooting, though hopefully not on the same evening. €–€€

CITY CENTRE

A22 [72 D1] (20 rooms) 22 Ausekļa iela; w a22hotel.com. Elegant boutique hotel in an early 20th-century building over the road from the Viesturdārzs park, its interior décor seeking to give the place a 1930s feel, when it housed the US embassy in Rīga. Future US President John F Kennedy briefly stayed here in 1939, & the hotel milks the connection for all it's worth. Its restaurant (€€€€€) is named John, offering such restrained dishes as black pasta with crayfish & caviar, & the cocktail bar is called Jackie. The hotel's name is just an abbreviation of the street address. €€€€€

Grand Poet Hotel [77 A5] (168 rooms) Raiņa bulvāris 5/6; w grandpoet.semarahotels.com. This is a top-end hotel with plush rooms, a spa & fitness centre. An assertiveness has gone into its interior design, with loud colours & a restaurant called SNOB (€€€€€). With a cheeseburger priced at €25, served with truffle-flavoured chips, the latter lives up to its name. It sits across Bastejkalns Park, in a building that witnessed the most violent episode of the 1991 Barricades as the then location of the Interior Ministry, attacked by Soviet OMON special forces. €€€€

Radisson Blu Latvija [77 C5] (571 rooms) Elizabetes iela 55; w radissonhotels.com. There are several hotels across Rīga carrying the Radisson brand. This 27-storey block just to the side of Esplanade Park is the largest, & a city landmark in its own right. It opened in 1979 as the Hotel Latvija, but has long shaken off its Soviet origins to embrace international business hotel standards, with spa & fitness centre. The Skyline Bar on the 26th floor, accessed by a glass-sided elevator, offers a great view across the city. Don't confuse this hotel with its sister, the Radisson Blu Elizabete, further south along the same street at Elizabetes iela 73. €€€€

Tallink Hotel Rīga [77 D7] (256 rooms) Elizabetes iela 24; **w** hotels.tallink.com. Although at time of writing the Tallink ferry company no longer serves Rīga, they do maintain a hotel here. The city centre location is good, & the place is comfortable, if not brimming with character. **€€€**

Jakob Lenz Guesthouse [76 A2] (25 rooms) Lenču iela 2; **** 6733 3343; **e** reservation@ guesthouselenz.lv. A couple of blocks north of the Art Nouveau showcase of Alberta iela, this guesthouse offers basic rooms, not all with en suites, & a communal kitchen. **€€**

Cinnamon Sally Hostel [77 C7] (58 bed spaces) Merķeļa iela 1; **w** cinnamonsally.com. Next to the McDonald's restaurant over the road from the railway station, this is a German-owned backpackers hostel with dorms (1 female-only), & 2 private rooms. They have a fully equipped kitchen & free coffee. **€–€€**

OUTSIDE THE CENTRE

Dodo Hotel [69 F7] (109 rooms) Jersikas iela 1; **** 6724 0220; **e** sales@dodohotel.com. While this place is outside the centre in Maskavas forštate, it deserves a listing as one of the few decent no-frills budget options in Rīga. You can get to the centre easily enough via the tram stop on nearby Latgales iela. **€€**

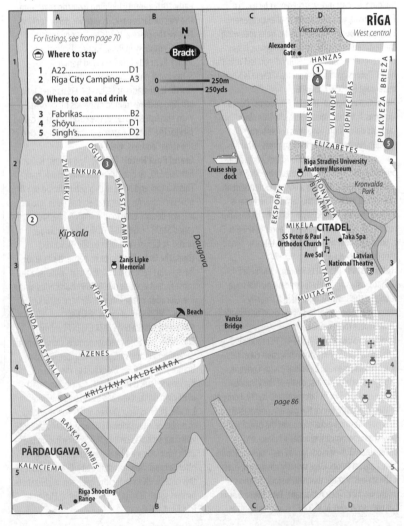

Hanza Hotel [111 C2] (80 rooms) Elijas iela 7; w hanzahotel.lv. In Maskavas forštate, but within easy walking distance of the centre, a block east of the Academy of Sciences building. The hotel occupies a former residential apartment building built in 1901, & offers functional rooms, many looking out on to the charming wooden Church of Jesus. There is a spa with sauna & steam bath. €€

Rīga City Camping [72 A3] Ķīpsalas iela 8; w rigacamping.lv; ⊕ 15 May–15 Oct. On Ķīpsala, across the Daugava from the Old Town, this grass-covered campsite is pretty close to the city centre, offering tent & trailer pitches with shower & toilet block & Wi-Fi. The site can get crowded, though, giving it the feel of a car park. €

✗ WHERE TO EAT AND DRINK

The city centre has increasingly taken over from Vecrīga as the centre of gravity of the restaurant scene in Rīga, with the streets of the Quiet Centre offering a particularly strong cluster of worthwhile places. The area around Miera iela is known more for its bars and clubs (page 81) than restaurants, but there are some good places to eat here too to soak up the booze.

VECRĪGA

3 pavāru [86 E2] Torņa iela 4; w 3pavari.lv. Housed in Jacob's Barracks, with tables arranged around a kitchen area with chefs at work preparing your dishes, the 'Three Chefs' is an innovative restaurant, announcing its flair with an artistic complimentary starter of colourful sauces flavoured with local ingredients, painted on a sheet of greaseproof paper, which you then demolish with your bread. There is a 6-course tasting menu, or a good short à la carte list. The restaurant also goes by the name 'Tam labam būs augt' ('It will grow well'). €€€€€

Barents [86 E2] Smilšu iela 3; w barents.lv; ⊕ closed Sun–Mon. One of the smartest (& priciest) restaurants in town, offering an 11-course tasting menu & an à la carte selection, with seafood a particular strength. You can book a seat at the chef's table, to watch chief choreographer Dzintars Kristovskis in action. The Barents Cocktail & Seafood Bar next door (€€€€) offers cocktails featuring local herbs, as well as a lighter menu ranging from oysters to a chanterelle burger. €€€€€

Domini Canes [87 F5] Skārņu iela 10; w dominicanes.lv. Elegant Old Town restaurant from the owners of the Pļavas restaurant near Ainaži. Sit at dark wooden tables inside or at outdoor tables, & sample a menu drawing on local ingredients. €€€€

Milda [87 F6] Kungu iela 8; w restoransmilda. lv; ⊕ closed Mon. Focuses on the flavours of the Baltic, with Latvian classics like grey peas with bacon, as well as the Lithuanian mince-filled potato dumplings known as *cepelinai*. €€€€

Zviedru vārti [86 D2] Aldaru iela 11; w zviedruvarti.lv. Standing in front of the Swedish Gate, which gives the restaurant its name, this is run by a family from Kurzeme, & offers Latvian dishes like grey peas with smoked meat & eel braised in a leek sauce, as well as a wider international menu. The restaurant is small, but they also have outdoor tables. There is a 2nd branch nearby at Torņa iela 4-1. €€€€

Nāc un ēd [87 G5] Audēju iela 15; ☎2921 1131; ⊕ closed Sun. The Old Town branch of this chain of canteens, 'Come & Eat' offers a cheap, no-frills place for lunch at functional tables. There are plenty of Latvian dishes on offer. €€

CITY CENTRE

Tails [76 A4] Antonijas iela 6A; w tails.lv. A smart fish restaurant in the Quiet Centre, offering a soothing brown-toned interior. A fish-drying room open to view makes for an unusual decoration. They offer a 'raw bar' of ceviche, tartare & oysters, as well as cooked fare, from seafood risotto to dry-aged tuna steak. The 'non-Caesar' salad turns out to be prawns. €€€€€

Andalūzijas Suns [77 D7] Elizabetes iela 83; w andaluzijassuns.lv. Popular place in the renovated Berga bazārs shopping arcade, the 'Andalusian Dog' takes its name from Buñuel's surrealist masterpiece, & maintains the theme through the illustration of a dog sporting a Dali-esque moustache on the menus. These dip in & out of various cuisines, from fish & chips to chimichanga. The menu includes dishes for dogs – mostly beef patties. They also serve b/fast

& business lunches, & have tables on the terrace outside. €€€€

Café Osiris [77 E5] Krišjāņa Barona iela 31; w cafeosiris.lv; ⊕ closed Sun. This place started out in 1994 under the helm of actor Andrejs Žagars as the culinary wing of the Soros Foundation activities in Latvia, a place for writers & intellectuals. With its green stone tabletops, it still retains something of this feel, & offers both full meals & sandwiches, as well as good cakes. €€€€

COD [76 E4] Tērbatas iela 45; w cod.lv. Contemporary Japanese restaurant, offering beautifully presented sashimi & dishes cooked over a robata grill. They also have a cocktail bar. €€€€

Kolonāde [76 G2] Brīvības bulvāris 26; w kolonade.lv. Occupying an Ionic-columned pavilion close to the Freedom Monument, & large glass-walled annexe behind it, festooned with pot plants, this is a smart place with an international menu. Extensive, & pricey, wine list. €€€€

Lidojošā varde [76 A4] Elizabetes iela 31A; w lidojosavarde.lv. The 'Flying Frog' is a popular Quiet Centre option, with a summer terrace & interior crammed with frog-related knick-knacks. The menu is wide-ranging, spanning pasta, burgers, wok dishes & more Latvian-inspired choices like sorrel soup. Yes, they do offer frogs' legs. €€€€

Shōyu [72 D1] Auseklā iela 20; w shoyu.lv. This diminutive place close to Viesturdārzs specialises in appetising & hearty bowls of ramen, though also serves poke bowls, with the gooey *mochi* rice cakes for dessert. €€€€

RĪGA'S TOP CAFÉS

The Latvian capital sometimes seems to have a café on every street corner. There are numerous places to stop for coffee and cake. Among the chains, **Sala** are at the cheaper end of the market, and found in some of Rīga's most popular parks. **Cadets de Gascogne** are a small chain of French bakeries, offering excellent croissants, both savoury and sweet. **Caffeine** are Norwegian-owned, and ape the better-known international coffeehouses, which are otherwise quite thinly represented in the city. There are also places tracking the latest sweet fad, such as **Cruffins**, housed within the Konventa Sēta Hotel in Vecrīga, doling out the eponymous cruffin – a croissant shaped like a muffin, filled with flavoured creams. Among the more atmospheric places for that coffee break, the following are some of the standouts.

Amalija Cake House [77 C6] Tērbatas iela 2D, Vērmanes dārzs; ☏ 2780 3907. This place in Vērmane Garden stands out from the other cafés of the Sala chain through its exuberant interior decoration, its walls filled with colourful murals of cakes, & for some reason a crowned flamingo, the work of artist & photographer Amalija Andersone.

Black Magic [86 E4] Kaļķu iela 10; w blackmagic.lv. This place bills itself as the birthplace of Rīga Black Balsam, offering tastings daily at 19.00 (€18; advance booking required) in the basement room they claim may have been the original apothecary of Abraham Kunze. This hardly seems likely, but they spin a good yarn, & your entry to the basement through a secret door in the bookcase is memorable, as are the interruptions to the tastings from the resident ghost. The café is atmospheric, if touristy, with wooden ceilings & old pharmaceutical bottles decorating the place. They offer fine handmade chocolates, & have the full range of black balsams to go with your coffee.

Kūkotava [77 D5] Tērbatas iela 12-1; w kukotava.eu. With French bistro-style tables & plenty of wrought ironwork, Kūkotava has 2 cafés side by side. Kūkotava Passage offers great cakes. Kūkotavas Épicerie majors on croissants, bread & delicatessen goods.

MiiT [76 D4] Lāčplēša iela 10; ☏ 2729 2424; e info@miit.lv. A vegan café named MiiT? Apparently, they retained the name of the bike shop that once

Siļķītes un Dillītes [111 A2] Nēģu iela 7; ☎2639 1122; e normundsmalinovskis@gmail.com. Located within Rīga Central Market, in the corridor between the fish & vegetable pavilions, 'Herring & Dill' is an excellent fish restaurant, in cramped premises with a no-frills vibe, taking cash only. It promotes a Latvian pescatarian cuisine: try the herring baked in paper. €€€€

Singh's [72 D2] Pulkveža Brieža iela 2; ☎6331 1909; e info@singhs.lv. A rarity in the low-spice environment of Latvia; an authentic Indian restaurant, focusing on Punjabi cuisine but ranging more widely. Offers a good-value business lunch on weekdays. There is another branch at Ģertrūdes iela 32 (☎6622 0000). €€€€

Snatch [76 B4] Elizabetes iela 39; w snatch.lv. Italian restaurant in the Quiet Centre, with a lively décor & a menu incorporating a tempting range of homemade pasta, from tagliolini with black truffle to spaghetti & red prawns. €€€€

Space Falafel [76 B4] Antonijas iela 8; ☎2736 6166. An Israeli restaurant in the Quiet Centre, with an interior enlivened by bawdy artworks, & a line of tables along the street outside. Offers both light & more substantial fare, from pastrami sandwiches & *sabich* to Mozambique-style octopus. They also offer meze. €€€€

Zivju lete [76 B4] Dzirnavu iela 41; w zivjulete. lv. A fish restaurant, with smartly functional décor, offering a sauté of seafood of your choice, as well as more standard mains like baked sea bass & the classic fish & chips. €€€€

Big Bad Bagels [76 C4] Baznīcas iela 8 w bigbadbagels.lv. Subterranean bagel bar, with occupied the building. It attracts a hip crowd sipping cappuccinos while working on their laptops at the wooden benches. They offer soups, salads, sandwiches & nice cakes, as well as a set weekday vegan lunch & good b/fast. €€

Mīkla [76 B4] Dzirnavu iela 42; ☎2577 8333. This Quiet Centre bakery offers fresh-baked bread, croissants, muffins & pastries & good coffee, with a functional interior and outside courtyard. There is another branch at the Grand Hotel Kempinski Rīga in the Old Town.

Parunāsim [86 C2] Mazā Pils iela 4; ☎2566 3533. Tucked away in an Old Town courtyard, this place advertises itself as 'the most romantic café in Rīga', & with its cozy furniture, kitsch lighting & tables spilling into the yard, it would be hard to disagree. You'll either love or hate the witty signage ('I dieted for a month & all I lost was 30 days'). It is priced at the tourist market, but the cakes are excellent, & they offer quiche & soup for something fuller.

Pie Pulvertorņa [86 E2] Vaļņu iela 2; ☎6722 0032. An unassuming but friendly café across the road from the Powder Tower in Vecrīga, they offer cakes & pastries, b/fast options of omelettes & porridge, & light lunches of savoury pancakes.

Rocket Bean Roastery [76 F1] Miera iela 29/31; w rocketbeanroastery. com. Both the location & ethos of this speciality coffee roastery aim at a hip young crowd. With cafés at 2 more locations, among them a central site at Dzirnavu iela 39, they also serve light lunches, with a refreshing kombucha to wash down your avocado burger.

Tabu Tea House [77 C6] Tērbatas iela 2G, Vērmanes dārzs; ☎6721 2436; e tabu.tearoom@gmail.com. Housed in a 2-storey wooden pavilion in Vērmane Garden, this place invites you to take a mindful break from sightseeing with a good selection of teas, & even (with advance booking) a full Chinese tea ceremony.

V Ķuze [86 C1] Jēkaba iela 20/22; w kuze.lv. Vilhelms Ķuze was a Latvian chocolatier, deported to Siberia in 1941, where he died in a labour camp. This Old Town café was established in 2004 bearing his name, & enchants with its Art Deco interior & exquisite objects fashioned from chocolate & marzipan. Also offers light bites like pancakes & salads, & good cakes.

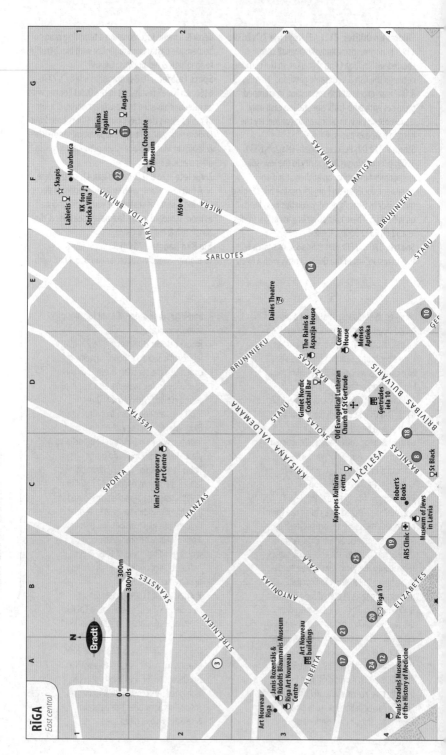

Bradt

0   300m
0   300yds

Art Nouveau
Rīga

Jānis Rozentāls &
Rūdolfs Blaumanis Museum

Rīga Art Nouveau
Centre

Art Nouveau
buildings

Pauls Stradiņš Museum
of the History of Medicine

Kim? Contemporary
Art Centre

Kaņepes Kultūras
centrs

Rīga 10

Robert's
Books

ARS Clinic

Museum of Jews
in Latvia

St Black

Old Evangelical Lutheran
Church of St Gertrude

Ģertrūdes
iela 10

Gimlet Nordic
Cocktail Bar

The Rainis &
Aspazija House

Corner
House

Mēness
Aptieka

Dailes Theatre

Labietis ☆ ☆ Skapis
KK fon ♫
Strička Villa ●

M/Darbnīca

M50 ●

Laima Chocolate
Museum

Tallinas
Pagalms

Angārs

Streets: STRĒLNIEKU, SKANSTES, SPORTA, HANZAS, VESTAS, KRIŠJĀŅA VALDEMĀRA, ANTONIJAS, ZAĻĀ, ALBERTA, ELIZABETES, STABU, SKOLAS, BRUŅINIEKU, LĀČPLĒŠA, BAZNĪCAS, BRĪVĪBAS BULVĀRIS, ŠARLOTES, STRĪDA BRIĀNA, MIERA, TĒRBATAS, MATISA, BRUŅINIEKU, STABU, GER

3, 17, 21, 24, 12, 20, 25, 19, 8, 18, 10, 14, 22, 11

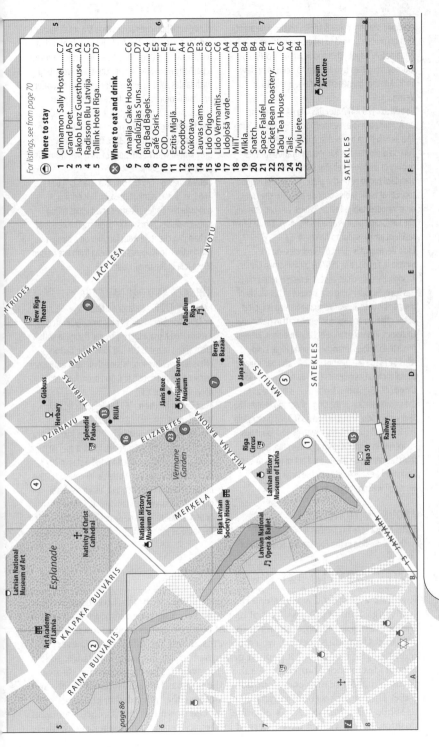

For listings, see from page 70

Where to stay

1 Cinnamon Sally Hostel......C7
2 Grand Poet.......................A5
3 Jakob Lenz Guesthouse.....A2
4 Radisson Blu Latvija.........C5
5 Tallink Hotel Rīga.............D7

Where to eat and drink

6   Amālija Cake House.........C6
7   Andalūzijas Suns.............D7
8   Big Bad Bagels................C4
9   Café Osiris.......................E5
10 COD................................E4
11 Ēzītis Miglā.....................F1
12 Foodbox.........................A4
13 Kūkotava........................D5
14 Lauvas nams...................E3
15 Lido Origo.......................C8
16 Lido Vērmanītis...............C6
17 Lidojošā varde................A4
18 MiiT................................D4
19 Mikla..............................B4
20 Snatch............................B4
21 Space Falafel..................B4
22 Rocket Bean Roastery......F1
23 Tabu Tea House..............C6
24 Tails................................A4
25 Zivju lete........................B4

✪ Zuzeum Art Centre

page 86

Esplanade

Vērmane Garden

Latvian National Museum of Art

Art Academy of Latvia

Nativity of Christ Cathedral

New Rīga Theatre

Globuss

Herbary

Splendid Palace

RIIJA

Jānis Roze

Krišjānis Barons Museum

Bergs Bazaar

Jāņa sēta

Palladium Rīga

National History Museum of Latvia

Rīga Latvian Society House

Latvian History Museum of Latvia

Rīga Circus

Latvian National Opera & Ballet

Rīga 50

Railway station

TĒRBATAS

ĢERTRŪDES

BLAUMAŅA

LĀČPLĒŠA

AVOTU

DZIRNAVU

ELIZABETES

KRIŠJĀŅA BARONA

MĀRIJAS

SATEKLES

SATEKLES

MERĶEĻA

KAĻĶA BULVĀRIS

KALPAKA BULVĀRIS

RAIŅA BULVĀRIS

13. JANVĀRA

cramped seating inside & tables on the pavement, though mostly geared to take-away. Offers imaginative bagels, themed as a global culinary journey from 'bacon in Mexico' to 'salmon in New York'. Another branch sits at Audēju iela 10 in Vecrīga. €€

Foodbox [76 A4] Antonijas iela 6A – entrance on A. Pumpura iela; w foodbox.lv; ☺ closed Sun. This kebab shop opened in 2008 by the son of a Turkish diplomat has earnt a reputation for the quality of its döner kebabs, served in lavash or standard bread or on the plate. The falafel is good too. Eat at basic tables outside beneath the trees, or at wooden tables inside, where you can admire the landscape photos of Ivars Pundurs, Latvia's first resident ambassador to Turkey. €€

Lido Vērmanītis [77 C6] Elizabetes iela 65; w lido.lv. Founded in 1987 by businessman Gunārs Ķirsons, the Lido chain of canteen-style restaurants has become something of a symbol of Latvia. The Vērmanītis branch near Vērmane Garden is typical of the offer: an engaging interior, staff in traditional costumes, & a wide range of Latvian dishes. Among more than a dozen branches around Rīga, **Lido Alus Sēta** [86 D4] (Krāmu iela 2) is also particularly useful for tourists given its Old Town location. **Lido Origo** [77 C8] (Stacijas laukums 2) is right next to the railway station in the Origo shopping centre. The faux rustic **Lido Atpūtas Centrs** [69 F8] (Krasta iela 76) is huge & child-friendly, with playful fountains, an ice rink in winter & even a petting zoo, but is far from the centre, on the A6 road out of town towards Daugavpils, easily spotted by the large model windmill welcoming you in. €€

AROUND MIERA IELA

Ezītis Miglā [76 F1] Tallinas iela 10; w ezitis. lv. The 'Hedgehog in the Fog' is a bar & restaurant chain, with branches across Rīga & a small number outside the capital. The Tallinas kvartāls branch has a particularly grungy feel, reflecting its location in a partially renovated former car repair workshop, with tables spilling out into the courtyard. It offers an unadventurous but reliable mix of burgers, wraps, salads & pasta dishes, though one hopes the 'hedgehog solyanka' refers to the chain rather than the contents of the dish. The outside walls are painted with hedgehogs of all types, from cute prickly balls to Sonic. €€

Lauvas nams [76 E3] Brīvības iela 82; ☎6731 2661; e lauvas.nams@inbox.lv. This ēdnīca opposite the Dailes Theatre serves up its filling canteen dishes 24hrs a day, meeting the needs of a changing clientele from families on a budget in the daytime to students returning from the bars of Miera iela in the small hours. €€

ĶĪPSALA AND PĀRDAUGAVA

Fabrikas [72 B2] Balasta dambis 70; w fabrikasrestorans.lv. Photogenically located in a renovated Ķīpsala factory by the Daugava with great views towards the Old Town, the 'factory' offers an inventive international menu & a summer terrace over the river. Sat & Sun brunch served noon–14.00. €€€€

Max Cekot Kitchen [69 E8] Jelgavas iela 42; w maxcekot.com; ☺ 18.00–23.00 Thu–Sat. Housed in an old industrial building in Pārdaugava, this is a restaurant you need to make a special trip to visit. Awarded a coveted Michelin star in 2023, chef Max Cekot has but 1 offer: a 10-course tasting menu, served 3 nights a week, using seasonal dishes in a modern Latvian cuisine. A vegetarian option is available. Some dishes are finished off at the table as you watch. Booking required. €€€€€

ENTERTAINMENT AND NIGHTLIFE

Rīga has a busy and vibrant entertainment scene, with the Live Rīga website (w liveriga.com) offering a digest of major forthcoming attractions. Pick up one of the free listings magazines from the tourist office or venues around town, like *Riga This Week* (w rigathisweek.lv), which notwithstanding the title is printed every two months. Note that the most popular performances sell out well in advance, so it is a good idea to book your tickets via the venue websites before you come. Be aware, though, that for many venues, including the popular Latvian National Opera and Ballet Theatre, tickets once purchased cannot be either refunded or changed.

While still a focus of Rīga's nightlife, the Old Town has lost its once dominant position as new venues have emerged in the city centre and further afield. There are, though, some great bars and clubs within its atmospheric streets, if you avoid the tourist traps.

The streets around **Miera iela** northeast of the city centre are a favoured hangout for a hip, student crowd, offering a mix of bars, restaurants, clubs and cultural spaces, sometimes combined within a single venue. There are two main clusters. **Tallinas kvartāls** (Tallinas iela 10) is based around that tried-and-tested formula of a collection of crumbling buildings, in this case once home to the city ambulance service, grouped around an open courtyard, brightened up with a liberal application of street art and now accommodating restaurants, bars and event venues. The second cluster is **Briāna kvartāls**, just off Aristida Briāna iela, and the adjacent Valdemāra Pasāža, an office and commercial block occupying the reconstructed brewery of Karl Christoph von Strick, dating from the second half of the 19th century. The brewery building, which is home to bars, restaurants and clubs, sits behind a pair of once smart brick buildings connected by an arched gate on which stands a statue of Mercury, patron of merchants. One was a residential building, now home to events venue the **K. K. fon Stricka Villa** [76 F1] (Aristida Briāna iela 9; w fonstrickavilla.lv). The other, the former administration building of the brewery, houses the culture space known as **M/Darbnīca** [76 F1] (Aristida Briāna iela 9; w mdarbnica.lv).

CONCERT VENUES

Arena Rīga [69 E6] Skanstes iela 21; w arenariga.com. This 11,000-seat indoor arena opened in 2006 for the International Ice Hockey Federation World Championship that year. As well as hosting matches of the national ice hockey & basketball teams, it is the venue for the largest concerts, featuring international names, though the building is charmless.

Ave Sol [72 D3] Citadeles iela 7; w avesol.riga. lv. Housed in the 18th-century St Peter & St Paul Orthodox Church, built in the former Rīga Citadel north of Vecrīga, it became a concert hall in the Soviet period. Unlike the many churches used for secular purposes during the Soviet occupation before being returned to ecclesiastical ones, this has remained a concert hall. From its wooden-panelled foyer to the rows of tatty chairs under the star-studded, blue-painted ceiling, the place looks like it has been untouched since Soviet times. It is home to the Ave Sol chamber choir, founded in 1969. Some concerts here are free of charge.

Great Guild [86 E3] Lielā ģilde; Amatu iela 6; w lnso.lv. The former home of the guild-house of Rīga's wealthy German-speaking merchants, the building was remodelled in the Soviet period as a concert hall & now houses the Latvian National Symphony Orchestra.

Latvian National Opera & Ballet [77 B7] Latvijas Nacionālā Opera un Balets; Aspazijas bulvāris 3; w opera.lv. As part of the redesign of Rīga's city centre following the removal of the fortifications, a grand new building was opened in 1863 close to the City Canal to house the German-language Rīga City Theatre, relocated here from unsatisfactory premises in the Old Town. Damaged by fire in 1882, it was reconstructed in 1887. The place is now home to both the Latvian National Opera, first performing here in 1919, & Latvian National Ballet, with a season running Sep–Jun. With its Ionic-columned Neoclassical façade, the building is a Rīga landmark, & with performances of a high quality & much cheaper than at a similar venue back home, comes highly recommended. Book well in advance. There is a jarring modern appendage to the building, housing the smaller New Hall.

Palladium Rīga [77 E6] Marijas iela 21; w palladium.lv. This concert venue, with a capacity of 2,000, housed in the building of the old Palladium cinema, hosts concerts of international & Latvian pop & rock performers.

VEF Culture Palace [69 G5] VEF Kultūras pils; Ropažu iela 2; w vefkp.lv. Some 5km northeast of the centre, along Brīvības iela, the building is a throwback to Soviet days. Opened in 1960, it embodies the socialist realism of the architecture of 1950s USSR, with 8 tall columns presiding over the façade & a sweeping staircase at the back of the huge foyer within. It was built to service the cultural needs of the workers of the State Electrotechnical Factory (VEF), though has now been modernised & falls under the control of the city administration. With a Grand Hall seating 800 & a smaller Chamber Hall accommodating 250, it offers pop, jazz & classical concerts, as well as acting as home for numerous amateur choirs & dance groups.

THEATRES AND CINEMAS

Dailes Theatre [76 E3] Dailes teātris; Brīvības iela 75; w dailesteatris.lv. The largest professional theatre in the Baltic States, it was founded by Eduards Smiļģis, a key figure in Latvian theatre, who remained its director until 1965. Its current premises are a purpose-built modernist building, designed by architect Marta Staņa in 1959, though not completed until 1977. Note the stylised concrete flames on the top of the façade. The building has 3 halls, the largest with a capacity of more than 900. Performances are in Latvian, but some productions (indicated on their website) offer English surtitles.

Latvian National Theatre [72 D3] Latvijas Nacionālais teātris; Kronvalda bulvāris 2; w teatris.lv. This exuberant building, with an eclectic façade incorporating Art Nouveau elements, holds a crucial place in Latvian history as the proclamation of the country's independence was read from its stage on 18 November 1918. It was opened in 1902 as Rīga's Second (Russian) Theatre, its construction funded by local Russian merchants, a counterweight to the German-language First Theatre. It became the Latvian National Theatre in 1919, though renamed Rīga Drama Theatre in the Soviet period. Its main hall seats close to 700, & there are 2 further small halls. Performances are in Latvian.

Mikhail Chekov Rīga Russian Theatre [86 E4] Mihaila Čehova Rīgas Krievu teātris; Kaļķu iela 16; w mct.lv. Tracing its origins to 1883, making it the oldest Russian-language drama theatre outside Russia itself, it has since 2006 borne the name of Michael Chekov, the Russian actor & director & nephew of playwright Anton Chekov, who spent 2 years here from 1932. It is located in the heart of the Old Town. Performances are in Russian, with Latvian & often English surtitles.

New Rīga Theatre [77 E5] Jaunais Rīgas teātris; Lāčplēša iela 25; w jrt.lv. Repertory theatre with a reputation for innovative productions, founded in 1992 & under the artistic direction of Alvis Hermanis since 1997.

Performances are generally in Latvian, though some have English surtitles (indicated on the website). In March 2024, the theatre relocated to its historic premises on Lāčplēša iela, after a 7-year stay in an old tobacco factory while that building was renovated.

Rīga Circus [77 C7] Rīgas cirks; Merķeļa iela 4; w cirks.lv. A veteran institution dating from the 1880s, the circus building is progressively being restored, & offers a modern circus experience, without performing animals, focused on dance, acrobatics & comedy. Children sit on mats at the front of the circular auditorium, with parents on seats behind.

Splendid Palace [77 C5] Elizabetes iela 61; w splendidpalace.lv. This historic cinema, dating from 1924 & exuberantly built in a neo-Baroque style, hides away from pedestrians scurrying along Elizabetes iela behind a spectacularly ugly block. Its focus is on Art House cinema rather than the mainstream multiplex diet, with films frequently subtitled in English. They also offer guided tours of the building (€10).

BARS AND CLUBS
Vecrīga

The Banshee [87 E5] Skārņu iela 11; ✆2685 4696; ◷ closed Mon–Tue. Despite the location in an unattractive building on an attractive street, this is a good choice, with craft beers on draught, the range displayed on digital screens above the bar, friendly staff, & the chance to try out your skills on the Latvian table game *novuss*.

Clayton McNamaras Drinking Emporium [87 G6] Vaļņu iela 41; ✆2001 2800; e info@ claytonmcnamaras.com. The place is packed out with models & other memorabilia in honour of the heroes of action movies & comic books, from Star Wars to Superman.

Folkklubs Ala Pagrabs [87 E6] Peldu iela 19; w folkklubs.lv. This brick-columned vaulted cavern is simultaneously bar, restaurant (€€€) & music venue, & does all 3 well. The menu includes local dishes like grey peas & bacon served in a hollowed-out loaf of rye bread, they have Latvian beers on tap & home-distilled spirits, & showcase local bands.

Kiwi Bar [87 E5] Skārņu iela 7; w kiwibar.lv. Every city needs its expat-focused sports bar, & this spot close to St Peter's Church is the best of the bunch in Rīga. A friendly place, managed by New Zealanders, with live sport on TV & a summer terrace.

City centre

Gimlet Nordic Cocktail Bar [76 D3] Baznīcas iela 37; w gimletnordic.com; ⊕ closed Sun–Mon. Specialises in cocktails created using plants of the Nordic & Baltic region, served in a small bar with a suitably Nordic minimalist décor.

Herbary [77 D5] Dzirnavu iela 67; w herbary. lv. Cocktail bar with a restaurant (€€€€) on the open top floor of the Galleria Rīga shopping mall, offering a nice spot for a sunset drink overlooking city rooftops.

Kaņepes Kultūras centrs [76 C4] Skolas iela 15; w kanepes.lv. The 'Hemp Cultural Centre' inhabits a once grand but more recently abandoned building. It provides a platform for a range of social organisations, & offers a LGBTQIA+-friendly bar with craft beers & a varied mix of events exploiting its shady terrace.

St Black [76 C4] Dzirnavu iela 57A, entrance on Baznīcas iela; ☎2863 5605; e st.black.booking@ gmail.com. The décor is indeed dark in this city centre venue offering live music, & while they bill themselves as a rock café, the music tends to be at the softer end of the genre. Also a restaurant (€€€€), with a menu ranging across Tex Mex, burgers & poke bowls.

Around Miera iela

Angārs [76 G1] Tallinas iela 10; w kvartalaangars.lv. The 'hangar' is an appropriately shed-like bar & entertainment venue in Tallinas kvartāls. The food (€€€), ordered from an open kitchen in the venue, sets out to create a street-food atmosphere, with burgers offered under the 'Fat Popo' brand (including the 'Royal Big Fat Popo' for the ravenous), as well as sushi & poke bowls under the 'Koi Sushi' label. Attracts a student clientele.

Labietis [76 F1] Aristida Briāna iela 9A-2; w labietis.lv. A temple to their home-brewed craft beer, including varieties flavoured with various herbs & berries. For the brave, they offer a braggot, a hybrid of mead & beer, named 'beekeeper's widow', with an alcohol content of 14%. The walls are decorated with murals of fighting Latvian tribesmen.

Skapis [76 F1] Aristida Briāna iela 9A; ☎2026 9669; ⊕ Thu–Sat. LGBTQIA+-friendly club, with frequent drag nights & karaoke.

Tallinas Pagalms [76 F1] Tallinas iela 10; ☎2556 7349; e pagalmsfest@gmail.com. A place that perfectly sets the tone of Tallinas kvartāls: a derelict-looking building daubed with murals & graffiti, offering a mix of bar, basic restaurant (€€€), club & cultural space.

SHOPPING

Rīga's **markets** are one of the city's great draws. The vibrant and fascinating **Rīga Central Market** [111 A1] (Rīgas Centrāltirgus; Nēģu iela 7; ☎6722 9985; e centraltirgus@rigasnami.lv; ⊕ 07.30–18.00 Mon–Sat, 07.30–17.00 Sun) sits south of the Old Town beyond the railway track. It was opened in 1930, and is based around five large pavilions that started out life as German Zeppelin hangars in Vaiņode in Kurzeme, their upper parts transferred here and repurposed. The pavilion on the Daugava River side of the complex houses the fish hall, its neighbour is the place for vegetables, and the third pavilion combines sweets and cakes with a food hall. The fourth pavilion, the least interesting of the bunch, is mostly clothes, while the fifth pavilion, oriented at 90 degrees to the others and longer than its neighbours, is the meat hall. More stalls spill outside the pavilions, including areas devoted to flowers and fruit. You will hear more Russian spoken here than at the Kalnciems or Āgenskalns markets; prices here are lower, the service brusquer. Latvian specialities to look out for include plastic bottles of birch juice in the springtime, Jāņi cheese in the summer, smoked chickens year-round and mountains of dill. A bakery in the corridor between the fish and vegetable pavilions serving up fresh Uzbek *non* bread and triangular filled samsa pastries points to the trading links between Central Asia and Latvia, though the quantity of items from Russia on sale declined sharply following the Russian invasion of Ukraine.

Kalnciems Quarter [69 D7] (Kalnciema kvartāls; Kalnciema iela 35; w kalnciemaiela.lv; ⊕ 10.00–16.00 Sat), a cluster of renovated wooden buildings in Pārdaugava houses, offices occupied by creative types around a courtyard and small orchard. This hosts an excellent farmers' market each Saturday, offering high-quality Latvian food products, clothing and handicrafts. Children love the carousel operated manually by a lady dressed as a town crier who emits various snorts and whinnying noises in imitation of the carousel animals. In the run up to Christmas, the market opens on Sundays too. A small car park (€2) opens on market days across adjacent Melnsila iela. Many bus and trolleybus routes run here from the centre along Kalnciema iela, including the number 22 airport bus. Get off at the Melnsila iela stop.

In the Pārdaugava district of the left bank of the Daugava, **Āgenskalns Market** [69 D7] (Āgenskalna tirgus; Nometņu iela 64; w agenskalnatirgus.lv; ⊕ 08.00–19.00 Tue–Sat, 09.00–17.00 Sun–Mon) is housed in one of the distinctive 'red-and-white'-style Art Nouveau buildings of Rīga city architect Reinhold Schmaeling, involving the juxtaposition of red brick and light-coloured plastered areas. Construction started in 1911, but was completed only in 1923 following the turmoil of World War I. It was reopened in 2022 after a smart restoration and is under the same management as the Kalnciems Quarter. The food and drink products on sale here are similar to those at the Kalnciems market, with an emphasis on high-quality local producers. The galleried upper floor is a good lunch option, with branches of some of the more innovative Latvian eateries, including Ausmeņa Kebabs and Vīnkalni pizza. Buses 4, 7 and 8 bring you here from central Rīga.

BOOKSHOPS
Globuss [77 D5] Dzirnavu iela 67; w eglobuss.lv. Located on the 6th floor of the Galleria Rīga shopping mall, it displays the sentence 'In the beginning was the word' in a range of languages on the window. 'Iesākumā bija vārds' in Latvian, as you were asking. It has a reasonable range of English-language novels. There is another branch at Vaļņu iela 26 in the Old Town.

Jāņa seta [77 D7] Elizabetes iela 85A; w karsuveikals.lv. The shop of Latvian cartographers Jāņa seta, they have a great collection of maps & travel guides, many in English, among them Bradt guides & a strong selection of maps on Baltic subjects. Making a fascinating souvenir, they also stock old Soviet army topographical maps, potentially including your hometown, rescued as they were about to be pulped.

Jānis Roze [77 D6] Krišjāņa Barona iela 5; w janisroze.lv. Founded in 1914 by the eponymous Jānis Roze, a bookseller & publisher deported to Siberia following the arrival of the Soviets, where he died in 1942, the company now operates a chain of bookstores. The branch on Krišjāņa Barona iela has a reasonably large English selection. There are toys & children's books downstairs.

Robert's Books [76 C4] Dzirnavu iela 51-1; w robertsbooks.lv. English-language bookstore in a courtyard behind Dzirnavu iela, established by journalist Robert Cottrell, offering a quirky selection of books & a pleasant café.

Valters un Rapa [86 G4] Aspazijas bulvāris 24; w valtersunrapa.lv. This veteran Latvian company was founded in 1912 by Artur Walters & Jānis Rapa, & was once both publishing house & bookstore. Nationalised by the Soviets in 1941, an act that prompted Jānis Rapa's suicide, it reappeared in the 1990s. The entrance is guarded by a couple of wise owls perching on piles of books. It has a small selection of books in English, & a good collection of publications about Rīga. Also sells stationery.

HANDICRAFTS AND DESIGN
Art Nouveau Rīga [76 A3] Strēlnieku iela 9; w artnouveauriga.lv. If exploring the Art Nouveau buildings of Rīga has whetted your appetite for a souvenir in the style, this store is conveniently located just across the road from the Rīga Art Nouveau Centre. It offers Art Nouveau-themed items, from mugs, notebooks & greetings cards to more expensive ornaments.

Baltu rotas [87 E5] Grēcinieku iela 11; w balturotas.lv. Sigulda-based jewellers Inita & Vitauts Straupe produce designs based on Baltic themes. The Vecrīga store incorporates a small museum of Baltic jewellery. They have another branch in the Sigulda Castle complex.

ETMO [86 E2] Torņa iela 4-3A; w etmo.lv. Located in Jacob's Barracks in the Old Town, this place aims to fuse the ideas of 'ethnographic' & 'modern' – hence 'ETMO'. It offers stylish Latvian-made scarves, slippers, tablecloths & porcelain.

Hobbywool [86 C2] Mazā Pils iela 6; w hobbywool.com. This family-run Old Town business is found in an alleyway off Jēkaba iela, identifiable by the bicycle with a knitted frame over the entrance. They offer woollen socks, gloves & bobble hats in Latvian-style designs, as well as special kits, with instructions, to enable you to knit your own pair of Latvian mittens.

M50 [76 F2] Miera iela 17; w m50.lv. Located on hip Miera iela, this offers clothing, accessories, home décor items & gifts, showcasing both local artists & well-known brands.

RIIJA [77 D6] Terbatas iela 6/8; w riija.lv. Offers beautiful items from Latvian designers, from candles to jumpers, ceramics to blankets. They have a particularly strong focus on items featuring traditional Latvian signs, & the store's symbol is the Jumis sign, a mark of fertility & abundance.

ACTIVITIES

For an unusual way to enjoy the great outdoors in Latvia, **Purvu bridēji** (Slokas iela 61–7, Kurzemes rajons; w purvubrideji.lv) organises bogshoe hikes, providing transport from Rīga, bogshoes and rubber boots, and the service of a guide. They also organise group hikes, which are a much cheaper option for the solo traveller or a couple, though these do not typically include transport to the starting point, and you have to bring your own rubber boots or hiking boots with a waterproof membrane.

A shooting range is not for everyone, but the various ranges around Rīga are popular with visitors. **Rīga Shooting Range** [72 A5] (Meža iela 1 K-5, Zemgales priekšpilsēta; w rigashootingrange.com) in the Āgenskalns neighbourhood of Pārdaugava is the best known of the bunch, offering packages incorporating a mix of semi-automatic pistols, rifles and hunting rifles, including Russian assault rifles in the Kalashnikov series, and the presence of an English-speaking instructor.

Several of the top-end hotels in Rīga have good spas open to non-guests, but for something different, the elegant **Taka Spa** [72 D3] (Kronvalda bulvāris 3A; w takaspa.lv) in the Citadel area offers a relaxing series of rituals lasting between 1 and 3 hours, combining massage, bathing and tea.

OTHER PRACTICALITIES

There are branches of both the main Swedish-owned **banks** at the junction of Kaļķu iela and Vaļņu iela in Vecrīga: Swedbank [86 F3] (Kaļķu iela 26; w swedbank.lv) and SEB Bank [86 F3] (Vaļņu iela 11; w seb.lv). Both have ATMs, and there are ATM terminals in many places across the city centre.

Two city-centre **post offices** are worthy of note. Rīga 50 Post Office [77 C8] (Rīgas 50 pasta nodaļa; Stacijas laukums 2; ☎6700 8001) is in the Origo shopping centre close to the railway station, and is open at weekends. Rīga 10 Post Office [76 B4] (Rīgas 10 pasta nodaļa; Elizabetes iela 41/43; ☎6733 1609) is a flagship 'concept post office', offering souvenirs and a coffee machine, as well as the usual postal services, in a soothingly decorated environment.

To call an **ambulance** in the event of a medical emergency, dial ☎113 or ☎112. The private **ARS Clinic** [76 C4] (Medicīnas centrs ARS; Skolas iela 5; w arsmed.lv) is centrally located, has English-speaking doctors and can provide a range of diagnostic services. There are numerous **pharmacies** across town. The branch of Mēness Aptieka [76 D4] (Brīvības iela 74–26; ✆2037 7466) is worthy of note as it is open round the clock.

WHAT TO SEE AND DO

VECRĪGA The district of 'Old Rīga' is the historical centre of the city, and indeed was the city, protected by a defensive wall, for much of its history before the 19th-century urban expansion. It is compact and walkable, with cobbled streets radiating from a series of squares, which form the best orientation points. Many of the main sights are here, as well as a lively restaurant scene and nightlife, and you are likely to spend a good portion of your time in Rīga in this part of town. It is not a picture-box medieval city; rather, it assembles buildings from a range of periods and styles reflecting the city's complex and often troubled history. Together with the neighbouring districts of the city centre developed in the Art Nouveau style in the early 20th century, it was inscribed as a UNESCO World Heritage site in 1997.

Around Pils laukums At the northern end of the Old Town, in the shadow of the Vanšu Bridge over the Daugava, the 'Castle Square' neighbourhood is focused on Rīga Castle.

Rīga Castle [86 A2] (Rīgas pils; Pils laukums 3) Long an important seat of power, its history owes much to the intermittent feuding between the Livonian Order and the inhabitants of Rīga. The latter had destroyed the original 13th-century castle of the order, but following a peace agreement between the two groups, construction of a new castle was begun in its present location in 1330. It served as the residence of the Master of the Livonian Order, until renewed conflicts with the Rīgans led the Master to relocate to Cēsis. The Rīgans eventually destroyed the castle in 1484, only to be forced to rebuild it again under their treaty of surrender, a task completed in 1515. Following the demise of the Livonian Order, the castle became the seat of Polish–Lithuanian and Swedish administrations, housed the administration of the Rīga Governorate of the Tsarist Empire, and in 1922 became the residence of the President of Latvia.

Rebuilding from the 17th century largely removed its medieval appearance, and the four-storey façade it presents onto Pils laukums, with the balcony in the centre, is that of a place of administrative rather than military power. The two circular towers, one with crenellations, diagonally opposite each other at the northwest and southeast corners of the building, are more suggestive of its antiquity. Following a Soviet interlude when it hosted the Young Pioneer organisation, it is again the official residence of the President of Latvia (hence the sentry boxes and a long line of flagpoles out front). Most of the building is not open to the public, but at the time of writing the castle was preparing to welcome back the National History Museum of Latvia, long in temporary premises following a 2013 fire at the castle. The museum entrance will be along Daugavas gāte on the southern side of the castle.

Our Lady of Sorrows Church [86 B3] (Rīgas Sāpju Dievmātes baznīca; Pils iela 5; ✆2027 5175) At the southern end of Pils laukums, the 'sorrows' in the name of this powder-blue walled church are a reference to the embattled state of the Catholic faith in post-Reformation Livonia. The church owes its existence to Holy Roman Emperor Joseph II, who on a visit to Rīga in 1780 was horrified at the meagre wooden Catholic chapel on the site, and requested the permission of Russian Empress Catherine the Great to build a grander Catholic church. The church was completed in 1785, adopting the Neoclassical style of the rest of the square, and was for many years the only Roman Catholic church in Rīga. It was rebuilt in the late 1850s by Rīga's chief architect, Johann Felsko.

St Saviour's Church [86 B3] (Anglikāņu Sv. Pestītāja baznīca; Anglikāņu iela 2A; ℄2517 1989) Lying appropriately enough at the end of Anglikāņu iela, the product of an initiative of the British business community in Latvia, Rīga's Anglican church was consecrated in 1859. It is a red-brick building with a tall spire, built in the favoured neo-Gothic style of Johann Felsko, chief architect of Rīga at the time. The funky stained-glass windows in polychrome geometrical designs recall its days as the student club of the Rīga Polytechnical Institute during the Soviet period. Note the plaque recalling the 112 men of the Royal Navy and Royal Air Force killed in action in the Baltic in 1918 and 1919, supporting the independence struggles of the Baltic States. They include nine sailors of the British cruiser HMS *Dragon*, killed off Rīga on 17 October 1919 while helping Latvian forces protect the city.

Big Christopher [86 A3] (Lielais Kristaps) On the river embankment opposite the Anglican Church, a polychrome statue of St Christopher bearing the naked Christ on his shoulder stands in a glass-sided case. The statue represents Big Christopher, a distinctively Latvian take on the tale. A kind, huge and strong man lived on the banks of the Daugava, and would ferry travellers across the river. One day he carried a small child across, but to his surprise the child became heavier and heavier, and he only just managed to get to the other bank. The child was Christ; and the weight was great because he bore the sins of the world. The child baptised the man Christopher, or 'bearer of Christ'. On his departure, Christopher found he had left a great chest of gold. With this money was founded the city of Rīga. The original statue, dating from 1683, resides in the Museum of the History of Rīga and Navigation. The version on the riverbank is a 1997 copy.

Around Doma laukums
Cobbled and expansive Doma laukums ('Cathedral Square') hosts various open-air events and exhibitions through the year. Note the children's playground on a sunken corner of the square. Opened in 2017, and taking the form of a wooden maze around which disport bronze animals based on a medieval bestiary, it is the work of sculptor Liene Mackus and bears the name **Labirints** ('Labyrinth'). An armadillo emerges at the top of a flight of steps. There is a dragon, a unicorn, an owl and a relief on a manhole cover of a fish with legs.

Rīga Cathedral [86 C4] (Rīgas Doms; Herdera laukums 6; w doms.lv; ⊕ 10.00–17.00 Mon–Sat, 14.00–17.00 Sun; adult/child €5/3) Dominating the square, the cathedral is the seat of the Archbishop of the Evangelical Lutheran Church of Latvia, and a building closely entwined with the city's history. It was founded in 1211 by the city's founder, Bishop Albert of Rīga. The cathedral, though, has been remodelled and enlarged many times since then, and the present-day red-brick building filling the southern side of Doma laukums is a mix of Romanesque, Gothic, Baroque and Art Nouveau styles. An exterior gable marked with the year 1727 records the date of one of those reconstructions, following severe damage during the 1710 siege of the city.

The interior is airy and overfilled with wooden pews. Note the fine stained-glass windows dating from the late 19th and early 20th centuries, some depicting Biblical scenes, others historical events such as Bishop Albert laying the foundation stone

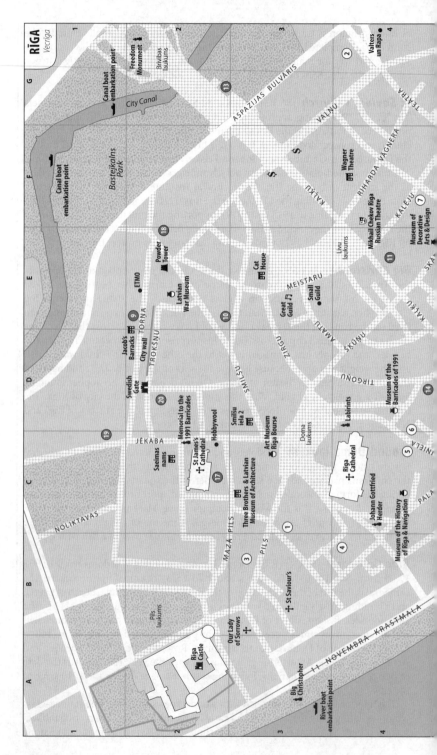

G 1
F
E
D
C
B
A

Canal boat
embarkation point

Freedom
Monument

Brīvības
laukums

City Canal

Canal boat
embarkation point

Bastejkalns
Park

ASPAZIJAS BULVĀRIS

VALŅU

2

Valters
un Rapa

13

Powder
Tower

18

ETMO

Latvian
War Museum

Cat
House

$

$

Wagner
Theatre

RIHARDA VAGNERA

TEĀTRA

Mikhail Chekov Riga
Russian Theatre

KALĒJU

Museum of
Decorative
Arts & Design

7

Jacob's
Barracks

9

City wall

TORŅU

10

MEISTARU

Great
Guild

Small
Guild

Līvu
laukums

11

SKĀ

Swedish
Gate

20

Memorial to the
1991 Barricades

Hobbywool

JĒKABA

19

Saeimas
nams

St James's
Cathedral

17

SMILŠU

Smilšu
iela 2

Art Museum
Riga Bourse

ZIRGU

AMATU

ŠĶŪŅU

TIRGOŅU

Museum of the
Barricades of 1991

14

Three Brothers & Latvian
Museum of Architecture

Johann Gottfried
Herder

Doma
laukums

Labirints

Rīga
Cathedral

6

5

PINELA

PALA

NOLIKTAVAS

MAZĀ PILS

PILS

St Saviour's

3

1

4

Museum of the History
of Rīga & Navigation

Pils
laukums

Our Lady
of Sorrows

Rīga
Castle

Big
Christopher

11 NOVEMBRA KRASTMALA

River boat
embarkation point

KALĒJU

KALĒJU

86

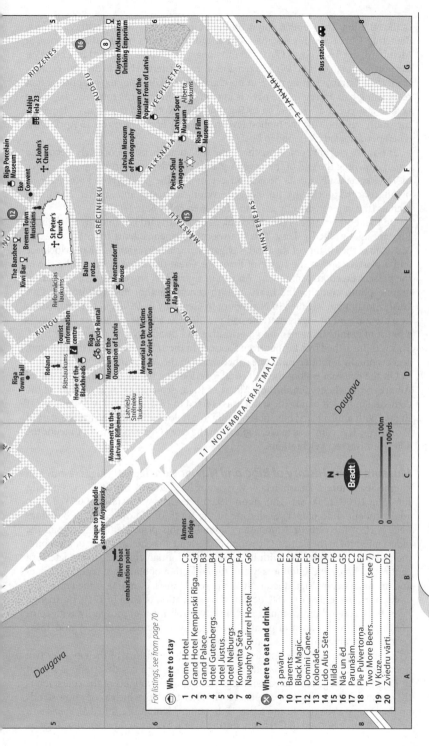

Daugava

RIDZENES

AUDÉJU

Kaļķu iela 23

Clayton McNamaras Drinking Emporium

The Banshee
Kiwi Bar

Riga Porcelain Museum

Bremen Town Musicians

Eke Convent

St John's Church

St Peter's Church

Museum of the Popular Front of Latvia

VECPILSĒTAS

Latvian Museum of Photography

ALKSNĀJA

Latvian Sport Museum

Alberta laukums

Riga Film Museum

Reformācijas laukums

KUNGU

Baltu rotas

Mentzendorff House

GRĒCINIEKU

MĀRSTAĻU

Peitav-Shul Synagogue

Riga Town Hall

Roland

Rātslaukums

Tourist information centre

House of the Blackheads

Riga Bicycle Rental

Museum of the Occupation of Latvia

Folkklubs Ala Pagrabs

PELDU

Memorial to the Victims of the Soviet Occupation

MINSTEREJAS

Monument to the Latvian Riflemen

Latviešu Strēlnieku laukums

Plaque to the paddle steamer *Moykovsky*

River boat embarkation point

Akmens Bridge

Daugava

11 NOVEMBRA KRASTMALA

Daugava

JĀŅA TĀ EL

Bus station

N

Bradt

0   100m
0   100yds

For listings, see from page 70

Where to stay

1   Dome Hotel............................C3
2   Grand Hotel Kempinski Riga......G4
3   Grand Palace.........................B3
4   Hotel Gutenbergs...................B4
5   Hotel Justus..........................C4
6   Hotel Neiburgs.......................D4
7   Konventa Sēta.......................F4
8   Naughty Squirrel Hostel............G6

Where to eat and drink

9   3 pavāru.............................E2
10   Barents..............................E2
11   Black Magic.........................E4
12   Domini Canes.......................F5
13   Kolonāde............................G2
14   Lido Alus Sēta.......................D4
15   Milda.................................F6
16   Nāc un ēd............................G5
17   Parunāsim...........................C2
18   Pie Pulvertorņa.....................E2
19   Two More Beers.................(see 7)
20   V Ķuze...............................C1
     Zviedru vārti.......................D2

of the building. The wooden pulpit, dating from 1641, is festooned with sculptures, depicting Christ and his disciples and allegorical figures of Christian virtues. St Meinhard, the first known Christian missionary in Livonia, is buried in a niche on the northern wall of the choir. His remains were transferred here in the 14th century from their original resting place in his church in Ikšķile. The stone baptismal font resembling half an egg in the nave is known as St Meinhard's font, also sat in the Ikšķile church, and was moved to Rīga in 1893. Note also the bronze plaque on the south wall showing the highest level reached by flood waters on 13 April 1709, when pews floated like wooden boats.

The most glorious object in the cathedral, though, is the ornately decorated organ crowning the end of the nave. A plaque records that Liszt composed a piece in 1884 specifically for its dedication ceremony. The cathedral is known for its organ concerts, including full-fledged evening concerts and shorter 20-minute recitals (the latter frequently at noon Mon, Wed & Sat & 15.00 Sun).

On the southern side of the cathedral, a large courtyard is framed by a delightful Romanesque vaulted gallery. This houses miscellaneous items from the adjacent Museum of the History of Rīga and Navigation, including cannons, an old clockface and a plaster copy of the statue of Peter the Great that once stood on the site of the present Freedom Monument. An urn in a glass bell jar resting on a cylindrical granite plinth contains the heart of 19th-century author and philosopher Carl Gustav Jochmann. He died in Naumburg in Germany in 1830, but bequeathed his heart to a friend in Rīga, where he had practised as a lawyer. Another curiosity is a block of granite fashioned into a primitive and decidedly grimacing stone head. This was unearthed by a farmer from Salaspils in the 1850s, handed to the museum, and eventually forgotten until unearthed again in the courtyard in 2000.

On the external wall of the cathedral, overlooking the courtyard, is a statue of Albert von Buxhoeveden, Bishop Albert of Rīga, depicted holding a model of the cathedral in his left hand. The statue was erected in 1897 as part of preparations for Rīga's 700th anniversary, but subsequently lost following its removal at the start of World War I. A copy was made, a gift from the city's German Balts, in time for the 800th anniversary celebrations.

Museum of the History of Rīga and Navigation [86 C4] (Rīgas vēstures un kuģniecības muzejs; Palasta iela 4; w rigamuz.lv; ⊕ May & Sep 10.00–17.00 daily, Jun–Aug 10.00–17.00 Sat–Thu, noon–19.00 Fri, Oct–Apr 10.00–17.00 Wed–Sun; adult/student/child €5/3/1) Sheltering to the south of the cathedral, in buildings once part of the cathedral monastery complex, this place claims the title of the oldest museum in the Baltics. Christoph Haberland, the chief architect of Rīga, built the galleried Column Hall, with its marbled Corinthian columns, in the late 18th century, to house the City Library and the collection of objects of natural sciences and art amassed by Rīga doctor Nikolaus von Himsel. A mural at the end of the Column Hall, painted in 1788, depicts the occupation of Rīga in 1710, portraying Peter the Great as both conqueror of the city and bringer of prosperity, with coins pouring out from a horn of plenty, tipped up by a celestial cherub. A mid-18th-century portrait of von Himsel surveys the hall.

The museum today offers a detailed survey of the history of the city over two floors, with labelling in Latvian throughout, though with key descriptions set out in English-language laminated booklets. Among the highlights of the collection is the original statue of Big Christopher (Lielais Kristaps), of which a copy now stands on the Daugava riverbank, and a late-15th-century sculpture entitled *Madonna on a Crescent Moon*, removed to Germany during World War II and returned to Rīga by the authorities in Lübeck in 2001. It is one of the finest medieval wooden sculptures in Latvia. Note also the Silver Cabinet, displaying silver artefacts made by the masters of the Rīga Goldsmiths' Guild, such as the welcome goblets used by each guild. There are also a couple of halls filled with model ships and dedicated to the story of navigation in Latvia.

The small square in front of the museum, abutting Doma laukums, is named Herdera laukums, home to a bust of German philosopher and theologian **Johann Gottfried Herder**, who taught in Rīga Cathedral in the 1760s.

Art Museum Rīga Bourse [86 C4] (Mākslas muzejs Rīgas Birža; Doma laukums 6; w lnmm.lv; ⊕ 10.00–18.00 Tue–Thu & Sat–Sun, 10.00–20.00 Fri; adult/student/child €6/3/2) Opposite the cathedral on Doma laukums is the old Rīga Stock Exchange building, built in the 1850s by St Petersburg-based architect Harald Julius von Bosse in the style of a Renaissance palace of Venice, its external statues and interior gilding all exuding an image of wealth. The building has been restored, and now houses the Rīga Bourse Museum, a showcase of non-Latvian art. The genesis of the museum lies in the collections of well-to-do Rīga merchants, mostly acquired in the 19th century. Particularly notable are the works gathered by Friedrich Wilhelm Brederlo, wine merchant and head of the Bourse Committee in the early 1840s, including paintings from the Dutch Golden Age and German and Austrian Romantic period. From the collection of Paul von Transehe-Roseneck come several works from the 19th-century Austrian artist Hans Makart.

As well as European painting, the museum includes some fine porcelain, including Meissen, Sèvres, Wedgwood, and Japanese Satsuma ware, as well as some Ancient Greek pottery and a small Egyptian collection, including the sarcophagus and mummy of a Theban priest from around 900BCE. Of particular note is a room dedicated to the paintings of spiritual-minded Russian artist, philosopher, traveller and writer Nicholas Roerich, who was drawn to Central Asia, eventually settling in the Kullu Valley in India. The paintings in the collection, striking blue-toned mountainscapes often incorporating Buddhist themes, were sent by Roerich to the Latvian Roerich Society in Rīga, a group dedicated to promoting his ideas, where they arrived in 1937. The society was disbanded with the Soviet occupation in 1940, and the paintings eventually ended up in the collection of the Latvian National Museum of Art.

Around the Saeima
Head north from Doma laukums along Jēkaba iela. The first road leading off this on your left is Mazā Pils iela, in one of the most scenic parts of the Old Town.

Three Brothers [86 C3] (Trīs brāļi) At numbers 17, 19 and 21 Mazā Pils iela sit a trio of historic buildings in a photogenic line. They have been collectively christened the Three Brothers. On the right, the white-painted house at number 17 with the stepped gable is the senior-looking of the three, and so it proves. The façade dates from the late 15th or early 16th century, and this is the oldest surviving stone building in Rīga. Note the tiny windows on the upper floors, and the stone benches on either side of the main entrance, which is set back from the road, reflecting the fact that at its time of construction this part of Rīga was still on the outskirts of the city, and there was less pressure on builders to pack their dwellings tightly. The middle brother, painted pale yellow, proclaims its age in iron numbers across its façade spelling out '1646'. It is topped with a curving Dutch-style gable. The grand stone portal is an 18th-century addition. The pale-green painted house

3

on the left of the ensemble at number 21 is a slither of a building, and dates from the late 17th or early 18th century.

The Three Brothers now accommodate the Latvian State Inspection for Heritage Protection, together with the **Latvian Museum of Architecture** (Latvijas Arhitektūras muzejs; Mazā Pils iela 19; w archmuseum.lv; ⊕ 09.00–18.00 Mon, 09.00–17.00 Tue & Thu, 09.00–19.00 Wed, 09.00–16.00 Fri). Admission is free, and you get what you pay for: there is no permanent exhibition, just one room offering temporary exhibitions of varying degrees of interest.

St James's Cathedral [86 C2] (Svētā Jēkaba katedrāle; Jēkaba iela 9 – entry from Klostera iela; ☎ 6732 6419; ⊕ 07.00–13.00 & 14.30–18.00 Mon–Sat, 07.00–19.30 Sun; admission free) Along the street heading north from the Three Brothers, its green spire piercing skyward atop a square-based brick tower, is the Roman Catholic cathedral in Rīga. It has served several faiths over the course of a complex history. It is also sometimes referred to in English as St Jacob's Cathedral, a confusion arising because the Latvian name Jēkabs corresponds to both the English Jacob and James. It dates from 1225, though at the start of its life was not a cathedral, that role being held by Rīgas Doms. It became a Lutheran church in 1522, and was the first Lutheran church to hold services in Latvian in the following year. It switched to Jesuit control in 1582 during the Counter-Reformation, though went back to the Lutherans some 40 years later under Swedish rule. Following Latvia's independence, with Rīgas Doms now a Lutheran cathedral, St James's Church was handed to the Catholics to use as their cathedral. The transfer was the subject of Latvia's first ever referendum in 1923, called by Baltic-German politician Paul Schiemann, who opposed the transfer. Voters sided with Schiemann, but the low turnout meant that it went ahead. A plaque near the entrance records the visit of Pope John Paul II in 1993.

Behind the cathedral, on Jēkaba iela, stands a **Memorial to the 1991 Barricades** [86 C2], recalling the concrete defences hastily erected in January 1991 to protect public buildings and defend the re-establishment of Latvian independence (page 94). The memorial incorporates concrete blocks from the original barricades, daubed with slogans like 'Freedom for Baltic'.

Saeimas nams [86 C2] (Jēkaba iela 11) The seat of Latvia's parliament stands opposite St James's Cathedral in a monumental caramel-coloured building. It was built in the 1860s, in the style of a Renaissance palace, to house the Landtag of the Livonian Noble Corporation, the body of representatives of the German-Baltic nobility who owed fealty to the Russian emperor but made up the local ruling class. In 1920, the building housed the Constitutional Assembly of Latvia, tasked with elaborating the constitution of the newly independent state, and which made way for the first Saeima on 7 November 1922. During the Soviet occupation, the building housed the Supreme Soviet of the Latvian Soviet Socialist Republic. A plaque next to the entrance records the declaration on the restoration of independence of the Republic of Latvia made by deputies of the Supreme Soviet on 4 May 1990, heralding the country's independence from the Soviet Union. The building is once again the home of the Saeima. Note in a niche on an external wall, the statue of mythical Latvian hero Lāčplēsis, his bear ears hidden by wavy locks. The original occupant of the niche was Wolter von Plettenberg, Master of the Livonian Order in the early 16th century and a key figure for German Balts. Lāčplēsis replaced him in 1922, before being in turn destroyed in the 1950s during the Soviet occupation. The present statue is a reconstructed version installed in 2007.

Around the Swedish Gate Running eastwards off Jēkaba iela, the narrow, curving western stretch of Trokšņu iela is among the most atmospheric streets of the Old Town. As it crosses Aldaru iela (Brewer's Street), you encounter the **Swedish Gate** [86 D2] (Zviedru vārti), the only surviving gate of the old city wall. It dates from 1698, during the period of Swedish control of the city. Cannons are embedded into the walls, and the house over the gate has thoughtfully decorated its windows with plant pots, making for a photogenic spot. There is, though, a dark legend around the place, telling of a young local girl who developed a forbidden romantic relationship with a Swedish soldier. Local citizens, as a warning to other girls who might be similarly tempted, built her into the wall of the gate. It is said that she still cries out at night, affirming her enduring love for the soldier.

The eastern end of Trokšņu iela is marred by an over-restored section of the **city wall** [86 D2] running between it and the parallel Torņa iela, its fresh red bricks jarring against the nearby genuine antiquity. The restored wall ends in rather bizarre fashion in mid-arch, instead of colliding against the building beyond. Standing in the shadow of the northernmost arch is the bronze statue of a shrouded female figure. Titled *The Ghost*, it is a 2015 work by Ieva Rubeze. Along the other side of Torņa iela runs the long, yellow-walled **Jacob's Barracks** [86 D2] (Jēkaba kazarmas), built in the late 18th century. They now accommodate restaurants and upmarket shops.

Powder Tower [86 E2] (Pulvertornis) At the eastern end of Torņa iela, at the junction with Smilšu iela, stands one of the most striking remnants of the medieval defences, the circular-based brick Powder Tower, with cannonballs embedded in its walls in commemoration of the Second Northern War. First mentioned in 1330, when it was known as the Sand Tower, it was destroyed in 1621 during the Polish–Swedish War, and the current version dates from 1650. It was used as a gunpowder store, later a prison, and then a lodge for a German student fraternity, before being incorporated into the **Latvian War Museum** [86 E2] (Latvijas Kara muzejs; Smilšu iela 20; w karamuzejs.lv; ⊕ 10.00–17.00 Wed–Sun; admission free). Tracing the history of warfare in Latvia from the 9th century to the present day, the displays are of varying levels of interest, with signage over much of the earlier period in Latvian only, with laminated summaries in English. A well-presented exhibition on Latvia in World War I, focusing on the role of the Latvian Riflemen battalions, has English signage and some compelling items, such as a display of rings crafted by soldiers from the heads of artillery shells.

Smilšu iela Running back westwards from here towards Doma laukums [86 D3], Smilšu iela has some fine Art Nouveau buildings. Note in particular the exuberant creation of Konstantīns Pēkšēns at **Smilšu iela 2** [86 D3]. Dating from 1902, it is among the earlier Art Nouveau blocks of the city. A protruding part of the façade is held up by three columns; the central one takes the form of a spreading tree, while those to either side are female and male figures, emerging organically from tree trunks.

Around Līvu laukums The spacious **Līvu laukums** [86 E4] (Livs' Square) is among the more bustling parts of the Old Town, accommodating restaurant tables from adjacent eateries. It is not a historic square, but was laid out in the Soviet period on the site of buildings destroyed during World War II.

Guildhalls The western side of the square is dominated by the buildings of Rīga's two guildhalls, institutions that reflected the social hierarchy of the city and

3

were both made up largely of German speakers. The larger of the two is, logically enough, the **Great Guild** [86 E3] (Lielā ģilde; Amatu iela 6), which represented the merchants of the city. Also admitted to its exclusive ranks were goldsmiths, lawyers and theologians. Its origins lie in the 13th century, but the current building, in a neo-Gothic style with a crenellated roof, dates from the 1850s. It is now a concert venue, home to the Latvian National Symphony Orchestra. Next door is the **Small Guild** [86 E3] (Mazā ģilde; Amatu iela 5), housed in another neo-Gothic building, this one dating from the 1860s, the façade embellished by an octagonal tower. The Small Guild, which was less prestigious, represented the artisans of Rīga. The importance of both organisations declined after 1877, as the Russian Empire exerted its political control over the city.

Cat House [86 E3] (Kaķu nams; Meistaru iela 10) Note the yellow-walled apartment block dating from 1909 in an Art Nouveau style across the road from the Great Guild. This is popularly known as the Cat House in honour of the two sculptures of cats, their backs arched, on top of the two spired corner towers. Tourist guides will spin you the tale that the building was commissioned by a merchant who, not being an ethnic German, was refused membership of the Great Guild, and expressed his anger at that state of affairs by positioning the cat sculptures so that their rear quarters faced the guild building. Peace evidently intervened at some point, as the cats now face forwards. A plaque on the building records that this was the workplace of film director Juris Podnieks, who drowned in 1992 while scuba diving in a lake in Kurzeme.

Wagner Theatre [86 F4] (Vāgnera teātris; Riharda Vāgnera iela 4; w vagneriga. lv; not open to the public) Taking Riharda Vāgnera iela southeastwards from Līvu laukums, you reach at number 4 the façade of the former Rīga City Theatre, opened in 1782 on the commission of Baron Otto Hermann von Vietinghoff to a design by the architect Christoph Haberland, a stalwart exponent of Neoclassical architecture. The theatre quickly established itself as a centre of Rīga cultural life. The young Richard Wagner worked as music director from 1837 until 1839. It was creatively a productive period for the composer, who started work on his opera *Rienzi*. He and his wife Minna had, however, amassed such large debts while in Rīga that they were forced to flee the place to stay ahead of their creditors. A particularly stormy sea crossing to London during his escape inspired his opera *The Flying Dutchman*. From 1863, on the construction of the present-day National Opera House, the place was no longer used for performances. Its upper floor hosted chamber music concerts from 1988 to 2007, but at that stage, with the condition of the building deteriorating, it was abandoned. The Rīga Richard Wagner Society has been established with the aim of renovating the theatre and establishing a Richard Wagner museum. Until its work is realised, the visitor must be content with a plaque on the façade recording Wagner's presence here. It also records the guest performances given in the 1840s by, among others, Franz Liszt, Clara Schumann and Hector Berlioz.

Around Rātslaukums Curving southwards past the cathedral, **Jauniela** [86 C4] is among the most picturesque lanes of the Old Town, with its polychrome buildings abutting the cobbled street. It was evidently determined that this was the spot in the then Soviet Union most closely resembling Victorian London, as it doubled as Baker Street in the television series *The Adventures of Sherlock Holmes and Dr Watson*; a great success among Soviet audiences. Rīga still commemorates the great detective's birthday in or around January each year with a parade of costumed characters.

Museum of the Barricades of 1991 [86 D4] (1991 gada barikāžu muzejs; Krāmu iela 3; w barikades.lv; ⊕ 10.00–17.00 Mon–Fri, 11.00–17.00 Sat; donations welcome) Taking Krāmu iela to the left, you reach almost immediately this well-presented and absorbing small museum developed by veterans of the events of the Barricades of 1991 (page 94). It is housed on the first floor of an 18th-century building. The exhibition starts with a mocked-up Soviet kitchen. Peer through a keyhole to view images of the wealthy and decadent west, out of reach on the other side. A room dedicated to the organisation of the Barricades features a diorama of Doma laukums showing the fires burning across the square to provide warmth for those defending Rīga's strategic sites. The international impact of the Barricades, the role of the press, and the attack on the Interior Ministry on 20 January 1991 are all highlighted.

Rātslaukums [87 D5] (Town Hall Square) Further down Jauniela, Mazā Jauniela, also running off to the left, brings you into cobbled Rātslaukums. This is fronted, logically enough, by the columned façade of **Rīga Town Hall** [87 D5] (Rīgas rātsnams). The building is a 2003 reconstruction; the old town hall was destroyed in World War II. In the centre of the square stands a **Statue of Roland** [87 D5], the semi-fictional Frankish hero whose presence in city squares in Germany and the Baltic region signified medieval city privileges. This statue, which depicts the coat of arms of Rīga on the shield, is though far from medieval: it was installed in 1896, though that statue is now in St Peter's Church and what you see in the square today is a modern replica.

House of the Blackheads [87 D5] (Melngalvju nams; Rātslaukums 7; w melngalvjunams.lv; ⊕ 10.00–17.00 daily; adult/student €7/5) All eyes focus on the House of the Blackheads, the showiest building in Rīga, across the square from the Town Hall. The Brotherhood of the Blackheads was an association of unmarried and foreign merchants who were not yet eligible for membership of the Great Guild. Thriving across Livonia from the 14th century, The Brotherhood chose as their patron Saint Maurice, the black Egyptian military leader from whom they took the symbol of a black head. The building was constructed in the early 14th century, but heavily bombed by the Germans in 1941, its ruins demolished in 1948 during the Soviet occupation. The building you see today is a reconstruction from the 1990s. Pay a little more for your entrance ticket and get a glass of sparkling wine or a cup of coffee to accompany your walk round the building.

The brick cellars are the only survivals from the original building, and you can still see the hypocaust, a warm-air heating system below the floor. This part of the building today hosts an exhibition devoted to the history of the Brotherhood. Above this are the historical cabinets, laid out in a 19th-century style and incorporating displays of snuffboxes and silverware. The latter includes some of the large and fantastical works of silversmith Oļegs Auzers. The Latvian President worked from these rooms from 2012 to 2016 while Rīga Castle was being restored. The largest room in the building is the extravagant Celebration Hall, an *Apotheosis of St Maurice* painted on the ceiling. Note also the busts of Latvian and foreign composers on your way up. Another large room, furnished in a Rococo style, has been named the Blue Guard Hall in honour of the company of cavalrymen founded in 1720 by merchant journeymen, whose light-blue uniforms gave them their title. The guards were disbanded in the 1880s.

Rīga tour guides will claim that the Brotherhood gave the world the first decorated Christmas tree, with documents suggesting that in 1510 they put up a tree in the square and embellished it festively before setting fire to the thing. Their

THE BARRICADES

The Supreme Soviet of the Latvian Soviet Socialist Republic adopted a declaration on the restoration of independence on 4 May 1990. Ten days later, Soviet leader Mikhail Gorbachev responded with a decree announcing that the declaration was void since it violated the Soviet Constitution. An increasingly tense period followed, characterised by friction both between Latvia and the Soviet Union, and within Latvia itself between the independence movement, represented by the Popular Front of Latvia (Latvijas Tautas fronte), and pro-Soviet forces. Bomb explosions in December 1990 accentuated concerns that the latter were planning to provoke violence as a pretext for seizing power. On 2 January 1991, Soviet special forces within the Ministry of Internal Affairs, a unit known as OMON, seized the Press House, the national printing house of Latvia.

Events in Lithuania to the south then spiralled out of control. On 10 January, Gorbachev demanded the restoration of the Soviet constitution in Lithuania. With the risk of Soviet military intervention looming, Lithuanian citizens encircled key strategic buildings to protect them. In the early morning of Sunday 13 January, Soviet tanks arrived at one of these key sites, the TV tower in Vilnius, and soldiers fired into the crowd gathered around it. Thirteen Lithuanians were killed, another died of a heart attack, and a Soviet soldier was killed by fire from his own side. The date became known as Bloody Sunday in Lithuania.

Learning of the attack in Lithuania, the Popular Front in Latvia called on citizens to gather together to defend strategic sites. A large demonstration was centred on Rīga Cathedral Square, and the Front called for the construction of barricades. As night fell, a remarkable episode of non-violent popular resistance took shape, with agricultural machinery and trucks, the latter loaded with construction waste and logs, brought into the city to block streets. Three fishing vessels were even deployed in the Daugava River in the defence of the Latvian Television Centre. Large concrete blocks and wire obstacles were also used. Cathedral Square, which occupied an important site in the Old Town adjacent to the Latvian Radio headquarters, became the organisational hub of the Barricades movement.

opposite numbers in Tallinn make the same claim for that city. An octagonal stone plaque on the square concretises Rīga's pitch in several languages.

Museum of the Occupation of Latvia [87 D5] (Latvijas Okupācijas muzejs; Latviešu strēlnieku laukums 1; w okupacijasmuzejs.lv; ⊕ 10.00–18.00 Sat–Wed; adult/student €5/3). Rātslaukums is separated from the adjacent square, Latviešu Strēlnieku laukums, by an ugly Soviet-era building resembling a black box raised off the ground by pillars. This housed a Soviet museum honouring the Latvian Red Riflemen, but now holds one of the most important, and sobering, museums in Rīga. It highlights the depredations faced by the Latvian people under the occupations of Nazi Germany and the Soviet Union. The academic underpinning to the well-presented displays is that of US academic Timothy Snyder's *Bloodlands*: the idea that Latvia was part of a region in which the evils of the regimes of Hitler and Stalin reinforced each other to create truly appalling levels of suffering. The permanent exhibition proceeds historically, the colours of the walls at each point giving a measure of the distress faced by the Latvian people.

A tour of the museum starts upstairs, in a white-walled space dedicated to the flowering of independent Latvia in the interwar period. You then descend into the

Volunteers staffed the barricades in shifts. Food and drink were organised. A bonfire burned in the square. Barricades were also organised to protect important sites in other Latvian towns.

In the following days, OMON forces attacked bridges on the outskirts of the city. During an attack on 16 January at the Vecmīlgrāvis Bridge in the north of Rīga, a driver working for the Latvian Transport Ministry named Roberts Mūrnieks was fatally shot, becoming the first victim of the events of the Barricades.

The bloodiest episode, though, took place on the evening of 20 January, when OMON and other groups attacked the Latvian Interior Ministry. During shooting centred on the footbridge across the City Canal in Bastejkalns Park over the road, five people lost their lives: two militia officers, two documentary film cameramen and a student. There was another fatality on the following day when Ilgvars Grieziņš, on his way to volunteer his services as an English-language translator, was killed in an accident near the parliament building as heavy concrete blocks were being moved.

Following the funerals of those killed on 20 January, the immediate threat appeared to have dissipated, although tensions remained and there were further flare-ups, notably at the time of the Soviet coup attempt in August, when a driver named Raimonds Salmiņš was killed in Rīga. Latvia's independence was finally recognised by the Soviet Union, which itself had only three months to live, on 6 September 1991. Some of the barricades were not though finally dismantled until 1992.

Rīga is full of reminders of the events of the Barricades, including concrete blocks from that period preserved near the Saeima and in Kronvalda Park, where they are symbolically united with a chunk of the Berlin Wall. There are memorials at the death sites of those killed in the violence, from engraved pink stones in Bastejkalns Park to a cross near Vecmīlgrāvis Bridge where Roberts Mūrnieks was shot. Every year on 20 January, the day of commemoration of the participants of the Barricades, a bonfire burns symbolically on Cathedral Square.

darkness with the signature of the Molotov-Ribbentrop Pact on 23 August 1939. Displays examine the parallels between the evils of the two powers: Nazi Holocaust and Soviet Holodomor. There are moving displays on the Soviet mass deportations of 1941 and 1949, including a mock-up of a rail truck, with projected images of deportees crowded on to it. Coverage of the German Occupation includes the massacre of Jews in Latvia, with the collaboration of some Latvians in the atrocities acknowledged. The end of World War II simply marked a different occupation: fabric strips hanging from the ceiling represent Latvia's forests, and the partisan resistance against the Soviet Union. A display on the Gulag labour camps, a Soviet system designed to dehumanise those sent here, deliberately rehumanises them through a focus on personal reminiscences.

As the exhibition turns red, the focus moves to the subjection of Latvia to Soviet totalitarianism, including through collectivisation, the militarisation of society, and the importation of ethnic Russians, diluting Latvian cultural identity. KGB surveillance is highlighted: note the listening device unearthed during the renovation of the Hotel Rīga in 1999. The story then takes a positive turn, with a focus on Latvians in exile, and of the domestic struggles of the Singing Revolution in confronting the Soviet Union, with striking footage of the human chain of the Baltic Way. You climb back upstairs, and into the light.

Latviešu Strēlnieku laukums [87 D6] (Latvian Riflemen's Square) This centres on a pink granite **Monument to the Latvian Riflemen** [87 D6] dating from 1971. The monument started out in support of the Soviet cult of the Latvian Red Riflemen, the members of the Latvian regiments who supported the Bolsheviks. Its origins are still apparent both in the overall Soviet style of the monument and in the stars decorating the caps of the three great-coated figures who stand back-to-back, their gazes covering the square. Following the restoration of Latvian independence, the monument was retitled to embrace all Latvian Riflemen, the emphasis now on the role of these units in fighting for the Latvian cause during World War I, rather than on those elements supporting the Soviet Union.

Another monument in the square stands more unequivocally as a rejoinder to the evils of the Soviet Union. The **Memorial to the Victims of the Soviet Occupation** [87 D6] takes the form of a wall, one side patterned with small red and white pieces of granite to resemble a Latvian blanket. On the reverse side, the design reproduces a handkerchief embroidered by deportee Mērija Stakle with the names of others deported with her to Siberia. The wall is the venue for wreath-layings in commemorative events linked to the Soviet occupation and in remembrance of its victims.

On the embankment close to Akmens Bridge, note the plaque recalling the nearby sinking on 13 August 1950 of the overloaded **paddle steamer** *Mayakovsky* [87 B6]. Some 147 people were killed, a disaster hushed up in Stalin's Soviet Union. The plaque was put up in 2011, ironically at the landing place for present-day river cruise vessels.

Around Reformācijas laukums
A couple of blocks to the east of Rātslaukums, over Kungu iela, cobbled Reformation Square [87 E5] takes its name from the role played by the adjacent St Peter's Church in the early adoption of the Reformation in Rīga through the work of pastor Andreas Knöpken, who set out 24 theses of the new movement in a disputation in the church on 12 June 1522.

St Peter's Church [87 E5] (Svētā Pētera Evaņģēliski luteriskā baznīca; Reformācijas laukums 1; ✆6718 1430; ☉ summer 10.00–18.00 Tue–Sun, winter 10.00–18.00 daily; tower & church adult/student/child €9/7/3, church-only €3/2/1) First mentioned in 1209, the church is a landmark of the Old Town. Its metal Baroque-style spire, with alternating cupolas and galleries, rises 123m, and its observation deck at 72m, reached by an elevator running every 10 minutes, offers a great view across old Rīga and the Daugava. Signs warn against standing, sitting, climbing or putting children on the railings, or indeed bending over the railings. Avoid going near the railings, basically.

The spire has had a challenging history. A 136m version was built in 1491, which collapsed in 1666, burying eight people in the process. A fire damaged its replacement in 1677, with a new version completed in 1690, which at 148m was then the tallest wooden structure in Europe. It was sadly destroyed by lightning in 1721. Visiting Russian Tsar Peter the Great apparently helped to put the fire out. A new spire was built in 1746. It is said that, to avoid the misfortunes faced by previous versions, master builder Johann Wilbern downed a goblet of wine while sitting astride the golden cockerel at its top. He threw the goblet down on to the ground, the spire destined to last as many years as the number of pieces the goblet shattered into. Unfortunately, it landed on a cartload of hay passing below and failed to break. The spire did not, though, immediately collapse, surviving until World War II, when artillery fire again brought it down. Cockerel number seven was placed at the top of the reconstructed tower in 1970.

The façade has three identical portals, flanked by Baroque-style sculptures in niches. The interior impresses for its soaring vaulted nave, pushed aloft by red brick columns. It is relatively spartan, save for the elaborate gold-framed shields on the columns. There is currently a large empty space above the gallery at the back of the nave where the organ should be, though a joint Latvian–German project aims to reconstruct the Baroque organ of 1734 that once stood here. Items of statuary in a corner of the church include the original statue of Roland that once stood in Rātslaukums and, topped by a small equestrian statue, the Blue Guard Chapel, named for the 18th-century voluntary city guard. Note also the plaque in the nave recalling the presence of Johann Gottfried Müthel, German composer and student of Bach, church organist here for more than 20 years until his death in 1788. There are frequent temporary exhibitions in the aisles.

Bremen Town Musicians [87 E5] Behind St Peter's Church, on Skārņu iela, stands one of Rīga's most popular sculptures, a 1990 work by Bremen artist Christa Baumgärtel, based on a Brothers Grimm fairy story, and involving four creatures, a donkey, a dog, a cat and a cockerel, standing on each other's backs. The statue was a gift from Bremen to its twin city of Rīga. The version in Rīga differs, though, in one important characteristic from that found in Bremen. In Rīga, the animals are peering through an iron curtain, evidently amazed at the riches on the other side, a setting inspired by the then ongoing process of Perestroika and the imminent break-up of the Soviet Union. Visitors rub snouts and beaks for good luck.

Museum of Decorative Arts and Design [87 E4] (Dekoratīvās mākslas un dizaina muzejs; Skārņu iela 10; w lnmm.lv; ⊕ 11.00–17.00 Tue, Thu–Sun, 11.00–19.00 Wed; adult/student/child €6/3/2) Standing opposite the back of St Peter's Church on Skārņu iela, the building of the former St George's Church has a chequered history even for a city characterised by tribulations. It was built at the start of the 13th century as the chapel of the Castle of the Livonian Brothers of the Sword. In 1297, a particularly bad year in the always fraught relations between the townsfolk of Rīga and the Livonian Order, the castle was sacked, with only St George's Chapel unscathed. The new castle was built in its present location close to the Daugava, and the site of the old castle was turned over to the Convent of the Holy Spirit. In 1554, in the wake of the Reformation in Rīga, St George's Church was given over to warehousing. In 1989, it became home for the Museum of Decorative Arts and Design. The temporary exhibition space on the ground floor is particularly evocative, within the thick walls of the Romanesque church.

The permanent collection is laid out over two floors upstairs. One display looks at Latvian decorative applied art from the late 19th century until the 1960s. Detailed information is received by downloading an app on your phone. Note the 1920s brightly coloured ceramic plates of the Baltars porcelain painting workshop, combining traditional Latvian motifs and modernist styles. The furniture designed by Ansis Cīrulis in the 1930s used an Art Deco style adapted to suit the patriotic focus of the Ulmanis government. The top floor focuses on design since the 1960s. Note the model of the concrete 'RĪGA' city sign, designed by Valdis Celms in the 1980s, and still found at entrances to the city.

Eke Convent [87 F5] (Ekes Konvents; Skārņu iela 22) The yellow-walled building a little further to the east along Skārņu iela was built in 1435, to accommodate travellers entering the city. In the late 16th century, the mayor of Rīga, Nikolajs Eke, found himself in need of improving his image, having been on the wrong side of the Calendar Riots of 1584, when Rīga's Lutheran citizens had protested against the City Council's support for the new calendar approved by Pope Gregory. He was also accused of appropriating public money for his own needs. Needing to demonstrate his positive credentials, he established in this building in the 1590s a refuge for indigent old women. More recently, the building has housed a wax museum and a hotel. A relief on the façade, dating from the early 17th century, depicts Christ and the Sinner.

Rīga Porcelain Museum [87 F5] (Rīgas Porcelāna muzejs; Kalēju iela 9/11; w porcelanamuzejs.riga.lv; ⊕ 11.00–18.00 Tue–Sun; adult/student €5/3.50) Tucked into the Konventa sēta courtyard behind Skārņu iela, the museum offers a history of porcelain manufacture in the city. This kicked off in the 19th century with the factories opened by two entrepreneurs, the Russian Sergei Kuznetsov and the German Jacob Carl Jessen. In the Soviet period their production was brought together in the Rīga Porcelain Factory, one of the largest producers in the Soviet Union, but like so many Soviet industrial enterprises it was unable to compete in a Latvia opened up to the west, and collapsed in the 1990s. Note the room devoted to Soviet ideological production, focused on large vases with portraits of Stalin, hammer-and-sickle designs and scenes of booming industrial and agricultural enterprise. The museum also runs creative workshops (advance booking essential).

St John's Church [87 F5] (Svētā Jāņa baznīca; Skārņu iela 24; w janabaznica. lv; ⊕ May–Sep 10.00–18.00 Mon–Sat, 13.00–18.00 Sun) Dating from the 13th century, when the chapel of a Dominican monastery was located on the site, the church has had an eventful history. The Dominicans were ousted in 1523 during the Reformation. After periods of service as stables and an ammunition store, the place fell to the Evangelical Lutheran Church.

The present Gothic design largely dates from the 15th and 16th centuries, with the tower added in 1849. The interior impresses for its intricate vaulted ceiling. It is said that two 15th-century monks opted to be sealed into the southern wall as a demonstration of their piety in a bid for immortalisation as saints. They were fed by passers-by through a grate. They never, however, achieved their dream of sainthood, it being judged that they had acted for their own glory rather than for that of God. A brick gate beside the church leads into the picturesque **St John's Courtyard** (Jāņa sēta), occupied with the tables of adjacent eateries.

Kalēju iela Kalēju iela runs parallel to Skārņu iela, one block to the north. Among the most photogenic Art Nouveau buildings in the Old Town is the polychrome confection at Kalēju iela 23 [87 F5], the work of Jewish architect Paul Mandelstamm, who was later a victim of the Holocaust. Its entrance is decorated with a hood featuring painted trees and a line of daisies. A lamp in the form of a drooping plant curls forward over the top. Around the window above, the rays of a golden sun, together with the window itself, form the keyhole shape so beloved of Rīga's Art Nouveau architects.

Mentzendorff House [87 E6] (Mencendorfa nams; Grēcinieku iela 18; w rigamuz.lv; ⊕ May–Sep 10.00–17.00 Sat–Thu, noon–19.00 Fri, Oct–Apr 10.00–17.00 Wed–Sun; adult/student €3/2) A block to the south of St Peter's Church, this white-walled building with a steeply pitched roof was built in 1695 by a glass cutter named Jirgen Helm. It takes its name from its last pre-war owner, August Mentzendorff, whose family held the place in the early 20th century. Now part of the Rīga Museum of History and Navigation, it aims to offer a feel of the life of a wealthy family in, roughly, the 18th century, with furniture taken from the collection of its parent museum. There are restored wall and ceiling paintings, including a bucolic woodland scene in the dancing hall. There is a room devoted to Dietrich André Loeber, a German law professor and grandson of Mentzendorff, who did much to support the museum's establishment. The cellar houses an exhibition of modern glass art, continuing the building's association with glassmaking.

The southern streets of Vecrīga
The southern part of the Old Town is the area least visited by tourists. Its main square, **Alberta laukums** [87 G6], or Albert Square, making all British visitors immediately think of the soap opera *Eastenders*, is named in honour of Bishop Albert, and was the site of a Liv village predating the arrival of the Crusaders. It is now a desolate place, with an unattractive view towards the railway tracks. There are though some pleasant streets around it, such as Alksnāja iela, lined with former warehouses dating from the 16th to the 18th centuries, and there are several worthwhile museums dotted among the narrow lanes.

Museum of the Popular Front of Latvia [87 G6] (Tautas fronts muzejs;
Vecpilsētas iela 13/15; w lnvm.lv; ⊕ 10.00–17.00 Tue–Sat; admission free) A branch of the National History Museum of Latvia, the museum is housed in a 17th-century building close to Alberta laukums given to the Latvian Popular Front in February 1989 by the Council of Ministers of the Latvian Soviet Socialist Republic. The organisation's newsletter, *Atmoda*, was published here. Over three floors, the building tells the story of the front, an umbrella organisation bringing together people with a common vision of a democratic and free Latvia, in helping to secure the restoration of independence from the Soviet Union. It is an atmospheric and worthwhile presentation, even if it does go into more detail than the casual visitor may be seeking. Note the film of the dismantling of the Lenin monument in Rīga in August 1991, theatrically displayed on a screen set up in the base of a mock-up of a toppled Lenin monument.

Latvian Sport Museum [87 F6] (Latvijas Sporta muzejs; Alksnāja iela 9;
w sportamuzejs.lv; ⊕ 10.00–17.00 Tue–Fri, 10.00–16.00 Sat; adult/student €2.50/1.50) A block to the southwest, much of this museum is devoted to an exhaustive collection of the medals and other memorabilia of Latvian sporting champions. Note the wooden bobsleigh built in Cēsis in the 1920s, and the Misha the bear, mascot of the 1980 Moscow Olympics, belonging to the 2.13m-tall basketball player Uļjana Semjonova, a key figure of the gold-medal-winning Soviet women's team in both the 1976 and 1980 Olympics.

Rīga Film Museum [87 F6] (Rīgas Kino muzejs; Peitavas iela 10, but entry from
Alksnāja iela; w kinomuzejs.lv; ⊕ 11.00–18.00 Tue, Wed, Fri, 11.00–20.00 Thu, 11.00–17.00 Sat; adult/student €3.50/1.80) This is a small museum, appropriately reflecting the diminutive scale of the Latvian film industry, but well presented, housed in an 18th-century building. There is an account of the connections of Soviet director Sergei Eisenstein with the city. He was born here in 1898, the son of prominent architect Mikhail Eisenstein, though left for St Petersburg, where he would initially follow his father's footsteps before turning to theatre and then film. There is also a display on animation, and another highlighting the most significant Latvian documentaries.

Peitav-Shul Synagogue [87 F6] (Sinagoga Peitav-Shul; Peitavas iela 6/8; w jews.
lv/en/riga-synagogue; ⊕ 10.00–17.00 Sun–Fri) Built in 1905 in an Art Nouveau

style with motifs inspired by Assyrian and Egyptian art, this was the only one of the synagogues of Rīga to escape the burning orchestrated by the Nazis in July 1941. Given its Old Town location, tightly packed against neighbouring buildings, it was considered too risky to burn it down, lest the fire spread. The building was used as a warehouse instead. In the Soviet era, it was one of the few functioning synagogues across the USSR.

Latvian Museum of Photography [87 F6] (Latvijas Fotogrāfijas muzejs; Mārstaļu iela 8 – entry from Alksnāja iela; w rigamuz.lv; ⏱ 10.00–17.00 Wed & Fri–Sun, noon–19.00 Thu; adult/student/child €4.50/3.50/1.50) Housed in a 16th-century merchant's building, this offers a learned exhibition on the development of photography in Latvia, set against global advances in the use of the medium. You are invited to photograph yourself against the decorative backgrounds of photo salons of the early years of the 20th century. Note the display on the tiny Minox camera and its inventor, Walter Zapp. It was produced from 1938 by the State Electrotechnical Factory (VEF) in Rīga. Weighing 125g, it was small enough to put in your pocket, like a cigarette lighter. Zapp moved to Germany in 1941 as part of the resettlement of German Balts, founding a new Minox company in that country after the war. Another display focuses on Latvian-born George Benjamin, who later settled in Canada, developing a passion for the exploration and photography of 'blue holes', large marine caverns formed in limestone through karst processes. The museum also hosts temporary exhibitions showcasing contemporary photographers. At the time of writing, the museum was preparing to relocate to a temporary location at Kronvalda bulvāris 4, while its building is restored.

CITY CENTRE When in 1997 the historic centre of Rīga was inscribed as a UNESCO World Heritage site, the historic centre of Tallinn, capital of Estonia, also made the list. Both cities were praised for their medieval cores, a legacy of their history as important ports of the Hanseatic League. While Tallinn's inscription covered just the 113ha of the medieval town, that for Rīga covered 438ha, stretching out of the medieval core to encompass the districts beyond. These were built up with residential blocks at the beginning of the 20th century when the Art Nouveau movement was at its peak, a key factor behind the inclusion of the area in the UNESCO listing. Now the centre of the modern city of Rīga, this is a cityscape of parks, Art Nouveau apartment blocks and public buildings reflecting the Latvian national consciousness that emerged during the Tsarist era. It makes for worthwhile exploration, and a fine complement to Vecrīga.

Around the City Canal With the Daugava River forming the boundary of Vecrīga to the west, the City Canal [86 G2] (Pilsētas kanāls) to its east completes the encirclement of the Old City. The canal has its origins in the moats defending the historic city.

Bastejkalns Park [86 F1] (Bastejkalna parks) Separating Vecrīga from the modern city centre, this is an inviting elongated stretch of greenery centred on the canal. It was laid out in the late 19th century by landscape architect Georg Kuphaldt on the site of demolished city ramparts. A low hill gives the park its name, 'Bastion Hill', though the view from the top to the Old Town and Freedom Monument is impeded by trees. There are various pieces of statuary in the park. At the northern end, across the road from the Ionic-columned façade of the building now housing the Ministry of Foreign Affairs, is a 2003 statue to Kārlis Ulmanis, a controversial addition in some quarters given the authoritarian nature of his regime. To the south is a seated statue of writer

Rūdolfs Blaumanis. Either side of the footbridge across the canal, note the five polished pink granite stones, dedicated to victims of the violence of 20 January 1991, when Soviet forces attacked the building then housing the Ministry of Interior just over the road. A sixth stone in grey granite honours driver Raimonds Salmiņš, killed later that year. Rather different emotions are engendered by one of those little footbridges festooned with locks of fidelity that seem to be appearing in cities everywhere.

Freedom Monument [86 G2] (Brīvības piemineklis) A symbol of Latvian independence, the monument is a column rising 42m, topped with a female figure holding up three golden stars. Unveiled in 1935, it is the work of sculptor Kārlis Zāle. While originating in a proposal for a war memorial, its imagery, focused on the statue of freedom holding up stars representing the historic regions of Kurzeme, Vidzeme and Latgale, focuses less on those killed than about what they had been fighting for: the creation of independent Latvia. The inscription on the base, *Tēvzemei un Brīvībai*, 'For Fatherland and Freedom', is a quotation from Latvian writer Kārlis Skalbe. The sculptures seek to build a collective identity for Latvia, through stylised depictions of attributes such as family, reliefs bearing scenes of Latvian fighting in the uprising of 1905 and the War of Independence, and figures associated with Latvian folklore like Lāčplēsis, the furry-eared heroic 'bear-slayer', and pagan priest Vaidelotis, shown holding a *kokle*, a traditional Latvian instrument. Imbued with a Latvian national ideology, the monument served during the Soviet occupation as a symbol of the independence enjoyed by Latvia in the interwar years. In late-1980s Rīga, in the wake of Gorbachev's policy of *glasnost*, the monument became the venue for protest activity, and increasingly, calls for independence. The Freedom Monument today thus symbolises both independence won and independence regained. An honour guard stands at its base.

National History Museum of Latvia [77 B6] (Latvijas Nacionālais vēstures muzejs; Brīvības bulvāris 32; w lnvm.lv; ⊕ Sep–May 10.00–17.00 Tue–Sun, Jun–Aug 11.00–19.00 Tue, 10.00–17.00 Wed–Sun; adult/student/child €3/1.50/0.75) A block northeast of the Freedom Monument, along Brīvības bulvāris, this is one of the country's most venerable museums, its origins lying in the items assembled from the 1870s by the Rīga Latvian Society's Science Commission with the aim of strengthening national consciousness. It was long housed in Rīga Castle, and is scheduled to return there. Following a castle fire in 2013, it has, however, occupied temporary premises in a building originally constructed in 1875 for the German-Baltic Transehe-Roseneck family. Its long stay in temporary accommodation appears to have hindered innovation, and the museum today offers a comprehensive but tired canter through Latvian history from the Palaeolithic to the 20th century. Descriptions are in Latvian only, though there are summary cards in English. Note the mocked-up domestic interiors including the living room of an 1830s manor house, decorated in the inviting Biedermeyer style, and city apartments furnished in the styles of the Art Nouveau and Art Deco. The latter is given a sense of atmosphere by background music gloriously including a Latvian-language version of 'The Lambeth Walk'. The tough history of World War II and the Soviet occupation is told better in the Occupation Museum.

Latvian Museum of Natural History [77 C7] (Latvijas Nacionālais dabas muzejs; Krišjāņa Barona iela 4; w dabasmuzejs.gov.lv; ⊕ 10.00–17.00 Wed, Fri, 10.00–19.00 Thu, 11.00–17.00 Sat–Sun; adult/student/child €3.50/2.50/1.50) Located three blocks to the southeast of the National History Museum, and spread over four floors, this museum focuses on plants and animals native to Latvia. Your enjoyment of the place will depend heavily on your attitude to stuffed animals. It also covers palaeontology and geology, as well as human interactions with the environment. The place is popular with families and offers a good selection of child-friendly exhibits alongside the rocks and taxidermy, but most signage is in Latvian only, save for some touchscreen exhibits and laminated overviews of the collections.

Around the Esplanade
There is a second line of greenery, comprising the parks of the Esplanade and Vērmane Garden, running parallel to Bastejkalns Park two blocks to the northeast.

Latvian National Museum of Art [77 B5] (Latvijas Nacionālais mākslas muzejs; Jaņa Rozentāla laukums 1; w lnmm.lv; ◑ 10.00–18.00 Tue–Thu, 10.00–20.00 Fri; 10.00–17.00 Sat–Sun; adult/student/child €8/4.50/3.50) The most important repository of Latvian art is housed in an impressive building with an Ionic-columned façade atop a grand external staircase along the main Krišjāņa Valdemāra iela. Purpose-built to house the museum, the building was the 1905 work of architect Wilhelm Neumann. The museum is firmly focused on Latvia. Its permanent exhibition provides an excellent overview of the development of Latvian art, and its relationship to the building of a national identity, between 1780 and 1940. Coverage of the Soviet occupation is patchier. Many of the most important Latvian paintings are here. Janis Rozentāls is well represented, including through his diploma work *Pēc dievkalpojuma* (*After the Service*), showing the varied parishioners of his hometown of Saldus as they leave the church, and his 1913 painting *Princese ar pērtiķi* (*Princess with a Monkey*), strongly influenced by the Art Nouveau style, seen in the clothing of the red-headed princess and ornament of the carpet. There are wintry landscapes by Vilhelms Purvītis, and *Peldētāji zēni* (*Bathing Boys*), the best-known work of Johann Walter. An interesting display highlights the work of Constructivist artist Gustavs Klucis, who combined photographs with slogans in the service of the Stalinist regime in Moscow. The museum offers frequent, high-quality, temporary exhibitions.

Esplanade [77 B5] (Esplanāde) A stretch of parkland running behind the Latvian National Museum of Art as far as the domed Orthodox Cathedral. There was once a hill on this site, but it was levelled in 1784 out of fear that this offered a potentially advantageous point for enemy attacks, and it later served as a military parade ground. It hosted the exhibition to mark the 700th anniversary of Rīga in 1901, and is now somewhere between park and promenade. It is the home for several contrasting pieces of sculpture. There is a large pink granite statue of the poet Jānis Pliekšāns, better known by his pseudonym Rainis, dating from 1965, the centenary of his birth. Poetry readings are held at the monument each year on Rainis's birthday, 11 September. Just north of the Orthodox Cathedral stands Field Marshal Prince Michael Barclay de Tolly, a German-speaking Livonian aristocrat of Scottish descent, one of the main Russian military commanders countering Napoleon's invasion of 1812. The monument in Rīga commemorates the centenary of that campaign, and the sides of the plinth are inscribed with the dates '1812' and '1912'. The current statue is a 2002 reconstruction: the original was removed in 1915, the bronze being required for the war effort. Nearby stands a very different monument to another military commander, Oskars Kalpaks, Commander-in-Chief of the Latvian armed units during the War of Independence, in which he was killed in 1919. Kalpaks' face is etched on a triangular piece of metal, resembling a shark's fin emerging from a wavy stone sea. Note also the exuberant red-brick neo-Gothic building at the western corner of the park. This houses the **Art Academy of Latvia** [77 B5] (Latvijas Mākslas akadēmija; Kalpaka bulvāris 13), the work of architect Wilhelm Bockslaff, and completed in 1905, originally to house the Commerce School of the Rīga Stock Exchange.

Nativity of Christ Cathedral [77 B5] (Kristus Piedzimšanas pareizticīgo katedrāle; Brīvības bulvāris 23; \6721 2901; ⊕ 07.00–18.30 Mon–Fri, 07.00–19.00 Sat, 06.00–18.30 Sun) This Russian Orthodox cathedral was built from 1876 to 1884, while Latvia was part of the Russian Empire, in a neo-Byzantine style, with four smaller domes grouped around a large central dome atop a cylindrical tower. The entrance is beneath a belfry, partly detached from the main body of the cathedral. It served as a planetarium during the Soviet occupation. Its painted, icon-festooned interior is as exuberant as Latvia's Lutheran churches are restrained.

Vērmane Garden [77 C6] (Vērmanes dārzs) A genteel park, with an open-air stage and a charming fountain incorporating sculptures of children at play. The garden was laid out in 1814 on an area burned down in 1812 as part of a scorched-earth policy against the threatened Napoleonic invasion, its land and financing sponsored by the Prussian Consul-General to Rīga and his mother, Anna Gertrud Wöhrmann. The name of the park is a Latvian rendering of her surname, and her generosity is commemorated by a small obelisk, flanked by a pair of lions. There is also a statue of Latvian chess grandmaster Mikhail Tal, a world champion in the 1960s. It provides the venue for frequent fairs.

Rīga Latvian Society House [77 C7] (Rīgas Latviešu biedrības nams; Merķeļa iela 13; w rlb.lv) Across Merķeļa iela from Vērmane Garden, this Neoclassical building was constructed in 1909 after the previous Latvian Society headquarters burned down. Note the decorative panels on the façade by Janis Rozentāls. The society, founded in 1868, played an important role in developing Latvian national consciousness, and continues today to promote Latvian culture.

North of Vecrīga The stretch of the city centre north of Krišjāņa Valdemāra iela alongside the Daugava houses the passenger terminal for cruise ships coming into Rīga, as well as the port district of Andrejosta and a scattering of worthwhile sights.

Kronvalda Park [72 D2] (Kronvalda parks) Behind the National Theatre, this is another of the parks straddling the City Canal, in this case taking in the northern stretch of the canal. It was developed in the 1860s as Riflemen's Garden (Strēlnieku dārzs) by the German Rifle Association of Rīga. It was purchased by the city of Rīga and renamed in the 1930s to honour Latvian writer and language advocate Atis Kronvalds. The park houses the modernist multi-storey block built in 1974 for the Central Committee of the Communist Party of Latvia, a building apparently inspired by the UNESCO headquarters in Paris. Later known as the World Trade Centre, it now stands derelict. The park is also home to a chunk of the Berlin Wall, presented in an ensemble combined with one of the Rīga Barricades of 1991. It also has several gifted monuments and statues, among them a pavilion donated by China and a statue of Timurid Sultan Ulugh Beg from Uzbekistan.

Pauls Stradiņš Museum of the History of Medicine [76 A4] (Paula Stradiņa Medicīnas vēstures muzejs; Antonijas iela 1; w mvm.lv; ⊕ 11.00–17.00 Tue–Wed & Fri–Sat, 11.00–19.00 Thu, 11.00–16.00 Sun; adult/student/child €5/3/2, free entry 17.00–19.00 Thu) Over the road sits this specialised medical museum, built from the collection of Latvian surgeon and oncologist Pauls Stradiņš, who also gives his name to Latvia's medical university and the Clinical University Hospital. Among the fascinating and occasionally gruesome exhibits note the stuffed two-headed dog, the result of a transplantation experiment by Soviet scientist Vladimir Demikhov, who grafted the head and forepaws of a small dog on to the neck of a much larger one and established a single circulatory system using the heart of the larger dog. Such experiments were to pave the way eventually for human heart transplantation, but the poor dog survived only four days post-operation. There is a room devoted to space medicine, with exhibits highlighting the Soviet space programme, including another stuffed dog, Chernushka, a three-year-old sent into space in 1961. There's also a stuffed monkey, strapped into a centrifugal seat.

Citadel [72 D3] (Citadele) The area between the western edge of Kronvalda Park and the Daugava is the site of the former citadel of Rīga. This was constructed from the mid 17th century, and connected to Vecrīga by a drawbridge. The citadel helped see off Russian and Lithuanian attacks during the Second Northern War in the 17th century, but was heavily damaged in 1709 by the troops of Peter the Great. It was later reconstructed, but by the mid 19th century the citadel had had its day, along with the rest of the city fortifications. The area was the site of a Soviet plan to create a modern government centre for the Latvian Soviet Socialist Republic, which would involve the construction of three high-rise buildings. Only one of these was realised, which today accommodates the Latvian Ministry of Agriculture.

The most interesting building in the citadel today is the **St Peter and St Paul Orthodox Church** [72 D3] (Sv Pētera un Pāvila pareizticīgo baznīca; Citadeles iela 7), built in the 1780s in a Neoclassical style, and originally intended as the garrison church. It became the main Orthodox place of worship in Rīga until the Nativity of Christ Cathedral was completed in 1884. During the Soviet period, it was handed over to the city administration for use as a concert hall, which is still its function today. Note the bust of a young woman just outside the church. This is **Anna Kern**, a Russian socialite with whom Pushkin had an affair in St Petersburg, and who later moved to Rīga with her husband, the general in charge of the garrison.

Rīga Stradiņš University Anatomy Museum [72 C2] (RSU Anatomijas muzejs; Kronvalda bulvāris 9; w am.rsu.lv; ⊕ 11.00–18.00 Tue–Wed, Fri–Sat, 13.00–20.00 Thu; adult/student/child €5/3.50/2) If your interest in the subject has been piqued by the nearby Museum of the History of Medicine, you might want to cross Kronvalda Park to this well-presented showcase of the anatomical collection of Rīga Stradiņš University. The upper floor takes you through the anatomy of human organs, and offers a sizeable collection of craniums. The story turns darker in the basement, with a display of congenital abnormalities. Photography is not permitted in this area. The museum collection, particularly that in the basement, may be distressing for younger visitors.

Viesturdārzs [72 D1] Lying immediately to the north of Hanzas iela, this is Rīga's oldest park, named after the 13th-century Semigallian ruler Viesturs. It is a tranquil place containing several objects of historical interest. The most immediately obvious is the **Alexander Gate** [72 C1] (Aleksandra Vārti), Rīga's triumphal arch, albeit a pretty modest example of the genre, with a single arch bordered by Ionic columns. It was installed in 1818 to celebrate the Russian victory over Napoleon. Tsar Alexander I himself attended the opening ceremony. It originally stood in a city centre site, but was shunted out here in 1936. The origins of the park lie in

Peter the Great's ambition to build a summer residence here. He came personally to supervise construction, and a memorial stone recalls the elm tree planted here by Peter in 1721 in commemoration of the end of the Great Northern War. That tree is long gone, though a young elm has been planted in its place.

The park, a favourite spot for relaxation, was gifted to the city by Tsar Nicholas I in 1841. In 1873, the arena for the first All-Latvian Song Festival was built here. A monument was erected in 1973, on its centenary, based around a rectangular sunken pool on one side of which stands sculpted reliefs of notable composers, with fragments from their compositions. Kārlis Baumanis, composer of the Latvian national anthem, was deliberately excluded by the Soviets – his likeness was added in 2003.

Alberta iela [76 A3] A modestly sized street in a part of the city known appropriately as the Quiet Centre, Alberta iela is the target for visitors in search of the best of Rīga's Art Nouveau. The central draw is a line of apartment blocks along the northern side of the street built at the beginning of the 20th century by architect Mikhail Eisenstein, whose son Sergei was the celebrated film director known for the silent masterpiece *Battleship Potemkin*. The buildings are exuberant, festooned with decoration including human figures, both real and mythological, and floral motifs and masks, giving the whole side of the street the feel of an elaborate stage set. Highlights include the five-storey building at **Alberta iela 2A** with a façade that extends a further floor just to provide a canvas for yet more ornamentation. A pair of sphinxes flank the entrance to the building, which was the early childhood home of philosopher Sir Isaiah Berlin. Reliefs of winged lions guard the entrance to **Alberta iela 4**, and there are more statues of lions on top of the building, staring out in opposite directions. The framing of the windows of the fifth floor forms a keyhole shape, a common feature of Rīga's Art Nouveau buildings. The façade at **Alberta iela 8** centres on a protruding semi-cylindrical structure, offering two floors of bay windows. Vertical lines of light-blue brickwork colour a façade rich in ornament, with reliefs filling the spaces between lines of windows.

Another Eisenstein concoction is at **Alberta iela 13**, on the corner with Strēlnieku iela, with a particularly varied range of depictions of female figures: as statues, reliefs and faces – smiling, serene and shocked. Next door, at **Strēlnieku iela 4A**, is another Eisenstein apartment block, today housing the Stockholm School of Economics. What look rather like imagined space helmets sit above the ground-floor windows. On another corner of Alberta and Strēlnieku streets is the yellow-painted block at **Alberta iela 12**, with a sharply pointed corner tower, and Renaissance-inspired loggias. It was the work of prolific Latvian architect Konstantīns Pēkšēns, who liked the building so much, he made it his home.

Rīga Art Nouveau Centre [76 A3] (Rīgas Jūgendstila centrs; Alberta iela 12; w jugendstils.riga.lv; ⊕ 10.00–18.00 Tue–Sun; adult/student €9/5 May–Sep, €5/3 Oct–Apr) Occupying the ground floor and basement of Alberta iela 12, this is a museum dedicated to the Art Nouveau style. A hologram of Konstantīns Pēkšēns welcomes you into his home. It neatly complements a walking tour of Rīga's Art Nouveau buildings by offering a reconstruction of an apartment kitted out in all things Art Nouveau. There is a plant-festooned bay window in the living room, whose walls are decorated by an ornamental band studded with daisy motifs. The room is watched over by a photograph of Pēkšēns, as if to ensure that visitors don't become over-familiar with the place. A poky maid's room off the kitchen reminds of the social stratification at the turn of the 20th century. The apartment was kitted out with the latest personal hygiene technologies, including an enamel bath and,

in the smallest room of the flat, a state-of-the-art latrine immodestly titled 'The Incomparable Closet', imported from England. On the floor below, multimedia presentations offer further information on Rīga's Art Nouveau buildings.

Janis Rozentāls and Rūdolfs Blaumanis Museum [76 A3] (Jaņa Rozentāla un Rūdolfa Blaumaņa muzejs; Alberta iela 12–9; w memorialiemuzeji.lv; ⊕ Sep–May 11.00–18.00 Wed–Sun, Jun–Aug noon–19.00 Wed, 11.00–18.00 Thu–Sun; adult/student €2/1) A second museum in the same building, this one on the fifth floor, offers two Latvian cultural figures in one. It was the apartment home of painter Janis Rozentāls, whose versatile output embraced the Art Nouveau style. His airy studio sits in the attic above, reached up some wooden stairs. The then ailing writer Rūdolfs Blaumanis also lived here as a tenant for a couple of years, and has a room dedicated to his works. The museum is atmospheric, though there is little information on offer, with a sign at the entrance warning darkly that those who would like to learn more should book a guided tour.

ART NOUVEAU RĪGA

Rīga offers what is described by UNESCO as 'the finest collection of Art Nouveau buildings in Europe'. Art Nouveau emerged in the 1890s as a reaction against the prevailing currents of historicism and eclecticism. The functionality of objects and buildings was central to Art Nouveau, but they were turned into works of art through the use of sinuosity of line, motifs taking inspiration from sources ranging from nature to the Orient, and by the innovative use of materials such as iron and glass. The movement took different names in different parts of the continent. In Italy, for example, it was known as Liberty style, a name that has nothing to do with the awakening of political consciousness but was instead drawn from the London department store known for bringing in textiles and other objects from the Far East. In Germany, it took the name Jugendstil, deriving from an art magazine that promoted the movement, and it is as *Jūgendstils* that the movement is known in Latvia.

But why is there such a concentration of Art Nouveau buildings in Rīga? The answer lies in the rapid growth of the city, an important port and industrial centre of Imperial Russia, at the turn of the 20th century – exactly when Art Nouveau was in vogue. An exhibition in 1901 marking the celebrations of the 700th anniversary of Rīga helped promote Art Nouveau designs, in the same way the Paris Exposition had done a year earlier.

Visitors in search of Art Nouveau in Rīga head to the extravagantly decorated confections along Alberta iela, but while these are some of the showiest examples of the style, they are but the tip of the iceberg, and not really representative of Rīga's Art Nouveau as a whole. Jānis Krastiņš, professor at Rīga Technical University and an authority on the Art Nouveau architecture of the city, identifies three distinct phases in the evolution of Art Nouveau in Rīga.

The **Eclectic Decorative Art Nouveau** that characterises Eisenstein's buildings along Alberta iela ran from the turn of the century until around 1907 and, according to Krastiņš, often featured the Art Nouveau ornamentation of buildings whose composition otherwise harks back to earlier architectural styles. Other examples include two stunning buildings in the Old Town, the Konstantīns Pēkšēns-creation at Smilšu iela 2 (page 91) and the polychrome delight at Kalēju iela 23 (page 98).

From around 1907, these eclectically decorated buildings made way for a new style, **Perpendicular Art Nouveau**, which features a strongly emphasised

There is no lift, but the climb is made more pleasurable by the delightful spiral staircase, itself an Art Nouveau masterpiece.

Eastern city centre East of the Esplanāde and Vērmane Garden is a busy central area of shops, offices and restaurants, with some attractive Art Nouveau apartment blocks. The main artery is Brīvības iela, spearing northeastwards from the Freedom Monument.

Museum of Jews in Latvia [76 C4] (Muzejs Ebreji Latvijā; Skolas iela 6; w ebrejumuzejs.lv; ⊕ Oct–Apr 11.00–17.00 Sun–Thu, May–Sep 11.00–17.00 Sun–Fri; admission free) This sits on the third floor of a large white-fronted building at Skolas iela 6, the work of Jewish architect Paul Mandelstamm. Completed in 1925, the building accommodated the interwar Jewish theatre, then a house of political education in the Soviet period. Now restored to the Rīga Jewish community, it is home to several Jewish organisations. Across three rooms, dedicated respectively to the

verticality, frequently achieved through bands and building projections accommodating bay windows. Ornamentation is less pronounced, though will still frequently be present, for example, in filling the spaces between rows of windows. The architect Jānis Alksnis was among the champions of Perpendicular Art Nouveau, and the apartment building at Lāčplēša iela 18 is an early example. Verticality is emphasised by projections running up and down for three storeys on either side of the façade, as well as by the decoration around the windows.

By the turn of the 20th century, Rīga was becoming rapidly more Latvian in feel, through the rural to urban migration of predominantly ethnic Latvians. A third current of Rīga's Art Nouveau architecture, **National Romanticism**, was influenced by, and in turn supported, the developing Latvian national consciousness. Architects sought to draw on the traditions and spirit of the Latvian people in a style that emphasised natural building materials like stone, drew on ethnographic patterns, characteristically featured steep roofs, and whose buildings were often bulky in feel. There was some cross-fertilisation with similarly inspired styles emerging in other countries on the peripheries of empire, notably Finland.

A young architect named Eižens Laube was among those to champion the style, and one of Laube's most notable works forms the odd building out on Alberta iela, at number 11. Sitting among Eisenstein's eclectically decorated concoctions, the apartment house features heavy blocks of stone at the base of the façade, surmounted by plasterwork in grey and brown, rising to a strongly pointed roof. There are ethnographic motifs above the doorways and semi-cylindrical projections accommodate bay windows.

Art Nouveau had petered out in Rīga even before the travails of World War I. Other architectural currents had moved in, though in some cases in a hybrid form that for a while retained elements of Art Nouveau, such as a Neoclassical Art Nouveau that characterises the rebuilt Rīga Latvian Society House at Merķeļa iela 13 (page 103), a building whose façade is enlivened by murals painted by Janis Rozentāls. The legacy of those few years of the intensive construction of Art Nouveau buildings at the turn of the 20th century is, however, a remarkable cityscape in a place that knows how to put on the Jugendstil.

Jewish community before World War I, the period of independent Latvia before 1941 and the Holocaust, the museum chronicles Jewish resilience in Latvia in the face of appalling tribulations. While the displays in the first two rooms need modernisation, the power of their story overcomes any weaknesses in presentation. There is video footage of the burning of the Choral Synagogue in Rīga, as well as a grainy amateur film shockingly recording the murder of a group of Jewish men in Liepāja.

Old Evangelical Lutheran Church of St Gertrude [76 D4] (Vecā Svētās Ģertrūdes evaņģēliski luteriskā baznīca; Ģertrūdes iela 8; w gertrude.lv) St Gertrude of Nivelles, patron saint of travellers, gave her name in the Middle Ages to churches located outside the protection of city walls, where travellers arriving late, after the walls had been locked for the night, could give thanks for the completion of their journey. A church has existed on the site since at least the 15th century, though these were of wood until in 1864 when, with stone structures finally allowed outside the centre, construction of a new church began under the direction of Rīga's chief architect, Johann Felsko. This was the first neo-Gothic red-brick church to be built in the outskirts of Rīga. The interior features a wooden neo-Gothic altar and pulpit, a fan-vaulted ceiling and an early-20th-century organ. The church still hosts occasional organ concerts. With the growth in population at the start of the 20th century, a second red-brick church was built nearby on Brīvības iela: this accommodated Latvian-language congregations and was known as St Gertrude New Church. Hence the original church, used by the German community, became known as Old St Gertrude.

The church sits on an island in the traffic. Some of the apartment blocks overlooking the church are fine examples of the Art Nouveau style. Note the residential block at **Ģertrūdes iela 10** [76 D4], peppered by faces, some looking out nervously between approaching snakes.

Corner House [76 D4] (Stūra māja; Brīvības iela 61; w okupacijasmuzejs.lv; ⊕ 10.30–17.30 daily; adult/student €15/5) A block at the corner of Brīvības iela and Stabu iela, at first sight typical of Rīga's early-20th-century apartment complexes, the Corner House holds a dark secret. It housed the Rīga headquarters of the Soviet security agency, the KGB, and its forerunners from the autumn of 1940 until the restoration of Latvian independence, save for the brief period under German occupation. This was the scene of the interrogation and imprisonment of those suspected of opposition to the regime. Display panels tell the history of the building, which is visitable beyond the entrance area only with a guided tour (book through their website). The tour is a salutary experience. Visitors are shown plainly furnished interrogation rooms, then taken to the basement where prison cells house hard beds behind heavy metal doors, and finally to the execution chamber, a small room with a wooden-panelled wall studded with bullet holes; the venue for executions in the 1940s. The exhibition is run by the Museum of the Occupation of Latvia. English-speaking guides are knowledgeable and keen to convey the tragic history of the place. There are question marks over the building's future, but let us hope it continues its role of ensuring that the horrors of Soviet occupation are not forgotten.

The Rainis and Aspazija House [76 D3] (Raiņa un Aspazijas māja; Baznīcas iela 30; w memorialiemuzeji.lv; ⊕ Jun–Aug 10.00–17.00 Tue & Thu–Sat, noon–19.00 Wed, Sep–May 10.00–17.00 Tue–Sat; adult/student €2/1) One of five memorial museums across Latvia dedicated to one or both members of the country's most famous literary couple, this is a two-storey wooden house, just a block away from the Corner House, though a world apart in subject matter. It was purchased by the poets in 1924, four years after their return from exile, when Rainis was active in political and public life and in need of a city-centre home that could support his required socialising. They did not, however, move in until 1926, when they lived in the upstairs apartments, tenants occupying both the rooms downstairs and an outbuilding in the yard. A video on the couple's entwined lives and works is screened in the basement.

Upstairs, the flat has been furnished as far as possible as they would have known it. Note the bread wrapped in pages from *Faust*. These illustrate the story that Rainis was able to translate *Faust* while in detention and deprived of books, by Aspazija getting the pages to him in this fashion. On the ground floor, stored in modern cabinets, is their library. Under their will, written in 1926, they left the house to the city of Rīga and stipulated that the library must be made accessible to all. The outhouse in the courtyard at the back hosts temporary exhibitions.

Kim? Contemporary Art Centre [76 C2] (Kim? Laikmetīgās mākslas centrs; Sporta iela 2; w kim.lv; ⊕ noon–18.00 Tue–Sun; admission free) Founded in 2009, its name an acronym of the question 'what is art?' ('kas ir maksla?'), this well-regarded centre hosts exhibitions, screenings and performances, particularly showcasing emerging Latvian artists. It is in the '**Sporta 2' Quarter** ('Sporta 2' kvartāls), a creative island set around a courtyard within the Skanste neighbourhood northeast of the centre. The area was once home to the Uzvara ('Victory') sweet factory, and offers a couple of places to eat and drink in the courtyard after all that art. Take the number 11 bus to the Bruņinieku iela stop, and then walk around 300m along Sporta iela to get here.

Laima Chocolate Museum [76 F2] (Laimas Šokolādes muzejs; Miera iela 22; w laimasokoladesmuzejs.lv; ⊕ 10.00–18.00 Wed–Sun; adult/student €7/5) Out of the centre, along Miera iela, stands this temple to Latvia's best-known brand of chocolate, Laima, named after the Latvian goddess of fate. A well-presented exhibition retells both the story of chocolate and that of the Laima company, which traces its origins to the Theodor Riegert confectionery and chocolate company, founded in 1870, the name Laima first appearing on the scene in 1925. A factory was built in 1938 on the site of the present museum, though the main production centre these days is the town of Ādaži, outside Rīga. The Norwegian Orkla group now owns the company.

The exhibition covers the story of the Laima Clock, which stands to this day close to the Freedom Monument in central Rīga and has become a symbol of the city. This being a pro-chocolate museum, displays emphasise the health-giving qualities of the stuff, which apparently include a sharp mind and strong bones. For added health-giving benefit, you get to taste a sample. There is a Laima shop on the site. The number 11 tram will get you here from the city centre – alight at the Laima stop.

Krišjānis Barons Museum [77 D6] (Krišjāņa Barona muzejs; Krišjāņa Barona iela 3–5; w memorialiemuzeji.lv; ⊕ 13.00–19.00 Wed, 11.00–18.00 Thu–Sun; adult/student €2/1) Krišjānis Barons played an important role in the development of a Latvian national identity through the painstaking collation of *dainas*. These were four-line poems, often based around pre-Christian deities or events in rural life, which formed the heart of Latvian folk songs. Barons' magisterial *Latvju dainas* was published in six volumes between 1894 and 1915, including more than 200,000 poems. This small museum is housed in the apartment in which Barons spent the last four years of his life until his death in 1923, living with his son Kārlis, a university professor. Note the replica of Barons' Cabinet of Dainas (Dainu skapis), a piece of furniture he designed himself in order better to organise his collection of texts, each handwritten on paper slips stored in the many drawers.

Bergs Bazaar [77 D7] (Berga bazars; Elizabetes iela 83–85; w bergabazars. lv) This smartly renovated shopping arcade was built around 1887 as Rīga's first modern shopping centre. The developer was an ethnic Latvian named Kristaps Kalniņš, who Germanised his name as Christoph Berg, to fit in with the city's German-Baltic elite, who had hitherto monopolised the circles into which ethnic Latvians were starting to gain a foothold. He engaged architect Konstantīns Pēkšēns, whose covered walkway designs took inspiration from the Grand Bazaar of Istanbul. Neglected during the Soviet occupation, the area was returned to his heirs following the restoration of independence, and it is now home to high-end shops, offices and apartments.

Zuzeum Art Centre [77 G8] (Mākslas centrs 'Zuzeum'; Lāčplēša iela 101; w zuzeum.com; ⊕ 11.00–19.00 Mon–Wed & Fri–Sat, 11.00–20.00 Thu, 11.00–17.00 Sun; adult/student €10/5) In an otherwise nondescript corner of town close to the railway track, this is a vibrant art space occupying a former cork-factory building. The centre houses the extensive modern art collection of Latvian businessman Jānis Zuzāns, though what you will see depends on the temporary exhibitions on offer in its two halls. There is also a shop, café and rooftop terrace. A large skeletal bronze sculpture from British artist Thomas Houseago in the courtyard outside serves as a marker to the place.

Maskavas forštate

Colloquially known by locals as Maskačka, the 'Moscow Suburb' runs from the southern edge of the Old Town along the historic road between Rīga and Moscow, hence its name. It was long associated with Russian and Jewish migrants into the city, houses the largest Old Believer house of prayer in the world and was the site of the Jewish ghetto during the Nazi occupation. It is still home to a high proportion of native Russian speakers, giving it a different atmosphere to other central districts. Separated from the Old Town by railway lines, it precisely embodies an 'other side of the tracks' feel. Many Latvians living in other parts of the city still caution about criminality here. But it is no longer markedly less safe than other central districts, its Tsarist-era wooden houses are gradually being refurbished, and it makes for an interesting and atmospheric visit. The Rīga Central Market (page 81) at its northwestern end is a good place to start. The Rīga municipal authorities announced in February 2024 that many of the streets in the district would be renamed, dropping their previous celebration of Russian historical figures like Pushkin, Turgenev and Lomonosov in favour of Latvian ones. The main thoroughfare of the district, formerly Maskavas iela, is now Latgales iela, and the area is part of the wider Latgales priekšpilsēta (Latgale Suburb).

Spīķeri [111 A2] (w spikeri.lv) Between the hangars of Rīga Central Market and the Daugava sits Spīķeri, the historic warehouse district, located just outside the former city walls, a place where cargoes were loaded and unloaded. Until the demolition of the fortifications in the mid 19th century, the buildings here were required to be made of wood. As part of his reconstruction plan following the demise of the fortifications, Rīga's chief architect, Johann Felsko, decided on a new district of brick-built warehouses. In total, some 58 were built, with

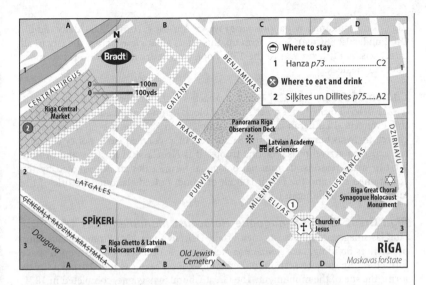

Where to stay
1 Hanza *p73*............................C2
Where to eat and drink
2 Siļķites un Dillītes *p75*.....A2

matching façades. By the early 20th century, the requirement for warehouses in this area had declined, and some of the buildings were destroyed to make room for the Rīga Central Market. Those that remain today are favoured as premises of entrepreneurial tech companies, making for a district of trendy young professionals during the working week.

Rīga Ghetto and Latvian Holocaust Museum

[111 A3] (Rīgas geto un Latvijas holokausta muzejs; Latgales iela 14a; w rgm.lv; ⊕ 10.00–18.00 Sun–Fri; suggested donation adult/child €5/3) It is located in an atmospheric 19th-century block originally built as stables and a courtyard area in front, although not actually on the territory of the former Rīga ghetto. They have ambitious plans to develop a permanent exhibition in a reconstructed building, but until then the museum offers self-contained displays on aspects of the Holocaust in Latvia. These include a chronicle of the lives of Czech Jews deported in 1942 from the Theresienstadt transit camp to Rīga. Many were shot soon after their arrival.

A moving collection of drawings by Aleksandra Beļcova offers a sympathetic portrayal of the ghetto by an artist living in Rīga at the time. In one self-portrait, she wears a headscarf resembling a *tallit* prayer shawl. In the courtyard outside, boards display a long list of Jews transported into Rīga from Germany and elsewhere, and there is one of the railway wagons in which they arrived. Very few were to survive. Note also the reconstructed wooden house that once stood in the ghetto on Mazā Kalna iela. Up to 13 people were crammed in each of its small rooms.

Latvian Academy of Sciences

[111 C2] (Latvijas Zinātņu akadēmija; Akadēmijas laukums 1) This occupies one of the most distinctive buildings in Rīga: a tiered skyscraper in the Stalinist style, resembling one of the Seven Sisters in Moscow. In 1951, the Central Committee of the Latvian Communist Party decided on the construction of a Collective Farmers' House as the first skyscraper of Rīga, a reflection of the importance of collective farms within the Soviet system. In 1958, the Latvian Academy of Sciences took over the project and financed its completion. Note the hammer-and-sickle symbols still visible high up on the outside of the building. The place houses the **Panorama Rīga Observation Deck** (Panorama

Rīga skatu laukums; **w** panoramariga.lv; ⊕ Apr–Nov 10.00–22.00 daily; adult/child under 12 €8/free). Some 65m up, this offers great views across the city in all directions. A lift takes you to the 15th floor, with stairs taking you up two more floors to the deck.

Church of Jesus [111 C3] (Jēzus evaņģēliski luteriskā baznīca; Elijas iela 18; ☎6721 0185) Located in a quiet square a block behind the Academy of Sciences, this Evangelical Lutheran church was completed in 1822, on the site of an earlier church that was burned down in 1812 as part of a scorched-earth policy ahead of the expected arrival of Napoleon's troops. It is Neoclassical in style, and of note for two main reasons: its unusual octagonal form, a design necessitated by the constrained site, and the fact it is built of wood, indeed claiming the title of the tallest wooden building in Latvia.

Rīga Great Choral Synagogue Holocaust Monument [111 D2] (Rīgas Horālās sinagogas Holokausta memoriāls; Dzirnavu iela 124) From the Academy of Sciences building, take Benjamiņas iela a couple of blocks east. An open space formed within the intersections of Benjamiņas, Jēzusbaznīcas and Dzirnavu streets forms the site of the monument. The Great Choral Synagogue, completed in 1871, was the largest in Rīga. Just three days after German forces had entered the city on 4 July 1941, under Nazi orders, the auxiliary unit set up by Latvian Nazi collaborator Viktors Arājs and his thugs set fire to the synagogue, reportedly burning alive Jewish Lithuanian refugees trapped in the building. Other synagogues in the city were also burned or ransacked. The ruins of the Great Choral Synagogue were demolished after the war, but in 1993, a memorial symbolically recreated the bases of the walls, set into the square. A boulder placed on one wall is marked with the date of 4 July 1941, and 4 July is the date chosen annually to remember those killed in the Holocaust in Latvia. Close by is a concrete memorial, erected in 2007. It takes the form of a toppling concrete wall, symbolising the threat of extermination of the Jewish people, which is, however, prevented from falling completely by concrete pillars bearing the names of 270 Latvians who risked their lives to protect Jews. The silhouette of Žanis Lipke reflects his particularly significant role.

Old Jewish Cemetery [69 F7] (Vecie ebreju kapi; Līksnas iela 1) Latgales iela runs eastwards through the Maskavas forštate neighbourhood. Some 3km east of the Academy of Sciences, turn up the hill on to Ebreju iela to reach the Old Jewish Cemetery, nowadays a wooded park of undulating ground. Opened in 1725 in what was then the edge of the city, this was the first spot in Rīga in which Jews were allowed to bury their dead. It was used for burials until the late 1930s. With the German occupation, the prayer house and mortuary were burned down, and the place was the site for the mass burial of more than 1,000 Jews killed in the Rīga Ghetto. It was razed in the Soviet period, the tombstones removed, and renamed the Park of the Communist Brigades. It was given its current name in 1992. From central Rīga, take the number 7 tram to the Balvu iela stop to get here.

PĀRDAUGAVA Literally the district 'over the Daugava', the left bank of the Daugava offers far less to detain the tourist than the right. There are nonetheless some good reasons to cross the Daugava, and not just en route to and from the airport. The area contains the atmospheric Āgenskalns and Kalnciems markets (page 82), the attractive island of Ķīpsala, and a cluster of sights around the iconic National Library of Latvia.

Ķīpsala [72 A3] The island of Ķīpsala lies a short walk over the Daugava from the city centre via Vanšu tilts ('Shroud Bridge' – the name refers to the shroud-like cables that support it). A little less than 3km long and some 500m wide, it lies on the left bank of the Daugava, with only small channels separating it from the Pārdaugava mainland. It was traditionally home to fishermen, and then, in the Soviet period, parts of the Rīga Polytechnic Institute arrived. The opening of Vanšu Bridge in 1981 suddenly brought the place much closer to central Rīga, paving the way for its rapid development, now becoming one of the most desirable addresses in Rīga. Cobbled Balasta dambis, running alongside the Daugava, offers a great view across towards the Old Town. In summer, there is a river **beach** (Ķīpsalas pludmale) in the shadow of Vanšu Bridge.

Žanis Lipke Memorial [72 B3] (Žaņa Lipkes memoriāls; Mazais Balasta dambis 9; w lipke.lv; ⏲ noon–18.00 Tue–Wed & Fri, noon–20.00 Thu, 10.00–16.00 Sat; donation requested) The major sight on Ķīpsala is the memorial museum to Žanis Lipke, a Rīga dock worker incensed by what he saw of the treatment of Jews during the Nazi occupation. Lipke retrained to be able to help Jews, becoming a contractor for the Luftwaffe, where he was responsible for bringing Jews from the ghetto to their place of work at the Luftwaffe warehouses. Through a mix of bribery and subterfuge, Lipke managed to smuggle out Jews in this way, and then conceal them in various hiding places, including in a bunker under the woodshed of his Ķīpsala garden, accommodating up to 12 people at a time. Safer onward hiding places were arranged through friends in the Dobele area. Žanis and his wife, Johanna, helped save the lives of at least 40 Jews. The memorial was opened in 2012. It was designed by architect Zaiga Gaile, its windowless dark wooden form like an overturned boat aping the fishing history of Ķīpsala.

Next door to Lipke's house on Ķīpsala, still inhabited by his descendants, the memorial tells the story of the bravery of Žanis and his family. You can look down to a stylised bunker measuring roughly 3m², nine bunks on its sides. Above the bunker, a fragile wooden construction has been installed to represent a *sukkah*, a temporary hut built for the Jewish Sukkot festival as a symbol of shelter in the wilderness.

Around the National Library of Latvia
A cluster of Pārdaugava sights lies just beyond the western end of the Akmens tilts, the 'Stone Bridge' connecting the area with Vecrīga.

National Library of Latvia [69 E7] (Latvijas Nacionālā bibliotēka; Mūkusalas iela 3; w lnb.lv; ⏲ 11.00–19.00 Mon–Fri, 10.00–17.00 Sat; admission free) It says much about the importance of Latvian language and literature to the national consciousness that a library should be among the grandest of the public buildings erected since the restoration of independence. The library is seen as the repository of the cultural DNA of the Latvian people. The striking building, its curving form variously likened to a mountain, wave, or ski slope, sits on the left bank of the Daugava overlooking the Old Town. The building is the work of Latvian-American architect Gunnar Birkerts, its design taking its nickname and inspiration, Castle of Light (Gaismas pils), from the Auseklis poem of that name, telling of a castle which is lost, but will rise again. Commissioned at the end of the 1980s, the library was finally opened in 2014. A human chain was formed to carry some of the holdings from the old main library building to the new one.

The interior is centred on a huge atrium, which in turn is dominated by a vast bookshelf rising upwards over five stories. This hosts the People's Bookshelf initiative (**w** tautasgramatuplaukts.lv), in which all are invited to donate a book, writing a message in it to explain the importance of the book to them. The building includes conference and reading rooms and some temporary exhibition space. Note the unusual sculpture outside, showing two statues of the writer Rainis, identical in all respects except size, one 3m in height, the other 1m. They sit at either end of a long sloping bench. The sculpture, *Divi Raiņi* ('Two Rainises'), is by Aigars Bikše, and is apparently intended to demonstrate that education spurs growth.

Railway Museum [69 D7] (Dzelzceļa muzejs; Uzvaras bulvāris 2A; **w** railwaymuseum.lv; ⊕ 10.00–17.00 Tue–Wed & Fri–Sat, 10.00–20.00 Thu; adult/student €5/3) Sitting behind the National Library and housed in spacious former railway repair shops, the museum offers a dry account in Latvian-only of the history of Latvian railways from 1858 to 1940 alongside more child-friendly exhibits, including a large model railway and an exhibition on the 'life of a train station'. The largest hall is given over to temporary exhibitions. Outside, there are interwar and Soviet locomotives, including some specialist vehicles, among them a snowplough, a car full of equipment for measuring track parameters, and a carriage built for the transport of prisoners.

Uzvaras Park [69 D7] (Uzvaras parks) Further down Uzvaras bulvāris, the park, 'Victory Park', is one of the most politically contested spaces in Latvia. It was opened in 1910, on the 200th anniversary of Russia's securing of Livonia, and named Pētera parks in honour of Peter the Great, the Russian ruler who secured it. It was renamed Victory Park in 1923 to celebrate instead Latvia's defeat of Bermondt's West Russian Volunteer Army in its War of Independence. In 1985, a Monument to the Liberators of Soviet Russia and Rīga from the German Fascist Invaders was put up in the park, a structure as ungainly as its title, centred on a 79m pillar consisting of five bunched columns, each topped by a Soviet star. In the wake of Russia's invasion of Ukraine in 2022, the monument was demolished in August that year. With the central pillar alone weighing some 2,000 tonnes, this was no easy undertaking.

Other Pārdaugava sights A few other attractions are further afield.

University of Latvia Botanical Garden [69 C7] (Latvijas Universitātes Botāniskais dārzs; Kandavas iela 2; **w** botanika.lu.lv; ⊕ Oct–Mar 10.00–16.00 daily, Apr & Sep 10.00–19.00, May–Aug 10.00–21.00; adult/student/child Oct–Mar €3.50/2.50/2, Apr & Sep €4/3/2.50, May–Aug €5/4/3) Founded in 1922, it has occupied its current site on the grounds of the former Volfschmidt Manor since 1926. It offers a pleasant place for a stroll or summer picnic, with its dahlias, rhododendrons and magnolias all splendid in season. The garden buildings are gradually being renovated. In the tropical butterfly house, co-located with a greenhouse filled with azaleas, the garden staff have added several canaries. The gardens are also enlivened by some large modern artworks: particularly striking is *The Girl with the Shoe*, a 2017 work by Aigars Bikše, in which a giant pigtailed girl is in the process of tearing the roof off a wooden house in search of her lost footwear. The Botāniskais dārzs/Rīgas Stradiņa universitāte public transport stop serves the place: trams 1 and 5 are among the routes that will get you here.

Sudrabkalniņš [69 C6] Far from the sights of the city, this wooded hill along Slokas iela, near the intersection with Kurzemes prospekts, owes its fame to the fierce defence of Rīga by the Latvian Army in November 1919 against the efforts of the West Russian Volunteer Army under Pavel Bermondt-Avalov to take the city. The decisive battle took place here on 11 November, a date commemorated ever since in Latvia as Lāčplēsis Day. A memorial was unveiled in 1937, designed by sculptor Kārlis Zāle, the author of the Freedom Monument. A wall comprised of blocks of granite taken from the Daugavgrīva Fortress juts out from the hillside, with a flight of steps to its side. A frieze on one side of the wall portrays Latvian warriors of old, and on the other side, soldiers of the Latvian Army. A plaque on the terrace at the top of the monument lists the names of 54 soldiers killed here. Buses 36 and 37 serve the Sudrabkalniņš stop on Kurzemes prospekts.

THE OUTER SUBURBS

Rīga's cemeteries Respect for the dead is taken seriously in Latvia, with families paying much attention to tending the graves of their departed relatives, and Rīga's cemeteries contain much of interest in relation to both the architectural and human histories of the city. They cluster in an area northeast of the centre, en route to the Mežaparks neighbourhood. Tram 11 will take you here from the centre, with stops for Lielie kapi, Brāļu kapi and Meža kapi.

Great Cemetery [69 F6] (Lielie kapi) The closest of the major cemeteries to the city centre, the Great Cemetery was established in 1773. An outbreak of bubonic plague across the Russian Empire led to a decree banning burials within churches, and Rīga set up its new cemetery outside the city. It covers 36ha and was used for burials until 1957. It was the place of burial for Rīga's German-Baltic elite as well as increasing numbers of well-to-do Latvians. Dominated by the graves of German-Baltic families whose heirs had left Latvia, and thus with nobody to tend many of the graves, and confronted with an anti-German spirit in Soviet Latvia, the place fell victim to neglect, vandalism and theft. In the late 1960s, the Soviet authorities cleared away many of the less prestigious graves, with the aim of keeping the most significant and transforming the place into a public memorial park, but they left the task only partially completed. The cemetery today houses a number of once grand family mausolea, many now in disrepair with some covered in scaffolding, in a wooded parkland setting. Two Lutheran churches still stand within the cemetery grounds.

Several figures associated with the Latvian National Awakening in the 19th century are buried here. A black obelisk marks the grave of Krišjānis Valdemārs, proponent of naval schools for Latvians. Next to this are plaques and relief panels marking the approximate sites of the graves of compiler of Latvian folk songs Krišjānis Barons and folklorist Fricis Brīvzemnieks. At the northern edge of the cemetery, a rough-hewn monument denotes the grave of Andrejs Pumpurs, author of the Lāčplēsis epic. Several tombs attest to the strength of the British community in the city. Note the tombstone, now fixed into a brick wall, of Edgar Browne, 'a native of England', who died in Rīga in 1833 at the age of 27.

The Great Cemetery is now divided into two parts by Senču iela, insensitively built across it in Soviet times. The southern section of the cemetery is itself divided into two. A fenced eastern part, the **Pokrov Cemetery** [69 F6] (Pokrova kapi), is used for Orthodox burials and still administered by the Latvian Orthodox Church. The western part is known as **St James's Cemetery** [69 F6] (Jēkaba kapi), as it was initially allocated to the parish of the church of St James. Graves here include that of Julie von Holtei, an actress married to Karl von Holtei, manager of the theatre in Rīga from 1837 to 1839, when Richard Wagner was its musical director. Julie died in 1839 in childbirth. Her funeral was the setting for the first performance of Wagner's song *Gesang am Grabe von Julies von Holtei.*

Rīga Brethren Cemetery [69 F6] (Brāļu kapi; Aizsaules iela 1B) The most visually impressive of the Rīga cemeteries is this military cemetery, striking through both the scale and the harmonious nature of its design. It was built between 1924 and 1936, the work of sculptor Kārlis Zāle, designer of the Freedom Monument. Some 2,000 Latvian soldiers are buried here, mostly from World War I and the Latvian War of Independence. The burials are marked by stone teeth in the low walls along the sides of the paths. Note those inscribed 'nezināms' – 'unknown'. The monumental statuary aims to express the gratitude of the Latvian people to those who fell while fighting for their cause. You enter beneath a large stone gate flanked by sculptures of horsemen, both men and horses bowing their heads to honour the dead. From the gate, a tree-lined avenue takes you to a raised terrace, with an eternal flame in the centre. The central burial ground lies on a lower level beyond this. Flights of stairs take you down, past sculptures of wounded horsemen. The burial ground ends at a wall supporting an imposing statue of a grieving Mother Latvia, her fallen sons at her feet. The wall below is protected by four sculptures of Latvian knights, heads bowed, behind shields representing the regions of Kurzeme, Zemgale, Vidzeme and Latgale. Kārlis Zāle himself is buried here, right at the back of the burial ground, in the centre in line with the Mother Latvia statue.

Rainis Cemetery [69 F5] (Raiņa kapi; Aizsaules iela 1A) Immediately across Varoņu iela from the Brethren Cemetery, the Rainis Cemetery is sometimes known as the 'cemetery of the godless' as it started life as a burial place for those who did not belong to a specific religious congregation. It is dominated by the grave of Latvian writer Rainis, who died in 1929. From the entrance, a broad alley takes you to Rainis's grave, a large pink stone sculpture of an agonised naked figure on a low wall, set within a circular retaining wall. The cemetery also houses many noted Latvian cultural figures, their plots identified on a map near the entrance, as well as various Soviet-era functionaries, seeking the prestige of a resting place close to Rainis.

Forest Cemetery [69 F5] (Meža kapi; Aizsaules iela 2) This large cemetery surrounds the Brethren Cemetery. The Forest Cemetery was inaugurated in 1913, as the Great Cemetery was running out of space. It is divided into two parts: First Forest Ceremony, entered from Aizsaules iela, and Second Forest Cemetery, entered from Gaujas iela. The former is of more interest to the casual visitor, with the long alley just beyond the entrance leading to the grave of Jānis Čakste, first president of independent Latvia, who died in 1927. It is an elaborate memorial, featuring a column bearing a relief of Čakste and a cross, flanked by a curved wall with weeping figures on the ends. The Soviet authorities were unimpressed by the grand vista in front of the grave of an independence-era politician and contrived to block the view towards Čakste by inserting an elaborate memorial marking the grave of Vilis Lācis, writer and chairman of the Council of Ministers of the Latvian Soviet Socialist Republic, who died in 1966. Soviet-era burials behind the Lācis memorial further tarnish the harmony of the alley in front of Čakste's grave.

Mežaparks [69 F5] One of the most well-to-do Rīga neighbourhoods, the district, then called Kaiserwald, was laid out in the early 20th century, inspired by the garden city movement. Kaiserwald also holds a darker significance as the name of a German concentration camp, operating near here from 1943 to 1944. **Mežaparks**

means literally 'Forest Park', and its heart is a forested area covering 424ha, on the western shore of the Ķišezers lake, logically if somewhat confusingly also bearing the name Mežaparks. The park, opened in 1949, is a popular place for joggers and recreational pursuits, including for its city beach in summer. The main entrance is at the Mežaparks/Zoo tram stop, served by tram 11 from the city centre. A broad paved promenade heads into the park from here. From brick pavilions near the entrance, **Mežaparka noma** (Kokneses prospekts 39; w mezaparkanoma.lv) offers rental of bicycles (€7 for the first hr; €3/hr subsequently), as well as roller-skates, scooters and skateboards, to facilitate your exploration of the park using whatever means you choose.

Rīga Zoo (Rīgas Nacionalais zooloģiskais dārzs; Meža prospekts 1; w rigazoo.lv; ⊕ 3 Apr–15 Oct 10.00–19.00, entry until 18.00; 16 Oct–2 Apr 10.00–17.00, entry until 16.00; adult/student/child May–Oct €15/10/8, Nov–Apr €12/8/5 Mon–Fri, €14/9/6 Sat–Sun) Its entrance to the side of the main Mežaparks park entrance, Rīga Zoo was founded in 1912, and offers the chance to get acquainted with both Latvian and exotic wildlife. Note that the tropical house and other indoor exhibits close 30 minutes earlier than the rest of the zoo, and that the tropical house opens only at 11.00.

Mežaparks Grand Stage (Mežaparka Lielā estrāde; Ostas prospekts 11) This is a place of great cultural significance for Latvians as the main venue of the five-yearly Song and Dance Festival (page 54). Until the 1950s, the festival had been held at different temporary venues across the city, but as its size increased, the decision was made to build a permanent venue in Mežaparks. The architect of the project was Vladimir Schitnikov, also responsible for Rīga's Daugava Stadium. He built a grand venue in the Stalinist Baroque style.

That Soviet construction has now given way to a new stage, first used for the Latvian Song and Dance Festival in 2023, reflecting the values of independent Latvia. It features rows of concrete steps for the choirs to stand on beneath a curving metal roof, loosely modelled on a forest, giving the stage the nicknames of the 'Silver Grove' or the 'Hill of Song'. The stage faces a banked grassy slope, on which temporary seats are placed for the audience during the song festival, but which is put to other uses outside it, including for tobogganing on rubber rings during the winter months.

Around the back of the stage is the entrance to the **Latvian Song and Dance Festival Exhibition** (Dziesmu un deju svētku ekspozīcija; Ostas prospekts 11; w dziesmusvetkutelpa.lv; ⊕ 11.00–17.00 Wed–Sun; adult/student/child €8/5/3), offering a well-presented introduction to the event. A history of the festival, from its first edition in 1873 to the present day, occupies one large wall on the ground floor. Opposite, a bank of television screens is filled with images of the massed festival choir performing classics such as the emotional *Saule, Pērkons, Daugava*. You can also listen through headphones to some of the best-known songs associated with the festival. Upstairs is a library of festival-related publications.

Mežciems The suburb of Mežciems on the eastern side of the city literally means 'Forest Village', a name that gives little clue to the character of the place, with its many Soviet-era apartment blocks. Two very different sights may bring you out here: the excellent Rīga Motor Museum and a sobering memorial to the Holocaust in Latvia.

Rīga Motor Museum (Rīgas Motormuzejs; S. Eizenšteina iela 8; w motormuzejs. lv; ⊕ 10.00–18.00 Tue–Sun; adult/child €10/5). Housed in a purpose-built complex over three floors, its entrance resembling a car grille, this is one of the most engrossing museums of Latvia. Its origins lie in the work of Viktors Kulbergs, who in 1972 founded the Latvian Antique Automobile Club, with a mission to track down and restore vintage cars. Through more than 100 cars on display, the museum charts the history of the automobile. Among the many fascinating exhibits note the Lincoln V12 gifted by the Soviet government to writer Maxim Gorky in 1934. He didn't drive. 'Frankenstein' is a BMW 326 kept going through the Soviet period with the help of spare parts from various Soviet automobiles, including headlights from a GAZ truck and a radiator grill from a Moskvitch. The BMW emblem is almost the only original feature about the car.

Upstairs is a display of the large, luxurious and almost invariably black cars used by Soviet leaders, who were 'not burdened by modesty' as the labelling puts it. Star of the show here is a 1966 Rolls Royce Silver Shadow that Brezhnev managed to crash in 1980. It is displayed with a startled Brezhnev mannequin at the wheel.

THE HOLOCAUST IN LATVIA

The German attack on the Soviet Union began on 22 June 1941, quickly reaching Latvia. The Holocaust started immediately, initially entrusted to Einsatzgruppe A of the Sicherheitsdienst (SD), a mobile death squad whose task was to kill members of those groups the Nazis regarded as 'undesirable', with Jews at the head of that list. An SD unit killed six Jews in Grobiņa already on the night of 23 June. An aspect of the Holocaust that remains controversial in Latvia was the involvement of Latvian citizens in much of the killing through Latvian auxiliary units of the SD. The most notorious was the Arājs Kommando, established by a one-time police-officer-cum-eternal-student named Viktors Arājs, who gathered recruits among students as well as organisations such as the anti-Semitic Pērkonkrusts. The Arājs Kommando led attacks on the Jews of Rīga at the beginning of July, including the burning of the Choral Synagogue. The Kommando took their orders from such German officers as Rudolf Lange, a particularly feared figure who shot one young man who failed to open a railway carriage door fast enough for his liking.

According to a Nazi activity report, by the middle of October 1941 some 30,000 Jews had been executed in Latvia. The Einsatzgruppe and its Latvian auxiliaries slaughtered Jewish communities across the country. The German occupation of the small town of Preiļi, some half of whose population was Jewish, is chronicled in the diary of a 15-year-old girl named Sheina Gram. Writing in Yiddish, she reports the arrival of the Germans in the town on 2 July. On the following day, they broke into the synagogue and trampled on the Torah scrolls. Jews were ordered to wear a six-pointed yellow star and were rounded up for forced labour. Sheina was made to cut peat. On 27 July, 'bloody Sunday', some 250 Jews of the town were shot. Jewish girls were, she wrote, sent to clean up Jewish apartments to accommodate those who had killed their previous occupants. The last entry in Sheina's diary is dated 8 August. She writes of her fears for what will come next. On the following day, Sheina, her parents and brother were among the hundreds of Jews from Preiļi and the surrounding area murdered in the Jewish cemetery.

At the end of July, Heinrich Lohse, the Nazi State Commissar overseeing the Baltic lands and Belarus, determined that Jews should be moved to ghettos and used as cheap labour, a policy disapproved of by Walter Stahlecker, commander of Einsatzgruppe A, who wanted to maintain the focus on extermination. The Rīga ghetto was established in the Maskavas forštate neighbourhood, with some

There is a fine display of more quotidian Soviet-era cars, including the Moskvitch and Zaporozhets. Pick up the telephone in the booth to hear a procession of Soviet-era jokes: 'Where did Adam and Eve come from? The USSR. Stark naked, one apple for two people, and they are convinced they are living in paradise.'

There are vehicles manufactured in Latvia in the basement, including minibuses produced by the Rīga Autobus Factory (RAF), which from its factory in Jelgava became one of the major minibus producers of the Soviet Union. The museum has a café offering a good-value set lunch, which is helpful as there is not much else in the immediate area. Bus number 5 gets you here from the city centre.

Biķernieki Memorial [69 G6] (Biķernieku memoriāls; Biķernieku iela 70) The forest of Biķernieki, today a large and tranquil space within the Mežciems district, holds an appalling secret. This was the largest mass murder site of the Holocaust in Latvia. Between July 1941 and October 1944, some 35,000 people were shot

30,000 Jews concentrated in the small area of 16 blocks by the end of October. It had, however, been in operation no more than a few weeks, when the designs of Heinrich Himmler, who controlled the SD, overruled those of Lohse. Himmler wanted to eliminate the Latvian Jews to free up space in the Rīga ghetto for Jews deported eastwards from Germany and Austria. He brought in Friedrich Jeckeln, architect of the Babi Yar massacre in Ukraine, to oversee the shooting of 25,000 Latvian Jews from the ghetto at specially dug pits in the forest of Rumbula just outside Rīga. Only around 5,000 Latvian Jews in Rīga were allowed to live: mostly skilled male workers and female seamstresses, who were rehoused in a 'small ghetto'. The occupants of the first train of Jews from Berlin, which arrived in Rīga on 30 November, were immediately shot at Rumbula. But from mid-December Jews from Germany were housed in the remaining area of the original ghetto, now known as the 'German ghetto', and administered separately from the 'small ghetto'. The Biķernieki forest north of Rīga was the single biggest Holocaust mass murder site in Latvia. Among those who died here were almost 4,000 Jews killed in March 1942 when the Nazi authorities decided that the German ghetto in Rīga was getting overcrowded and organised the so-called Dünamünde actions. They pretended that the older and weaker inhabitants of the ghetto were to be sent to a town called Dünamünde, for lighter work processing fish. Dünamünde did not exist. They were taken to Biķernieki and shot.

From March 1943, in the Mežaparks suburb of Rīga, the Germans began the construction of the Kaiserwald concentration camp. In June, the ghetto in Rīga, along with those in Liepāja and Daugavpils, were liquidated, and the Jews surviving in them brought to Kaiserwald. While conditions in the camp were tough, it was not an extermination camp, but was used as a source of forced labour for German companies. With the advance of the Red Army in August 1944, Jews aged under 18 or over 30 at Kaiserwald were killed, the rest evacuated to the camp at Stutthof in Poland.

In all, some 70,000 Latvian Jews were murdered during the Holocaust, as well as more than 20,000 Jews deported from Germany and other Nazi-occupied territories. The targets of systematic murder in Latvia also included Roma communities, homosexuals and communists. Monuments across Latvia to the victims of the Holocaust remember these lives so cruelly cut short.

Rīga WHAT TO SEE AND DO

3

119

here. Most victims were Jews, but those killed also included political prisoners and Soviet prisoners of war, as well as more than 700 patients from the Rīga psychiatric hospital. A memorial designed by Latvian architect Sergejs Rižs, funded by the governments of Germany and Austria, was opened in 2001. From a white concrete arch close to the road, a path runs to the monument focused on a cube of black granite, representing a symbolic altar, under a white concrete frame. Around this is a forest of jagged stones, carved with the names of hometowns of the victims. Around this central area are many burial sites in the forest, each marked by a rectangular platform with a single standing stone. Bus 16 from the central railway station serves the Biķernieku memorials bus stop, close to the entrance.

Latvian Ethnographic Open-Air Museum [69 G5] (Latvijas Etnogrāfiskais brīvdabas muzejs; Brīvdabas iela 21; w brivdabasmuzejs.lv; ⊕ May–Sep 10.00–18.00 Sun–Thu, 10.00–20.00 Fri–Sat, Oct & Apr 10.00–17.00 daily, Nov–Jan 10.00–16.00 daily, Feb–Mar 10.00–16.00 Tue–Sun; adult/student/child May–Sep €4/2/1.40, Oct–Apr €2/1.40/0.70) This was established in 1924, making it one of the oldest outdoor museums of its kind in Europe. Spread over 87ha of forest alongside the picturesque shore of Lake Jugla, its origins lay in the efforts to build a national identity in newly independent Latvia. It offers a collection of predominantly wooden rural buildings, dating from the end of the 17th century to the early 20th.

The buildings are grouped by the four main historic regions of Latvia, with each well represented. Farm assemblages are the bedrock of the place, usually involving a farmhouse and various outbuildings, the latter serving to demonstrate the considerable range of Latvian barn designs. There are several churches: note the painted ceiling and carved pulpit and altar of the Usma Lutheran Church from Kurzeme, dating from the early 18th century. A grand half-timbered warehouse bears the date of 1697, and once graced the harbourside in Liepāja. Some of the smaller buildings are fascinating too, including wooden sauna houses, net huts from the Kurzeme coast, incorporating lengthwise poles on which fishing nets were dried, and some 19th-century beehives resembling sarcophagi: hollowed blocks of pine, laid horizontally and covered with a roof of wooden planks.

The museum is a pleasant place to wander, though the explanatory text is limited, and many buildings are locked up outside peak season. The long wooden building near the entrance is the Priedes roadside pub, built in 1841 in Vecumnieki near Bauska. The central room would have served farmers and labourers, while the gentry drank in more exclusive surroundings at what was known as the 'German end' of the building. It today holds the Priedes tavern, as well as a souvenir shop offering jewellery, textiles and ceramics. During the summer season, from May to September, you may encounter artisans at the museum, offering the opportunity to try out their crafts. The museum also hosts interesting seasonal events linked to Latvian traditional festivals, including Easter and Midsummer. Trolleybus 31 and buses 28 and 29 come here: the stop is Brīvdabas muzejs.

Bolderāja A riparian suburb on the left bank of the Daugava as it approaches the Gulf of Rīga, Bolderāja is a district mixing wooden houses, Soviet-era apartment blocks and plenty of greenery, and has developed an exaggerated reputation as a lawless, end-of-the-line sort of place.

Daugavgrīva Fortress [68 C2] (Daugavgrīvas cietoksnis; Birzes iela 2; ☏ 2820 4051; ⊕ 10.00–16.00 Sat–Sun; admission free) Bolderāja owes its development to this fortress, laid out in a star-shaped design with six bastions, surrounded by a moat. There had long been a fortress protecting the mouth of the Daugava, but the current version took shape from 1682, the work of Swedish military engineer and future Governor-General of Livonia Erik Dahlbergh, who adopted the Vauban-type fortress design in vogue at the time. It was then known as Neumünde. In 1700, at the start of the Great Northern War, it was captured by the forces of Augustus II the Strong, ruler of Saxony, Poland and Lithuania, and was briefly known as Augustusburg before the Swedes retook it the next year. Russian forces under Count Boris Sheremetev then captured the place in 1710, ushering in a period of Russian control lasting until World War I. The military has long since left, though there is still a Latvian naval base nearby. The fortress now offers a landscape of decaying buildings being reclaimed by nature, making it a pleasant place for a stroll around the ramparts. Bus 3 brings you here from the city centre – the stop is Daugavgrīvas cietoksnis.

Mangaļsala Across the mouth of the Daugava from Bolderāja, Mangaļsala has a very different feel. It was once an island, formed in the 16th century when the Daugava created its current mouth as a new channel to the sea. The original channel gradually silted up, and became blocked in 1840, turning Mangaļsala into a sandy peninsula. It is a tranquil place, with a white sand beach backed by dunes, and pine forest behind these. This attractive coastal environment has been protected since 1962 as the **Piejūra Nature Park** [68 D1] (Piejūras dabas parks). The military importance of this area, guarding the approach to Rīga from the sea, means the woods are studded with remnants of former military installations from both Tsarist and Soviet times. These are now decaying, graffiti-covered concrete structures: exploring them can be dangerous. Another somewhat decrepit sight here is found offshore: the protruding hull of a Swedish-flagged ship, the *Lady Cotlin*, which ran aground here in 1951 to the alarm of the Soviet authorities. At the mouth of the Daugava, the **Mangaļsala Breakwater** (Mangaļsalas mols) dates from the second part of the 19th century. Stretching into the sea, it is a popular place for a promenade, known particularly for attractive views at sunset. There is a mirror-image breakwater across the Daugava at Bolderāja. The 24 bus will get you to Mangaļsala from the city centre.

Babīte On the western edge of Rīga, off the road towards Jūrmala, sits the dormitory village of Babīte. The main attraction is the **University of Latvia Experimental Rhododendron Breeding Nursery 'Babīte'** [68 A6] (Rododendru selekcijas un izmēģinājumu audzētava 'Babīte'; 'Rododendri', Spilve, Babītes pag.; w rododendri.lu.lv; ⊕ May–Jun 09.00–19.00 daily, Apr & Jul–Oct 09.00–18.00 daily, Nov–Mar 09.00–16.00 daily; adult/student/child May–Jun €5/4/3, Jul–Apr €2/2/2). Established in 1980, the nursery was the child of Professor Rihards Kondratovičs, who dedicated his professional career to rhododendron research and ran the place until his death in 2017. Kondratovičs started his research at the University of Latvia in 1957 at a time when rhododendrons were not widespread in Latvia, building a collection of the plants and creating new cultivars, focusing on winter-hardy varieties suitable for the Latvian climate. The nursery covers almost 12ha, with pine trees providing a half-shadow for the rhododendrons below. An asphalt path provides a 1.5km circuit. You pass both rhododendron cultivars and wild species, the latter including the single wild species native to Latvia – *Rhododendron tomentosum*, the marsh Labrador tea, a squat evergreen shrub with white flowers and a notably strong fragrance. The place is a riot of colour in May and June, when it gets most of its visitors. Babīte is served both by train from Rīga (it is a stop on the line to Tukums) and by the number 13 bus.

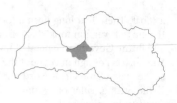

Around Rīga

The belt of small towns around the Latvian capital is an exception to the picture across much of Latvia of continuing depopulation in response to declining fertility and the lure of higher paid jobs elsewhere in the European Union. Here, numbers are growing, attracting families from Rīga looking for a home with a garden or simply more square metres for their euros. Towns like Mārupe are also bringing in light industry, attracted by their transport connections. This is all good news for the economy of the ring around the capital known as Pierīga, but for the most part these dormitory towns and industrial parks have little to offer the tourist. There is, however, one major exception: the long expanse of the beach resort of Jūrmala, Rīga's playground, with a compelling genteel townscape of wooden Art Nouveau villas. The town of Salaspils southeast of Rīga, while unattractive at first glance, also offers a varied mix of sights, from places connected with Nazi atrocities to Latvia's main botanic garden.

JŪRMALA

The combination of a long sandy beach and the prospect of curative waters have made the line of former fishing villages that collectively make up the resort of Jūrmala a popular place for recreation since Tsarist times. The resort still delivers a compelling offer. Its fine beach, strong accommodation and restaurant choices, attractive wooden architecture, historical connections to Latvian writers Rainis and Aspazija, breadth of entertainment options, and some great nature just outside the urban area add up to many reasons to linger. It is straightforwardly accessible from Rīga, and indeed it is perfectly possible to explore Rīga from an accommodation base in Jūrmala rather than the other way around.

HISTORY The modern resort of Jūrmala emerged from a string of fishing villages along the coast. From the late 18th century, these developed as popular bathing places for the well-to-do, a process accentuated through developments in transport, particularly the arrival of the railway in 1877. The first sanatorium, Marienbāde, opened its doors in Dubulti in 1870, and in 1881 the Dubulti Bathing Association ruled that men and women could bathe at the same time, provided that they were properly attired, the first such arrangement in Tsarist Russia. World War I caused a good deal of damage, but the development of the resort picked up again thereafter. The city of Jūrmala was formally established in 1959 when the seaside resort of Rīgas Jūrmala was amalgamated with the spa resort of Ķemeri and the town of Sloka. In the Soviet period, Jūrmala became a holiday and medical destination known throughout the USSR. Soviet institutions built their own sanatoria and guest houses here. The Jaunķemeri sanatorium, founded in 1967, is one of the few survivors from that period. Following the restoration of Latvian independence,

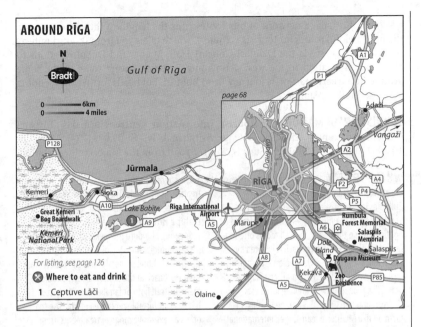

page 68

AROUND RĪGA

N

Gulf of Rīga

0 ——— 6km
0 ——— 4 miles

For listing, see page 126

❌ Where to eat and drink

1   Ceptuve Lāči

Jūrmala remained a popular holiday choice for Russian tourists, with many wealthy Russians buying up property in the city, but worsening relations between Latvia and Russia have challenged this model, and Jūrmala's businesses are anxiously eyeing western holidaymakers.

GETTING THERE AND AROUND Jūrmala is served by the Rīga to Tukums **railway** line. Note that there is no single railway station named Jūrmala: the resort stretches for 30km along the coast and encompasses 14 stations. Those of most use for the main sights and tourist areas are, from east to west, Lielupe, Bulduri, Dzintari, Majori, Dubulti and, much further to the west, Ķemeri. The service from Rīga as far as Dubulti is the most frequent on the Latvian Railways network and is cheap, with departures roughly every 30 minutes (€1.50). The train takes around 25 minutes to Lielupe, 32 minutes to Majori and 35 minutes to Dubulti. Frequency drops west of here, but there are still around 15 departures daily to Ķemeri (1hr; €2.10). There are also **bus** connections from Rīga to both Sloka railway station and the Jaunķemeri spa, stopping at Majori and Dubulti stations on the way, but service is less frequent than the train.

In the summer months, a more exotic form of transport is available between Rīga and Jūrmala by **river boat** with the company Rīga Ship (w rigaship.lv; ⊕ 15 May–15 Oct; adult/child €20/10 one-way, €30/15 return). The motorboat *New Way* leaves Rīga at 11.00, departing from the Daugava embankment close to the Big Christopher statue, taking 2 hours 30 minutes to reach Majori, via the Daugava, Buļļupe and Lielupe rivers. Departure from Majori is at 16.00.

If you are arriving in Jūrmala by private **car**, note that an entry fee is charged between 1 April and 30 September. Currently €3 per vehicle, this is payable at ticket machines located on the Rīga side of the Lielupe River as you come into the city. **Bicycle** is another option from Rīga: it is about 25km of mostly flat riding, with a bicycle path running alongside the railway line for much of your route once you have navigated your way out of the city.

Within Jūrmala, a network of **bus** routes runs the length of the resort. Among the most helpful routes for tourists is route 4, which takes you from Bulduri railway station in the east via the Dzintari Concert Hall, Majori and Dubulti stations to Sloka railway station in the west. Also route 5, which covers some of the same ground in the early part of its journey from Bulduri, but heads further west, ending at Ķemeri railway station.

TOURIST INFORMATION The **tourist information centre** (Jūrmalas Tūrisma informācijas centrs; Lienes iela 5; w visitjurmala.lv; ⊕ 09.00–17.00 Mon–Fri, 10.00–17.00 Sat, 10.00–15.00 Sun) is over the road from the Majori railway station.

WHERE TO STAY   *Map, page 127, unless otherwise stated*

Light House [map, opposite] (11 rooms) Gulbenes iela 1A; w lighthousejurmala.lv. This boutique hotel is, unusually for Jūrmala, located right alongside the beach, with all rooms offering sea views. The decoration of each is inspired by a different country or Latvian region – though some are easier to discern than others. Sunbeds, umbrellas & beach towels are free for guests. The restaurant (€€€€€) is among the best in town, with a Mediterranean-tinged international menu. €€€€€

Baltic Beach Hotel (165 rooms) Jūras iela 23/25; w balticbeach.lv. Top-end hotel & spa complex close to the beach. It has several dining options, including Italian dishes at the Il Sole restaurant (€€€€€) & seafood & steaks at VIEW (€€€€€). There are numerous treatments available at the spa, from massage & mud to full sauna rituals. Room rates give you access to seawater pool, sauna & steam bath for 2hrs/day. €€€€

Hotel Jūrmala Spa (190 rooms) Jomas iela 47/49; w hoteljurmala.com. Centrally located on Jomas iela, where it represents something of an eyesore, this large hotel offers a 'wellness oasis' of pools, saunas & a gym, with a range of spa

treatments available. The 11th floor Seaside Bar offers nice views over the town. €€€€

Lielupe Hotel by SemaraH [map, opposite] (264 rooms) Bulduru prospekts 64/68; w lielupe. semarahhotels.com. One of the behemoths of the Jūrmala hotel scene, this place is a short walk from the beach at the eastern district of Bulduri, markets itself both at families & conferences, but has comfortable renovated rooms. The spa offers an extensive range of treatments, from Asian-inspired massage to more home-grown offerings like a massage with Latvian herb-filled pouches. €€€€

Villa Joma (20 rooms) Jomas iela 90; w villajoma.lv. In a restored wooden villa, already a hotel in the 19th century, centrally located on Jomas iela, this is a characterful choice, although the 'small rooms' live up to their billing. Also has a good restaurant (€€€€) with an international menu. €€€€

Parus (12 rooms) Smilšu iela 2; w parus. lv. 3-star hotel in a 1920s wooden villa a block behind the beach, with a pleasant garden with a wooden gazebo. They offer beach towels & bicycle rentals. €€€

WHERE TO EAT AND DRINK   *Map, page 127, unless otherwise stated*

36.Line [map, opposite] Baznīcas iela 2B, Dubulti; w 36line.com. Amid the dunes overlooking the Dubulti beachfront, this smart restaurant is a Jūrmala institution, offering a tempting menu from duck breast in a ginger honey marinade to black cod. Line 36 was actually the name of the Lielupe street housing the original restaurant. €€€€€

Laivas [map, opposite] Vienības prospekts 36; w restoranslaivas.com. Picturesquely sited on the bank of the Lielupe River, close to a small marina, the 'Boats' demonstrates its maritime heritage with a small wooden boat in front of the restaurant,

nautical-styled lighting within & oars in the toilets. The menu heads in all directions, including a raw bar with venison tartare & oysters, Latvian dishes like black pudding, steak & pizza. It is, though, a pricey option. €€€€€

House of Light Jomas iela 63; w hol.lv. Housed in a glass-sided box on Jomas iela, this is a family-friendly central restaurant, with modern décor, grilled meat & fish dishes, a children's menu & a play area. There is no connection between this place & the Light House hotel & restaurant. €€€€

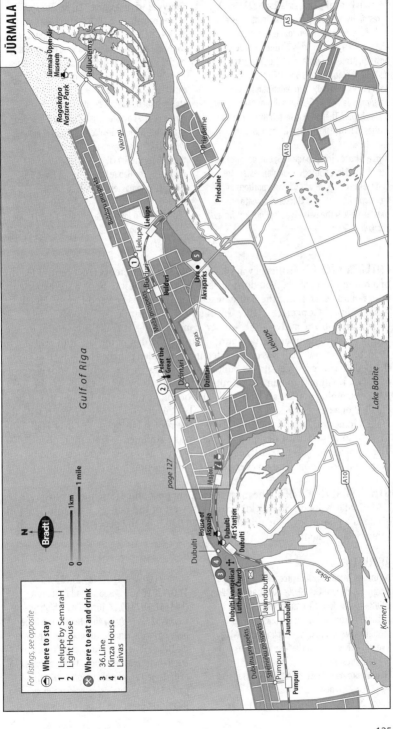

JŪRMALA

For listings, see opposite

Where to stay
1 Lielupe by SemaraH
2 Light House

Where to eat and drink
3 36.Line
4 Kinza House
5 Laivas

Gulf of Riga

Ragakāpa Nature Park

Jūrmala Open-Air Museum

Buļļuciems

Vikingu

Priedaine

Lielupe
Lielupe

Buļļuprospekts

Bulduri

Mežaprospekts

Bulduri

Rīgas

Lielupe

Lvu
Akvaparks

Priedaine

Dzintari

Peter the Great

Dzintari

Lake Babite

page 127

Majori

House of Aspazija

Dubulti
Art Station

Dubulti

Dubulti

Dubulti

Dubultu prospekts

Dubultu Evangelical
Lutheran Church

Jaundubulti

Jaundubulti

Slokas

Pumpuri

Strēlnieku prospekts

Pumpuri

Kemeri

A5

A10

A10

Yerevan Pandok Jomas iela 25; ✆2230 8579; e restorans@yerevanpandok.lv. On the western end of the pedestrianised Jomas iela, close to Majori railway station, this 2-storey wooden villa hosts an Armenian restaurant & delicatessen. The restaurant ranges across South Caucasus cuisines, with plenty of kebabs, Armenian staples such as *basturma*, as well as Georgian dishes like *khinkali* & *khachapuri*. The interior, tastefully decorated in shades of brown, includes a frieze of bygone Jomas iela. €€€€

Kinza House [map, page 125] Baznīcas iela 2, Dubulti; w kinzahouse.lv. Georgian restaurant behind the dunes, offering hearty portions of *khachapuri*, the stewed chicken & tomato dish *chakhokhbili*, & the twisted dumplings known as *khinkali*. €€€

Ceptuve Lāči [map, page 123] 'Benūžu-Skauģi', Babītes pagasts; w laci.lv. If the Liepkalni bakery shop & café is considered an almost compulsory stop by many Latvians heading east from Rīga on the road to Daugavpils, then the Lāči bakery performs a similar function for those heading west from the capital on the A9 route towards Liepāja. A canteen-style restaurant offers a good-value lunch; you can stock up at the store on Lāči bread & branded chocolates, & there are nicely landscaped grounds with a children's playground. It's around 13km up the A9 from the Rīga ring road, separated from Jūrmala by the Babīte Lake & Lielupe River. €€

De Gusto Jomas iela 46; ✆2920 3024; e odegusto@gmail.com. Popular pastry shop on pedestrianised Jomas iela, offering a good range of cakes, including the cream-filled Vecrīga & several gluten-free options.

ENTERTAINMENT As they always have been, **spa treatments** are a central feature of a holiday in Jūrmala. You don't have to be a hotel guest to book a spa experience at the main centres, like the Baltic Beach Hotel, Jūrmala Spa and Lielupe Hotel.

Dzintari Concert Hall (Dzintaru koncertzāle; Turaidas iela 1; w dzintarukoncertzale.lv) – the 'Amber' concert hall – is really two venues in one. The place started out as the Edinburgh Concert Garden in the late 19th century. In 1936, today's Small Hall was constructed in the wooden panelled building that sits on the pedestrianised street. It was built in a classical style but suffused with elements of Latvian national romanticism, notably the murals by Ansis Cīrulis in the foyer. Also welcoming you in is a large sculpture of conductor Arvīds Jansons in full flow. He died of a heart attack in Manchester in 1984 while conducting a concert with the Hallé Orchestra. Behind the Small Hall is the roofed but open-air Great Hall, built in 1960 in a modernist design and open in the summer. It seats more than 2,000. The complex has been smartly renovated, with a new glass entrance building and basement cloakroom, and hosts concerts covering genres from classical music to pop.

OTHER PRACTICALITIES The most convenient **post office** (Strēlnieku prospekts 16; ✆6776 2430) sits on Strēlnieku prospekts, west of the railway station in Dubulti. There is a **pharmacy** (Jomas iela 66; ✆2680 9302) on the pedestrianised stretch of Jomas iela in Majori.

ACTIVITIES

Jūrmalas Tarzāns Meža prospekts; w jurmala. tarzans.lv; ⊕ Jun–Oct 10.00–20.00; adult/child €20/8–15. The Jūrmala branch of the popular Tārzans network of adventure parks involves several routes of ropeways & ziplines of varying levels of difficulty strung between the trees of the Dzintari Forest Park.

Līvu Akvaparks Viestura iela 24; w akvaparks. lv; ⊕ Jun–Aug noon–21.00 Mon–Fri, 11.00–21.00 Sat, 11.00–20.00 Sun, Oct–May

noon–21.00 Wed–Fri, 11.00–21.00 Sat, 11.00–20.00 Sun, closed Sep; adult/student/ child €31.60/29.00/24.10 for 2hrs in high season, €35.60/32.10/27.70 for 4hrs. Housed in a large building on the Jūrmala side of the bridge across the Lielupe River, with a spaghetti of coloured water chutes protruding from its tower, this is one of the largest water parks in northern Europe. It is pitched at all age groups, with adrenalin-inducing slides, gentle river way tackled on a rubber ring,

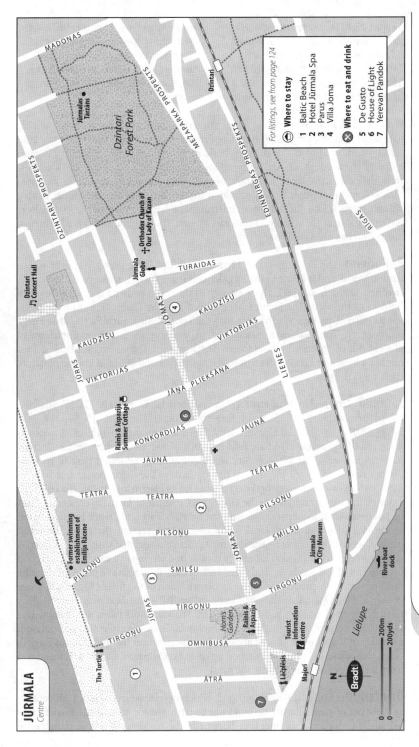

JŪRMALA
Centre

MADONAS

Dzintari Forest Park

● Jūrmalas Tarzāns

DZINTARU PROSPEKTS

MEŽAPARKA PROSPEKTS

Dzintari

EDINBURGAS PROSPEKTS

RIGAS

✝ Orthodox Church of Our Lady of Kazan

Dzintari Concert Hall 🎵

Jūrmala Globe 🎪

TURAIDAS

KAUDZĪŠU

JOMAS

④

VIKTORIJAS

JURAS

KAUDZĪŠU

LIENES

VIKTORIJAS

JĀNA PLIEKŠĀNA

Rainis & Aspazija Summer Cottage 🏛

⑥

KONKORDIJAS

JAUNĀ

JAUNĀ

✝

TEĀTRA

● Former swimming establishment of Emīlija Rācene

TEĀTRA

TEĀTRA

②

PILSOŅU

PILSOŅU

JOMAS

PILSOŅU

SMILŠU

SMILŠU

③

SMILŠU

Jūrmala City Museum ●

The Turtle ↟

TIRGOŅU

JURAS

TIRGOŅU

Horn's Garden

Rainis & Aspazija 🏛

⑤

TIRGOŅU

River boat dock

OMNIBUSA

Tourist information centre ℹ

ĀTRĀ

Lāčplēsis ↟

Majori

⑦

Lielupe

N ↑

Bradt

0   200m
0   200yds

& a pirate ship for the younger ones, who get a soaking when a huge bucket of water disguised as Captain Kidd's head tips over. For the adults there are saunas, a steam room & a Turkish bath, & for everyone a large wave pool. An outdoor area opens in summer with more slides & pools.

There are eateries on site: your wristband is loaded with credit, from which you settle up at the end. The admission charge is slightly lower in 'low season', but w/end, the summer months & school holidays are all 'high season'. Take care: floors can be slippery.

WHAT TO SEE AND DO The two major attractions of Jūrmala are its beach of soft, pale sand, backed by dunes, and its wooden houses and villas. Since the early 20th century coincided with a peak in the building of wooden villas for wealthy Rīgans, many of these adopt an Art Nouveau style, employing all manner of flourishes, from delicate lattice work to corner towers. With the resort stretching for more than 30km, orientation is best provided by the legacy of the individual fishing villages from which Jūrmala was constructed, a legacy preserved in the railway stations that bear their names. From east to west, the neighbourhoods of principal tourist interest are as follows.

Buļļuciems The eastern end of Jūrmala is still in large part given over to the natural world, and is home to the **Ragakāpa Nature Park** (Ragakāpas dabas parks), covering 150ha from the Lielupe estuary to the more built-up neighbourhood of Bulduri to the west. The Lielupe once flowed into the Daugava, but in the 1750s cut its current passage northwards into the Gulf of Rīga, turning the area into a promontory. The park was established to preserve its attractive environment of sand dunes covered by pine forest. The Ragakāpa Dune, largest of the dunes, reaches a height of 17m, with an overall length of around 800m. A couple of nature trails cross the place.

Jūrmala Open-Air Museum (Jūrmalas brīvdabas muzejs; Tīklu iela 1A; w visitjurmala.lv; ⏲ 15 May–14 Sep 10.00–18.00 Tue–Sun, 15 Sep–14 May 10.00–17.00 Tue–Sun; admission free) The museum dates from 1970, when it was established as the open-air folk museum of the local fishermen's collective. Its heart is a group of 19th-century wooden buildings relocated here to recreate the household of a well-to-do local fishing family. The living house was built in 1882, its first owner the appropriately named Ansis Fišermanis. Inside the building, mannequins are dressed up in the Honorary Costume of Jūrmala, created in 2021 on the demand of local participants in the Latvian Song and Dance Festival, bereft at the lack of a traditional local folk costume to represent the area. The result features a good deal of blue – suitable for a place so associated with sea and river. A straw-roofed barn is divided into three rooms: one serving as a cart house, a second for grain and food products, and a third for clothes, used also as a place for sleeping in summer. A fish-processing house displays models of the fish of Rīga Gulf. There is also a 'black sauna', with soot-blackened walls, where heat was generated by piled boulders beneath which a fire was lit. Wooden workshops are occupied by exhibitions on rope stranding and boat building. There is a collection of boats and a display of the wooden fragments of ships rescued from the gulf, like an English cargo ship some 200 years old washed up on the coast near Carnikava. It was dated from a 1799 penny found under the mast.

Dzintari The Dzintari neighbourhood, which developed in the late 19th century as a district of particularly fine buildings constructed for aristocratic owners, was originally known as Edinburga, in honour of the wedding of Maria, daughter of

Russian emperor Alexander II, to the Duke of Edinburgh. From here, pedestrianised **Jomas iela** runs westwards, parallel to the sea, the centre of the action in Jūrmala away from the beach. It is flanked with eateries and lively in summer, when your walk along the street will be accompanied by the sound of buskers. Overlooking its eastern end is the **Orthodox Church of Our Lady of Kazan** (Kazaņas Dievmātes ikonas Dzintaru pareizticīgo baznīca; Aizkraukles iela 2; \6767 7500), with colourful blue and gold domes and pastel-painted walls. It is a modern building, on the site of a wooden church built in 1896 but dismantled during the Soviet period. On the pavement in front of the church stands the copper-covered **Jūrmala Globe**, against which you can take a selfie, pointing out your home town. Behind the church lies the **Dzintari Forest Park** (Dzintaru mežaparks), a pleasant, forested area.

In a well-heeled residential area of detached villas in spacious grounds northeast of the park, there is the curious sight of an **equestrian statue of Peter the Great** standing in the garden of a private house on the corner of Dzintaru prospekts and Drustu iela. The statue was erected in 1910, to mark the 200th anniversary of the Russian conquest of Rīga, and originally installed in the heart of Rīga, on the site of the current Freedom Monument. It was being transported to St Petersburg in 1915 when the ship carrying it was torpedoed by a German submarine. It was recovered in pieces by Estonian divers in the 1930s, and after languishing in fragments for decades was restored by Latvian businessman Jevgeņijs Gombergs, who was, however, unable to persuade the Rīga municipality of the virtues of displaying a statue of a Russian leader in a prominent place. Peter the Great, therefore, currently rests in Gombergs' garden.

Majori The neighbourhood of Majori forms the heart of Jūrmala. A scrap of greenery opposite the station is home to a 1953 **statue of Lāčplēsis**, Latvia's bear-slaying national hero, here depicted despatching a dragon, metal sword held aloft as he prepares to deliver the final blow. As you begin your walk along Jomas iela from here, note **Horn's Garden** (Horna dārzs) on your left, a small park laid out by Albert Horn in 1870, once renowned as an open-air concert venue. The first Latvian symphonic music concert was held here in 1905. A diminutive statue of the Latvian writers Rainis and Aspazija, watched over by a raven in reference to Rainis' play *The Little Raven* (*Krauklītis*), celebrates their engagement with the garden.

Jūrmala City Museum (Jūrmalas muzejs; Tirgoņu iela 29; w visitjurmala.lv; ⊕ 15 May–14 Sep 10.00–18.00 Wed–Sun, 15 Sep–14 May 10.00–17.00 Wed–Sun; admission free) Housed in an ugly concrete building a block to the south, along Tirgoņu iela, it offers a well-presented exhibition on the ground floor on the history of Jūrmala as a resort. Temporary art exhibitions are held upstairs, and there is also a curious multimedia display entitled *Rainis' Space* (*Raiņa telpa*), in which you are invited to walk over wooden boards to reach the sandy shore, and to be as inspired as Rainis was by the coast of Jūrmala. The museum gift shop is a good place for souvenirs.

Rainis and Aspazija Summer Cottage (Raiņa un Aspazijas vasarnīca; Jāņa Pliekšāna iela 5/7; w memorialiemuzeji.lv; ⊕ Jun–Aug 10.00–17.00 Tue & Thu–Sat, noon–19.00 Wed, Sep–May 10.00–17.00 Tue–Sat; adult/student €2/1) Another of the Jūrmala locations associated with the husband-and-wife Latvian writers lies on Jānis Pliekšāns iela, the real name of Rainis, which runs off Jomas iela to the north. The property was built around 1895 and consisted of a wooden building close to the street and a little stone house behind it. Rainis and Aspazija purchased it in

1926 as their summer house. They generally rented out the wooden house and lived themselves in the stone building, drawing inspiration from the seaside. By autumn 1929, the family renting the wooden house had left, and an ailing Rainis settled in a room in that property where he died on 12 September. The place was developed as a museum complex in the Soviet period, when an adjacent building, now used primarily for temporary exhibitions, was added. A ground floor exhibition in the wooden house focuses on the love between Rainis and Aspazija in understanding their work. Upstairs you can see the little room in which he died, his medicines beside his bed. Their rooms in the stone garden house behind have also been furnished as the writers would have known them. They slept in adjacent rooms, each with a modest bed and a work desk for their writing.

Beach This is at its busiest along the Majori section of the coast, though compared to the Mediterranean, that still gives you a good deal of space. At the end of Pilsoņu iela, note the wooden green-walled **former swimming establishment of Emīlija Rācene**, its circular wooden tower looking straight over the beach. It was built in 1914 in an Art Nouveau style, and once offered a menu of therapeutic baths, though stood derelict at the time of writing. Along the beach to the west of here, guarding the flight of steps up to Tirgoņu iela, is a sculpture named **The Turtle** (Bruņurupucis). Installed in 1995, it has become a required photo opportunity for visitors to the city.

Dubulti This is the district to the west of Majori, where the urban area of Jūrmala is squeezed to its narrowest extent by a meander of the Lielupe River. The Dubulti railway station, built in 1977, creatively also houses the **Dubulti Art Station** (Zigfrīda Meierovica prospekts 3; ☎2954 8719; e dubulti.art.station@gmail.com; ⊕ 09.00–17.30 daily; admission free) which claims to be the only modern art space in Europe located within a functioning railway station. Down Baznīcas iela, just west of here, stands perhaps the most impressive of all Jūrmala's Art Nouveau buildings, the **Dubulti Evangelical Lutheran Church** (Dubultu evaņģēliski luteriskā baznīca; Baznīcas iela 13; ☎6775 5806). It was built between 1907 and 1909 to a design by architects Wilhelm Bockslaff and Edgar Friesendorf. Its tower, topped with a spire, features flourishes in a national romanticism style.

House of Aspazija (Aspazijas māja; Zigfrīda Meierovica prospekts 18/20; ☎6776 9445; e aspazijas.maja@jurmala.lv; ⊕ 15 May–14 Sep 10.00–18.00 Tue–Sat, 15 Sep–14 May 10.00–17.00 Tue–Sat; admission free) This is another of the many sites in Jūrmala linked to writers Rainis and Aspazija, though here it is Aspazija who takes centre stage. It is a delightful wooden two-storey building where the poetess spent the last ten years of her life from 1933, after Rainis' death, living here with her housekeeper and her brother's daughter. As well as her own output, she spent much time sorting out both her husband's literary legacy and the considerable debts he had left. The house is furnished as she would have known it, and eerily, in her bedroom, you are greeted with a hologram of Aspazija herself, deep in thought as she sits on her bed writing poetry, her beloved cat under the bed. It lies east from Dubulti railway station along Zigfrīda Meierovica prospekts, back towards Majori.

Ķemeri At the western end of Jūrmala, Ķemeri is different in feel to the rest of the resort, and indeed was once a separate town. It owes its fame to the raised bogs in the area, the source of the sulphurous mineral waters that burst out from the peat in more than 30 springs. The curative properties of the water here were known from the late 18th century, and the spa resort of Bad Kemmern was founded in 1838. The arrival of the railway from 1877 provided a further impetus to the development of the resort. It was heavily damaged in World War I, but the government of independent Latvia focused on the place, particularly with the opening in 1936 of the huge **Hotel Ķemeri**, designed by Eižens Laube, one of Latvia's most famous architects, and known as the 'White Ship' because of its liner-like form. The hotel became a sanatorium in the Soviet period, but following the restoration of Latvian independence and the collapse of the Soviet resort system, the 'White Ship' became a white elephant and has been closed since 1995. Ķemeri today echoes with the ghosts of its former spa glories. The long white façade of the Hotel Ķemeri remains the fulcrum of the place, notwithstanding that it is fenced off, awaiting a suitable investor. The central tower on its façade does indeed look rather like the funnel of an ocean liner.

Ķemeri Resort Park (Ķemeru kūrorta parks; Tūristu iela 2B) Lying behind the hotel, this park, first laid out in the 19th century in the new resort, is a pleasant place to wander, with numerous footbridges crossing the tranquil Vēršupīte River. There are several worthwhile sights within the park. The small wooden **St Peter and Paul Orthodox Church** (Sv Pētera un Pāvila Pareizticīgo Baznīca; Katedrāles laukums 1; \6776 5417), attractively painted in shades of green, red and brown, was built in 1893, making it the oldest church in Ķemeri. To signal the services, a shuttered window is opened in the bell tower above the entrance, followed by impressively enthusiastic bell ringing. Nearby, an artificial islet in a pond abutting the river is cutely known as the **Islet of Love** (Mīlestības saliņa) and accommodates a rotunda dating from the 1920s, its Doric columns supporting an observation platform accessed by a metal spiral staircase, and housing a welcome kiosk serving up coffee, pastries and ice cream.

The circular **Ķemeri Water Tower** (Ķemeru ūdenstornis; Tukuma iela 38; \6714 7900; ☉ May–Oct 10.00–18.00 daily; admission free) is an unmistakeable sight in the resort park. Dating from the 1920s, it was built to meet the needs of both resort and town, but from the outset combined tourism with the requirements of utility through the incorporation of an observation platform. This reopened in 2020, and now includes an exhibition on the history of Ķemeri. Nearby is the **'Little Lizard' Sulphur Spring** (Sēravots 'Ķirzaciņa'), a spring along the side of the Vēršupīte River, with a stone lizard taking the sulphurous waters which bubble up pungently here. The lizard dates from 1949, replacing an earlier sculpture of a boy on a dolphin, a victim of World War I. There's a wooden pavilion next to the spring, decorated with elegant latticework.

The settlement of Ķemeri alongside the park is nondescript, though is enlivened by the modern sculpture of **Anniņa of Ķemeri** (Ķemeru Anniņa; Senatnes iela 5), an elegant young woman promenading with her parasol by her side, a 3.5m work formed of layered aluminium plates. The sculpture references the song *Ķemermiestiņā*, associated with the Latvian Riflemen, whose heroine is the beautiful Anniņa living in a small hut in Ķemeri.

Ķemeri National Park (Ķemeru Nacionālais parks) At this end of Jūrmala the attractions of the natural environment eclipse those of the manmade one, and the Ķemeri National Park around the town offers a great range of walking trails. The park was established in 1997, to help preserve the raised bogs, shallow coastal lakes, deciduous forests and sulphurous springs of the area. The **Forest House** (Meža

4

mãja; Tūristu iela 1; w kemerunacionalaisparks.lv; ⊕ Jun–Aug 11.00–18.00 Tue–Sun, May & Sep 11.00–17.00 Sat–Sun), located logically enough in woodland some 900m from the resort park, contains the park information office and is the starting point for one of the trails.

The major lure of the park, however, is further afield. The **Great Ķemeri Bog Boardwalk** (Lielā Ķemeru tīreļa laipa) sits on the other side of the main A10 road. Heading towards Ventspils, the signposted turning is 200m west of the turning towards Ķemeri, and from there a 2km bumpy unpaved track brings you to the start of the boardwalk, where there is a car park (€3). If you don't have your own transport, the boardwalk is around 3.5km from Ķemeri railway station. It takes you across the Ķemeri Raised Bog (Lielais Ķemeru tīrelis), one of the largest such bogs in Latvia, covered in a network of pools, waterlogged areas of light-green moss, and relatively drier patches with heather and dwarf pine. In season, you may see berries such as cranberries, cloudberries and blueberries, and the bog is a breeding habitat for birds like the wood sandpiper and European golden plover. Wooden planking leads you safely over the bog, though you do have to watch your footing, as the planking is uneven in places. There are two looping circuits: the shorter version is 1.5km in total; the longer one, which takes you to a wooden observation tower, is 3.5km.

SALASPILS

Some 18km southeast of Rīga, Salaspils was an early centre of both human settlement in Latvia and of German missionary activity at the end of the 12th century. It was the site of the Battle of Kircholm of 1605 during the Polish–Swedish War, an encounter noted for the charge of the Polish–Lithuanian cavalry, helping to defeat a numerically far superior Swedish force. Previously a rural settlement, the place expanded rapidly during the Soviet occupation, with the construction of large housing blocks, and today it mostly has the feel of an undistinguished dormitory suburb of Rīga. There are, though, some interesting sights in and around the town, including Latvia's National Botanic Garden and the memorial to the Nazi concentration camp of Kurtenhof.

The **tourist information centre** (Salaspils novada Tūrisma informācijas centrs; Miera iela 1; w visit.salaspils.lv; ⊕ May–Sep 09.00–18.30 Mon–Fri, 10.00–16.00 Sat–Sun, Oct–Apr 09.00–17.30 Mon–Fri) shares the ticket office of the National Botanic Garden.

GETTING THERE AND AWAY Salaspils is a stop on the railway line from Rīga to Daugavpils, with more than 20 trains daily from the capital (25mins). The **railway station** (Salaspils dzelzceļa stacija; Miera iela; ✆ 8000 1181) is centrally located, across the road from the National Botanic Garden. **Buses** from Rīga depart from Riepnieku iela 2, roughly every 20 minutes.

✗ WHERE TO EAT AND DRINK Centrally located, just over the railway crossing from the botanical gardens, **4 Pēdas** ('Four Feet'; Līvzemes iela 2; w 4pedas.lv; €€€€) is a large restaurant with an outdoor terrace and good international menu from poke to grilled octopus. There is a café, **Kafejnīca Kruasāns**, in the same building, offering snacks and nice cakes.

WHAT TO SEE AND DO While the National Botanic Garden is right in the centre of town, Salaspils' other attractions are scattered.

National Botanic Garden (Nacionālais botāniskais dārzs; Miera iela 1; w nbd. gov.lv; ⊕ Oct–Mar 09.00–18.00 daily, Apr–Sep 09.00–20.00 daily, conservatory Oct–Mar 09.00–18.00 Wed–Sun, Apr–Sep 10.00–19.00 Wed–Sun; adult/child €8/5 inc conservatory, €5/3 gardens only) In the centre of town, its entrance across Miera iela from Salaspils railway station, the garden has its origins in the 19th-century nursery of Christian Wilhelm Schoch. It was established in 1956 as the Botanical Garden of the Academy of Sciences, and is substantial in size, covering 129ha. Since only those parts of the garden near the entrance have smart lawns and colourful flower beds, with wooded areas and fields further afield, hiring a bicycle at the entrance (€3 for the first hour; €1/hr thereafter) is potentially a good option for getting around. There is a large conservatory, with caged birds chirping among the tropical and subtropical plants.

Salaspils Memorial (Salaspils memorials; ✆6721 6367; ⊕ exhibition Apr–Oct 10.00–17.00 daily, Nov–Mar 10.00–15.00 daily; admission free) The memorial recalls a grim episode of Latvian history: the presence here of the Nazi German punishment camp known either as Salaspils or Kurtenhof, after the German name for the city. Construction of the camp started in November 1941, using Jews deported from Germany, Austria and Czechoslovakia to build it, many of whom died amid appalling conditions. The camp was opened in May 1942, and around 23,000 people were imprisoned here until its closure in September 1944 ahead of the Russian advance. It housed political prisoners, deserters and those who had failed to follow work regulations. They were put to work in quarries, peat bogs and a range of workshops, labouring 10 hours a day, six days a week. With meagre diets and little protection against outbreaks of disease, some 2,000 prisoners died.

With the Soviet Union keen to highlight German atrocities during World War II, the decision was made to mark the site with a grand memorial. Opened in 1967, this provides a striking example of Soviet brutalist architecture. A path from the car park at the site leads through forest, and you are confronted with a sloping concrete wall, raised up at one end on a large black plinth. The wall physically separates the territory of the camp from the outside world. An inscription above your head reads, in Latvian, 'the ground groans beneath these gates'. The wall conceals a long hollow space housing an exhibition, which includes both moving testimonies of those imprisoned at the camp and a display on the construction of the memorial. Four groups of large sculptural compositions are placed on the lawn behind the wall. A mother protects her children. A figure struggles to get up from the ground. The sculptures reflect an ideology of Soviet resistance to Nazi cruelty and ignore the complexity of the backgrounds of those who suffered at Salaspils. There was no reference in the original design of the memorial to Jews, for example, or to members of Polish or Latvian resistance movements. The eeriest feature of the memorial is a thudding noise designed to recall a heartbeat, produced by a metronome placed in a black tile-covered structure on the paved area in front of the lawn.

The memorial is located off the Rīga to Salaspils road, a couple of kilometres to the west of Salaspils town.

Rumbula Forest Memorial (Rumbulas meža memorials) Some 4km back towards Rīga on the same road is the turning to another testimony of Nazi atrocities during the occupation of Latvia: the Rumbula Forest Memorial. Located on higher ground a few hundred metres from the Rumbula railway station, this was the scene of massacres on 30 November and 8 December 1941, when some 25,000 Jews were murdered by the Nazi Einsatzgruppe A, abetted by Latvian collaborators.

The mass murder was carried out to depopulate the Rīga ghetto of Latvian Jews to free up space to allow for the deportation of Jews from Germany and Austria. An SS commander named Friedrich Jeckeln, who had overseen mass killings in Ukraine, was brought to Latvia to lead the operation, centred around murder pits designed such that the victims would be walked into their own graves. The memorial, focused on a sculpture of a menorah, surrounded by jagged stones, some engraved with the names of victims of the massacre, was erected in 2002. Large concrete platforms beneath the trees indicate the sites of the mass graves. There is also a simple inscribed stone of remembrance placed here in 1964, a rare example of a memorial to Holocaust victims installed during the Soviet period on the territory of the then USSR.

Dole Island (Doles sala) The largest island in the Daugava River is an attractive place, 5km long and covered in pine forest. A nature park was established here in 1987 to help protect its landscapes. The construction of the Rīga Hydroelectric Power Plant (Rīgas HES) in the 1970s dammed the river in the middle of the island, which had the effect of both reducing the size of the island, as the area upstream of the dam was flooded, and transforming it into a peninsula rather than a true island. The place is reached along the A5 road from Salaspils, which runs over the river at the power plant.

Daugava Museum (Daugavas muzejs; Dolesmuiža; w daugavasmuzejs.lv; ◷ 10.00–17.00 Wed–Mon; adult/student €2/1) The main sight on the island, the museum is attractively housed in the building of Dole Manor (Dolesmuiža), long the home of the von Löwis of Menar family, German Balts of Scottish descent. The current manor house building dates from 1898. The museum covers the history of settlement of the Daugava, its importance as a trade and communication route until the mid 19th century, and the construction of hydroelectric plants in the 20th century. Within the landscaped grounds are a late-19th-century fisherman's farmstead, together with wooden fishing weirs used to catch salmon and lamprey. An obelisk in the grounds is etched with dedications from the then owner Alexander von Löwis of Menar to his parents, wife and various relatives. Note also the modern sculpture, with little stone houses standing on the flattened tops of rocks, dedicated to the buildings destroyed by the flooding of the river to make way for the power plant. Three buses a day come to the museum from Skolas iela in Salaspils.

Zoo Rezidence (Stārasti; w zoorezidence.lv; ◷ 11.00–19.00 Tue–Sun; adult/child €7/5) This provides a contrasting attraction on the island: red and black cages set beneath white-barked birch trees, with goats, llamas, camels and peacocks, sharing the territory of the zoo with Soviet-era cars and motorbikes parked on the lawns.

5

Vidzeme

The name Vidzeme can be translated as 'Middle-earth', and in the same way that the setting for Tolkien's fantasies lay at the heart of the continent of earth, so in many ways is Vidzeme the cultural heartland of Latvia. Its territory runs from the Daugava River in the south to the border with Estonia. Inhabited by Latgalian and Livonian tribes prior to the arrival of the German Crusaders, the area today is the most solidly ethnically Latvian part of the country. It is a largely rural region, lacking a dominant city. Valmiera, with a population little higher than 20,000, is its largest settlement. It does, though, contain some of Latvia's main tourist attractions outside Rīga. The Gauja National Park, with its fast-flowing rivers, forests and (unusually for Latvia) undulating landscape, is an obvious draw, within which the towns of Sigulda and Cēsis compete for attention. The former markets itself as the centre for high-octane adventure tourism in Latvia, while the latter is a picturesque town centred on its Livonian Order castle. The sandy coast north of Rīga is another major draw, but Vidzeme also tempts with genteel hotels in manor houses of the German-Baltic nobility, echoes of the Cold War ranging from a secret bunker to a nuclear missile base, and connections with literary figures as diverse as Italian writer Giuseppe Tomasi di Lampedusa and the mendacious Baron Munchausen.

VIDZEME COAST

With sandy beaches, imposing dunes and coastal meadows, the Vidzeme coast presents a tempting tourist offer during the all-too-brief Latvian summer, especially as those beaches are rarely crowded. The main A1 road north from Rīga into Estonia runs parallel to the coast and provides a straightforward means of getting here. There is also a rail connection from Rīga as far as Skulte, just north of Saulkrasti.

SAULKRASTI Rather like Jūrmala, Saulkrasti is an elongated coastal settlement comprising several former fishing villages; its name, 'sunny coast', is suggestive of happy summer holidays at the seaside. It offers a good sandy beach, backed by forested dunes; but while it is indeed a popular summer vacation spot, it is much less developed than Jūrmala, and has a low-key feel. Beyond some changing cubicles, there is little beach infrastructure. The locals like it that way.

Getting there and away As Saulkrasti is so spread out, it is important to decide which of the several railway stations and bus stops best serve the sights you wish to visit. A few buses a day bring you to Saulkrasti from Rīga central bus station. The closest bus stop to the White Dune is at Inčupe. For the bicycle museum, get off at the Stacijas iela stop further north. By train from Rīga (50mins), Pabaži is a convenient stop for the bicycle museum. The White Dune is between Inčupe and Pabaži stations, around 1.5km from both. If you walk the Sunset Trail from the

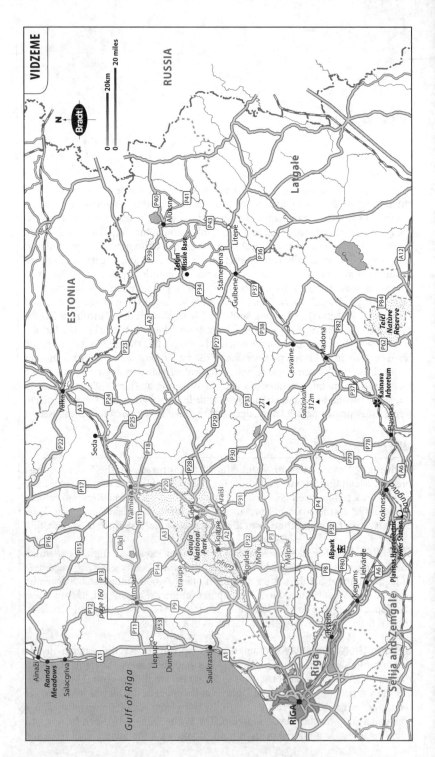

VIDZEME

20km

20 miles

Bradt

N

ESTONIA

RUSSIA

Latgale

Gulf of Riga

RĪGA

Riga

Sēlija and Zemgale

Ainaži
Randu
Meadows
Salacgrīva
Liepupe
Dunte
Saulkrasti

P22
P17
P16
P15
P13
P12
P11
P53
A1
A1

Seda

Valka

P23
P24
P25
P29
P18
P28
P30

Valmiera
Dikļi
Cēsis
Araiši
P20
P31
P11
A3
P14
Straupe
Ligatne
Gauja
National
Park
A2
Līgatne
Sigulda
Mori
Mālpils
P32
P3
P32
P9
Limbaži
page 160

Aluksne
P40
P41
P43
Litene
P39
Zeltiņi
Missile Base
Stāmeriena
Gulbene
P34
P37
P36
P38
P27
Cesvaine
271
Gaiziņkalns
312m
Madona
P33
P82
P62
Teiči
Nature
Reserve
P84
P12
A12

Kalsnava
Arborētum
Pļaviņas
P37
P78
P79
P4
P80
ABpark
P32
P8
Ķegums
Lielvārde
A6
Pļaviņas Hydroelectric
Power Station
Koknese
Daugava
A6
Ogre
Ikšķile

A2

dune, Saulkrasti railway station and bus stop are your best options to get back to Rīga. The car park at the White Dune charges €2 for the first hour, and a hefty €4 an hour after that. If you are coming for a day at the beach, the summer car park a short walk away over the main road will set you back a more reasonable €5 for the day.

✖ Where to eat and drink Conveniently located next to the White Dune car park, **Baltā kāpa** (Kāpu iela 1A; w baltakapa.lv; ⏰ Thu–Sun only, also Mon in summer; €€€€) is a grey-walled wooden chalet with terraces both outside and on top of the building. It offers brisk service and a nice menu of international dishes with occasional local touches, like Baltic herring and chips.

What to see and do The standout coastal feature at Saulkrasti is the **White Dune** (Baltā kāpa), an 18m-high coastal dune covered in pine forest. It offers good views of the meandering mouth of the Inčupe River as it crosses the beach below. Wooden boardwalks and steps guide your path over the dune and to the beach. Close to the car park, you pass **Catherine's Linden Trees** (Katrīnas liepas), reportedly planted by Russian Empress Catherine the Great when she visited the place in 1764. The dune is at the southern end of Saulkrasti, near the village of Inčupe. From it, the **Sunset Trail** (Saulrieta taka) offers a pleasant coastal walk, taking you northwards for 3.6km to the village of Pēterupe.

One of Latvia's quirky private museums, the **Saulkrasti Bicycle Museum** (Saulkrastu velosipēdu muzejs; Rīgas iela 44A; w velomuseum.lv; ⏰ Apr–Aug 10.00–18.00 daily, Sep–Mar by appt; adult/child €5/2.50) houses the collection of Guntis and Jānis Seregins in a two-room building behind the family home. It offers a display of bicycles laid out in approximate chronological order; the oldest example from 1870. The family began their collection in 1977, when it had an unstated political motivation: to demonstrate the wealth of bicycle production in independent Latvia in the pre-war period, at a time when the Soviet authorities were dismissive about Latvian achievements. The displays are in Latvian, but there is usually an English-speaking guide on hand. If the museum has whetted your appetite to take to two wheels, **bicycle rental** is also available here (€2.50/hr). The museum sits around 1km north of the White Dune, along Rīgas iela.

DUNTE The hamlet of Dunte, 17km north of Saulkrasti along the main A1, is on the tourist map based on its connections to the far-fetched world of Baron Munchausen. The baron, famed for the fantastic stories he told of his military career, was the fictional creation of German writer Rudolf Erich Raspe. The character was, however, based on a real-life figure, Hieronymus Karl Friedrich, Freiherr von Münchhausen, who had just such a reputation for weaving exaggerated tales of his military exploits. The real-life Münchhausen was deeply upset at the creation of this fictional alter ego and ended his days as a recluse, but it is in his earlier life that we find his connections to Latvia.

Münchhausen was born into an aristocratic family in the Electorate of Hanover in 1720. He served on the Russian side during the Russo-Turkish War of 1735–39, and from 1740 was stationed in Rīga. In that city, he befriended Georg Gustav von Dunten, who invited him to his country estate at Dunte. There, Münchhausen met and fell in love with his host's daughter, Jacobine, and the two were married in Liepupe in 1744. The young couple lived at Dunte for six years, before settling back at Münchhausen's estates at Bodenwerder, the venue for his exaggerated after-dinner stories. Jacobine died in 1790, after which Münchhausen married a girl some

57 years his junior, who gave birth to a daughter whose paternity Münchhausen denied. He died chafing at his fictional characterisation, embroiled in divorce proceedings, and presumably thinking longingly back to happier days at Dunte.

Those days are brought to life at the suitably eccentric **Munchausen's World** (Minhauzena pasaule; Duntes muiža; w minhauzens.lv; ⏲ 10.00–17.00 Mon–Fri, 10.00–18.00 Sat–Sun; combined ticket adult/child €12/7, museum-only adult/child €5/3). It is centred on a museum devoted to the man and his tales, on the site of the Dunte manor. Rooms on the ground floor aim to recreate the interior of the manor during Münchhausen's time, though with plenty of nods to the tales of the fictional baron. A mannequin depicts the baron holding a string on which four flying ducks are tied. This recalls a story in which the baron, lacking powder in his gun, fishes for ducks using bacon wrapped in a dog leash. He catches 13 ducks in this way. Their combined flapping causes him to rise from the ground. He steers his way home using his coat tails as rudders until he finds himself above his own chimney. At this point he twists the ducks' necks and all fall through the chimney, landing in the kitchen hearth where he presents a ready-cooked dinner. Upstairs, the museum changes tack, offering a display of wax models of celebrated figures in Latvian history, and a collection of 2,000 beer glasses from around the world. It then rediscovers its central theme with a display of books and films inspired by Münchhausen.

Your combined ticket also allows you to sample the other attractions of Munchausen's World, including various trails, notably one which takes you past wooden sculptures inspired by the baron's tales, under the A1 road, and ending at what the park's publicity material assures you is the world's largest beer stein. It is quite clearly a remodelled former windmill. There is also a children's playground centred on a model of Munchausen's sailing ship. The park is signposted from the main road: a statue of the baron in a red jacket flying homewards on a cannonball also guides you in. Buses plying the route along the A1 from Rīga to Ainaži stop at Dunte on the main road, not far from the park.

LIEPUPE Standing alongside the main A1 road, the **Liepupe Evangelical Lutheran Church** (Liepupes Evaņģēliski luteriskā baznīca; Jelgavkrasti; ☎2524 6865) dates from the late 18th century, and has an unusual form, with the bell tower and main entrance on the side of the church, behind which sits the altar with the pulpit directly above it. The Jelgavkrasti stop on the Rīga to Ainaži bus route is close to the church.

🏠 Where to stay and eat

Liepupe Manor (10 rooms) Liepupes muiža, Muižas iela 11, Liepupe; w liepupesmuiza.lv; ⏲ May–Aug Wed–Sun, Sep–Apr Fri–Sun. Smart hotel in a restored 18th-century manor house set in parkland, with a restaurant & spa complex offering a range of treatments. The manor is in the village of Liepupe, a couple of km off the main A1. €€€€

Sidrabiņi Jelgavkrasti; w sidrabini.lv. On the A1, directly to the south of the Evangelical Lutheran Church, this is a rustic pub/restaurant with a tempting menu rich in traditional Latvian dishes, from grey peas to cold beet soup. Their home-produced sausages & smoked meat are a speciality, & also sold from a store on the site. Eat in a log cabin or on outside tables. €€€

SALACGRĪVA This strategic location at the mouth of the Salaca River was the choice for a castle constructed by Bishop Albert of Rīga in 1226. That structure is but a distant memory, but the town reemerged in the 19th century as a port, sending North Vidzeme products like timber and linen on to Rīga and Pärnu. A fish-processing plant was established during the Soviet period, and lives on today as the Brīvais vilnis canned fish company. The town was also known as the venue for the annual Positivus Festival each July, but in 2022, following two years of cancellations during the Covid-19 pandemic, this moved to Rīga in search of easier accessibility. Motorists heading north on the A1 coastal road know the place for the battered bridge across the Salaca River, where traffic is reduced to a single lane, creating a bottleneck. The Rīga to Ainaži bus stops here: Salacgrīva is around 2 hours from Rīga.

Where to stay Slung around the south side of Kuiviži harbour, **Kapteiņu Osta** (5 rooms in hotel & 21 cottages; Pērnavas iela 49a; w kapteinuosta.lv; **€–€€€**) combines an ugly concrete hotel, a camping and caravan park and a cluster of wooden cottages, the latter bearing the names of sea captains, from Nemo to Morgan. The most expensive cottages have their own saunas. The beach is a short walk through the dunes.

What to see and do On the northern side of the river mouth is **Salacgrīva Lighthouse** (Salacgrīvas bāka), a small square-based brick lighthouse topped with a red lantern that serves as an unofficial symbol of the town. A few hundred metres to the north, along Pērnavas iela but also visible from the A1, is a 1986 memorial to seamen lost at sea, doubling as a Soviet war memorial, and universally known as '**Milda**'. A mother stands, arms raised, with a naked child standing on her shoulder. On the south side of the river, off Rīgas iela, one block seaward off the main road, is the **Salacgrīva Museum** (Salacgrīvas muzejs; Sila iela 2; w salacgriva.lv; ⊕ 10.00–17.00 Tue–Fri, 10.00–14.00 Sat; adult/child €1/0.60). This has exhibits related to the local pursuit of lamprey fishing on the Salaca River. A traditional **lamprey weir**, involving a footbridge of spruce boards, can still be seen on the river, a little way upstream from the bridge.

The small harbour of **Kuiviži** at the northern edge of Salacgrīva offers a nice sandy beach, backed by dunes. North of here, running 9km up to the town of Ainaži, are the **Randu Meadows** (Randu pļavas). Occupying a narrow stretch of coastal land running north for around 9km, they offer a landscape of meadows, reedy marshes and lagoons, protected as a nature reserve since 1962. The meadows owed their existence to cattle grazing and hay gathering among coastal communities. The decline of cattle farming in the area poses a risk that the meadows will become overgrown and eventually revert to forest, and grazing management is an important part of the work of the reserve. Even so, the areas of meadow given over to reed have considerably expanded in recent years. The moist meadows and lagoons provide great birdwatching opportunities, with such species to look out for as Baltic dunlin and Arctic tern. And they house many colourful and rare plant species. The meadows are conveniently appreciated by taking the signposted **Randu Meadows Trail** (Randu pļavu taka) on the side of the A1 road between Kuiviži and Ainaži, where there is a small car park. The 1.4km trail takes you through forest-covered dunes and the meadows to an observation tower, passing informative panels en route.

AINAŽI The sleepiest of small towns, lying just south of the Estonian border, it is hard to imagine today the significant role that Ainaži played in Latvia's naval and shipbuilding history. The idea of establishing a naval school here was the initiative of Krišjānis Valdemārs, a Latvian writer and politician closely associated with the First Latvian National Awakening of the second half of the 19th century. As the government of Tsarist Russia grappled with a shortage of trained seamen to service its expanding maritime trade, Valdemārs saw an opportunity to set up a school for poor Latvian and Estonian youngsters living in coastal areas. He believed that learning seamanship would provide a means for young Latvians to expand their horizons, become wealthy and contribute to the National Awakening. Existing naval schools in Rīga and Liepāja were expensive and provided tuition in German only. Valdemārs alighted on Ainaži, which already had a tradition of small-scale boatbuilding. Local ship-owners put up the money, and in 1864 the naval school was opened. Its success was to spawn another 40 seafaring schools for the peasantry across the Russian Empire.

The development of the school went hand in hand with that of the construction of sailing ships in Ainaži and the wider Vidzeme region in the late 19th century, an industry facilitated by abundant timber resources and cheap labour. Vidzeme became noted for the building of two- and three-masted wooden sailing ships. In 1870 the three-masted Ainaži-built *Georg* reached Montevideo. But with the arrival of steamships at the start of the 20th century, the industry quickly fell into decline. The town was claimed by both Estonia and Latvia as they emerged from their independence wars. Under the arbitration led by British colonel Stephen Tallents, Ainaži was awarded to Latvia, in part as compensation for the allocation of the lion's share of Valka/Valga to Estonia. Its border location is most visible today in the proliferation of large alcohol stores around the town, mainly serving visitors from Estonia enticed across the border by the prospect of cheaper booze.

Where to stay and eat A grey-walled building alongside the main A1 on the southern edge of Ainaži, **Pļavas** (13 rooms; Valdemāra iela 121; w plavashotel. lv; €€€) is named for the nearby Randu Meadows, and offers a functional but unexciting place to stay, but an excellent place to eat. The restaurant (€€€€) spills on to a covered terrace and well-tended garden, offering an enticing menu.

What to see and do The maritime history of the place is well told in the **Ainaži Naval School Museum** (Ainažu Jūrskolas muzejs; K. Valdemāra iela 47; w rigamuz. lv; ⏱ 10.00–17.00 Wed–Sun; adult/student/child €2/1.50/1). It is housed in the original home of the naval school, restored in 1968. A rustic red-painted wooden building, it is surrounded by a well-tended garden studded with anchors and other maritime detritus, as well as a bust of Valdemārs. The museum tells the story of the school, with a wax model of the white-bearded Christian Dahl, its first head teacher, a Swede who worked here for almost 30 years and ensured the success of the place. There are also displays on the history of shipbuilding in the town.

A few metres north of the museum along Valdemāra iela, the road passing for the main drag in this quiet place, stands the octagonal brick **Ainaži Lighthouse** (Ainažu bāka), built in 1930. Narrow Kuģu iela opposite leads down to the **sandy beach**.

A short walk south along Valdemāra iela is the **Ainaži Firefighting Museum** (Ainažu Ugunsdzēsības muzejs; Valdemāra iela 69; ☎2921 3784; e ainazu.muzejs@ limbazunovads.lv; ⏱ 10.00–17.00 Mon–Fri; adult/child €1/0.60). This chronicles the work of the Ainaži Volunteer Firefighters' Association over almost a century through a slightly twee-sounding exhibition called 'shiny buttons and helmets', as well as a display of fire engines whose cabins the young and not so young are welcome to clamber into.

There are some 11 buses a day to Rīga (2hrs 20mins) and infrequent connections to Valmiera and Limbaži.

LIMBAŽI AND WESTERN VIDZEME

The area of western Vidzeme away from the coast and north of the Gauja National Park is off the main tourist track, but the district capital of Limbaži makes for a worthwhile spot. This attractive rural area boasts reconstructed aristocratic manor houses, some converted into boutique hotels, which may encourage you to linger.

LIMBAŽI Today a pleasant low-key district capital with some 7,000 inhabitants, Limbaži was in medieval times an important trading town and member of the Hanseatic League. A stone castle was built here in the 13th century by the Bishopric of Rīga, and then fought over during the next two centuries by the Archbishops of Rīga and the Livonian Order. It served in the early 16th century as the spring residence of the archbishop. Limbaži, however, began its long decline from around this period with the silting up of the Svētupe River and the loss of its international trading connections. Town and castle suffered grievously during the 16th-century Livonian War, attacked variously by Russia, Sweden and Poland, and it was said that only three houses remained intact by the end of the long war. Further calamities followed, culminating in a devastating fire in 1747, and the town that reemerged had much more provincial ambitions than medieval Limbaži.

The **tourist information centre** (Limbažu Tūrisma informācijas centrs; Torņa iela 3; w visitlimbazi.lv; ⏲ 10.00–17.00 Mon–Sat, 11.00–16.00 Sun) is centrally located. Note the newly restored wooden town centre kiosk over the road, filled with items that might have been purchased by a 1930s consumer.

Getting there and away
The **bus station** (Limbažu autoosta; Stacijas iela 7; ☏ 6402 1045) is about a kilometre southeast of the historic centre. Connections include a dozen or more buses daily to Rīga (from 1hr 40mins), five a day to Valmiera (around 1hr) and a couple to Ainaži (1hr 25mins).

✗ Where to eat and drink *Map, below*
Housed in an atmospheric knick-knack-filled cellar, **Trīs kambari** (Baumaņu Kārļa laukums 3; w kambari.lv; €€€) is a good choice for a reasonably priced meal, once you get past the comedy menu (soups, for example, are listed under 'let's take the spoons'). In summer, they offer outside tables on a neighbouring lawn.

What to see and do
The main sights are grouped close to each other in the historic town centre. The **Limbaži Museum** (Limbažu muzejs; Burtnieku iela 7; w limbazumuzejs.lv; ⏲ May–Sep 10.00–18.00 Wed–Fri, 11.00–17.00 Sat–Sun, Oct–Apr 10.00–17.00 Tue–Sat; adult/child €1/0.50) is located in the two-storey red-walled new castle building. One room highlights the life and career of Limbaži's best-known resident,

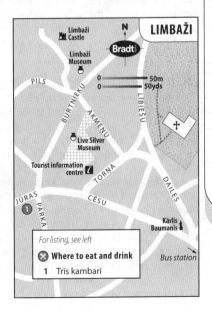

19th-century composer Kārlis Baumanis, author of the country's national anthem. He spent much of his career as a German teacher in St Petersburg, before returning to Limbaži, where he died in 1905. The museum also offers a canter through the town's history from the 13th to the 19th century, and temporary exhibitions usually exploring different aspects of the 20th century story. The signage, however, is almost entirely in Latvian. The ruins of **Limbaži Castle** are to be found round the back, though given the predations suffered by the castle, there is understandably not a great deal to see, amounting to a couple of restored walls, including a gate. Above the latter, on the site of one of the castle towers, a wooden **observation tower** (⊕ as for the museum, from where tickets can be purchased; €0.30) has been constructed.

A more unexpected attraction is the **Live Silver Museum** (Dzīvā sudraba muzejs; Burtnieku iela 4; w sudrabamuzejs.lv; ⊕ 11.00–17.00 Wed–Sat, 11.00–15.00 Sun; adult/child €5/2.50). Entered from the courtyard around the back of the old town hall building a few doors from the city museum, this is one of the private museums in which Latvia excels. It showcases the extravagant work of silversmith Olegs Auzers, who died in 2021, and is maintained by his widow. The most intricate of all the silver sculptures on display is a *Castle of the Future*, set in an imagined 3001, in which religious harmony is forecast to have broken out, symbolised by castle turrets decorated with the symbols of different religions. Despite all this harmony, the castle defenders are still depicted spearing attackers on the battlements. You are invited to spot seven monks in the castle, as well as 14 men and one woman aboard the ship *The Flying Dutchman*. The latter model is an allegory of human life, whose crew are variously engaged in productive things like steering and climbing the rigging, or less productive ones like getting drunk and falling off. The ship's sails are torn, its hull holed, symbolising the ageing process. Auzers was commissioned by the Latvian president to make diplomatic gifts for visiting heads of state: there is a copy of the silver rose brooch gifted to Queen Elizabeth II during her State Visit in 2006.

Erected in 1998 at the junction of Dailes iela and Cēsu iela is a **statue of Kārlis Baumanis**, depicting the bearded composer in a long cloak, conductor's baton behind his back. On the plinth are inscribed the words *Dievs, svētī Latviju* (God bless Latvia!), the title of the national anthem. On the puffy pink rock at the base of the plinth is a carving of a rat – the lady at the tourist information office told me there was a funny story about that rat, but she had forgotten it. I never did find out what it was.

DIKĻI The green and widely spaced village of Dikļi, 23km northwest of Valmiera, holds an unexpectedly important place in Latvian cultural life as both the venue of the first play performed in the Latvian language and as the host of the forerunner of the Latvian Song Festival. The village centres on **Dikļi Palace** (Dikļu pils; Dikļi; w diklupils.lv), whose present neo-Baroque building dates from 1896, under the ownership of Baron Paul von Wolff, on the site of an earlier manor. Following the departure of its aristocratic owners on Latvian independence, the building served as a children's home and sanatorium through the interwar and Soviet periods, until it was purchased by businessman Egons Mednis, who restored it as a hotel. Mednis filled the place with a collection of paintings by Latvian artists and with his hunting trophies, as well as a fine assemblage of tiled stoves. The challenges of the Covid-19 pandemic forced the hotel to close its doors to all but weddings and conference bookings, and at the time of writing it had not yet reopened. It was in the threshing barn here in 1818 that the first play was performed in Latvian, a translation of Schiller's *The Robbers*, done by a servant at the manor who had been inspired by the play on seeing it performed in German in Rīga.

Immediately to the west of the palace gate sits a small park laid out on an island in the gentle Mazbriede River. This is **Viks' Fairy Tale Park** (Vika pasaku parks), filled with wooden statues depicting animal characters of the children's stories of local writer Viktors Kalniņš, better known as Viks. They include his take on the Loch Ness monster, involving two dinosaurs, Ness and Nessie, finally reunited after Nessie is freed by the digging of the Mud Dwarf from the muddy lake in which she languished.

A kilometre further west, in a tranquil riverside spot, is the **Neikenkalns Natural Stage** (Neikenkalna dabas koncertzāle), a wooden stage with stepped rows cut into the slopes above it for choral singers or audience members. It was here in 1864 that local pastor and teacher Juris Neikens, inspired by local youths singing songs together after a long day's work, brought together six male choirs from across the region as well as 120 children of the local parish to create Latvia's first song festival, a forerunner of the first national event that would be held in Rīga nine years later. The white-walled building over the road from the car park has a portrait of Neikens in a boarded-up window, recording that he lived in that building for ten years from 1857. The village is served by buses from Valmiera.

BĪRIŅI Some 20km northwest of Sigulda, Bīriņi centres on **Bīriņi Castle** (Bīriņu pils), a manor house built in the neo-Gothic style between 1857 and 1860 for German-Baltic aristocrat August von Pistohlkors. On high ground above a lake, amid spacious parkland, with its crenellations, prominent southwest tower, and pink-and-white-painted façade, it makes for a romantic sight. The Bīriņi bus stop on the P9 road a few hundred metres from the castle sits on a route between Rīga (1hr 10mins) and Limbaži (35mins).

The castle now operates as a **hotel** (24 rooms; w birinupils.lv; €€€–€€€€) and conference venue, and is among the more successful of the many attempts in Latvia to convert former aristocratic country residences into smart hotels. Rooms range from characterful suites in the tower to quite functional affairs, some in the gardener's house in the grounds. There is a good restaurant (€€€€) in the brick-columned castle basement. If you just want to visit the park, there is a €3 entrance fee. Bicycle and boat rental are also available.

VALMIERA

Valmiera, a small city on a meandering stretch of the Gauja River, is the largest settlement in Vidzeme. Its considerable historical tribulations have weakened the tourist appeal of the place, though it does have some worthwhile sights. It is also particularly well endowed with sports stadia, reflecting a proud local sporting tradition. Valmiera-born race walker Jānis Daliņš, who gives his name to the largest of the stadia, was the first athlete from independent Latvia to win an Olympic medal: silver in the 50km walk in 1932.

HISTORY Part of the Latgalian land of Tālava until the 13th century, it was secured by Bishop Albert of Rīga. The place then fell under the control of the Livonian Brothers of the Sword, who set about building a castle here. Well sited on trade routes along the Gauja, the town, known as Wolmar in German, became a member of the Hanseatic League between the 14th and 16th centuries. It was heavily damaged in the Livonian War in the late 16th century and again in the Great Northern War at the start of the 18th, but arrested from a long period of decline by first the building of a bridge over the Gauja in the 1860s, and later the arrival of the railway at the end of the century. Its particularly brutal history, even by Latvian standards, with repeated cycles of destruction and rebuilding, culminated in devastation in the later stages of World War II. Soviet-era industrialisation included the building of a fibreglass factory and another producing metal fuel cans.

GETTING THERE AND AWAY The **bus station** (Valmieras autoosta; Stacijas iela 1; ☏9000 6677) is centrally located, just to the south of the bridge across the Gauja. There are buses roughly every 30 minutes to Rīga, at least six a day to Valka and up to 13 a day to Cēsis. The **railway station** (Valmiera dzelzceļa stacija; Stacijas laukums 1) is further out, at the southern end of Stacijas iela. There are five connections daily to Rīga (around 2hrs), and two to Valga.

TOURIST INFORMATION The **tourist information centre** (Valmieras Tūrisma informācijas centrs; Bruņinieku iela 1; w visit.valmiera.lv; ⊕ 10.00–18.00 Tue–Wed & Fri–Sat, 10.00–19.00 Thu, 10.00–16.00 Sun) is in the Valmiera Museum complex.

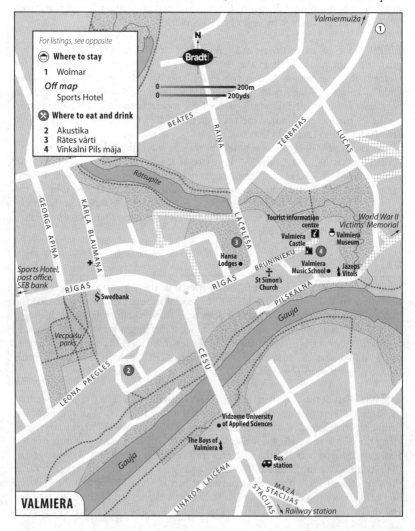

WHERE TO STAY *Map, opposite*

Sports Hotel (40 rooms) Vaidavas iela 15;
w sportshotel.lv. On the western edge of town,
this functional 3-star hotel, like so much in the city
geared towards athletic pursuits, sits close to the
Valmiera Olympic Centre. A bland option, but fine
if the Wolmar is full. €€

Wolmar (30 rooms) Tērbatas iela 16a;
w hotelwolmar.lv. A comfortable, smartly
renovated hotel on the northern edge of the town
centre. A parrot squawks you in to the restaurant,
& the rooms are decorated with slogan boards
welcoming you to 'home sweet home'. €€

 WHERE TO EAT AND DRINK *Map, opposite*

Akustika Diakonāta iela 6; w akustikavalmiera.lv.
Housed in a former post office, this place combines
a bare-brick interior & unadorned concrete ceiling
with laid-back music, outdoor seating in summer &
a short, inventive menu. €€€€
Rātes vārti Lāčplēša iela 1; w ratesvarti.lv.
Reliable central restaurant, offering burgers, wok-
cooked noodles & grilled meat & fish dishes, with
some more adventurous options, like ostrich meat
tartare. €€€€

Vīnkalni Pils māja Bruņinieku iela 4; 2554
3123; e info@vinkaniesi.lv. Cosily located in
a rustic building appended to the ruins of the
Livonian Order castle, this family-run pizzeria
has established a reputation as one of the best
in Latvia, with a branch in the Āgenskalns
market in Rīga. Choose between a Romana or
Napoletana base. Also offers salads, pasta & poke
bowls. €€€

OTHER PRACTICALITIES Rīgas iela, north of the Gauja River and running parallel
to it, is the main thoroughfare. It is home to a **post office** (Rīgas iela 34; 6422
1404), branches of both Swedish banks **Swedbank** (Rīgas iela 15; 6744 5555) and
SEB (Rīgas iela 40; 2666 8777) and a **pharmacy** (Rīgas iela 16; 6428 1160).

WHAT TO SEE AND DO The surviving historical buildings of the town are nicely
signposted by the square-based red-brick tower of **St Simon's Church** (Svētā
Sīmaņa evaņģēliski luteriskā baznīca; Bruņinieku iela 2; w simanadraudze.lv;
⊕ 11.00–18.00 Tue–Fri, 11.00–17.00 Sat, 10.00–13.00 Sun; tower adult/child
€2.50/0.50). It dates from the late 13th century and is one of the largest Gothic
churches outside Rīga, though has been damaged and rebuilt on various occasions,
and during the Soviet occupation served as a concert hall. You can climb the tower
for a view over the town or, for those who can't manage the steps up, look at the
same view from a screen in the church.

Immediately behind the church, along Bruņinieku iela, stand the few remaining
walls of **Valmiera Castle** (Valmieras Viduslaiku pils), built by the Livonian
Order in the 13th century, and once a fortress of some significance occupying a
strategic location on the Gauja River and playing host to *Landtags* of the Livonian
Confederation. It was destroyed by the Russians in 1702 during the Great Northern
War and never restored after that, serving instead as a source of building materials
for the town. The castle is part of the territory of the **Valmiera Museum** (Valmieras
muzejs; Bruņinieku iela 3; w valmierasmuzejs.lv; ⊕ de Woldemer exhibition 10.00–
18.00 Tue–Sat, 10.00–17.00 Sun, art exhibition hall 10.00–17.00 Tue–Sat, adult/
student de Woldemer exhibition €5/3, art exhibition hall €3/2), which incorporates
eight historic buildings set in attractive parkland close to the river. The Old Pharmacy
dates from 1735, and adjacent to this, standing on 17th-century foundations, is a
new glass-sided building hosting the de Woldemer exhibition on the history of the
castle and on Valmiera as a Hanseatic town. Another building combines temporary
art exhibitions on the ground floor with ethnographic displays in the basement
ordered by activity: laundering clothes, making bread and producing milk. Close to
the river is an 18th-century house, with a herb garden in its courtyard.

5

The large yellow-walled building adjacent to this is the **Valmiera Music School** (Valmieras Mūzikas skola), which has in its grounds a coin-shaped monument honouring composer Jāzeps Vītols, who founded the first Latvian Conservatory of Music. He was born in the town somewhat by accident: his parents were transiting the place when his mother went into labour. Across the car park, note the derelict building in the shadow of the castle ruins enlivened by colourful paintings on boards fixed to its walls, gargoyles, and the skeleton of a fish protruding from a satellite dish on the roof. The artworks are products of a 2018 German-Latvian art symposium.

The Gauja runs through the centre of town: its green banks make for a pleasant stroll. Take the river path eastwards from the museum, and head inland over the footbridge, crossing the small stream known as the Rātsupīte, which would once have provided the castle with additional defensive protection. After 200m or so, you reach the **World War II Victims' Memorial** (Valmieras memoriāls II Pasaules karā kritušajiem karavīriem; Lucas iela 2A). Erected in 1985, its dominant sculpture features a stone backdrop said to evoke a split linden tree, in front of which a bronze soldier whose pose resembles that of an outstretched goalkeeper covers his fallen comrade. Lines of graves, mostly of fallen Soviet soldiers, fill the terrace in front of the sculpture.

Heading in the opposite direction from St Simon's Church, immediately across the main Rīgas iela, is a large mural declaring Valmiera a Hanseatic city, next to which is a gathering of little slope-roofed kiosks, the **Hansa Lodges**, used to host occasional Medieval-themed markets, but mostly standing closed. A few hundred metres along Rīgas iela you reach **Vecpuišu parks** (Bachelors' Park), founded on the eve of World War I by eight bachelors of the town to create a place of leisure for its citizens. The pavilion in the park dates from this period, and now houses the Valmiera concert hall and a restaurant. The wooden lattice box in the park is a sculpture titled *Dinamiskā Pilsēta* (*Dynamic City*), a tribute to the 1919 work of Constructivist artist Gustavs Klucis, born near Valmiera in 1895. The sculpture was a symbol of Valmiera's imaginative if unsuccessful bid for nomination as European Capital of Culture for 2027.

Cēsu iela takes you over the Gauja River in the town centre: the modern bridge here has become a symbol of the town, with the structures at its sides resembling ribs, giving the feel of driving through a skeleton. The southern side of the river is of interest mainly because both bus and train stations lie here. The modern buildings of the **Vidzeme University of Applied Sciences** (Vidzemes Augstskola; Cēsu iela 4) are the first you encounter after the bridge. Note the statue outside the university, presenting three barefooted young men with flowing locks and flared trousers, dancing exuberantly in an outward-facing circle. This is known as *Valmieras puikas* (*The Boys of Valmiera*), and depicts characters from Pāvils Rozītis's autobiographical novel of the same name.

On the northern edge of town, a couple of kilometres from the centre, is the park of **Valmiermuiža**. This is the site of a Baroque hunting lodge, built in 1764 by Peter August Friedrich, Duke of Schleswig-Holstein-Sonderburg-Beck, who received the place as a reward for his service to Russia. But for one lonely tower, little remains of the lodge, and the real reason for visiting the place today is the **Valmiermuiža Brewery** (Valmiermuiža Alus Darītava; Dzirnavu iela 2; w valmiermuiza.lv). Set up by local brewer Aigars Ruņģis, this fine craft brewery offers tours and tastings by appointment. The **Alus Virtuve** (Beer Kitchen; \ 2866 4424; e alusvirtuve@ valmiermuiza.lv; ⊕ noon–20.00 Fri, 10.00–21.00 Sat, 10.00–16.00 Sun; €€), scenically housed in the granary of the former manor, gives you the chance to pair their products with hearty snacks and more substantial dishes.

SEDA The small town of Seda, 3km off the main road between Valmiera and Valka, is a place lost in time. It owes its existence to the Seda peat bog (Sedas purvs). A company named Kūdra ('Peat') was established in the late 1930s to extract peat from the bog, but the business didn't get going in a major way until 1954. At the tail end of the Stalinist period a purpose-built town appeared here, to accommodate workers brought from across the Soviet Union to join the enterprise of peat removal.

Seda today echoes with the ghosts of the Soviet occupation. Its central square is now called Skolas laukums: a conifer surrounded by greenery stands in the centre in a place once occupied by Lenin. The square is dominated by the Seda secondary school, built in 1955. From here streets lined with birch and linden trees fan out between two-storey yellow-walled 1950s housing blocks, many only partially inhabited. To the right, Uzvaras iela leads to the **Seda Cultural Centre** (Sedas kultūras nams; Parka iela 21; ☎ 2832 3986), a building in Soviet Classical style, fronted by four large Doric columns; the pediment bearing the date 1959, as well as a five-pointed Soviet star. To the left of the square, the same road takes you to the diminutive **St Archangel Michael Orthodox Church** (Svētā Erceņģeļa pareizticīgo baznīca; Uzvaras iela 12), built in 2004 from a remodelled grocery store, there having been no church envisioned in the atheist Soviet town. The first church bell here was apparently fashioned from a gas cylinder, though this has been replaced by arrivals from Russia. The low mound over the street with a couple of concrete vents protruding out of the top is a Soviet-era underground bomb shelter. Paths from the town take you to the peat bogs, crossing the tracks of a narrow-gauge railway line used for peat extraction. These are far from pristine bog habitats, but do have attractions of their own. The shallow, overgrown ponds are favoured sites for migratory birds, and there is a **birdwatching tower** (skatu tornis) in the bog some 4km from the town.

Buses stop in the central square. There are five connections a day to Rīga, up to eight to Valmiera and up to seven to Valka. The place also features a large population of stray cats.

VALKA This district capital is of interest as a geopolitical curiosity: sitting directly on the border with Estonia it forms part of a larger settlement. It is united with the neighbouring Estonian town of Valga under the slogan 'One City, Two States'.

History Known in German as Walk, the place developed from the 13th century as a single settlement, receiving city rights in 1584 from Stephen Báthory, the ruler of Poland–Lithuania. It became a significant railway junction in the late 19th century.

At the start of World War I, as the German army invaded Courland and later Vidzeme, refugees arrived in the town, then situated away from the front line. It was in the turbulence of that war that Valka achieved a claim to historical fame in late 1917 as the venue of the first session of the Latvian Provisional National Council, a body comprising representatives of various Latvian organisations that had been formed in Petrograd a few weeks previously. The resolutions adopted at that session proclaimed the unity of a Latvia comprising Vidzeme, Kurzeme and Latgale, a decision which fell short of a full declaration of independence but was nonetheless an important step on the path to Latvian statehood, and one which included the region of Latgale. The resolutions put the council on a collision course with the Bolshevik-dominated Iskolat administration, also based in the town, which had just declared the establishment of Soviet power in those parts of Latvia, including north Vidzeme, not occupied by the Germans. The council was forced to relocate back to Petrograd. The Republic of Iskolat ceased to exist in March 1918 with the signature of the Treaty of Brest-Litovsk, under which Russia renounced its claims to Latvia. Following the Armistice in November 1918, and the annulment of the Treaty of Brest-Litovsk, the Bolsheviks sought control, and in December took Valka. The Provisional Soviet Government of Latvia headed by Pēteris Stučka was briefly based in Valka at the end of 1918, before moving to Rīga. Shortly thereafter, the Estonian army liberated Valka from the Bolsheviks, and with Estonian support Latvians in freed areas were mobilised into Latvian army units, forming the Latvian Northern Brigade under Jorģis Zemitāns.

Having played a distinguished role in the wars of independence of both Latvia and Estonia, Valka faced a problematic situation in the peace. With a population comprising both Latvians and Estonians, it was claimed by both new states. Unable to agree on the fate of the city, Latvia and Estonia concluded that a joint commission headed by British colonel Stephen Tallents would decide on its future. With neither side willing to compromise, the commission eventually decided on 1 July 1920 to divide the place into two, along the little Varžupīte River. This gave Estonia the largest part of the city, including the historical town centre. This now bears the Estonian name Valga. Latvia was allocated the suburb of Lugaži, emerging with around 80 buildings, mostly wooden. Tallents' decision satisfied neither side, perhaps an indication that it was indeed an impartial one. Latvia offered to give its portion of the city to Estonia in exchange for the island of Ruhnu in the Gulf of Rīga, but Estonia was not to be moved. In the end, unable to come up with any better alternative, the two sides agreed Tallents' plan in a border treaty signed in 1923.

Getting there and away
The **Valga railway station** (Jaama pst 12; \+372 616 0245) is a grand affair in the Estonian part of town, with a massive vaulted ticket hall supported by golden-topped columns. As well as trains to various destinations in Estonia, including Tallinn and Tartu, there are two trains daily to Rīga run by Latvian Railways, and taking just under 3 hours. There are two bus stations, one on each side of the border. **Valga bus station** (Jaama pst 12; \+372 512 0295) is immediately in front of the railway station and serves Estonian destinations. **Valka bus station** (Valkas autoosta; Rīgas iela 7; \6472 3538) is centrally located and has six buses daily to Rīga (3hrs–3hrs 40mins), up to nine a day to Valmiera (1hr–1hr 20mins) and up to five a day to Smiltene (1hr).

Tourist information
The **Valka tourist information centre** (Valkas Tūrisma un informācijas birojs; Semināra iela 1; w visitvalgavalka.com; ⊕ 09.00–17.00 Mon–Fri, 09.00–14.00 Sat) sits just on the Latvian side of the border.

Where to stay and eat

Metsis (18 rooms) Kuperjanovi 63; w hotellmetsis.com. The best accommodation option sits in Estonian Valga, in well-tended gardens & offering comfortable if slightly tired rooms, some with saunas. The restaurant (€€€€) has an enticing menu, but is home to an overwhelming collection of stuffed animals. While many Baltic restaurants display hunting trophies, this one takes it to a whole new level. You are welcomed into the dining room by a baboon, a bear prowls in search of scraps, & a hedgehog sniffs at your dessert. €€

Walk Café Raiņa iela 1; \2000 3516. An unpretentious place on the Latvian side of town, with a menu ranging from burgers to sushi. The 'One City, Two States' theme is captured on the cocktails list, where you are invited to choose between a Valka Slammer & a Valga Breeze. Both involve rum. €€€

What to see and do The Latvian and Estonian towns each have their own mayors and local administrations, so the extent to which Valka/Valga really is viewed as one city should not be overstated, but with the entry of both countries into the Schengen area in 2007 the border no longer involves any immigration or customs formalities. Indeed, among the sights of the place are several installations designed to celebrate the openness of the frontier. In the centre of town sits the cutest **border crossing** you are ever likely to see. A footbridge over the diminutive river Varžupīte is identified by a little wooden sentry box marked 'Valga-Valka Estonia-Latvia'. A couple of benches painted respectively in Latvian and Estonian colours are further evidence of the border. A black and white border post and lots of flags complete the ensemble. A few metres away, a large swing installed on another footbridge over the river gives the visitor the surely unique experience of being able to swing from one country to the other.

At the intersection between Raiņa and Rīgas iela on the Latvian side of town is the **Monument to the Latvian Provisional National Council** (Monuments 'Veltījums Latviešu Pagaidu Nacionālajai padomei'; Raiņa iela 9A). A modern sculpture commemorating the first session of the council and its proclamation of Latvian unity, this comprises three entwined curving concrete columns, representing the three regions of Kurzeme, Vidzeme and Latgale, topped by what looks for all the world like Harry Potter's golden snitch.

The **Valka Local History Museum** (Valkas Novadpētniecības muzejs; Rīgas iela 64; w muzejs.valka.lv; ⊕ 15 May–1 Oct 11.00–18.00 Tue–Fri, 10.00–16.00 Sat–Sun, 2 Oct–14 May 10.00–17.00 Mon–Fri, 10.00–16.00 Sat; adult/student €2/1) is housed in the building which in the second half of the 19th century held the teachers' seminary run by Latvian pedagogue Jānis Cimze, training up future Latvian and Estonian teachers. The ground floor is devoted to Cimze and his school. Organ music plays in the background, reflecting the importance of music in the life of the seminary. Cimze is noted as the founder of the Latvian tradition of choral singing and was a major force behind the establishment of the first All-Estonian and All-Latvian Song Festivals. Upstairs is a well-produced exhibition with labelling in Latvian, Estonian and English on the role of Valka during the complex process of the birth of independent Latvia after World War I, incorporating some engaging interactive elements. The museum also hosts temporary exhibitions of local artists. It is a couple of kilometres out of the centre, just off the main road towards Valmiera.

With the historic centre of the pre-1920 city on the Estonian side of the border, there are some worthwhile sights a short stroll into Estonia. Note the former **Town Hall** (Valga raekoda; Kesk 11), an elegant two-storey wooden building dating from 1865 with an octagonal tower. Over the road is **St John's Church** (Valga Jaani kirik; Kesk 21), the work of Christoph Haberland, chief architect of Rīga in the late 18th century, favouring a style of classicism. St John's was completed only in 1816, long after Haberland's death, and is apparently the only church in Estonia with an oval plan.

Across the roundabout from the church, looking down Kesk, the main central thoroughfare, with a double row of trees along its centre, is a plaque to **Stephen Báthory**, King of Poland and Grand Duke of Lithuania in the late 16th century. It celebrates the latter's role in granting town rights to the place. Beyond the roundabout at the other end of Kesk, in a scrap of tree-covered park, is a bust of local hero **Alfred Neuland**, whose weightlifting gold medal in the 1920 Olympic Games in Antwerp was Estonia's first. Close by, the history of the city is told in the **Valga Museum** (Valga Muuseum; Vabaduse 8; w valgamuuseum.ee; ⊕ 11.00–18.00 Tue–Fri, 10.00–15.00 Sat; adult/child €8/5), which takes you from prehistory to the Soviet era.

SIGULDA

Some 50km from Rīga, this town of 15,000 people to the south of a picturesque stretch of the Gauja River is a significant tourist destination, with a combination of attractions. First, the natural beauty of its setting, which has given rise to misleading descriptions as 'the Switzerland of Vidzeme' (you are not about to spot the Matterhorn anytime soon). Second, its historical importance, including the castles in Sigulda itself and on the opposite bank of the Gauja at Turaida. And third, a series of adventure sports offerings, making Sigulda the adrenaline capital of Latvia. The place can be straightforwardly visited as a day trip from Rīga, but merits a longer stay.

HISTORY The banks of the Gauja River valley were home to the Livonian people. The chieftain of Turaida, Kaupo, was among the first prominent Livonians to convert to Christianity, around 1191. He became a friend of Bishop Albert of Rīga, who took him to Rome where this converted pagan chieftain impressed Pope Innocent III. His tribe rebelled against him in his absence, and on return he was forced to besiege his own fortress. He was later killed while fighting the pagan Estonians. The area fell directly under the control of the German Crusaders by 1207, when the Livonian Brothers of the Sword began construction of a castle on the left bank of the Gauja, naming the site Segewald, the future Sigulda. The proliferation of castles in the area is largely down to the fact that, while the Livonian Brothers of the Sword controlled the left bank of the Gauja, the right bank was ruled by a different crusading power, the Bishopric of Rīga, which commenced construction of a stone castle at Turaida, on the site of Kaupo's castle, in 1214, and built another castle at Krimulda in the mid 13th century.

Sigulda was for centuries a small settlement around the Livonian Order Castle. The place fell in the late 18th century into the ownership of the Borch family, and in 1867 came an event that would be crucial to the later development of Sigulda. Olga Borch, daughter of the owner of Sigulda manor, married Prince Dmitry Kropotkin. Dmitry was a Russian aristocrat who was to become governor of two Russian governorates before being assassinated in 1879 by a member of the 'People's Will' revolutionary organisation. Olga received Sigulda manor as part of her dowry, and used her influence to transform Sigulda into a spa resort for aristocratic families, including through lobbying in 1886 to ensure that the Rīga to Pskov railway line incorporated a stop at Sigulda. Her son, Prince Nikolai Kropotkin, took over the running of the place in 1893 and continued her work, promoting the local mineral waters in the manner of fashionable European spas, and even installing a bobsleigh and luge track. The Kropotkin family lost ownership of the manor in the agrarian reforms of 1922, and Nikolai emigrated to Germany, where he died in 1937.

Sigulda continued to develop as one of the most important tourist destinations in Latvia, with its place as a winter sports centre cemented by the construction of the Sigulda Bobsleigh, Luge and Skeleton Track in 1986.

GETTING THERE AND AWAY Sigulda's expansive orange and white-painted **railway station** (Siguldas dzelzceļa stacija; Ausekļa iela 6; \6723 8232) dates from the early 1950s: its columned hall has ticket counters for both the railway station and the bus station in front. There are 15 trains daily to Rīga (around 1hr), five a day to Cēsis (40mins) and two to Valga (1hr 40mins). The **bus station** (Siguldas autoosta; Ausekļa iela 6; \2544 5573) offers a frequent connection to Rīga (around 1hr 10mins) and a patchier one to other destinations in Vidzeme. There is also a particularly useful local bus route, roughly hourly, from Sigulda station to Turaida, with some buses going on to Krimulda. Taking the bus up the hill to the reserve, returning on foot via Gutman's Cave, Krimulda, and then taking the cable car across the Gauja, makes for an enjoyable and varied day.

One scenic, if pricey, transportation option is the **Sigulda Cable Car** (Siguldas vagoniņš; 14 Jāņa Poruka iela; **w** siguldaadventures.com; ⊕ Nov–Mar 10.00–17.00 daily, Apr 10.00–17.00 Mon–Fri, 10.00–18.20 Sat–Sun, May–Aug 10.00–18.20 daily, Sep 10.00–18.20 Mon–Sat, noon–18.20 Sun, Oct 10.00–18.20 Mon–Fri, noon–18.20 Sat–Sun; adult/child €16/12 return, €12/8 one-way). It runs for 1,020m

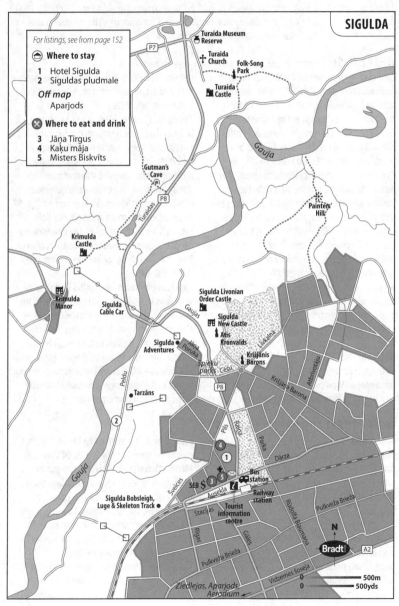

SIGULDA

For listings, see from page 152

🏠 **Where to stay**
1 Hotel Sigulda
2 Siguldas pludmale
Off map
Aparjods

❌ **Where to eat and drink**
3 Jāņa Tirgus
4 Kaķu māja
5 Misters Biskvīts

over the Gauja valley, reaching a height of 43m above the ground, between Sigulda and Krimulda (Krimuldas iela 3). There are departures every 20 or 30 minutes and the ride takes 7 minutes. It was opened in 1969, following a sustained lobbying campaign by local man Aivars Janelsītis, who apparently came up with the idea when frustrated by the effort required to meet up with his girlfriend, who worked at the Krimulda sanatorium across the valley.

TOURIST INFORMATION Sigulda's **tourist information centre** (Siguldas novada Tūrisma informācijas centrs; Ausekļa iela 6; w tourism.sigulda.lv; ⊕ 09.00–18.00 daily) is on the side of the railway station. As well as offering the usual masses of leaflets, they sell tasteful Sigulda-themed souvenirs.

⌂ WHERE TO STAY   *Map, page 151, unless otherwise stated*

Ziedlejas [map, page 160] (4 cabins) Ziedlejas Gaujmaļi, Krimulda; ✆2949 1087; e info@ziedlejas. lv; w ziedlejas.lv. An upmarket wellness retreat 7km to the west of Sigulda, in forest close to the Gauja River, this offers funky modern cabins with one wall & part of the roof made of glass to bring you closer to nature. The bed folds up during the day, & a table rises from the floor at the touch of a button. The main focus of the place is the Latvian traditional sauna, the *pirts*. A Pirts Master guides you through a session typically lasting around 3 hours, involving heat, swatting with bundles of twigs, massage & a dip in a cold pool. There are 3 types available: the glass pirts provides a contemporary Latvian sauna experience; the smoke pirts involves similar procedures in a darker, smokier setting; the woollen pirts, housed in a yurt, offers a gentler, more meditative programme. A pirts session costs around €250 per head, though this cost drops with a larger family size. There is no restaurant on site. €€€€
Hotel Sigulda (43 rooms) Pils iela 6; w hotelsigulda.lv. Centrally located hotel, combining a 19th-century stone building with an adjacent modern block. There is a decent

restaurant (€€€€), & they have a spa, with steam bath & sauna, though use of these is not included in the room rate. €€€
Aparjods (30 rooms) Ventas iela 1A; w aparjods. lv. Around a central courtyard, this array of sympathetic wooden buildings with shingle or reed roofs includes a hotel, restaurant, sauna & conference facilities. The standard rooms are simply furnished, though they also have more spacious 'comfort' rooms, & the restaurant (✆6797 4414; €€€€) is a smart affair, offering both Latvian & international dishes. The downside is a peripheral location in the southwest part of town, 2km from the railway station & away from the sights. €€–€€€
Siguldas pludmale (Campsite) Peldu iela 2; w makars.lv. A well-located campsite run by the Makars travel agency alongside the Gauja River close to Sigulda's river beach, below the Tarzāns adventure park. It offers tent, caravan & camper spots, & they have tents available for rent, as well as canoe, raft & SUP board rental for those looking to take to the river. They can organise transport pick-ups for canoeing expeditions. €

✕ WHERE TO EAT AND DRINK   *Map, page 151*

Jāņa Tirgus Krišjāņa Valdemāra iela 2; w janatirgus.lv. Housed in a black-walled wooden building resembling a vast shed, this gastromarket combines high-end produce outlets & a selection of eateries, with a focus on local businesses rather than chains. Good options include **Melnais Pipars** (✆2488 9457; €€€€), offering steak & ribs, & **Lielais Loms** (✆2488 9457; €€€), where the focus is on fish & sushi. Catch the smoked fish at the latter place, usually made weekly at 14.00 Sat & selling out quickly. Rounding out the offer here are great cakes & pastries at **GUSTAVbeķereja**, & ice cream,

coffee & herbal tea at **Piens un Ledus**. Note that the market closes at 18.00 Sun (20.00 Mon–Sat).
Misters Biskvīts Ausekļa iela 9; w mrbiskvits. lv. Centrally located opposite the railway station, this popular spot offers some main meals, as well as soups, salads, pancakes & burgers, but is particularly sought out for its great cakes & pastries. Also has a branch (Apr–Nov only) at the Turaida museum complex. €€€
Kaķu māja Pils iela 8; w cathouse.lv. The 'Cat House', a name that provides a potential source of confusion to American visitors, is a popular central

canteen-style option with a terrace & Latvian dishes on the menu. Continuing the cat theme, they also run the Kaķis Hotel just round the back (€€). The rooms are basic, though the central location is great. €€

SPORTS AND ACTIVITIES Sigulda has developed a reputation as the Latvian heartland of extreme adventure experiences. I confess that I have not tested out any of the following, but if this is your bag, here you are.

Aerodium Vidzemes šosejas 47km; w aerodium. lv; ⊕ 14.00–18.00 Mon–Fri, noon–18.00 Sat–Sun; adult/child under 12 €59–119/€19–39. Don the overalls, goggles & helmet provided, & take to the air in a vertical wind tunnel. Various packages are available, from taster to more elaborate options – all include an instructor. It's just south of the A2 road from Rīga, around 5km west of town.

Sigulda Adventures Jāņa Poruka iela 14; w siguldaadventures.com; ⊕ Apr–Oct, eves only; solo €89, tandem €139. Not satisfied with the gentle pleasures offered by a cable car ride over the Gauja, Sigulda claims to be the only place in Europe offering the visitor the option of a **bungee jump from a cable car**. Jumps take place late in the day, after the usual cable car transfers have finished. Also on offer is a **zipline** (May–Oct; solo €69, tandem €119) along the cable-car track, reaching speeds of 60km/h.

Sigulda Bobsleigh, Luge and Skeleton Track Šveices iela 13; w bobtrase.lv; visit-only adult/child €3/0.60; summer bob ⊕ May–Sep noon–17.00 Sat–Sun, adult/student/child €30/27/24; soft bob ⊕ Nov–Mar noon–17.00 Sat–Sun, adult/student/child €25/22.50/20; taxi bob ⊕ Nov–Mar noon–17.00 Sat–Sun, adult €85. Bobsleigh & luge were practised in Sigulda from the late 19th century, when Prince Nikolai Kropotkin installed a 900m ice lane with a single turn. It became internationally known for the sports following the construction of the present track in 1986, to service the Soviet teams. It is an impressive structure, with a men's track 1,200m in length, involving 16 turns. It is an interesting place to visit, but for those seeking real adventure, there are summer & winter options to speed down it. The winter options are a padded 'soft bob', which descends at up to 80km/h, & for the truly daring the 'taxi bob', where you are taken down in a standard bobsleigh by an expert. Summer brings a bobsleigh on wheels, with riders encased in a metal cage.

Tarzāns Peldu iela 1; w tarzans.lv; ⊕ 10.00–20.00 daily; obstacle park adult/child €20/8–15. The company runs obstacle parks in several places around Latvia, but thrill-seeking Sigulda is the largest of them all. The focus is on a series of obstacle courses up in the trees, including rope swings & ziplines. There are other attractions (priced separately), from small-child-friendly pursuits like trampolining, bouncy castles & water-gun squirting bumper boats, to the scarier giant swing, catapult & the 'crazy roller', in which you are launched downhill in a cage inside giant wheels. Given that there are many separately priced short-duration attractions here, it can get expensive. It is located on the western side of town, at the top of the Gauja valley.

OTHER PRACTICALITIES The **post office** (Pils iela 2; ✆6797 1740) is centrally located, across the main Ausekļa iela from the railway station. There is a **pharmacy** (Pils iela 3A; ✆6797 0910) a little further up Pils iela. The Sigulda branch of **SEB Bank** (Krišjāņa Valdemāra iela 1A; ✆2666 8777; ⊕ Tue, Wed & Fri only) near Jāņa Tirgus has an ATM, which is just as well, as the bank is only open three days a week.

WHAT TO SEE AND DO Unlike Cēsis or Kuldīga, the town centre of Sigulda is rather functional, and lacks picture-postcard cobbled streets flanked by historic buildings. The main sights are on or beyond the northern edge of town, on both sides of the Gauja River, which here forms a deep ravine. A couple of sights are worth a glance if walking through the town to reach the Castle Quarter. A patch of greenery has been enlivened with sculptures of the painted curved-topped walking sticks that have become a symbol of the place, and named **Spieķu parks** (Walking Stick Park; Jāņa Poruka iela 1). To the east of here along Cēsu iela, at the front of a large park, is a seated **statue of Krišjānis Barons**, classifier of the four-line Latvian folk songs known as *dainas*. Barons spent his last summer, 1922, in Turaida across the river from here. The statue was erected in 1985, marking the 150th year of his birth.

Sigulda Castle Quarter (Siguldas Pils kvartāls) Within a walled complex entered through a brick gate, the town's main historical attractions are displayed in a nicely presented package. A stable block and other former outbuildings of the New Castle contain craft workshops, a café and an ice-cream shop. They are surrounded by pleasant lawns, which also accommodate a **statue of Atis Kronvalds**, a 19th-century Latvian writer who sought to challenge the view of the German-Baltic aristocracy that Latvian was not a suitable language for serious literature or scientific discourse. The statue was commissioned by the Latvian Press Society in 1937 to mark the centenary of his birth, and depicts Kronvalds in full flow during a speech at the Vidzeme Teachers' Conference in 1869 when he spoke in Latvian to highlight his case.

Sigulda New Castle (Siguldas Jaunā pils; Pils iela 16; w tourism.sigulda.lv; ⊕ Oct–Apr 09.00–17.00 daily, May–Sep 09.00–19.00 Mon–Fri, 10.00–19.00 Sat–Sun; adult/student €4.50/2.50, combined ticket with Livonian Order Castle adult/student €6/3) Standing at the end of the formal gardens, the New Castle was built from 1878 to 1881 as the summer residence of the Kropotkins. It was granted to the Latvian Writers and Journalists Trade Union after the Kropotkin family were dispossessed in the agrarian reforms of 1922. Renamed the Writers' Palace, it became the property of the Latvian Press Society in 1934 after the union was dissolved following Ulmanis's coup. The interior was comprehensively remodelled in 1937 in the Latvian national romanticism style. After years as a sanatorium during the Soviet occupation, the castle has been restored in the style of the 1937 remodelling. Note the inlaid wooden mosaics of such Latvian characters as a *kokle* player, the use of Latvian ethnographic symbols, the stained-glass depiction of *The Four Seasons* in National Romanticism style at the base of the spiral stairs and the Art Deco ceramic fireplace in the dining hall. The most curious exhibit in the restored castle is a ghost taking a bath. Complete with an appropriately spooky soundtrack, you find it on the first floor in a small room behind a door conveniently labelled 'ghost'. The most architecturally striking feature of the castle is an octagonal brick tower. Climb this for good views across the Gauja valley below. The castle also houses the district registry office and plays host to wedding ceremonies.

Sigulda Livonian Order Castle (Pils iela 18; ℡6797 0263; e info@sigulda.lv; ⊕ Nov–Apr 09.00–17.00 daily, May–Sep 09.00–19.00 daily, Oct 09.00–17.00 Mon–Fri, 09.00–19.00 Sat–Sun; adult/student €2/1, combined ticket with New Castle adult/student €6/3) Lurking behind the New Castle are the partially restored ruins of the Livonian Order Castle. This was the castle of the Livonian Brothers of the Sword, who in the territorial division with the Bishop of Rīga agreed in 1207, were allocated the land on the left bank of the Gauja, the Bishopric taking the right bank. The castle was a means simultaneously of quelling Livonian revolt, controlling the Gauja, and keeping the Bishopric in its place on the other side of the river. In 1432, it became the residence of the Land Marshal of the Livonian Order, the second most senior officer of the order. The castle was damaged in the Livonian War, and in 1566 became the residence of Jan Hieronimowicz Chodkiewicz, Governor of Livonia. It was damaged again in fighting between Poland and Sweden, and by the 19th century its role was a touristic rather than military one, serving as a romantic ruin. The side of the Livonian Castle looking towards the New Castle is the best preserved, and you can climb a couple of towers. Behind this, an open-air stage provides the atmospheric setting for the **Sigulda Opera Music Festival**, held annually at the end of July.

Painters' Hill (Gleznotāju kalns) There are well-marked trails around the Gauja valley. One of the best known and most straightforward brings you to Painters' Hill, a viewpoint which also goes by the name of Paradise Hill (Paradīzes kalns). On high ground 80m above the Gauja River, it offers the view across the valley to Turaida Castle and beyond that has inspired such notable Latvian artists as Jūlijs Feders and Vilhelms Purvītis. It is an easy and flat walk of 860m from a car park at the northeastern edge of town.

Turaida Museum Reserve (Turaidas muzejrezervāts; Turaidas iela 10; w turaida-muzejs.lv; ⊕ May–Sep 09.00–20.00 daily, Oct 09.00–19.00 daily, Nov–Mar 10.00–17.00 daily, Apr 10.00–19.00 daily; adult/student/child €6/3/1.15 May–Oct, €3.50/1.50/0.70 Nov–Apr) Established in 1988, the reserve covers 40ha of parkland at Turaida, 5km north of Sigulda on the opposite side of the Gauja. While the obvious focus of the reserve lies in the reconstructed red-brick Turaida Castle of the Archbishopric of Rīga, the objectives of the reserve administration are much broader than that, and consist, according to billboards here, of nothing less than 'to establish a harmonic society by demonstrating the development of Latvian wisdom and experience of life and universal human values through the environmental, cultural and historical heritage accumulated in and around the historical centre of Turaida in the past millennium'. Rather than focusing on the castle in isolation, as much attention is given to the earlier occupation of the area by the Livonian, or Liv, people, who built a hill fort at Turaida, and to its more recent history as an aristocratic estate. And some parts of the reserve, notably the Folk-Song Park and Memorial to the Rose of Turaida, depart from the historical story in favour of a wider commentary of Latvian cultural identity. There is a charge for the car park, currently €1.50. You can also get here by bus from Sigulda station.

Turaida estate Turning left from the ticket office as you enter the museum reserve, you reach a selection of buildings of the estate, grouped around photogenic ponds. The estate had a series of aristocratic owners, culminating with Alexander Stahl von Holstein, who took over the place in 1907. With the agrarian reforms of the 1920s, von Holstein was allowed to retain just 55ha, the rest divided up into 106 new small farms, and in 1939, when the von Holstein family left for Germany, the Latvian state took over the remainder. Several of the buildings contain exhibitions, notably a renovated house of corvée peasants, given over to politically charged multimedia displays of the securing by peasant farmers of the mastery of their land in independent Latvia. Other exhibitions are less ambitious in scope, such as an interesting display in the wooden bath house of the sauna tradition in Latvia. And some buildings feature craftsmen in action in high season.

Turaida Church In the other direction from the ticket office, a path heads towards the medieval castle. Before reaching this, you pass the Evangelical Lutheran Turaida Church, on an area of high ground which is, appropriately enough, known as Church Hill. It was built in 1750 on the site of an earlier church, making it one of the oldest surviving wooden churches in Latvia. Close by is a memorial stone to **The Rose of Turaida** (Turaidas roze; page 156), her year of birth given as 1601, that

THE ROSE OF TURAIDA

One of the best-known Latvian tales, the tragic story of the Rose of Turaida has its origins in court documents of 1620 unearthed in 1848 by Magnus von Wolffeldt, his retelling of the court case providing the inspiration for a poem, *Die Jungfrau von Treiden*, by Adelbert Cammerer. Further literary efforts based with various degrees of fidelity on the original story followed, most notably two works in the 1920s: a play by Rainis entitled *Mīla stiprāka par nāvi* (*Love is Stronger than Death*), and the ballet by Emilis Melngailis, *Maija* (*Turaidas roze*).

The story starts with a battle. In 1601, during the Polish–Swedish wars, Swedish troops took Turaida Castle. A clerk of the castle named Greif, looking for survivors, found a baby girl alive among the fallen. He took her home and resolved to bring her up as his own. It being the month of May, he named her Maija. She grew to be a beautiful young woman, and was known as the 'Rose of Turaida'. Maija fell in love with a young man named Viktor Heil, a gardener at Sigulda Castle on the opposite side of the Daugava, and in the fateful year of 1620 they would meet at Gutman's Cave, planning their wedding.

Unfortunately, there were two Polish army deserters serving at Turaida Castle, named Adam Jakubowski and Peter Skudritz. Jakubowski desired Maija, but was rejected by her. Jakubowski, assisted by Skudritz, tricked her into an assignation at Gutman's Cave where, instead of Viktor, it was Jakubowski who was there to meet her, intent on forcing her to be his bride. Maija was wearing a red scarf around her neck Viktor had given her. She told Jakubowski that this was a magical scarf, protecting the wearer from injury. She would give him the scarf if only he would let her go. She suggested that he test its power on her. He struck her with his sword and Maija, her honour protected, fell dead to the ground.

But it was Viktor who was arrested, his guilt assumed by the discovery of an axe belonging to him in the vicinity. The truth of the tale was, however, revealed by a repentant Skudritz and by a young girl called Lenta, the daughter of Maija's adoptive father, who had accompanied Maija to the cave, and Jakubowski was caught and hanged for the crime. Or according to some versions of the tale, Jakubowski was overcome by horror at what he had done and hanged himself in the forest. Viktor buried Maija near the castle, planted a linden tree on her grave, and left the area, never to return.

of her death 1620. It is a favourite photo stop for newlyweds, who place flowers at the base of the stone.

Continuing along the path you reach on your left the 19th-century building of the estate gardener's house, now given over to an exhibition devoted to the **Gauja Livs**, the Finnic-speaking tribe that flourished in the area in the 11th and 12th centuries. Turaida apparently means 'Garden of God' in the Livonian language. The exhibition includes archaeological finds of the Livonian period, including a bone pipe and an impressive collection of silver coins and jewellery.

Turaida Castle Next, the path brings you to the heavily reconstructed red-brick Turaida Castle (Turaidas pils). Building started in 1214 on the orders of Albert, Bishop of Rīga, on the site of the Livonian hill fort. It was among the most important of the castles belonging to the Bishopric, later Archbishopric, of Rīga, and frequently accommodated the Archbishop. Under Swedish rule from the beginning of the 17th century, it gradually lost its military significance and went into decline. A fire in 1776 destroyed many of the wooden parts, and these were not replaced. Extensive restorations in the Soviet period, even if perhaps not conducted with the greatest of care, have resulted in a structure that is undeniably impressive. The cylindrical main tower, also known as the Bergfried, was originally entered through a door 9.5m up, accessed by a wooden ladder which could easily be removed in the event of attack. The tower served as the castle's last line of defence. Restored during the Soviet period, it now offers an excellent view across the Gauja valley. The western block and great semicircular tower date from the 15th century, while the southern block, a square-based lower tower in form, has its origins in the 13th. All house exhibitions inside their reconstructed rooms, including an interesting display of decorated ceramic tiles from stoves in the castle.

Folk-Song Park (Tautasdziesmu parks) To the northeast of Turaida Castle, part of the museum reserve is devoted to Folk-Song Park. This is home to 26 bulky granite sculptures, the work of Indulis Ranka. It was inaugurated in 1985, initially with 15 sculptures set out across an area of high elevation baptised Folk-Song Hill, as part of the celebrations of the 150th anniversary of the birth of folk-song collector Krišjānis Barons. The performances of Latvian folk songs in the park formed part of the National Reawakening that presaged the reestablishment of independence in 1991. The park expanded into an amphitheatre-like stretch of ground below the hill, which has been named Folk-Song Garden, containing further sculptures. There is no explanatory signage, and it seems that the sculptures allude generally to the Latvian folk-song tradition, rather than each portraying a particular song.

Gutman's Cave (Gūtmaņa ala; Turaidas iela 2A) A kilometre or so back down the hill from Turaida Museum Reserve, just off Turaidas iela, linking Turaida with Sigulda, sits Gutman's Cave. It vies with Alekšupīte Waterfall in Kuldīga for the title of most over-hyped site in all of Latvia. The tourist literature will tell you that this cave, fashioned by a previous course of the Gauja River at the site of an underground spring at the base of a sandstone outcrop, is the widest and highest in all the Baltics. What this rather glosses over is that, extending just 18m back into the rock, it barely qualifies for the name 'cave' at all. Yet the place has considerable antiquity as a tourist destination, as evidenced by the graffiti inscribed into its walls. The oldest identified inscription dates from 1667, recording the visit of one Anna Magdalena von Tiesenhaven. The older graffiti impresses for the particularly fine handwriting, and was professionally done by local craftsmen, who would take commissions from rich visitors to have their names placed in a prominent spot.

Tourists initially came for the reputed healing properties of the spring: the cave is reportedly named from the German for a '*gut Mann*' ('good man'), who would use the spring waters to help cure people of their ills. Its fame was cemented by the legend of the Rose of Turaida (see opposite), as the place at which Maija met her end at the hands of the dastardly Adam.

There are several smaller caves nearby, including **Viktor's Cave** (Viktora ala), taking its name from Maija's true love. There is a car park, and you can also get here on a boardwalk trail from Turaida, avoiding the need to walk alongside the road.

Krimulda Situated on high ground on the opposite bank of the Gauja from Sigulda, around 3km southwest of Turaida, Krimulda is today most visited as the western terminus of the cable car across the Gauja valley. It attracts for its views and for a couple of historic buildings. On a wooded hilltop northeast of the cable-car terminal sits ruined **Krimulda Castle** (Krimuldas pilsdrupas), built by the Archbishopric of Rīga in a well-protected site with the Gauja valley on one side, and that of the Vikmeste River on the other. It was destroyed in 1601 by Polish troops, to avoid the risk of it falling into Swedish hands, and never rebuilt. Only a few fragments of wall remain, having been refashioned as a romantic ruin in the 19th century by the owners of Krimulda Manor. There is a well-marked trail from the castle to Gutman's Cave, 1km away.

Some 400m from the medieval castle, on the other side of the cable-car terminal, is **Krimulda Manor** (Krimuldas muiža; Mednieku iela 3; w krimuldasmuiza.lv). Built in a Neoclassical style in the early 19th century by its new aristocratic owner Johan Georg von Lieven, it impresses for its four-columned portico. And there are vestiges remaining of the romantic manor park enjoyed by Tsar Alexander II during a visit in 1862. The von Lieven family departed Latvia in 1921 in the wake of the agrarian reforms, and in the following year a bone tuberculosis sanatorium was established here by the Latvian Red Cross. The place remains a rehabilitation centre, though is now privately run. The 'sunning porch', a semicircular wooden structure where tuberculosis patients would receive sun baths, still frames the lawn in front of the manor. It is possible to stay here, though the basic hotel and hostel rooms (**€–€€**) offer more the feel of a Soviet sanatorium than an aristocratic palace.

SOUTH OF SIGULDA

MORE The parish of More southeast of Sigulda was the scene of a fierce battle in 1944. A Red Army assault had reached the German defence lines in More on 25 September. The lines were defended by troops of the 19th Division of the Latvian Legion, one of the two divisions of mainly conscripted Latvian personnel subordinated to the German Waffen-SS. Although heavily outnumbered, the Latvian troops managed to fend off the Russian attacks until they were required to abandon their positions on 5 October as part of a wider German withdrawal. The **Battle of More Memorial Park**, the creation of former soldiers of the Latvian Legion as a tribute to their fallen comrades, lies on the eastern side of the village, close to the More elementary school, which served as a command post during the battle. Trench lines can still be discerned in the park, and a granite memorial lists the names of 186 Latvian soldiers killed or declared missing.

A couple of kilometres to the west, on the road to Sigulda, a signposted turn to the left brings you to the **More Museum** (Mores kauju muzejs; 'Kalna Kaņēni', Mores pag.; w moresmuzejs.lv; ◷ May–Oct 10.00–16.00 daily, Nov–Apr by appt; adult/child €5/3). The ground floor has exhibits relating to World War I fighting in the region, but majors on the World War II Battle of More, with separate rooms devoted to Russian and German weaponry and other objects unearthed from the battlefield. Upstairs, unexpectedly, there is a display of jewellery for sale. A miscellaneous collection of military vehicles sits outside, including a Soviet T-34 tank. Some visitors will find the signage at both museum and memorial park disconcerting, in casting the forces on the German side of this World War II battle as the heroes. The actions of the Latvian troops at More are depicted as helping to delay the Red Army's advance to Rīga and thereby facilitate civilian escapes from Soviet rule.

A couple of hundred metres beyond the More Museum is a very different attraction, the **More Safari Park** (Safari parks More; 'Saulstari', Mores pag.; w safariparks.lv; ◷ call ahead; adult/child €6/4). The name is misleading, as the only animals you will encounter are deer. But it is nonetheless a diverting place, particularly for children. Pay €2 for a bucket of fruit, and walk round a 1.5km trail between fenced enclosures full of red and fallow deer. You can stay here at the **More Guest House** (6 rooms; 📞2025 2844; **€€**), whose restaurant (**€€€€**) is squarely focused on deer meat, from burgers to venison steak. Watch live deer grazing outside the windows as you consume their less fortunate relatives.

MĀLPILS A village of 2,000 people in the southern part of Sigulda district, Mālpils, known in German as Lemburg, grew up around a fortress of the Livonian Order. That castle was destroyed by retreating Polish troops during the war with Sweden in the early part of the 17th century. After several changes of ownership, the manor of Mālpils fell in the late 18th century into the hands of Gustav von Taube, Governor of Vidzeme, who built the manor house and landscaped the adjacent park. Heavily damaged by fire during the 1905 Revolution, the manor house was remodelled by German-Baltic architect Wilhelm Bockslaff in a Neoclassical style. After serving variously as a school, state farm administration and agricultural museum, the manor house was acquired in 2003 by businessman Aldis Plaudis, who has converted it into a smart hotel.

🏠 **Where to stay and eat** Mālpils Manor (Mālpils muiža; 22 rooms; Pils iela 6; **w** malpilsmuiza.lv; **€€–€€€€**) is set in landscaped gardens, and has been restored in the style of the Neoclassical country house of the early 20th century. The rooms are very different in quality (and price), from elegantly furnished suites to basic attic rooms. The fine rooms have been expensively restored, though have a newly minted rather than lived-in feel. The restaurant (**€€€€**) has an imaginative menu, with a particular penchant for game, recalling Aldis Plaudis' hunting trophies on display in the fine rooms.

LĪGATNE

The town of Līgatne – though with a population of little more than 1,000 its feel is more that of a village – sits at the heart of the Gauja National Park. Its picturesque setting, diverse attractions in and around the town, and some good restaurants have combined to make the place a popular choice for day trippers from Rīga, and it also serves as a fine base for deeper explorations of the Gauja. The Līgatne River, a tributary of the Gauja, is one of the fastest flowing streams in Latvia. The speed of the water here is at the root of the prosperity and indeed existence of the place: providing a suitable location for the construction of a paper mill in 1815. The golden age of paper production in Līgatne came at the end of the 19th century, when it produced paper with the watermark of the double-headed eagle of Tsarist Russia. The owners of the mill built houses for their workers and public buildings to meet their needs. While the paper mill closed in 2016, the town itself retains its atmosphere as a place fashioned by its principal employer.

The **tourist information centre** (Līgatnes Tūrisma informācijas centrs; Spriņģu iela 2; **w** visitligatne.lv; ⏱ May–Oct 09.00–18.00 daily, Nov–Apr 09.00–17.00 daily) is centrally located in a small wooden building constructed in 1889 as a guardhouse for the paper mill.

GETTING THERE AND AWAY Līgatne is a stop on the **railway** line between Rīga and Valga, but the station is in the village of Augšlīgatne to the south, and not convenient for the historic centre of Līgatne itself. The **bus** is a better option, with

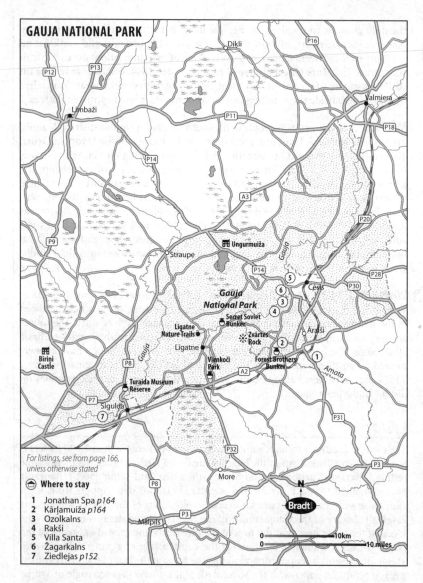

GAUJA NATIONAL PARK

Dikli

Valmiera

Limbaži

Ungurmuiža

Straupe

Gauja National Park

Secret Soviet Bunker

Cēsis

Ligatne Nature Trails

Zvārtes Rock

Ligatne

Āraiši

Biriņi Castle

Vienkoči Park

Forest Brothers Bunker

Amata

Turaida Museum Reserve

Sigulda

More

Mālpils

For listings, see from page 166, unless otherwise stated

Where to stay

1 Jonathan Spa *p164*
2 Kārļamuiža *p164*
3 Ozolkalns
4 Rakši
5 Villa Santa
6 Žagarkalns
7 Ziedlejas *p152*

N

Bradt

0   10km
0   10 miles

connections to Cēsis (30mins), Sigulda (15mins) and Rīga (1hr 20mins). Given that many of the most interesting sites here lie outside the town, coming with your own transport is a distinct advantage.

 WHERE TO STAY AND EAT

Zeit (9 rooms) Gaujas iela 4; w zeit.lv. On high ground above the town, this is a family-oriented hotel in the red-brick building of a former motorcycle helmet factory. A net park (tīklu parks; ⏰ noon–19.00 Thu, 10.00–21.00 Fri–Sat, 10.00–19.00 Sun; €5–10/hr depending on child's age) offering trampolining in the tree canopy is a particular draw, & there is also an indoor play area. The functional restaurant, which spills out on to an expansive terrace, offers family-friendly choices like grilled chicken & chips (€€€). Hosts concerts (usually Fri eve), attracting popular Latvian artists. €€€

Pavāru māja Pilsoņu iela 2; w pavarumaja.lv. Housed in a red-brick building constructed at the turn of the 20th century by the owner of the paper mill as a maternity hospital, this restaurant run by chef & ornithologist Ēriks Dreibants focuses on locally grown & wild products, receiving a Michelin green star in 2023. Its walls are decorated with ceramic rhubarb stalks & watercolours of birds. Open only for a set 6-course dinner menu Fri & Sat, & 4-course lunch menu Sat & Sun. Booking required. €€€€€

Pie Jančuka Spriņģu iela 4; ☏ 2914 9596; e info@piejancuka.lv. Housed in the basement of the large brick building in the centre of town, built in 1897 as a club for the paper mill workers & now serving as a culture centre & library. It is an unassuming pub, offering hearty dishes like *karbonāde* & chicken fillet, with wooden tables attractively located alongside the Līgatne River in summer. Closes in the early evening. €€€

WHAT TO SEE AND DO The brick buildings and chimneys of the **paper mill** (Līgatnes papīrfabrika; Spriņģu iela 4A) are at the northern edge of town, though the mill is only visitable as part of a group guided tour (ask about availability at the tourist information centre). The town itself is a well-preserved late-19th-century factory village. The tourist information centre provides details of a 3.5km walking trail, taking in the most impressive buildings of its industrial heritage. Note the terraced rows of wooden buildings, the oldest dating from the 1880s, built for the mill workers. Married workers would be given an apartment with one bedroom, while single workers were entitled to just one upstairs room. Managers were given two- or three-room houses at the end of each row. All did, though, receive free water, electricity and firewood.

The valley of the Līgatne River in the town is characterised by sandstone outcrops, and these give rise to its most unusual feature, a series of manmade caves, mostly used as cellars by the locals for the storage of vegetables over the winter. A sandstone cliff in the town centre known as **Lustūzis**, peppered with cellar caves, is among the most photogenic spots. The most macabre is a line of three cellar caves along Spriņģu iela, over the road from the brick building, now a retirement home, built in 1897 as the community hospital. While one of the three caves was used by the hospital to store vegetables, the other two served as its morgue.

Secret Soviet Bunker
(Padomju slepenais bunkurs; Rehabilitācijas centrs 'Līgatne', Skaļupes; w bunkurs.lv; ⊕ reservations required: tours generally May–Oct noon, 14.00 & 16.00 Sat–Sun, 15.00 Mon–Fri, Nov–Apr noon & 14.00 Sat–Sun; adult/child €18.50/15.50) Līgatne's most unexpected attraction lies beneath a rundown sanatorium 4km northeast of town at Skaļupes, close to the Gauja River. It is a fascinating piece of Cold War history: a Soviet-era civil protection bunker, 9m underground, covering 2,000m². Opened in 1980, it was intended to house senior government officials in the event of nuclear war or other serious threat, and takes the form of a large subterranean network of green-walled rooms and corridors. The Līgatne rehabilitation centre was built on top of it, a centre for government officials to relax and take medical treatments, but essentially serving as camouflage for the secret installation below.

Guides will show you rooms full of ageing communications equipment, diesel generators and the air purification system. A toilet block has cubicle doors marked 'men', 'women' and 'not working' – the latter were reportedly perfectly functional, but reserved for senior government officials. Some of the rooms are now occupied by assorted Soviet-era memorabilia, from record players to abacuses. In normal times there were just 20 people working here.

While a certain theatrical licence has crept in – the bust of Lenin making for a photo-opportunity in the main conference room is actually a film prop – the place gives a clear feel for the work of the bunker in the last years of the Cold War. The bunker only once operated to full activity; during a civil protection training exercise in 1984, when 300 officials arrived here for three days. Local people were ordered to stay indoors and not to look out of their windows. The tour includes a Soviet canteen lunch of *pelmeni* and juice.

The parquet-floored Līgatne rehabilitation centre above the bunker, and from where the tours depart, is still in service for programmes of medical rehabilitation. It is in itself a throwback to the Soviet era. There are footpaths in the woods around the centre, including the **Mythology Trail** (Mitoloģiskā taka), which runs to the Gauja River, and in highlighting themes from Latvian mythology almost feels like it is making an apology for the Soviet bunker. There is a bus stop (Skaļupe) directly in front of the rehabilitation centre with connections to Līgatne and occasionally Cēsis, but there are only a few buses daily.

Līgatne Nature Trails (Līgatnes dabas takas; w ligatnesdabastakas.lv; ⊕ Nov–Mar 09.00–16.00 Mon–Fri, 09.00–17.00 Sat–Sun, Apr–Oct 09.00–18.00 Mon–Fri, 09.00–19.00 Sat–Sun; adult/student/child €7/6/5) Another popular attraction outside town, lying 4km north of Līgatne, again close to the Gauja River, is somewhere between a wildlife park and a nature trail, involving a signposted path through the forest around 4km long. You pass large, fenced enclosures that are home to the pick of Latvia's wildlife: brown bear, lynx, wild boar and red deer. A 22m observation tower part of the way round sits between the wild boar and red deer enclosures. There are plaques along the route with information about tracks, diet and the like, but the signage is in Latvian only. The place is worthwhile, but can get packed at weekends when the weather is fine. From Līgatne, take Dārza iela northwards, and follow the signposts. There is an additional car park charge of €2.50 for those visiting the trails.

Vienkoči Park (Vienkoču parks; Vienkoči; w vienkoci.lv; ⊕ 10.00–18.00 daily – closes at dusk in winter; adult/student €5/3) Some 5km south of Līgatne, just north of the A2 road, this is one of those fantasies driven by the passion of one individual in which Latvia so excels. Over almost 10ha, the park showcases the wooden sculpture of woodcarver Rihards Vidzickis. The name *vienkoči* refers to the carving of a sculpture from a single piece of wood, although not all the sculptures in the park conform to this stringent requirement. The sculptures are varied in style, from models of historical manor houses of the area, and of the Līgatne paper mill, to a forest of wooden mushrooms. A wooden toad is covered with small coins, reflecting the Latvian superstition that a toad provides a blessing for the house. The trail through the park also takes you to the delightful banks of the Līgatne River. Wooden owls stare at you from the trees. There is a small museum, arranged as a historic workshop and stuffed full of woodworking tools. It abuts Rihards' own workshop. A children's play area near the entrance features imaginatively carved games such as an all-wooden version of Twister.

AROUND THE AMATA RIVER

Rising in the Vidzeme Uplands, the Amata flows 66km northwestwards to join the Gauja River. It is another of the fastest and most picturesque rivers in Latvia, known for the sandstone and dolomite cliffs and rock outcrops on its banks. The **Amata Trail**, along its right bank, runs for 21km from the village of Amata, westwards past Kārļi to end at the Veclaučū Bridge on the road between Kārļi and Līgatne. For those not contemplating hiking the whole trail, one place to aim for is the **Zvārtes Rock** (Zvārtes iezis), signposted off the road between Kārļi and Līgatne. There is a car park, charging €2. The rock is an attractive sandstone outcrop around 20m high jutting out over the Amata River, standing in front of the larger Zvārtes Cliffs, which reach a height of 45m. An easy path of wooden steps takes you up to the top of the latter. This area, they say, was once a gathering place for witches. It now gathers picnickers.

FOREST BROTHERS BUNKER (Mežabrāļu bunkurs; Amadas, Melturi; w mezabrali. wordpress.com; ⊕ call ahead; €3) Signposted from the A2 road, and just to the north of it a couple of kilometres west of the exit for Cēsis, sits a Forest Brothers bunker. It is one of the log-built subterranean shelters in which Latvian partisans known as Forest Brothers hid out from the Soviet authorities in the aftermath of World War II. The last of the Forest Brothers did not surrender until 1956. The bunker could accommodate up to 25 people. A hollowed-out tree stump attached to the roof served as a chimney, and there were two concealed entrances. The surrounding area was mined with pairs of mines, connected by wires, which would detonate when disturbed. You are taken round by the English-speaking custodian of the place.

ĀRAIŠI Some 7km south of Cēsis, the main attraction of this small village is the **Āraiši Lake Fortress Archaeological Park** (Āraišu ezerpils Arheoloģiskais parks; Drabešu pag.; ✆ 2566 9935; e ezerpils@cesunovads.lv; ⊕ May–Sep 09.00–19.00 daily, Oct–Apr 09.00–17.00 Wed–Sat, 10.00–16.00 Sun; adult/student €5/4), centred around a reconstructed wooden lake village, home to a Latgalian community of the 9th and 10th centuries. The well-presented visitor information centre is something of a shrine to Latvian archaeologist Jānis Apals, incorporating a reconstruction of his study. Apals' research focused on the theory that the Latgalian tribes relied for their defence not just on hillforts but also on villages built on log platforms on lakes, whose waters would have protected against attack. Apals learned to dive to further his research, identified some ten lake fortresses across Latvia, and carried out excavations in Āraiši between 1965 and 1979. The remains of 150 wooden buildings were discovered, belonging to five separate building phases. Wet and airtight conditions helped preserve wooden and textile items, some of which are on display in the information centre.

Apals also promoted the scheme to reconstruct the Latgalian village. It is an atmospheric place. A rectangular lattice of logs creates a platform, built over a low island in the lake, and accessed along a wooden walkway between the reeds. Log houses are arranged on the platform, their entrances facing towards the centre. Stoop to enter. On higher ground, occupying a peninsula extending into the lake, stand the ruins of the Livonian Order Āraiši Castle, inhabited between the 14th and 17th centuries. Beyond the Livonian castle, a path to the lakeshore brings you to some reconstructed Stone and Bronze Age dwellings.

On a hilltop west of the lake, **Āraiši Windmill** (Āraišu vējdzirnavas; Drabešu pag.; ✆ 2923 8208; e vineta.cipe@inbox.lv; ⊕ 10.00–19.00 daily; adult/student €2/1) is a working mill dating from 1852, with an exhibition across its four floors. They host a Bread Day festival here on the last Sunday in July. From the lake fortress, take the Cēsis road northwards for 400m, turning left on to a signposted track, reaching the windmill after 1km.

If you are here in the winter months, husky club **Dodkepu.lv** (Papardes 2, Drabešu pag.; w dodkepu.lv; €60–70 per person) provides the opportunity to try out dog sledging through the Latvian forests. Advance booking essential: they will give you a meeting point.

 ## Where to stay and eat *Map, page 160*

Jonathan Spa (11 rooms) 'Ezerputni', Amatciems; w jonathanspahotel.com. This is a pricey but relaxing spa resort in a large wooden chalet within the Amatciems development, a planned residential community set amid numerous artificial lakes, offering wooden walled & reed-roofed homes for the well-heeled. The spa includes pool, sauna, jacuzzi & some more unusual facilities, such as a mineral-walled shungite room. The larger suites are in a neighbouring chalet. There is a good restaurant (€€€€) offering a limited international menu & expensive wine list. €€€€€

Kārļamuiža (10 rooms) Kārļi; w karlamuiza.lv. The manor house of Kārļamuiža was developed in the 18th century by the von Sievers family, who purchased it along with Cēsis manor, before selling it in 1795 to Scottish merchant James Pierson & his wife Angela, who remodelled the place. The manor later ended up back in the von Sievers family, was burnt down in the 1905 revolution, & rebuilt only to be destroyed again in 1919 during the Latvian War of Independence. The hotel occupies the restored 2-storey building of the servants' quarters of the old manor. It is a tranquil place, close to the village of Kārļi, backed by orchards, & an 800m walk from the Amata River, where you can join the Amata Trail. Bedrooms are named after former owners of the manor, like 'James' & 'Angela'. 'Annmarie' is an adjacent cottage. B/fast & a good 3-course set dinner are provided on prior reservation. €€–€€€

THE NORTHERN GAUJA

There is a worthwhile manor house in the northern part of the Gauja National Park.

UNGURMUIŽA (Raiskuma pag.; w ungurmuiza.lv; ⊕ May–Sep 10.00–18.00 Tue–Sat, 10.00–16.00 Sun, Oct–Apr call ahead; adult/student €5/3) This is a rare example of a well-preserved wooden Baroque manor house dating from the 18th century. The estate of Ungurmuiža, which takes its name from earlier owners the Ungern family, was purchased in 1728 by Lt Gen Balthazar von Campenhausen, who was dissatisfied with the existing buildings and ordered the construction of the new wooden manor. A large clock stands above the entrance of the red-painted building. The interior is enlivened by mid-18th-century wall paintings from Limbaži artist Georg Dietrich Hinsch, which range from abstract designs and landscapes to a pair of grenadiers, guarding the entrance to an upstairs room. There are also period furnishings and poignant photographs of members of the von Campenhausen family working in the gardens, riding through the grounds or simply staring forward at the viewer. The manor was not nationalised during the agrarian reforms of the 1920s, and the family owned the estate until 1939. It served as a school in the Soviet period, and has gradually been renovated following the restoration of Latvian independence.

In the pleasant gardens behind the manor note the wooden tea pavilion, a Baroque delight with a distinctive curved roof looking rather like a helmet. The weathervane records the date of its restoration in 1977. There is also a children's playhouse dating from the mid 19th century, curiously the only brick building in the place. The old wooden schoolhouse serving the manor, founded in 1734, now houses a characterful **restaurant** (closed Mon & Sun eve; €€€€) with wooden-panelled walls. The place also runs as a hotel (5 rooms; €€€), with two rooms on the first floor of the manor and another three above the restaurant. Ungurmuiža is around 15km northwest of Cēsis. The Unguri stop on the Limbaži to Cēsis and Straupe to Cēsis bus routes is on the main P14 road close to the turning for Ungurmuiža, a couple of kilometres away.

CĒSIS

One of Latvia's most picturesque towns, centred on a major castle of the Livonian Order in a fine setting close to the Gauja River, Cēsis is doable as a day trip from Rīga but warrants a more relaxed stay. It is enticing creative professionals away from the Latvian capital, and has something of a hipster reputation, fuelled by the hosting of summer gatherings such as the political discussion forum LAMPA and the Cēsis Art Festival. Its offer combines history and culture with forest walks and kayaking in summer, and skiing in winter.

HISTORY The origins of Cēsis lie in a wooden hill fort on Riekstu Hill built by a tribe known as the Vends, after whom the German name for Cēsis, Wenden, takes its inspiration. The Vends converted to Christianity during the Livonian Crusade of 1206, and the Livonian Brothers of the Sword took up residence here shortly thereafter. The Livonian Brothers opted to build their new stone castle close to the hill fort of the Vends, and their successors, the Livonian Order, enlarged the place, which became one of their mightiest castles. From 1481, as relations between the order and the town of Rīga became strained, Cēsis Castle became the headquarters of the Livonian Masters, a status it retained until the order was dissolved. The wealth of Cēsis reached a peak in the early 16th century, when the Livonian Order was led by the capable Master Wolter von Plettenberg, who strengthened the castle's fortifications. The town, a member of the Hanseatic League, developed as an important trading centre.

Tragedy was to strike in 1577 when the troops of Ivan the Terrible laid siege to the castle. The Russian and Tatar troops had a massive numerical superiority, and the story runs that the last of those sheltering in the castle opted to blow themselves up with gunpowder in a mass suicide rather than be taken by the Russians. Ivan did not retain Cēsis Castle long. In December of that year, Johann Biering, castellan of Turaida Castle, retook it from the Russian garrison. The Russians attacked again in October 1578, but in a battle in an open field outside the town were defeated by a combined Swedish and Polish force, marking a turning point in the Livonian War. Cēsis Castle was in the hands of Poland–Lithuania until the early 17th century, when it fell to Sweden. By the end of that century, damaged by the soldiers of a Swedish unit stationed there, and having lost much of its military significance, Cēsis Castle was in decline. As the castle itself descended into ruin, the old gatehouse of the outer bailey was rebuilt as a manor house in the 1760s.

In 1777 Cēsis Castle manor was purchased by a Russian army officer named Count Karl Eberhard von Sievers. The von Sievers family owned the place until the agrarian reform of 1920 stripped it from them. In 1889 the railway arrived, spurring on the town's development. Cēsis played an important role in the Latvian War of Independence, when a combined Latvian and Estonian force defeated German troops near here in June 1919. In the Soviet period, Cēsis developed as a touristic and health resort, with cures offered at the Cīrulīši Sanatorium. It remains one of Latvia's most important tourist towns.

GETTING THERE AND AWAY The **railway station** (Cēsu dzelzceļa stacija; Stacijas laukums 1; ☎6418 6445) is at the eastern edge of the town centre, at the end of Raunas iela, which runs east from the central Vienības laukums. It is served by five trains a day running between Rīga (around 1hr 40mins) and Valmiera, with two of them going on to Valga. The **bus station** (Cēsu autoosta; Stacijas laukums 5;

6412 2762) is outside the railway station, offering roughly hourly buses to Rīga (1hr 50mins) with stops at Līgatne and Sigulda en route.

TOURIST INFORMATION The **tourist information centre** (Cēsu Tūrisma informācijas centrs; Baznīcas laukums 1; w turisms.cesis.lv; ⊕ 10.00–17.00 Tue–Fri) is centrally located, between St John's Church and the castle.

 WHERE TO STAY *Map, page 160, unless otherwise stated*

Hotel Cēsis [map, below] (39 rooms) Vienības laukums 1; w hotelcesis.lv. Built in 1939, this is a comfortable enough if somewhat bland 3-star option, its rooms decorated in varying shades of brown. It does, though, enjoy a plum location right in the town centre. **€€€**

Villa Santa (30 rooms) Gaujas iela 88; w villasanta.lv. Santa was the name of a Latvian women's magazine & its founder, Santa Anča,

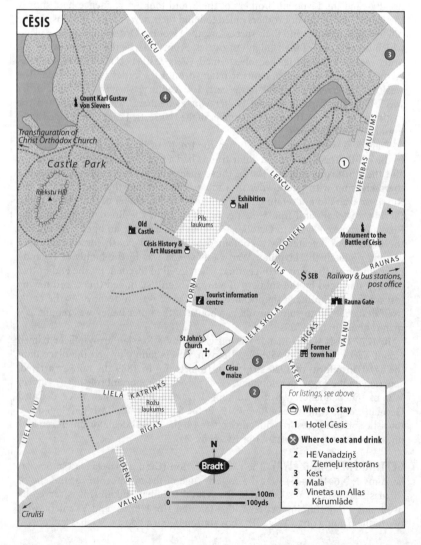

CĒSIS

LENČU

Count Karl Gustav von Sievers ④

Transfiguration of Christ Orthodox Church

Castle Park

Riekstu Hill

LENČU

VIENĪBAS LAUKUMS

①

Exhibition hall

Pils laukums

Old Castle

Cēsis History & Art Museum

PODNIEKU

Monument to the Battle of Cēsis

PILS

RAUNAS

$ SEB

Railway & bus stations, post office

Tourist information centre

TORŅA

LIELĀ SKOLAS

Rauna Gate

RĪGAS

VALŅU

St John's Church

Former town hall ⑤

Cēsu maize

KASES

LIELĀ KATRĪNAS

Rožu laukums

②

For listings, see above

⊖ **Where to stay**
1 Hotel Cēsis

✖ **Where to eat and drink**
2 HE Vanadziņš Ziemeļu restorāns
3 Kest
4 Mala
5 Vinetas un Allas Kārumlāde

LIELĀ LĪVU

RĪGAS

UDENS

N

Bradt

0 ———— 100m
0 ———— 100yds

VALŅU

Cirulīši

whose publishing company purchased in 2014 a wooded area above the Gauja River which had offered summer guesthouses for Russian nobles at the turn of the 20th century. They have built 3 smart wooden villas in the style of those buildings, making for a tranquil, upmarket hotel complex. The restaurant (€€€€) offers a tempting international menu & a nice terrace. It's 3km west of the centre. €€€

Rakši (18 rooms & 2 apartments) Drabešu pag.; w kamieli.lv. One of Latvia's quirkier accommodation options, this log-built hotel sits in the middle of a camel park 7km southwest of Cēsis. Its rooms are furnished in Moroccan style, giving a curious feel somewhere between coniferous forest & Sahara Desert. The cheaper rooms have shared bathrooms. Its restaurant, the Camel Café (€€), is mostly child-friendly fast food, though also offers tajine in keeping with the Moroccan theme. Note that the restaurant is not open evenings. You are surrounded by pens housing camels, llamas &

ostriches, & even a lemur house. Those not staying at the hotel can visit the camel park on a day ticket (⏰ 10.00–18.00 daily; adult/child €7/5 basic ticket or €20/15 with lemur feeding & other attractions included). €€–€€€

Ozolkalns w ozolkalns.lv. Downstream of the Žagarkalns campsite, this offers a largely similar menu of wooden holiday cottages sleeping 4 or 5, tent spots, kayak hire, & a winter skiing & snowboarding resort (closed Mon) in the slopes above. €–€€

Žagarkalns Mūrlejas iela 12; w zagarkalns. lv. Well-maintained campsite on the banks of the Gauja around 3km from the centre of town. Offers trailer spots with electricity supply, places for tents, & small wooden cottages. They also have various river craft & bicycles for hire. Up the hill, on the edge of the suburb of Cīrulīši, is the Žagarkalns ski resort (closed Mon), offering 1.4km of easy slopes & a ski school for winter visitors. €–€€

✕ WHERE TO EAT AND DRINK *Map, opposite*

Kest Valmieras iela 1; w kest.lv. Housed in a former fire station, chef Māris Jansons serves up a set 5-course menu, paired with an equal number of either alcoholic or non-alcoholic drinks. After the meal you are ushered to a dark lounge bar for coffee & liqueurs. Altogether a memorable dining experience, though only open for sittings on Fri at 20.00 & Sat 15.00 & 19.00. €€€€€

H. E. Vanadziņš Ziemeļu restorāns Rīgas iela 15; w vanadzinarestorans.lv. Housed in a red-painted wooden building that is a reconstruction of the former home of Cēsis mayor Kārlis Vanadziņš, the 'Northern Restaurant' offers Arctic-inspired dishes, from Arctic trout to Swedish flatbreads served with a lingonberry ketchup. Its terrace contains a chunk of medieval wall. Also has a few smartly furnished rooms (€€€), making for a good central option. €€€€

Mala Lenču iela 11; ☎2610 1945; e telpamala@gmail.com. Located in a partially renovated old brewery, this is a vegetarian café & bar, with a bohemian atmosphere. The menu is short & also includes vegan dishes. Tables & chairs are scattered here & there in the large grounds, where they also host music & arts events. €€

Vinetas un Allas Kārumlāde Rīgas iela 12; ☎2837 5579; e karumlade@inbox.lv. A nice central option for a light lunch of soup or salad, or an afternoon coffee & cake. There are enticing sweet treats on sale too, from a marzipan Winnie the Pooh to a chocolate horseshoe. The outside tables along Rīgas iela are a perfect spot for people watching in good weather. €€

SHOPPING AND OTHER PRACTICALITIES Displaying the green diamond mark of Latvian cultural heritage, bakery **Cēsu maize** (Rīgas iela 18; w cesumaize.lv; ⏰ closed Sun) offers an excellent range of sourdough bread, made variously from spelt wheat, buckwheat, oats and barley. The entrance is on Lielā Skolas iela, close to St John's Church.

There is a **post office** (Stacijas laukums 5; ☎6412 2008) close to the railway station. The central Vienības laukums hosts a **pharmacy** (Vienības laukums 2A; ☎6410 7158), and there is a branch of **SEB Bank** (Pils iela 4; ☎2666 8777) on nearby Pils iela.

WHAT TO SEE AND DO

Town centre The main square, Vienības laukums, centres on an obelisk topped with a golden ball, a **monument to the Battle of Cēsis** of 1919. It was erected in 1924, blown up during the Soviet occupation in 1951 and then rebuilt in 1998. The inscriptions on the monument are in Estonian as well as Latvian, reflecting the role of Estonian troops in helping Latvia defeat the German forces and turn the tide of the Independence War.

From Vienības laukums, cobbled Rīgas iela curves down the hill. As you leave the square, the low stone walls either side of you, topped with plant beds, mark out the position of the **Rauna Gate**, historic entrance to the Old Town. Heading down Rīgas iela, at number 7 on your left is the 18th-century building of the **former town hall**. Its front wall bears the former coat of arms of Cēsis; an oversized knight fiercely defending the castle. The building now houses various non-governmental organisations.

St John's Church (Sv Jāṇa evaņģēliski luteriskā baznīca; Lielā Skolas iela 8; \6412 1549; ⊕ noon–18.00 Tue–Sun) Lielā Skolas iela, running in parallel one block to the north, is dominated by the impressive, heavily buttressed bulk of St John's Church. Dating from the 13th century, it was built to serve the Livonian Order, and is the largest medieval church in Latvia outside Rīga, reflecting Cēsis's importance. The interior contains tomb slabs of several Masters of the Order, including fragments of that of Wolter von Plettenberg. Note also, in a side room, the wall tomb of Bishop of Wenden and Polish humanist Andrzej Patrycy Nidecki, who died in 1587. The tomb has a relief of the departed bishop portrayed as if in slumber. You can climb the bell tower (adult/student €3/2), passing early-20th-century graffiti on the way, though the view is obstructed by a metal grille. Signs warn you to avoid being on the sixth floor when the church bell rings on the hour. This is good advice.

Cēsis Castle Complex (Cēsu pils komplekss; Pils laukums 9; w cesupils.lv; ⊕ May–Sep 10.00–18.00 daily (museum closed on Mon), Oct–Apr 10.00–17.00 Wed–Sun; adult/student €10/6 May–Sep, €6/4 Oct–Apr) This is the town's major sight, incorporating both the medieval stone castle and the Cēsis History and Art Museum sited in the manor house of the von Sievers family. In summer, the castle grounds host workshops, with medieval-attired artisans demonstrating the techniques of bone carving, basket making and the like. Their presence accounts for the higher ticket price in the summer months. Your Castle Complex ticket also gives you entry to the **exhibition hall** (Pils laukums 3) housed in a former stable block and coach house across Pils laukums, which displays the work of local artists.

The Old Castle Surrounded by a dry moat, the Old Castle is an impressive ruin, living up to its billing as the once mightiest fortress of Livonia. Arranged around a central courtyard, the western and northern sides of the castle are reduced to low remnant walls, but the eastern and southern walls have largely survived. Take the wooden footbridge across the moat to enter the castle. Your first port of call before venturing into the circular Western Tower, the best preserved of the towers, is to take a lantern from a lady in medieval garb doling them out from a booth in the courtyard. After an eerie climb in the darkness, you emerge into a large room with reticulated vaulting that was once the Livonian Master's Chamber. One flight further up, another room houses a video presentation, taking you through the history of the castle from the 13th century to the present day.

Within the ruined walls of the western range below the tower, a rectangular metal plate, torn open as if with a can opener in the form of a cross, was installed here in 2021 to commemorate those 300 inhabitants of the castle who blew themselves up rather than fall into the hands of Ivan the Terrible's forces in 1577. Another multimedia exhibition in the basement of the Southern Tower uses the stories of some of those imprisoned in the castle to give a feel for the dying years of the Livonian Order, assailed by the greed of its own Brothers, the plotting of Russia and the ideas of the Reformation.

Cēsis History and Art Museum The museum sits in the castle manor house, dating from the 1760s though substantially reconstructed by Count Karl Gustav von Sievers in the 19th century. Displays cover the occupation of the area by the Vends, including finds unearthed from Riekstu Hill, and the daily lives of the Brothers of the Livonian Order. A room devoted to the history of the Latvian flag draws inspiration from the fact that the red-white-red horizontally banded flag adopted in the early 20th century as the flag of independent Latvia was based on one mentioned in the medieval *Rhymed Chronicle of Livonia*, which talks of such a flag used around 1279 by Latgalian tribes from the Cēsis area. It is said that a wounded Latgalian leader was wrapped in a white sheet: the edges of the sheet were stained red with his blood, while the central portion where he lay remained white. Other rooms set out the role played by Cēsis in the Latvian War of Independence, the history of the town under the rule of the Livonian Order, Poles and Swedes, and its contribution to the Latvian National Awakening.

Further rooms reconstruct manor interiors as they may have looked under the von Sievers family, including a Biedermeier-style coffee room with walls decorated in overpowering green and white vertical stripes which continue on to the ceiling, rather giving the impression of standing beneath a marquee. The most distinctive feature of von Sievers' reconstruction of the manor house was the remodelling of what had been the eastern tower of the outer bailey into a crenelated neo-Gothic tower, known as Lademacher's Tower. You can climb to the top for a good view across the town.

Castle Park (Pils parks) From Pils laukums, a flight of stone steps takes you down to the Castle Park. This was laid out about 1830 by Count Karl Gustav von Sievers around a small lake at the foot of the castle, whose ruins served to give the park an additional romantic appeal. A bust of von Sievers surrounded by railings recalls his role both as the founder of the park and his military service with Russia, when he fought against the army of Napoleon. The park incorporates Riekstu Hill, site of the hill fort of the Vends. On another piece of high ground overlooking the park stands the small blue-domed **Transfiguration of Christ Orthodox Church** (Kristus Apskaidrošanas pareizticīgo baznīca; Palasta iela 22; \2960 8697), dating from 1845. Graves of members of the von Sievers family, surrounded by railings, lie in the grounds.

Cīrulīši A suburb southwest of the town centre, Cīrulīši ('Skylarks') takes its name from a local manor, served in the Tsarist period as a summer resort for members of the Russian nobility, and housed a major sanatorium in Soviet times. Wooded slopes running down to the Gauja River once hosted a wooden toboggan track, built in the 1960s but superseded a couple of decades later by the construction of the Sigulda bobsleigh and luge track. The area is still, though, a centre for winter sports in Latvia, focused on the slopes of the Žagarkalns ski complex. A new **Space**

Exploration Centre is under construction close to the sanatorium, the brainchild of Latvian space enthusiast Pauls Irbins. Bus 3005 brings you here from the centre of town.

Along the bank of the Gauja River beneath here, the **Cīrulīši Nature Trails** (Cīrulīšu dabas takas) offer easy walking through an attractive wooded landscape. To get here, take the winding Gaujas iela westwards from the town centre. After around 3km, just before the bridge over the Gauja, a turning to the left is signposted to the nature trails. Take this turning, and almost immediately to your left a boardwalk leads you on a short detour to the **Zvanu Cliffs**, a moss-covered sandstone outcrop reaching a height of 30m, with an area of moist fenland below. The nature trails connect the Žagarkalns and Ozolkalns campsites, running alongside the placidly flowing Gauja. There are route options of varying lengths, including 3.5km and 6.2km trails, with interesting natural features signposted in Latvian and English. One place to make for is the **Spoguļu Cliffs**, a sandstone cliff-face pockmarked with niches above an oxbow lake created in a former channel of the Gauja. The name of the rocks, 'Mirror', comes from the allegedly perfect reflection they made in the clear waters of the oxbow lake. The water quality has evidently deteriorated since they received their name.

ALONG THE DAUGAVA

The Daugava River, flowing through the heart of Latvia, long a vital trade and communication route and now serving, through its hydroelectric plants, as the source of much of the country's electricity, is central to the Latvian national consciousness. There are some interesting sites along its banks.

IKŠĶILE Nowadays a verdant dormitory town of Rīga, 30km to the west, Ikšķile holds an important place in Latvian history as the first capital of the Bishopric of Livonia, the site of the church of the Augustinian priest Meinhard, who arrived here in the late 12th century on a mission to convert the local pagans to Christianity. Meinhard had some slow success in converting the resident Livs and, noting their vulnerability to Lithuanian raiding parties, promised to build them stronger fortifications if they would embrace the new religion. He enlisted the help of stonemasons from Gotland in constructing a castle at Ikšķile with a church in around 1185: the oldest stone building in the Baltic States. When in the following year Meinhard was made bishop, it became his cathedral. At the start of the 13th century, Albert of Buxhoeveden, determining Ikšķile to be poorly sited for his needs of conversion and conquest, founded the city of Rīga, and moved his centre of operations there. Ikšķile rapidly declined in importance.

The castle at Ikšķile was destroyed in the 16th century, and the church was rebuilt on several occasions, including a comprehensive revamp in the late 19th century, only to be reduced to ruins in World War I. The ruins now sit, topped by a red protective roof, on St Meinhard Island (Sv. Meinarda sala) in the Daugava River, created during the damming of the river for the construction of the Rīga Hydroelectric Plant in the 1970s. The ruins can be viewed from the green embankment of the Daugava, though if you want to explore them from closer quarters, boat rentals are available at **Ikšķiles laivu noma** (Peldu iela 28; w udensprieks.lv). Ikšķile **railway station** (Ikšķiles dzelzceļa stacija; Pārbrauktuves iela 2; ☎6723 1805) is on the Rīga to Daugavpils line, with around 25 trains daily to Rīga (35mins). **Buses** to Rīga are less frequent but also take around 35 minutes.

ĶEGUMS The name of this small town on the right bank of the Daugava is synonymous with that of the hydroelectric power station whose construction in the late 1930s provided the motor for its development. The 1930s power station sits on the right side of the river. A second plant was added alongside it in the 1970s, closer to the left bank. They are part of the network of hydroelectric plants run by the state utility company Latvenergo, which maintains here a small **Museum of Energy** (Enerģētikas muzeja ekspozīcija; Ķeguma prospekts 7/9; w latvenergo. lv; ⊕ 09.00–17.00 Tue–Sun, but ring ahead; adult/student €2/1, children free). Housed within the power station complex, the entrance is on the left bank of the Daugava. There are some impressively sized turbines in the garden outside, and within a rather dry display on the history of electricity generation in Latvia, with photographs of the construction of the various hydroelectric plants. There is also a collection of Soviet-era household appliances. Note the vacuum cleaners themed around the space race, designed to resemble rockets or even the planet Saturn, complete with rings.

LIELVĀRDE A small town on the right bank of the Daugava River, strung along the A6 road, Lielvārde holds a cultural importance as both the home of the *Lielvārdes josta*, a red and white belt comprising individually crafted combinations of some 22 different cultural symbols, and as the setting of parts of the *Lāčplēsis* epic. It also housed a Soviet airbase, now the home of the Latvian air force.

If you're looking for somewhere to eat, try **Kante** (Laimdotas iela 1; ✆ 2214 3143; e 96kante@gmail.com; €€) on the main road through the town. This place describes itself as a 'comfort food restaurant', which is quite apt, serving up groaning plates of hearty fare in bland surroundings. There's also an outdoor play area for children and a large car park.

What to see and do The main sights are grouped together in the **Lielvārde Park** (Lielvārdes parks), on the bank of the Daugava, where a brook named the Rumbiņa joins the larger river. To get here, take a signposted right turn off the main road just beyond a concrete sign bearing the word 'Lāčplēsis'. This is a remnant of the former Lāčplēsis kolkhoz, one of the best-known collective farms in Soviet-occupied Latvia. Its founding director, Edgars Kauliņš, was a local political heavyweight today remembered rather fondly in Latvia for his efforts to ensure that the locals were not included in the deportations of 1949. The collective farm was the original home of Latvia's Lāčplēsis beer, though this is now brewed elsewhere.

A small hillock accommodates the ruins of the 13th-century **Lielvārde Castle**, built by the Bishopric of Rīga but destroyed by Russian troops during the Livonian War in 1577. A manor house, built in the early 19th century, was comprehensively destroyed during World War I. In its place now stands a **sculpture garden** dating from 1988, comprising wooden sculptures resembling totem poles, illustrating characters from the Lāčplēsis epic. Other sculptures dotted around the place represent motifs found in the Lielvārde belt. The **Lielvārde Evangelical Lutheran Church** (Lielvārdes Evaņģēliski luteriskā baznīca; Edgara Kauliņa aleja 21; ✆ 2912 8534) also stands within the park. Two dates are inscribed at the top of the tower: 1747, the year of its construction, and 1932, that of its rebuilding, following extensive damage in World War I.

Opposite the church, housed in the former granary of the Lielvārde estate, is the **Andrejs Pumpurs Museum** (Andreja Pumpura Lielvārdes muzejs; E. Kauliņa aleja 20; ✆ 6505 3759; e muzejs@lielvarde.lv; ⊕ 10.00–17.00 Tue–Sat, 10.00–15.00 Sun). It honours the author of the Lāčplēsis epic, who studied in the town and used

THE LIELVĀRDE BELT

When describing the red and white patterned belt that forms a central part of the local traditional costume, the guide at the Andrejs Pumpurs museum quickly embraces the language of the mystical. The white colour symbolises the soul, goodness and purity. The red represents blood, energy and strength. Each belt is unique. The symbols found on it are not symmetrical, but change along the belt, telling a story that is individual to its owner. Only those who are at peace with both the past and future can weave a Lielvārde belt. If correctly woven, to match the character of the wearer, it can give the wearer great energy and help protect them from evil. It should never be tied with a knot, and should run around the waist at least twice, helping the energy to flow.

The guide tells me that many visitors to the museum come to identify their personal symbol on the belt. If you place your hand just above the belt, running it just over the surface, stop when you feel a change in your hand, like a slight warming. The symbol on the belt below your hand will be a personally fortifying one for you. Loving couples engrave the chosen symbol on their wedding rings.

The belt is traditionally 3m long, though the museum also has a 10m version. It is one of the items inscribed on the Latvian Cultural Canon, and its design adorns numerous Latvian souvenirs, from mugs to bobble hats. It even runs down the side of an apartment block close to the museum.

its Daugava River setting as the backdrop to the exploits of his hero. The museum holds numerous copies of the epic, including one of its first edition of 1888, as well as sculptures and paintings illustrating themes from the tale. There is also a display case offering examples of the Lielvārde belt and, upstairs, a display about Edgars Kauliņš and the Lāčplēsis kolkhoz, including the director's battered chair and Lenin paperweight. There is little information in English.

Two large rocks standing between the museum and the river are said to be the bed and blanket of Lāčplēsis, who clearly was not accustomed to restful sleep. A fallen segment of tree trunk to the side of these is known as Spīdala's Log, claimed to have been used by Spīdala, the witch of the Lāčplēsis epic, as a means of transportation, though this would make it a behemoth of broomsticks.

ABPARK (Lēdmanes pag.; w abpark.lv; ⊕ Apr–Sep daily, hours vary; €25) The largest amusement park in the Baltics, ABpark opened its doors in 2017. The park's name is inspired by Latvian animated film series Avārijas Brigāde, but other than one play area based on the characters from that series, the theme is not strongly developed, and the park instead comes across as a mish-mash of ideas. A large red robot, the ABpark guardian, welcomes you in from the road. Once inside there are dodgems, lasertag, tube sliding, carousels, a shooting range and virtual reality experiences to keep the children amused for the day, though Disneyland this is not. Among the more unusual attractions are a dinosaur trail, with model dinosaurs dotted about the woods, some making a roar as you pass. And a display of dolls in glass-sided wooden booths illustrating tales like the Wizard of Oz. On-site cafés keep the little ones fuelled with pasta and chicken nuggets. The park is located on the side of road E22, the more direct road from Rīga towards Daugavpils, rather than the A6 hugging the Daugava. It has a large car park, but is not easy to reach without your own wheels. There is, however, a bus to the park on summer weekends, leaving the bus station in the nearest district capital of Ogre in the morning, returning late afternoon.

KOKNESE Some 50km east of Lielvārde, at a bend of the Daugava River, Koknese makes a worthwhile stop, offering both historical and modern attractions. The town's historical attractions centre on the **Koknese Castle Ruins** (Kokneses pilsdrupas; Kokneses parks; \ 2927 5412; e turisms@aizkraukle.lv; ⊕ May–Oct 09.00–19.00 daily; adult/student €2/1.50). These romantically sited ruins jut out on a promontory between the Daugava and its tributary, the Pērse River. Walls are studded with arched windows, and a cannon has been placed artistically pointing downriver. A torture chamber has been mocked up in one of the few largely intact rooms. While the waters of the rivers now lap at the base of the castle, this is not how things would have looked at the time of its foundation, when it stood over the rivers at an imposing height. The damming of the Daugava to create the Pļaviņas Hydroelectric Station explains the castle's relegation to water level.

It was built in 1209 by Bishop Albert on the site of a Livonian wooden castle. Enjoying a strategic position on the trade routes of the Daugava, Koknese, then known as Kokenhusen, secured city rights in 1277 and joined the Hanseatic League. The place was ransacked by Ivan the Terrible in 1577, and dealt a further blow during the Great Northern War in 1701 when a retreating Polish-Saxon army blew up the place to avoid it falling into Russian hands. The castle has remained a ruin ever since. It is set in the wooded **Koknese Park**, landscaped in 1900, which makes for a pleasant stroll.

The modern attraction is a memorial park named **Likteņdārzs** (w liktendarzs. lv; ⊕ May–Oct 08.00–17.00 Mon–Fri, 09.30–18.00 Sat–Sun, Nov & Apr 09.30–16.00 Sat–Sun; car park €2), lying on the right bank of the Daugava just east of the town, with a signposted turning off the A6 a couple of kilometres out of town. There is also a footpath, the **Kokneses dabas taka**, running scenically along the riverbank from Likteņdārzs to the castle ruins. Likteņdārzs means 'the Garden of Destiny', and the memorial garden, still under construction, honours Latvians who suffered or died during the traumatic events of the 20th century. Japanese monk and garden designer Shunmyō Masuno has developed the overall concept for the garden.

It centres on an amphitheatre of stones and soil, surrounded by a moat which is said to represent the tears of the perished. Friends Alley, running to the amphitheatre, is made of stones bearing the names of supporters of the project. The garden impresses as a collective undertaking, with evidence of the contributions of Latvian citizens and organisations, from stones to soil to bridges, at every turn. A wooden observation terrace provides a good spot to contemplate the river. Nearby are the remnants of trenches from World War I, with rocks sculpted by Ojārs Feldbergs serving as a memorial to the Latvian Riflemen. A winding Alley of Destiny features pillars with QR codes describing significant moments of Latvian 20th-century history. An Assembly House, with a slanted roof doubling as a viewing platform, offers conference facilities. Other planned elements of the garden, such as a House of Silence which will celebrate the lives of those who created independent Latvia, have at the time of writing yet to materialise, and it is currently not straightforward to envisage how this rich collection of symbolic elements will hang together.

Koknese is a stop on the railway line between Daugavpils (2hrs) and Rīga (1.5hrs). There are also bus connections to Rīga (1.5hrs) and other destinations along the Daugava.

PĻAVIŅAS This small town is attractively sited on the banks of the Daugava. It gives its name to the Pļaviņas Hydroelectric Power Station, the largest in the Baltic States, and opened in 1968 in the face of considerable local opposition, given the loss of both habitats and iconic natural features, notably the 18m-high Staburags cliff. Despite the name, the power station is located almost 40km to the west, at Aizkraukle.

Lying to the west of the town alongside the main A6 road between Rīga and Daugavpils, **Liepkalni maiznīca** ('Liepsalas', Klintaines pag.; w liepkalni.lv; €€€), a branch of the Liepkalni bakery, is an institution and a favoured stopping place to break up that journey. There is a shop focused on Liepkalni bread and bakery products, an upmarket souvenir shop in a separate pavilion, and a café with a terrace and children's play area. The menu ranges from *karbonāde* to baked salmon. It is always busy and fronts a particularly attractive stretch of the Daugava. The island just offshore houses a small temple (Lokstenes dievturu svētnīca) devoted to the pagan Latvian religion of Dievturība, though this is not usually accessible to visitors.

CENTRAL VIDZEME

The central part of Vidzeme has some of the highest ground in Latvia, though with the highest point in the country just 312m above sea level, the hills here are gentle and undulating rather than mountainous. This has not prevented the area from becoming a favoured winter destination for Latvians in search of ski slopes, but it is rarely visited by international travellers. The main district capital in the area, Madona, has little of tourist interest, but there are some worthwhile stops in the surrounding region.

CESVAINE A small town with a population barely above 1,000, Cesvaine is of interest as the home of one of the showiest palaces in Latvia. Across the road in front of the palace, the former palace stables, attractively decorated with carved timbers, now serve as home to the **tourist information centre** (Cesvaines Tūrisma centrs; Pils iela 2; w cesvaine.lv; ⊕ summer 10.00–18.00 Tue–Sat, 10.00–17.00 Sun, winter 09.00–17.00 Tue–Fri, 10.00–17.00 Sat).

There are frequent **bus** connections to Madona (25mins), the closest district capital, and more sporadic ones to other Vidzeme destinations, including Valmiera and Gulbene.

 Where to stay and eat

Grašu Pils (10 rooms & a separate house) Graši, Cesvaine; w hotelgrasupils.lv. Some 4km outside Cesvaine along unmetalled roads, this is a former aristocratic residence dating from the 18th century, now converted into a hotel linked to the Children's Village of Graši charitable foundation. It is a comfortable & welcoming place, but note that no meals other than b/fast are available. €€

Kuilis krodziņš Augusta Saulieša iela 2B; ✆2648 9404. Cesvaine does not offer a wide choice of eateries, but this centrally located wooden building close to the Sūla River serves up hearty platefuls, even if most of the dishes are variants of *karbonāde*. €€

What to see and do **Cesvaine Palace** (Cesvaines pils; Pils iela 1; ✆2833 7703; e pils@cesvaine.lv; ⊕ 10.00–18.00 Tue–Thu & Sun, 10.00–19.00 Fri–Sat; adult/ student €6/3) was built between 1893 and 1896 for Baron Adolf von Wulf, owner of the Cesvaine manor, in an eclectic style combining Gothic, Romanesque, Renaissance and Art Nouveau elements. Forming a U-shape, with an open yard in which stands the main entrance, it features a circular tower with a spire topped with an impressive weathervane, loggias, steep tiled roofs and a proliferation of tall chimneys. It was used as a school from 1919, was damaged by a fire in 2002, and is now gradually being restored. As such, the interior is less impressive than the grand exterior, but there are some nice features, including the fireplace in the dining room propped up by carved bears. A spiral staircase off the dining room takes you up the tower, where a balcony offers good views over the palace park. Most of the rooms remain largely bare, save for temporary art exhibitions, though several feature murals and painted stucco ceilings.

In the shadow of the palace stand a few remnants of the **medieval castle** of Cesvaine, constructed by the Archbishopric of Rīga in the late 14th century. Behind and below the castle, a landscaped park covers 30ha, the Sūla River flowing picturesquely through it. The park incorporates an ancient castle mound, known locally as **Baron's Hill** (Baronkalns), for on the top of it lies the grave of Adolf von Wulf, marked with a metal cross on top of a simple tombstone. He died in 1904 at the age of 46, having had just a few years in which to enjoy his remarkable palace.

GAIZIŅKALNS The ascent of the highest peak in Latvia is not the most challenging of climbs. Gaiziņkalns stands just 312m above sea level, and the walk up from the car park on its slopes is but a pleasant stroll. The 2km **Gaiziņkalns nature trail** offers an enjoyable circuit encompassing the car park, summit and the Gaiziņš ski complex at the base. The hill takes its name from the Latvian word *gaišzinis*, meaning 'clairvoyant', as it is said that the peak is able to forecast the weather. If it is covered in mist, rain will follow within the next three days. The sides of the hill are punctuated by ski slopes and lifts, and the summit is topped by a Latvian flag as well as a wooden mock-up of the red-brick observation tower built here in 1981 during the Soviet occupation, though never completed and later demolished. The hill was one of the triangulation points of the Struve Geodetic Arc (page 216), though the original marker dating from 1824 was apparently demolished when the observation tower was built. Gaiziņkalns is 20km west of the district capital, Madona. Roads are unmetalled close to the hill. The nearest bus stop is about 2km away, at Garkāji, served by infrequent buses from Madona (about 30mins).

KALSNAVA ARBORETUM Run by the Latvian State Forests organisation, the **Kalsnava Arboretum** (Kalsnavas arboretums; 'Ogu īves', Jaunkalsnava; w mammadaba.lv; ⊕ 16 Oct–30 Apr 10.00–15.00 Mon–Fri, 1 May–15 Oct 09.00–18.00 Tue–Fri, 10.00–17.00 Sat, 10.00–15.00 Sun; adult/student/child €8/4/3) was established in 1975 to develop a collection of foreign shrubs and trees potentially suitable for planting in these climes, as well as to conduct forestry research. Covering 144ha and fenced for the better protection of its woody inhabitants, the arboretum has stands of various trees and shrubs, with a rhododendron trail beneath the pines and a collection of peonies among the highlights in season. There is an observation tower for a bird's-eye view over the site, and a small activity centre for children. With a modern ticket office and large car park, the place is immaculate. It lies 30km southwest of Madona, just off the P37 road running between Madona and Pļaviņas. The village of Jaunkalsnava is a stop on the train route between Rīga and Madona (around 2hrs from Rīga), though served only by one or two trains daily. There are also bus connections from Jaunkalsnava to Madona, Pļaviņas and Rīga.

TEIČI NATURE RESERVE Established in 1982 and covering almost 20,000ha, the nature reserve is focused around the Teiči Bog, one of the largest and best preserved in the Baltic States. This is a raised bog, which reaches heights up to 7m above the surrounding area through peat formation. Since the peat lies above the groundwater, the bog is fed solely by rainwater, which is low in minerals, providing an environment dominated by sphagnum moss, though other plant species here include ferns and orchids. Lakes are often found around the moss domes, and the reserve contains 18 lakes larger than 1ha, making it an important bird site. The black-throated loon, more usually found in lands to the north of Latvia, is a symbol of Teiči, building its nests on islands in the lakes. The reserve is also important as a breeding ground for black grouse and wood grouse.

Teiči is a wetland site of international importance designated under the Ramsar Convention, and is protected in Latvia as a 'strict nature reserve', the highest level of protection available. This means that visits are only allowed in certain areas, only in summer months, and only if accompanied by an inspector of the Nature Conservation Agency (call ✆2913 9677 at least 3 days in advance; Jun–Oct only). Casual visitors can, however, get a glimpse of the place by climbing an **observation tower** (Skatu tornis, Teiču dabas rezervāts) at the side of the A12 road at Kristakrūgs between Jekabpils and Rēzekne. The tower takes you above the line of trees flanking the road for a sight of the bog beyond.

ALŪKSNE

Alūksne is a district capital of some 6,000 people in a relatively elevated area of eastern Latvia, close to the borders of Estonia and Russia. This part of the country, sometimes known as Maliena, has a reputation for the longest winters and shortest summers in Latvia, but Alūksne, attractively sited along the shore of a lake of the same name and with historic buildings linked to the Livonian Order and to the aristocratic von Vietinghoff family, makes for an enjoyable destination.

HISTORY Settled by Latgalians, Alūksne was conquered by the Livonian Order in 1224 and became known as Marienburg in honour of Mary, mother of Jesus. A stone castle was built on Lake Alūksne in 1342. Marienburg fell to Russia in 1560, became part of the Polish–Lithuanian Commonwealth in 1582 and then the Swedish Empire from 1629. In 1702, during the Great Northern War, Russian forces under Count Boris Sheremetev took the town, its Swedish defenders destroying much of the castle rather than let it fall into Russian hands. When in 1721 Vidzeme became part of the Russian Empire, Alūksne lost its military importance as a border fortress. The manor of Alūksne was acquired in 1753 by Otto Hermann von Vietinghoff, a member of a Baltic aristocratic family with long connections to the place. Otto was an influential figure within the Russian Empire, his possessions and authority in the Vidzeme region so great that he was dubbed the 'Half-King of Livonia'. The von Vietinghoff family played a central role in the affairs of Alūksne until their departure for Germany in the wake of World War I. A fire in 1940 damaged the town centre, but Alūksne today is a prosperous and attractive place, the hub of the Maliena region.

GETTING THERE AND AWAY Alūksne's **bus station** (Alūksnes autoosta; Pils iela 72; ✆6432 2157) is centrally located, sharing its building with a Rimi supermarket. There are at least five departures daily to Rīga (3hrs 10mins for the fastest buses).

One form of transport which is also one of Alūksne's biggest attractions is the **Gulbene–Alūksne Narrow-Gauge Railway** (Gulbene-Alūksne bānītis; Jāņkalna iela 52; w banitis.lv). This is a 33km stretch of 750mm gauge railway running

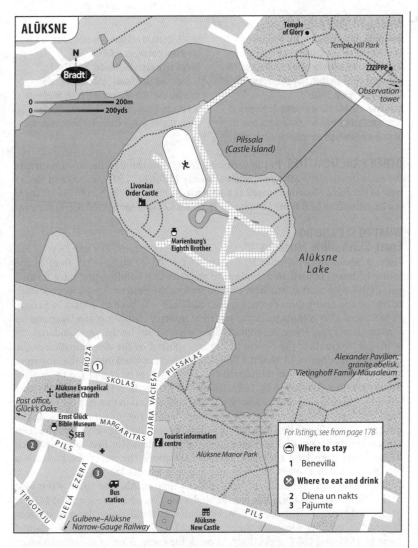

ALŪKSNE

N

Bradt

0 — 200m
0 — 200yds

Temple of Glory ●

Temple Hill Park

ZZZiPPP ●

Observation tower

Pilssala
(Castle Island)

Livonian
Order Castle

Marienburg's
Eighth Brother

Alūksne
Lake

BRŪŽA

①

SKOLAS

PILSSALAS

Alexander Pavilion;
granite obelisk,
Vietinghoff Family Mausoleum

Alūksne Evangelical
Lutheran Church

Post office,
Glück's Oaks

Ernst Glück
Bible Museum

$ SEB

OJĀRA VĀCIEŠA

MARGARITAS

PILS

②

Tourist information
centre

Alūksne Manor Park

TIRGOTĀJU

LIELĀ EZERA

③

Bus
station

Gulbene–Alūksne
Narrow-Gauge Railway

Alūksne
New Castle

PILS

For listings, see from page 178

⊖ **Where to stay**

1   Benevilla

⊗ **Where to eat and drink**

2   Diena un nakts
3   Pajumte

between Alūksne and the neighbouring district capital of Gulbene, the last surviving remnant of the much longer Pļaviņas to Valka line, built in 1903 when narrow-gauge railways were used to connect rural settlements to the broad-gauge network. The train runs twice daily in each direction (€5), using a diesel locomotive. Buy your ticket on the train. Additionally, a steam train is run on selected Saturdays in summer. There is an interesting exhibition on the history of the line at the Alūksne station, in a large wooden building that once housed a luggage shed (⊕ May–Oct 10.00–18.00 Tue–Sun, Nov–Apr 10.00–17.00 Tue–Sun).

TOURIST INFORMATION   Alūksne's **tourist information centre** (Alūksnes Tūrisma informācijas centrs; Ojāra Vācieša iela 1; w visitaluksne.lv; ⊕ 09.00–17.00 Mon–Fri, 10.00–15.00 Sat–Sun) is in a modern wooden chalet at the town centre end of the Alūksnes muižas parks.

Benevilla (6 rooms) Brūža iela 8; w benevilla.lv. This small hotel close to the Evangelical Lutheran Church provides a comfortable central option. Its restaurant (€€€) is open only on evenings Tue–Fri & all day Sat. €€€

Pajumte Pils iela 68; w pajumte.lv. Brightly lit central restaurant with functional décor over 2 floors & a surprisingly adventurous menu, from

catfish steaks to red deer. Also offers pizza & a good range of salads. €€€€

Diena un nakts Pils iela 58; ☎2922 6073; e eevita.kalnina@inbox.lv. This central café opposite the Bible Museum is cheerily filled with pot plants. Alongside cakes & pastries, it offers filling staples such as *karbonāde* & pancakes. €€

OTHER PRACTICALITIES Pils iela, running east–west through the town centre, is the main drag, hosting the **post office** (Pils iela 21; ☎6432 2501), a couple of blocks west of the Bible Museum, as well as a **pharmacy** (Pils iela 27A; ☎2037 7471). There is a branch of the **SEB Bank** (Brūža iela 1; ☎2666 8777; ⊕ Mon, Wed & Fri) close by.

WHAT TO SEE AND DO

Ernst Glück Bible Museum (Ernsta Glika Bībeles muzejs; Pils iela 25A; ☎2562 7589; e bibeles.muzejs@inbox.lv; ⊕ May–Oct 10.00–17.00 Tue–Sat; free) In the centre of town, housed in a diminutive pavilion-like building that once formed part of the town market, and later a petrol station, the museum showcases the work of one of the town's most famous residents. Glück was born in Wettin in Saxony in 1652, and after coming to Latvia served as military chaplain of the Daugavgrīva fortress near Rīga. There, he embarked on what would be the great undertaking of his life, to translate the Bible into Latvian, spurred by the determination of the Swedish king, Charles XI, that the Bible should be translated into all the languages of his domains. Glück was transferred to Alūksne where he completed the bulk of the work of the translation by 1689. Glück and his family were taken to Moscow when the Russians captured Alūksne in 1704, and he died in that city the following year. His foster daughter, Marta Skowrońska, would rise to greater fame as the future bride of Peter the Great, on his death becoming Empress Catherine I of Russia. The one-room museum has a couple of examples of the first Latvian printed Bible, dating from 1694 and using Glück's translation. The rest of the museum is mostly devoted to a collection of donated Bibles in various languages.

There is another reminder of Ernst Glück's time in Alūksne some 600m west of the Bible Museum along Pils iela. Behind a long wooden house named Mācītāj muiža (Pils iela 15), the site of Glück's residence, stand two oak trees, in front of which a boulder identifies them as **Glück's Oaks** (Glika ozoli). He planted these in 1685 and 1689 respectively, to mark the completion of the translation of each Testament.

Alūksne Evangelical Lutheran Church (Alūksnes evaņģēliski luteriskā baznīca; Pils iela 25) Behind the Bible Museum stands this Neoclassical church, built in the 1780s by Rīga architect Christoph Haberland, at the instigation of Baron Otto Hermann von Vietinghoff. If the church is open, ask to climb the stairs to the tower for a fine view across the lake. Taking in the view has been a feature of the church from the outset: the Baron instructed that an unusually sturdy wooden tower staircase be constructed to facilitate his guests' enjoyment of it.

Alūksne New Castle (Alūksnes Jaunā pils; Pils iela 74) The most impressive building in town stands on the eastern side of the centre: the crenellated New Castle, commissioned in 1864 by Baron Alexander von Vietinghoff in a Tudor neo-Gothic style. In the interwar period it housed the Seventh Sigulda Infantry Regiment, and is now home to two museums.

Alūksne District Museum (Alūksnes novada muzejs; Pils iela 74; w aluksnespils.lv; ⊕ Jun–Aug 10.00–17.00 Tue–Wed & Fri–Sat, 10.00–18.00 Thu, 10.00–16.00 Sun, Sep–May 10.00–17.00 Tue–Wed & Fri–Sat, 10.00–18.00 Thu; adult/student €6/4) This packages the history of the town into an exhibition entitled 'feast of centuries', focused on a huge wooden dining table into which exhibits ranging from 12th-century jewellery to a Soviet Pioneer tie have been studded. There is a room dedicated to local-born artist Leo Kokle and his portraits of bright young ladies of the early 1960s. Kokle died in Rīga in 1964 at the age of just 40. Also here is a room showcasing 120 dolls, each wearing the traditional ladies' dress of a different settlement in Latvia. They are the work of Austra Linde, a local woman living in exile in the USA in the Soviet period, who created the dolls as an affirmation of her Latvian identity.

'Environment Labyrinth' Nature Museum (Dabas muzeja 'Vides labirints'; Pils iela 74; ☏2862 4196; e aldis.verners@inbox.lv; ⊕ 11.00–14.00 Tue & Fri–Sat, 14.00–18.00 Wed; adult/student €5/3) The other museum in the castle is a privately run nature museum, whose owners are passionate about their collection, which includes a display of fluorescent minerals.

Alūksne Manor Park (Alūksnes muižas parks) Running down the slope between the New Castle and the shores of Alūksne Lake, and extending along the lakeshore to the east, the park was laid out in the late 18th and early 19th centuries. Secreted within its wooded grounds, pavilions and pieces of statuary give a good feel for the stately life of the von Vietinghoff family. The wooden **Alexander Pavilion** (Aleksandra paviljons) overlooking the lake was named in honour of Tsar Alexander I, who visited the town, and was a favourite tea-drinking spot for the von Vietinghoffs. A little further on, a granite **obelisk** was erected in 1799 by Christoph Burchard von Vietinghoff in honour of his father Otto, whose relief is depicted on the front. In a corner of the park is the circular metal-domed **Vietinghoff Family Mausoleum** (Fītinghofu dzimtas mausolejs), dating from 1831. The interior can be viewed through a metal grille, but is bare. More unexpectedly, a video projected on to the walls tells you the story of the family in a range of languages. Other small temples in the grounds were dedicated to Aeolus, Greek ruler of the winds, and Pomona, Roman goddess of fruitful abundance. There is also a Bird Pavilion, with grilles for walls, though no longer any caged birds.

Alūksne Lake (Alūksnes ezers) The lake provides the town with its playground. A bridge at the western edge of Alūksne Manor Park takes you across to **Pilssala** (Castle Island), a place dedicated to recreation, and housing Alūksne's summer beach. Here also stand the ruins of the **Livonian Order Castle** (Livonijas ordeņa pilsdrupas), whose crumbling romance is dented by the ugly concrete stage built in the middle of the place. One circular tower has been reconstructed and now accommodates a 30-minute sound and light performance entitled **Marienburg's Eighth Brother** (Marienburgas astotais brālis; Pilssalas iela 5; ☏ 2914 9810; e astotaisbralis@aluksne.lv; ⊕ May–Oct 11.00–17.00 Wed–Sun, Nov–Apr 10.00–16.00 Wed–Sun; adult/child €6/4). With performances running every 40 minutes, this tells in music and spoken word a convoluted story involving the eight towers of the castle as brothers, each in love with a girl named Maria. The eighth brother

eventually woos Maria by dint of his wondrous singing when transformed into a Moon Bird, but this singing has the unfortunate effect of putting the defenders of the castle to sleep. The eighth brother blows up the fortress rather than allowing it to fall to the invaders, a reference to the historical destruction of the castle in 1702 to prevent it falling into Russian hands. But the eighth brother has now been reawakened by the sound of Maria's voice, and both live on happily.

Temple Hill Park (Templakalna parks) On the far side of Pilssala, a wooden footbridge takes you over Alūksne Lake to this further attractive expanse of wooded parkland. The bridge plays romantic music at the start of every hour, so don't be entirely surprised to find yourself crossing the lake to the strains of 'My Way'. Temple Hill was the site of a Latgalian fortification from the 9th to 13th centuries, and now offers a network of paths over a wooded hill with views down to the lake. Among the attractions is the **Temple of Glory** (Slavas templis), a rotunda supported by six Doric columns, placed on the spot where in 1702 the Livonian Order Castle on Pilssala was fired upon. The rotunda was erected in 1807 at the initiative of Baron Christoph Burchard von Vietinghoff to honour the commander of the Russian forces in the 1702 battle, Count Boris Sheremetev, but also the Swedish commander, Captain Wolf, for his refusal to allow the Russians to take the castle intact. Further east is an **observation tower** (skatu tornis; Miera iela 34; \2913 0280; ⊕ May–Oct 11.00–19.00 Tue–Sun; €1). Built of tree trunks, at 37.8 metres it is among the tallest such towers in Latvia, and offers, as you would expect, a good view across the lake to the town beyond. Braver visitors, or perhaps those wishing to avoid another burst of 'My Way', can return to Pilssala by a zipline across the lake, courtesy of **ZZZIPPP** (Templakalna iela 6A; \2871 8728; e ziplinealuksne@ gmail.com; ⊕ 11.00–19.00 daily in summer but weather dependent; Mon–Tue €15, Wed–Sun €20). Take-off is close to the observation tower.

GULBENE

The town at the southern end of the Gulbene–Alūksne Narrow-Gauge Railway is overshadowed tourism-wise by the attractions of Alūksne, its northern partner, but Gulbene has some sights of its own. The Archbishopric of Rīga constructed a castle here in the 14th century on the mound of an earlier Latgalian fortress, though this is long destroyed. The manor of Vecgulbene came into the hands of the von Wolff family in 1802, and much of the touristic interest of Gulbene today has, as we shall see, been fuelled by the romantic acts of Baron Heinrich von Wolff. The modern town centre lies to the north of the manor buildings and contains little of touristic interest. It was known in German as Schwanenburg, and that bird also provides the town's Latvian name – 'gulbis' meaning swan.

GETTING THERE AND AWAY Gulbene **railway station** (Dzelzceļa stacija; Dzelzceļa iela 8; \6441 6371) is an imposing building, the work of architect Pēteris Feders and dating from 1926. It was bombed in 1944 and later reconstructed. The large size of the station building gives, however, an inaccurate picture of its actual importance, as there are at the time of writing but three passenger trains a week to Rīga, focused on the weekend. There is no longer a ticket office – you need to buy tickets online or on the train.

Gulbene is, though, a special place for railway enthusiasts as the southern terminus of the Gulbene–Alūksne Narrow-Gauge Railway (page 176). All that space in the railway station building is now occupied by the **'Railway and**

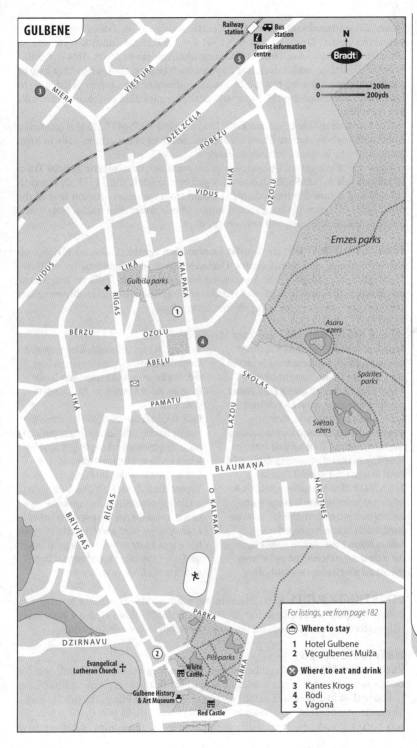

GULBENE

Railway station
Bus station
Tourist information centre

N

Bradt

0 _____ 200m
0 _____ 200yds

MIERA
VIESTURA
DZELZCEĻA
ROBEŽU
VIDUS
LIKĀ
OZOLU

Emzes parks

VIDUS
LIKĀ
O KALPAKA
Gulbišu parks

BĒRZU
OZOLU
ĀBEĻU

Asaru ezers

Spārītes parks

SKOLAS
LAZDU

RIGAS
LIKA
PAMATU

Svētais ezers

BLAUMAŅA

O KALPAKA
NĀKOTNES

BRĪVĪBAS
RIGAS

PARKA

For listings, see from page 182

🛏 Where to stay
1 Hotel Gulbene
2 Vecgulbenes Muiža

DZIRNAVU

Evangelical Lutheran Church ✝

Gulbene History & Art Museum 🏛

Pils parks

White Castle 🏰

PARKA

✖ Where to eat and drink
3 Kantes Krogs
4 Rodi
5 Vagonā

Red Castle 🏰

Steam' Educational and Interactive Centre ('Dzelzceļš un Tvaiks' izglītojošs un interaktīvs centrs; Dzelzceļa iela 8; ☏2544 8661; e dzelzcelsuntvaiks@gulbene.lv; ⏰ 10.00–18.00 Mon–Sat, 10.00–15.00 Sun; adult/student €6.50/5). This is a child-oriented exhibition with interactive displays, each bearing the sponsorship logo of a local company, showing how pulleys work, warning of the dangers of listening to loud music while walking close to a railway track, or inviting you to test your skills as a train driver.

The **bus station** (Gulbenes autoosta; Dzelzceļa iela 6B; ☏6447 1788) is located in front of the railway station. There are approximately eight departures daily to Rīga, two or three to Valmiera and five to Balvi.

Given that the sights of Gulbene are quite spread out, the **Gulbene Tourist Train** (Dzelzceļa iela 8; ☏2655 7582; e turists@gulbene.lv; adult/child €5/3.50) is worth considering. It runs five times daily (3 on Sun) from the railway station around the main sights of the town, though travelling on wheels rather than tracks. Note that it only operates in summer, and only on dry days.

TOURIST INFORMATION The **tourist information centre** (Gulbenes tūrisma un kultūrvēsturiskā mantojuma centrs; Dzelzceļa iela 8; w visitgulbene.lv; ⏰ 10.00–18.00 Mon–Sat, 10.00–15.00 Sun) is co-housed with the 'railway and steam' exhibition in the cavernous railway station building. They also sell locally produced ceramics and jewellery, and offer electric bicycle hire.

WHERE TO STAY AND EAT   *Map, page 181*

Vecgulbenes Muiža (14 rooms & 10 dorms) Brīvības iela 18; w vecgulbenesmuiza.lv. Located in the refurbished former riding school of the manor, this is the smartest hotel in town. Rooms run off a gallery above a large brick conference facility. Rooms are characterful, though the absence of curtains over some irregularly shaped windows is awkward. There is a good restaurant (€€€€) with a mix of international dishes. €€€
Hotel Gulbene (23 rooms) O. Kalpaka iela 27A; ☏2942 8585; e hotelgulbene@inbox.lv. A refurbished Soviet-era hotel in an ugly 4-storey concrete block in the town centre. The rooms are bland, but the location is good. €€
Kantes Krogs Miera iela 5; w kanteskrogs.lv. Out of the centre in the northern part of town, this popular place is a large wooden building,

with large wooden tables inside & large swings in the garden. Everything about the place is large, including the menu, which ranges from Latvian favourites like *karbonāde* & potato pancakes to sushi. €€€
Rodi O. Kalpaka iela 60; ☏2560 3460. Within the concrete building of the Gulbene Cultural Centre, this is a central pizzeria also offering burgers, pancakes, kebabs & *pelmeni*, served up at American-diner-style booths or an outdoor terrace. €€€
Vagona Dzelzceļa iela 8A; ☏2000 7650; e cafevagona@gmail.com. Just outside the railway station, this café is appropriately housed in a railway wagon. Sit on one of the tables crammed inside, or on a table on the lawn nearby. As well as good coffee, they offer a limited menu of burgers, chicken tortilla & Belgian waffles. €€

OTHER PRACTICALITIES Rīgas iela, running north–south through the town centre, houses the **post office** (Rīgas iela 28/30; ☏6449 7690). There is also a **pharmacy** (Rīgas iela 55A; ☏2037 7163) on the same street, opposite Gulbišu parks.

WHAT TO SEE AND DO

Vecgulbene Manor (Vecgulbenes muiža) The historic centre of Gulbene lies on the southern edge of the modern town, and is focused on a series of buildings linked to the old aristocratic manor in the green setting of **Pils parks** (Castle Park). The main manor building, known as the **White Castle** (Baltā pils; Brīvības iela 12), was once a grand neo-Renaissance palace, but the depredations of history have weighed heavy, and it is now in a parlous state, its ruined walls mostly exposed red brick rather than white.

More rewarding is the former orangery of the manor, which now houses the **Gulbene History and Art Museum** (Gulbenes novada vēstures un mākslas muzejs; Pils iels 3; w gulbenesmuzejs.lv; ⊕ 16 Sep–14 May 10.00–17.00 Tue–Fri, 10.00–16.00 Sat; 15 May–15 Sep also 10.00–16.00 Sun; adult/student €6/3 including barn & Red Castle). There are photographs showing the former splendour of the Red and White castles, as well as some of their occupants, notably the bushy bearded Heinrich von Wolff and his beloved wife Marisa, also known as Maria.

The permanent exhibits of the museum focus, though, on two prominent local artists, both named Jūlijs. There is a collection of furniture designed in the early 20th century by Jūlijs Madernieks in a national romantic style. And a display of modern carpets made in Iran but inspired by the designs of Madernieks and our second Jūlijs, Straume, a specialist in textile art who spent 16 years in Georgia from 1907. The museum also has a miscellaneous ethnographic collection, ranging from looms to scythes via an old movie projector, in a converted barn across Brīvības iela, and offers temporary art exhibitions in both their main building and in the Red Castle. Note that a refurbishment of the orangery building was planned at the time of writing, so the location of the collections may change.

The neo-Gothic **Red Castle** (Sarkanā pils; Parka iela 10) lies to the east, its bricks slightly redder in hue than those of the White Castle. It is better preserved than that building, though still but a shadow of its former glories. It was built in the late 19th century as a gift from Baron Heinrich von Wolff for his beloved wife, Marisa. As you approach the castle you may hear it talking to itself, for speakers project a 30-minute imagined dialogue in Latvian between Heinrich and Marisa, as they admire the splendour of the manor and talk about the future. Nearby, note the statue of cupid on a cylindrical plinth, a modern work inspired by the statues that adorned the park in its heyday. There are also two empty plinths, with metal steps, to allow you and your beloved to pose for a romantic photo as human statues. Perfect for the statuesque couple.

On the other side of Brīvības iela from the Castle Park stands the **Evangelical Lutheran Church** (Gulbenes Evaņģēliski luteriskā baznīca; Brīvības iela 12; ☏2643 3632; ⊕ 10.00–20.00 daily). Dating from 1843, the church currently lacks a tower, a victim of World War II. There is an ongoing campaign to restore it. A statue of Martin Luther stands in front of the entrance. It was put up in 1883, on the 400th anniversary of the birth of the leader of the Protestant Reformation. The church occupies the site of both the Latgalian hill fort and the castle of the Archbishopric of Rīga, and thus marks the historic centre of the town.

Town centre Swan motifs are everywhere in Gulbene. Swans feature on the coats of arms of both town and district, there are swan murals and swan-themed flower beds. There is even a swan-themed sundial (a swandial?) in the grounds of one of the schools. The centre of gravity of all this swan worship is **Gulbišu parks** (Swan Park) in the centre of town. There is a pond here overlooked by a large bronze swan in the process of feeding its cygnet, and a series of benches featuring swan-themed designs of different styles and antiquities. What the park lacks, however, is actual living swans.

To spot a real swan you have to head to a different area of parkland on the eastern side of town. This large, wooded park was originally known as Marijas parks, and was laid out by Baron Heinrich von Wolff to honour his wife. It today has two names. The smaller southern part is named **Spārites parks**, and it is here at the pond known as **Svētais ezers** (Holy Lake) that Gulbene's one remaining live swan is to be found, a black swan rather touchingly named Heinrich. The authorities are taking no chances with his safety. He swims in a section of the pond protected by a fence and guarded by CCTV. Baron Heinrich built the pond following his wife's early death in 1883: it is said that a letter of Marisa's name was inscribed in stone on each of the islets. Just beyond a Soviet-era war memorial, **Asaru ezers** (Tear Lake) is even more mournful – it is named for the island in the middle which has the shape of a tear. The larger and wilder northern part of the park is named **Emzes parks**, now a protected dendrological plantation. In keeping with the theme of Heinrich's love for Marisa, this park features a lake shaped in the form of a letter 'M'. (The name of the park is a Latvian transliteration of the German 'M-See', or 'M Lake'.) The 3.2km-long **Heinrich's Forest Trail** (Heinriha meža taka) takes you through both parks.

EASTERN VIDZEME

While Alūksne is the main draw in this part of the country, there are some interesting destinations amid the fields and forests in the wider area.

ZELTIŅI MISSILE BASE An abandoned nuclear missile base at Zeltiņi offers fascinating if decaying reminders of the Cold War hidden within its forest setting. A secret site during the Soviet period, construction of the base began in 1958 and missiles with nuclear warheads were located here from 1962 until the end of the 1980s. The last Soviet troops left the base in 1991. The base comprised two zones. A military base accommodated troops of the Alūksne Missile Regiment. Beyond this was an even more strongly protected missile launch zone, with four launch pads. Driving or walking into the territory of the former base, you first pass a derelict brick building that was the checkpoint for the base, before reaching the crumbling apartment blocks of the base itself. Beyond this is the checkpoint building into the launch zone. When the base was in operation this was protected by a high electric fence and mines. The roads in the base are paved with concrete slabs.

There are four rocket hangars, and adjacent rocket launch sites. On one of these a huge **head of Lenin** makes an incongruous site. It once stood in Alūksne, but was moved here during the wave of demolition of Lenin monuments marking Latvia's National Reawakening. One notable structure within the launch zone is the earth-covered reinforced-concrete Signallers' Hangar. The largest room within it still has a drawing on one wall of a signaller in action, a large missile standing behind him. On the opposite wall are inscriptions in Russian warning of possible threats to the base: 'paratrooper attack'; 'radioactive cloud approaching'; 'air strike'. Note that although you are free to wander across the base, many of the structures are in parlous condition, so take care and pay heed to warning signs.

The base is 25km southwest of Alūksne, just off road P34 beyond the village of Zeltiņi. The village, from where the base is walkable, is served by a couple of buses a day from Alūksne. If you have your own transport you can drive right into the site. A downloadable audio guide is available (see w izi.travel).

STĀMERIENA Some 26km south of Alūksne, towards the adjacent district capital of Gulbene, the village of Stāmeriena is of interest for the **Stāmeriena Palace** (Stāmerienas pils; Vecstāmeriena; w stamerienaspils.eu; ⏰ 10.00–18.00 Tue–Fri, 10.00–20.00 Sat, 10.00–17.00 Sun; adult/student €6/3), formerly owned by the von Wolff family, not to be confused with the von Wulfs, proprietors of Cesvaine.

The grand Baroque Rundāle Palace is the work of Russian court architect Francesco Bartolomeo Rastrelli PAGE 221

above (DG/S)

Stāmeriena Palace was a summer retreat of Giuseppe Tomasi di Lampedusa, celebrated Italian author of *Il Gattopardo* PAGE 184

below (Y/S)

above
(KT/S)
The Peitav-Shul Synagogue in Rīga was built in 1905 in an Art Nouveau style PAGE 99

left
(P/S)
Soviet statues at the Salaspils Memorial tower over the site of a Nazi German concentration camp PAGE 133

below left
(AIB)
The Orthodox Church of the Holy Spirit in Jēkabpils, home to the Wonder-Working Icon of the Mother of God of Jakobstadt PAGE 215

below
(SM/S)
Bauska Castle commands an imposing position at the confluence of the Mūsa and Mēmele rivers PAGE 219

Cēsis Castle was once the mightiest fortress of Livonia PAGE 168   top (A/S)

Picturesque Kuldīga, inscribed on the UNESCO World Heritage list in 2023 PAGE 259   above (B/S)

Following the damming of the Daugava River, water laps at the ruins of Koknese Castle PAGE 173   below (VJ/S)

above and top left
(AP/S & LL/S)
Weaving traditions are maintained at craft centres across Latvia; the ethnographic signs woven into Latvian belts have complex meanings PAGE 20

above right
(AIB)
Groups prepare for the Latvian Song and Dance Festival at a regional event in Dobele PAGES 54 & 231

below
(LT)
Celebrated with gusto, Midsummer is the most uninhibited festival in the Latvian calendar PAGE 53

Built in 1852, the Āraiši Windmill still operates today PAGE 163 above left (AIB)

Caves fashioned by hand in the sandstone outcrops around Līgatne are used to store vegetables PAGE 161 above right (AIB)

Bread is at the heart of the Latvian diet: learn all about it at the Aglona Bread Museum PAGE 208 right (JB)

Museums across Latvia offer re-creations of bygone rural living. Pictured here: Pāvilosta Local History Museum PAGE 268 below (JB)

<table>
<tr><td>above
(AIB)</td><td>Take the Great Ķemeri Bog Boardwalk over one of the largest raised bogs in Latvia PAGE 132</td></tr>
<tr><td>left
(VTIC)</td><td>The grazing of wild horses helps defend Latvia's meadowlands from forest encroachment</td></tr>
<tr><td>below
(DS/S)</td><td>Sunset from the White Dune at Saulkrasti PAGE 137</td></tr>
</table>

The Daugava River is at the heart of Latvian identity PAGE 170

above
(OK)

Birdwatching at the Venta Rapid – Europe's widest waterfall – in Kuldīga PAGE 263

right
(IS/S)

Kayaking on the Gauja River

below
(SS)

above
(IK/S)

Latvia has hundreds of kilometres of sandy beaches: Jūrmala (pictured) is the best known PAGE 130

below
(AKu/S)

Crumbling military fortifications along the coast at Karosta, north of Liepāja PAGE 277

Construction of the palace began in 1835, but the place was burned down in the 1905 Revolution, and the present building is largely a 1908 reconstruction, adding Neoclassical and Art Nouveau elements to the earlier neo-Gothic and neo-Renaissance design. The exterior is impressive, with a square-based central tower and steep tiled roofs.

Much of the fascination of Stāmeriena stems from the European connections by marriage made by members of the family. Then owner Boris von Wolff married in 1894 the Italian mezzo-soprano Alice Barbi, a close friend of German composer Brahms in the latter's final years. The Italian connections continued into the next generation: their eldest daughter Alexandra married Giuseppe Tomasi di Lampedusa, celebrated author of the 1958 novel *Il Gattopardo* (*The Leopard*). Stāmeriena was among the few aristocratic mansions not to be nationalised in the Latvian agrarian reforms of the 1920s, and di Lampedusa spent several summers here in the 1930s. The place housed an agriculture school and then a state farm administration during the Soviet period. It is now in the hands of the Gulbene municipality, and its interior is gradually being restored.

The use of candles and piped music gives a romantic feel to tours of the building, which has been made to seem more homely through a miscellaneous collection of donated furniture and ceramics. The grand oak staircase centred on a fireplace which greets you as you enter the building is a highlight of the interior. Also here is an exhibition on local-born artist Leo Svemps, a family tree of the von Wolffs, and even a cardboard cut-out di Lampedusa, wrapped up well in winter coats. The attic houses temporary exhibition space.

The village of Stāmeriena also boasts a fine Orthodox church, scenically positioned along the shore of Lake Stāmeriena. The **St Alexander Nevsky Orthodox Church** (Sv Ņevas Aleksandra pareizticīgo baznīca; Vecstāmeriena; ☏2917 8536) owes its origins to the marriage of Baron Johann Gottlieb Eduard von Wolff with Sofia Potemkina, who was of the Orthodox faith, and at her insistence, a wooden Orthodox church was built here in 1851. The present stone church dates from 1904, and features a tall bell tower above the main entrance and a cluster of silver onion domes. Stāmeriena is served by buses from Gulbene and is also a stop on the Gulbene–Alūksne Narrow-Gauge Railway.

LITENE The village of Litene, 17km east of Gulbene on the P35 road towards Balvi, is known as the scene of a particularly brutal episode of the deportations carried out by the occupying Soviet authorities on 14 June 1941. It targeted the officers of the former Latvian army, which following the Soviet occupation had been merged into the Red Army 24th Territorial Corps. The Latvian troops were brought in early June to Litene and nearby Ostrovieši, developed in the late 1930s as summer camps for the Latgale Division of the Latvian army, in what was billed as a training exercise. On 14 June, Latvian officers were taken in groups into different parts of the forest, on the pretext that this was all part of the exercise. There they were disarmed by the Red Army and NKVD forces, and taken to Gulbene railway station, from where they were sent to labour camps in Siberia. A group of senior Latvian officers at the camp headquarters, set up in the Litene primary school that had in happier times served as a manor house of the Barons von Wolff, were similarly disarmed. Anyone showing resistance was shot on the spot. More than 500 Latvian officers from the two camps were deported. Less than 100 would return.

The remains of 11 Latvian officers were uncovered at one site in the forest in 1988. Their reburial at the **Litene Cemetery** (Litenes kapi) formed part of the Latvian National Reawakening of the late 1980s. The site is now marked by a memorial comprising a wall of stone blocks in the shape of crosses. Inaugurated in 2001, it is known as the 'Wall of Pain', and is the scene of a remembrance event on 14 June each year. There is an Art Deco-style chapel nearby, built in 1937. The cemetery is signposted from the Balvi road, and lies 6km from it on an unmetalled lane.

The fragmentary remains of the **Latvian Army Summer Camp** (Latvijas armijas vasaras nometnes vieta) have been turned into a place of recollection of the tragic events. A clearing in the forest is decorated with an anti-tank gun dating from the 1950s, as well as a small wooden observation tower with a Latvian flag on top. The only surviving structure from the camp is, though, a food storage facility, a windowless basement structure covered by moss, somewhat resembling a nuclear bunker. A campfire next to this, surrounded by wooden benches, is lit each year at the 14 June commemorations. The army camp is also signposted from the P35, the turning east of that to the cemetery. The camp is 3km along an unmetalled road. It is a 4km walk between camp and cemetery.

6

Latgale

The Latgale region of eastern Latvia is distinctive. It takes its name from the Latgalian tribe that inhabited the area before the coming of the crusaders, ruling through the principalities of Jersika and Atzele. Its history took a different path from that of the rest of Latvia when, in 1621, it remained under the control of the Polish–Lithuanian Commonwealth as the Inflanty Voivodeship, rather than forming part of the Swedish Empire as was the fate of the rest of Livonia following the Swedish victory in their war with Poland. This had several important consequences. Under the influence of Catholic Poland rather than Lutheran Sweden, Roman Catholicism remained the dominant faith, a fact still true today, evidenced by the roadside crosses seen throughout the region, though rarely in other parts of Latvia. Another important area of Latgalian distinctiveness is language. The Latgalian tribe spoke the language that has emerged as present-day Latvian, after assimilation with the languages of neighbouring Baltic tribes. But a Latgalian language, related to but distinct from Latvian, emerged through the separate later development of the Latgale region. It now counts around 150,000 speakers, mostly in Latgale. Abutting the Russian border, the ethnic mix of Latgale is different, too, from that of other parts of Latvia, with a large proportion of ethnic Russians, especially in the region's largest city, Daugavpils. Polish and Belarusian minorities are also significant. Historically part of the Pale of Settlement within the Russian Empire in which permanent residency by Jews was allowed, the region was once home to large Jewish communities.

This different ethnic, linguistic and religious mix lies at the root of other areas of distinctiveness between Latgale and other parts of Latvia. Among local crafts, Latgalian pottery has earned a strong reputation (page 194). There are dishes specific to the region, among them *guļbišnīki*, fried potato croquettes with a stuffing of minced meat and onion, *kļockas*, cottage-cheese-filled dumplings, and *asuškas*, dumplings served in a milk and sweet cream sauce. And the people of Latgale have a reputation as the least reserved of Latvia, though this does not mean a Latvian ebullience. Latgale is the poorest region of Latvia, and the tourism industry is less developed than in other areas. Hotels and restaurants tend to be more basic, fewer in number and cheaper than those in other parts of the country. But it is a worthwhile region to visit. Highlights include the lakes that pepper the central part of the region, the meandering Daugava River between Daugavpils and Krāslava, the Tsarist fortress of Daugavpils with its impressive art centre showcasing the work of local-born artist Mark Rothko, and the Roman Catholic centre of pilgrimage at Aglona.

NORTHERN LATGALE

Northern Latgale is well off most tourist itineraries. There are fewer native Russian speakers here than in other parts of the region, but the Latgalian language and culture are strongly embedded.

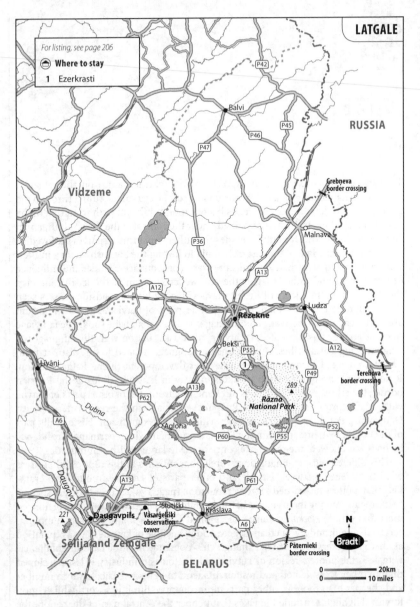

For listing, see page 206

⌂ **Where to stay**

1   Ezerkrasti

RUSSIA

P42

Balvi

P45

P46

Grebņeva
border crossing

P47

Vidzeme

Malnava

P36

A13

A12

Ludza

Rēzekne

Bekši

P55

①

Terehova
border crossing

P49

289

*Rāzna
National Park*

Līvāni

A13

P62

Dubna

P60

P55

P52

Aglona

A6

P61

A12

Daugava

A13

Slutiški

Krāslava

221

Daugavpils

Vasaŗģeliški
observation
tower

A6

N

Bradt

Sēlija and Zemgale

Pāternieki
border crossing

BELARUS

0 ——————— 20km
0 ——————— 10 miles

BALVI The capital of the district covering the northern part of the Latgale region, Balvi is a small town, attractively sited beside the adjacent Balvu and Pērkonu lakes, which are in turn connected by the Bolupe River. The town itself was largely destroyed in July 1944, and its centre bears the marks of Soviet rebuilding, with apartment blocks and a Corinthian-columned cultural centre.

The **tourist information centre** (Balvu novada Tūrisma informācijas centrs; Brīvības iela 46; **w** visit.balvi.lv; ⊕ 08.30–18.00 Mon, 08.30–17.00 Tue–Thu, 08.30–16.00 Fri, but closed for lunch noon–12.30) is housed in the same building as the district museum.

Getting there and away The **bus station** (Balvu autoosta; Brīvības iela 57; ☏ 6452 1707) is centrally located if somewhat hidden away at the back of the Planēta mall. There are seven departures a day to Rīga, three to Alūksne and five to Rēzekne.

What to see and do **Balvi Manor** (Balvu muiža; Brīvības iela 47) was built in the late 18th century, but rebuilt in a Neoclassical style in the 19th. It has suffered various depredations, and now houses a school, showing few signs of its earlier glories. Across the road, its former granary now accommodates the **Balvi District Museum** (Balvu novada muzejs; Brīvības iela 46; ☏ 6452 1430; e muzejs@balvi.lv; ⊕ 10.00–17.00 Tue–Fri, 11.00–16.00 Sat; adult/student €2/0.50). Making extensive use of touch-screen displays, this offers a nicely presented overview of rural life, including local crafts, together with photographs and exhibits recreating Balvi town as it looked before the destruction of World War II. There is also a room devoted to the Latgale Partisan Regiment, formed in 1919 from the Balvu Partisan Regiment, which became a key component of the Latvian army during the War of Independence. Behind the museum is a park known as the **Bear Garden** (Lāča dārzs; Brīvības iela 52) on the site of the manor orchards. It now has the appearance of a meadow criss-crossed with paths and studded with large boulders. There is a pond in the centre with an islet on which stands a boulder fashioned like a throne. An oak tree with a 1.3m circumference, a line of benches around its trunk, stands guard at the edge of the park.

Another park, immediately to the east of Balvi Manor, **Balvi City Park** (Balvu Pilsētas parks; Partizānu iela 2) contains a couple of noteworthy pieces of sculpture. A metal tree-like structure named **Gaiss** ('Air') has numerous wind chimes hanging from it, some embellished with metal shields representing local authorities in Latgale. In the corner of the park is a symbol of the town, the **Monument to the Fallen Soldiers of the Latgale Partisan Regiment**. It features the statue of a young soldier of noble bearing, stepping forward, a rifle by his side. The soldier is known as Staņislavs, for some reason. The statue was erected in 1938, torn down during the Soviet period, but restored in 1993, the latest version the work of Andrejs Jansons, son of original sculptor Kārlis Jansons.

MALNAVA The small village of Malnava, just off the A13 highway a few kilometres south of the Grebņeva border crossing with Russia, has developed around the eponymous **Malnava Manor** (Malnavas muiža). This was once the home of the noble Szadurski family, but has housed an agricultural college since the interwar period. The manor was visited by Adolf Hitler in July 1941, who came to view the headquarters of the German Army Group North, at that point stationed in the house. Mounds occupied by reinforced concrete bunkers in the grounds behind the main building are still referred to by the locals as 'Hitler's bunkers'. There is a bus stop in the centre of the village served by infrequent **buses** from Ludza.

Close by is the **'Latgolys Šmakovka' Distillery** (Latgolys šmakovka muzejs Malnavā; Kļavu iela 11; w latgalessmakovka.lv; ⊕ ring ahead; tour €7, with tasting €10). Šmakovka is Latgalian moonshine, and this place, in an atmospheric white-walled building centred on an ancient-looking still, appears to be of some antiquity. Appearances, however, can be deceptive, and the operation was actually set up just a few years back by spirits enthusiast Jānis Krivtežs in a former dairy. Jānis offers a passionate guided tour of the place, which includes a small museum of hooch-related artefacts.

✗ Where to eat and drink Dzīles (Zaļā iela 9; ☎2653 8016; e dzileslv@gmail.com; €€€€) is a 'home restaurant' which sits around the back of host Ainas family home. She will prepare a hearty and high-quality Latgalian menu, typically running from a starter of salmon pickled in beetroot to a traditional desert of *asuškas*. Booking is essential, at least a day in advance.

WESTERN LATGALE

LĪVĀNI A district capital of 7,000 people at the western edge of the Latgale region on the right bank of the Daugava, near the point at which it is joined by the smaller Dubna River, Līvāni is a linear town strung out along the central Rīgas iela, which is also the main A6 road between Rīga and Daugavpils. Here in 1533, a manor was established by a landowner named Lieven, from whom the place took its name. It is not a tourist town, its name mainly associated in Latvia with glass production. The first glassworks was established here in 1887. In the Soviet period, the Līvāni Glass Factory was a significant operation, employing 1,250 people by 1980. Following the restoration of Latvian independence, the factory soldiered on for a while as a private enterprise, before its liquidation in 2009. The glassmaking tradition continues in the town through a German-owned company, Ceram Optec, producing optical fibres. Unfinished apartment blocks from the end of the Soviet period flank the main street.

The **tourist information centre** (Līvānu novada Tūrisma informācijas centrs; Domes iela 1B; w visitlivani.lv; ⏰ 08.00–12.00 & 13.00–17.00 Mon–Fri, 10.00–14.00 Sat) is next door to the glass and craft centre. It is often shut, understandably given the average tourist flow in Līvāni, in which event the reception at the glass and craft centre takes on the role.

Getting there and away The **railway station** (Līvānu dzelzceļa stacija; Dzelzceļa iela 16; ☎6531 6401) is centrally located. It sits on the line between Rīga and Daugavpils, with around five departures a day in each direction. The **bus station** (Līvānu autoosta; Dzelzceļa iela 21A) is located just outside the railway station. There are three or more buses a day to Rīga and around two to Daugavpils.

What to see and do The well-presented **Līvāni Glass and Craft Centre** (Domes iela 1; w livanustikls.lv; ⏰ Jun–Aug 09.00–18.00 Tue–Fri, 10.00–16.00 Sat, 11.00–15.00 Sun, May & Sep–Oct 09.00–18.00 Tue–Fri, 10.00–16.00 Sat; Nov–Apr 09.00–17.00 Tue–Fri, 10.00–16.00 Sat; adult/student €4/2), signposted 800m off the main road, makes for a worthwhile stop. It sits on the right bank of the Daugava. A large room is filled with examples of Līvāni glass production through the decades, including coloured glassware sets like the 'Arctic' design produced in the 1980s, its blue-tinged ashtrays, candy dishes and vases a feature of homes in Soviet Latvia. Desperate attempts to innovate in the 1990s included the use of opaque, milky-white glass, but by then demand was declining fast.

Another room offers a change of tone, with a display on artisans in Latgale in the 19th and 20th centuries, organised thematically by craft, from blacksmiths to weavers. Highlights include what is claimed to be the longest belt in Latvia, running to 94m, and weaved as a gift to Līvāni town on its birthday. It is wrapped around a large bobbin. Note also the *puzuris* suspended from the ceiling: a mobile made from straw, fashioned into complex geometric shapes, used as a Christmas decoration. For an extra €4 you can see glassblowing in action, as the centres in-house glassmakers produce little glass birds for the souvenir shop.

RĒZEKNE

The city of Rēzekne, with a population a little under 30,000, likes to call itself 'the Heart of Latgale', contrasting itself with Daugavpils, which is geographically on the edge of the Latgale region, and culturally dominated by Russian-speakers. Its position as a railway hub was to prove disastrous for Rēzekne in World War II, when it was subjected to both Nazi and Soviet bombardments, destroying much of the city. Like Valmiera and Jelgava, the legacy of this bombardment is a largely post-war cityscape of no immediately obvious touristic appeal. There are, however, some worthwhile sights amid the concrete.

The **tourist information centre** (Rēzeknes Tūrisma informācijas centrs; Krasta iela 31; ☏ 2633 2249; e tic@rezekne.lv; ☉ 10.00–18.00 Mon–Fri, 10.00–16.00 Sat) is housed in a pavilion within the funky Zeimuļs centre, close to the castle ruins.

HISTORY The city was the site of a Latgalian hill fort, destroyed by the Livonian Order, who replaced it with their own stone fortress of Rositten in 1285, marking the eastern frontier of the order's territories. During the Livonian War, Ivan the Terrible took the castle in 1577, but under the Truce of Jam Zapolski in 1582, Russia renounced its claims in favour of the Polish–Lithuanian Commonwealth. Rēzekne fell to Russia under the First Partition of Poland in 1772, and received city rights the following year, when it was known as Rezhitsa. Its economic fortunes rose with the arrival of the first railway in 1860. Rēzekne lay on both the Moscow to Ventspils and St Petersburg to Warsaw lines, making it an important hub. With some two-thirds of its buildings destroyed in World War II, Rēzekne emerged from the war with a population of only around 5,000. Post-war reconstruction put the emphasis on industrial development and brought in many Russian-speaking workers from other parts of the Soviet Union. Ethnic Russians today comprise some 40% of the population.

GETTING THERE AND AWAY The **bus station** (Rēzeknes autoosta; Latgales iela 17; ☏ 6462 4656) is centrally located, just south of the Rēzekne River. There are five to six buses a day to Rīga, around six to Daugavpils, four to Alūksne, two to Valmiera, two or three to Jēkabpils and between five and nine to Ludza. The passenger **railway station** (Rēzekne-2 dzelzceļa stacija; Stacijas iela 9; ☏ 6723 2135) is Rēzekne 2, on the northern side of town. There is one fast train daily to Rīga (2hrs 45mins) and two slow trains (approx. 3hrs 30mins). The latter go on to Zilupe, close to the Russian border. Note that the Rēzekne 1 railway station, on the west side of town on the railway line built between St Petersburg and Warsaw, currently serves freight traffic only.

🏠 **WHERE TO STAY** *Map, page 192*

Hotel Kolonna (41 rooms) Brīvības iela 2; w hotelkolonna.com. Centrally located, close to the bus station & GORS concert venue, the rooms are, however, quite tired & spartan. Its restaurant walls are covered with a long tale in Latvian about the fiery & beautiful Rozālija, daughter of the owner of a hostelry on this spot, who kept the place in order through a strict set of rules: no shouting, & booze only in moderation. Evidently a subtle hint for modern-day patrons. €€

Restart (29 rooms) Stacijas iela 30b; w restarthotel.lv. Part of the Rēzekne Olympic Centre & surrounded by sports facilities, you may well share your stay with a visiting sports team, but this is probably the most comfortable, albeit not most central, option in town. €€

✖ WHERE TO EAT AND DRINK *Map, below*

Marijas kafija Atbrīvošanas aleja 88; 📞2651 4420; e marijaskafija@inbox.lv. With a vaulted brick interior & a long menu ranging across Latvian specialities & international standards, this is among the smartest options in town, notwithstanding the pool table at the entrance. €€€

Zīds Pils iela 4; w latgalesgors.lv. Smart restaurant within the GORS concert hall, whose enticing international menu includes a particular penchant

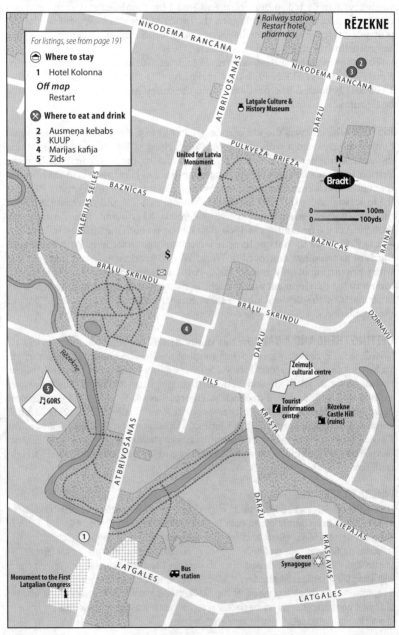

RĒZEKNE

For listings, see from page 191

🛏 **Where to stay**
1   Hotel Kolonna
Off map
    Restart

✖ **Where to eat and drink**
2   Ausmeņa kebabs
3   KUUP
4   Marijas kafija
5   Zīds

NIKODEMA RANCĀNA

Railway station, Restart hotel, pharmacy

NIKODEMA RANCĀNA

ATBRĪVOŠANAS

DARZU

Latgale Culture & History Museum

PULKVEŽA BRIEŽA

United for Latvia Monument

VALĒRIJAS SEILES

BAZNĪCAS

N

Bradt

0 _____ 100m
0 _____ 100yds

BAZNĪCAS

RAINA

BRĀĻU SKRINDU

$

BRĀĻU SKRINDU

DZIRNAVU

Rēzekne

DARZU

4

Zeimuļs cultural centre

PILS

GORS

5

Tourist information centre

Rēzekne Castle Hill (ruins)

ATBRĪVOŠANAS

KRASTA

DARZU

1

LIEPĀJAS

KRASLAVAS

LATGALES

Bus station

Green Synagogue

Monument to the First Latgalian Congress

LATGALES

for avocado, from the avocado tartare starter to the avocado cake dessert. Closed Mon. €€€

Ausmeņa kebabs Nikodema Rancāna iela 41; ☎2011 2200. With its rough-beamed wooden ceilings & summer terrace this place serves up not only a good range of kebabs, but also serves as an unlikely culinary vehicle for the promotion of Latgalian culture, with its menu written in Latgalian & use of ethnographic symbols in its marketing. It has taken the formula to Rīga. €€

KUUP Nikodema Rancāna iela 41; w kuup.lv. In the same complex as Ausmeņa kebabs, but under different management, the folks at KUUP ('steam') grind their own coffee, offer salads, soup, sandwiches & cakes, plus a range of coffee-related merchandise. Closed Mon. €

ENTERTAINMENT Billing itself as 'the Embassy of Latgale', **GORS** (Pils iela 4; w latgalesgors.lv) is an airy modern concert venue, completed in 2013, and is the pride of Rēzekne. Its 1,000-seat main hall attracts visitors from as far afield as Rīga. The complex includes a smaller 200-seat hall, an art gallery space and good restaurant.

OTHER PRACTICALITIES There is a **post office** (Atbrīvošanas aleja 81; ☎6700 8001) a block to the south of the United for Latvia Monument on the main Atbrīvošanas aleja. A branch of **SEB Bank** (Atbrīvošanas aleja 81; ☎2666 8777) is in the same building. There is a **pharmacy** (Atbrīvošanas aleja 114; ☎6462 2753) two blocks to the north of the monument, on the same main road.

WHAT TO SEE AND DO
United for Latvia Monument (Vienoti Latvijai) A symbol of the city, the monument sits on the main drag, Atbrīvošanas aleja, which runs north–south through the centre. Next to the local administration building in the heart of town, the traffic parts to leave space for the monument. It depicts a female figure, universally known as Māra, in Latvian folk costume holding aloft a golden cross. At her feet are two further figures: a soldier breaking chains and a virginal figure offering an oak crown to the liberator. The monument, unveiled in 1939, commemorates the liberation of Latgale in the Latvian War of Independence, and the wider liberation of Latgale from centuries of conquest by foreign powers. It was replaced by a statue of Lenin during the Soviet occupation, but following the restoration of Latvian independence, a replica of the original was restored to the plinth, the work of Andrejs Jansons, son of the original sculptor.

The monument is an interesting combination of Latvian folk traditions, seen particularly in the dress of the central character, and the Catholic church, represented by the golden cross. She seems simultaneously to be the Māra of Pagan Latvian traditions and the Mary of the Christian one. These strands together illuminate the theme of Catholic Latgale uniting with Latvia as a whole.

A few metres to the north, the **Latgale Culture and History Museum** (Latgales Kultūrvēstures muzejs; Atbrīvošanas aleja 102; w rezekne.lv; ⊕ Sep–May 10.00–18.00 Tue–Sat, Jun–Aug 10.00–18.00 Wed–Sat, 11.00–17.00 Sun; adult/student €4/1) offers an introduction to Latgalian culture spread over three floors, including through what is billed as the world's largest permanent display of Latgalian pottery (page 194).

Rēzekne Castle Hill (Rēzeknes pinskalns) A block to the east of Atbrīvošanas aleja, overlooking the Rēzekne River, stands a grassy mound topped by no longer particularly impressive ruins of the Livonian Order castle. Heavily damaged through its challenging history, by the start of the 18th century the castle had lost its military importance and was simply left as a ruined quarry for building materials.

The Latgale region is renowned within Latvia for its ceramics. Important figures who helped to develop an international reputation for the pottery during the interwar period included Andrejs Paulāns and Polikarps Vilcāns. They are associated with the complex ceramic candlestick holders, somewhat resembling menorahs, which have become a symbol of Latgalian pottery. Both were awarded gold medals at the 1937 Paris exhibition. The Latgalian art historian Jānis Pujāts was influential in popularising the ceramics of the region during the Soviet period, through the organisation of exhibitions to showcase the work of local potters. Pujāts also helped organise the Latgale Ceramics Studio in Rēzekne, bringing together many local potters. It has since been renamed in honour of Paulāns.

In the Soviet era, Latgalian pottery was to be found in almost every Latvian home, with a ceramic vase or milk jug placed on a linen tablecloth on the dining table, and a candlestick holder on the sideboard. Fashions changed, but through the continuing innovations of local potters, imaginative Latgalian designs remain popular and make an excellent souvenir. Unglazed ceramics are now more sought after than the glazed designs favoured in the Soviet era, with some potters focusing on more minimalistic blackened ceramic plates and bowls, echoing the pottery unearthed in archaeological finds. A workshop named the Pūdnīku skūla (Potters' School), founded in 1990, was a major promoter of this move to blackened ceramics. Several potters have workshops around Rēzekne to which visitors are welcome, though call in advance. You will need your own transport to get to them, however, as they are almost all in isolated farms. One good choice is the workshop of husband-and-wife team **Staņislavs Viļums and Viola Anna Bīriņa** (Bekši, Ozolaines pagasts; w cukrasata.lv), whose output includes stylish, unglazed dark grey items with a wood grain finish. Their workshop is signposted 'Cukrasāta' from the hamlet of Bekši, south of Rēzekne on the A13 road towards Daugavpils.

The building beneath the castle hill with a higgledy-piggledy grass-covered roof with two slanted towers protruding from the top is a creative centre known as **Zeimuļs** (Krasta iela 31; w zeimuls.lv). Opened in 2012 to much architectural acclaim, it is focused on youth activities. Its name means 'pencil' in Latgalian, and the towers have something of the appearance of giant pencil holders.

Monument to the First Latgalian Congress (Piemineklis 'Latgales kongresam 100')

A block south of the bridge across the Rēzekne River on Atbrīvošanas aleja, situated on your right, is the modern monument inaugurated in 2017 in honour of the 100th anniversary of the First Latgalian Congress. At a meeting at the 'Diana' cinema located on this spot in April 1917, the congress determined that Latgale should unite with the Latvians of Vidzeme and Kurzeme to form a unitary Latvian state. Its design resembles a millstone, divided into three segments, on the top of which lies a relief map of Latvia, with Rēzekne marked. The motif of the monument seems to be that only with these three constituent regions together can Latvia rise. Black rays extending from the monument indicate the towns from which delegates came to the congress.

Green Synagogue (Rēzeknes Zaļā sinagoga; Krāslavas iela 5; ☎ 2661 5683; ⏲ 10.00–15.00 Wed & Sat; admission free, but donations accepted) Head east from the First Latgalian Congress Monument along Latgales iela past the bus station. Take Krāslavas iela a block to the north to reach the synagogue. Built in 1845, this is the oldest surviving wooden building in the city, part of a small area around Latgales iela that largely survived the bombardments of World War II. It is also one of the few timber synagogues in Latvia to have survived roughly in its original form, though there have been some modifications along the way, such as the large matzo bread oven, a rather ungainly Soviet-period addition to the building. In the late 19th century, around half the population of Rēzekne were Yiddish-speaking Ashkenazi Jews. Only a few Jews remained in the city following the horrors of the Holocaust, and the building, in a critical state, was abandoned in the late 1980s. It has been sensitively restored and now offers an insight into the history of the Jewish community of Rēzekne.

LUDZA

With a population under 8,000, Ludza is the green and quiet capital of a district of eastern Latvia abutting the Russian border. It claims the title of the oldest town in Latvia, a claim crystallised in sculptural form in the modern square in front of the municipal administration, with a large sundial formed of a key opening a box labelled 'Ludza 1177'. Three stones alongside bear the inscriptions 'Lyuchin 1177', 'Lyutsin 1777' (the date of its receipt of town rights from Catherine the Great) and 'Ludza 1900', reflecting the change in name of the town over time. It has an attractive location, with two lakes, the Lielais Ludzas ezers and Mazais Ludzas ezers (Big and Small Ludza Lakes), framing the northern edge of the town centre.

HISTORY The place receives a mention, as Lyuchin, in historical sources dated to 1177. Dating its foundation to that year is, however, doing itself down, as the surroundings of the lakes here have been settled since around 1000BCE. On the site of an earlier Latgalian fortress, the Livonian Order constructed Ludza Castle at the end of the 14th century, strategically located on a strip of high ground between two lakes, though its defensive position was evidently not as strong as first seemed, given a subsequent history of repeated conquest of the place. It served as an outpost at the eastern borders of the order, guarding trade routes with Russia. In 1480, Master of the Livonian Order Bernd von der Borch moved unsuccessfully against Pskov, an action that helped precipitate the Russian invasion of Livonia in 1481. Ludza Castle was destroyed, and only rebuilt by the Livonian Order in 1525 on the back of improved relations with Moscow. Ludza Castle was again occupied by Russian troops in 1558, and captured yet again in 1577 by Russian forces under Ivan the Terrible.

In 1582, Ludza passed to the control of the Polish–Lithuanian king, Stephen Báthory. The castle was taken by Swedish troops in 1625 during the Polish–Swedish war, but the Swedish commander lacked reinforcements and it was swiftly returned to Poland–Lithuania. The castle fell again to invading forces in 1654, when it was surrounded by the troops of Russian voivode Lev Saltikov during the Russian–Polish war. Poland took a decision in 1667 to maintain only Daugavpils Castle in the province of Inflanty, and Ludza Castle was allowed quietly to fall into ruin. By the time Ludza was incorporated into the Russian Empire in 1772, the ruins were already rather picturesque. Jews formed the majority of the town's population in the early 19th century, though following the ghettoization and then murder of Ludza's Jews during the Holocaust, few remain today.

GETTING THERE AND AWAY The **bus station** (Ludzas autoosta; Kr. Barona iela 47; ✆6572 2281) is central, offering some eight departures daily to Rēzekne, two of these going on to Rīga and two to Daugavpils. The **railway station** (Ludzas dzelzceļa stacija; Stacijas iela 90; ✆6571 6403) is less convenient, on the southern side of town, around 1km to the centre. It is served by two trains daily, running between Rīga (4hrs) and Zilupe close to the Russian border (35mins). The trains also pass through Rēzekne (30mins).

TOURIST INFORMATION The **tourist information centre** (Ludzas novada Tūrisma informācijas centrs; Baznīcas iela 42; w visitludza.lv; ⊕ May–Sep 08.00–17.00 Mon–Fri, 10.00–18.00 Sat, 10.00–14.00 Sun) is centrally located.

 WHERE TO STAY AND EAT *Map, opposite*

Lucia (22 rooms) Kr. Barona iela 20/18; ✆2625 3535; e hotellucia@inbox.lv. This 2-storey hotel in the town centre is the best of the uninspiring accommodation options, though rooms are pretty spartan. €€

Kristīne Baznīcas iela 25; ✆2652 7888. Next to a clothes store also named Kristīne, this central café is decorated in yellow inside & out, & offers an insistent soundtrack of popular music. The menu is heavy with stews & cutlets, & features local standbys like *solyanka* & pancakes. €€

SHOPPING AND OTHER PRACTICALITIES Spread over two floors of a ramshackle brick building, the **Ludza Craftworkers' Centre** (Ludzas Amatnieku Centrs; Tālavijas iela 27A; w ludzasamatnieki.lv) provides a home for specialists in all manner of traditional crafts, from belt makers to potters to tailors of folk costumes. Call ahead to arrange a briefing on local artisan traditions. The products of the craftworkers are for sale, making this a fine place for souvenirs. The **post office** (Raiņa iela 25; ✆6572 2290) is close to the municipal administration building. There is a **pharmacy** (Latgales iela 61; ✆2037 7630) west of the centre along the main Latgales iela. You can find a central **ATM** at the Maxima supermarket on Latgales iela 124.

WHAT TO SEE AND DO
Town centre The **Orthodox Church of the Assumption of Mary** (Vissvētās Dievmātes aizmigšanas pareizticīgo baznīca; Latgales iela 121; ✆2544 8825), built in 1843 in a Classical style, a bell tower above its Doric-columned façade, sits at the heart of town. The surrounding streets are characterised by one- and two-storey brick and wooden houses of the 19th century, though a fire in 1938 caused much damage. One block to the north stands the orange-painted wooden **Ludza Great Synagogue** (Ludzas Lielā sinagoga; 1 Maija iela 30; ✆6572 3931; ⊕ 11.00–15.00 Tue–Fri, 10.00–14.00 Sat; adult/student €2/1), built around 1800 and said to be the oldest wooden synagogue in the Baltics. It presents items on the history of the Jewish community of Ludza, as well as displays about local photographer Wolf Frank and his son, documentary-maker Herz Frank.

Baznīcas iela rises to the east, ascending to the twin-towered façade of the Roman Catholic **Church of the Assumption** (Jaunavas Marijas Debesīs uzņemšanas Romas katoļu baznīca; Baznīcas iela 54; w ludzasbaznica.lv). The first church was built on this spot, adjacent to the castle, during Polish rule in 1687, with the aim of strengthening adherence to Catholicism in the area, but was destroyed in a fire in 1736. It was replaced in 1738 by another wooden church, which, however, was largely destroyed in the devastating fire of 1938. The present building was the product of a renovation interrupted by the Soviet occupation and completed only

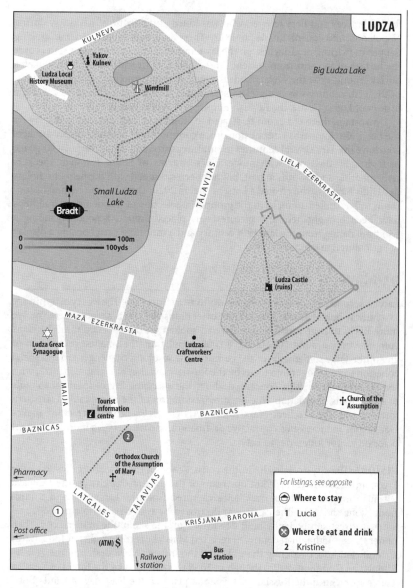

in 1995. Its interior is decorated in pastel shades of blue and white. To the side of the church, the brick and boulder ruins of **Ludza Castle** (Ludzas Viduslaiku pilsdrupas) stand picturesquely on the hill above Ludza's two lakes.

Ludza Local History Museum (Ludzas Novadpētniecības muzejs; Kuļņeva iela 2; w ludzasmuzejs.lv; ⊕ 08.00–17.00 Mon–Fri, 10.00–17.00 Sat; adult/student Apr–Oct €3/1, Nov–Mar €2/1) The museum lies a couple of blocks to the north of Baznīcas iela, beyond the bridge over the stream connecting the two lakes. It is housed in the building which served as the birthplace in 1763 of Yakov Kulnev, among the most popular Russian military leaders of the early 19th century, known

Latgale LUDZA

6

197

for his bravery and fiery temper, who was killed at the Battle of Klyastitsy during Napoleon's invasion of Russia in 1812. There is a bust of the general, looking dapper in twirling moustaches, on the lawn outside. Inside, displays upstairs cover the history of the area from ancient times, including treasures from the Odukalns burial ground near the Lielais Ludzas ezers. A reconstruction of a female burial of the 12th century shows a skeleton festooned with jewellery. Displays cover the history of Ludza Castle, the Russian Empire and World War II.

Downstairs there is a room dedicated to Kulnev, and an interesting display on the Lutsi, also known as Ludza Estonians, a community of South Estonian speakers who have lived for several centuries in rural areas around Ludza. The Lutsi language had virtually died out, with modern descendants of South Estonian speakers remembering a few words at best, but has been sustained with the help of scholars like Uldis Balodis, who created a Lutsi primer in 2020. There is also a natural history room full of stuffed animals. In the grounds, a selection of wooden rural buildings have been brought here and picturesquely placed around a pond, including a windmill dating from the late 19th century and a threshing barn housing a display of agricultural machinery.

DAUGAVPILS

Latvia's second city, Daugavpils feels a world away from Rīga. The legacy of its history as a railway hub of Tsarist Russia and Soviet industrial city is a place where you are more likely to hear Russian than Latvian spoken on the streets. Ethnic Latvians comprise only around 20% of the 80,000 population, the smallest proportion of any of the large settlements of the country. The resulting challenges around social cohesion were brought into focus by the Russian invasion of Ukraine in 2022, with the government in Rīga concerned about the susceptibility of local inhabitants to Russian disinformation. The ongoing restoration of the remarkable Tsarist-era fortress, with the excellent Mark Rothko Art Centre its central attraction, makes Daugavpils an increasingly attractive destination, and it deserves a more prominent place on visitor itineraries to Latvia.

HISTORY The city's origins lie in the construction of the Dünaburg Castle by the Livonian Order in 1275, 19km upstream of the present-day city on the Daugava River, to maintain control over lands captured from the Latgalians and control trade along the river. The castle was destroyed by Ivan the Terrible in 1577, and a new fortress subsequently built downriver, on the site of the modern city. Then under Polish–Lithuanian control, it received Magdeburg town rights in 1582. It was a significant hub, becoming the capital of the Inflanty Voivodeship of the Polish–Lithuanian Commonwealth, though in 1656 was captured by the forces of Russian Tsar Alexis. Since the Russian victory took place on the feast day of Saints Boris and Gleb, the city was renamed Borisoglebsk, but returned to Polish–Lithuanian control under the Treaty of Andrusovo in 1667, reverting to its former name.

In 1772, the city became part of the Russian Empire following the First Partition of Poland. With concerns growing about the threat of Napoleon, construction of a new military fortress commenced in 1810, the still-unfinished fortress playing its role in the defence of Russia's western borders during the War of 1812. The city, renamed Dvinsk in 1893, had become an important railway hub in the late 19th century, and by 1913 had a population of 113,000. Yiddish-speaking Jews had arrived in the city from the 17th century, initially fleeing the massacres of Bohdan Khmelnytsky in Ukraine, and by the eve of World War I Jews comprised almost half

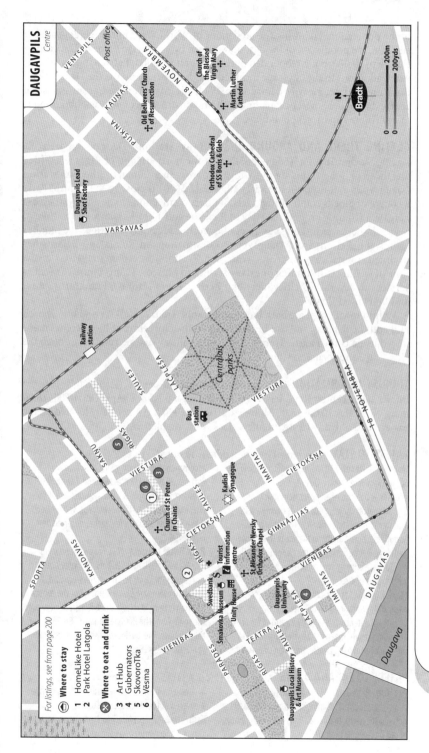

DAUGAVPILS
Centre

For listings, see from page 200

Where to stay
1 HomeLike Hotel
2 Park Hotel Latgola

Where to eat and drink
3 Art Hub
4 Gubernators
5 SkovoroTka
6 Vēsma

VENTSPILS
KAUNAS
PUŠKINA
PUŠKINA
VARŠAVAS
SAULES
RĪGAS
SAULES
SAKŅU
VIESTURA
LĀČPLĒŠA
KANDAVAS
SPORTA
PARĀDES
RĪGAS
TEĀTRA
VIENĪBAS
RĪGAS
RĪGAS
SAULES
CIETOKŠŅA
CIETOKŠŅA
CIETOKŠŅA
IMANTAS
IMANTAS
IMANTAS
GIMNĀZIJAS
VIENĪBAS
LĀČPLĒŠA
DAUGAVAS
18 NOVEMBRA
18 NOVEMBRA
18 NOVEMBRA

Post office
Church of the Blessed Virgin Mary
Martin Luther Cathedral
Old Believers' Church of Resurrection
Orthodox Cathedral of SS Boris & Gleb
Daugavpils Lead Shot Factory
Railway station
Centrālais parks
Bus station
Kadish Synagogue
Church of St Peter in Chains
Tourist information centre
St Alexander Nevsky Orthodox Chapel
Swedbank
Smakovka Museum
Unity House
Daugavpils University
Daugavpils Local History & Art Museum

Daugava

0   200m
0   200yds

N

Bradt

Latgale DAUGAVPILS

6

199

of the population. Following the predations of World War I and the independence struggle, the population of the city, now known by its Latvian name of Daugavpils, shrank to 29,000, but it rebounded during the period of first Latvian independence, when additions to the cityscape included the Unity Bridge across the Daugava and the Unity House. Heavily damaged in 1944, the city developed as an industrial centre during the Soviet occupation, with the construction of new neighbourhoods of multistorey apartment buildings.

GETTING THERE AND AROUND The **railway station** (Daugavpils dzelzceļa stacija; Stacijas iela 44; \6548 7263) sits at the northern end of Rīgas iela. There are three or four trains daily to Rīga (approx 3hrs 20mins). The **bus station** (Daugavpils autoosta; Viestura iela 10; \6542 5270) is close to the Central Park, a couple of blocks south of Rīgas iela. It offers connections to destinations across Latgale, including around six a day to Rēzekne and 11 to Krāslava. At the time of research there was just one bus a week between Daugavpils and Rīga. The number of bus connections from Daugavpils to destinations in Russia and Belarus has declined dramatically in recent years, but Ecolines (w ecolines.net) was at the time of writing still running one daily service to Moscow (25hrs 5mins) as well as services to several EU cities including Berlin (24hrs 15mins), Frankfurt (30hrs) and Warsaw (17hrs).

Within town, there are both **buses and trams**. Tram route 3 serves both Church Hill and the fortress, and can be picked up in the city centre at the Vienības nams stop outside Unity House. Tram 1 starts at the railway station, running through the city centre and thence to Church Hill.

TOURIST INFORMATION The **tourist information centre** (Daugavpils Tūrisma informācijas centrs; Rīgas iela 22A; w visitdaugavpils.lv; ⊕ Apr–Oct 10.00–18.00 daily, Nov–Mar 10.00–18.00 Mon–Sat, 10.00–16.00 Sun) is centrally located on the eastern end of Unity House. It offers stacks of pamphlets.

 WHERE TO STAY Map, page 199, unless otherwise stated

HomeLike Hotel (10 rooms) S. Mihoelsa iela 66; w homelikehotel.lv. Despite the unpromising exterior at the end of an apartment block, this is a good central choice, with rooms decorated in a contemporary style, albeit with rather grating homilies to domesticity on the walls. 'Fill a house with love & it becomes a home'; a sentiment that would work equally well replacing the word 'love' with 'laundry'. €€

Mark Rothko Art Centre residences [map, page 204] (10 rooms) Mihaila iela 3; w rothkocenter.com. Primarily intended for artists attending residential programmes organised by the Mark Rothko Art Centre, this is an unusual accommodation option inside the Daugavpils Fortress, in the Art Centre building. The vaulted bedrooms are simply & smartly furnished, & there is a shared kitchen. No meals are served though, & the fortress area can feel rather deserted at night. €€

Park Hotel Latgola (116 rooms) Ģimnāzijas iela 46; w hotellatgola.lv. This 10-storey hotel can't quite shake off its Communist-era past, & standard rooms are bland & poky, but the central location is unbeatable, & there is a great view over the town from the Plaza restaurant (€€€) on the top floor. The 'business class' rooms are more spacious. €€–€€€

WHERE TO EAT AND DRINK Map, page 199, unless otherwise stated

Art Hub Rīgas iela 54A; w arthub.lv. This city-centre basement restaurant is decorated in pastel green latticework to offer a 1930s feel, with photos of old Daugavpils projected on a screen. The menu is strong on steaks & homemade pasta. They have a covered outdoor terrace. €€€€

Gubernators Lāčplēša iela 10; w gubernators.lv. Offers a hearty menu in vaulted basements filled with knick-knacks, from samovars to stuffed toys, carriage wheels to clocks. €€€

SkovoroTka Rīgas iela 65; w skovorotka. business.site. The name is a corruption of the Russian word for frying pan, in homage to Daugavpils' most famous son, Mark Rothko. The décor recalls the artist's 'multiform' paintings, & the hearty menu stretches from burgers to borscht. They open up a yard round the back in summer. €€€

Arsenāls [map, page 204] Mihaila iela 3; w sanmari.lv. In a vaulted space adjacent to the Mark Rothko Art Centre, this offers a broad range of mains, salads & pancakes, but service is slow & the rendition uninspiring. The place warrants a

listing for its reasonable prices & because of the dearth of alternatives in & around the fortress. €€

Vēsma Rīgas iela 49; w vesma.lv. Occupying a prime spot on the pedestrianised Rīga iela, with a functional interior & large terrace, this is a survivor of the Soviet period, established in 1963, & offering a menu rich with Baltic & Russian dishes, including the pink *aukstā zupa*, shashlik & the Lithuanian speciality of meat-filled potato dumplings known as *cepelīni* because they look Zeppelin-like in form. They also have pizzas named after local cities. A 'Daugavpils' is covered with canned pineapple for some reason. This is a good place to try *šmakovka*, the local firewater. €€

OTHER PRACTICALITIES The most central post office having recently closed, the best option was at the time of writing a **post office** (18 novembra iela 136; ↘6543 1016) northeast of the centre beyond Church Hill. There is a branch of **Swedbank** (Rīgas iela 22A; ↘6744 5555) in the city centre within the Unity House building. There is a **pharmacy** (Rīgas iela 9; ↘6542 4774) close to the Park Hotel Latgola, on Rīgas iela.

WHAT TO SEE AND DO
City centre Pedestrianised **Rīgas iela**, running southwestwards from the railway station, is the main central street. Note the Roman Catholic **Church of St Peter in Chains** (Svētā Pētera Ķēdēs Romas katoļu baznīca; Rīgas iela 39). With its sweeping columned arcades either side of the domed church, it takes inspiration from the larger church dedicated to St Peter in Rome. It was built in 1849, but comprehensively remodelled in the interwar period. In the scrap of park alongside the church, a heart-shaped sculpture with 'Daugavpils' written on it provides a suitable Instagram opportunity.

Another sculptural composition on Rīgas iela involves a collection of ceramic jars encased in a clear column: a reminder of the importance of ceramics in the artistic life of Latgale. Beyond the Park Hotel Latgola, Rīgas iela runs into **Vienības laukums** (Unity Square), a bleak expanse, partly turned over to car parking, though also a venue for open-air concerts.

Unity House (Vienības nams; Rīgas iela 22A) Lying along the southern side of Vienības laukums, the bulky grey Unity House presents a Corinthian-columned Neoclassical façade on its west side. Built in 1937, it was a project instigated by Latvian president Kārlis Ulmanis, who sought to strengthen unity within ethnically diverse Daugavpils, and housed a range of organisations, including the Daugavpils Theatre, Latvian Society and a library. The Daugavpils Theatre is still there, offering plays in Latvian, Russian and Latgalian. The central library and tourist information centre are entered from the opposite end of the building.

Šmakovka Museum (Šmakovkas muzejs; Rīgas iela 22A; w smakovka.lv; ⊕ Apr–Oct 11.00–19.00 daily, Nov–Mar 11.00–19.00 Tue–Sun; adult/student €5/3.50) Also in Unity House, entered from the Rīgas iela side, is this museum to *šmakovka*, the local moonshine, its name deriving from the Polish word for 'taste'. Descend the steps to a glitzily laid out temple to the stuff. The displays start with some Latgalian cultural context, before moving to the business of illicit spirit production. There is a jokey style to the displays: peer through the spyhole of an old police station door to see a glass of hooch under arrest. There is relatively little explanatory signage, but free audio-guides are available. *Šmakovka* tastings are offered at the end of the tour, at €1.50 a glass, and a bargain (though not necessarily a wise one) €2.50 for three.

A block to the south is a small park laid out in the 19th century, dedicated to poet Andrejs Pumpurs, to whom there is a bust here. In the park, the diminutive blue-domed **St Alexander Nevsky Orthodox Chapel** (Sv. Aleksandra Nevska pareizticīgo kapela; Saules iela 20; ☏2211 9610) dates from 2004, and honours the former St Alexander Nevsky Cathedral, which lay on this site until its demolition under Soviet occupation in 1969. There are photographs of the old cathedral in the chapel. On the southern side of the park is the imposing Corinthian-columned façade of Daugavpils University, formerly a teacher-training institute.

Daugavpils Local History and Art Museum
Daugavpils Local History and Art Museum (Daugavpils Novadpētniecibas un mākslas muzejs; Rīgas iela 8; w dnmm.lv; ☉ 10.00–18.00 Tue–Sat, 10.00–16.00 Sun–Mon; adult/student €5/2) Further along Rīgas iela, the museum is housed in a grand building, its entrance guarded by a pair of lions. Its permanent exhibition offers a tour through the city's history, though most of the labelling is in Latvian and Russian. Note the model of the Livonian Order Dünaburg Castle, the massive lock of the Mikhailovsky Gate of the Tsarist fortress, and the mock-up of a Soviet-era living room, with a Latgalian ceramic vase proudly standing on the bookcase. A room rather grandly named 'Past Reverence' turns out to be a mocked-up Art Nouveau interior. The museum also hosts temporary exhibitions of local artists.

Kadish Synagogue
Kadish Synagogue (Daugavpils sinagoga; Cietokšņa iela 38; w jewishlatgale.lv; ☉ call ahead; donation welcomed) Lāčplēša iela runs parallel to Rīgas iela, two blocks to the south. At the junction with Cietokšņa iela sits the Kadish Synagogue. Built in 1850, this is the only one of the 40 synagogues that populated Daugavpils on the eve of World War I still in use. It was restored in 2005 with funds donated by the children of artist Mark Rothko. The first floor, formerly reserved for women, has been turned into a small museum by chronicler of the Jewish history of the city Josifs Ročko, who is an enthusiastic guide. The museum displays are poignant: photographs of smiling children at interwar summer camps followed by those of lines of Jews awaiting execution at Mežciems just outside the city.

Church Hill
Church Hill The multi-faith character of Daugavpils is neatly demonstrated by Church Hill (Baznīcu kalns) in the Jaunbūve neighbourhood across the railway a kilometre or so east of the centre. The neighbourhood was a product of urban expansion after the 1860s when the railway arrived, and the place is notable for the close juxtaposition of four churches representing different Christian denominations. The Evangelical Lutheran church, the neo-Gothic **Martin Luther Cathedral** (Mārtiņa Lutera katedrāle; 18 Novembra iela 66; ☏2631 5707; e info@ luterakatedrale.lv; ☉ 15 Apr–30 Sep 10.00–16.00 Mon–Sat, 10.00–14.00 Sun; 1 Oct–14 Apr by appt) is a red-brick building dating from 1893 with a tall spire. In the Soviet period, it served variously as a warehouse and boxing club. The interior is plain, with a programme underway to install an organ gifted by the Swiss city of Basel. You can climb to a viewing platform, offering a view to the adjacent churches. Nearby, the white-walled Catholic **Church of the Blessed Virgin Mary** (Jaunavas Marijas bezvainīgās ieņemšanas Romas katoļu baznīca; A. Pumpura iela 11A;

‎6543 9187) was the 1905 work of the same architect, Wilhelm Neimanis. Its neo-Baroque façade has twin towers, and the altar is adorned with a copy of Murillo's *Immaculate Conception*. Unlike the Lutheran church, it remained open through the Soviet period.

The other two religious buildings on Church Hill are across busy 18 Novembra iela. The **Old Believers' Church of Resurrection** (Jaunbūves vecticībnieku draudzes Augšāmcelšanās, Dievmātes Piedzimšanas un Svētītāja Nikolas dievnams; Puškina iela 16A; ‎6543 6307) was consecrated in 1928, the largest of four houses of prayer of the Old Believers' community in Daugavpils. It is not usually open to visitors. The **Orthodox Cathedral of Saints Boris and Gleb** (Svēto mocekļu Borisa un Gļeba pareizticīgo katedrāle; Tautas iela 2; ‎6545 3544), named in recollection of the date of the Russian conquest of the city in 1656, was built in 1905 on the site of an older iron church, which was moved to the present-day village of Jersika. It was built as a garrison church: the proliferation of lateral doors apparently ensured that troops could exit the place quickly in the event of attack.

Trams 1 and 3 bring you here (get off at the Baznīcu kalns stop), as do numerous buses.

Daugavpils Lead Shot Factory (Daugavpils Skrošu rūpnīca; Varsāvas iela 28; w dsr.lv; ⊕ 10.00–16.00 Sat–Sun, call to arrange tours at other times; adult/student €12/9) A few hundred metres northwest of Church Hill, along Varsāvas iela, this is a fascinating piece of industrial heritage. It centres on a tall square-based brick tower, the focus of an ingenious method for the production of lead shot based on a technique devised in 1782 by William Watts of Bristol. Lead is lifted to the top of the tower, where it is melted. The molten lead is passed through a sieve and poured down the tower. As it falls, it breaks into droplets, which are rendered spherical because of surface tension, like droplets of rain. The tower must be tall enough to facilitate this process. In Daugavpils the lead falls 37m into a water-filled cooling well at its base. The Daugavpils factory dates from 1885: it originally used a wooden tower, with the current brick version dating from the early 20th century.

The factory is still in operation, today producing shotgun cartridges and pellets for pneumatic rifles. The tour includes only the old part of the factory, focused on lead shot, which now is poured just once a year. The equipment is all of considerable antiquity, and you are also taken up the 120 steps of the tower, whose interior staircase looks for all the world like an inspiration for an M C Escher woodcut. The tour ends with the opportunity to try your marksmanship skills with a pneumatic rifle at the factory's range. Note that programmed tours are all in Latvian: the factory will arrange tours in English, and during weekdays, but for a higher cost of €65 per tour.

Daugavpils Fortress The fortress, which claims the dubious distinction of being the last bastion-type fortress built anywhere, based around a technology that was already becoming obsolete at the time of its construction, sits on the right bank of the Daugava, a couple of kilometres north of the city centre. Construction started in 1810, but the place was not completed until 1878. It was laid out as a typical military town of the 19th century, with a parade ground in the centre and blocks for administration and living quarters around it. It later served as a Latvian army base, and during the German occupation in World War II housed a prisoner of war camp, Stalag-340, with the Jewish Ghetto occupying a smaller part of the fortress across the Daugava, now home to the Daugavgrīva Prison. The fortress is an atmospheric place. It is gradually being renovated, an enormous undertaking,

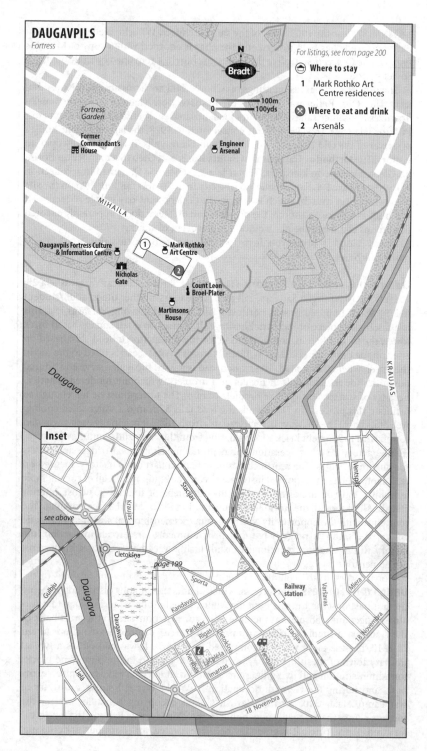

DAUGAVPILS
Fortress

N

Bradt

0 ——————— 100m
0 ——————— 100yds

Fortress
Garden

Former
Commandant's
House

Engineer
Arsenal

MIHAILA

Daugavpils Fortress Culture
& Information Centre

1

Mark Rothko
Art Centre

2

Nicholas
Gate

Count Leon
Broel-Plater

Martinsons
House

Daugava

KRAUJAS

For listings, see from page 200

Where to stay

1 Mark Rothko Art
   Centre residences

Where to eat and drink

2 Arsenāls

Inset

see above

Stacijas

Kraujas

Ventspils

Cietoksņa

page 199

Sporta

Gulbju

Daugava

Daugavas

Kandavas

Parades

Rīgas

Vienības

Lāčplēša

Imantas

Cietoksņa

Vienība

Railway
station

Varšavas

Miera

Stacijas

18 Novembra

Liela

18 Novembra

and its territory currently includes both smartly reconstructed streets, buildings and squares, especially in the southeastern part of the fortress, and areas of derelict-looking apartment blocks. The latter still recall a time not too many years back when the place was a byword for social deprivation.

The story of the place is told in the **Daugavpils Fortress Culture and Information Centre** (Daugavpils cietokšņa Kultūras un informācijas centrs; Nikolaja iela 5; \6542 4043; e cietoksnis@daugavpils.lv; ⊕ Apr–Oct 10.00–19.00 daily, Nov–Mar 10.00–18.00 daily; admission free). It is housed in the former water-lifting tower, a distinctive red-brick building dating from the 1860s built to secure the water supply for the fortress with a steam-powered machine filling a water tank from wells on the banks of the Daugava. There is a one-room exhibition centre, with mannequins in period dress and, oddly, collections of cameras and suitcases. Nearby stands the restored **Nicholas Gate** (Nikolaja vārti), the most impressively monumental of the original four gates into the fortress, named after Tsar Alexander I and his brothers. It has lateral rooms on either side of the central archway, one now hosting a souvenir shop. The double-headed eagle stands at the top of the gate, which is also decorated with pairs of double-headed axes.

Mark Rothko Art Centre (Marka Rotko Mākslas centrs; Mihaila iela 3; w rothkocenter.com; ⊕ 11.00–17.00 Sun & Tue–Thu, 11.00–19.00 Fri–Sat; adult/child €10/5) A short stroll from the Nicholas Gate lies a long yellow-painted building with stepped staircases at each end, the artillery arsenal of the fortress dating from the 1830s. It now houses Daugavpils' star attraction, the Mark Rothko Art Centre. The great abstract expressionist painter Mark Rothko was born Markus Yakovlevich Rothkowitz into a Jewish family in Daugavpils in 1903. The family moved to the United States in 1913, over fears that Markus's elder brothers would be drafted into the Russian army. In America Markus would eventually become Mark, an artist known particularly for his 'multiforms', involving two or three bright blocks of colour, with soft edges that blend into the background colour. The city of Daugavpils, looking to highlight its connections with Rothko, made contact with Rothko's children, Kate and Christopher, who agreed to loan out original works of the artist and to become co-founders of the centre, which opened in 2013.

The centrepiece of the exhibition is a room displaying half a dozen original Rothko works, received on temporary loan from his children. The loaned works are periodically changed, though typically involve paintings from different stages of his career, in different styles. These are supplemented by a well-produced exhibition tracing Rothko's life and work. The centre is also a wider hub for contemporary art. It organises Mark Rothko painting symposia, whose participants are required to donate work to the centre, and another permanent exhibition, 'Found in the Collection', showcases the best of these, alongside purchased works. There are also temporary exhibitions, impeccably presented.

Across the courtyard, the former gunpowder magazine of the fortress has been converted into the **Martinsons House** (Martinsona māja; 1 Nikolaja iela; adult/child €6/3), a long, vaulted gallery showcasing Daugavpils-born Latvian ceramicist Pēteris Martinsons, who donated much of his work to the Art Centre just before his death in 2013. Purchase your ticket at the Art Centre reception. Close by, at the foot of the fortress wall, the sculpture of a barred window honours **Count Leon Broel-Plater**, a Latgalian nobleman executed in the fortress for his part in the January Uprising of 1863 against the Russian Empire, with the objective of restoring the Polish–Lithuanian Commonwealth. The sculpture was unveiled in 2013 by the presidents of Poland and Latvia in commemoration of the 150th anniversary of the uprising.

Engineer Arsenal (Inženieru arsenals; Imperatora iela 8; ☏ 2803 3133; e inzenieruarsenals@daugavpils.lv; ⏰ 10.00–19.00 Wed–Sun; adult/student €10/5). Two blocks north of the Mark Rothko Art Centre, arranged around a central courtyard, is the Engineer Arsenal. Billing itself as a centre of technology and industrial design, it is really focused on historic automobiles, with a particularly strong showing of Soviet models, from the proletarian Zaporozhets to the Volga beloved by the nomenklatura. Mopeds and motorbikes are showcased upstairs. They plan to expand the collection to include more foreign vehicles, though have already made a start with a London taxi. The collection is atmospherically displayed in a brick-built Tsarist arsenal dating from the 1840s.

Fortress Garden A couple of blocks to the west, the central garden was laid out in the late 19th century on the site of the former parade ground. A fountain with three upright cannons, leaning against each other, is the centrepiece. This was installed in 1912 to mark the centenary of the victory over Napoleon. A long yellow-walled building, its entrance guarded by a couple of cannons, runs along the southern side of the garden. This is the former **Commandant's House**, dating from 1818, now a regional police headquarters. A plaque on the rear wall, in front of the car park along Mihaila iela, records that **Wilhelm Küchelbecker**, Russian poet, friend of Pushkin and supporter of the Decembrist revolt of 1825, was imprisoned in the fortress between 1827 and 1831.

Buses 4, 13 and 13A, and tram 3 bring you to the fortress from the city centre.

SOUTHERN AND EASTERN LATGALE

RĀZNA NATIONAL PARK (Rāznas nacionālais parks) Of the many lakes dotting Latgale, the largest in the region, and the second largest in all Latvia, is Lake Rāzna, with a surface area close to 58km^2 and a maximum depth of 17m. The lake sits in the heart of the Latgale Upland. Concerns around the despoliation of the lake and surrounding countryside led to the creation in 2007 of the Rāzna National Park, covering some 530km^2, to help protect both Lake Rāzna and other water bodies in the area, notably Lake Ežezers to the south, whose numerous islands are adorned with a distinctive deciduous forest cover.

Beautifully located on the northern shore of Lake Rāzna is **Ezerkrasti** [map, page 188] (Dukstigals, s. Tiliši, Čornajas pag.; w raznasezerkrasti.lv; €–€€), a recreation complex with wooden cottages set amid well-tended lawns that run down to the lake. With a large group you can rent out a whole cottage (sleeping between 7 & 34 people), but you can also book a single room. The cheapest have shared showers and toilets. There is also a campsite and places for trailer parking. Activities include volleyball courts and a playground, the option of hiring SUP boards and windsurfers, and a nearby rope course in the trees. There is an on-site café (€€), open only during the summer, which serves a good set breakfast and hearty lunch. On advance order, they will prepare a special lunch of local dishes like Rāzna eel soup and the cottage-cheese-filled dumplings known as *asuškas*.

AGLONA Some 40km northeast of Daugavpils, sited picturesquely between two lakes, Ciriš and Egles (also known as Lake Aglona), this village becomes the focus of attention on 15 August each year when thousands of Catholic pilgrims descend on the Basilica of the Assumption for the commemoration of the Assumption of Mary. It all kicks off on 14 August with an evening mass, followed at 22.00 with a slow candlelit procession around the perimeter of the basilica compound, ending with a climb to a raised area of ground topped by three crosses. There is another mass on the following morning, typically attended by senior members of the Latvian government. A market outside the compound offers stalls selling candles for the procession, along with other religious items, bread, hats, furniture, soft toys and revolutionary vegetable graters. There are food stalls in a separate area.

Getting there and away The **bus stop** is on Somersēta iela, opposite the café of the same name. There are a couple of buses a day to Daugavpils (approx. 1hr 10mins), one to Rezekne (1hr) and two to Krāslava (45mins). Aglona **railway station** is inconveniently located several kilometres northwest of the village, and sits on the barely used line between Daugavpils and Rēzekne. It only really comes into play around the Assumption celebrations, when special trains are laid on from Rīga, with buses also organised between the railway station and basilica.

🏠 **Where to stay and eat** With no conventional hotels in Aglona, and demand during the Assumption festival far outstripping the supply of homestay accommodation, many pilgrims camp or sleep in their cars, but it may also be possible to book a room in advance at the **Pilgrims' House**, operating from the Catholic school and bookable through the basilica. Rooms (**€€**) are basic but clean, with single beds. On the main Somersētas iela, **Somersēta** (Somersētas iela 36a; 🖉 2911 9965; e somerseeta@gmail.com; ⏱ closes 18.00 Sun–Thu; **€€**) is an unpretentious place offering canteen-style goulash, ribs, *karbonāde* and kebabs, with wooden tables outside and a soundtrack of cheery Latvian music.

What to see and do
Basilica of the Assumption (Ciriša iela 8; w aglonasbazilika.lv) Dominating the village, this white-walled church was built in an Italian Baroque style with two square-based towers framing its façade. A Dominican monastery had been founded here in the late 17th century. The current church dates from the late 18th century. It was granted the status of 'Basilica minoris' on its 200th anniversary celebrations in 1980, and is one of the international shrines recognised by the Holy See. The vaulted interior, with its Rococo ornamentation and imitation marble walls, looks fresh and new, and indeed was restored heavily from 2011 to 2013.

The focus of the church is the golden icon of Our Lady of Aglona, standing above the altar. Its perceived healing abilities have been central to the emergence of Aglona as a place of pilgrimage, though it is probably a copy of the icon of the Mother of God of Trakai in Lithuania. Steps at the side of the nave allow you to view the icon close up, along with the votive images of silver hearts, heads and legs displayed under glass below it, the grateful offerings of those healed of their maladies. A bronze-coloured plaster statue of Pope John Paul II recalls his visit in 1993. Among those buried in the basement are Julijans Vaivods, the first Latvian cardinal, who died in 1990. Also Boļeslavs Sloskāns, a bishop incarcerated in the remote Solovki prison camp in the White Sea in the 1920s, and who later served in Belgium. Sloskāns is currently being considered for potential beatification.

A huge green lawn in front of the church, criss-crossed by paths and surrounded by a fence, was laid out in advance of the papal visit of 1993 and accommodates the pilgrims arriving here on 15 August. There is a statue of **King Mindaugas and Queen Morta of Lithuania**, dating from 2015. Mindaugas was baptised a Catholic around

1250, allowing him to make peace with the Livonian Order, and he became the only ever crowned king of Lithuania in 1253. He later broke with the order, and according to some accounts, may have reverted to paganism. He was assassinated in 1263: by tradition, Aglona is said to be the place of his death. Behind the church, alongside Lake Egles, is the **Holy Spring of Aglona**, a small stone well, with water spouts on either side, set into a circular brick depression. Previously known as St Anton's Spring, it has lost its once pungent smell of hydrogen sulphide, and with it many of its medicinal qualities, but the faithful still come to fill their water bottles here.

Aglona Bread Museum (Maizes muzejs; Daugavpils iela 7; ✎ 2928 7044; e maizesmuzejs@inbox.lv; ⊕ by appt; €8 with tea & bread, adult/child €18/16 with meal) This place is less a museum in the conventional sense than a guided presentation about bread-making, incorporating a tasting. You can bake your own bread for an additional €3. They have a good bakery store (⊕ 08.30–16.00 Mon–Fri, 09.30–14.00 Sat–Sun) round the back.

Christ the King Hill (Kristus Karaļa kalns; w agkk.lv; ⊕ 09.00–18.00 daily; admission free) Located a kilometre east of the Basilica of the Assumption, at the eastern end of Lake Egles, this place represents a very different manifestation of Christian faith. It is a sculpture park established in 2006, with wooden sculptures illustrating Christian themes scattered over the slopes and around artificial ponds. At the top of the hill, a tall engraved sculpture resembling a totem pole represents Jesus Christ the Conqueror. Smaller columns signifying the disciples stand facing him. There are sculptures of sinners, like the avaricious man clutching a bag of dollars. Angels have elongated wings resembling tall antlers. And there are non-religious sculptures here and there, with bears a favourite.

DAUGAVAS LOKI NATURE PARK The Daugava River between Krāslava and Daugavpils is characterised by nine large meanders, and offers both a rich flora and fauna and a cultural significance borne of the important role played by the Daugava as an early trade route. The area was threatened in the 1980s by Soviet plans for the Daugavpils Hydro-Electric Station. A 1986 article by literary critic Dainis Īvāns and engineer Artūrs Snips in the magazine *Literatūra un māksla* criticising the proposed plant generated huge public support, prompted the abandonment of the project the following year, and helped stimulate the emerging Latvian movement against Soviet occupation. The Daugavas Loki ('Bends of the Daugava') Nature Park was founded in 1990 to give more concrete protection to the area. In 2011, Latvia submitted the park for consideration as a possible future UNESCO World Heritage site. At **Vasarģeļiški**, a 21m wooden observation tower a couple of kilometres south of the A6 road between Daugavpils and Krāslava offers a nice view over the meandering river.

Slutišķi One place to aim for in the park is the picturesque hamlet of Slutišķi on the Daugava, comprised largely of log-built houses. At the time of writing, it was a permanent home to just one family, the other houses serving as summer residences. Slutišķi, first mentioned as a village in 1785, was established as a community of Old Believers, and you can learn more about this community at the rewarding **Slutišķi Old-Believers' Farmstead** (Slutišķu vecticībnieku lauku seta; ✎ 2653 2508; e naujenesmuzejs@augsdaugavasnovads.lv; ⊕ May–Sep 10.00–18.00 Wed–Sun, Oct–Apr 08.00–17.00 Mon–Fri by prior appt, guided tours only; adult/child €1.50/1). Managed by the local history museum in the nearby village of Naujene, this is centred on two log-walled farmsteads dating from the late 19th century, the elegant carving around their windows a means of conveying architectural beauty in otherwise poor Old Believer families.

The building closest to the entrance was the property of an Old Believer family named Jermolajev until 2007, when it was acquired by the local authority. Note the 'red corner' of the main room, centred on an icon in a silver frame. The large stove would have kept warm all day. The children of the family would sleep on the top of it. The adults slept in beds along the walls. A second set of buildings, formerly owned by the brother of the owner of the first, accommodates a newer museum display with more multimedia elements. You are welcomed into this room by a mannequin of the lady of the house, Fedosija, offering a commentary on the lives of the Old Believers. In a carpenters' workshop opposite, her husband, Isajs, describes the importance of carpentry to the community. In the stable, somewhat surreally, a model lamb takes up the storytelling role.

Slutiški is 2km south of the A6 road between Daugavpils and Krāslava. Buses plying between these two centres stop at several places along the A6, including Vasarģeļišķi, and Židino, around 3km from Slutiški, but be prepared for much walking and waiting without your own transport.

KRĀSLAVA A quiet district capital on a meandering stretch of the Daugava River just a few kilometres from the border with Belarus, Krāslava offers an attractive townscape of single-storey wooden houses mostly built in the early 20th century. The presence of Latgalian castle mounds is indicative of a long history of human settlement here. Falling to the Livonian Order in the 13th century, the place languished for several centuries as the seat of a small rural manor, until in 1729 it was purchased by a nobleman with ambitions, Johann Ludwig Plater. The estate remained in the hands of the Plater family for close to 200 years, as they sought with varying success to turn Krāslava into a major centre in Latgale. The coat of arms of the town features a silver boat with five oars floating across a blue background. The boat is suggestive of the role of the Daugava in the economic development of the place, the oars symbolising the five nationalities that made up its mixed population: Latvians, Russians, Poles, Belarusians and Jews.

The **tourist information centre** (Krāslavas novada Tūrisma informācijas centrs; Pils iela 2; w visitkraslava.com; ⊕ 15 May–15 Sep 09.30–18.00 Mon–Fri, 10.30–19.00 Sat–Sun, 16 Sep–14 May 08.45–17.15 Mon–Fri, 10.00–15.00 Sat–Sun) is found within the Krāslava Castle Complex, in the old governor's house to the left of the entrance.

Getting there and away Krāslava **railway station** (Krāslavas dzelzceļa stacija; Ūdrīšu pag.; ✆6561 6203) sits 4km north of town, on the P62 road towards Aglona. It is currently served by one train daily in each direction on the line between Indra to the east and Rīga, via Daugavpils. The **bus station** (Krāslavas autoosta; Rīgas iela 55; ✆6562 2423) is centrally located on the main Rīgas iela, close to the castle complex. There are around nine buses a day to Daugavpils.

What to see and do The main attraction is the **Krāslava Castle Complex** (Krāslavas pils komplekss), lying in a walled compound on high ground overlooking the town. It centres on the three-storey manor of the Plater family completed in 1791 in a Baroque style, though rebuilt in the 1820s in a more Neoclassical manner. Following the agrarian reforms of the 1920s, and the death in 1923 of the manor's last owner, Count Gustav Christoph Plater, the building played host to a school,

6

though is now in a parlous condition and not open to visitors. Outbuildings within the castle complex do, however, host a range of attractions. The low-slung former servants' house beside the manor accommodates the **Krāslava Museum of History and Art** (Krāslavas vēstures un mākslas muzejs; Pils iela 8; w kraslavaspils.lv; ☉ May–Oct 10.00–17.00 Wed–Fri, 10.00–16.00 Sat, 10.00–14.00 Sun; Nov–Apr 10.00–17.00 Tue–Fri, 10.00–16.00 Sat; adult/child €1/0.50). An exhibition based around the town coat of arms covers the lives of the five major ethnic communities to have shaped the place. Another exhibition tells the story of the manor, and there are temporary exhibitions on local themes. The former stables are now home to **craft workshops**. The manor gardens, sloping down to the town below, make for a pleasant stroll. They include a grotto, built to give the Platers a picturesque ruin within their park.

7

Sēlija and Zemgale

The swathe of lands between the Daugava River and the Lithuanian border, Sēlija and Zemgale, have cause to feel neglected. The three gilded stars lifted by the female figure at the top of the Freedom Monument in Rīga represent the three Latvian regions of Vidzeme, Latgale and Kurzeme. Poor Sēlija and Zemgale are omitted altogether, reflecting the fact that these lands were grouped with Kurzeme for much of the period from the 16th century until 1917, first within the Duchy of Courland and Semigallia and then as part of the Courland Governorate of the Russian Empire. The disappearance of these regions feels particularly galling to the locals since Mitau, today's Jelgava, the capital of both duchy and governorate, is a city of Zemgale, not Kurzeme. Yet the Semigallian tribes from whom the region of Zemgale takes its name held out most fiercely against the German crusaders, almost to the end of the 13th century, their stories playing an important part in Latvian cultural identity. Sēlija, also known as Selonia after the Selonian tribes who once called the area their home, forms the eastern part of the region, around Jēkabpils. It is sometimes subsumed into Zemgale, giving the locals a double reason to feel ignored. Zemgale lies to the west.

The top tourist attraction is the Baroque Rundāle Palace, work of the Italian architect of the Russian court Francesco Bartolomeo Rastrelli. A visit there combines nicely with a stop at Bauska, with its restored castle. Jelgava is a city of major historic importance, though its attractions are rather dimmed by the legacy of brutal bombardment in World War II and unsympathetic Soviet-era reconstruction. The village of Tērvete is a good child-friendly destination, combining the chance to learn more about the Semigallian tribal chiefs with a nature park filled with fairy-tale statues. Dobele is a draw during the lilac festival in early summer. Sēlija is well off the tourist trail, but its principal town, Jēkabpils, has some worthwhile sights.

JĒKABPILS

With a population of some 21,000, Jēkabpils is really a tale of two cities, separated by the Daugava River. Krustpils on the right bank and Jēkabpils on the left developed separately, and were long part of different countries, before being gathered together as a single municipality named Jēkabpils in the Soviet period. Developed as an industrial town under Soviet occupation, and prone to flooding of the Daugava in winter and spring, it is not a major tourist destination, but a mix of attractions, including the restored Krustpils Castle and sights linked to the Struve Geodetic Arc UNESCO World Heritage site, make Jēkabpils a worthwhile place to break the journey between Rīga and Daugavpils.

HISTORY On the right bank, Krustpils developed thanks to a castle built in the 1230s by the Archbishop of Rīga, protecting the route from Rīga to Daugavpils.

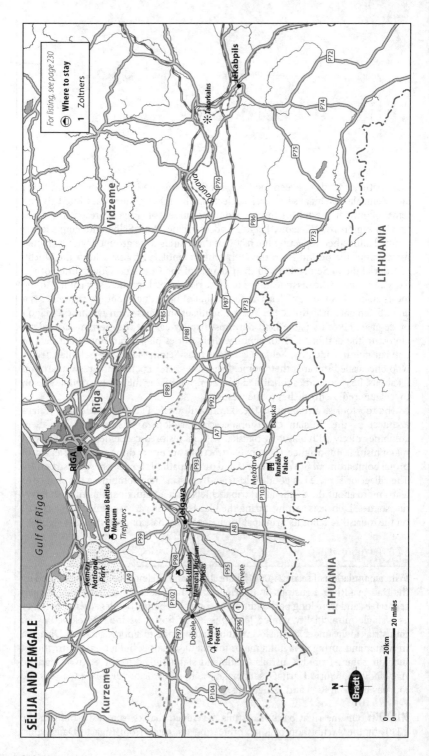

SĒLIJA AND ZEMGALE

For listing, see page 230

Where to stay

1 Zoltners

Gulf of Riga

Kurzeme

Ķemeri National Park

Christmas Battles Museum
Tīrelpurvs

RĪGA

Rīga

Vidzeme

Daugava

Jēkabpils

Jūdžkalns

P72

P74

P75

P76

P86

P73

P85

P87

P73

P88

P89

P92

P93

A7

Bauska

Mežotne

Rundāle Palace

P103

Jelgava

A8

P98

P99

P95

P102

Kārlis Ulmanis Memorial Museum Pikšas

Tērvete

P97

Dobele

Pokaiņi Forest

P96

1

P104

LITHUANIA

LITHUANIA

N

Bradt

0   20km
0   20 miles

In 1585 the castle, then known as Kreitzburg, was given by Polish king Stephen Báthory to Baron Nikolauss von Korff for meritorious service during the war with Russia, and the place remained in the von Korff family until the Latvian War of Independence. In 1921, the castle was turned over to military use, hosting the Latgale Artillery Regiment and later units of the Soviet army. Following the restoration of Latvian independence it passed to the Jēkabpils History Museum in 1994 and renovation works commenced.

Jēkabpils over the river developed following the arrival in the 17th century of Old Believers fleeing persecution in Russia. The place grew economically thanks to the presence of rapids along the Daugava, which forced barges to offload their cargoes here, take them a short distance by land, and then return them to the water. In 1670, Jacob Kettler, Duke of Courland and Semigallia, bestowed town rights upon the place, and it was promptly named Jakobstadt, later Jēkabpils, in his honour. A local tale concerning the duke provides the background to the coat of arms of Jēkabpils – a lynx beneath a fir tree. It is said that the duke became lost while out hunting until he spotted a lynx standing beneath a tree and at that very instant discerned the town beyond, and hence his salvation. The incorporation of Courland and Semigallia into the Russian Empire in 1795 meant that Krustpils and Jēkabpils found themselves part of the same nation, but they continued to develop as two separate towns. The opening of the Krustpils station on the Rīga to Daugavpils railway in 1861 altered the balance of advantage between the two towns by giving an economic boost to Krustpils while reducing the importance of the Daugava, and therefore Jēkabpils, as a means of transport.

The two towns were finally united by a bridge built in 1936, one of the major public works projects of the Kārlis Ulmanis government. This was, however, blown up in 1944 by retreating German troops and rebuilt only in 1962. In that year, the two towns were merged to create a single city with the name Jēkabpils. The Soviet authorities promoted the development of plants manufacturing building materials, such as the romantically named Krustpils Reinforced Concrete Constructions Manufacturing Facility, and new residential blocks to accommodate their employees.

GETTING THERE AND AWAY The **Krustpils Railway Station** (Krustpils dzelzceļa stacija; Stacijas laukums; ✆6521 6264) has a peripheral location on the northern edge of town, more convenient for Krustpils Castle, lying about a kilometre north of the latter. There are around nine trains daily to Rīga (2hrs), five to Daugavpils (90mins) and three to Rēzekne (90mins). The **Jēkabpils bus station** (Jēkabpils autoosta; Vienības iela 1; w jekabpilsap.lv) is on the left bank of the river and more convenient for sights around Jēkabpils town centre. There are up to eight buses a day to Rīga (2.5hrs) and up to four to Daugavpils (2hrs). Another group of long-distance buses, particularly those for which Jēkabpils is not the terminus, don't go to the bus station. Instead, they use a stop at the corner of Kurzemes iela and Rīgas iela on the Krustpils side of the river.

TOURIST INFORMATION The **tourist information centre** (Jēkabpils novada Tūrisma informācijas centrs; w visit.jekabpils.lv; ⊕ 08.30–17.00 Mon–Fri) was at the time of writing moving from the Krustpils side of town to a new, more central location in the Old Town Square.

 WHERE TO STAY AND EAT *Map, page 214*

RŪMĪ (7 rooms) Brīvības iela 187; ✆2561 0000; e info@rumihotel.lv. Probably the best of the limited range of hotel options in Jēkabpils, this is a clean, central place. Some rooms have a

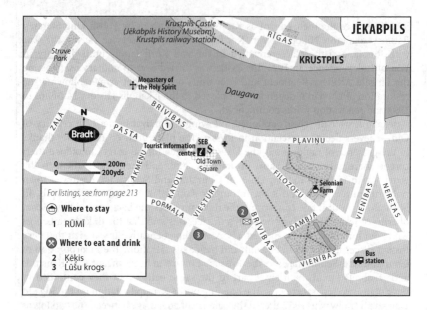

kitchenette. There is no reception: you are given access-code information when you book. €€

Lūšu krogs A. Pormaļa iela 27; 2913 3388; e lusukrogs@gmail.com. Named after the emblematic animal of Jēkabpils, the 'Lynx Pub' is a central place with an outdoor terrace, offering a hearty if unadventurous menu ranging from *karbonāde* to wok-cooked noodles to pizza. €€€

Ķēķis Brīvības iela 131; 2642 4543; e kafejnica. a12@inbox.lv. A canteen-style place, serving Latvian staples like *karbonāde*. Has a good-value set lunch, & also serves b/fast. The décor is shades of brown throughout, from the bare brick walls to the curtains. €

OTHER PRACTICALITIES The **post office** (Brīvības iela 131; 6700 8001) is centrally located, in the same block as the Ķēķis café. There is a branch of **SEB Bank** (Vecpilsētas laukums 3A; 2666 8777) on the Old Town Square, and a **pharmacy** (Brīvības iela 144; 6523 2255) just off it.

WHAT TO SEE AND DO
Jēkabpils The historic town of Jēkabpils on the left bank of the Daugava provides the modern town with its centre. Its heart is the **Old Town Square** (Vecpilsētas laukums), partly given over to a car park. Several sculptures were installed here in 2010. There is a concrete fountain with a bronze lynx, the symbol of the town, playing at the water spout. Another composition, a see-saw resembling a giant set of market scales, represents the origins of the place as the old market square. One moving artwork is called *Pilsētas stāsts* (Town Story), featuring characters drawn from old photographs, who have been reproduced in life-sized silhouette form. There is a young couple on their wedding day. A soldier carrying a small child. A girl in a wheelchair pulled by a rocking horse. One wonders what became of them. Did the couple have a long and happy marriage? Did the soldier return safely from the war? And what fate befell the girl?

Selonian Farm (Sēļu seta; Filozofu iela 6; w jekabpilsmuzejs.lv; ⊕ May–Sep 10.00–18.00 Mon–Fri, 10.00–17.00 Sat–Sun, Oct 10.00–17.00 Mon–Fri, 10.00–16.00

Sat–Sun, Nov–May 10.00–17.00 Tue–Fri, 10.00–16.00 Sat–Sun; adult/student €3/1.50) The open-air display of the Jēkabpils History Museum is a collection of 19th-century wooden rural buildings, including a farmhouse, windmill and bathhouse, offering an insight into the life and work of a moderately wealthy Selonian farmer of that period.

Monastery of the Holy Spirit (Svētā Gara klosteris; Brīvības iela 200; \6523 1486; e svetagaraklosteris@inbox.lv) This Orthodox monastery sits in a walled compound on the western side of the town centre, entered beneath a brick bell tower built in 1887. The monastery dates from the mid 17th century. Of the two churches on the site, the diminutive white-walled **Church of St Nicholas the Wonder-Worker** (Svētā Nikolaja Brīnumdara pareizticīgo baznīca) dates from 1774, replacing a wooden church on the same site. To the side is the much larger **Church of the Holy Spirit** (Svētā Gara pareizticīgo baznīca), built in a Baroque style with neo-Byzantine touches in 1888. Its external decoration combines lines of red and lighter-coloured bricks and a ceramic frieze made at the Kuznetsov porcelain factory in Rīga.

Within the icon-rich interior in the form of a cross, the main object of veneration is the **Wonder-Working Icon of the Mother of God of Jakobstadt**. This small icon is said to have been found miraculously during the wars of the mid 17th century, when a Swedish soldier, crossing the Daugava, noticed a plank of wood floating on the water and retrieved it by spearing it. On picking it up, he realised both that blood was streaming from the wood and that it bore an image of the Virgin and Child. He took it to the Orthodox monastery in Jēkabpils, where he himself converted to the Orthodox faith and remained as a monk. The icon was, however, lost in the turmoil of World War I. What you see today is a copy, made in Russia in 2008. The small icon is set into a larger scene, depicting angels holding the icon above the monastery. On a chain at the base of the icon are threaded rings given as votive offerings. It is the subject of a feast of veneration on 26 July each year, the anniversary of the arrival of the copy from Moscow.

Struve Park (Strūves parks) A few blocks further west, this small park owes its place in history to the presence of a triangulation point of the Struve Geodetic Arc (page 216). A flat stone marks the point from which Struve's observations were made in 1826. This was also part of the Latvian triangulation network created in 1931. A 42m-tall wooden tower was built at this time by teachers and students of the University of Latvia to support their observations. While this no longer survives, a metal sculpture was installed here in 2008, in the form of a model of the old tower, linked by a line of cobbles to the Struve point. The park started out life in the 19th century as the City Garden, a place for the well-heeled with a fee charged to enter the place. It was renamed to honour Pushkin in the Soviet period, and the name was changed again in 1992 in favour of Struve.

Krustpils The side of town on the right bank of the Daugava contains just one sight of major interest, but it is the major draw of the place: the impressive Krustpils Castle.

Krustpils Castle (Krustpils pils; Rīgas iela 216B; w jekabpilsmuzejs.lv; ⏲ May–Sep 09.00–18.00 Mon–Fri, 10.00–17.00 Sat–Sun, Oct–Apr 09.00–17.00 Mon–Fri, 10.00–16.00 Sat–Sun; adult/student €6/4) The castle is entered beneath a square-based tower, which brings you into the cobbled courtyard. There is a suite of restored rooms, offering something of a feel of the castle following its reconstruction in the

There are today three Latvian sites on the UNESCO World Heritage List, though a further three sites currently on the tentative list aspire to join this exclusive club. All visitors would identify straightforwardly that one of Latvia's World Heritage sites is the remarkable historic centre of Rīga. Many would guess correctly that the picture-postcard old town of Kuldīga is the second. Most would struggle, though, to identify the third, a listing shared with nine other countries, from Norway in the north to Moldova in the south. It is the Struve Geodetic Arc, a long chain of survey triangulations running for more than 2,820km from Hammerfest in northern Norway to the Black Sea. Its purpose was no less than to establish the exact size and shape of the earth, including to clarify the extent of flattening of the earth at the Poles as Newton had theorised. There were more directly practical motivations, too, including to provide data for the mapping of Tsarist Russia.

Friedrich Georg Wilhelm von Struve was a German-born scientist, a professor of astronomy at the University of Tartu in present-day Estonia, and authority on double stars. He also developed a more terrestrial interest in geodetic surveying, beginning his observations along the arc, which stretches near the 25th meridian east, in 1816. In 1828, he concluded an agreement with the Baltic-German geodesist Carl Friedrich Tenner, as a result of which Struve led the measurements in the northern part of the arc, while Tenner conducted the surveys further south. Latvia was the only part of the arc in which both made measurements, the source of some specific problems, as Struve and Tenner adopted two different standards in making their calculations, which had to be reconciled. Their observations were completed in 1855.

The original arc included 258 main survey triangulations, of which the UNESCO listing alighted on a selection of 34 where station marks have survived, including at least one from each of the countries traversed by the arc. These include two sites in Latvia. The 216m hill of Sestu-Kalns in Madona district in the Vidzeme uplands was marked in 1824. A site in the town of Jēkabpils, then Jakobstadt, marked in 1826, was the southernmost point measured by Struve himself. It was here that the issues related to the different units of length employed by Struve and Tenner had to be addressed. Both of these two triangulation points remained important in Latvian national mapping activities, thus preserving their identities.

early part of the 19th century. QR codes provide English-language audio recordings to guide you round. Note the panelled oak ceiling in the dining room, the beautiful tiled stoves, and photographs of members of the von Korff family. The small amount of furniture on display is, though, not original to the castle. The audio guide tries to make up for this absence, for example, by adding snoring sounds to designate when a bedroom has been reached.

A warren of rooms downstairs includes the reconstructed manor kitchen. Also here is the well-presented **Jēkabpils History Museum**, centred on a corridor down which flows the Daugava River. On the wall to your right is a timeline showing the development of Krustpils, while that of Jēkabpils over the river is set out to your left. There are rooms devoted to the arrival and faith of Old Believers, the Struve Geodetic Arc and the achievements of local people, the latter including a mock-up of a hot-air balloon, which ascends at the touch of a button, to commemorate the flight by balloon over the Daugava by Kārlis Skaubitis in 1911.

You can also climb the tower for a good view over the Daugava. The **Visitor Centre** across the car park from the entrance has a souvenir shop and an exhibition on the history of tourism in Jēkabpils in the basement.

AROUND JĒKABPILS: TABORKALNS   Tracking down the triangulation points of the Struve Geodetic Arc can prove a curiously addictive pursuit. One is located 15km northwest of Jēkabpils at the top of the hill known as Taborkalns or Dāburkalns, which at 157.8m is the highest in the area. This upland was created 14,000 years ago at the end of the last Ice Age, as a moraine embankment formed between the tongues of two glaciers. A path leads up from the small car park. A 33m metal observation tower was built in 2021 next to the stone marking the location of the Struve geodetic point. It was measured in 1824 and 1826, then again in 1828 by Lt Hodzjko, whose measurements from this and neighbouring points facilitated the connection of the Struve and Tenner triangulation networks. The tower offers a view of a forest canopy on all sides, with patches of farmland and glimpses of the Daugava the only leavening features. Note that the closest bus stop to the site is not the Taborkalns stop but Dābori, around 500m from the hill. Bus 6938 from Jēkabpils will bring you here (35mins), but there are only around three departures daily.

BAUSKA

A district capital of some 10,000 people, Bauska was formed around its Livonian Order castle, built in an excellent defensive location on the peninsula at the confluence of the Mūsa and Mēmele rivers where they join together to form the Lielupe. The castle is the town's main draw, but its rivers, the wooden buildings in the streets around the reconstructed Town Hall and a couple of museums also justify spending more time here than a simple change of buses en route to Rundāle Palace. The only dent in the charm of the place comes from the lorries tearing through the centre on the busy A7 road, heading to and from Lithuania.

HISTORY   Bauska Castle was constructed by the Livonian Order in the 15th century to protect their southern border and control trade between Rīga and Lithuania. It was one of the last major castles built by the order. On the creation of the Duchy of Courland and Semigallia in the 16th century, it fell into the possession of the first duke, Gotthard Kettler, and became one of his residences. Under his son, Friedrich, it was expanded, creating a more modern residence in the Renaissance style.

The town of Bauska grew up initially to the west of the castle, and sheltered by it, at the end of the peninsula formed by the rivers. This location appears to have been somewhat incommodious for Gotthard Kettler, involving the continuous traipsing of townsfolk around his castle, and in the 1580s he instructed that the town be resettled to its present location to the northeast, along the left bank of the Mēmele River. The castle was captured by Swedes during their wars with Poland–Lithuania in 1625, but a more fatal blow came during the Great Northern War at the start of the 18th century. The castle had surrendered in 1701 to Swedish forces under King Charles XII, and the Swedes extended the fortifications. Their works, however, proved insufficient to see off the Russians, who besieged it in 1705. In 1706, the Russians retreated from the castle, blowing the place up on their departure to ensure that their enemies could not take advantage of it. No longer holding any great strategic value, the castle was not restored, and developed into romantic

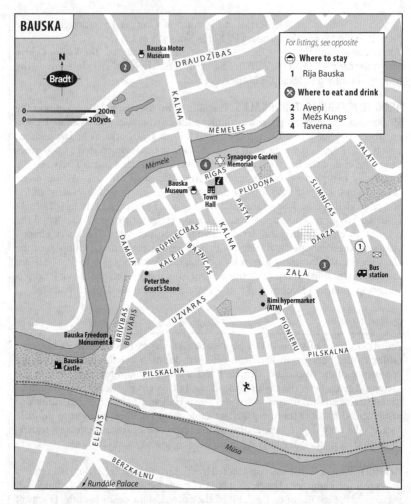

BAUSKA

N

For listings, see opposite

Where to stay

1 Rija Bauska

Where to eat and drink

2 Aveņi
3 Mežs Kungs
4 Taverna

0 ————————— 200m
0 ————————— 200yds

Bauska Motor Museum

DRAUDZĪBAS

KALNA

MĒMELES

Mēmele

RĪGAS

Synagogue Garden Memorial

Bauska Museum

Town Hall

PLŪDONA

SALATU

SLIMNĪCAS

PASTA

KALNA

DARZA

RŪPNIECĪBAS

KALĒJU

BAZNĪCAS

DAMBJA

Peter the Great's Stone

ZAĻĀ

Bus station

Rimi hypermarket (ATM)

UZVARAS

PIONIERU

Bauska Freedom Monument

BRĪVĪBAS

BULVĀRIS

Bauska Castle

PILSKALNA

PILSKALNA

PILSKALNA

ELEJAS

BĒRZKALNU

Mūsa

Rundāle Palace

ruins, attracting the attention of artists. The town of Bauska developed through the 19th century, taking advantage of its position on the trade route between Rīga and Lithuania. The Jewish population of the town grew during the century, with Jews eventually comprising the majority of townsfolk.

GETTING THERE AND AWAY The **bus station** (Bauskas autoosta; Slimnīcas iela 11; ✆2837 6006) is east of the centre, just off the main A7 road, known in town as Zaļā iela. There are up to 36 buses a day to Rīga (from 1hr 20mins), and around a dozen to Pilsrundāle (from 15mins). Bauska's location on the main road south from Rīga also makes it a stop on international routes run by FlixBus (w global.flixbus.com), with departures to Tallinn, Vilnius, Prague, Vienna, Warsaw and Berlin. You cannot buy tickets for this service at the bus station – they must be purchased online.

TOURIST INFORMATION The **tourist information centre** (Bauskas Tūrisma informācijas centrs; Rātslaukums 1; w visit.bauska.lv; ⏲ Jun–Aug 09.00–17.00 Mon–Fri, 10.00–14.00 Sat–Sun, Sep–May 09.00–17.00 Mon–Fri, 10.00–14.00 Sat) is on the ground floor of the Town Hall building on the central square. A QR code on the door provides access to an audio guide walking tour of the town, rather over-comprehensively offering 33 different stops.

WHERE TO STAY AND EAT *Map, opposite*

Rija Bauska Hotel (72 rooms) Slimnīcas iela 7; w rijahotels.com. This 5-storey block close to the bus station has the unmistakeable look of a former Soviet hotel, but the place has been renovated to a comfortable enough if unexciting level. €€
Aveņi Aveņmuiza; w aveni.lv. In a wooden building on the edge of town next to the motor museum, it boasts an interior laid out in the style of an old town square, with booths for private dining, loads of plants & a cute children's corner. The menu is wide ranging & includes some good vegan options. There is also a list of local wines, the product of various fruits & berries. €€€€

Mežs Kungs Zaļā iela 1; w mezs-kungs.lv. This large airy restaurant close to the bus station has antlers over the entrance & a game-heavy menu ranging from venison ragout to an *ukha* fish soup served with a vodka shot accompanying the paintings of duck & deer on the walls. €€€€
Taverna Rīgas iela 27; ℘ 2630 6309. In a centrally located wooden-fronted building on Town Hall Square, this place serves huge portions of Latvian standbys such as *karbonāde* & chicken fillet. There are tables outside & garish red-upholstered furniture within. Half portions are available, & recommended. €€€

OTHER PRACTICALITIES The **post office** (Slimnīcas iela 9A; ℘ 6392 2588) is behind the Rija Bauska Hotel. There is a **pharmacy** (Pionieru iela 2; ℘ 2036 6389) among the cluster of supermarkets at the western end of Zaļā iela, and you will also find an **ATM** in the Rimi hypermarket here.

WHAT TO SEE AND DO

Bauska Castle (Bauskas pils; Pilskalns; w bauskaspils.lv; ⊕ May–Sep 09.00–19.00 daily, Oct 09.00–18.00 daily, Nov–Apr 11.00–17.00 Tue–Sun; adult/student €9/4.50) Accessed by a path crossing a deep ditch guarded by cannons, Bauska Castle is essentially two castles in one, easily distinguishable from each other by their different states of repair. On the west side stands the 15th-century Livonian Order castle. Once comprising five towers built around a central courtyard, this is now in ruins, the remains of its walls protected by cappings of grass-covered turf, giving the whole place a picturesque air. The circular main tower has been reconstructed and can be ascended up brick and wooden stairways. The second floor housed the apartment of the Vogt, the administrator of the Bauska area in the days of the Livonian Order. From here, you can look down to view a rotating 3D video display chronicling the expansion of the castle over time.

Immediately to the east, around a cobbled central courtyard, stands the heavily reconstructed 16th-century Renaissance castle, a residence of Dukes of Courland and Semigallia. The sgraffito decoration on the external walls is striking, forming a trompe-l'œil effect in which the flat walls appear to be covered by protuberances. This has been painstakingly reconstructed, based on small patches of original sgraffito design. A history exhibition inside has a room devoted to the Semigallian tribes that were masters of the area before the arrival of the Livonian Order, with displays of jewellery and spearheads unearthed from grave sites. Then come displays on the Livonian Order, and on the Renaissance castle. The discovery of oyster shells among the archaeological finds here hints at the relative sophistication of the diet of the ducal court. Another room covers the wars of the 17th century, and the castle's gradual descent into romantic ruins in the 18th.

You are then invited to put on some slippers to view a suite of rooms furnished as the apartments of the duke and duchess. The slippers aim to protect the striking polychrome tiles, reconstructed on the basis of a small surviving area of original tiling. In mid-July, the castle holds the **Vivat Curlandia!** festival of early music (w earlymusic.lv).

The castle is surrounded by wooded parkland offering fine strolls above the Mūsa and Mēmele rivers. Heading back towards the town, note the **Bauska Freedom Monument** (Bauskas Brīvības piemineklis), dating from the 1920s. A bronze sculpture of an axe-wielding Semigallian warrior was added in 1992. Four soldiers are buried at its base.

Town centre Bauska town centre, on the left bank of the Mēmele River and characterised by a mix of both stone and wooden buildings, radiates from a large brick-paved square, Rātslaukums, with at its heart the delightful **Town Hall** (Bauskas rātsnams; Rātslaukums 1). With terracotta-painted walls and topped by a half-timbered clock tower, the origins of the building lie in the granting of city rights to Bauska by Duke Friedrich Kettler in 1609. The construction of a town hall in the centre of the market square followed. The building had fallen into decay by the mid 19th century, but has been sympathetically restored, and now houses both the civic registry office and the tourist information centre.

In the northeast corner of the square, close to the river, stands the **Synagogue Garden Memorial** (Bauskas ebreju kopienas memorials 'Sinagogas dārzs'). Bauska's Grand Synagogue stood on this site. Built in 1844, it contained a magnificently carved Torah Ark, a reconstructed fragment of which can be seen in the Jews in Latvia museum in Rīga. Abraham Isaac Kook, a leading proponent of religious Zionism who became the first Ashkenazi Chief Rabbi of British Mandatory Palestine, served here as rabbi early in his career. The synagogue was burned to the ground by the Nazis in July 1941. Most of the remaining Jews in Bauska were executed in Likvertenu Forest outside the town in early August. Stones encased in wire mesh suggest the walls of the synagogue, as well as forming five human figures, depicted leaving a service.

Bauska Museum (Bauskas muzejs; Kalna iela 6; w bauskasmuzejs.lv; ⊕ May–Oct 10.00–18.00 Tue–Fri, 10.00–16.00 Sat–Sun, Nov–Apr 10.00–17.00 Tue–Fri, 10.00–16.00 Sat–Sun; adult/student €3/1.50) A visually appealing museum just across Kalna iela from the Town Hall, this takes you through the 20th-century history of the town by reconstructions of shop interiors. A grocery, photo studio and smithy of the turn of the century are followed by an interwar hairdresser's shop, complete with moustache curlers, stationers and sewing workshop. There is a mock-up of a living room of the Soviet period, with the daughter of the house dressed in a Young Pioneer uniform. Upstairs there is a display on the contribution of Jews to the history of the town, and a large display of dolls and other toys from the late 19th century to the start of the 21st. There is also a space for temporary art exhibitions.

Along **Rīgas iela** to the side of the museum, note the fabric flowers fashioned on metal mesh hung on the wooden walls of the houses. They were installed here in 2017 to help brighten the place up. Head west from the town centre along the unmetalled and rustic Kalēju iela and you reach after a few hundred metres a wooded area with a moss-covered boulder taking centre stage. This is known as **Peter the Great's Stone** (Petera akmens). Legend has it that, during the fighting for the castle in the Great Northern War, two adversaries, Peter the Great of Russia and Augustus the Strong of Poland, had lunch on the stone in 1701. After their meal, they decided, for reasons left unrecorded by legend, to bury their spoons under the rock.

Bauska Motor Museum (Bauskas motormuzejs; Derpeles iela 2.; w motormuzejs. lv; ☉ 10.00–18.00 Tue–Sun; adult/student €5/3) In a hangar-like building on the northern edge of town, this is a branch of the Rīga Motor Museum, and while nothing like as comprehensive as its parent museum is interesting in its own right. It has two main displays of vehicles. The first focuses on motorcars and motorbikes found in Latvia between 1920 and 1990. There is a good range of Soviet-era vehicles, from the compact Zaporozhets, to the luxury GAZ-13 Chaika, destined for high-ranking party leaders. The latter is, of course, black.

The second hall features a mixed range of vehicles, including several products of the Latvian RAF factory, one of the main producers of vans and minibuses in the USSR. A RAF caravan trailer from 1978 is one of just two known surviving examples. Upstairs there are a few hands-on exhibits and a children's play area.

AROUND BAUSKA

RUNDĀLE PALACE (Rundāles pils; Pilsrundāle; w rundale.net; ☉ Jun–Aug palace 10.00–18.00 daily, garden 10.00–19.00 Mon–Thu, 10.00–21.00 Fri–Sun; Sep palace 10.00–18.00, garden 10.00–19.00; May & Oct palace & garden 10.00–18.00; Nov–Apr palace & garden 10.00–17.00; adult/student/child Apr-Oct €17/10.50/5.50, Nov–Mar 12/8.50/3.50 – separate palace & garden tickets are also available, & there are 2 further exhibitions within the palace charged additionally) One of Latvia's major sights, this Baroque palace was the work of Francesco Bartolomeo Rastrelli, the Italian architect best known for his work for the Russian court, including the Winter Palace in St Petersburg. The story of how such a grand palace appeared in the Latvian countryside has its origins in the meteoric rise of Ernst Johann von Biron. Biron had secured a place at the court of Anna Ioannovna, regent of Courland, becoming Anna's favourite and confidant. When in 1730 Anna was elevated to the throne of Russia, Biron moved with her, retaining his place as her trusted advisor. When the post of Duke of Courland and Semigallia fell vacant in 1737 on the death of childless Duke Ferdinand, Anna proposed Biron, a choice accepted by Augustus III, King of Poland, who had relied on Russian support to secure his office.

Biron had already purchased the estate at Rundāle in 1735. That year, in anticipation of his appointment as duke, Biron engaged Rastrelli to build him a grand summer residence. Rastrelli ordered the demolition of the old castle, to be replaced by a palace in the form of a quadrangle, with a stable block to the north. The foundation stone of the new palace was laid in 1736, though work slowed somewhat in 1738, when Biron engaged Rastrelli simultaneously to build Jelgava Palace. But with the death of his protector Empress Anna in 1740, and Biron's deportation to Siberia, work at Rundāle immediately stopped. Biron's restoration to the duchy by Empress Catherine the Great in 1763 marked the occasion for work on the palace to recommence. Rastrelli returned to Rundāle. The existing Baroque interior decoration by then considered outmoded, Rastrelli set about remodelling the interiors in a more modern Rococo style. Duke Ernst Johann loved Rundāle, but his son and successor Duke Peter favoured Vircava Palace, closer to Jelgava, as his summer residence.

Following the annexation of the duchy by Russia in 1795, Catherine presented the palace to Count Valerian Zubov. On his death, it fell to his brother, Prince Platon Zubov, the last favourite of Catherine the Great. Platon died in 1822, and his widow later married Count Andrey Shuvalov. Rundāle Palace was then owned by the Shuvalov family until the agrarian reforms introduced by the new

Latvian government in 1920 when the palace, damaged during the Latvian War of Independence, was transferred to the control of the Ministry of Agriculture. After a difficult few decades in which parts of the palace were used variously as museum, school and even grain storehouse, a Rundāle Palace Museum was established in 1972, and restoration began in earnest.

Getting there and away The Rundāles Pils **bus stop** is conveniently sited on the road in front of the palace. It is served by a dozen or so buses a day from Bauska (from 15mins), a couple of which carry on to Rīga. There are up to five buses a day to Jelgava (1hr 10mins) and a couple to Dobele (1hr 25mins). Rundāle Palace is also a favoured day trip destination for Rīga-based tour operators.

Where to stay and eat

Baltā māja (11 rooms) Pilsrundāle; ☎6396 2140; e baltamaja@inbox.lv. Housed in an 18th-century building which originally accommodated palace servants, this is an atmospheric place close to one of the palace car parks, though rooms are small & the cheapest have shared bathrooms. Its restaurant (€€€) is a good option, with tables outside around a pond. The menu seeks to evoke a medieval feel, including snails & blood sausage, as well as classic Latvian dishes like the dessert *maizes zupa*. €–€€

Ozollāde Pilsrundāle; w ozollade.lv. Located on the ground floor of the palace, the 'Oak Chest'

serves up a tempting range of dishes, such as catfish stewed in double cream & leek, on wooden tables beneath a vaulted ceiling. It is also a good place just for coffee & cake after a tour of the palace. It is not open for dinner. €€€

Pils Krogs Pilsrundāle; ☎2922 4624; e kommats@inbox.lv. Housed in a yellow-walled outbuilding in the palace grounds, this place has a disappointingly bland interior, an outdoor terrace & a fine if unadventurous menu ranging from *karbonāde* to pasta. 'Octopus sausages' turned out to be a children's dish of sausages cut into octopus shapes. €€€

What to see and do Approaching the palace, you first pass between the orange-painted former stable blocks, arranged in a semicircle, in one of which the ticket office is located. The courtyard of the palace itself is entered through imposing gates, whose pillars are topped with stone lions sporting crowns. Note the monogram 'EJ', Ernst Johann, on the railings to the side of the gates. Cross the cobbled courtyard and ascend the grand balustraded staircase to start the tour of palace rooms.

The tour starts with the **state rooms** used for lavish entertainment. One of the first rooms you reach is the most luxurious, the Gold Hall, with a ceiling painting by Francesco Martini and Carlo Zucchi, Italian artists invited to Rundāle in the 1760s. The painting, *The Apotheosis of Duke Ernst Johann*, is packed with figures symbolising the virtues of the duke. The golden stucco decorations overlaying the stucco marble walls adds to a general sumptuousness. Note the 'EJ' monograms in gold. The porcelain cabinet just off the Gold Hall, one of two such rooms in the palace, features 34 elaborately carved consoles on the walls, specifically built to show off the duke's porcelain collection. The 30m-long Grand Gallery once accommodated a lengthy banquet table. It leads into another large room, the White Hall, the palace ballroom. The white-painted walls and ceiling here are decorated with stucco reliefs, the work of Johann Michael Graff, brought here from Berlin in 1765 to help provide a Rococo-style interior. Among the reliefs, illustrating pastoral scenes, seasons and elements through the liberal deployment of putti, note the stork's nest on the ceiling, made of real twigs coated with gypsum. There is another porcelain cabinet off this room.

The next series of rooms visited along the set route are the 20 rooms of the **duke's apartments**, running as an 86m-long enfilade, an arrangement characteristic of Baroque architecture. The apartments were themselves an important part of court life, and covered both private quarters and more public rooms. Note the way that contrasting schemes are used to decorate adjoining rooms, such that silk wall coverings alternate with stucco marble, and exuberant ceiling paintings with white stucco ceilings. For a duke's apartments, the decoration of the Rose Room is remarkably feminine, with pink stucco marble panels on the walls adorned with trailing garlands of stucco flowers, and on the ceiling a painting of Flora, Roman goddess of flowers, with her attendants. Note also the room with walls decorated in pink silk damask on which are hung portraits of the Biron family as well as those of European rulers of the time. The portrait of Duke Ernst Johann is set below that of Polish King Stanisław August Poniatowski, with Russian Tsar Peter the Great to his right and Prussian King Frederick the Great to his left, an arrangement that deftly summarises the geopolitical challenges faced by Courland as it navigated its independence between the ambitions of major powers. The duke's bedroom, at the centre of the suite of apartments following a tradition established at Versailles, features another ceiling painting drawing on mythological themes, and of course a bed, its canopy decorated with plumes of feathers, sitting in a large niche. The monogram 'EJ' above the niche reminds the visitor whose bed it was.

In the reception room next door, note the large painting of Duke Peter, depicted in the garden of his favourite Vircava Palace. The duke presented the portrait to the Academia Petrina in Jelgava, but in 1791, a student at the college named Ulrich von Schlippenbach, influenced by the French Revolution, slashed the portrait with a knife. The offended duke took the portrait back and gave it to his doctor. Von Schlippenbach became a Romantic poet.

The final suite of visitable rooms is that of the **duchess' apartments**, occupying 11 rooms. Its antechamber now displays portraits together with a Biron family tree, better to understand the family relationships underpinning the history of the palace. The duchess' boudoir stands out for the elaborate niche in the form of a shell, with stucco trees framing it, the work of Johann Michael Graff. The chaise longue occupying the niche is made of two parts that can be used separately or together, a piece of furniture that rejoices in the name *duchesse brisée* ('broken duchess'). Behind the duchess' bedroom, note the splendid toilet room, with wood-panelled walls and an elaborate stucco ceiling. There follow several rooms that now accommodate displays: of 18th-century ladies' fashion; of the von Behr and von Medem families, prominent members of the Courland aristocracy; and of 18th-century Courland society.

Also in the palace are exhibitions not included in the main admission charge. These are of more specialist interest and none is unmissable, though the best of the bunch is the exhibition entitled 'from the Gothic Style to Art Nouveau', which covers developments in the decorative arts. You should, however, not miss the formal **park**, also designed by Rastrelli, to the south of the palace. It covers 10ha and features a network of alleys radiating from three fountains in front of the palace. The flowering of tulips in the spring and roses in summer brings many visitors to the park. The Green Theatre, a grass-covered amphitheatre in the park, is the venue for recitals.

MEŽOTNE Some 10km to the west of Bauska, on the right bank of the Lielupe River, the parish of Mežotne centres on the Neoclassical **Mežotne Palace** (Mežotnes pils). Following the Russian annexation of the Duchy of Courland and Semigallia in 1795, Empress Catherine the Great granted the lifetime use of the estate at Mežotne to Charlotte von Lieven, tutor to her grandchildren. The deal improved still further under Catherine's son, Paul I, who in 1797 made her the hereditary owner of the estate, and later made her a countess to boot. She was elevated still further in 1826 to the title of princess by Paul's son, Nicholas I. Giacomo Quarenghi, the Italian architect at the Russian court, produced a Neoclassical design for a manor house at Mežotne to befit its new owner, and this was executed by Johann Georg Adam Berlitz. An English-style park was laid out around the manor, and the manor complex included a wide range of buildings, such as dairy and distillery.

Charlotte von Lieven, who was based with the Russian court in St Petersburg, only spent one night in her palace, when accompanying Paul I's widow Maria Feodorovna to Germany in 1818. She returned only on her death in 1828, to be buried in the churchyard. Later in the 19th century, her son Johann Georg von Lieven and grandson Paul von Lieven expanded the family holdings by obtaining Bauska Manor, including the ruined Bauska Castle, as well as properties in Vidzeme, such as Krimulda Manor. Paul's son, Anatol von Lieven, led the Liepāja Volunteer Rifle detachment during the Latvian War of Independence, made up largely of former Russian Imperial army officers fighting in support of independent Latvia. This patriotism did not prevent him from being dispossessed of the Mežotne estate under the agrarian reform of 1920, and the palace became an agriculture school. Following extensive restoration, a hotel opened here at the start of the 21st century, but this sadly failed, and at the time of writing, the palace is closed. The property of the state, there is an ongoing debate as to what should be done with it.

You can thus admire no more than the exterior, including its portico with four Ionic columns. You are, though, free to wander the grounds, which run to the bank of the Lielupe River. The **Mazā Mežotnes pils** (**w** mazamezotnespils.lv), based in the former dairy of the manor complex, smartly restored by sculptor Regina Deičmane, hosts occasional piano concerts. A pontoon bridge over the river in summer allows you to walk to the wooded hill on the opposite bank, the site of a Semigallian hillfort. The Mežotne **bus stop** is close to the palace, offering around three buses a day to Bauska (20mins).

JELGAVA

Latvia's fourth city by population, Jelgava has a great historic pedigree as the capital of the Duchy of Courland and Semigallia, when the place was known as Mitau. Unfortunately, brutal bombardment during World War II, followed by an uninspired reconstruction during the Soviet period, when the focus was on industrialisation rather than aesthetics, have given Jelgava an unappealing cityscape of concrete apartment blocks. With only a few historic buildings still standing, many visitors bypass the place altogether. But since those buildings include Jelgava Palace, the work of Russian court architect Francesco Bartolomeo Rastrelli, and the Academia Petrina, the product of Duke Peter von Biron's dream of a great Latvian university, the city deserves a look.

HISTORY Known by the German name Mitau until 1917, Jelgava grew around a Livonian Order castle, built in 1265 on the island of Pilssala in the Lielupe River to benefit from added natural protection against the surrounding Livonian and Semigallian tribes. The real flourishing of the place came with the establishment of the Duchy of Courland and Semigallia, of which Mitau became capital in 1578. Following the partitioning of the duchy in 1596, Mitau was the place of residence of Friedrich Kettler, ruler of Semigallia, and from 1617, with the duchy once more

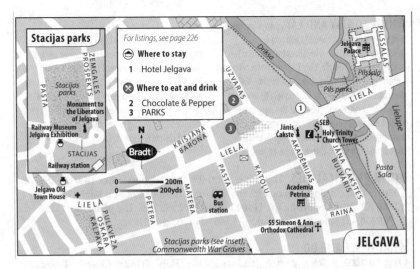

For listings, see page 226

Where to stay

1 Hotel Jelgava

Where to eat and drink

2 Chocolate & Pepper
3 PARKS

Stacijas parks

Stacijas parks

Monument to the Liberators of Jelgava

Railway Museum Jelgava Exhibition

STACIJAS

Railway station

Jelgava Old Town House

0   200m
0   200yds

JELGAVA

Stacijas parks (see inset),
Commonwealth War Graves

united, Mitau again became its capital. In the 18th century, the duchy increasingly fell under the influence of Russia, and Mitau's fortunes depended on the relations of its rulers to the Russian court. Following the death at the age of 18 of Duke Friedrich Wilhelm in 1711, on the way back to Courland from his wedding to the Russian princess Anna Ioannovna, Anna ruled the place as regent until 1730. She was elevated to the Russian throne in 1730 on the death of Tsar Peter II, and in 1737, on the extinction of the Kettler line, Anna persuaded the nobles of Courland to elect her advisor and confidante Ernst Johann von Biron as the new duke. With financial support from Russia, von Biron embarked upon the magnificent Jelgava Palace. His son Peter, the last Duke of Courland and Semigallia, further embellished the city, including through the foundation of the Academia Petrina, which he hoped would become a great university.

Following annexation by Russia in 1795, Mitau remained the capital of the Courland Governorate, and the arrival of the railway in 1868 brought further expansion. The city was damaged heavily during World War I and the Latvian War of Independence, but its growth renewed in independent Latvia. In the summer of 1944, however, the effects of a Soviet attack and German counterattack left the city in ruins, its historic centre destroyed. In the Soviet period new factories arrived such as the Rīga Autobus Factory (RAF), a major producer of Soviet minibuses.

GETTING THERE AND AWAY The **railway station** (Jelgavas dzelzceļa stacija; Stacijas iela 1; ☎6723 2135), dating from 1870, sits at the southern edge of the city centre. There are more than 20 departures a day to Rīga (30–55mins), but only one or two daily to stations further west, including Dobele (22mins), Saldus (1hr 10mins) and Liepāja (2hrs 30mins). The **bus station** (Jelgavas autoosta; Pasta iela 26; ☎6302 2639) is in the city centre, offering buses to Rīga (55mins) every few minutes. Dobele (35mins) is served by two or more buses an hour, and there are around eight a day to Bauska (1hr 15mins).

TOURIST INFORMATION The **tourist information centre** (Jelgavas Tūrisma informācijas centrs; Akadēmijas iela 1; w visit.jelgava.lv; ⊕ 10.00–18.00 Tue, 10.00–20.00 Wed–Sat, 11.00–18.00 Sun) is housed in the ground floor of the Holy Trinity Church Tower.

Sēlija and Zemgale   JELGAVA

7

⌂ WHERE TO STAY AND EAT *Map, page 225*

Hotel Jelgava (41 rooms) Lielā iela 6;
w hoteljelgava.lv. In an ideal central location next
to the bridge to Pilssala, this 3-storey hotel offers a
comfortable if unremarkable place to stay. €€€
Chocolate & Pepper Kr Barona iela 6; **w** choco-
pepper.lv. Located on the side of the ugly green-
walled House of Culture next to Hercoga Jēkaba
laukums, this place has a wide-ranging menu
stretching from sushi, through wok-cooked dishes

& burgers to such fare as Lake Peipus pikeperch.
Pepper was the nickname of the former owner,
apparently. Not sure about Chocolate. €€€€
PARKS Kr Barona iela 3 – 1A; **w** parksrestorans.
lv. Located logically enough beside a park, the
central Hercoga Jēkaba laukums, this offers a broad
menu encompassing poke bowls, pizza, wok-
cooked dishes & steak. €€€€

OTHER PRACTICALITIES There is a centrally located **post office** (Katoļu iela 2B;
⚞6301 2402) close to Hercoga Jēkaba laukums. A branch of **SEB Bank** (Lielā iela 1;
⚞2666 8777) sits opposite the Hotel Jelgava on Lielā iela. The **pharmacy** (Lielā iela
36; ⚞6308 4218) west of here, along Lielā iela is open 24 hours a day.

WHAT TO SEE AND DO

City centre A city centre landmark, the **Holy Trinity Church Tower** (Sv
Trīsvienības baznīcas tornis; **w** visit.jelgava.lv; ⊕ 10.00–18.00 Tue, 10.00–20.00
Wed–Sat, 11.00–18.00 Sun; adult/student €4/1.50 inc exhibition hall, €1.50/0.80
sightseeing platform only) is all that remains of a church built in 1574, one of the
first purpose-built Lutheran churches in Europe. Destroyed in 1944, red bricks
on the pavement mark the location of former columns. Defiantly, the square-
based tower has survived. As well as the tourist office, the interior accommodates
displays on the history of Jelgava, and there is a glass pyramid at the top of the
tower offering views across the city. In front of the tower, at the corner of Lielā iela
and Akadēmijas iela, is a 2003 **statue of Jānis Čakste**, the first president of Latvia,
who went to school in the city.

Academia Petrina A couple of blocks south, along Akadēmijas iela, the
Academia Petrina was built in 1775, making it the first higher education institute
in Latvia. It was an initiative of Duke Peter von Biron, who envisaged a great
university in Mitau, and set about inviting distinguished scholars like Immanuel
Kant and John Gottfried Herder, only to be rebuffed by them. One of the few
survivals of Mitau's golden age, its pink-and-white building with a Corinthian-
columned façade and central tower now houses the **Ģederts Eliass Jelgava History
and Art Museum** (Ģ Eliasa Jelgavas vēstures un mākslas muzejs; Akadēmijas iela
10; **w** jvmm.lv; ⊕ 10.00–17.00 Tue–Sun; adult/student €4/1). Rather cluttered
displays cover the history of the region. In a room dedicated to the Duchy of
Courland and Semigallia, a mannequin representing Duke Jacob sits wistfully at
a table dreaming of colonial glories. Note also the trophy from the 1895 Latvian
Song and Dance Festival, held in Jelgava, the only time the festival has ventured
outside Rīga.

There are sobering photographs of the destruction wrought in World War II,
and the chance to try on a virtual reality headset to relive the conflict between
Semigallians and brothers of the Livonian Order. A hall upstairs showcases the
paintings of Ģederts Eliass, who was involved in the 1905 revolutionary movement
before becoming a noted artist, famed particularly for unsentimental portraits of
rural life. *Mēslu vešana* (Carrying of Manure) from the 1930s pictures a woman
transporting a large quantity of dung. The museum has, though, little signage
in English.

St Simeon and St Ann Orthodox Cathedral (Sv Simeona un Sv Annas pareizticīgo baznīca; Raiņa iela 5; `\`6302 0207) Continuing south from the Academia Petrina, at the junction of Raiņa iela and Akadēmijas iela stand the turquoise domes and spire of the cathedral of St Simeon and St Ann. On his marriage to Anna Ioannovna, niece of Peter the Great, Duke Friedrich Wilhelm promised that an Orthodox Church would be built in Jelgava. While the duke's early death prevented him from having any part in the matter, a wooden church was built in 1726, replaced in the 1770s by a stone church built to the design of Rastrelli. With the financial support of Tsar Alexander III, the church, now designated a cathedral, was rebuilt to enlarged dimensions in 1892. Damaged in World War II, there were threats during the Soviet period to demolish the building altogether, and a couple of holes drilled in the walls in 1983 to set explosive charges have been preserved as a demonstration of how close the cathedral came to destruction. The protests of local people forced the authorities to reconsider. It was renovated following the restoration of Latvian independence, and now sports a colourful interior of new icons and murals.

Islands in the Lielupe
From the Holy Trinity Church Tower, take Lielā iela eastwards over the bridge to reach the long island of **Pilssala** in the Lielupe River and the city's major attraction, Jelgava Palace.

Jelgava Palace (Jelgavas pils; Lielā iela 2; w jelgavaspils.lv; ⊕ Jun–Aug 09.00–17.00 Mon–Fri, 09.00–18.00 Sat, 11.00–16.00 Sun, Sep–May 09.00–17.00 Mon–Fri) The place impresses for its size: a rectangular three-storey building around a central courtyard, it claims the title of the largest Baroque palace in the Baltics. Construction started in 1738, as a palace fit for the ambitions of the new Duke of Courland and Semigallia, Duke Ernst Johann von Biron. It was built on the site of the Livonian Order castle, demolished to make way for the new palace: the work, like Rundāle, of architect Francesco Bartolomeo Rastrelli. On Biron's fall from grace in 1740, work on the palace was promptly stopped, though picked up again after Biron's return from exile in 1762.

Plaques put up in 2019 record a French episode in the palace's history, when Louis XVIII of France, exiled by the Revolution, was granted the use of Jelgava Palace by Tsar Paul I of Russia in 1798. He attempted to reproduce an elaborate court life modelled on that of Versailles. In 1799, the palace was the venue for the wedding of his niece Marie-Thérèse, eldest child of the executed King Louis XVI, and Louis Antione, Duke of Angoulême. After Paul I tired of his Bourbon guests, Louis XVIII and his court moved to Warsaw in 1801, though returned to Jelgava in 1805 when Paul's successor, Alexander I, proved more accommodating. Louis left Jelgava Palace definitively in 1807, moving to the safer destination of England. A plaque also records the death in 1807 of Henry Essex Edgeworth, Irish Catholic priest and confessor of Louis XVI. He had accompanied Louis XVIII to Jelgava, but died of a fever contracted while visiting French prisoners.

In the 19th century, the palace accommodated the administration of the Courland Governorate. It was damaged during the War of Independence in 1919, but in the late 1930s was renovated to accommodate the new Latvia Agricultural Academy. The renovation added a new west wing, enclosing the central courtyard. It remains the home of the academy's successor, the Latvia University of Life Sciences and Technologies, and its institutional interiors only hint at the palace's former Rococo glories. A basement in the southeast wing does, however, hold one fascinating link to its past life. It houses the **Vault of the Dukes of Courland and Semigallia** (Kurzemes hercogu kapenes; ⊕ Jun–Oct 10.00–17.00 Wed–Sun,

7

Nov–May 10.00–16.00 Wed–Sun; adult/student/child €3/2/1), comprising 21 metal sarcophagi and nine wooden coffins; the final resting place of dukes and their immediate families who died between 1569 and 1791. The sarcophagi containing the remains of the first dukes were moved here following the construction of the new Jelgava Palace. They are intricately decorated: resting on feet comprised either of eagles' claws clutching cannonballs or lions. There is a landscaped park around the palace, and meadows in the northern part of Pilssala which provide a home for wild horses. There is also an observation tower here.

Pasta Sala ('Post Island') A smaller island to the south of Pilssala, and connected to it by bridge, Pasta Sala is a favoured place for outdoor recreation. A collection of mostly abstract sculptures is the legacy of an annual chamotte ceramics symposium. Pasta Sala also plays host to an annual ice sculpture festival in early February and sand sculpture festival in early June. There is a river beach with changing rooms. A curving pedestrian bridge links the island directly with the town centre.

Around the railway station
On the southern edge of the city centre, there are a couple of places of interest around the railway station.

Railway Museum Jelgava Exhibition (Dzelzceļa muzejs ekspozīcija Jelgavā; Stacijas iela 3; w railwaymuseum.lv; ⊕ 10.00–17.00 Wed & Fri–Sat, 11.00–19.00 Thu; adult/student €2/1) The Jelgava branch of the Latvian Railway Museum is sited in a green-painted wooden house built in the early 20th century for railway station workers. It is full of interesting memorabilia, such as a 'spravochnaya', an automatic information machine from the 1970s, now used to display photographs of locomotives and station buildings. You can also watch a video of Latvian rapper Ansis visiting the narrow-gauge railway in Gulbene in order to sample steam engine noises for his, er, tracks.

Monument to the Liberators of Jelgava Standing in front of the railway station, in a stretch of park known as Stacijas parks, this monument depicts Latvian epic hero Lāčplēsis standing solemnly, head bowed, following victory over the vanquished Dark Knight. The work of sculptor Andrejs Jansons, it was unveiled on 21 November 1992 to mark the anniversary of Jelgava's liberation from Bermondt-Avalov's West Russian Volunteer Army in 1919. The monument is a copy of one made in 1932 by the sculptor's father, Kārlis Jansons, dismantled in 1951 to make way for a statue of Lenin.

Vecpilsētas iela Quarter
One small area of characterful wooden houses on the northwestern edge of the centre was largely spared the bombardments of World War II. The buildings here are gradually being restored to make a historic quarter, centred on the showcase Old Town House.

Jelgava Old Town House (Jelgavas Vecpilsētas māja; Vecpilsētas iela 14; w visit. jelgava.lv; ⊕ 10.00–18.00 Tue–Sat, 11.00–17.00 Sun; adult/student €4/1.50) This large wooden house, dating from the late 18th century and inhabited until the 1980s, once housed a shop, laundry, bicycle repair workshop and cobbler's store in addition to residential apartments. The place had fallen into decrepitude, but has been painstakingly restored, a process which required raising the building by 30cm and creating new foundations. It now houses an exhibition telling the story of the building and its restoration, and through this the wider history of Jelgava. Each room of the exhibition has a golden chest in the middle. Press a button on the wall, and the chest comes apart to reveal displays in drawers and under lids, including the quotidian items found during the restoration, from a 1960s skin-softening cream to a lice comb. A soundtrack of household noises, from footsteps to piano music, plays as you walk round.

Commonwealth War Graves On the edge of town, off a large roundabout on the A8 road bypassing Jelgava to the east, take the turning signposted to Meža kapi (Forest Cemetery). After 300m, the entrance to the cemetery falls on your right. Here you will find the British plot, marked with a war cross, and 36 white headstones marking Commonwealth burials. Most of those buried here were prisoners of war of the Germans, who died in 1917. The Meža kapi bus stop is close to the entrance to the cemetery. Bus 5 serves it from Jēlgava bus station.

NORTH OF JELGAVA

TĪREĻPURVS The marshland known as the Tīreļpurvs lying between Jelgava and Lake Babīte was the focus of the Christmas Battles of World War I, a brutal engagement commemorated actively today because of the central role in the fighting of the Latvian Riflemen brigades, all-Latvian volunteer units set up with the approval of the Tsarist authorities, and the consequent importance of the battles in forging a Latvian national consciousness. The Battles were focused on a surprise Russian attack on the German lines around Christmas 1916. The Tīreļpurvs marshland was chosen because the area was all but impassable in summer, and thus relatively less heavily defended by the Germans, while the freezing of the marsh waters in winter made an attack possible. Latvian Riflemen in white winter camouflage were used to cut the German barbed wire defences, to allow the main body of Latvian troops to advance through to the main German defence. Fighting was tough. On 25 December, Latvian and Siberian forces took the fortified Machine-gun Hill (Ložmetēkalns), a sand dune on the northern part of the marshes. This was the clearest single success of the battle, and a memorial on the hill, some 6km north of the Christmas Battles museum, is the focus of annual commemorations of the battle each January. But overall, as with so many of the battles of World War I, territorial gains were insignificant and fleeting. A counterattack by the German Eighth Army regained most of their lost positions.

There are memorial stones, graves and remnants of the German fortifications dotted across the area, but the best place to learn more about the battles is the **Christmas Battles Museum** (Ziemassvētku kauju muzejs; Mangaļi, Valgundes pagasts; w karamuzejs.lv; ⏰ 10.00–16.00 Tue–Sun; admission free) housed in the Mangaļi homestead which was at the centre of the action. A branch of the Latvian War Museum, this offers a two-room exhibition about the battles, focusing on the role of the Latvian Riflemen, with a diorama of part of the battle site, and a collection of bullets, barbed wire and other accoutrements of warfare found in the local area. Displays are in Latvian, though with laminated explanatory cards in English and German. Outside are reconstructions of German fortifications, including a section of log-lined ramparts and one of the formidable concrete pillboxes that proved a huge challenge for attacking Latvian Riflemen. A 7km trail includes various sites linked to the battles. The area today is more forest than marsh; the consequence of post-war drainage works. The museum is accessed along signposted forest tracks, running 6km east from the P99 road between Jelgava and Tireļi. Getting here requires your own transport.

TĒRVETE The green village of Tērvete has an important place in Latvian history, as the capital of Semigallian leaders Viestards, who first allied with and then opposed the Livonian Brothers of the Sword in the early 13th century, and Namejs, who led a Semigallian rising against the Livonian Order from 1279 to 1281. It is thus regarded as the centre of Semigallian resistance against the German crusaders in the 13th century. The memorial house of Latvian children's author Anna Brigadere and the charming sculpture-encrusted Tērvete Nature Park round out its tourist offer. There are around eight **buses** a day from Dobele. The bus stop named Sprīdīši, after Anna Brigadere's best-known character, is convenient for the castle mound.

 ## Where to stay and eat

Zoltners [map, page 212] (13 rooms) Kroņauce; w zoltners.lv. In an attractive rural setting to the northwest of Tērvete, a signposted 3km off the main Tērvete to Dobele road, this is a smartly furnished hotel & restaurant, with shades of grey favoured. Hotel rooms are in 2 of the buildings arranged around a courtyard, with the restaurant in a 3rd & a venue for receptions in a 4th. The restaurant combines prompt service & an enticing menu (€€€€). They have their own microbrewery. **€€€**

Sprīdīši (5 rooms, 5 cabins & pavilion); w spridisi.lv. Around the back of the Anna Brigadere Museum stands a guest house in a wooden building. They also have 5 wooden huts in the woods, looking like upturned boats, with toilets, showers & a kitchenette in a shared block, & a charming if tiny pavilion converted into accommodation by the addition of mattresses up a ladder in the attic. The restaurant (€€) has a shaded outdoor terrace, & offers an unadventurous menu featuring *karbonāde*, burgers & ribs. **€€**

What to see and do

Tērvete Castle Mound (Tērvetes pilskalns) Tērvete's relatively hilly terrain within flat Latvia does much to explain its military importance at the time of the Semigallian rulers, and the site of their hill fort still impresses today, a steep-sided hill, rising 19m. It is accessed from the P103 road running through the village. At the small car park opposite a Spar supermarket, signposts lead you down across a meadow, over a wooden bridge across the diminutive Tērvete River, and then to the far side of the mound where there is a flight of wooden steps up.

Immediately southeast of the castle mound, on another area of high ground which would have been part of the forecourt of the Semigallian fortifications, separated from the hill fort by a steep ditch, stand the **Kalnamuiža Castle Ruins** (Kalnamuižas pilsdrupas). There are some ruined walls of the Livonian Order castle, built in the 14th century in what was then a border area, to protect against attacks from Lithuania.

To the northwest stands **Svētkalns**, the Sacred Hill, the site of a wooden castle of the Livonian Order built following the death of Namejs, with the objective of subjugating the Semigallians. This hill also goes by the name of Swedish Hill, apparently because Swedish troops during the Great Northern War inflicted great damage on Kalnamuiža Castle by firing on to it from this point. Back close to the car park, another area of higher ground, **Klosterkalns**, bears evidence of settlement since the 1st century BCE. It is now decorated by a collection of metal animals, illustrating the writings of Anna Brigadere. The metal hedgehog looks particularly prickly.

Tērvete Wooden Castle (Tērvetes koka pils; w lielkenins.lv; ⊕ May–Oct 10.00–17.00 Wed–Sun; adult/child €5/3) This is an attempt to reconstruct a grand Semigallian fortress, on a nearby site just above the main road on the western edge of the village. The initiative of historian Normunds Jērums, construction is proceeding intermittently, with the eastern side complete, and accommodating a museum in a series of low-ceilinged wooden rooms accessed up rickety wooden staircases. The museum consists largely of reproductions of weaponry and jewellery of the period in glass display cases. The female mannequins used to display period costumes sport glamorous modern make-up and hairstyles, giving the medieval period an unexpectedly alluring feel. There is also a mannequin depicting the white-bearded Viestards on his throne.

Anna Brigadere Museum 'Sprīdīši' (Annas Brigaderes muzejs 'Sprīdīši'; w spridisi.lv; ◷ 1 May–15 Oct 10.00–17.00 Wed–Sun; adult/child €3/2) This charming building was built in 1840 as the watermill for the local manor. It later served as a schoolhouse. Tērvete-born writer Anna Brigadere had made a name for herself as a popular children's author, her most famous work the play *Sprīdītis*, a Tom Thumb-like tale of a diminutive hero who heads into the world looking for happiness, discovering after a long series of adventures that it is to be found at home. She was unmarried and lived with her brother's family in Rīga. In 1922, at celebrations marking her 25th anniversary as an author, she was gifted this house in the village of her birth. She spent summers here until her death in 1933, remaining in Rīga during the winter months. The house is preserved as a memorial museum, retaining much of her furniture and personal items. A corner room contains both her bed and writing desk, and one suspects that it was here she spent a good deal of her time. There is also a display of her books, including several copies of *Sprīdītis* as well as her autobiographical work *Dievs, daba, darbs* (God, Nature, Work), the three pillars of her life.

Tērvete Nature Park (Dabas parks Tērvetē; 'Tērvetes sils'; ✆ 2830 9394; e tervete@lvm.lv; ◷ Oct–Mar 09.00–17.00 daily, Apr–Sep 09.00–19.00 daily; adult/student €6.50/5) Sitting along the main P103 road a couple of kilometres northwest of the village, the Tērvete Nature Park, managed by Latvian State Forests, provides for a family-oriented day in the forest, on the trail of wooden sculptures of fairy-tale folk. The park dates from the Soviet period and was set up with the noble aim of encouraging children to respect Latvia's forests. This messaging is maintained through display panels in Latvian stressing the importance of not picking flowers, as well as through a cape-wearing pig called Cūkmens, immortalised in a wooden statue.

The wooden sculptures are clustered into two main groups. The Dwarves' Forest is full of little wooden buildings that offer great clambering for young ones. The Fairy Tale Forest centres on a tall statue of the forest king, to whom his wooden subjects bring gifts of wooden flowers. Some statues are based on characters created by Anna Brigadere. The diminutive Sprīdītis plays the flute to defeat the giant Lutausis by making him dance. At peak times, costumed actors supplement the wooden characters. As distances are quite large, there is a 'Fairy Tale Train' (€1.50–€3 per ride), of the wheeled variety, to ferry wearier visitors between park entrance, an observation tower beyond the Dwarves' Forest and an excellent playground near the Fairy Tale Forest. There is also bicycle hire available at the entrance. Note that the small car park at the entrance costs a hefty €10, while a much larger car park 5 minutes' walk away over the wooden bridge across the road in front is free.

DOBELE The administrative centre of Dobele district (Dobeles novads) is a pleasant small town, with a worthwhile Livonian Order castle, though comes into its own in late May and early June, when thousands of Latvian tourists descend on the place for the annual lilac festival.

The **tourist information centre** (Dobeles novada Tūrisma informācijas centrs; Dobeles Amatu māja, Baznīcas iela 8; w dobele.lv; ⊕ 09.00–17.30 Tue–Fri, 09.00–15.00 Sat) is located in the wooden house of crafts (amatu māja), close to Tirgus Laukums, which also showcases the work of local artisans.

Getting there and away The **railway station** (Dobeles dzelzceļa stacija; Stacijas iela 2; ☎6371 6203) stands northwest of the centre. It is on the Rīga to Liepāja line, currently served by one train daily; two on Sundays. The **bus station** (Dobeles autoosta; Stacijas iela 1; ☎6372 3501; e autoosta@dobele.lv) serves at least 20 buses daily to Rīga, most stopping also in Jelgava.

 Where to stay The three-storey **Hotel Dobele** (29 rooms; Uzvaras iela 2; w hoteldobele.lv; €€) has its roots unmistakeably in the Soviet period and offers basic but central accommodation.

What to see and do
Town centre The place centres on a spacious cobbled square, **Tirgus Laukums**, the former market square. Note the fountain built in the form of a well: water drops into the bucket, eventually causing it to tip over with a loud crack. The **Dobele Evangelical Lutheran Church** (Dobeles Evanģēliski-Luteriskā baznīca) along one side of the square, with its square tower topped by a green spire, dates from 1495, though has been rebuilt several times. A couple of hundred metres west, Brīvības iela runs over the gentle Bērze River, which ambles through the town enlivened by occasional fountains.

Dobele Castle (Dobeles pils; Brīvības iela 2C; w dobele.lv; ⊕ 15 May–15 Sep 10.00–18.00 Tue–Sat, 11.00–16.00 Sun, 16 Sep–14 May 10.00–18.00 Tue–Fri, 11.00–16.00 Sat; adult/student €5/3) The ruined castle stands on higher ground across the river. You can wander freely around the external walls, beyond which runs a partially dry moat on the landward side. The entrance charge is levied for the museum housed in the restored building of the convention house. The main hall on the ground floor offers a display of fragments of ceramic stove tiles dating from the 16th to 18th centuries, supplemented with temporary art exhibitions. Exhibits in the basement tell the story of the castle, with good English-language labelling.
   The exhibits highlight the Semigallian tribe that first put a wooden castle on the site and held out for ten years against the Livonian Order before finally abandoning the place in 1289. They first burned down their castle so it would not fall into the hands of the attackers before heading south to modern-day Lithuania. The origins of the current castle lie in the stone building built by the Livonian Order from 1335 until 1347. With the demise of the order in the 16th century, the castle came into possession of Gotthard Kettler, the first Duke of Courland and Semigallia. It was rebuilt in the early 17th century. A room highlights the collection of medicinal herbs of Elisabeth Magdalena of Pomerania, who settled here on the death of her husband, Friedrich Kettler, the then Duke of Courland and Semigallia, in 1642. The castle was damaged in the Great Northern War, and much of the population of Dobele perished in a plague epidemic between 1710 and 1713. The castle began a slow process of decay thereafter. The convention house also has a roof terrace offering nice views across to Dobele town.

Institute of Horticulture (Dārzkopības institūts; Graudu iela 1, Ceriņi, Krimūnu pag.; w darzkopibasinstituts.lv; ⊕ lilac season: mid-May–mid-Jun 09.00–21.00

daily; adult/student €7/5; hours & prices differ for other seasonal events) Dobele's other main sight lies on the edge of town, a couple of kilometres south of the centre along Zaļā iela. The institute is closely associated with horticulturalist Pēteris Upītis, a researcher at the Latvian Academy of Agriculture, who came here in 1957, attracted by the relatively benign climate in Dobele, to cultivate fruit crops that would be compatible with Latvian winters. He died in 1976. The institute's orchards and gardens cover 43ha, and it continues to develop cultivars suitable for the Baltic region. There is a small museum devoted to Upītis' work, with some of his personal items including, poignantly, his crutches hanging on a wall.

Upītis is particularly known for the cultivation of lilacs. The **lilac garden** at the institute, covering 4.5ha, is an internationally important collection. When the lilacs blossom in early summer, Dobele and the institute become a centre of attention, attracting thousands of visitors daily for the **Dobele Lilac Festival** (Dobeles Ceriņu festivals). The lilac garden becomes a riot of purple and white blossoms, with display panels telling the stories of different cultivars, like the Kristīne Baltpurviņa, named after the object of Upītis' affections. Realising that he was a workaholic, she turned him down. This white lilac cultivar is particularly known for blossoms bearing five petals rather than the usual four: finding one is considered lucky. Visitors sit on chairs beneath the lilac trees and consume tubs of the ice cream made from fruits from the institute. Cherry and apple seasons also bring more modest quantities of visitors to the place.

Rūķīšu tēja (Rūķīši, Krimūnu pag.; w rukisuteja.lv) Continuing out of Dobele along the same road, Zaļā iela, you encounter on your left, after a couple more kilometres, a farm producing herbal tea. It is easily identified by the brightly coloured mural of herbs on the wall of the main building. There is a giant statue of a gnome out the front with a blue flower to his lips. An on-site shop (call ahead to check they are open) offers a range of herbal teas, both loose and in bags, and there is a display of herbs in the front garden.

POKAIŅI FOREST Southwest of Dobele, Pokaiņi forest (Pokaiņu mežs) embodies the upsurge of interest in Latvia following the restoration of its independence in 1991 in reconnecting with the pagan origins of the country. The forest, offering an undulating terrain of low hills and valleys, is an attractive place, but what sets it apart from the rest of Latvia's forested landscapes are the piles of stones found scattered around its floor. In the 1990s, researcher Ivars Vīks popularised the idea that Pokaiņi might represent a complex of ancient sanctuaries. He argued that this was a place of energy and healing, and volunteers have since worked to clean the piles of stones, as well as an array of standing stones of various forms, giving them names drawn from Latvian mythology, like Laima's Table and Māra's Eye. New features have been added, such as a wooden pole decorated with the symbols of the traditional Lielvārde Belt. Visitors are drawn to the place for its purported healing qualities: some lay small coins on the stones for luck. Not all researchers are convinced about the mystical connections of the place: at least one archaeologist has suggested that the stones may simply have been piled up from earlier attempts to clear fields for agriculture. But it makes for an enjoyable walk in the woods. Take the road towards Auce from Dobele. The forest is 300m down a signposted unpaved road on the left, 14km from Dobele. There is a car park with an information centre (✆2639 2564). A track running around the edge of the forest offers further parking places, providing a useful means of accessing some of the outlying stones. Pokaiņi is also served by an infrequent bus from Dobele.

PIKŠAS This farm between Jelgava and Dobele has been preserved as a memorial museum to its most famous, and controversial resident, Latvian politician Kārlis Ulmanis (page 12). The **Kārlis Ulmanis Memorial Museum 'Pikšas'** (Kārļa Ulmaņa piemiņas muzejs 'Pikšas'; Pikšas, Bērzes pag.; w piksas.gov.lv; ⏰ 09.00–16.00 daily; adult/student €4/2) is housed in a beautifully tended complex of stone and wooden farm buildings. Falling under the purview of the Ministry of Agriculture, it combines displays about the life and legacy of Ulmanis with exhibitions about agricultural machinery and husbandry in Latvia's first independence period. It was the place of Ulmanis's birth and childhood, and remained a second home to him as he built his political career, when it was run by his elder brother Jānis.

The museum fascinates for the way in which it preserves a changing interpretation of Ulmanis's role over time. It was founded in 1993 by Gunārs Ulmanis, the grandson of Kārlis's brother Jānis. Gunārs remained director until his death in 2017. An exhibition of Ulmanis's life curated by Gunārs, the text in Latvian only, is exhibited in a wooden residential building on the site. It is hagiographic in tone, reflecting both the family ties and the spirit of the time, soon after the restoration of independence, when the period before Soviet occupation was viewed through rose-tinted glasses. This exhibition has been retained, although a more modern exhibition in the main building now offers a thoughtful and balanced account of Ulmanis's life, acknowledging the controversies and presenting both positive and critical assessments. This again is in Latvian, though a booklet of English-language texts of the displays is available. Other buildings on the site house agricultural machinery, ranging from a 1930s Fordson tractor to an enormous wooden barrel used for churning butter.

8

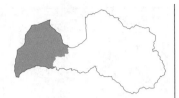

Kurzeme

The Kurzeme region of western Latvia, known in English as Courland, takes its name from the Curonians, or Cours, a tribe living on the shores of the Baltic, known for their skills as sailors and ferocity as pirates. As with the Semigallians to the east, they long resisted the German crusaders in the 13th century. The history of the region diverged with the rest of modern Latvia in 1561, on the collapse of the Livonian Order, when its last Master, Gotthard Kettler, became the first Duke of Courland and Semigallia, a vassal state of the grand Duchy of Lithuania and later of the Polish–Lithuanian Commonwealth. During its 17th-century heyday under Duke Jacob Kettler, Courland and Semigallia became a prosperous force, even becoming a colonial power with the securing of territories in Tobago and at the mouth of the Gambia River. On its annexation by Russia in 1795, Courland and Semigallia came under the rule of the same power as the rest of present-day Latvia, though was still administered separately as the Courland Governorate. The name of Courland again reached the world stage in the dying months of World War II, when some 200,000 troops of German Army Group North were cut off in the Kurzeme Peninsula by advancing Red Army forces. The German troops, including forces of the Latvian Legion, remained in what became known as the Courland pocket for close to a year, from summer 1944 until 10 May 1945, capitulating only after the fall of Germany itself.

Kurzeme has some significant tourist draws. Its coast offers sandy beaches and the lure of wild places such as Cape Kolka, alongside its two port cities, Ventspils and Liepāja. The latter merits an extended stay, studded with elegant Art Nouveau buildings, the northern suburb of Karosta emerging from its past as a Tsarist and Soviet military port, and the city looking forward to a spell as European Capital of Culture in 2027. Pāvilosta, summer playground of well-heeled Latvians, also merits attention. There is much fascination in exploring the cultures of the minority Livonians in the northern coastal villages and the Suiti around Alsunga. The UNESCO World Heritage-listed picture-postcard town of Kuldīga is another major attraction.

TUKUMS

The gateway to Kurzeme, Tukums is a district capital of around 16,000 people, 70km west of Rīga. It is a pleasant location, and although its sights are not unmissable it packages them well, especially through the work of the Tukums Museum, covering seven small museums, which can be seen on a combined ticket (€5). The local authorities are endeavouring to cast the place as Latvia's town of roses, and the Rose Festival in mid-July includes the creation of a giant crown of roses.

HISTORY The first written mention of the place came in 1253, in the partition of Courland between the Livonian Order and the Bishopric of Courland, Tukums

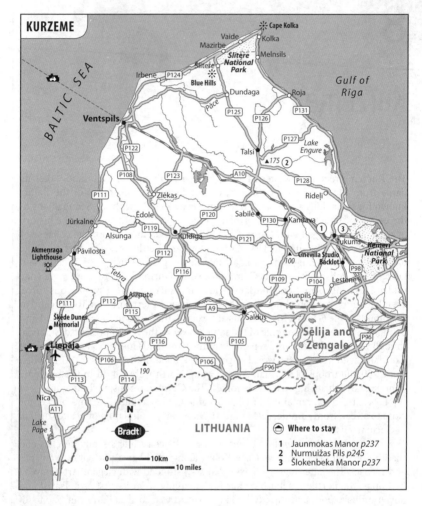

KURZEME

Baltic Sea

Cape Kolka
Vaide
Mazirbe · Kolka
Slitere National Park · Melnsils
Irbene P124
Slitere
Blue Hills
Dundaga · Roja
Pace
Gulf of Rīga

Ventspils
P125
P126
P131
P122
P127 · Lake Engure
Talsi · ▲175 (2)
P108 P123 A10
Zlēkas P128
P120 Rideļi
Jūrkalne Edole
P119 Sabile · Kandava (1) (3)
Alsunga · Kuldīga · P130 · Tukums · Ķemeri National Park
Akmeņraga Lighthouse · Pāvilosta P112 P121
Tebra P116 Cinevilla Studio Backlot (100) · P98
P109 P104 Lestene
Aizpute P112 P115 Jaunpils
Skēde Dunes Memorial · Saldus · Selija and Zemgale
P116 P107 P105 · P96
Liepāja P106 ▲190 P106 · P96
P113 P114
Nīca A11
Lake Pape
N
Bradt
LITHUANIA

0 ━━━ 10km
0 ━━━ 10 miles

Where to stay
1 Jaunmokas Manor p237
2 Nurmuižas Pils p245
3 Šlokenbeka Manor p237

falling to the order. A settlement of German merchants grew up around the Livonian Order castle. In the 17th century, Tukums experienced rapid growth during the rule of Jacob Kettler, Duke of Courland and Semigallia, and in 1877, the opening of the railway line to Rīga provided a spur to further growth. There was a Soviet Navy airbase just outside the town, flying Sukhoi Su-24 'Fencer' bombers. The airbase is now privately owned and has been rebranded as Jūrmala Airport, presumably in a bid to capitalise on the renown of the seaside resort. Tukums today is a laid-back town, with food processing and construction plants.

GETTING THERE AND AWAY The **railway station Tukums 1** (Dzelzceļa stacija Tukums 1; Dzelzceļa iela 3; ✆6311 6249) sits in a Tsarist-era red-brick building at the bottom of the hill below the town centre. There are some 15 trains a day to Rīga (1hr 20mins). Note there are two railway stations in Tukums: you need the Tukums 1 station for the town, not Tukums 2, which is the terminus of the passenger line from Rīga and sets you down in the eastern outskirts. The **bus station** (Tukuma autoosta; Dzelzceļa iela 2A; ✆8070 0002) is over the road from Tukums 1 railway station. Connections include Rīga (5–6 daily), Kuldīga (4 daily), Ventspils (4 daily) and Jelgava (3–4 daily).

TOURIST INFORMATION The **tourist information centre** (Tukuma Tūrisma informācijas centrs; Talsu iela 5; w visittukums.lv; ⏰ 09.00–18.00 Mon–Fri, additionally May–Sep 09.00–15.00 Sat & Jun–Aug 10.00–14.00 Sun) is centrally located, a couple of blocks north of Brīvības laukums.

🏠 **WHERE TO STAY AND EAT** *Map, page 238, unless otherwise stated*
Several of the historic manor houses around Tukums (page 238) provide accommodation. Pick of the bunch is **Jaunmokas Manor** [map, opposite] (22 rooms & 1 house; €€–€€€) which offers two Art Nouveau-themed rooms in the main manor itself, as well as cheaper and more spartan rooms in a converted stable block. **Šlokenbeka Manor** [map, opposite] (15 rooms; ☎2515 5225; €–€€) has quite basic rooms, and a pub with outdoor seating in the manor courtyard.

Hotel Tukums (24 rooms; Pils iela 9; w hoteltukums.lv). If you are looking for accommodation in town, this place offers spartan rooms in a renovated 19th-century building 300m from Brīvības laukums. It also has a restaurant with brick columns & a beamed ceiling &, unexpectedly, a bowling alley. €€

Kvazi Pizza Katrīnas laukums 1; w kvazi.lv. There is not a particularly wide range of eateries in town, though this place does claim to offer the best pizza in Tukums. €€

OTHER PRACTICALITIES The **post office** (Pils iela 20; ☎6318 1168) is east of the centre along Pils iela. A branch of **Swedbank** (Pils iela 15A; ☎6744 5555) sits just over the road. There is a centrally located **pharmacy** (Elizabetes iela 8; ☎6312 5695) a couple of blocks north of Brīvības laukums.

WHAT TO SEE AND DO The heart of the town is Brīvības laukums, a spacious concrete-covered square. Its western side is dominated by the **Tukums Evangelical Lutheran Church** (Tukuma evaņģēliski luteriskā baznīca; Brīvības laukums 1; ☎2022 1951), with a square-based clock tower topped with a spire, and buttressed walls. It dates from the 17th century, though the spire was built in 1754. A few metres further to the west, along Lielā iela, a modern square contains a relief **monument to Zigfrīds Anna Meierovics**, the first foreign minister of independent Latvia and also a prime minister of the country, who went to school in Tukums. He was killed in a car accident just outside the town in 1925, aged only 38.

Castle Tower (Pils tornis; Brīvības laukums 19A; w tukumamuzejs.lv; ⏰ 20 Apr–20 Oct 10.00–17.00 Tue–Sat, 11.00–16.00 Sun, 21 Oct–19 Apr 10.00–17.00 Tue–Fri, 11.00–16.00 Sat–Sun; adult/student €1.50/free) At the back of Brīvības laukums, this two-storey square-sided tower with a steep tiled roof is a heavily remodelled remnant of the Livonian Order castle. It has seen more recent service as a prison and a store, and now houses a small museum devoted to the history of the town.

Tukums Art Museum (Tukuma Mākslas muzejs; Harmonijas iela 7; w tukumamuzejs.lv; ⏰ 11.00–17.00 Tue–Fri, 11.00–16.00 Sat–Sun; adult/student €1.50/free) Just north of the Meierovics monument, in a former bank building on Harmonijas iela, sits the Tukums Art Museum. This was founded in 1935 through

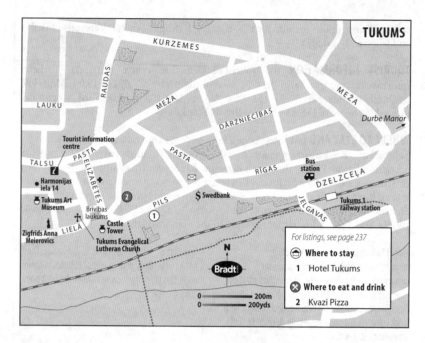

the work of painter Leonīds Āriņš, who donated his collection of canvases from some of the masters of Latvian art, including Janis Rozentāls, Vilhelms Purvītis and Valdemārs Tone, giving the museum one of the best art collections outside Rīga. Given the small size of the building, only a limited sample of its collection is on display at any one time. There is also a room devoted to the paintings of Leonīds Āriņš himself, featuring bright canvases from the Soviet period. The art museum is at the heart of the historic centre of Tukums: cobbled Harmonijas iela and Dārza iela are particularly attractive, with wooden buildings dating from the late 19th and early 20th centuries. Unable to display more than a fraction of its collection, the art museum has found a way to highlight its treasures – by showcasing these on billboards attached to the street lights in this area. The wooden house at **14 Harmonijas iela** opposite the Art Museum was the home of Zigfrīds Anna Meierovics as a schoolboy at the turn of the 20th century.

Around Tukums There is an interesting range of manor houses close to the town.

Durbe Manor (Durbes pils; Mazā Parka iela 7; w tukumamuzejs.lv; ⊕ 20 Apr–20 Oct 10.00–17.00 Tue–Thu, 10.00–19.00 Fri–Sat, 11.00–16.00 Sun, 21 Oct–19 Apr 10.00–17.00 Tue–Fri, 11.00–16.00 Sat–Sun; adult/student €2.50/1.50) On the eastern edge of Tukums, a couple of kilometres from the centre, sits Durbe Manor. Once a sub-estate of the Šlokenbeka Manor, it came into the possession of the German-Baltic von der Recke family, and the current Neoclassical building, with an Ionic-columned façade, dates from a 1904 remodelling. In the wake of the agrarian reforms following Latvia's independence, the manor was presented to Latvian playwright Rainis, who, however, only occupied it for brief periods before his death in 1929. The place was later a sanatorium, and now falls under the management of the Tukums Museum. It can be visited with the combined ticket valid for all of the museum's properties. Rooms on the ground floor are furnished in the comfortable if formal style of the German-Baltic nobility at the turn of the 20th century. Upstairs there are exhibits on the history of the manor, including its use as a hospital of the Baltic Landeswehr in 1919 and its later ownership by Rainis. There are also temporary exhibitions.

Šlokenbeka Manor (Šlokenbekas muiža; Milzkalne; w slokenbeka.lv) In the village of Milzkalne, 5km east of Tukums, Šlokenbeka Manor dates from the 15th century. Its distinctive form, with buildings arranged in a fortified outer wall around a large central courtyard, makes this a rare surviving Latvian example of an enclosed fortified manor. In the Soviet period, it served as the headquarters of Road Construction District No 5, and one echo of that phase in its history is that, as well as a hotel, it now accommodates the **Latvian Road Museum** (Latvijas Ceļu muzejs; ☏ 6318 2354; e muzejs@lvceli.lv; ⊕ May–Oct 09.00–16.00 Tue–Fri, 10.00–17.00 Sat–Sun, Nov–Apr 09.00–16.00 Mon–Fri; admission free). The manor's courtyard houses bulldozers, lorries, road signs and other assorted artefacts of the road construction industry.

Jaunmokas Manor (Jaunmoku pils; Tumes pag.; w jaunmokupils.lv; ⊕ 09.00–19.00 daily; adult/student/child €5/3/2) This large red-brick building mixes neo-Gothic and Art Nouveau styles, just off the A10 road 10km west of Tukums. The old manor building having burned down, this one was built in 1901 by architect Wilhelm Bockslaff to serve as a hunting and recreation lodge for influential Rīga mayor George Armitstead, who, however, sold the place in 1904 after inheriting another manor house nearby. The manor went through a range of uses in the ensuing decades, including a children's sanatorium in the interwar period, and is now managed by Latvia's State Forests. That explains the presence of a forestry museum on the first floor. There are displays about hunting in the tower, and rooms on the ground floor are furnished to give a feel for the period of George Armitstead's occupancy. One original item is a stove made in 1901, decorated with tiles offering scenes of Rīga and Jūrmala. It was created for the exhibition of Rīga's 700th anniversary and presented to Armitstead at the end of it.

SOUTH OF TUKUMS

The countryside to the south of Tukums, culturally on the boundary between Courland and Semigallia, contains an interesting mix of sights.

CINEVILLA Some 16km southeast of Tukums, a signposted 4km off the P98 road between Tukums and Jelgava, sits the **Cinevilla Studio Backlot** (Kinopilsētiņa 'Cinevilla'; Vidusvecvagari, Slampes pag.; w cinevillastudios.com; ⊕ 10.00–19.00 daily; adult/child €5/3). This is a film set, theatrically located in the Latvian countryside, its artificial streets recreating ancient Rome, a battle-scarred 20th-century European town and a Livonian village. Some of the sets will, though, leave you puzzling as to the nature of the film shot here, like a lorry scaling the side of a building. There are film posters and set photographs of some of the productions, though you will look in vain for international blockbusters. It is all rather fun, if crumbling in places.

LESTENE the village of Lestene is known for its **Brothers' Cemetery** (Lestenes Brāļu kapi), a place of commemoration for the fallen soldiers of the Latvian Legion, whose nature remains controversial today (page 52). The cemetery was dedicated in 2003. Plaques along the wall at the back, either side of an abstract sculpture of Mother Latvia depicting a mother grieving for her son, record the names of 18,000 fallen members of the Legion. Grey plaques mark the reburials of 1,300 Legionnaires. Explanatory signage acknowledges the controversies around the commemoration of the members of a unit subordinated to the Waffen SS, but argues that the Latvian soldiers commemorated here 'were forced to fight on the side of Nazi Germany – a foreign power hostile to Latvia, against another equally hostile power'. While there is continuing disagreement among historians around the Latvian Legion, the cemetery offers a striking reminder of the losses suffered by so many Latvian families. The fact that their fallen sons died fighting a Red Army that also included conscripted Latvian soldiers adds to the sense of tragedy. The cemetery is adjacent to the **Lestene Evangelical Lutheran Church** (Lestenes evaņģēliski luteriskā baznīca), dating from 1670, and once known for its Baroque woodcarvings. It was badly damaged in fighting for the Courland Pocket at the end of World War II and is usually locked. Lestene is served by up to five buses daily from Tukums (40mins).

JAUNPILS Most of Latvia's medieval castles now stand either in ruins, or have been so transformed over the ensuing centuries that they no longer offer a medieval atmosphere. **Jaunpils Castle** (Jaunpils pils; w jaunpilspils.lv) is an exception. It is an impressive structure, with four wings around a cobbled courtyard, a circular tower in its southern corner, and water surrounding the place on three sides.

Its first known written mention comes in 1411, in a list of the castles of the Livonian Order, but it probably dates from the 14th century. It fell under the purview of the *komtur* of the more important castle at Dobele. In 1576 it came into the possession of the last *komtur*, Thies von der Recke, in a deal with Gotthard Kettler, the first Duke of Courland and Semigallia, under which Kettler secured Dobele but von der Recke was granted Jaunpils as a free property, directly subordinate to the King of Poland. This began more than 330 years of continuous possession of Jaunpils by the von der Recke family, even if the place did come under the rule of the Duke of Courland and Semigallia on Thies's death in 1580. The von der Recke dynasty had some illustrious moments. In 1605, at the Battle of Salaspils, Matthias von der Recke engaged in hand-to-hand combat with King Carl IX of Sweden, securing the king's silver sword and royal hat. The Swedes took their revenge, heavily damaging the castle in 1625. It was rebuilt in 1646, and by the end of the 18th century was focused more on aristocratic life than military defence. It suffered damage during the 1905 Revolution and was rebuilt by Baltic-German architect Wilhelm Bockslaff. The last von der Recke to own Jaunpils left for Germany in 1919. Through all these rebuildings and reconstructions much of its original atmosphere was retained.

A **museum** (⊕ 10.00–17.00 Mon–Thu, 10.00–18.00 Fri–Sun; adult/child €5/3.50), entered from the central courtyard, tells the history of the place. Note the bust of Elisa von der Recke, a German-Baltic writer who lived here for a few years as the wife of castle owner Georg von der Recke. Her literary successes came after their divorce, notably an account of her months with self-styled Count Alessandro di Cagliostro, Italian occultist to the royal courts of Europe. One narrow staircase up, exhibits focus on the von der Recke family as the lords of Jaunpils. One equally narrow staircase down, there is a display on the knights of the Livonian Order in the vaulted windowless basement.

There are up to four buses a day to Dobele (45mins) and three to Tukums (50mins), though at the time of writing there were no Dobele buses on Sunday.

The castle also incorporates a **hotel** (Jaunpils Castle; 12 rooms; **€-€€€€**), which offers rooms of varying standards and prices, from the 'Baron's Room', with a four-poster bed in the former bedroom of the lord of the manor, to spartan dormitories with shared showers and toilets. The **restaurant** (**€€€€**) is housed in a vaulted, candlelit space with medieval-inspired music to add to the atmosphere. 'Many visitors from near and far come here to enjoy the fried blood pudding', proclaims the menu, an announcement which may or may not entice you, but the food is good. If you book two days in advance you can order a medieval-themed meal, from the sumptuous 'Baron's feast' to the more modest 'servant's meal'.

THE ABAVA VALLEY

Flowing westwards across the central Kurzeme region until it meets the Venta River, the Abava River takes a winding course, with several rapids. The presence of modest slopes prompts tourist industry references to the 'Switzerland of Kurzeme', which is overdoing it, but the Abava Valley Nature Park is a picturesque place, with the attractive small towns of Sabile and Kandava worthwhile stops.

SABILE Stretching along the Abava Valley, the small town of Sabile was built around a Livonian Order castle. It is today known for its wine production, something of a feat at this latitude, and locals will tell you that the place once secured a *Guinness Book of Records* listing as the world's most northerly vineyard. This is, logically enough, known as **Wine Hill** (Vīna kalns), sitting above the centre of town off Rīgas iela. Cider production has also been added to Sabile's alcoholic accomplishments.

Sabile is served by **buses** from Kuldīga (40mins) to Rīga (2hrs), which also pass through Kandava (20mins).

✘ Where to eat and drink Right in the centre of town, with an outdoor terrace on decking, **Resto Terase** (Ventspils iela 1/3; w restoterase.lv; **€€€€**) offers a menu ranging from salmon fillet to pizzas and burgers, with the opportunity to try the local Abavas wines, ciders and spirits.

What to see and do The **Sabile Cider House** (Sabiles Sidra Nams; Rīgas iela 11; w gardeners.lv; ⊕ May–Oct) is a good place to sample the products of the cider plant just over the road, as well as local wines.

Also in the town centre, the orange-painted former synagogue building accommodates the **Sabile Art, Culture and Tourism Centre** (Sabiles mākslas, kultūras un tūrisma centrs; Strautu iela 4; ✆2784 1827; e tic.sabile@talsi.lv; ⊕ Oct–Apr 10.00–17.00 Tue–Fri, 10.00–16.00 Sat, May–Sep 10.00–17.00 Tue–Sat, 11.00–16.00 Sun). The Jewish community of Sabile were exterminated on 6 August 1941. The building was used as a sports hall in the Soviet period, and has now been converted to a combined exhibition space and tourist information office. The most unexpected sight of Sabile, though, sits in a front garden along Rīgas iela, the main road heading east towards Kandava. The **Doll Garden** (Leļļu dārzs; Rīgas iela 17) is full of straw-filled dolls dressed up in all manner of outfits. A band of musicians; a couple of guys sawing a log; Superman. Some of the dolls are a little the worse for wear, but they make for an arresting sight – either charming or disconcerting, according to the viewer's mood.

The **Pedvāle Art Park** (Pedvāles mākslas parks; Pedvāle; w pedvale.lv; ⊕ 10.00–18.00 daily; 1 May–23 Oct adult/student €3.50/3; 24 Oct–30 Apr adult/student €2.50/1.50) sits 2km out of town, across the river, in the settlement of Pedvāle. It is the initiative of sculptor Ojārs Arvīds Feldbergs, who in 1991 acquired the manors of Firkspedvāles and Brinkenpedvāles and their extensive grounds. Firkspedvāles Manor has been restored and now hosts an artists' residency, while the parkland is home to sculptures from Feldbergs and some of the visiting artists. These are scattered over two meadows behind the manor house, with more across the valley beyond, covering a total of almost 100ha. Many of the sculptures involve large boulders, bearing embellishments or incisions, though the most colourful piece is a big armchair made out of bright blue oil drums. Note also the rocks on sticks placed in painted oil drums close to the manor house; works described by Feldbergs as *Petraflora Pedvalensis*. There is no labelling.

KANDAVA Kandava is positively cosmopolitan in comparison to Sabile, but is another sleepy small town on the right bank of the Abava River. Its historic centre makes for a pleasant stroll, even if its sights are low key. Most buildings date from the late 19th century, following a fire in 1872 that destroyed the earlier wooden structures.

The **tourist information centre** (Kandavas Tūrisma informācijas centrs; Ūdens iela 2; **w** visitkandava.lv; ⊕ Oct–Apr 10.00–17.00 Tue–Fri, 10.00–15.00 Sat, May–Sep 10.00–17.00 Tue–Wed, 10.00–18.00 Thu–Fri, 10.00–16.00 Sat, 10.00–14.00 Sun) sits just off Tirgus laukums, and doubles as a souvenir shop.

Getting there and away Kandava is served by the Rīga to Kuldīga bus route. The **bus station** (Kandavas autoosta; Kūrorta iela) is on the main road through the town, just south of the junction with Lielā iela.

Where to stay *Map, below*
An unremarkable but centrally located guesthouse close to the Powder Tower, **Pils** (6 rooms; Pils iela 7; ☎6312 4919; **€€**), makes a convenient place from which to

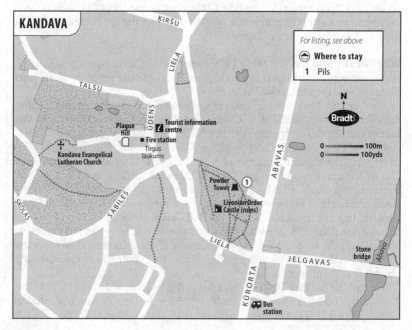

explore both Kandava and the Abava Valley. It has a nice outdoor terrace looking towards the castle.

What to see and do The **Livonian Order Castle** dates from 1253, but only a few low walls still stand on high ground overlooking the Abava. The solitary more substantial reminder of the castle is a square-based tower with a tiled roof on the slope of the castle mound. It was used for the storage of gunpowder during the rule of Duke Jacob Kettler, and is still referred to as the **Powder Tower** (Pulvertornis; Pils iela 4). A sculpture next to it depicts a cheery acorn dressed as a knight of the Livonian Order: a reference to the acorn-studded oak branch that forms Kandava's coat of arms. There is a model of how the castle might have looked in the park below.

Central Tirgus laukums is dominated by the historic building of the town **fire station** (Kandavas ugunsdzēsēju depo; Tirgus laukums 7) built, in a case of closing the stable door behind the bolting horse, in the wake of the late-19th-century fire that destroyed the place. A cobbled path behind the fire station takes you past **Plague Hill** (Mēra kalniņš), reputedly used as a place of burial of those killed during the plague of 1710, which hit the town particularly hard. Above this, at the top of the path, stands the **Kandava Evangelical Lutheran Church** (Kandavas evaņģēliski luteriskā baznīca; Baznīcas iela 5; ✆2827 7286) dating from 1736.

Just outside the centre, along Jelgavas iela, is the **stone bridge** across the Abava River, built in 1873 at the initiative of local landowner Karl von Fircks, reportedly after his horse broke its leg on the plank-way previously in use. It has four elegant arches, and is apparently the oldest of its kind in Latvia. There is another acorn sculpture here, this one embarking on a kayaking adventure, next to a wooden walkway leading down to the river.

THE GULF OF RĪGA COAST

RIDEĻI This hamlet on the P128 road between Rīga and Talsi is home to the stone **Rideļi Watermill** (Rideļu dzirnavas; w ridveludzirnavas.lv; ⊕ Jun–Aug 10.00–18.00 daily, Sep–May call ahead; adult/child €2/1). The mill is driven by the waters of the Kalnupe River, which flows into Lake Engure. It dates from 1759, though the present building is the product of an 1860s enlargement to take advantage of the lowering of Lake Engure following the connection of the latter to the sea. The mill is no longer used for the commercial processing of grain and now houses a museum telling the story of milling. The millpond over the road, **Rideļu dzirnavezers**, at 37ha more lake than pond, is a delightful spot fringed by reeds. A billboard proclaims this to have been a favoured fishing spot of Soviet singer-songwriter Viktor Tsoi, front man of the rock group Kino, the voice of Russian youth of the *glasnost* generation.

The poignancy of that sign is demonstrated by another site 6km southeast along the P128. Here, on the western side of the road, is a **statue of Viktor Tsoi** (w 35km. lv), depicted in an open-necked shirt, looking defiantly to his right, wrapping his arms around his body. At the base are flowers, portraits of Tsoi drawn by fans and cigarette butts. For it was at this spot on 15 August 1990 that Viktor Tsoi was killed in a car crash when, possibly having fallen asleep at the wheel, he drove his Moskvitch-2141 into the path of an oncoming bus. Tsoi had been in Latvia not just fishing but also recording Kino's next album, posthumously released as the band's final one and colloquially known as the Black Album. The monument was erected in 2002, and the site is maintained by the 35km.lv organisation, relying on support from the singer's fans.

Where to stay and eat Run by the owners of the Rideļi Watermill, **Kafejnīca Cope** (Rideļi; w rideludzirnavas.lv; €) offers four basic rooms, as well as tent spaces. The café (€€€) serves carp from Rideļi millpond and a wide range of sweet and savoury pancakes. It has a terrace overlooking the millpond and also provides boat rental.

LAKE ENGURE The third largest lake in Latvia, Lake Engure (Engures ezers) is a former coastal lagoon, now separated from the sea by a bar 2km wide along which runs the P131 coast road. It has an outlet to the sea provided by the 4km-long Mērsrags Canal, excavated in 1842 to expand the area of agricultural land. The lake is shallow and overgrown with reeds, making it a particularly important spot for waterfowl, and it has hosted an ornithological research centre since the 1950s. It has been protected as the Lake Engure Nature Park since the late 1990s. The lake can be accessed along a signposted unpaved road off the P131 just north of the village of Bērzciems. Wild cattle and horses are being introduced in a fenced area in a programme to help restore lakeside meadows, which had been the victim of a decline in cattle farming and hay cutting. Also here is a 3.5km-long **Orchid Trail** (Orhideju taka) which in late June offers the possibility of seeing some of the 32 species of wild orchids to be found in Latvia.

ROJA A small fishing port at the mouth of the Roja River, this was one of the Latvian settlements accommodating a naval school from 1873, as part of the identity-building initiative of Krišjānis Valdemārs. The focus of the village during the Soviet time was the fish-canning business of the Banga collective farm, whose derelict offices line Ostas iela north of the harbour. Lovers of smoked sprats in oil should fret not, however, as the Banga name and production lives on. There is a good sandy **beach** at the end of Ostas iela, with toilets, changing cubicles and a small playground. Each summer, a sculpture of a blue pig is moved into position on the beach. Apparently, it symbolises hope.

The **Roja River** offers riverside walking and cycling. At the mouth of the Roja, on the landward side of the bridge at the port, is **Spura** (Jūras iela 1A; w spura.lv), offering kayak and stand-up paddleboard tours along the river, ranging from basic rentals to more elaborate expeditions. They also have a laid-back café (⊕ Wed–Sun), where you sup your latte on a beanbag on the riverfront terrace.

The **bus station** (Rojas autoosta; Selgas iela 16) is centrally located on the main road. There are around six buses daily to Rīga, four or more to Kolka, and up to 13 a day to Talsi.

 Where to stay and eat

Hotel Roja (6 rooms) Jūras iela 6; w rojahotel.lv. Clean if blandly decorated centrally located hotel, in a nice setting close to the port & surrounded by lawns. €€

Otra puse Jūras iela 8; ℓ 2947 7602. Part of the Hotel Roja next door, this offers a menu with plenty of nods to the local fishing industry, such as the 'Made in Roja' starter of 3 locally produced fish products. Large terrace, attracting a 10% additional charge. €€€

TALSI AND AROUND

TALSI The local tourist authorities make much of the fact that Talsi, capital of the district covering northeast Kurzeme, is built around nine hills. Think Latvian proportions, however: these are more large mounds than Matterhorns. Adding to the picturesque setting are the two small lakes nestling within the hills, and an attractive Old Town with 19th-century buildings and some cobbled streets. Lielā iela, which curves scenically through the centre of town, is the main drag.

The area was inhabited by Livonians in the 9th century, but these were displaced by Curonians in the 10th, who established a hill fort here. The first written mention of the place came in 1231, in a reference to a contact between the papal envoy and Curonian elders. The Livonian Order built a castle here, destroyed during the Polish–Swedish conflicts of the 17th century. The town further suffered from outbreaks of the plague in 1657 and 1710, and a major fire in 1733, and was hit hard by both the 1905 Revolution and World War I. With an economy focused on agricultural and wood processing, it is today a charming if low-key destination.

Getting there and away The **bus station** (Talsu autoosta; Dundagas iela 15; ☎6322 2105) is a few hundred metres northwest of the centre. There are at least 17 departures daily to Rīga (2hrs 10mins), around six to Ventspils (from 1hr 15mins), and around five a day to Kolka, whose journey time varies markedly according to the circuitousness of the route taken.

Tourist information The **tourist information centre** (Talsu novada Tūrisma informācijas centrs; Lielā iela 19/21; w visittalsi.com; ⊕ May–Sep 09.00–18.00 Mon–Fri, 10.00–16.00 Sat. 10.00–14.00 Sun, Oct–Apr 09.00–18.00 Mon–Fri, 10.00–14.00 Sat) is co-located in the building of the Talsi Cultural Centre in the heart of town.

🏠 **Where to stay and eat** *Map, page 246, unless otherwise stated*

Nurmuižas pils [map, page 236] (22 rooms) Lauciene, Talsu nov.; w nurmuiza.lv. Some 11km east of Talsi on the P128, this is a large complex of manor buildings, whose origins lay in a 16th-century Livonian Order castle that was later the property of the von Fircks family. The buildings housed a collective farm in the Soviet period, & had settled into a state of decrepitude by the 1990s. The estate was purchased in 2004 by businessman Olegs Fiļs who set about restoring it, & now accommodates a hotel, restaurant & spa. There are rooms in both the main castle building & restaurant building: all have en suites. The restaurant (€€€€) offers a short but enticing menu, & the former smithy has been converted into a spa (€35 pp/2hrs) with both Finnish sauna & Turkish bath. €€€–€€€€

Hotel Talsi (53 rooms) Kareivju iela 16; w hoteltalsi.lv. In a potentially attractive setting overlooking Talsi's second lake, Vilkmuižas ezers, this is an ugly 4-storey block, whose interior offers echoes of Soviet period décor, like the carved wooden column dominating the reception. Rooms are as dated as you would expect, but clean enough. €€

Jazz Coffee Lielā iela 31; ☎2967 3095; e jazzcaffe@inbox.lv. This place confusingly has 2 names, Jazz Coffee & Jazz Café, which seem to be used interchangeably. Despite the address on Lielā iela, the entrance is from the back of the building, on the shore of Lake Talsi. The terrace, overlooking the lake, is delightful on a fine day, with a soft jazz soundtrack playing soothingly. The menu ranges from simple wraps to more elaborate offerings like venison steak. €€€

Ie-pauzē Lielā iela 8A; ☎2625 4554; e sajutuharmonija@gmail.com; ⊕ closed Sun. With a counter crammed full of sweet offerings in little packets & a selection of teas & coffees in jars on the shelves behind, this charming tearoom just off Lielā iela has a few tables upstairs.

Other practicalities The **post office** (Lielā iela 20; ☎6700 8001) is centrally located, immediately opposite the tourist information office. There is a branch of **SEB Bank** (Lielā iela 17; ☎6777 9988) a few doors up Lielā iela, with an ATM, and a **pharmacy** (Lielā iela 5; ☎2881 4504) near the western end of Lielā iela.

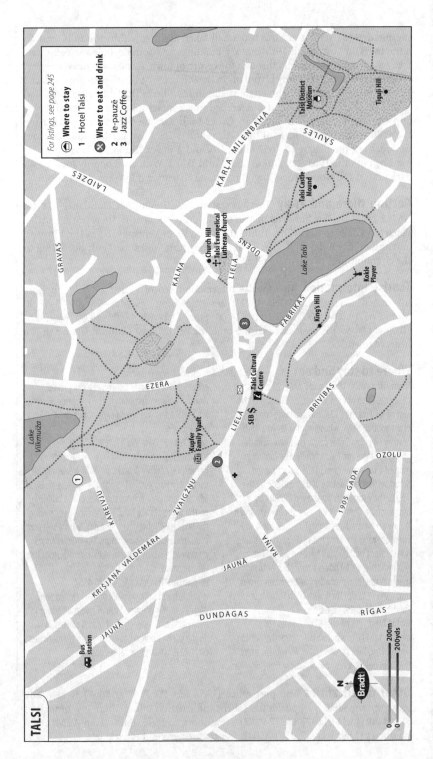

TALSI

For listings, see page 245

Where to stay
1 Hotel Talsi

Where to eat and drink
2 Ie-pauzē
3 Jazz Coffee

Talsi District Museum
Tiguļi Hill
Talsi Castle Mound
Church Hill
Talsi Evangelical Lutheran Church
Lake Talsi
Kokle Player
King's Hill
Talsi Cultural Centre
SEB
Kupfer Family Vault
Lake Vilkmuiža
Bus station

LAIDZES
KARĻA MILENBAHA
SAULES
GRAVAS
KALNA
UDENS
LIELA
FABRIKAS
EZERA
LIELA
BRĪVĪBAS
OZOLU
KAREIVJU
ZVAIGZNU
KRIŠJĀŅA VALDEMĀRA
JAUNĀ
RAŅA
1905. GADA
JAUNĀ
DUNDAGAS
RĪGAS

N
Bradt

0   200m
0   200yds

What to see and do The kidney-shaped **Lake Talsi** (Talsu ezers) makes an attractive central backdrop. A sign proclaiming 'Esi Talsi' ('Be Talsi') in the lake offers the place's Instagram moment, with the framing of the Old Town climbing to the Lutheran Church. There is also a fountain, and a pleasant walk to be had around the lake, partly along boardwalks. The eastern side of the lake rises to **Talsi Castle Mound** (Talsu pilskalns), one of Talsi's nine hills, a grass-covered mound reaching 32m above the lake. This was the site of the Curonian hill fort, and grassy ramparts can still be discerned at the summit.

There is another grassy hill on the opposite side of the lake. This one, **King's Hill** (Ķēniņkalns), is said to be the place of burial of Lamekinas, ruler of West Courland. Lamekinas was the signatory of the agreement with papal legate Baldwin of Alna, under which the Curonians had the right to remain free, provided they adhered to the Catholic faith, paid taxes and participated in wars against the pagans. The agreement was undone by a Curonian rebellion a few years later. Legend has it that the hill was formed from soil brought here in the hats of the local people when Lamekinas was buried. At the base of the hill, overlooking the lake, is the stone **statue of a Kokle Player** (Koklētājs). It has come to symbolise Latvian perseverance in the face of oppression. The statue was commissioned in the 1930s to the memory of those who had fought for Latvian independence. Sculptor Kārlis Zemdegs made a plaster model, portraying a naked young man with flowing hair playing the *kokle*, with the instrument held to his body rather like a harp. The Soviet occupation intervened, but the sculpture was finally realised in stone in 1996 by Vilnis Titāns. Further along the bank of Lake Talsi at the base of King's Hill, in the direction of the town centre, the large white building is the **Talsi Cultural Centre** (Talsu tautas nams; Lielā iela 19/21; w tautasnams.lv; ⊕ call in advance to request a visit). This accommodates a variety of music and dance clubs, as well as art and crafts workshops, arranged around a central courtyard.

On Zvaigžņu iela, just off Lielā iela in the town centre, note the **Kupfer Family Vault** (Kupfern dzimtas kaplīča; Zvaigžņu iela 2), a triangular Neoclassical mausoleum with Doric columns at the corners, the burial site of members of the Kupfer and Heinz families, well-to-do German-Baltic merchants of the town.

From the northern end of Lake Talsi, cobbled Ūdens iela runs up a third of the nine hills of town. **Church Hill** (Baznīckalns) is named, logically enough, for the **Talsi Evangelical Lutheran Church** (Talsu evaņģēliski luteriskā baznīca; Baznīcas laukums 4; ☏ 2939 2287) standing at the top, a white-walled building with a square-based tower at the western end. The church dates from 1567, though has been several times rebuilt. Its main claim to fame is that violinist and theologian Carl Amenda was pastor here in the early 19th century. Amenda had worked in Vienna as a music teacher for Mozart's children, and befriended Beethoven. The latter composer is celebrated with a bench not far from the District Museum that plays *Ode to Joy*.

The **Talsi District Museum** (Talsu novada muzejs; K Milenbaha iela 19; w talsumuzejs.lv; ⊕ 09.00–16.00 Tue–Sun; adult/student €2/1) stands on the eastern side of the town centre on Tiguļi Hill, highest of all the nine hills of the town, in the late 19th-century mansion of Baron Georg von Fircks. There is a well-presented display of Curonian archaeological finds, including twisted neckrings and weaponry, many extracted from Lake Vilkmuiža, which served as a burial place for the Curonians. The dead were cremated, and their remains sunk in the lake together with their most precious belongings. A display of local costumes highlights the skirts with brightly coloured vertical stripes typical of the area. There is a range of temporary exhibitions, with a separate building in the grounds given over to art.

DUNDAGA This quiet village in the northern part of Talsi district centres, as it always has done, on its impressive castle, which sits on a peninsula surrounded on three sides by ponds formed in the Pāce River. **Dundaga Castle** (Dundagas pils; Pils iela 14; w dundagaspils.lv; ⊕ 15 May–15 Oct 08.30–noon & 12.30–17.00 Mon–Fri, 11.00–17.00 Sat–Sun, 16 Oct–14 May call ahead, weekdays only; guided tour adult/ child €3/0.85) dates from the 13th century, when the first castle was built by the Chapter of Priests of the Bishop of Rīga. It changed form and hands several times until coming in the 17th century into the ownership of the Osten-Sacken family, who transformed it from a medieval castle to a residence befitting country nobility. It was burnt down in 1872, and again during the 1905 revolution. After being taken over by the state following the agrarian reforms of 1920, it housed the town hall, and during the Soviet occupation was used as a school.

The castle externally has a charming feel, particularly when viewed from its cobbled courtyard, but the interior has been so heavily restored that much of its character has been lost. It now serves a range of functions, housing an art and music school, the local tourist information centre, a stage for events and a venue for weddings. It is visitable only through a guided tour.

There are small exhibitions within the castle covering its history, local handicrafts, crocodile hunter Arvīds Blūmentāls, and the work of local sculptor Jānis Mikāns, whose collection of medals is on display. It is also possible to stay here in one of eight simple twin- or four-bed rooms with shared bathrooms (**€€**). The castle is surrounded by a pleasant landscaped park.

A short walk away, at the corner of Dinsberga iela and Talsu iela, sits a **concrete crocodile** on a pile of stones. A 1995 gift to Dundaga from the Latvian Honorary Consul in Chicago, it commemorates the life of Dundaga-born crocodile hunter Arvīds Blūmentāls.

CROCODILE HARRY

Arvīds Blūmentāls was born in Dundaga in 1925, emigrating to Australia in 1951. While the journey Down Under was one taken by many Latvians in the turbulent aftermath of World War II, Arvīds' choice of career was decidedly unusual: he became a crocodile hunter. Becoming known as Crocodile Harry, he could take smaller crocodiles with his bare hands, and it was said, how accurately is debatable, that he despatched tens of thousands of the creatures during his career. Everyone in Dundaga will tell you that Arvīds provided the inspiration for the character of Mick Dundee, rugged hero of the 1980s *Crocodile Dundee* film series. The filmmakers themselves, however, cited the Outback exploits of one Rod Ansell as their source of inspiration. But if Arvīds was not the central model for Dundee, his life story was perhaps even more remarkable than anything dreamed up by the filmmakers. With opportunities for crocodile hunting increasingly restricted, Arvīds changed his career to that of opal miner, settling in the mining town of Coober Pedy in the 1970s. There he excavated himself an underground home, Crocodile Nest, photographs of which can be seen in the exhibition of his life in Dundaga Castle. It is distinctive and then some, not least in the collection of ladies' underwear, apparently gifts from his admirers, hanging from the ceiling. It also featured his own decidedly politically incorrect sculptures and, actually giving him a definitive link with Hollywood, featured in the film *Mad Max Beyond Thunderdome*. He died in 2006 at the age of 81.

The **bus stop** is centrally located, close to the junction of Pils iela and Talsu iela. There are around eight buses a day to Talsi, two to Kolka, and even a couple to Rīga, via Talsi.

THE LIVONIAN COAST

The northern coastal tip of Kurzeme is a geographically and culturally distinctive area, centred on a string of a dozen fishing villages associated with the Livonian people (page 251). It is part of the **Slītere National Park**, established in 2000 on the basis of a much older nature reserve, and includes a few kilometres inland a ridge known as the **Blue Hills** (Zilie Kalni), marking the ancient shoreline of the Baltic ice lake. The landscape coastwards of these hills, developed as the sea receded, is a distinctive one, comprising a series of long forested dune banks known as *kangari*, separated by marshy depressions called *vigas*. This challenging topography contributed to the cultural isolation of the fishing villages.

MELNSILS One of the few Livonian fishing villages lying at the northern end of the Gulf of Rīga coast, rather than the Baltic coast to the west, Melnsils is known today for its sandy beach and large campsite, the latter offering a range of accommodation options. It is served by around five **buses** a day running between Rīga and Kolka.

Where to stay and eat
Melnsils (w melnsils.lv; €–€€€) is a large beachside complex offering a campsite for both tents and trailers, together with various structures converted into unusual accommodation, among them large wooden barrels, former military bunkers and an old motorboat. There's even a pink-toned 'love boudoir'. For most of these, shared toilets and showers are located separately. There is a **pub** (Krogs Melnsils; 2871 1911; e krogs.melnsils@gmail.com; ⊕ May–Sep daily, Oct–May Fri–Sun), offering both burgers and more local fare, such as herring with cottage cheese and boiled potatoes (€€). It's a family-friendly place, with kayak and bicycle rental, and can be noisy in peak season.

KOLKA The largest of the Livonian fishing villages, Kolka, originally known as Domesnes and mentioned in a court judgement of 1387, is the only one of the villages that actually expanded during the Soviet occupation. That it did so owed much to the presence of its fish-processing factory, and its influential director Jevgenijs Morozovs. Its fish-canning operation became a major source of income for the Banga fishing collective based in Roja, to which it was eventually subordinated, providing canned sprats for consumers across the Soviet bloc. Fish processing is still important to the village, though at much reduced levels.

That Soviet expansion means that Kolka is not the most attractive village in Latvia, and most visitors speed through the place en route to Cape Kolka. It does, though, have one recommended stop. The **Livonian Community House** (Lībiešu saieta nams; 'Pastnieki'; 2940 2093; e lsn@kolka.lv; ⊕ 09.30–17.00 daily; admission free), in a smartly modernised building on the main road through the village, is a cross between tourist information centre, exhibition space, museum and home for civil society organisations. It offers display materials in four languages: Latvian, English, Livonian, and the local Dundžiņ dialect of Latvian, which features many Livonian influences. The display offers a good introduction to Livonians, to the history of Kolka and its cape, and to the local fishing industry. There is a replica of the Mervalla Rune Stone in Sweden, dating from the 11th century, commissioned by one Sigrid and recording the exploits of her husband, Sven, in sailing around Cape Kolka to Zemgale with expensively laden ships. These are apparently the first two Latvian place names mentioned specifically in writings. The inscription suggests that travelling around Cape Kolka was considered a dangerous undertaking, worthy of record.

Buses stop on the P131 road, just a few metres north of the Livonian Community House. There are around five buses a day to Rīga.

Cape Kolka (Kolkasrags) is the northernmost tip of Kurzeme, the point at which the curving shoreline of the Gulf of Rīga meets the Baltic Sea. Standing here certainly feels remote, though its charms are understated: those expecting dramatic cliffs befitting the dangerous reputation of the place for mariners will be disappointed. Instead, two sandy beaches backed by pine forest come gently to a point. The many fallen trees are, though, testament to the storms that periodically batter this spot. A jumble of boulders at the cape mark the ruins of the old lighthouse. The modern **Kolka Lighthouse** (Kolkas bāka) is visible out to sea, sitting on an artificial island some 6km from the shore. This was constructed in the 1870s, and now holds the title of Latvia's only sea island. The lighthouse has operated fully automatically since 1979. Its purpose is to guide shipping away from the dangerous shoal that extends seawards from Cape Kolka, making the area a maritime graveyard. Signs here warn that the currents at the cape mean that the area is also dangerous for swimming.

Cape Kolka is a kilometre north of the village of Kolka. Driving north from the village on the P131, take the signposted turn to the right at the roundabout, which brings you after 300m to a car park (€1.50/hr), where there is also an information-centre-cum-gift-shop and a summer café. If you are planning to do more than pay a quick visit to the cape, one money-saving tip is to take the second rather than first turning at the roundabout, signposted to 'Kolkas raga priežu taka' (Cape Kolka Pine Trail), which brings you after 200m to a free car park. A short walk past a wooden **birdwatching tower** takes you to the beach some 600m west of the cape. The **Pine Trail** starting at this car park is 1.2km long, crossing pine-covered dunes with a springy undergrowth below. Look out here for the little pit traps constructed by antlion larvae, which wait at the bottom for passing ants to fall in. The latter will be despatched mercilessly: held in the larva's jaws and injected with venom.

VAIDE Some 11km west of Kolka, Vaide provides a contrasting and more typical example of the Livonian fishing villages: one that declined in the Soviet period and now comprises a few houses scattered among the trees. Aside from its beach, it offers one of those private museum collections that so enrich Latvia, the **'Purvziedi' Antler Collection** (Ragu kolekcija 'Purvziedos'; 'Purvziedi'; ☎ 6320 0179; e livahausmane@gmail.com; ⊕ call in advance; adult €1). Housed in the wooden loft of a rural home, there are more than 600 antlers here, collected over several decades from the 1960s by a forest guard named Edgars Hausmanis, a collection maintained by members of his family following his death in 2017. There are both elk and deer antlers, some fashioned into chairs, others hanging from every beam and wall, accompanied by stuffed animals, skulls and a bear skin. The place is signposted, along unmetalled tracks about 3km from the main road. The family also run a basic campsite around the back of their home.

MAZIRBE Continuing west along the P124 coast road, 21km from Kolka, lies Mazirbe, the village most closely associated with efforts to protect the Livonian language and culture. Around 1km seaward of the main road lies the **Livonian Community House** (Lībiešu tautas nams; Mazirbe; w livones.net; ⊕ Jun–Aug

The Livonians are a people indigenous to Latvia, but whose language, unlike Latvian, is a Uralic one related to Estonian and Finnish. They settled in two distinct areas of modern Latvia, on the north coast of Kurzeme and in Vidzeme, along both the Daugava and Gauja rivers. They were named in historical records from the 12th century. From the 14th, the Livonians of Vidzeme began a long process of assimilation with the other Baltic tribes of the area, forming the modern-day Latvian people. The Livonian language had died out in most of Vidzeme by the 17th century, though it held out in the area around Skulte and Liepupe until the mid 19th.

In the isolated fishing villages of the north Kurzeme coast, however, the Livonian language survived, and this area forms the current heartland of the Livonian culture. But do not assume that you are likely to hear Livonian spoken in the street. The 20th century was a challenging time for the Livonians of north Kurzeme. Following a period of population decline and linguistic assimilation accelerated by World War I, the interwar period saw a concerted attempt to organise and protect the Livonian culture, with the establishment in 1923 in Mazirbe of the Livonian Union (Līvõd Īt). A Livonian flag was created in the same year, now to be seen hanging from public buildings in the area. It consists of three unequal horizontal stripes: a narrow central white stripe, with a broader green one above and blue below. It is a stylised view of the coastal landscape when viewed from a fishing vessel: forest overlying the beach, with the sea below. A Livonian anthem written to mark the first raising of the flag shares its melody with the national anthems of Estonia and Finland, and those countries, along with Hungary whose language also shares linguistic affinities with Livonian, have long supported the Livonian community of Latvia. All three, alongside Latvia itself, provided funding for the Livonian community house in Mazirbe, opened in 1939. A monthly Livonian-language newspaper, *Līvli*, was published through most of the 1930s, with financial support from the Helsinki Academic Kindred Nations Club.

During the Soviet occupation, the Livonian Coast was subject to special restrictions as a frontier region of the USSR. Barbed wire in the dunes blocked access to the sea and beaches were raked in attempts to stop local people trying to escape to the west. Restrictions were placed on fishing, and many local people moved to Ventspils or Rīga to find jobs. Together with an influx of military personnel, this accelerated a decline in the Livonian language and culture. There are now but a handful of fluent Livonian speakers, although a range of organisations and initiatives promote knowledge of the language, including the Livonian Institute at the University of Latvia, established in 2018. Livonians are recognised as an indigenous ethnic minority in Latvia. There is renewed interest in Livonian choral singing, traditional dress and folklore.

One local delicacy associated with the Livonian community, though also baked by ethnic Latvians in the region, is the *sklandrausis*, known as *sūrkak* in Livonian, a circular sweet open pie made from rye dough and filled with a potato and carrot paste. The rye crust gives them a taste rather reminiscent of the Karelian pasties popular in Finland and Estonia. You can find these on menus in some local restaurants and on sale at markets in the area.

11.00–16.00 daily; admission free). Dedicated in 1939, it is a white-walled functionalist building, constructed to the design of Finnish architect Erkki Huttunen. Housing a theatre, it hosts events celebrating the Livonian language and culture, notably the annual Livonian Festival on the first Saturday of August. Outside of these, it offers a few panels on aspects of Livonian culture and a café in the foyer. The sandy **beach** is 1.3km from here (signposted).

There are two **buses** a day to Mazirbe from Rīga, and a couple of buses from Ventspils between May and September only, though these don't run every day.

Where to stay Opposite the Livonian Community House, **Branki and Stūrīši** (4 rooms; 'Branki', Mazirbe; **w** branki.weebly.com; **€–€€**) offers lodgings in rustic buildings. The most striking is Stūrīši, a wooden cottage filled with assorted bric-a-brac, from woodworking tools to a child's cot. Note, though, that historical authenticity means that the toilet is outside and the shower in a separate building. Giving a feel of bygone Livonian life, Stūrīši can also be visited without staying (donation expected). Intriguing sculptures, like a mace-wielding warrior, pepper the gardens. A three-night minimum stay is not always enforced.

ŠLĪTERE

At the top of the escarpment of the Blue Hills, the tiny village of Šlītere is home to the **Šlītere Lighthouse** (Šlīteres bāka; **w** slitere.lv; ☉ 1 May–15 Oct 10.00–18.00; adult/child €3/1.50). A red-walled cylinder, 102.2m high, it stands 5km from the sea, and bears plaques with the dates of 1849, the date of its construction as a daytime landmark for sailors, and 2002, that of its restoration. The lighthouse was apparently required in the first place because deforestation activities of the baron of Dundaga in the early 19th century deprived sailors of the trees traditionally used as navigation landmarks. Immediately behind the lighthouse is the 2.2km **Šlītere Nature Path** (Šlīteres dabas taka), involving a steep wooden staircase down the escarpment to boardwalks below, crossing marshy and forested land. The village is 11km from Mazirbe, inland along the P125 road towards Dundaga.

IRBENE

Some 33km west of Mazirbe along the P124, a signposted turning takes you to a fascinating legacy of the Cold War now playing an important role in astronomical research. The **Ventspils International Radio Astronomy Centre** (Ventspils Starptautiskas radioastronomijas centrs; **w** virac.eu; ☉ book in advance; €80 per group) has its origins in a Soviet radio astronomy installation established in 1967 and maintained as a secret facility, used to spy on the west by intercepting communications. Known as Zvezdochka ('Little Star'), it comprised three radio telescopes, the largest of which was 32m in diameter, resembling a giant bowl. Following the restoration of Latvian independence, the Soviet personnel destroyed as much as they could before their departure, though could do little about the largest telescopes. There were calls within Latvia to demolish the place as an unwanted reminder of Soviet occupation, but it was saved by the petitioning of radio astronomers, who emphasised its research value. The site was handed over to the Latvian Academy of Sciences, and now forms part of the Ventspils University of Applied Sciences. Following extensive and ongoing renovations, there are now two working radio telescopes, of 32m and 16m diameters, as well as a new Low-Frequency Array (LOFAR), set out in a grid of numerous antennae.

Tourist visitors are not taken inside the working telescopes. You do, though, get to walk through an underground tunnel, and to see an exhibition in the tower that once held the smallest of the Soviet telescopes, at 8m diameter, now without an antenna and no longer operational. Through old equipment and photographs, it offers a feel of the place in Soviet times. Next to this, the old Soviet 16m antenna languishes on the ground. Also here is the stylised metal head of cosmonaut Yuri Gagarin, encased in a helmet, moved here from Ventspils in 2021. In the 'Kristal' building where visitors arrive, there is a small exhibition on the Rīga-born pioneer of rocketry Friedrich Zander, comprising items relocated here when a museum in Rīga dedicated to Zander was closed. Outside the facility stand the crumbling apartment blocks of a village that once accommodated Soviet personnel and their families, some 2,000 people at its peak. The buildings are now unsafe, so you should not get too close.

VENTSPILS

Ventspils, Latvia's sixth city, historically known in German as Windau, owes its prominence to its status as an ice-free port on the mouth of the Venta River. Its port has faced recent challenges stemming from the loss of much of its traditional business in the export of crude oil, following the development by Russia of its own Baltic oil terminals. But as a tourist destination, Ventspils has an attractive offer, combining an interesting historic centre, good beach and some high-quality new attractions such as the VIZIUM Science Centre. Ventspils takes tourism promotion seriously. It has made a speciality of repurposing workaday objects of its maritime industries into items of sculpture or minor tourist attractions: anchors, buoys and retired ships. And then there are the cows. The centre is liberally populated with cow statues, painted and sculpted into a wide range of different personalities, from 'At the Mirror' near the ferry terminal, with a pink-lipsticked cow checking her make-up, to the sinister 'Latvian Black' on the Ostas iela promenade, in which a black cow has been sawn in two, and then reconnected with a twisted section of oil pipeline. The cows are in part the legacy of Ventspils' hosting of International Cow Parade festivals in 2002 and 2012. People seem to like them.

HISTORY When in the 13th century Courland and its ports were divided between the Bishop of Courland and the Livonian Order, it was the order that received the harbour at Ventspils, then known as Vinda. The order constructed a castle on the south bank of the river, and the place became a trading city of the Hanseatic League. Its first golden age came in the 17th century, as the most important port of the Duchy of Courland and Semigallia. During the 40-year rule of Duke Jacob Kettler, the harbour and shipyard were modernised. Shipbuilding was overseen by master craftsmen brought in from the Netherlands, giving Courland the means to develop colonies in Tobago and the Gambia.

The era of prosperity was, however, curtailed by damage incurred in 1659 during a Swedish attack in the Polish–Swedish War, and then in 1710 an outbreak of plague during the Northern War further dented the city's fortunes. It was absorbed within the Russian Empire in 1795, and in the late 19th century experienced a second golden age as a major modern port of Imperial Russia, with a railway connection to Moscow. During the Soviet occupation, an oil pipeline was built, and Ventspils became a major port for the export of crude oil from the USSR. Following the restoration of Latvia's independence in 1991, the sitting mayor of Ventspils, Aivars Lembergs, was repeatedly re-elected, dominating city politics until his conviction on bribery and money-laundering charges in 2021. Lembergs even got into the act with cow design. He was the co-author of the cow sculpture entitled Gaismas Govs ('Cow of Light') which stands in the middle of Kuldīgas iela, a cream-coloured cow with 'Ventspils' written all over its body and covered with light bulbs.

GETTING THERE AND AWAY The **bus station** (Ventspils autoosta; Kuldīgas iela 5; ☏6362 2789) is centrally located, in a building with a curved blue glass external wall on the corner of Kuldīgas iela and Lauku iela. There are around a dozen buses a day to Rīga, four to Kuldīga and four to Liepāja. A cow dressed as a police riot officer with a visor stands outside: a composition entitled 'There Must be Order!' There is a **ferry** service from Ventspils to Nynäshamn in Sweden operated by Stena Line, with one or two sailings daily (around 10hrs). The ferry terminal (Dārzu iela 6; w stenaline.lv; ⊕ 08.00–23.00 Mon, 07.00–23.00 Tue–Thu, 08.00–18.00 Fri, 08.00–20.00 Sat, noon–23.00 Sun) is centrally located, a block from Tirgus laukums.

TOURIST INFORMATION The **tourist information centre** (Ventspils Tūrisma informācijas centrs; Dārzu iela 6; w visitventspils.com; ⊕ 08.00–18.00 Mon–Fri, 10.00–16.00 Sat–Sun) sits in the ferry terminal. As well as the usual maps and leaflets, this is the place to pick up your Venti, a special tourist currency which can be earned through games on their website and give you a miniscule discount on the admission prices to some local attractions. They look pretty, though.

 WHERE TO STAY *Map, opposite*
Ventspils' tourism offer is blunted somewhat by the paucity of good accommodation options.

Dzintarjūra (67 rooms) Ganību iela 26; w dzintarjura.lv. The 'Amber Sea' is a 4-storey block opposite the Latvija concert hall a short walk south of the centre. The rooms are spartan; the restaurant majors on pizza. It wouldn't qualify for a listing in most cities, but in Ventspils the choice is limited. €€
Kupfernams (6 rooms) Kārļa iela 5; w hotelkupfernams.lv. Rooms are in the beamed upper floor of a 2-storey wooden building in a good location in the historic centre. There is a café (€€€) downstairs, across the corridor from the reception in a beauty salon. €€

Piejūras kempings Vasarnīcu iela 56; ☏2200 8805; e camping@ventspils.lv. A large centrally located wooded campsite, close to the Seaside Open-Air Museum. It has tent & trailer spots, with a service building offering showers & shared kitchen, as well as accommodation in wooden cottages sleeping 4. There are nicely landscaped grounds, a café, sports facilities & bicycle hire – the latter is a good option, as the main sights in Ventspils are quite scattered & there is a good network of cycle paths. €

 WHERE TO EAT AND DRINK *Map, opposite*
Rātsgalds Baznīcas iela 2; ☏6531 2999. Cozy central restaurant with an international menu ranging from beef goulash to duck leg; lounge music & outside tables on the cobbled Rātslaukums. €€€
Skroderkrogs Skroderu iela 6; ☏6362 7634; e skroderkrogs@inbox.lv. An inviting place in a wooden cottage with a homely interior, serving up hearty dishes from stewed lamb pieces in wine to cod with onions. The terrace outside fills the narrow Skroderu iela. €€€
Ērmanītis Saules iela 16; ☏2926 4748; e ermanitis.ventspils@inbox.lv; ⊕ closes 20.00.

This canteen-style place is a good option for something cheap & filling: pork or chicken cutlets with masses of potatoes get top billing here. €
Windau Coffee Pils iela 25; ☏6350 9855; e windaucoffee@windaucoffee.lv; ⊕ until 21.00. Cavernous central café, popular with students, & offering a good-value set lunch & nice range of cakes. Also has an outside terrace. €
Kārumnieks Lielā iela 20; ☏2942 4860; e ventspils.karumnieks@gmail.com; ⊕ closed Sun & Mon. A diminutive pastry shop offering good coffee & fine cakes with a particularly impressive range of macaroons.

ENTERTAINMENT The **Latvija Concert Hall** (Koncertzāle 'Latvija'; Lielais laukums 1; w koncertzalelatvija.lv; ⊕ box office noon–15.00 & 16.00–18.00 Tue–Sat) is an

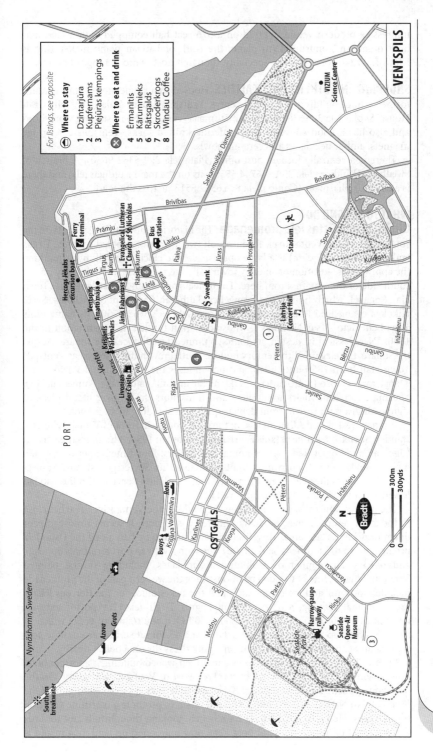

For listings, see opposite

Where to stay
1 Dzintarjūra
2 Kupfernams
3 Piejūras kempings

Where to eat and drink
4 Ērmanitis
5 Kārumnieks
6 Rātsgalds
7 Skroderkrogs
8 Windau Coffee

PORT

Nynäshamn, Sweden

Southern breakwater

Azova
Grots

Venta

Hercogs Jēkabs excursion boat

Ferry terminal

Prāmju

Tirgus

Ventspils Amatu māja

Jānis Fabriciuss

Krišjānis Valdemārs

Livonian Order Castle

Pils

Ostas

Rīgas

Avoti

Saules

Brīvibas

Tirgus laukums

Evangelical Lutheran Church of St Nicholas

Rātslaukums

Lielā

Bus station

Lauku

Raiņa

Jūras

Kuldigas

Swedbank

Ganibu

Kuldigas

Latvijas Concert Hall

Petera

Saules

Lielais Prospekts

Sarkanmuižas Dambis

Brīvibas

Stadium

Sporta

Kuldigas

Bērzu

Ganibu

Inženieru

Buoys

Krišjāna Valdemāra

Rota

Vasarnicu

Petera

J Poruka

Inženieru

OSTGALS

Karlines

Krona

Loču

Mednu

Parka

Vasarnicu

Narrow-gauge railway

Seaside Open-Air Museum

Seaside Park

Rinka

N Bradt

0   300m
0   300yds

VIZIUM Science Centre

impressive modern venue, centred on a 576-seat hall equipped with a German-built organ and unusual 4.7m piano, the work of Latvian piano-maker Dāvids Kļaviņš. Organ concerts are a speciality, though it hosts a broad range of events.

SHOPPING AND OTHER PRACTICALITIES Housed in a single-storey 18th-century former school building in the city centre, **Ventspils Amatu māja** (Ventspils Craft House; Skolas iela 3; ◥6362 0174; e amatumaja@ventspils.lv) hosts craft workshops and also has a good souvenir shop, offering knitted socks, Ventspils cow fridge magnets, amber necklaces and ceramic bowls.

There is a centrally located **post office** (Platā iela 8; ◥6362 9630). A branch of **Swedbank** (Kuldīgas iela 25A; ◥6744 5555) sits on the main Kuldīgas iela, and there is a 24-hour **pharmacy** (Ganību iela 8; ◥6362 5513) across the road.

WHAT TO SEE AND DO
Old Town and Ostas iela promenade The historic centre of Ventspils sits on the south bank of the Venta River. It centres on two attractive cobbled squares. **Tirgus laukums** (Market Square) is a large open space, the clock and bell tower marking the approximate location of an early town hall. The market is still held daily on the south side of the square. From here, Tirgus iela runs south to **Rātslaukums** (Town Hall Square), which houses the **Evangelical Lutheran Church of St Nicholas** (Svētā Nikolaja evaņģēliski luteriskā baznīca; Tirgus iela 4; ◥6362 2750). Its name hints at its benefactor, Tsar Nicholas I, whose donation funded its construction in the 1830s. Neoclassical in design, its Ionic-columned façade faces the square. Across the square, the elegant 18th-century building with grey shutters served as Ventspils Town Hall from 1850 until 1918, and now houses the International Writers' and Translators' House (Starptautiskā Rakstnieku un tulkotāju māja; Annas iela 13), offering short residencies for writers and translators. In an over-literal piece of signposting, a sculpture in front depicts quill pens standing in an inkpot.

A block west, along Akmeņu iela, in the small square in front of Ventspils library, stands a Soviet-era **statue of Jānis Fabriciuss**. Erected in 1954, it honours the Latvian Rifleman and Soviet Red Army commander, the first four-time holder of the then highest Soviet award, born near Ventspils. Given its Soviet genesis and subject matter, some would like to see it removed, but Fabriciuss' service with the Latvian Riflemen in World War I has so far saved it.

The port of Ventspils, running along the banks of the Venta River, reaches close to the town centre. When the Stena Line ferry is in port, it seems almost to peer down into Tirgus laukums. There is a pleasant stroll to be had along the **Ostas iela promenade** on the southern bank of the river, with a view to port terminals opposite and passing all manner of sculptural assemblages, including several painted Ventspils cows. A line of wooden pavilions along the western part of the promenade includes souvenir and ice-cream stalls and the ticket office for the **Hercogs Jēkabs excursion boat** (Hercogs Jēkabs ekskursiju kuģītis; Tirgus iela 12; w portofventspils. lv; sailings 10.00–19.00 May–Sep, 11.00–18.00 Oct; adult/student €5/2) which in summer offers up to seven departures daily for a 45-minute cruise around the port area, as far as the breakwaters. A cow in a pink dress sits on a bench nearby.

Overlooking the promenade, the elegant green-walled building is a former hotel now serving as the headquarters of the Free Port of Ventspils Authority. On the quayside opposite is a 2000 **statue of Krišjānis Valdemārs**, a prominent figure of the First Latvian National Awakening, who did much to promote a maritime vocation for Latvians. He is depicted sitting on a bench, looking thoughtfully out towards the sea. West of here is the pilot boat *Rota*, now marooned on land. Just inland is the **Ostgals** neighbourhood, established in the 19th century and characterised by narrow, quiet streets and wooden houses. Back on the promenade, its western end is decorated with colourful buoys emerging like little rockets from the pavement. The westernmost buoy is festooned with locks of romantic fidelity.

Livonian Order Castle (Ventspils Livonijas ordeņa pils; Jāņa iela 17; w muzejs. ventspils.lv; ☉ 10.00–18.00 Tue–Sun; adult/student May–Oct €5/2, Nov–Apr €3/2) The castle sits across the square in front of the Free Port of Ventspils Authority building. Along with Rīga Castle, it is one of the few Livonian Order castles to have survived as an occupied building to the present day, but for this reason, it has little feel of a medieval castle today. It was used as a prison from Tsarist times until 1959, and the galleried brick central courtyard still gives the sense of a place of incarceration. It thereafter accommodated a unit of Soviet border guards, and now houses the **Ventspils Museum**. Displays cover the history of the region from the earliest settlement. The castle chapel is one survivor from medieval times, serving successively as a Catholic, Lutheran and Russian Orthodox place of worship, and even housing a Lenin Room in the officially atheistic Soviet Union.

Around the beach From the town centre, Vasarnīcu iela ('Summerhouse Street') heads southwestwards, lined with grand and once grand wooden villas in spacious grounds.

Seaside Open-Air Museum (Piejūras brīvdabas muzejs; Riņķa iela 2; w muzejs. ventspils.lv; ☉ Mar–Oct 10.00–18.00 Tue–Sun, Nov–Feb by appt; adult/student €3/1.50). Dating from the 1950s, the museum offers a collection of wooden buildings of the 19th and early 20th centuries, relocated here from across Kurzeme to safeguard the rural architecture of the region. The buildings range from a windmill dating from 1864 to a fish smokehouse constructed from part of an old boat. A collection of fishing boats is preserved beneath a protective roof, among them one of the vessels on which Latvian refugees were taken to Sweden to escape a future in the Soviet Union.

The museum is also home to a **narrow-gauge railway** (Mazbānītis; trains May–Oct 11.15–16.30 Wed–Sun; adult/student €2/1), based around a reconstructed 1.4km ring of the 600mm track which originally arrived in Latvia with German forces in World War I, when it was used for military transport. An exhibition in the wooden station house tells the story of 600mm railways in Latvia, the last line not closing until 1972. The train makes a pleasant circuit of the adjacent Jūrmalas parks. A longer 3km line, serving an artificial ski hill at the southern edge of town nicknamed 'Lemberg's Trilby', was closed at the time of writing.

Seaside Park (Jūrmalas parks) Between the Seaside Open-Air Museum and the beach, this extensive park is decorated with anchors, including some real colossi, propped up with large rocks.

The predominantly sandy **beach** stretches for 1.2km, divided into zones for swimming, volleyball, windsurfing and naturism. There doesn't seem to be a naked volleyball option. It is well equipped, with changing cubicles shaped like blue dice with yellow spots, benches, lifeguard posts and children's swings. Metal steps take you up to the **southern breakwater** at the northern end of the beach. The breakwater and its northern partner shelter the mouth of the river, framing the entrance to the port of Ventspils. The walk to the end is atmospheric, passing through a forest of concrete tetrapods. Also here is the largest of the Ventspils cow sculptures, the blue-and-white sailor cow, sporting a little orange bobble hat. At the landward end, two fishing vessels stand on concrete blocks. You can climb aboard both the *Azova* and the *Grots*. Between the two is, for some reason, an oversized golden chair constructed from anchor chains. East of here, the rundown yacht harbour blocks direct access to the Ostas iela promenade.

VIZIUM Science Centre (Zinātnes centrs VIZIUM; Rūpniecības iela 2; w vizium. lv; ⏰ 10.00–19.00 Mon–Sat, 10.00–17.00 Sun; adult/child €15/5) Beside the roundabout south of the bridge across the Venta, a couple of kilometres east of the centre, the building presents a striking image, resembling a shimmering copper-coloured sand dune. Laid out in a series of zones, from physics and mathematics to geography and the world, it is an interactive child-oriented science museum, with loads of opportunities to test your skills in virtual reality contexts and learn something about science on the way. Be prepared to queue for the most popular exhibits, especially at weekends. There are 20-minute science shows two or three times a day for an additional fee. Note the mosaic map of the world on the floor of the circular foyer, with Ventspils at its centre. Even if you're not planning to visit the museum, you can climb on to the undulating roof, which has a viewing platform at its highest point with outlooks towards the city centre.

SOUTH OF VENTSPILS

The P108 and P122 roads run southwards from Ventspils to Kuldīga either side of the meandering course of the Venta River. The major sight here, though one that requires making advance arrangements, is the 17th-century church in the village of Zlēkas.

ZLĒKAS This outwardly unremarkable village is home to the **Zlēkas Evangelical Lutheran Church** (Zlēku evaņģēliski luteriskā baznīca; 📞 2920 3640; e gunita. zernevica@inbox.lv; ⏰ call ahead). Dating from 1645, the exterior, with its square-based tower topped by a green spire, is rather battered, but the interior contains some treasures. Zlēkas manor fell, like Ēdole Castle, into the possession of the von Behr family, who lavished attention on the church. The painted wooden pews give a fine indication of the social stratification of the village. At the top of the pile were the members of the von Behr family, who sat in the patrons' balcony on the right of the nave looking from the entrance. Dating from 1773, this wooden Rococo balcony stands on Corinthian columns. Either side of the altar are polychrome carved patrons' benches, one embellished by a wooden canopy further underlining the high social status of the occupants. The pews for ordinary parishioners in the main body of the church impress for the painted allegorical scenes on their doors, with figures representing virtues and vices. Note the allegory of Hatred, a Medusa-like figure with two faces and writhing snakes in lieu of hair.

The pulpit is a delight of polychrome-painted wooden carving. Note the angel at the base, holding up the whole structure, and the carving of John the Baptist on the door. The wooden altar is also a riot of colour. Polychrome reliefs depict the Agony in the Garden of Gethsemene and the Last Supper, and above these, a painting portrays the cruel torture of Christ. Beneath the altar, members of the von Behr family are buried in coffins in the crypt. This is sealed off, though there are some eerie photographs of the jumbled coffins at the back of the nave. The neo-Gothic organ was built in Liepāja in 1875. You can climb the tower – reconstructed in 1834 after lightning struck the spire – though when you see the rotten beams at the top you may wonder whether this was wise.

Leaving the village westwards along the P123, at the first crossroads out of the village, take the road to the north, in the direction of the hamlet of Palgas. You will soon see on your left a black obelisk on top of a mound, with some steps running up to it. The **Memorial to the Victims of the Zlēkas Tragedy** (Zlēku traģēdijas piemiņas vieta) recalls the darkest episode in the history of the village, the circumstances of which remain controversial. Notorious SS commander Friedrich Jeckeln, the organiser of massacres of Jews in Latvia, reportedly decided to teach a lesson to the local people, who he believed were providing support both to a Latvian military formation known as the Kurelians, established initially with German support but then suspected of conspiring against the Germans, and to Soviet partisans. He drew a circle around the village of Zlēkas and ordered the murder of all those inside it. The monument, with an inscription in Russian and Latvian, refers to the murder of 160 local people, their names inscribed on a ring of stones around the obelisk.

Back at the same crossroads, taking the opposite road, to the south, brings you swiftly to **Zlēkas Manor** (Zlēku muiža). The once grand complex of manor buildings, owned by the von Behr family until the agrarian reforms of 1920, burnt down in 1945 and lies now in ruin. There are hints of its former glory in the surrounding parkland. There is a **bus stop** in the village, with a couple of connections a day to Ventspils and Kuldīga.

KULDĪGA

One of Latvia's most picturesque small towns, Kuldīga became in September 2023 the third Latvian site to be awarded UNESCO World Heritage status, reflecting its fine state of conservation in comparison with the other major settlements of the Duchy of Courland and Semigallia. Its charm lies in wandering the attractive cobbled streets of its compact centre. Its houses have tiled roofs, decorated wooden doors and shutters, and there is a slight air of benign neglect about the place. The fish leaping over the Venta Rapid make for a memorable sight in spring.

HISTORY The administrative centre of the Curonian land of Bandava was located 3km downstream of present-day Kuldīga. The conquering Livonian Order started construction of a stone fortress on the bank of the Venta River, on the site of the present town, in 1242. This formed the nucleus of a settlement initially named Jesusberg and later Goldingen. In 1368, the settlement joined the Hanseatic League, obtaining city rights ten years later, the first place in Kurzeme to secure them. It was a frequent place of residence of the first Duke of Courland and Semigallia, Gotthard Kettler. And when in 1596 the duchy was divided into two parts, though overseen jointly by the Polish–Lithuanian Commonwealth, his elder son Friedrich Kettler ruled Semigallia from Mitau, now Jelgava, while younger son Wilhelm ruled Courland from Goldingen. Wilhelm, however, developed a frosty relationship with local landlords, and unfortunately for him the Polish–Lithuanian Commonwealth sided with the landlords. Wilhelm was ousted in 1616 and went into exile, Friedrich became the sole Duke of Courland and Semigallia, and Kuldīga's brief experience of capital city status was at an end.

It did, though, enjoy the fruits of the most prosperous period for the duchy under Wilhelm's son Jacob Kettler, who was born in Kuldīga and succeeded Friedrich in 1642. On acceding to the throne, Jacob had been required to sign a reconciliation agreement with the landlords, which inter alia stipulated that Jelgava would be the only capital of the duchy, but Jacob still spent much time in

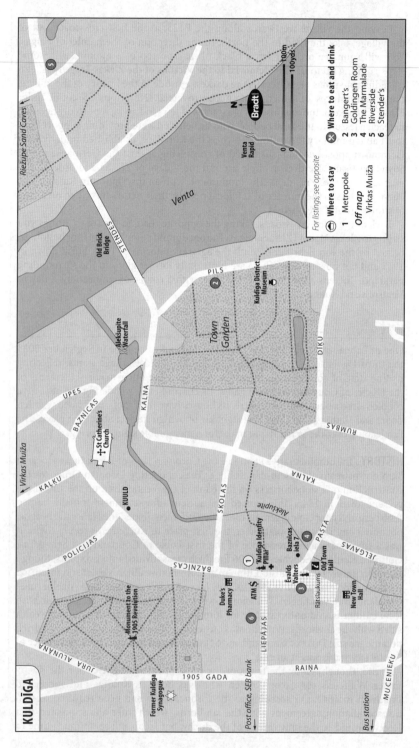

KULDĪGA

Riežupe Sand Caves

Venta

Old Brick Bridge

STENDES

Aleksupite Waterfall

UPES

BAZNICAS

KALNA

St Catherine's Church

Virkas Muiža

KALKU

KUULD

POLICIJAS

Monument to the 1905 Revolution

Duke's Pharmacy

ATM $

JURA ALUNANA

Former Kuldiga Synagogue

1905 GADA

Post office, SEB bank

LIEPAJAS

6

RAINA

MUCENIEKU

Bus station

SKOLAS

Aleksupite

'Kuldiga Identity Pillar'

1

Ēvalds Valters

Baznicas iela 7

3

Ratslaukums

Old Town Hall

New Town Hall

PASTA

JELGAVAS

KALNA

RUMBAS

DIKU

Town Garden

PILS

2

Kuldiga District Museum

Venta

N

Bradt

Venta Rapid

0   100m
0   100yds

For listings, see opposite

Where to stay
1 Metropole
Off map
Virkas Muiža

Where to eat and drink
2 Bangert's
3 Goldingen Room
4 The Marmalade
5 Riverside
6 Stender's

5

260

Kuldīga. Its fortunes suffered a reversal at the start of the 18th century. Swedish forces comprehensively damaged the castle in 1702 during the Great Northern War, and an outbreak of plague ravaged the town. The castle was demolished altogether later in the 18th century to provide a source of building materials. Following the annexation of Kurzeme by Russia in 1795, Kuldīga gradually lost importance, a relative decline that would be important in preserving its historic appearance. It did, though, partially revive in the late 19th century with the construction of the brick bridge over the Venta in 1874, and the establishment of the Vulkāns match factory in 1878.

GETTING THERE AND AWAY The **bus station** (Kuldīgas autoosta; Adatu iela 9; w kuldigasautoosta.lv) is west of the centre, a block south of Mucenieku iela. There are around nine buses a day to Rīga, four to Liepāja via Aizpute, and four to Ventspils.

TOURIST INFORMATION The **tourist information centre** (Kuldīgas Tūrisma informācijas centrs; Baznīcas iela 5; w visitkuldiga.com; ⏰ 9.00–17.00 Mon–Fri) is in the Old Town Hall building on central Rātslaukums.

 WHERE TO STAY *Map, opposite*

Virkas Muiža (22 rooms) Virkas iela 27; w virkasmuiza.lv. Housed in the renovated wooden manor house once owned by the von Fircks family, this place sits at the northern edge of town. The setting is charming, though rooms vary markedly in size & quality. They also run the adjacent Comfort Hotel, in a less glamorous building, as well as some 'boutique apartments' in town. €€–€€€€

Metropole (14 rooms) Baznīcas iela 11; ☎ 6335 0588; e reservations@hotel-metropole.lv. With a central location close to Rātslaukums, this hotel was founded in 1910, its foyer illustrated with the curious tale of a poor girl working here, spurned by a Russian officer. She committed suicide, but not before cursing the place with the warning that it would burn down in flames, a fate that did indeed befall it, before more recent renovation. Not perhaps the most enticing story for arriving guests. The rooms are somewhat tired, with the most expensive split over 2 levels. €€

✘ WHERE TO EAT AND DRINK *Map, opposite*

Bangert's Pils iela 1; w bangerts.lv. With a great location in the Town Garden, the menu includes locally sourced trout & venison, & there are both terraces & a balcony from which to admire the view over the Venta. The restaurant takes its name from Captain Bangert, who supposedly gifted the building now housing the District Museum as a present for his bride. €€€€

Goldingen Room Baznīcas iela 2; ☎ 6332 0721; e propellerfoodie@gmail.com. While the name of this restaurant on Rātslaukums is suggestive of traditional Kurzeme fare, the menu is Italian, the speciality pizza, served at wooden tables to a soundtrack of laid-back music. A popular place: advance booking advisable. Also has a terrace on the square. €€€

Riverside Stendes iela 2; ☎ 2549 4947; e riverside.kuldiga@gmail.com. On the eastern side of the Old Brick Bridge over the Venta, this is a glass-walled wooden pavilion with a terrace offering nice views down to the river. Advertising itself as 'cool café – cool people' it offers an international menu. €€€

Stender's Baznīcas iela 17 – entrance on Liepājas iela; w stenderspica.lv. Housed on the 2nd floor of a characterful wooden building that was once a granary, this place offers a cozy bar room & terrace overlooking the street. The menu is largely composed of variations on chicken fillet & pork *karbonāde*, served with fries & salad in huge portions. €€€

The Marmalade Pasta iela 5; ☎ 2606 0900; e skolasmaize@inbox.lv. Not a sixties pop rock band but a charming central Kuldīga café. Serves b/fast, salads, soups & pancakes. Sample from their cake selection as you reflect on your life. Closes at 18.00 (17.00 Sun). €

Kurzeme KULDĪGA

SHOPPING **Kuuld** (Baznīcas iela 27; ☏2631 1310; e info@kuuld.lv) is an inviting design shop with ceramics, candles, toys, mittens and scarves made by artisans from the Kurzeme region, making for an upmarket place to hunt out souvenirs.

OTHER PRACTICALITIES The **post office** (Liepājas iela 34; ☏6332 2190) lies west of the Old Town along Liepājas iela. There is a **pharmacy** (Baznīcas iela 9; ☏6332 2474) next door to the Metropole Hotel. A branch of **SEB Bank** (Plisētas laukums 5; ☏2666 8777; ⊕ Tue, Thu & Fri only) also sits to the west of the Old Town, close to Kuldīga City Square, though there is an ATM on Baznīcas iela, just opposite the Metropole Hotel.

WHAT TO SEE AND DO
Town Hall Square (Rātslaukums) A good place to start an exploration of the town, the square stands in front of the **New Town Hall**, a crenelated building of the late 19th century accommodating the local administration. On the side of the square is the wooden **Old Town Hall**, dating from the 17th century. Note the **statue of Ēvalds Valters** in front of the building. Valters, born in Kuldīga district, was a veteran Latvian actor who as a young man served as a Latvian Rifleman and who opened the founding congress of the Latvian People's Front in 1988. He died in 1994 at the age of 100. He is portrayed as a distinguished-looking gentleman in a suit sitting at a table, coffee cup in hand, while a small bird looks on.

Baznīcas iela Running north from Town Hall Square, Church Street is flanked by some of the most impressive historic buildings of the town. Note the green-painted wooden house at **Baznīcas iela** 7. Dating from 1670, it is the oldest wooden building in Kuldīga. It has a weathervane enlivened with a unicorn. Over the road at Baznīcas iela 10, the timber-framed building dates from 1622 and is known as the **Duke's Pharmacy** (Hercoga galma aptieka) as it originally housed a pharmacy, the permit for which had to be purchased from the duke. Outside the Metropole Hotel, an installation labouring under the name '**Kuldīga Identity Pillar**' (Kuldīgas Identitātes Pīlārs) includes video clips of local worthies gushing out lines like 'Kuldīga, you are an inspiration and good example to other towns'. It offers a list of Kuldīga's values. People, legacy, perseverance, creativity, honour, self-confidence, love and harmony, since you asked. Baznīcas iela runs, appropriately enough, to the cream-walled Evangelical Lutheran **St Catherine's Church** (Sv Katrīnas evaņģēliski luteriskā baznīca; Baznīcas iela 31; ☏2232 8283) which dates from 1252, though was rebuilt in the 17th century and subsequently. Duke Jacob Kettler was both baptised and married in this church.

Around Liepājas iela Pedestrianised Liepājas iela, running to the west off Baznīcas iela close to Rātslaukums, is the main shopping street. Turn right off here on to 1905 gada iela to reach the yellow-walled former **Kuldīga Synagogue** (1905 gada iela 6). Kuldīga's Jews were massacred in 1941, mainly at forest execution sites outside town, and the building today houses the central library. The park opposite centres on a 1955 Socialist Realist **monument to the 1905 Revolution** by Kuldīga sculptor Līvija Rezevska.

Alekšupīte Running through the town a block east of Baznīcas iela, the Alekšupīte is a small stream picturesquely flowing alongside historic buildings, a juxtaposition that has led to overenthusiastic attempts to depict the town as the 'Venice of Latvia'. Before depositing its waters in the larger Venta River, the Alekšupīte makes one more bid for fame. Just east of St Catherine's Church and over Baznīcas iela stands the **Alekšupīte Waterfall** (Alekšupītes ūdenskritums) billed as the highest in Latvia. It should perhaps be billed as the most over-hyped attraction in Latvia, for in reality this 4.5m drop was fashioned in the 17th century to facilitate the operation of a paper mill. With the water now flowing down a concrete channel, it is far from the most attractive spot in town.

Town Garden (Pilsētas dārzs) Also sometimes referred to as Castle Park (Pils parks), the garden sits on the left bank of the Venta River on the site of the Livonian Order Castle. There is little evidence of the latter save for a grassy mound in the centre of the park. The garden also provides a home for 22 sculptures by Līvija Rezevska. The sculpture park she developed here from 1976 emphasises Latvian themes, though sculpted in conformity with the changing dictates of Soviet art. Note the bulky *Suiti Folk Singers* from 1980 and the *Kokle Player* from 1975. Other statues portray characters from Rainis' plays, and abstract ideas such as *Nostalgia, Contemplation* and, of course, *Love*.

Kuldīga District Museum (Kuldīgas novada muzejs; w kuldigasmuzejs.lv; ⊕ 10.00–18.00 Wed–Sun, noon–18.00 Tue; admission free) Housed in a three-storey villa in the park, the museum offers a recreation of the apartment of a wealthy local at the turn of the 20th century, coupled with a three-room exhibition on the history of the town. Displays are in Latvian only, though laminated cards offer English highlights. One tale has it that the museum building was spotted at the Paris Exposition of 1900, where it was part of the Russian pavilion, by one Captain Bangert from Liepāja, who bought it and shipped it back to Liepāja as a wedding gift for his bride. It was moved again to Kuldīga in 1906, where it is still known as Villa Bangert. Whatever the truth of the story, it gives the museum the excuse to screen video footage of *fin de siècle* Paris.

Old Brick Bridge (Senais ķieģeļu tilts) Baznīcas iela crosses the Venta by way of this symbol of the town, with its seven red-brick arches. It was built in 1874, wide enough to allow two carriages to pass each other. It was damaged in World War I and rebuilt in 1926. On Midsummer night, the bridge traditionally plays host to a naked run, with oak wreaths sported to cover modesties. Just upstream is Kuldīga's second claim to waterfall glory, and a rather more credible one. This is the **Venta Rapid** (Ventas rumba), which lays claim, at 249m, to the title of Europe's widest waterfall. What this claim does not quite make clear is that, though indeed wide, it is far from Europe's highest waterfall. A curving band of Devonian dolomite, its height is just under 2m. While this gives the fall only a limited grandeur, it comes into its own in spring during the migration upriver of a silvery fish named the vimba. The sight of these fish determinedly trying to leap up and over the rapids, failing frequently only to try again, is a remarkable one. The migration of the fish inspired Duke Jacob Kettler to develop a novel way of fishing in the 17th century. He had wicker baskets placed on the waterfall, into which fish misjudging their jumps would end up. Kuldīga became known as the 'town where fish are caught in the air'.

Riežupe Sand Caves (Riežupes smilšu alas; Rumbas pag.; w smilsualas.lv; ⊕ Apr–Oct 11.00–17.00 daily; adult/child €6/5) This large network of caves, with a total length of 2km, is manmade, dug for several generations until the start of World War II for the fine quality white quartz sand found here, used in the glassmaking industry. The caves are still owned by the family that dug them, though are now used solely for tourism purposes. To get to the caves, take the signposted turning northwards on the right bank of the Venta just beyond the Old Brick Bridge. Head north for 4km, parallel to the Venta along Krasta iela. From the car park, walk for a few minutes through the forest, past glades dotted with painted wooden sculptures of cars, animals and fairy-tale characters. The ticket office is in a clearing, with the cave entrance down some wooden steps, along the side of the Riežupe stream, which flows into the Venta. Some 460m of the cave network is open to visitors. You are taken round by an English-speaking guide. The caves are closed in the winter months, when they are home to hibernating bats. They maintain an almost constant 8°C temperature year-round.

BETWEEN KULDĪGA AND LIEPĀJA

ĒDOLE This small village, along the P119 between Kuldīga and Alsunga, around 9km from the latter, sits in the shadow of **Ēdole Castle** (Ēdoles pils; Pils iela 1; w edolespils.lv; ⊕ museum 10.00–18.00 Mon–Sat, 09.00–18.00 Sun; museum adult/student/child €6/4/4, Fairy Tale Kingdom €6/4/4, combined ticket €10/7/6). It was built in the 13th or early 14th century by the Bishopric of Courland, before coming into the hands of the von Behr family in 1561. They owned the castle until the land reforms of 1920, and it was remodelled in the Gothic Revival style by Adolph Werner Behr in the 1830s, under whose ownership the surrounding park was also landscaped. Prince Joachim of Prussia, son of the German emperor, was a guest here during World War I. The castle is an atmospheric place, arranged around a central cobbled courtyard, its rooms decorated in the style of the German-Baltic aristocracy. The 'Fairy Tale Kingdom' turns out to be an exhibition in the cellars of dioramas depicting Latvian fairy stories and is not worth the additional entrance fee.

Ēdole is served by around four **buses** daily in each direction between Alsunga and Kuldīga. Ēdole Castle also houses an atmospheric **hotel** (9 rooms; €€–€€€). Note, though, that the cheaper rooms are basic and have shared bathrooms. The appealing **restaurant** (€€€) offers such suitably baronial dishes as crayfish soup, venison goulash and oven-baked trout.

ALSUNGA This village is the centre of Latvia's Suiti community (see opposite). There are around four **buses** daily to Kuldīga, one going on to Rīga.

🏠 **Where to stay and eat**

Spēlmaņu Krogs (5 rooms) Pils iela 7; w spelmanukrogs.lv. Centrally located between castle & Catholic church, this offers simply furnished & basic rooms on the 1st floor. They also offer cookery lessons in local dishes such as *sklandrausis*, for groups only. €€

Tējnīca Sapņotava Skolas iela 11a; ✆6001 1863; e tava@sapnotava.lv. Housed in a white octagonal pavilion in the garden in front of the craft house, this is billed as a teahouse, but alongside tea & cakes offers alcohol & light meals. An important part of the cultural life of Alsunga, it often has live music in the grounds outside on Sat. €€

What to see and do At the heart of the place sits **Alsunga Castle** (Alsungas pils; Pils iela 1; ✆2642 5015; e muzejs@alsunga.lv; ⊕ Apr–Oct 09.00–17.00 Tue–Fri, 11.00–16.00 Sat, 11.00–15.00 Sun; adult/child €2.30/1.15). Constructed by the Livonian Order in the 14th century, it was handed around 1560 by Gotthard Kettler, last Master of the Order (and first Duke of Courland and Semigallia), to his counsellor, Friedrich von Kanitz. In 1573, von Kanitz sold it on to Jacob von Schwerin, Marshal of Courland and Semigallia, whose son Johann was so to change the fortunes of the area through his marriage to a Catholic aristocrat. The castle was damaged during the Second Northern War between Sweden and the Polish–Lithuanian Commonwealth. In 1738, the von Schwerin family in turn sold it to Ernst Johann von Biron, Duke of Courland and Semigallia, and the castle was remodelled in the Baroque style shortly thereafter. It was taken over by the Russian State on their annexation of the duchy in 1795. Following World War I, the castle was managed by the parish, and occupied variously by a dairy and school. The place was in a sorry state during the Soviet occupation. It is slowly

THE SUITI

The Suiti is a small Catholic community of around 2,200 people, centred on the villages of Alsunga, Jūrkalne and Gudenieki. It is a religious outlier in this largely Lutheran region. Its story starts with a love affair. It was 1623. Johann Ulrich von Schwerin, son of the landowner of Alsunga, was on military service in Warsaw, for this was the heyday of the Polish–Lithuanian Commonwealth. At a court ball, he fell in love with a Polish aristocrat named Barbara Konarska. She was a Catholic, and the besotted Johann converted to that faith in order to marry her. This development did not impress his father, Jacob, and Johann and Barbara were forced to live in exile near Vilnius until 1632, when Jacob died. Returning home to Alsunga, Johann determined that all the peasants of his estate should follow his new faith, and brought in a group of Jesuits to help in the process of instilling the Catholic faith into the community. Johann's fate was, however, a sad one. Neighbouring Protestant landowners were unhappy both at his proselytising efforts and the treatment of Protestants on his territory. He had ruled, for example, that Catholics had right of way over Protestants on the road. In 1637, he was poisoned, according to some accounts, by a group of Protestant landowners who had invited him to a meeting.

Johann had required his peasants to dress distinctively, so that he could better distinguish them from neighbouring Protestants; the women in brightly coloured outfits involving checked shawls and red skirts, the men in grey jackets with shiny buttons. Because intermarriage between Catholics and Protestants was long strongly discouraged on both sides, the Suiti community developed in an isolated way from surrounding communities; for generations insulated from outside influences. This meant that not only were the differences promoted by Johann maintained, but the Suiti community tended to retain customs that died out elsewhere in the region through the impacts of modernisation. These included a form of drone singing performed by Suiti women, elaborate wedding traditions, the continued use of traditional musical instruments such as bagpipes, a local dialect and a large number of folk songs specific to the community.

With concerns building that this distinctive culture was under threat as younger generations were less familiar with the traditions of their parents and grandparents, the Suiti cultural space was inscribed in 2009 on the UNESCO List of Intangible Cultural Heritage in Need of Urgent Safeguarding. Local organisations promote Suiti music, singing, textiles and craft skills: these can be appreciated at the craft house in Alsunga.

8

being restored, and is currently semi-furnished to provide a vaguely 18th-century ambience. A plaque on the external wall of the round southeastern tower, along Pils iela, recalls the life of Johann Ulrich von Schwerin, concluding that he died for his faith. The Latvian word for faith, *ticība*, is etched into a wooden bench on the road opposite.

From the castle, take Pils iela eastward, passing on your left a low grassy hillock known as **Dižgabalkalns**, a former castle hill of the Curonians. It reportedly housed a cannon battery used by one General Berg of the Courland forces to secure Alsunga Castle in 1659, after it had been occupied by the Swedes during the Second Northern War. Carry on to the **Church of St Michael the Archangel** (Sv. Erceņģeļa Mihaēla Romas katoļu baznīca; Skolas iela 1). Built around 1623, it has been a Catholic church since the time of Johann Ulrich von Schwerin. Its two transepts, giving the church the form of a cross, were added in 1882. Members of the von Schwerin family are buried beneath the church.

From the church, Skolas iela takes you to the two-storey red-brick former school building now housing the **Alsunga Craft House** (Alsungas amatu māja; Skolas iela 11a; ✆ 2642 5015; e alsungasamatumaja@kuldigasnovads.lv; ⏰ Jun–Sep 09.00–17.00 Mon–Fri, 11.00–16.00 Sat–Sun, Oct–May 09.00–17.00 Tue–Fri, 11.00–16.00 Sat; adult/child €2.30/1.15). This combines the tourist information centre, a small museum featuring mocked-up interiors of bygone Suiti family life, and a series of rooms devoted to community organisations promoting Suiti culture, including ceramics and weaving workshops, with items available for purchase.

JŪRKALNE This coastal village between Pāvilosta and Ventspils was once known as Felixberg and is the only maritime settlement of Latvia's Suiti community (page 265). North of the village, near the hamlet of Ošvalki on the P111 coastal road, a signposted track takes you to impressive tall beachside dunes, at the top of which is a metal monument resembling a torn sail punctuated with holes. Known as the '**Sail of Hope**', or to give it the formal Latvian title used on the signpost, 'Piemiņas zīme latviešu bēgļiem uz Zviedriju 1944-45g', this commemorates the Latvian citizens who, in the dying days of German occupation at the end of World War II, fearing the advance of the Soviet army, sought passage on local fishing boats to take them the 170km to Gotland in neutral Sweden. The departures were partly organised through the Latvian Central Council, with the help of western allies, but others were privately organised affairs. This was a hazardous journey, with the refugees at risk from both German and Soviet forces, and travelling in often overloaded boats, but some 5,000 refugees made it across. The monument, by Ģirts Burvis, bears an inscription in Swedish and Latvian.

PĀVILOSTA Officially a town, Pāvilosta is a quiet settlement of low houses and mostly unmetalled roads at the mouth of the Saka River, with a population of under 1,000. It has grown in prominence in recent years as a watersports centre and as the summer residence of well-heeled Latvians.

The port in the Middle Ages was 6km further up the river. The development of the harbour in its current location dates from the second half of the 19th century, when local landlord Otto von Lilienfeld laid out a place he named Paulshafen, in honour of his brother Paul, governor of the Courland Governorate. The place really started to grow at the end of the 19th century, when the port became important in the shipment of stone to Liepāja for the building of the Karosta military base and also developed a shipbuilding industry. Following World War I, its focus switched to fisheries, and under the Soviet occupation, that industry was collectivised into

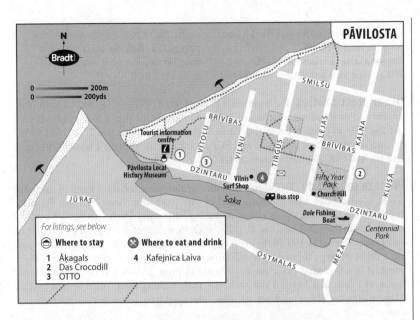

Bradt

0 — 200m
0 — 200yds

SMILŠU

BRĪVĪBAS

Tourist information
centre

Pāvilosta Local
History Museum

DZINTARU

VĪTOLU

VILŅU

TIRGUS

LEJAS

BRĪVĪBAS

KALNA

Vilnis
Surf Shop

Fifty Year
Park

Church Hill

KLUSA

JŪRAS

Saka

Bus stop

Dole Fishing
Boat

DZINTARU

Centennial
Park

OSTMALAS

MEŽA

For listings, see below

🏠 **Where to stay**   ✕ **Where to eat and drink**

1 Āķagals   4 Kafejnīca Laiva
2 Das Crocodill
3 OTTO

the Dzintarjūra fishermens' *kolkhoz*, later merged with that in Liepāja. While a small fishing industry remains, water-based tourism is now at the heart of its economy, yachts outnumbering the fishing boats lining the sides of the river, and in the summer months it embraces a laid-back beach-culture feel.

Getting there and away The **bus stop** is on Dzintaru iela, at the corner with Tirgus iela. There is one bus daily (Mon–Sat) from Rīga, via Kandava and Kuldīga, as well as four a day serving Pāvilosta on the route between Liepāja and Ventspils.

Tourist information The **tourist information centre** (Pāvilostas Tūrisma informācijas centrs; Dzintaru iela 1; **w** pavilosta.lv; ⏰ 10.00–17.00 Mon–Fri, 10.00–16.00 Sat, 10.00–15.00 Sun) is in the converted boat house behind the local history museum.

🏠 **Where to stay and eat** *Map, above*
Hotel restaurants comprise most of the Pāvilosta dining options.

OTTO (24 rooms) Dzintaru iela 7; **w** ottohotel. lv. The top of the range in Pāvilosta, a slick central hotel with use of the indoor pool & sauna included in the price. Its functional design occasionally comes at the expense of comfort – notably with its concrete-floored bedrooms, & the sombre dark grey exterior feels out of place in a resort town. Good b/fast, with all the hemp butter & chia pudding you would expect from a higher-end hotel in a place like Pāvilosta. The restaurant (€€€€) offers tables both indoors & around the garden, & a menu with nods to the local fishing tradition, like pickled herring. €€€€

Das Crocodill (8 rooms) Kalna iela 11; **w** dascrocodill.lv. Occupying one of the taller buildings in town, at 3 storeys, with a roof terrace, & more rooms in the outbuilding next to the outdoor pool, the rooms here are individually decorated apartments of varying sizes. They offer bicycles, surfboards, SUP boards & other watersports equipment for rent. €€€–€€€€

Āķagals (8 rooms) Dzintaru iela 3; 📞 2949 8899; **e** akagals.cafe@gmail.com. This 2-storey wooden guest house is well located, close to the beach, with some rooms offering balconies with river views. Rooms have wooden walls & floors, & there is a restaurant (€€€€).€€

Kafejnīca Laiva Dzintaru iela 31; ☏2926 7462. With a cooling white décor & tables along the road outside, this is a popular central place, offering pizza, pasta & salads, plus one or two fancier dishes like mussels in white wine sauce. Also serves b/fast. €€€

Other practicalities
The post office (Tirgus iela 1) is close to the bus stop. You are invited to stand on a surfboard displayed outside for that action photo. If you get the urge to catch a wave, the **Vilnis Surf Shop** (Dzintaru iela 27; ☏2644 4934; ⊘ closed Mon) offers surfboard and SUP board rentals. There is a **pharmacy** (Lejas iela 10; ☏6349 8222) in the town centre.

What to see and do
Dzintaru iela, running alongside the right bank of the Saka River, is what passes for the main road in this quiet spot. Arriving from the east, the first of Pāvilosta's sights encountered is **Centennial Park** (Simtgades parks), on the left of the road, laid out in 1979 for the town's centenary. A large boulder is inscribed: 'Pāvilosta 100 1879-1979'. A piece of higher ground nearby is accessed up a flight of steps topped by a millstone on its side looking like a concrete Polo mint. It is a favoured place for newlyweds to pose. Beside a millstone. With no sense of irony. Just beyond the park, the *Dole* **Fishing Boat**, once owned by the Dzintarjūra collective and set on concrete supports, offers a reminder of the town's past.

Over the road is the **Fifty-Year Park** (Piecdesmitgades parks; Dzintaru iela 47), laid out for the town's 50th anniversary in 1929. Local primary school head teacher Ernsts Šneiders led the effort to bring greenery to this windswept and sandy port, planting some 3,000 trees in total. The old market square in town, another appropriately green spot, is named in his honour. Next to the Fifty-Year Park stands Church Hill (Baznīckalns). So called because the building now housing the Culture House on top of it started out life in 1909 as an oratory. Evidence of a Mesolithic settlement has been discovered here, which accounts for the 'archaeological monument' sign.

Pāvilosta Local History Museum
(Pāvilostas novadpētniecības muzejs; Dzintaru iela 1; ☏6349 8276; e pavilosta.muzejs@tvnet.lv; ⊕ 15 May–14 Sep 09.00–17.00 Wed–Fri, noon–16.00 Sat–Sun, 15 Sep–14 May 09.00–17.00 Mon–Fri; adult/student €3/1) The museum sits in the stone building of the former sea pilots' house, close to the mouth of the river. There is a display on the history of Pāvilosta, starting with Mesolithic stone items from the Baznīckalns site, but with signage in Latvian only. A video installation offers a photographic history of Pāvilosta since 1918, though takes you into the minutiae of small-town life. Another room looks at the Soviet occupation, when the town lay in a restricted zone, the authorities so nervous about the risks of attempts by local citizens to flee to the west that the beach was adorned with a barbed-wire fence and its sands were raked to make it easier to spot tell-tale footprints.

There are temporary art exhibitions upstairs. Across the courtyard, a converted boathouse holds a display of fishing equipment as well as the museum's pride: VR headsets through which you can immerse yourself in three different fishing expeditions: upriver for lamprey, and out to sea for Baltic herring and the round goby, the latter an invasive species in the Baltic.

Beyond here, breakwaters extend either side of the river mouth into the Baltic, serving to elongate the river. There are sandy **beaches** either side of the breakwater, backed by dunes. White pods on the beach prove to be enclosed changing rooms, complete with their own mirror and sadly a fair amount of graffiti. Swimming close to the breakwaters is not permitted, and the tendency for rotting seaweed to collect behind them dissuades you from doing so. The beach south of the river is better quality.

AKMENSRAGS Occupying a muted cape as the coast southwest of Pāvilosta suddenly turns sharply south, the **Akmeņraga Lighthouse** (Akmeņraga bāka; Vērgale; \2835 0899; ☉ 10.00–16.00 Wed–Sun; €1) dates from the late 19th century, although the present brick cylinder, 38m in height, was built in 1921, with a major reconstruction in 1957 when the reinforced concrete shell was added. You can climb the 126 spiral stairs, lifting yourself through a hatch at the top to reach the light. A very short door gives access to a windy balcony, though the views are great. The lighthouse is signposted from the P111 road running south from Pāvilosta towards Liepāja. It is 11km from that road, and best to ring ahead to check the lighthouse is open, as its schedule can be affected by the weather. The beach here is sandy and uncrowded.

LIEPĀJA

The coastal city of Liepāja is the third largest in Latvia, with a population of some 68,000. It is an appealing place, with an enticing sandy beach, some of the best Art Nouveau architecture in Latvia outside Rīga, a cityscape in its northern suburbs that reflects the troubled history of the Tsarist and Soviet military bases here, and a lively entertainment scene, ranging from its status as a cradle of Latvian rock music to the swanky Great Amber Concert Hall. It will have the opportunity to showcase its charms as European Capital of Culture in 2027.

HISTORY A settlement named Libau was established here by the Teutonic Order in 1263 on the site of the earlier village of Līva. It suffered from various predations, including attack by Sweden during the Livonian War in the late 16th century. But in the 17th century there was a marked upswing in the town's fortunes linked to the maritime ambitions of the Duchy of Courland and Semigallia. The fine location of the city between sea and lake meant that the port here was well suited to delivering those ambitions, and Libau started to grow. In 1697, work began on a canal linking lake with sea, further to develop the port. The Great Northern War brought more challenges and capture of the town by Charles XII of Sweden, though it ended the war in Polish hands. The city, along with Courland as a whole, passed to Russian control in 1795, and Libau grew in the following century as the westernmost port of the Russian Empire, especially following the arrival of the railway in 1871.

Located just 70km from the border with Germany, the Russian authorities were preoccupied with the need to defend the city, and Tsar Alexander III ordered in 1890 the building of a new, heavily fortified, military port immediately north of town. It has acquired the name Karosta ('war port'). In the early 20th century, the city also served as an important embarkation point for migrants seeking a new life in North America: 40,000 migrants per year were taking the route by 1906.

The city, increasingly referred to by its Latvian name of Liepāja rather than the German Libau, played an important role in the creation of independent Latvia. Following the proclamation of Latvian independence on 18 November 1918 and the establishment of a provisional government under Kārlis Ulmanis, Russian advances forced that government to relocate from Rīga to Liepāja, arriving on 6 January 1919. On 16 April, a coup organised by the Germans installed Andrievs

Niedra as head of a puppet government, requiring Ulmanis to seek shelter on the steamship *Saratov* on the Commercial Canal, protected by British naval units on either side. This ship was briefly at this point the only part of Latvia held by the Latvian Provisional Government; the rest of the country being under either German or Russian control. The German-supported puppet government failed to maintain control, particularly after the German defeat against a combined Latvian and Estonian force at the Battle of Cēsis on 23 June, and by 27 June the situation in Liepāja was safe enough for Ulmanis and his ministers to disembark. In July the *Saratov* sailed to Rīga with the provisional government, and Liepāja's brief stint as de facto capital of the country was at an end.

During the Soviet occupation, Karosta military port was repurposed as a Soviet naval base, and Liepāja became a closed city. The arrival of ethnic Russians to staff the port and new industries necessitated the building of new apartment blocks and changed the ethnic character of the city. By 1989, ethnic Russians outnumbered Latvians. The Russians departed from the naval base only in 1994, three years after the restoration of Latvia's independence, and while their departure was warmly welcomed, this has required Liepāja to grapple with resulting challenges arising from population loss and the abandonment of many buildings, especially in Karosta. Its focus has been on the development of the commercial port, attraction of new industries and promotion of tourism.

GETTING THERE AND AROUND Liepāja **airport** (Liepājas lidosta; Lidostas iela 8, Cimdenieki, Grobiņas pag.; w Liepaja-airport.lv) is 5km east of the town centre, but unfortunately at the time of writing offered no scheduled services. The closest airport to Liepāja offering international flight connections is Palanga in Lithuania, 70km to the south, which may be a more convenient choice than Rīga if your travel plans are focused on western Kurzeme. The other transport links into Liepāja are all to be found north of the Commercial Canal. There is a **ferry** service operated by Stena Line daily between Liepāja and Travemünde (around 22hrs) on Germany's Baltic coast. The ferry terminal (Brīvostas iela 14A; w stenaline.lv) is north of the centre, just off Oskara Kalpaka iela.

The **railway station** (Liepājas dzelzceļa stacija; Rīgas iela 71; \6341 6284) dates from 1871, but notwithstanding the grand station building there is little passenger traffic: just one train a day between Liepāja and Rīga (3hrs 15mins). Bus travel is the main intercity public transport option. The **bus station** (Liepājas autoosta; Rīgas iela 71; \6342 2754) is outside the railway station, with 14 or more departures daily to Rīga (approx. 3hrs 30mins), four to Kuldīga (1hr 45mins) via Aizpute (50mins) and four to Ventspils (2hrs 10mins) via Pāvilosta (1hr).

There is a single **tram** line, served by modern red-and-white-painted trams, running north–south through the city, which connects the bus and railway stations with city centre locations. There are also several **bus** routes around town (w liepajastransports.lv). Tickets can be purchased from the driver, but are cheaper if bought in advance or, for those planning an extended stay, for ten trips. There are also one-, three- and five-day unlimited-use options.

TOURIST INFORMATION The **tourist information centre** (Liepājas reģiona tūrisma informācijas birojs; Rožu laukums 5/6; w liepaja.travel; ⊕ 09.00–18.00 Mon–Fri, 10.00–18.00 Sat, 10.00–16.00 Sun) is centrally located on Rožu laukums. Pick up the 'Follow the Notes' walking route map for a choice of 3.5km and 5.1km self-guided trails around the town centre, following metal musical notes embedded into the pavements.

LIEPĀJA

For listings, see from page 272

Where to stay
1 Art Hotel Roma
2 Boutique Hotel Roze
3 Liva
4 MORE
5 Promenade

Off map
BB Camping

Where to eat and drink
6 Darbnīca
7 MO
8 Parka Paviljons
9 Pastnieka māja
10 Red Sun Buffet
   Beach Bar
11 Rosemary

Ferry terminal,
railway & bus stations,
BB Camping, Karosta

Commercial Canal

Amber
Clock (5)

Great Amber
♪ Concert Hall

Holy Trinity
✝ Cathedral

Tourist information
ℹ centre

Madame Hoyer's
Guest House

Amatnieku
nams

St Anne's
✝ Church

Eduarda Veidenbauma

Bārtu

Rose
Square

Swedbank

St Joseph's
✝ Cathedral

Peter's
Market

Kūrmājas
prospekts 2/6

Graudu iela
36/38

Liepāja
Museum

Kūrmājas Prospekts

Jānis
Čakste
Square

Peldu iela
44

Vites

The Tree
of Ghosts

Mikeļa Valtera

"Pūt, vējiņi"

Seaside
Park

Zvejnieku Aleja

Monument to Sailors &
Fishermen Lost at Sea

Kurzeme   LIEPĀJA

Bradt

N

0   300m
0   300yds

Zvirbuļu · Jūras · Lielā · Baznīcas · Skolas · Zivju · Kungu · Radio · Graudu · Avotu · Tirgoņu · Siena · Kuršu · Republikas · Ludvika · Alejas · Rožu · Uliha · Dzintaru · Krišjāņa Barona · Liepu · Hika · Sporta · Celtnieku · Frīča Brīvzemnieka · Pasta · Vītolu · Toma · Peldu

8

WHERE TO STAY *Map, page 271*

Art Hotel Roma (28 rooms) Zivju iela 3;
w arthotelroma.lv. Arranged around a paved
courtyard, with shops & eateries on the ground
floor & the hotel above, this central place started
out life in 1882 as the Hotel de Rome, the work of
city architect Paul Max Bertschy. It has been smartly
restored, with a liberal sprinkling of artworks in
the rooms & corridors. A Capitoline wolf above the
reception desk underlines the Rome connection.
There is the Romas Dārzs Art Gallery & Museum of
Doll Art & Design (Galerija Romas dārzs un Leļļu
mākslas un dizaina muzejs; adult/child €5/2, free
to hotel guests) in the warren-like basement, with
works by 20th-century Liepāja artists & display
cases containing battered suitcases out of which
pour dolls & other toys of a bygone age. €€€€
Promenade (58 rooms) Veca Ostmala 40;
w promenadehotel.lv. The smartest hotel in
Liepāja, the Promenade has been tastefully
converted from a red-brick port warehouse along
the south bank of the Commercial Canal. The best
rooms have balconies overlooking the canal. There
are artworks in the foyer, & the restaurant is called
Piano. Because it has a piano in it. €€€€
Boutique Hotel Roze (8 rooms) Rožu iela 37;
w parkhotelliepaja.lv. Occupying a grey-painted

historic wooden building close to Seaside Park &
nicely located for the beach, this is a characterful
choice. There is a good restaurant (€€€€), with
meals served in the spacious garden in summer.
It is one of several hotels run by the Roze hotel
group, all bearing the name Roze, so specify the
address if taking a taxi here. €€€
MORE (20 rooms) Palmu iela 5; **w** morehotel.
lv. Occupying a wooden-walled building dating
from 1899 in a quiet part of the Old Town, this is
a comfortable & pretty good-value option. Locals
still know it by its old name, Poriņš. €€€
Līva (115 rooms) Lielā iela 11; **w** livahotel.lv.
With a good central location, this 5-storey concrete
block retains echoes of its Soviet-era origins, but
the rooms are fine. They proudly advertise their
3½ stars. €€
BB Camping Lībiešiu iela 2/6; **w** bbcamping.lv.
In the trees on the north side of Karosta, they offer
a range of accommodation options, from basic tent
pitches & camper sites to wooden huts resembling
overturned boats & fully equipped 'glamping tents'.
They also rent out tents. There is a wake park, with
wakeboard & SUP board rental, sauna rental & an
on-site café. The site is, though, 7km from the city
centre. €–€€€

✗ **WHERE TO EAT AND DRINK** *Map, page 271*

In an interesting effort to promote local cuisine, participating restaurants across the
city offer a dish called Liepājas menciņi, comprising small pieces of smoked cod,
cooked with potatoes and onions. It is served in a clay pot inscribed with the name
of the dish in most of the restaurants taking part in the scheme.

MO Friča Brīvzemnieka iela 7; **w** tiamo.lv. Part
of the TIAMO group, which owns a selection of
eateries in the city & likes capital letters, MO is
located in the rehabilitated former industrial
space of Julianna's Courtyard (Juliannas pagalms),
housing a range of bars & restaurants close to
the Commercial Canal. The interior is sombre, but
service & food are good, the menu ranging from
rabbit leg to pasta with tiger prawns. €€€€
Parka Paviljons Miķeļa Valtera iela 3; ☎ 2880
0887; **e** info@parkapaviljons.lv. In leafy Jūrmalas
parks, the restaurant sits in a glorious Art
Nouveau pavilion, with curving latticed windows.
Originally built in 1903, the building burnt down
in the 1970s, & what you see today is a modern
reconstruction. The food is good, though plays
second fiddle to the nicely recreated early-20th-

century atmosphere. There is a large outdoor
terrace. €€€€
Rosemary Zivju iela 3; ☎ 2037 3144;
e siagunilp@gmail.com. This basement restaurant
off the courtyard of the Art Hotel Roma also has
summer tables in the courtyard, & a menu ranging
geographically from burritos to paella, though
coming back home for Liepājas menciņi. Scenes of
bygone Liepāja are painted on the walls. €€€€
Pastnieka māja Friča Brīvzemnieka iela 53;
w pastniekamaja.lv. The 'Postman's House' is a
wooden building with an outside terrace. The
polychrome interior is less rustic than the exterior
leads you to expect, & the menu, served in an
envelope, takes you in strange directions with
anecdotes about the life of Arvids the postman
& curiously named dishes. 'Wishy-washy squish',

anyone? Get beyond the language, & the food is good, with plenty of nods to local cuisine, including Liepājas menciņi. €€€

Red Sun Buffet Beach Bar Peldu iela 59A; w redsunbuffet.lv. The most substantial of Liepāja's beach bars, in a white-painted wooden building with a rooftop terrace perfect for watching late evening summer sunsets over a cocktail. The menu is an unadventurous mix of ribs, fish & chips & burgers. The deal here & at the other

bar/cafés along the beach is similar: order & collect your food & drinks at the bar. €€€

Darbnīca Lielā iela 8; ☏ 2681 1313; e darbnicacafe@gmail.com; ◷ until 16.00, closed Sun & Mon. A laid-back central place, with bare brick columns, exposed pipework, distressed wooden tables & probably Neil Young playing on the music system. Offering noodles, salads, burgers & wraps, this is a good place for a light lunch or afternoon coffee. €€

ENTERTAINMENT Liepāja has since 2011 played host to the **Summer Sound Festival** (w summersound.lv), held on the beach at the beginning of August, and usually attracting some international performers along with the local names.

Multifunctional arts centre **Great Amber Concert Hall** (Koncertzāle 'Lielais dzintars'; Radio iela 8; w lielaisdzintars.lv; ◷ 11.00–14.00 & 14.30–17.00 Mon–Fri, 10.00–15.00 Sat–Sun, & for concerts) opened in 2015, and hosts the Liepāja Symphony Orchestra and a music school, and with its amber-toned glass façade, curving walls and irregular angles became an instant landmark. It somewhat resembles a large piece of amber. The white-toned Great Hall is the heart of the building, seating almost 1,000 and hosting a wide range of cultural events.

SHOPPING

Amatnieku nams Dārza iela 4/8; ☏ 2654 1424; e amatniekunams@inbox.lv; ◷ May–Sep 10.00–17.00 Mon–Sat, Oct–Apr 10.00–17.00 Mon–Fri. As with similar Houses of Craftworkers in other Latvian towns, this accommodates various artisans, from weavers to potters. There is also on display what is said to be Latvia's longest amber necklace: at 123m it is evidently in search of a particularly large neck. It is wound on to a wooden frame, giving it the appearance of a giant spider's web. The shop here is a good place to

buy authentic craft items, with amber jewellery a favourite.

Peter's Market Pētertirgus; Kuršu iela 5/7/9; w petertirgus.lv. The brightly illuminated brick building was completed in 1910 in an eclectic style incorporating Art Nouveau touches, the work of architect Ludwig Melville. It is the largest market building in Latvia outside Rīga. Note the fish stalls in the pungent basement. Further stalls selling fruit, vegetables & flowers spread out beyond the main market pavilion. It is open every day.

OTHER PRACTICALITIES There is a central **post office** (Radio iela 13; ☏ 2700 8001) close to the Great Amber Concert Hall. Pedestrianised Tirgoņu iela south of Rose Square houses a branch of **Swedbank** (Tirgoņu iela 18; ☏ 6744 5555) as well as a **pharmacy** (Tirgoņu iela 24; ☏ 2037 7467).

WHAT TO SEE AND DO

Vecliepāja Liepāja has an attractive Old Town. The red-brick neo-Gothic and neo-Romanesque buildings designed by Paul Max Bertschy, city architect for more than 30 years from 1871, give the centre some of its character. It is also dotted with a larger collection of Art Nouveau buildings than anywhere in Latvia outside Rīga. Many of these were built shortly after the relaxation of building restrictions in 1908, when the Tsarist authorities relieved the naval base of its fortress status. The Old Town sits to the south of the **Commercial Canal** (Tirdzniecības kanāls), the 3km-long waterway excavated at the end of the 17th century connecting the Baltic Sea with Lake Liepāja. The canal is closely associated with Liepāja's maritime prosperity and was necessitated by the silting of the Līva River which had previously been the focus of the port. The promenade on the south side of the canal makes for a pleasant stroll. Note the **Amber Clock** (Dzintara pulkstenis), an hourglass filled with small pieces of amber that were donated by local residents.

From the bridge across the Commercial Canal, Lielā iela heads southwards towards **Rose Square** (Rožu laukums; Zivju iela 9), the central square of the city, its focus a circular rose bed decorated with the coats of arms of Liepāja's sister cities. The Ionic-columned façade of Liepāja University overlooks it.

Holy Trinity Cathedral (Svētās Trīsvienības katedrāle; Lielā iela 9; ☎2591 4456; ☉ 10.00–18.00 Tue–Sat, noon–15.00 Sun) You pass on the way towards Rose Square this fine Baroque church completed in 1758. It has been a cathedral only since 2007. The Rococo interior, festooned with golden angels, is unlike most of the rather austere Lutheran churches of Latvia. The altar, the largest among Latvian Lutheran churches, centres on a sculptural representation of the Holy Trinity. Looking towards the altar, there is an elaborate pulpit on the left, and behind this, an equally ornate confessional box. To the right of the altar, raised above the floor and reached by a short spiral staircase, is a sumptuous glass-sided box, built for Ernest Johann von Biron, the then Duke of Courland, and topped with the coat of arms of Courland flanked by assorted weaponry. Dominating the back of the church is a huge organ, which claims the title of the largest mechanical organ in the world, with some 7,000 pipes. Its story is one of progressive enlargement from more modest beginnings in the 18th century, an effort aimed to eclipse the organ of Rīga Cathedral. The golden angels decorating the organ are, logically enough, holding musical instruments. You can climb the tower for good views across the city.

Beneath a plaque inside the church stand two small flags: the Finnish flag to the left and, to the right, the flag of the Finnish Jäger Battalion. This ensemble commemorates the swearing of loyalty in this church on 13 February 1918 to the legal parliament of Finland by the Royal Prussian 27th Jäger Battalion. The unit consisted mainly of Finnish volunteers serving in the German army during World War I. They were released to join the anti-communist side in the Finnish Civil War, making an important contribution in the struggle for Finnish independence.

Graudu iela Running northwest from Rožu laukums, Graudu iela is lined with a rich collection of Art Nouveau buildings, among them the green-painted apartment block at **Graudu iela 36/38**, built in 1913 in a Perpendicular Art Nouveau style by Max Theodor Bertschy, the son of Paul Max.

Madame Hoyer's Guest House (Hoijeres kundzes viesu nams; Kungu iela 24; ☎2990 5180; e interjeramuzejs@liepaja.lv; ☉ Sep–May 10.00–18.00 Wed–Sun, Jun–Aug 10.00–18.00 Tue–Sun; adult €3) One block south of Rožu laukums, just beyond the Kurzeme Shopping Centre, turn left on to Kungu iela. After about 400m, at the corner with Bāriņu iela, is the house at which Peter the Great stayed during his 'Grand Embassy' of 1697. The Russian Tsar was officially travelling incognito, though one suspects this would have fooled no-one. A branch of Liepāja Museum, the building was opened to the public in 2022 after extensive restoration, and now bears the name Madame Hoyer's Guest House. The authorities decided to focus the restoration around Peter the Great's landlady during his visit, rather than around the Russian emperor himself, a choice perhaps dictated by the poor state of Latvian–Russian relations.

The ground floor has been restored in the style of a 17th-century guest house, and is entered through a tavern, which serves a lunch of vaguely 17th-century dishes. A couple of guest rooms have been furnished, the guides telling you hopefully that these might have been the very rooms used by Peter the Great and his friend Menshikov. Next to these are, we are told, the private living room and bedroom of the widowed Margarethe Hoyer and her daughter. The floor upstairs, which probably served as a storeroom in Madame Hoyer's time, has been decorated in 19th-century style, and attempts to replicate the apartment of notary Christoph Stender, who owned the building from 1835. While none of the furnishings are original, there are many interesting touches, from the train set in the children's bedroom to the wooden mousetrap in the kitchen. In the basement is an exhibition (in Latvian only) on the restoration of the building.

This is a part of town with royal connections. The house next door across Bāriņu iela, proclaiming its year of construction as 1699, bears a plaque recording that Charles XII of Sweden stayed here in 1701 during the Great Northern War.

Around Peter's Market Retracing your steps back along Kungu iela, and at the end of it turning left towards the south, brings you after a couple of blocks to the elegant Peter's Market. This is flanked by two churches. To the west stands **St Joseph's Cathedral** (Svētā Jāzepa Romas katoļu katedrāle; Rakstvežu iela 13; \6342 9775; e katedrale@gmail.com), built in 1896 in a neo-Romantic style on the site of a smaller 18th-century church which was incorporated into the new building as the first chapel to your left as you enter, down some steps. Above those steps note the silver ship suspended from the ceiling, which appears to be a particularly elaborate votive offering, presumably in thanks for a storm quelled. The interior is decorated with soothing pastel paintings on walls and ceiling. On the other side of the market is the red-brick Lutheran **St Anne's Church** (Svētās Annas Evaņģēliski luteriskā baznīca; Veidenbauma iela 1; \2922 5332; e sv.annas. draudze@apollo.lv), the oldest church in Liepāja, tracing its foundation to the 16th century, though the building has been reconstructed several times, the present version the work of Paul Max Bertschy in the 1890s. The spire rises to 60m. Its carved wooden altar dates from the late 17th century, but the church is usually locked up outside services.

Jānis Čakste Square (Jāņa Čakstes laukums) A couple of blocks southwest of St Joseph's Cathedral sits Jānis Čakste Square, a park which started out life as a parade ground. Known as Pioneer Square in the Soviet period, it was remodelled in 2013 in honour of the first president of independent Latvia, Jānis Čakste. It is distinguished by an enormous Latvian flag, flying from a 35m pole, beneath which an inscription on a pink marble wall is a quote from Čakste: 'defend your country, cultivate it, because if there is no Latvia, there will be no you either.' A line of waterspouts down the middle of the park playfully throws up jets of varying heights. Note the red-brick apartment complex a block north of here at **Peldu iela 44**. One of the most striking compositions of architect Paul Max Bertschy, it features a neo-Gothic turret at the corner of the building.

Around the seafront Smart Kūrmājas prospekts heads west from the south bank of the Commercial Canal towards the seafront. At the start of its journey, the long building with an eclectically decorated Art Nouveau façade at **Kūrmājas prospekts 2/6**, dating from 1908, is the former headquarters of the Russian East Asiatic Steamship Company, which operated passenger services to New York on which many migrants reached America in the early 20th century. It is now home to the regional court.

Note a series of **bronze sculptures** along Kūrmājas prospekts. These illustrate the verses of the song composed in 1973 by musician Imants Kalniņš which has become the anthem of the city. *Pilsētā, kurā piedzimst vējš* (*In the City Where Wind Is Born*) reflects the fact that Liepāja, like Chicago, is a city known for its strong breezes. The lyrics describe the lives being lived while the wind is blowing, and the sculptures illustrate them: a shipwright planing his boat, a telephone engineer waving from his precarious place on a pole, a crow on a branch, and a pub table behind which the visitor can take the role of the 'amber Latvians' mentioned in the song.

Liepāja Museum (Liepājas muzejs; Kūrmājas prospekts 16/18; w liepajasmuzejs. lv; ⊕ Sep–May 10.00–18.00 Wed–Sun, Jun–Aug 10.00–18.00 daily; admission free) There are some fine early-20th-century mansions along Kūrmājas prospekts. One, built by Paul Max Bertschy, with a neo-Gothic exterior and interiors drawing from styles ranging from German Renaissance to Rococo, houses the Liepāja Museum. The historical displays on the ground floor are rather cluttered, with labelling in Latvian only. There is a room dedicated to the work of wood sculptor Miķelis Pankoks, who spent the latter part of his life in a psychiatric hospital in Chur in Switzerland, dying there in 1983. Upstairs is a more modern exhibition, with signage in English, highlighting the role of Liepāja in securing Latvian independence, as the seat of the provisional government in early 1919. The basement houses an ethnographic exhibition dedicated to the lives and work of the people of South Kurzeme.

Seaside Park (Jūrmalas parks) Kūrmājas prospekts takes you to Seaside Park, a 3km stretch of greenery behind the beach, dating to the late 19th century. There are some stately Art Nouveau buildings fringing it, hinting at elegant bygone times, particularly around Hika iela and Vites iela and centred on a circular duckpond. The open-air stage in the park, known as '**Pūt, vējiņi!**', was the venue in 1964 for the *Liepājas dzintars* rock festival, the first such event in the USSR, though the present-day arena has been modernised. Its name, 'Blow, Winds', is that of a Latvian folk song which served during the Soviet occupation as a surrogate anthem for Latvians. Close by is a stainless-steel statue of a tree, known as **The Tree of Ghosts** (Spoku koks), another monument linked to Liepāja's place at the heart of the emergence of rock music in Latvia during the Soviet period. The tree is a tribute to rock band Līvi, founded in 1976. *Spoku koks* is the name of one of the band's albums. Several past members of the group met with untimely ends: their names are engraved on the roots. Press a button on the benches around the tree and you (together with everyone nearby) are treated to a recording selected from the band's best-known songs. For example, *Ozolam* (*Song to the Oak*), which in singing of a dead-looking oak tree whose roots are nonetheless alive and will help generate millions of acorns speaks to the resilience of the Latvian people in the face of occupation.

A short walk north, on the edge of the beach, is a distinctly Soviet-era monument: a bronze statue of a woman tearfully holding her arm over her eyes on a tall, slanting plinth. This is the **Monument to Sailors and Fishermen Lost at Sea** (Piemineklis bojā gājušajiem jūrniekiem un zvejniekiem), erected in 1977. It is locally nicknamed 'Crocodile' for a supposed resemblance to Gena the Crocodile, star of a Soviet cartoon series. A plaque was added in 2000, dedicated to the ten crewmen of the US Navy PB4Y-2 Privateer aircraft, which had been conducting an electronic surveillance mission, shot down off Liepāja in 1950 by Soviet forces.

Liepāja's **beach** is sandy, and equipped with changing cubicles, toilets, showers and even bicycle racks in the form of penny farthings.

Karosta The territory of the Tsarist and Soviet military base immediately north of the city has a different feel to the rest of Liepāja. Initially bearing the name of its founder, Alexander III, it gradually took on the title of Karosta, a literal rendering of its role as a military port. Its southern edge is marked by the Karosta Canal, itself a core element of the late-19th-century engineering works establishing the base. From central Liepāja, you arrive over the **swing bridge**, built in 1906, which now takes the name of Oskars Kalpaks, commander of the 1st Latvian Independent Battalion. Karosta was designed as a self-contained town, with its own power station, water supply, schools and apartments, and its grid-patterned layout is today dominated by a mix of red-brick Tsarist-era buildings, many of them officers' living quarters with four flats in each block, and Soviet apartment blocks, most in various degrees of disrepair. On the departure of the Russian forces in 1994, the place was in a ruinous state, and Karosta became a byword for urban deprivation. With the gradual renovation of the better properties, and the demolition of those beyond salvation, an early-stage gentrification is taking place, and it is now easier to appreciate the attractions of the place, even if many of these have a dark side. With its greenery and broad boulevards, Karosta is rather spread out, making the bicycle a better option for exploring it than walking, especially if you plan to investigate the fortifications in its northern reaches.

St Nicholas Orthodox Naval Cathedral (Sv. Nikolaja Jūras katedrāle; Studentu rotas iela 7; \6345 7634) The most striking building in Karosta is a spiritual one. The cathedral has a large central golden dome atop a round tower, representing Christ, with four smaller domes around it, representing the evangelists. Tsar Nicholas II attended the opening ceremony in 1903. The shabby apartment blocks surrounding the building serve to accentuate its glittering exterior.

Karosta Prison (Karostas cietums; Invalīdu iela 4; w karostascietums.lv; ⊕ Jun–Aug 09.00–19.00 daily, May & Sep 10.00–18.00 daily, Oct–Apr noon–16.00 Sat–Sun; adult/child €7/3.50). In southeastern Karosta, close to the canal, sits Karosta Prison. A two-storey red-brick Tsarist building, it was originally planned as a hospital. From the outset, however, it became a prison, serving largely as a detention facility for sailors found guilty of minor disciplinary offences, who would typically spend a few days here. You visit on a guided tour, which usually start on the hour, taking you along black-painted corridors to prison cells, some bearing plaintive graffiti from former inmates: 'forgive me for everything'; 'I want to go home'. Various other activities are on offer, though all must be pre-booked, ranging from an escape room to a tour to the Northern Fort, and those seeking something different can even spend the night here, either on an iron bed in a cell, or with more comfort in a double bed in the chief officer's room (€–€€). For groups of at least ten, they will even organise an 'extreme night', in which guests take on the role of a prisoner and look forward to being humiliated. Buses 3 or 4 from Liepāja will bring you here.

Fortifications dating from Tsarist times can be reached with your own transport. Do, though, be careful exploring them: many are unstable and at risk of collapse. The most visually impressive is the **Northern Fort** (Ziemeļu forts; Jātnieku iela 25), historically known as No 1 Artillery Battery, offering graffiti-covered concrete bunkers gradually being reclaimed by the sea. It sits 3km north of Karosta, signposted from Lībiešu iela, the main road running in that direction.

Šķēde Dunes Memorial (Šķēdes memoriāls) A kilometre north of the fort lies a sobering reminder of the horrors of the Holocaust in Latvia. The Šķēde Dunes

Memorial marks the site of execution of the Jewish community of Liepāja, with some 2,800 Jews murdered during mass shootings between 15 and 17 December 1941. There were other executions here up to 1945, both of Jews and other groups targeted by the Nazis, including members of the Roma community, suspected communists and Soviet prisoners of war. A plaque records that from 1941 to 1945, 3,640 Jews were murdered here, including 1,048 children, alongside 2,000 Soviet prisoners of war and 1,000 Latvian citizens, the latter including those who had helped Jews and prisoners and resisted the occupation.

There are two memorials on the site. A white obelisk, bearing red stars and dating from the Soviet period, tells you in Latvian and Russian that between 1941 and 1945 more than 19,000 inhabitants of Liepāja were murdered by the Nazis, and proclaiming 'eternal memory to Soviet patriots!' Note both the figure quoted here far exceeding the already horrendous number of those killed at Šķēde and the absence of any specific reference to Jews. Both are typical features of Soviet commemorative monuments at such places of execution. The Soviet monument is dwarfed by one opened in 2005, the work of local sculptor Raimonds Gabaliņš, which takes the shape of a giant menorah laid out on the ground and built of local boulders. Representing the menorah lights are granite columns inscribed with passages from the Torah. Reaching the monument from the small car park, you pass along the Righteous among the Nations Alley, flanked with posts bearing the names of local people who risked their lives to save Jews.

SOUTHERN KURZEME

NĪCA A village on the main A11 road south from Liepāja towards the Lithuanian border, Nīca is of interest as a base for exploring the wedge of land in Latvia's southwest abutting Lithuania. For some reason, the village has a **tourist information centre** (Nīcas Tūrisma informācijas centrs; Bārtas iela 6; w dienvidkurzeme.travel; ◷ 10.00–17.00 Tue–Fri, 10.00–15.00 Sat), with a small collection of antiques and curios in the same building (☏2646 1735; ◷ 08.00–15.00 Mon & Wed, 08.00–14.00 Fri). Nearby is a comedy signpost telling you that it is 2,061km from the village to its near namesake, the French resort of Nice (Nīca in Latvian).

⌂ **Where to stay and eat** A pleasant guest house with a part timber-framed exterior, **Nīcava** (6 rooms; Nīcas pag.; w hotelnicava.lv; €€) is set in a small park with a pond and children's play area. The largest bedroom has a safari theme, with photos of African wildlife on the walls. Other rooms honour British pop groups: the Beatles, Queen and Pink Floyd. A small glass-walled restaurant (€€€) offers local dishes, including Liepājas menciņi, along with more standard fare like pork chops.

LAKE PAPE A shallow coastal lagoon lake in the southwestern corner of Latvia, Lake Pape (Papes ezers) runs 8km from north to south, with an average depth of just 0.5m. It is broken up by numerous reed beds. A canal dug in 1834 connects the lake with the sea, from which it is otherwise separated by a strip of dunes up to 2km wide. It is an important spot for migratory birds and is today protected within the Pape Nature Park (Papes dabas parks).

It is the site of an interesting **rewilding project** (w pdf-pape.lv; ◷ 10.00–18.00, but book ahead at least 3 days in advance; adult/student €4/2), the initiative of Pasaules Dabas Fonds, the Latvian arm of the WWF. A herd of small grey-coloured wild horses, bred to resemble the tarpan that once roamed the Eurasian steppe, and another of Heck cattle, the product of an attempt in 1920s Germany to breed back the extinct auroch, were introduced here from 1999. At that time much of the agricultural land around the lake had been abandoned, and without intervention would over time revert to forest. The introduction of grazing animals was an attempt to sustain a more open and biodiverse landscape. The wild horses and cattle occupy 400ha of enclosed plant-rich meadows. A warden will guide you close to the herds, but touching the animals is not allowed. Bison have also been introduced, but these now roam outside the enclosed areas and are rarely seen by visitors. The rewilding project is accessed from the A11 road to the landward side of the lake. Follow signs bearing the WWF logo to the 'wild horses' (Savvaļas zirgi). The small village of Pape lies on the other side of the lake, next to the coastal dunes. Many of the cottages here serve as summer residences of Lithuanian tourists.

AIZPUTE Bisected by the Tebra River, the small town of Aizpute is a tranquil place. Originally settled by Cours, who built a fort here on the site of the present-day Lutheran church, it was conquered by German crusaders in the 13th century, who knew the place as Hasenpoth and commenced building a castle in 1249. Aizpute obtained city rights in 1378, and for a time flourished as a commercial centre thanks to the navigability of the Tebra River, with goods reaching the sea at present-day Pāvilosta along the Saka River, of which the Tebra is a tributary. But from the 17th century it became an increasingly provincial backwater. Aizpute is on the **bus** route between Liepāja and Kuldīga, with four buses daily to each place.

The **tourist information centre** (Aizputes Tūrisma informācijas centrs; Atmodas iela 16; w visitaizpute.lv; ⊕ 10.00–18.00 Tue–Fri, 10.00-15.00 Sat) sits in a pink-walled building in the centre of town.

What to see and do An arched **stone bridge** across the Tebra River, built in 1907, acts as the fulcrum of the town. Overlooking the river immediately to the west of the bridge are the ruins of the **Livonian Order Castle** (Aizputes Livonijas ordeņa pilsdrupas; Liepājas iela 9). The castle, which has been destroyed and rebuilt over the centuries, and progressively converted from military to residential uses, is laid out as a square. Buildings survive along two walls, though these are in a parlous state, with blocked-up windows. An attempt has been made to recall the heyday of the place with the addition in 2017 of a statue of a knight of the Livonian Order. It is one of those statues that locals love to dress up: he was seen sporting a facemask at the peak of Covid restrictions, and a crown of oak leaves for Midsummer.

On the eastern side of the bridge is another hill, this one topped by **St John's Evangelical Lutheran Church** (Svētā Jāņa evaņģēliski luteriskā baznīca; Liepājas iela 3; ☏ 2844 6787). Dating from the 1250s, it is one of the oldest churches in Kurzeme. It has, however, been remodelled several times and the present look largely dates from 1860. Below Church Hill there is an 18th-century **watermill** (Ūdensdzirnavas; Liepājas iela 10A), with the Tebra River widened into an attractive millpond below it. From the base of the Church Hill, the main road runs uphill to the centre of town, where there are some appealing wooden buildings from the late 19th century.

SALDUS A quiet district capital sitting at the base of a gentle bowl, it was the site of the Livonian Order Castle of Frauenburg, destroyed during the Great Northern War at the start of the 18th century. Saldus died out thereafter, re-emerging as a market town in the 1850s. Its tourism effort focuses on the connections of the place to two very different figures: painter Janis Rozentāls and rock musician Ēriks Ķiģelis.

The **tourist information centre** (Saldus Tūrisma informācijas centrs; Striķu iela 3; w turisms.saldus.lv; ⊕ 08.00–18.00 Mon–Fri, 10.00–14.00 Sat) is on the central Oskara Kalpaka laukums, on the corner of Striķu iela.

Getting there and away
The **bus station** (Saldus autoosta; Jelgavas iela 2; ✆6382 2107) is centrally located, just off Oskara Kalpaka laukums, offering frequent connections to Rīga (just under 2hrs) and Liepāja (1hr 30mins). There is a **railway station** (Saldus dzelzceļa stacija; Stacijas iela; ✆6381 6203), a couple of kilometres north of town, on the Rīga to Liepāja line, though with just one train daily in each direction.

Where to stay and eat
Demians (10 rooms; Rīgas iela 10A; ✆6388 1596; e hotel. demians@gmail.com; €€) is a centrally located three-star hotel, taking its name from a Hermann Hesse novel. The Hesse theme is continued in its restaurant, **Stikla Pērlīšu Spēle** (€€€), named after Hesse's novel *The Glass Bead Game*. The restaurant is ebulliently decorated in blue and yellow mosaic designs and offers a plush menu.

What to see and do
The town centres on **Oskara Kalpaka laukums**, named after the first commander-in-chief of the Latvian forces during the War of Independence, and commemorating the fact that Saldus was the first Latvian town liberated by Kalpaks' battalion in 1919.

Janis Rozentāls History and Art Museum
(Jaņa Rozentāla vēstures un mākslas muzejs; Striķu iela 22; w muzejs.saldus.lv; ⊕ 09.00–17.00 Tue, Thu–Sat, 09.00–18.00 Wed; adult/student €5/2) Heading down Striķu iela, you reach after a few hundred metres the museum, spread across three adjacent buildings. The main building mixes a display in Latvian-only on the history of the town with temporary art exhibitions. Behind this, a second building houses the Latvian art collection of Saldus-born businessman Guntis Priedaiks. The real attraction is the third building, a house where Janis Rozentāls, who was born in the district, set up his art studio and lived for a couple of years until moving to Rīga in 1901. A well-presented exhibition highlights the places in Saldus and Kurzeme that featured in his paintings, and there are several Rozentāls canvases on display. If you are minded to skip the exhibitions in the first two buildings, entry to the Rozentāls exhibition alone is available at a reduced price (adult/student €3/1.50). There is a seated statue of the painter in front of the building.

St John's Evangelical Lutheran Church
(Sv Jāņa Evaņģēliski luteriskā baznīca; Kuldīgas iela 2; w saldusbaznica.lv) On higher ground overlooking Oskara Kalpaka laukums, the church stands on a site first occupied by a wooden church in 1461 and a stone one in 1615, although the present building is the late-19th-century work of architect Wilhelm Neumann. The flight of steps leading up from the square formed the setting of one of Rozentāls' most famous works, his diploma piece *Pēc dievkalpojuma* (*After the Service*). The painting depicts the varied parishioners leaving the church, heading off to their everyday lives. Seven of the characters in that painting, including Rozentāls' parents, have been immortalised in bronze sculptures placed on the steps. An adjacent signboard displays a copy of the painting itself. Indeed, Saldus has done a fine job of spotlighting the locations around town painted by Rozentāls by putting copies of his paintings on signboards at the places that inspired them.

Kalnsētas Park Heading east from Oskara Kalpaka laukums along the main Jelgavas iela brings you to the park, arrayed along the picturesque banks of the Ciecere River a kilometre out of the centre. The park was laid out in the late 19th century by Baron von der Recke, owner of Kalnamuiža Manor, which sits on the hill above the park and now houses a technical school. At the western end of the park, near the Jelgava iela bridge, a moss-covered boulder on the side of the river is known as **Rozentāls' Stone** (Rozentāla akmens), reportedly a favoured spot of the artist. A little further on, a tranquil spot has been named **Ēriks' Meadow** (Ērika pļava) in honour of Saldus-born musician Ēriks Ķiģelis, guitarist and composer with the Liepāja-based rock group Līvi, an influential Latvian musical voice in the later years of the Soviet Union. Ķiģelis was killed in a car accident in 1985, and two years later the ***Saldus Saule* rock festival** (w saldussaule.lv) was first organised in his honour in the town of his birth. It is still held annually in Kalnsētas Park, usually on the last weekend in July.

Appendix 1

LANGUAGE *With Adriana Ivama Brummell and Intra Liepiņa*

PRONUNCIATION Latvian is by and large pronounced as it is written. Stress is placed on the first syllable, with a few exceptions, such as the word for 'thank you' – pal**dies** ('thank you') and ne**viens** ('no-one').

The alphabet

A, a	as in b**u**t
Ā, 'ā'	the straight line appearing above Latvian vowels is a *garumzīme*, indicating pronunciation should be lengthened, as in f**a**ther
B, b	as in **b**ad
C, c	like 'ts' as in sho**ts**
Č, č	like 'ch' as in **ch**ick
D, d	as in **d**ark
E, e	pronounced either as a 'closed e' as in b**e**st or 'open e' as in c**a**t
Ē, ē	a lengthened version of either the 'closed e', as in gl**a**re or 'open e', as in fl**a**n, but longer
F, f	appears only in loanwords, as in **f**ox
G, g	as in **g**arden. Unlike the English, its sound does not change when followed by an 'e' or 'I', so it is not pronounced as in **g**erbil
Ģ, ģ	no direct English counterpart. It is rather like a 'd' and 'j' sounded together
H, h	appears only in loanwords, as in **H**olland
I, i	as in **i**nformation
Ī, ī	a lengthened version of 'i' as in b**ee**n
J, j	like 'y' as in **y**oung
K, k	as in **k**ick
Ķ, ķ	no direct English counterpart, but somewhat like a 't' and 'j' sounded together
L, l	as in **l**ife
Ļ, ļ	like 'll' as in mi**lli**on
M, m	as in **m**ark
N, n	as in **n**ine
Ņ, ņ	softer, as in **n**ew
O, o	may be pronounced in several different ways, though native Latvian words are typically pronounced as the diphthong 'oa', as in m**or**ning. Loanwords may be pronounced with a shorter sound, as in b**o**y
P, p	as in **p**ark
R, r	a rolled or trilled 'r' with no direct English counterpart
S, s	as in **s**afe

Š, š	like 'sh' as in **sh**are
T, t	as in ca**t**
U, u	as in p**u**t
Ū, ū	a lengthened version of 'u', rather like 'oo' as in f**oo**l
V,v	as in **v**ale
Z,z	as in **z**ip
Ž, ž	like the 's' in plea**s**ure

Note also the following two digraphs, letter combinations that represent single consonant sounds:

| Dz | like 'dz' in English, as in a**dz**e |
| Dž | like 'j' as in **J**ohn 'g' as in **G**eorge |

Diphthongs are pronounced as follows:

Ai	like 'ai' as in f**i**ne
Au	like 'ow' as in h**ow**. In Latvian, 'av' tends to be pronounced as 'au', as in the negating term 'nav'
Ei	rather like 'ay', as in d**ay**, though there is not an exact counterpart in English
Ie	May be pronounced in either a short or long form, like 'ia' as in Philadelph**ia** or 'ea' as in **ea**r
Iu	No exact counterpart in English, but approximates a combination of 'e' and 'oo'
Ui	No exact counterpart in English, but approximates a combination of 'oo' and 'y'

Other diphthongs appear only in foreign loanwords.

BASIC GRAMMAR Latvian nouns take either the masculine or feminine gender. Nouns, as well as adjectives, pronouns and numerals, all decline. There are seven cases: nominative, accusative, genitive, dative, instrumental, locative and vocative. There are three masculine declensions, with nominative endings -*s*, -*is* or -*us*. The three feminine declensions have nominative endings of -*a*, -*e* or, rarely, -*s*. To conform to these declensions, foreign proper names tend to be Latvianised, by giving them an -*s* or -*a* ending for male and female names, respectively. Thus, I tend to be referred to in Latvia as Pols Bramels. And you might see in Latvian bookstores tales of the child wizard Harijs Poters.

Latvian verbs fall into three conjugation classes, with some additional irregular verbs. Present, past and future tenses are used, as well as present perfect, past perfect and future perfect constructions. Verbs are used in five moods – indicative, imperative, conditional, conjunctive and debitive. Both active and passive voices are used.

USEFUL WORDS AND PHRASES
Essentials

Good morning	*Labrīt*
Good afternoon	*Labdien*
Good evening	*Labvakar*
Hello	*Sveiki*

Goodbye	*Uz redzēšanos* (formal)
	Visu labu/Atā (informal)
My name is…	*Mani sauc…/Mans vārds ir…*
What is your name?	*Kā jūs sauc?/Kāds ir jūsu vards?* (formal)
	Kā tevi sauc?/Kāds ir tavs vārds? (informal)
I am from…	*Es esmu no…*
Britain/America/Australia	*Lielbritānijas/Amerikas/Austrālijas*
How are you?	*Kā (jums/tev) iet?*
(Very) well	*(Ļoti) labi*
And you?	*Un jūs?*
Well too	*Arī labi*
Pleased to meet you	*Prieks iepazīties/Ļoti patīkami*
Thank you	*Paldies*
Don't mention it	*Lūdzu* (note that 'lūdzu is a versatile word in Latvian, whose meaning changes according to context, including 'please' 'here you are', 'excuse-me' and 'you're welcome')
Cheers!	*Priekā!*
yes	*jā*
no	*nē*
I don't understand	*Es nesaprotu*
Please would you speak more slowly	*Lūdzu, runājiet lēnāk*
Do you understand?	*Vai jūs saprotat?* (formal)
	Vai tu saproti? (informal)
Excuse-me	*Atvainojiet*

Questions

How?	*Kā?*
What?	*Kas?*
Where?	*Kur?*
What is it?	*Kas tas ir?*
Which?	*Kurš?*
When?	*Kad?*
Why?	*Kāpēc?*
Who?	*Kas?*
How much?	*Cik daudz?* (quantity)
	Cik maksā? (cost/price)

Numbers

0	*nulle*
1	*viens* (masculine)/*viena* (feminine)
2	*divi/divas*
3	*trīs*
4	*četri/četras*
5	*pieci/piecas*
6	*seši/sešas*
7	*septiņi/septiņas*
8	*astoņi/astoņas*
9	*deviņi/deviņas*
10	*desmit*

11	*vienspadsmit*
12	*divpadsmit*
13	*trīspadsmit*
14	*četrpadsmit*
15	*piecpadsmit*
16	*sešpadsmit*
17	*septiņpadsmit*
18	*astoņpadsmit*
19	*deviņpadsmit*
20	*divdesmit*
21	*divdesmit viens*
30	*trīsdesmit*
40	*četrdesmit*
50	*piecdesmit*
60	*sešdesmit*
70	*septiņdesmit*
80	*astoņdesmit*
90	*deviņdesmit*
100	*simts/simt*
1,000	*tūkstotis/tūkstoš*

Time

What time is it?	*Cik ir pulkstenis?*
It's…am/pm	*pulkstenis ir…rītā/vakarā*
today	*šodien*
tonight	*šovakar*
tomorrow	*rīt*
yesterday	*vakar*
morning	*rīts*
evening	*vakars*

Days

Monday	*pirmdiena*
Tuesday	*otrdiena*
Wednesday	*trešdiena*
Thursday	*ceturtdiena*
Friday	*piektdiena*
Saturday	*sestdiena*
Sunday	*svētdiena*

Months

January	*janvāris*
February	*februāris*
March	*marts*
April	*aprīlis*
May	*maijs*
June	*jūnijs*
July	*jūlijs*
August	*augusts*
September	*septembris*
October	*oktobris*

| November | *novembris* |
| December | *decembris* |

Seasons and the weather

Winter	*ziema*
Spring	*pavasaris*
Summer	*vasara*
Autumn	*rudens*
Today is…	*Šodien ir…*
sunny	*saulains*
rainy	*lietains*
cloudy	*mākoņains*
windy	*vējains*

Getting around
Public transport

I'd like…	*Es gribētu…*
a ticket to…	*lūdzu, biļeti uz…*
a one-way ticket	*lūdzu, biļeti vienā virzienā*
a return ticket.	*lūdzu, turp-atpakaļ biļeti*
I want to go to…	*Es gribu iet* (walking)/*braukt* (with any means of transport) *uz…*
How much is it?	*Cik maksā?*
What time does it leave?	*Cikos tas atiet?*
What time is it now?	*Cik ir pulkstenis?*
The train has been…	*Vilciens ir…*
delayed	*aizkavējies*
cancelled	*atcelts*
4x4	*4x4*
airport	*lidosta*
bicycle	*velosipēds*
boat	*laiva*
bus	*autobuss*
bus station	*autoosta*
bus stop	*autobusa pietura*
car	*auto/mašina*
ferry	*prāmis*
plane	*lidmašīna*
platform	*perons/ceļś*
port	*osta*
railway station	*dzelzceļa stacija*
ship	*kuģis*
sleeper	*kupeja/guļamvagons*
ticket office	*kase*
timetable	*saraksts*
train	*vilciens*
tram	*tramvajs*
trolleybus	*trolejbuss*
taxi	*taksometrs/taksi*
minibus	*mikroautobuss*
motorbike/moped	*motocikls/mopēds*

arrival	*ierašanās/pienāk* (bus/train station)
	lielidošana (airport)
departure	*izbraukšana/atiet* (bus/train station)
	izlidośana (airport)
first class	*pirmā klase*
second class	*otrā klase*
from / to	*no / uz*
here / there	*šeit / tur*
bon voyage!	*laimīgu ceļu! / labu ceļojumu!*

Private transport

Is this the road to…?	*Vai tas ir ceļš uz…?*
I have broken down	*Mana maśina salūza*
Where is the service station?	*Kur ir degvielas uzpildes stacija?*
diesel	*dīzeļdegviela*
leaded petrol	*svina benzīns*
unleaded petrol	*bezsvina benzīns*

Road signs

caution	*uzmanību*
danger	*briesmas*
detour	*apvedceļš*
entry	*ieeja*
exit	*izeja*
give way	*dot ceļu*
keep clear	*nestāvēt*
no entry	*iebraukt aizliegts*
one way	*vienvirziena*
toll	*nodeva*

Directions

Where is it?	*Kur tas ir?*
Go straight ahead	*Ej taisni uz priekšu*
turn left	*pagriezieties pa kreisi*
turn right	*pagriezieties pa labi*
…at the traffic lights	*…pie luksoforiem*
…at the roundabout	*…apļveida krustojumā*
north	*ziemeļi/uz ziemeļiem*
south	*dienvidi/uz dienvidiem*
east	*austrumi/uz austrumiem*
west	*rietumi/uz rietumiem*
behind	*aiz muguras*
in front of	*priekšā*
near	*tuvu*
opposite	*pretī*

Street signs

entrance	*ieeja*
exit	*izeja*
open	*atvērts*
closed	*slēgts*

toilets – men/women	*tualetes – vīrieši/sievietes*
information	*informācija*

Accommodation

Where is a cheap/good hotel?	*Kur ir lēta/laba viesnīca?*
Could you please write the address?	*Vai vari lūdzu uzrakstīt adresi?*
Do you have any rooms available?	*Vai jums ir brīvas istabas?*
I'd like…	*Es gribētu…*
a single room	*vienvietīgu istabu*
a double room	*divvietīgu istabu*
a room with two beds	*istabu ar divām gultām*
a room with a bathroom	*istabu ar vannas istabu*
to share a dorm	*kopmītni*
How much it is per night/person?	*Cik maksā par nakti/personu?*
Where is the toilet?	*Kur ir tualete?*
Where is the bathroom?	*Kur ir vannasistaba?*
Is there hot water?	*Vai ir karstais ūdens?*
Is there electricity?	*Vai ir elektrība?*
Is breakfast included?	*Vai brokastis ir iekļautas?*
I am leaving today	*Es šodien dodos prom*

Eating out

Do you have…	*Vai jums ir…*
a table for…people?	*galdiņš…cilvēkiem?*
a children's menu?	*bērnu ēdienkarte?*
I am a vegetarian	*Es esmu veģetāriete*
I am vegan	*Es esmu vegāns*
Do you have any…	*Vai jums ir kādi…*
vegetarian dishes?	*veģetārie ēdieni?*
gluten-free/lactose-free dishes?	*bezglutēna/bez laktozes ēdieni?*
Please bring me…	*Lūdzu, atnesiet man…*
a fork/knife/spoon	*dakšiņu/nazi/karoti*
I like…/I don't like…	*Man garšo…/Man negarśo* (of food)
Please may I have the bill?	*Lūdzu, rēķinu!*

Food and drink basics

bread	*maize*
butter	*sviests*
cheese	*siers*
oil	*eļļa*
pepper	*pipari*
salt	*sāls*
sugar	*cukurs*

Fruit

apples	*āboli*
bananas	*banāni*
grapes	*vīnogas*
oranges	*apelsīni*
pears	*bumbieri*

Vegetables

broccoli	*brokoļi*
carrots	*burkāni*
garlic	*ķiploki*
onions	*sīpoli*
peppers	*paprika*
potatoes	*kartupeļi*

Fish

mackerel	*makrele*
mussels	*mīdijas*
salmon	*lasis*
tuna	*tuncis*

Meat

beef	*liellopu gaļa*
chicken	*vista*
goat	*kazas gaļa*
lamb	*jērs*
pork	*cūkgaļa*
sausage	*desa*

Drinks

beer	*alus*
coffee	*kafija*
fruit juice	*augļu sula*
milk	*piens*
tea	*tēja*
water	*ūdens*
wine	*vīns*

Shopping

I'd like to buy…	*Vēlos iegādāties…*
How much is it?	*Cik maksā?*
I don't like it	*Man tas nepatīk*
I'm just looking	*Es tikai skatos*
It's too expensive	*Tas ir pārāk dārgs*
I'll take it	*Es to ņemšu*
Please may I have…	*Lūdzu, vai es varu…?*
Do you accept…?	*Vai Jūs pieņemat…?*
credit cards	*kredītkartes*
cash	*skaidru naudu*
more	*vairāk*
less	*mazāk*
bigger	*lielāks*
smaller	*mazāks*

Communications

I am looking for…	*Es meklēju…*
bank	*banka*
church	*baznīca*

Help!	*Palīdziet!*
Call a doctor!	*Zvaniet ārstam!*
There's been an accident	*Ir noticis negadījums*
I'm lost	*Esmu pazudis*
Go away!	*Ej prom!*
police	*policija*
fire	*uguns/ugunsgrēks*
ambulance	*ātrā palīdzība*
thief	*zaglis*
hospital	*slimnīca*
I am ill	*Es esmu slims*

embassy	*vēstniecība*
exchange office	*valūtas maiņas punkts*
post office	*pasts*
telephone centre	*telefonu centrs*
tourist information centre	*tūrisma informācijas centrs*

Health

I am…	*Es esmu…*
asthmatic	*astmatiķis*
epileptic	*epileptiķis*
diabetic	*diabētiķis*
I'm allergic to…	*Man ir alerģija pret…*
penicillin	*penicilīnu*
nuts	*riekstiem*
bees	*bitēm*
antibiotics	*antibiotikas*
antiseptic	*antiseptisks*
condoms	*prezervatīvi*
contraceptive	*kontracepcijas līdzeklis*
diarrhoea	*caureja*
doctor	*ārsts*
nausea	*slikta dūša*
over-the-counter medicine	*bezrecepšu zāles*
paracetamol	*paracetamols*
pharmacy	*aptieka*
prescription	*recepte*
prescription medicine	*recepšu zāles*
sun cream	*sauļošanās krēms*
tampons	*tamponi*

Travel with children

Are children allowed?	*Vai bērni ir atļauti?*
Is there a…?	*Vai ir…?*
baby changing room?	*bērnu pārģērbšanās istaba?*
a children's menu?	*bērnu ēdienkarte?*
Do you have infant milk formula?	*Vai tev ir piena formula zīdaiņiem?*

babysitter	*aukle*
highchair	*augsts krēsls*
nappies	*autiņbiksītes*
potty	*podiņš*

Other

and/some/but	*un/daži/bet*
beautiful/ugly	*skaists/neglīts*
boring/interesting	*garlaicīgi/interesanti*
difficult/easy	*grūti/viegli*
early/late	*agri/vēlu*
expensive/cheap	*dārgi/lēti*
good/bad	*labs/slikts*
hot/cold	*karsts/auksts*
my/ours/yours	*mans/mūsu/tavs* (inf.)/*jūsu* (form.)
old/new	*vecs/jauns*
this/that	*šis/tas*

Appendix 2

FURTHER INFORMATION

BOOKS
Non-fiction

Benton, Peggie *Baltic Countdown* Centaur, 1984. This is a fascinating first-hand account of Rīga during the first Soviet Occupation in 1940, written from the perspective of an employee of the British Consulate. A sobering read, but full of diverting details, like Soviet efforts to boost rabbit production, and ending with the family's departure from the city, via the Trans-Siberian Railway to Vladivostok.

Bergman, Una *Politics of Uncertainty: The United States, the Baltic Question, and the Collapse of the Soviet Union* Oxford University Press, 2023. Academic account looking at the collapse of the Soviet Union, not from the perspective of Moscow but from that of the Baltic States.

Clarke, Charles (ed.) *Understanding the Baltic States: Estonia, Latvia and Lithuania since 1991* Hurst, 2023. The Cambridge University Baltic Geopolitics Programme, launched in 2021, attempts to bring together researchers from the UK and across the Baltic region in examining the history and geopolitics of the Baltics. This edited volume focuses on the role of the three Baltic States in the dissolution of the USSR, and their own re-emergence as independent states.

Eksteins, Modris *Walking since Daybreak: a Story of Eastern Europe, World War II, and the Heart of Our Century* Mariner Books, 2000. Through the lens of his family autobiography, he tells the story of the impact on the Baltic States of World War II and occupation.

Garokalna, Daina *Latvian Ethnic Symbols for Strength and Protection* Apgāds Pūce, 2015. This short volume, available at bookstores in Latvia, offers an introduction to the meanings of 20 of the most commonly encountered Latvian traditional signs.

Hiden, John and Salmon, Patrick *The Baltic Nations and Europe: Estonia, Latvia and Lithuania in the Twentieth Century* Routledge, 1994. Academic account of the efforts of the Baltic States to secure the restoration of their independence, set against their 20th-century histories.

Hunt, Vincent *The Road of Slaughter: the Latvian 15th SS Division in Pomerania, January–March 1945* Helion, 2023. Vincent Hunt has written several books on Latvian military history. Here he tells the story of the death of up to 5,000 Latvian soldiers in northwestern Poland in 1945, trapped by the Red Army.

Kalnins, Mara *Latvia: A Short History* Hurst, 2015. A readable canter through Latvia's challenging history of occupation, written firmly from a Latvian perspective, and more forgiving than some would be of controversial episodes like the Ulmanis dictatorship.

Kolbergs, Andris *Rīga for the Curious Traveller* A K A Jūrmala, 2003. Tells the history of Rīga through a series of suggested walking tours, full of quirky anecdotes. Difficult to track down, but you may be able to find a copy in a Rīga bookstore.

Krastiņš, Jānis *Art Nouveau Architecture in Latvia* Madris, 2018. Richly illustrated survey of the Art Nouveau buildings across the country from the acknowledged expert on the subject.

Lieven, Anatol *The Baltic Revolution: Estonia, Latvia, Lithuania and the Path to Independence* Yale University Press, 1994. Written shortly after the restoration of independence of the Baltic States, this is a good account of that process and of the underpinning history of the region.

O'Connor, Kevin C *The House of Hemp and Butter: A History of Old Rīga* Northern Illinois University Press, 2019. Scholarly account of the history of Rīga until the Russian conquest of 1710, examining the impact on the city of different occupying powers as well as events such as the Reformation.

Salmon, Patrick and Barrow, Tony (eds) *Britain and the Baltic: Studies in Commercial, Political and Cultural Relations 1500–2000* University of Sunderland Press, 2003. Collection of academic essays underlining the strength of the historical connections between the UK and the Baltic region.

Taylor, Neil, with Laats, Juhan-Markus *Estonia: the Bradt Guide* Bradt Guides, 2021. Excellent and informative travel guide to Latvia's neighbour to the north, for those looking to spend time in both countries.

Fiction

Collier, Mike *Baltic Byline* Baltic Features, 2016. The fictional account of a journalist struggling to make a living as a foreign correspondent in the Baltic States, written by a Latvia-based British journalist.

Collier, Mike *Up the Baltick* Baltic Features, 2017. An account of 'the rediscovered journey of James Boswell and Samuel Johnson to Esthonia, Livonia and Kurland in the year 1778.' Quite a feat to maintain this pastiche over 348 pages.

Eglāja-Kristsone, Eva and Parkinsdon, Becca (eds) *The Book of Rīga: a City in Short Fiction* Comma Press, 2018. Ten short stories linked by the Latvian capital, with a foreword by former Latvian president Vaira Vīķe-Freiberga.

Ikstena, Nora *Soviet Milk* Peirene Press, 2018. One of the most successful Latvian novels of recent years, presenting an engaging look at the Soviet occupation through the lives of three generations of women.

Joņevs, Jānis *Doom 94* Wrecking Ball Press, 2018. A story set in Jelgava in the early 1990s, as our 14-year-old hero adjusts to life outside the Soviet Union, assisted by heavy metal music.

Mankell, Henning *The Dogs of Rīga* Vintage Crime/Black Lizard, 2004. This crime novel featuring Swedish detective Inspector Kurt Wallander is largely set in Rīga, and makes for a pacey read, although the lawless city of 1991 described in the book is a far cry from the Rīga of today.

Pastore, Luīze *Dog Town* Firefly Press, 2018. A charming and fantastical children's book, though one which will also be enjoyed by adults, involving a small boy's efforts to save Rīga with the help of some talking dogs.

WEBSITES

1188 (w 1188.lv) Contains Latvian-language news, but also helpfully public transport schedules and business listings.

The Baltic Times (w baltictimes.com) News stories from across the Baltic States.

A2

ENG.LSM.lv (**w** eng.lsm.lv) The official English-language news portal of Latvian Radio and Television provides a good source of information for the latest Latvian news, as well as entertainingly written background articles.

Investment and Development Agency of Latvia (**w** liaa.gov.lv) Focused on those looking to do business with Latvia.

Latvia Travel (**w** latvia.travel) Tourism portal of the Latvian Investment and Development Agency, with descriptions of the country's main attractions, advice on upcoming events and some useful themed articles.

Latvian Literature (**w** latvianliterature.lv). A platform established to promote Latvian literature abroad, with English-language biographies of the country's major writers, past and present, and suggested reading among contemporary Latvian literature.

Latvijas kultūras kanons (**w** kulturaskanons.lv) An initiative of the Latvian National Library, with brief descriptions in Latvian, English and German of highlights of Latvian culture, including architecture, literature, film and landscapes.

Latvijas Putni (**w** latvijasputni.lv) Run by the Latvia Birds Fund (Latvijas Putnu Fonds), this is a useful source of information for birdwatchers, although the site is updated rather infrequently.

Mammadaba (**w** mammadaba.lv) 'Mother nature' is a website run by the Latvia's State Forests organisation, devoted to tourism and recreation opportunities within the forests they manage. The site contains links to a series of 'Mammadaba' brochures, delightfully written by resident British journalist Mike Collier, and full of good ideas for a day out in the forest.

Mission Latvia (**w** latvia.eu) Promotional website about the country, focused on the efforts of the Mission Latvia campaign to develop the country as a hub of sustainable innovation.

Index

Page numbers in **bold** indicate main entries; those in *italics* indicate maps.

INDEX OF ADVERTISERS